IN THE RED

D0111833

WITHDRAWN

IN THE RED

On Contemporary Chinese Culture

Geremie R. Barmé

COLUMBIA UNIVERSITY PRESS

NEW YORK

Columbia University Press
Publishers Since 1893
New York   Chichester, West Sussex

Copyright © 1999 Geremie R. Barmé
All rights reserved

Library of Congress Cataloging-in-Publication Data
Barmé, Geremie R.
In the red : on contemporary Chinese culture / Geremie R. Barmé.
p.   cm.
Includes bibliographical references and index.
ISBN 0-231-10614-9 (alk. paper)
1. China—Civilization—1949–   2. China—Politics and
government—1976–   3. China—History—Cultural Revolution,
1966–1976. I. Title. II. title: Contemporary Chinese culture.
DS777.6.B37   1999
306'.0951'09045—DC21   98-39734

Casebound editions of Columbia University Press books are
printed on permanent and durable acid-free paper.
Printed in the United States of America
c 10 9 8 7 6 5 4 3 2

For John Minford

CONTENTS

A Culture in the Red

In October 1986, at the height of the *Pax* Hu Yaobang, a time of relatively benign cultural and political rule in China, the state-controlled Chinese Writers' Association organized an international symposium on contemporary literature at Jinshan, the steel town outside Shanghai. Hosted by Wang Meng, a prominent novelist and the recently appointed minister of culture, the gathering was a canny effort at arts public relations. Many of the international participants were leading translators of Chinese letters and Sinologists; one was even a member of the Nobel Academy. Some of China's most popular and faddish writers—men and women who had risen to prominence as pathbreaking novelists, poets, and essayists in the 1980s—also were present, although there were a few notable absences.[1] Over the ensuing days, much of the discussion centered on a common obsession on the mainland: the Nobel Prize for literature, that international stamp of cultural approval. Amid the lobbying of the Nobel academician, there also were recriminations from among disgruntled local participants that the Chinese arts— which, they contended, had come of age in the decade since the end of the Cultural Revolution in 1976—had been badly served by the academics and professionals who translated mainland literature into Western languages. If only Sinologues could do justice to the cutting-edge Chinese works through their translations and critiques, it was argued, then mainland culture would be sure to find the international recognition it so richly deserved.

In their speeches, many of my overseas colleagues concentrated on the literary innovations that had led to the appeal of post-Maoist literature to an increasingly sophisticated and demanding audience in China. For my part, I chose to reflect on the revival of individualistic prose, in particular the casual essay, from the late 1970s. This was a development that showed how more intimate and personal concerns in literature were being overwhelmed by newly unleashed market forces and literary sensationalism. Having just spent a year in Hong Kong working with the translator John Minford to edit a volume of contemporary Chinese writing,[2] I felt that the publishing furor and writing fever that had followed in the train of political relaxation and the recent commercialization of the arts had led, among other things, to a wave of national graphomania. In my concluding remarks, I quoted a passage from Milan Kundera, a writer who was then relatively unknown in China (although after 1989, much of his work was published in translation, and he become something of a literary paragon, if not a cliché):

> The irresistible proliferation of graphomania among politicians, taxi drivers, childbearers, lovers, murderers, thieves, prostitutes, officials, doctors, and patients shows me that everyone without exception bears a potential writer within them, so that the entire human species has good reason to go down into the streets and shout: "We are all writers!"
>
> For everyone is pained by the thought of disappearing, unheard and unseen, into an indifferent universe, and because of that everyone wants, while there is still time, to turn himself into a universe of words.
>
> One morning (and it will be soon), when everyone wakes up as a writer, the age of universal deafness and incomprehension will have arrived.[3]

When my speech was reprinted in *Literary Gazette* (Wenyi bao), the main official cultural newspaper in Beijing at the end of 1986, the Kundera quotation was inexplicably deleted.

In the Red is a study of the graphomania that has once more made China one of the greatest writing and publishing nations on the planet. It is the continuation of more than a decade of work on contemporary Chinese cultural issues. The earlier products of this endeavor can be found in four anthologies, and some of the material that supports the arguments of this book is contained therein.[4] *In the Red* provides also a summary and, by necessity, a highly selective history of cultural politics and purges in China from the late 1970s to the present. It highlights certain individuals and incidents that have illuminated, for me at least, some of the most intriguing aspects of cultural development on the mainland. Although the words *contemporary Chinese culture* appear in its title, this book can claim to be neither inclusive nor exhaustive. In admitting to its serious limitations, I am reminded of a derisive characterization by the Beijing intelligentsia of the sway that official culture held in 1990s China: at best, it covers a few people, incidents, and cultural phenomena within the Fourth Ring Road of Beijing and the First Ring Road of Shanghai.

Two decades of personal contact and involvement with many of the cultural figures and literary incidents described in this book, as well as a part-time career as a commentator on current Chinese events, have greatly influenced my work and analysis. As a result, *In the Red* is not an attempt to study the culture of the mainland from a purely academic or Olympian keep. Whereas I do not abjure the personal approach and am unabashed about my judgment of the works discussed here, my central fascination is with the production of post–Cultural Revolution Chinese culture and the dilemmas of attempting such a description, no matter how limited its history, while also evaluating that evolution.

Born in Sydney, Australia, in the 1950s, I grew up in the thrall of three cultural empires: the Anglo-European, North American, and Sino-Japanese. A half-caste member of a displaced tribe of Anglo-Celts (English and Scottish) and German Jewish refugees, I was excluded from both groups because of the hybridity of my bloodlines. In addition to this nagging state of internalized exile, I was lumbered with an ethnically other name, Barmé, with an acute accent, one that did not become multiculturally cool in Australia until the late 1970s, by which time I was too old to care.

Moving to Canberra to attend the Australian National University, I majored in Buddhist studies and Chinese. My teacher of modern Chinese and art history was Pierre Ryckmans (Simon Leys), and I studied the Confucian classics and poetry with the scholar, novelist, playwright, and critic Liu Ts'un-yan; the philosopher Julia Ching; Svetlana Dyer; Donald Leslie; Colin Mackerras; and the dilettante Chiang Yee, renowned for his writings as the Silent Traveler. From there I went to China, at the age of twenty already deeply imbued with Cultural Revolution indoctrination (having become an ironic fan of Peking Foreign Languages Press publications at the age of thirteen) and staggering equally under the weight of residual hippydom and Eastern mysticism. During the mid-1970s, along with a clutch of other foreign students in the People's Republic, I studied things that were paraded under the rubrics of culture and political science at Maoist universities in Beijing, Shanghai, and Shenyang. Some of us took badly the fall of the "Gang of Four" in October 1976 when we heard about it in the commune in the Liaodong Peninsula where we had been sent to pick apples for export to the Soviet Revisionists. It was a labor that didn't make us free, although hard currency from the Soviets had its revolutionary payoffs.

I stopped going to classes after we were instructed to blacken out all the offending, politically incorrect, and defunct "Gang of Four" jargon in our textbooks. Finally, in 1977, the delirium of rewriting history became so excessive that we were instructed to hand in the texts for pulping (I kept mine as mementos of the dumbing down of China). Although still sequestered in Shenyang, during R&R trips to Beijing I was befriended by the translators Yang Xianyi and Gladys Yang and, through them, met the fossil-poet (his expression) Ai Qing; the long-exiled party writer Ding Ling (who taught me the Chinese maxim: you have to live long enough to see the bodies of your enemies float by you in the river); the critic Qin Zhaoyang; Feng Xiaoxiong, the son of Feng Xuefeng, a party cultural stalwart purged in the 1950s; and the surviving members of the Louts' Hall, Erliu tang—a 1940s salon of writers, artists, and leftist bons vivants whose numbers included the playwright Wu Zuguang, the cartoonist Ding Cong, the calligrapher Huang Miaozi, and the essayist-artist Yu Feng, among others—as they were rehabilitated and resurfacing after ten to twenty years of isolation.

My application to the educational authorities in Beijing to quit the grim gulag of Shenyang and transfer my studies to Nanjing, a city newly opened to foreign students, was refused on the grounds that I had been classified as an "anarchic bourgeois element," one of the many representatives of inimical international forces hell-bent on undermining the People's Democratic Dictatorship. Thus rejected, I gave up my never-to-be completed mainland education and moved on to Hong Kong to work for the *Seventies Monthly*, a pro-mainland Chinese periodical edited by Lee Yee, where I became an English editor-translator with Jan Wong and Bennett Lee, schoolmates from my Beijing days. It was at this time of de-Maoification that I also started writing regular columns in Chinese for the Beijing-controlled Hong Kong daily *Ta Kung Pao* as a pseudomainland university graduate who had lived the slogans and who was something of a cultural curiosity in a colony that still had little truck with the motherland over the border. In 1979 Bennett and I struck out on our own to translate a volume of post–Cultural Revolution stories, examples of "the literature of the wounded," that were changing the face of mainland culture, and I learned about the incendiary wall posters of the "Li Yizhe" group and shuttled to Beijing and Guangzhou during the Democracy Wall period of 1978–1979. Appalled by the framing of Wei Jingsheng in 1980, I decided to take leave of things Chinese and pursue instead the study of Japanese. My three years in Tokyo and Kyoto, mostly living on Mombushō (Ministry of Education) largesse, were punctuated with frequent trips to Hong Kong and China to work on film projects, translate contemporary literature, and write satires and cultural criticism for the Hong Kong press.

It was through those youthful feuilletons that I first became embroiled in a series of minor fracas with Chinese literary figures.[5] For these efforts, I have been awarded over the years with the sometimes playful and occasionally earnest enmity of people like the pulp fiction writer Yi Shu in Hong Kong, as well as right-thinking figures on the mainland like the philosopher Li Zehou, the critic Li Tuo, journalists like Liu Binyan, and the conservative He Xin (who kindly thought of me as a CIA agent, an academic with a counterrevolutionary agenda, at the beck and call of the American imperium). My Chinese writings, in particular satires on post–4 June 1989 official culture and alternative art, led me to enjoy anew the discomfort of police surveillance and harassment in Beijing and Shanghai. Meanwhile, my academic writing in English, including "To Screw Foreigners Is Patriotic" (a chapter in this book), often annoyed po-mo (postmodern) colleagues and validated mainland suspicions of my heinous political sympathies. One of the things that these exchanges with mainland critics, men and women who rarely regard ideological disagreements as a tea party, have taught me over the years is the language of totalitarianism, an esoteric code of communication, and the vocabulary of power play. These were lessons that have been of considerable help to me in coming to an understanding of contemporary Chinese cultural change. Whether it be the fulminations of He Xin, Xiao Xialin, or Zhang Chengzhi, or even the more measured but equally barbed works of born-again Confucianites like Liu Dong, Frankfurtians like Li Tuo, or patriots like Wang Xiaodong, when denounced for one's "whitey," *laowai*, bourgeois sympathies and Western mind-set, I always feel myself to be in a familiar linguistic universe.

Having worked in the Hong Kong press and also in the film and theater worlds during the 1980s when mainland films, fiction, poems, plays, and literary criticism were often made into causes célèbres by the zeal of party censors and wily merchants in both China and the British colony, I was thrilled and dejected in turn as mainland culture flourished and foundered at the whims of party leaders; I also learned more about the mechanics of manufactured dissent than probably is good, even for a healthy cynic. To witness famous critics of the party reach accommodations with the authorities in private while putting on the brave face of the dissident to foreign journalists and scholars was also an educational experience. I observed, often with considerable sympathy, that many of the cultural martyrs I encountered from the late 1970s onward were men and women who were willing to be crucified only if they could survive the process and eventually alight from the cross of persecution to enjoy the benefits of those who had played brinkmanship with the devil. This book follows, among other things, the progress of this cultural evolution in late-twentieth-century mainland life while also offering observations on the fate of those who have attempted to stake out a public middle ground for intellectual and artistic endeavor.

Over the past two decades, official, state-funded culture in China has been involved in a transformation whose history has been marked by political purges and commercial gambits. During the 1980s, these became increasingly intertwined in a symbiotic relationship that enmeshed cultural practitioners of all persuasions. Because of the immense size, fluidity, and complexity of the processes involved, this book can attempt to analyze only small segments of official culture: those who infiltrate, manipulate, and oppose it and those who try to chart a course between the two scales of cultural hierarchy, that of the state and that of the non-official. I am interested in what happens in the culture as it develops within its own structures of power and symbolic universe; how the impact, affirmation, and multifaceted exploitation of the outside world is used in the creation of cultural status both in China and overseas; and how global cultural norms suffuse a system that is all the while rejecting and adapting them. I also make forays into issues such as how superficially determined power relationships (between, say, the state and independent artists) are described internally for a local Chinese audience and then depicted for consumption (that is, packaged and exported), initially in the broader realm of Chinese-language culture (including Hong Kong, Taiwan, and the overseas Chinese press) and then internationally.

One of my central interests is the investigation of how, under the party's aegis, comrades have become consumers without necessarily also developing into citizens. For this reason, the progress of political and cultural purges features as a threnody through these pages. The intermittent denunciations of artists, ideas, and works are described not simply as political contractions germane to the Chinese Communist Party's tireless infighting and efforts to maintain its authority and in response to international (U.S. and other) pressures but as an integral part of a complex endogenous process central to understanding the way in which both artists and their audiences have been socialized since the 1970s and how they have socialized those who would observe them both at home and internationally.

In this context, two events in particular loom large in the narrative that follows: the 1989 mass protest movement (followed by the 4 June Beijing massacre and nationwide purge) and Deng Xiaoping's January 1992 "tour of the south" during which the aged leader gave a final impetus to the economic reform policies that had transformed China in the late 1970s. They are intimately related, and their influence extends to both the grand sweep and the minutiae of my argument. The 1997–1998 party push for further radical reform rounds off this book and my thesis.

The role of countercultures, especially the nonofficial urban youth culture and "dissident culture," is discussed in light of how they involve co-option and the establishment of either a number of status quos or a broader spectrum of the pre-existing and assumed official status quo. The term *nonofficial culture* covers a complex skein of interrelated phenomena. Depending on the angle from which it is observed, or the point at which it impinges on the observer, nonofficial culture can also be spoken of as a parallel or even parasite culture. As such, it is neither nonofficial nor necessarily antiofficial. Much of it was and still is produced with state funding and certain (often low-level) official or state involvement. It may not be directly sanctioned or beholden to the overculture, and it cannot simply be classified as oppositional. Whereas the term *nonofficial culture* has becoming increasingly modish outside the mainland since 1989 to describe the works—film, art, theater, literature—produced in this cultural *demi-monde* as antiofficial, dissident, or underground, in the 1990s when commercial culture came to reign even on the mainland, the term *nonmainstream* or *underculture* was more appropriate. There is, however, no adequate nomenclature to describe the disparate range of cultural material produced over the past twenty years, for it has grown, metamorphosed, and developed within the orbit of an avowedly socialist state whose gravitational pull is often all too irresistible and that has itself undergone an extraordinary transformation. Both have matured together and used each other, feeding each other's needs and developing ever new coalitions, understandings, and compromises. Thus, when I talk about the overculture of the state, I am not necessarily implying that the samizdat poetry, fringe art, club rock 'n' roll, and films—the plethora of works that make up the underculture, or alternative culture—should be seen thereby as weak, defenseless, or simply a victim of official fiat.

Generationalism, the subdivision of cultural activists according to their provenance in terms of both locale and age group, has been a distinguishing way in which perceptions about contemporary Chinese culture have been calibrated both in China and internationally. The division of individuals into age groups— artistic substrata identified by year of birth, schooling, and graduation—is central to the manner in which cultural meaning, worth, and innovation are described and ordered by elites in China and how those elites infect nonmainland analyses of them. A certain amorphous group, for example, the "fifth generation of filmmakers," whose numbers include Chen Kaige and Zhang Yimou and many others whose cinematic output is far less easily characterized, is pegged for its specific series of experiences and for having responded culturally to sociopolitical stimuli according to a presumed template of possibility. Thus fourth-generation filmmakers make a certain kind of film, and those of the fifth, another. This gradation of experience translated into cultural product has prompted critics and investors both in China and overseas to search out the new, the up-and-coming, and the six, seventh or X, Y, Z generation of cultural figures. The critical laying on of hands becomes an important part of the validation of these new creators, and the role of the international, Kong-Tai (Hong Kong–Taiwan), and other critics is inestimable. The generations not only react against one another but also are in a shifting, often sparing, dialogue with one another: those who achieve success and recognition create thereby a pedagogy of practice for those who follow in their footsteps, one that they attempt to emulate or from which they draw lessons so as to avoid the pitfalls of their failures.

Rebellion against the fustian socialist state may appear easy in contrast to opposing commercialization and the lure of global cultural style. Thomas Frank writes about the pervasive influence of business interests in the production and delivery of culture. He describes the "cultural trust" in the United States as the "five or six companies whose assorted vice-presidents now supervise a broad swathe of American public expression," that is, turning the country into an "information-and-entertainment superpower." Frank's observations about the cultural trust are elucidating as we meditate on the plangent fate of quixotic cultural adventurers in China.

> The Cultural Trust further rationalizes its operations through vertical integration, ensuring its access to the eternal new that drives the machine by invading the sanctum of every possible avant-garde. Responsible business newspapers print feature stories on the nation's hippest neighborhoods; sober TV programs air segments on the colorful world of "zines"; ad agencies hire young scenesters to penetrate and report back on the latest "underground" doings. Starry-eyed college students are signed up as unpaid representatives of record conglomerates, eager to push product, make connections, and gain valuable experience on the lower rungs of the corporate ladder; while music talent scouts, rare creatures once, are seen everywhere prospecting for the cultural fuel that only straight-off-the-street 'tude can provide.[6]

It has been fashionable to follow Antonio Gramsci, who described subcultures as "pockets of resistance to dominant social order, expressing their dissatisfaction symbolically through style."[7] Much cultural studies discourse is premised on this and similar ideas. Any number of scholars and commentators working on mainland Chinese urban culture in recent years have pursued with considerable vigor the application of these views. My study—though not denying the pertinence of such approaches—is more concerned with cultural production than reception, and I am skeptical about the nature of what is termed the dominant social order as well as the subcultures that are active within it.

In his work on the rise of hip consumerism in 1960s America, *The Conquest of Cool*, Thomas Frank speaks of cultural dissent, "its promise, its meaning, its possibilities, and most important, its limitations."[8] In a very different context, I attempt to follow the recent history of consumer socialism and cultural dissent in China and investigate the ways in which they have developed and been propagated. I will leave it to others to analyze the cultural trends described in this book in light of the way in which they are "consumed" by canny customers in China, as well as how they are subverted and used in a transgressive, even liberating, manner. The themes of my story are rebellion and co-option, attitude and accommodation.

Despite the theoretical concerns in these pages, rather than pursuing an argument in one of the many dialects of hoch-po-mo, I prefer to use platt-English. By so doing and avoiding the obvious deployment of disciplinary strategies—whether they be the paradigms of race and queer theory, sociology of youth, psychoanalysis, media studies, or literary criticism—it is inevitable that my work will be judged by some to be intellectually too flabby, a non-starter in the development of what Matt ffytche so aptly terms " 'neurobics' for intellectual fitness freaks." In steering a treacherous course in the two-line struggle between theory and empiricism I am guilty of too little of the former (being "undertheorized" is, after all, the cardinal sin of modern academe) and too much of the latter.

Although "Greater China"—the mainland, Hong Kong, and Taiwan— has been slow to develop its own cultural trust, in the following pages I identify the development of some of the new "collectives" that it comprises and observe the growth of alternative cultural hierarchies beyond the ambit but still within the orbit of the state's arts bureaucracy and its institutional habits and within the reach of the invisible hand of entrenched cultural practice. Much of my work is concerned with delineating aspects of the multipolar cultural scene of Greater China, mentioning the role of Hong Kong and Taiwan in particular but also recognizing the general impact of offshore investment from places like Japan, as well as the influence of the international media, foundations, and cultural circuit of film and writers' festivals, art exhibitions, and publishing deals. I note that international film and theater festivals, galleries, and writers' groups and publishers need to fill the China niche in their programs and lists and that there are mainland suppliers who are happy to provide the goods, even if they are often shoddy and shop soiled.

The public attitude toward the kinds of notoriety that have launched many mainland cultural careers internationally over the past decades was also transmogrified in the 1970s. The absurd mental acrobatics of the Cultural Revolution era, during which political friends and foes changed places with confusing speed, undermined confidence in the value of government pronouncements and denunciations of works of literature, films, artists, and writers; but they also prepared the ground for the transitory whims of fashion and the cultural ephemera of the marketplace. Although the state and party survived the upheavals of the age and reaffirmed their power by elaborating a public consensus after 1976, the disavowal of Marxism-Leninism and Mao Thought in its practice undermined official authority and increasingly stripped the party of its political and cultural charisma. The increasing impact of the economic reforms and the development of a commercial publishing industry, a tabloid press, and a pop mass-media culture meant that the market began to assume a greater role in cultural and political issues. Official cultural figures—having profited in terms of fame, status, and sales from controversy in the early 1980s—also began to play on the strengths of "creative censorship." Government interdictions no longer necessarily marked the end of a career but, when properly managed, could often add to the public profile of a controversial artist. While authors who lacked the guile to finesse an accommodation with the new regimen, the aggregate writer who appeared in a number of often contradictory guises now flourished: official artist, negotiated dissident, market weathervane, celebrity. Each element in the public persona of these mercurial figures reflected on and adumbrated the other.

In attempting to discuss this shifting cultural landscape, I have often had recourse to both the writings of China's small but significant group of "independent" or "liberal intellectuals," *ziyou zhishifenzi*, and works by (former) Eastern bloc and Soviet writers and scholars whose insights provide a refreshing, critical angle on the paradoxes of terminal socialism. Miklós Haraszti, Alexander Zinoviev, Norman Manea, Mikhail Epstein, and Svetlana Boym, as well as the South African novelist J. M. Coetzee and the Yugoslav writer Danilo Kiš, all find a place here as we discuss issues that are peculiar to reformist China but that also confront and confound a broader humanity.

Some people would argue that subversive cultural forces in an authoritarian or totalitarian environment are, regardless of their peculiarities, limitations, and quirks, a positive development insofar as they undermine monolithic power or at least allow for a greater spectrum of expression and the growth of private cultural space. While such contentions feed into a belief that elite cultures have a moral and transformative value for the society as a whole, they also tend to elide the two-way, or multidirectional, traffic among cultural elites, their constituencies, and their mutual infiltration. In the 1990s, the Chinese avant-garde often chose to bite the hand of the state that nurtured it; it could afford to do so because it was also being fed by the invisible hand of the international market.

For the avant-garde scout, the collector of radical Chinoiserie chic who is in search of the authentic dissident Other, there is something enticingly self-reaffirming in the embrace of the nonofficial artist, a *je sais quoi* that places one at a comfortable remove both from the bourgeoisie, the mere middle classes of one's own clime, and from the other, China-insensitive foreign residents of Beijing and Shanghai. Over the past two decades I have been excited, enthralled, and often appalled, by artists, writers, and filmmakers I have encountered. However, in my case, from the mid-1980s, skepticism has generally triumphed over sychophancy. In the alignment of the cultural adventurer with the progressive Chinese artist, there is, to quote Tom Wolfe, a "feeling that he is a fellow soldier, or at least an aide-de-camp or an honorary cong guerrilla in the vanguard march through the land of the philistines." This process of identification and validation through discovery is part of a "particularly modern need and a peculiarly modern kind of salvation." One can assuage a guilt about one's wealth, for "avant-garde art . . . takes the Mammon and the Moloch out of money"[9] while also allowing the individual to fight against a repressive socialist state that fails to recognize the artist's worth and to struggle with the bourgeois West in tempting it to embrace the talents of an Eastern terra incognita.

The artist as trickster, the idiot-savant, is a figure who appears many times and in many guises in these pages. The growth of irony as a cultural stance was one of the most noteworthy developments of the 1990s, but in China what began as a refreshing deconstructive impulse after the cataclysmic events of 1989 quickly deteriorated into a self-devouring and debased parody of opposition. In the early 1940s George Orwell described the Don Quixote and Sancho Panza "dualism of body and soul . . . noble folly and base wisdom, [which] exist side by side in nearly every human being."

> If you look into your own mind, which are you, Don Quixote or Sancho Panza? Almost certainly you are both. There is one part of you that wishes to be a hero or a saint, but another part of you is a little fat man who sees very clearly the advantages of staying alive with a whole skin. He is your unofficial self, the voice of the belly protesting against the soul.[10]

The tireless shadow boxing between these two impulses, between the idealistic and the venal, is a theme at the center of the history contained in this book. In the case of China, there is no dearth of critics who would argue that irony dissolves and collapses all such juxtapositions. Like Cosmo Landesman of the defunct *Modern Review*, however, "personally, I think irony is an over-rated virtue. It is the nervous tic of those too timid to hold true convictions."[11] The Romanian writer Norman Manea, whose experiences under the old socialist order in Europe parallel much experienced by his fellows in the Far East, asked: "How could one 'resist' in this world of the absurd? Isn't every attempt to be authentic, to rehabilitate the truth, inevitably prey to manipulation and defacement?"[12] His response is perhaps more understanding of the dilemmas of the would-be independent creative mind:

> The artist is not a buffoon, even if he is seen as such by others, even if society forces him to the distortion of makeup and farce. But given the pressures of his environment—itself divided, distorted, flattened, twisted—the ridiculous mask the artist wears is not a sign of acceptance, but of rejection, even if this rejection is dissimulated and he is beginning to prepare his revenge. The artist cannot "dignify" officialdom by opposing it in a solemn fashion, because that would mean taking it too seriously, and inadvertently reinforcing its authority, thus acknowledging its authority. He pushes the ridiculous to grotesque proportions, but artistically, he creates . . . a surfeit of meanings.
>   . . . In today's frenetic, mixed-up society, this chaos of consumerism and fear in which everything is scrambled and destroyed, the ridiculous runs the risk of "swallowing up" art too. But the artist, even if he has been relegated

to the position of buffoon, tries to assume—even at the price of an apparent, momentary abnegation of the self—an ambiguous stance, to place himself on a shaky seesaw, to transform the loss into gain, the void into expectation, into a sort of promise that hides the brilliance and density of his "unseen face unmasked."[13]

Chen Maiping, editor of the overseas literary journal *Today* (Jintian), used the word *grotesque* to describe the craven nonofficial cultural scene of mainland China in the 1990s.[14] Although for Chen this word encapsulated the repulsive posturings of fin-de-siècle Chinese culture, for me it is even more accurate a depiction than he may have realized. In the sixteenth-century, *grotte* described the underground vaults of unearthed Roman ruins, and *grottesche* was used for the mannered patterns and decorations of these man-made caves. The artificial cavern was "the creation of a cosmos in miniature, a nature that is cultivated and controlled,"[15] and grottoes were to become a feature of the Renaissance garden. So, too, the grotesque in China today promises through the disguised and elaborate veneer of the forbidden and its surreptitious charms something covert and alluring, just hidden but deliciously obtainable. Its fantastic interweaving of motifs from the post–Sino-socialist cultural palette are for many an illusionist delight, yet finally it is a contrived environment, an artful ruin that decorates the demesne of the state. *Grotesque* is thus an apt description for many of the operations and appearances of mainland Chinese culture, a culture that is, in more ways than one, still very much in the red.

G. R. B.
Canberra

ACKNOWLEDGMENTS

Over the years, many people have provided me with insights into the treacherously complex realm of Chinese letters on the mainland, as well as in Hong Kong and Taiwan. Some have done so as friends and colleagues, others as sparring partners or adversaries. Although none of them should be held even partially responsible for the opinions expressed in this book, I would like to acknowledge their influence and help here:

John Minford, Winne Yeung Li-kwan (Yang Lijun), Pan Jijiong, Charles Ng (Wu Chenghuan), Yang Xianyi, Gladys Yang, Sang Ye, Linda Jaivin, Nicholas Jose, Claire Roberts, Simon Leys, Lee Yee, Fong Su, W. J. F. Jenner, Luo Fu (Luo Chengxun), Wu Zuguang, Xin Fengxia, Jane Macartney, Shen Jiming, Liu Shugang, Jocelyn Chey, Hans Chey (Moon Lin), Wu Bin, Yang Lian, Hou Te-chien, He Yong, Wang Youshen, Dai Qing, Li Xianting, Liao Wen, Huang Miaozi, Yu Feng, Wang Shuo, Lu Jianhua, Xu Jilin, Kong Lingqin, Chen Xing, Gloria Davies, Francesca Dal Lago, Zhang Jianya, Liang Xiaoyan, He Ping, Lo Ta-yu, Zhu Xueqin, Xiao Gongqin, Liu Xiaobo, He Xin, Lu Yuegang, Fan Yong, Dong Xiuyu, Hsiao Tzu, Yin Hui, Xiao Xialin, Cui Jian, Richard Rigby, Kate McLean, Murray McLean, Don Cohn, Daniel Kane, Ye Xiaoqing, Wang Meng, Shen Rong, Chen Xiaoming, Zuo Shula, Gong Xiaoxia, Scott Savitt, Zhang Zebo, Zhang Zeming, Zhang Youdai, Ding Ling, Kong Yongqian, Zhang Yuan, Tang Xiaodu, Ouyang Jianghe, Nancy Berliner, Zhang Xinxin, Zhang Jie, Yang Jiang, Qian Zhongshu, Liu Yuan, Chin Heng-wei, Chang Wen-i, Danny Yung (Rong Nianzeng), Su Kei (Shu Qi), Chen Maiping, Tao Dongfeng, Li Hui, Ying Hong, Bei Dao, Chen Ying-chen, Liu Xinwu, Chen Kaige, Bonnie McDougall, Li Tuo, Poon Yiu-ming, Mao Shian, Chris Buckley, Ian Buruma, Frank Dikötter, Michael Dutton, Perry Link, Stephen FitzGerald, and Benjamin L. Liebman.

The support of my colleagues at the Australian National University—especially Jonathan Unger, Anita Chan, W. J. F. Jenner, Gavan McCormack, Mark Elvin, and Tessa Morris-Suzuki—have made it possible for me to pursue interests that less accommodating scholars may well have viewed with disquiet. Similarly, without the generous funding for much of my travel to China over the past eight years from the Research School of Pacific and Asian Studies of the Australian National University, this would have been a very different work.

Richard Gordon, Carma Hinton, Nora Chang, and Dong Hua of Long Bow Inc., Boston, have been a constant source of solace, and Marilyn Young of the Department of History, New York University, made my sojourn there during the spring of 1996, when I was working on the final text of this book, an inspiration, as did many of her colleagues and students. My deep gratitude also to David Winters and Marcia de Castro, as well as Neil Thompson and Zoe Wang (Wang Ziyin). My brother Scot Barmé, my mother Jane Duncan Brown, and Jonathan Hutt also offered many useful comments on the manuscript in its final stages.

Special thanks also to Andrew J. Nathan, Thomas B. Gold, and Jeffrey N. Wasserstrom for their enthusiastic support and contributions to the publication of this book, as well as to Kate Wittenberg of Columbia University Press for her patience and sangfroid in dealing with this tome and its all-too-tardy author. I am also very grateful to Margaret B. Yamashita for her painstaking copyediting of a bulky and, until the end, growing manuscript, and to Ron Harris, my editor at Columbia. My thanks also to Miriam Lang, who generously offered to proofread the final text prior to publication.

My thanks also to the Beijing artist Zhu Wei and Stephen McGuiness of Plum Blossoms Gallery in Hong Kong for their generous permission to use Zhu's painting *China! China!* for the cover of this book. For other illustrative material, my heartfelt thanks go to Lois Conner for laboring over my collection of T-shirts, Liu Da Hong and Manfred Schoeni of Schoeni Art Gallery Ltd., the Louisiana Museum of Modern Art, Feng Mengbo, and Ai Weiwei.

Much of the material contained in the following pages has appeared earlier in various guises. I would like to thank the following for their support: *The China Journal* (formerly *The Australian Journal of Chinese Affairs*), *China Review 1992*, *China News Analysis, Current History, Art AsiaPacific*, the Louisiana Museum of Modern Art, Schoeni Art Gallery Ltd., Johnston Chang of Hanart 2, *China Information, Problems of Communism*, and *Issues & Studies*.

IN THE RED

CHAPTER ONE

The Chinese Velvet Prison

Since 1949, culture in mainland China has shared the fate of virtually every other field of endeavor, prospering and suffering in turn according to the dictates of political leaders. Essentially, the Chinese arts under socialism have evolved in ways familiar to us from the history of its "sibling cultures" in the Eastern bloc. All weathered a period of extreme militarization during which crude political aims transmogrified not only the public face of literature and art but even the personae of artists in private. It was a situation that came about because culture was seen by the Communist Party as being merely another weapon in the arsenal of class struggle. The militaristic phase of Chinese cultural history was seeded in the 1930s and came to an early flourishing after 1942 when Mao Zedong officially formulated a cultural policy in his "Yan'an Forum Talks on Literature and Art" at which he admonished artists to create edifying works and serve the workers, peasants, and soldiers. It was in the period between 1949 and 1976, however, that "culture as cudgel" reached its apogee. During these three decades, artists learned to their great personal cost the price of becoming a member of a pedagogical elite empowered to educate and enlighten the masses. For some the passage to achieving the status of state artist was easy; for others it was a harrowing and unforgettable experience.[1]

After the death of Mao Zedong in 1976 and the gradual ideological demobilization of the country, the arts came increasingly under the sway of a new-style leader, the party technocrat. Indeed, in the late 1970s, China witnessed what the authorities dubbed "a new age," *xin shiqi*, in literature and art, a "renaissance." Some optimists even described the 1980s as being a second or more thoroughgoing "new culture movement," the first of which, in the 1920s, saw the rise of mass vernacular culture and committed art. My own analysis of 1980s mainland Chinese culture is less enthusiastic:

> After decades of rule by Proledic [the dictatorship of the proletariat], external political coercion and the internal pressures of the Chinese deep

structure[2] meld to create a new self-censoring cultural figure, the state artist. . . .

As mainland China enters the phase of "soft" technocratic socialism, the parameters of the cultural Velvet Prison are being measured out in everyday practice. But this does not mean that there is no resistance to a new, higher level of co-option, conformity within the deep structure of the State. Individual artists struggle to maintain or achieve their independence . . . they are faced with a choice of suffering complete cultural ostracism or accepting the State's efforts to incorporate them in a new social contract, one in which consensus replaces coercion, and complicity subverts criticism.[3]

THE INS AND OUTS OF THE VELVET PRISON

In her novel *Washing in Public*, published in late 1988, Yang Jiang tells a story of unrequited love against the backdrop of the "ideological reeducation" experienced by Chinese intellectuals in the early 1950s.[4] With an extraordinarily deft touch, Yang presents in this tragicomic tale a picture of a society undergoing what was then still a gradual process, a transformation mirrored in the actions of her characters, a process that may be described as the "socialization of socialism." The transmogrification of Chinese society in those early years of Communist rule unfolded in a myriad of ways: subtle shifts in language, new tastes in dress, and a clash of values marked its progress. Then, during the "three anti and five anti campaigns" of 1950–1951, mainland Chinese intellectuals were called on to "drop their pants and cut their [bourgeois] tails," *tuo kuzi, ge weiba*, and accept unconditionally the new ideological order.[5] While Yang Jiang's novel can be taken as a delectable story of frustrated love, it is also a not-so-fictional history of a group of translators in a research institute and how they come to terms with the new regime.

Yang Jiang is a master of understatement, something she proved beyond doubt in her subtle Cultural Revolution memoirs.[6] *Washing in Public* handles with considerable wit the question of thought remolding and "self-renewal," *xi xin ge mian*, as the process was sometimes called,[7] depicting thought reform as an inexorable passage away from individual will to group consciousness under collective state tutelage. Individuals were subjected, in turn, to overt coercion and caring consultation, with the end result often being willing and, at times, even eager self-abnegation. The almost playful humor and irony employed by the writer make this excoriating process all the more chilling. For Zhu Qianli, a scholar of French literature and one of the central characters of the book, self-renewal is a scarifying ordeal. Only after being "struggled" does he realize the subtle difference between excessive self-flagellation—what he imagined was a necessarily humiliating shortcut into the ranks of the People—and a soul-felt personal deconstruction that allows his inquisitors to scavenge through the rubble of his life in search of elements of his past that are suited to the new era.[8] Zhu's fellow academic, Ding Baogui, learns from his colleagues' experience and makes a self-criticism that sees him readily accepted into the ranks of intellectuals in the New Society.[9]

Something of the reverse process is limned in the Beijing novelist Shen Rong's 1980 novella *Snakes and Ladders*.[10] The story is set in post–Cultural Revolution China, some three decades after the action depicted in Yang Jiang's book. A group of researchers in a local academy of social sciences are organized to denounce one of their colleagues. It turns out that a provincial party official had discovered elements of "bourgeois thinking" in the fellow's research work on Western modernist literature, in particular in his assessment of black humor. The meetings, political harassment, and lobbying by the party functionaries reveal a world much changed from the one evoked by Yang Jiang.[11] Whereas in Shen's story, the authority of the party is still considerable, no one is as obedient or dogmatic as in the past, and the intellectuals in the novel openly bargain with the party men to undermine the purge of their research institute, eventually negotiating a new and mutually acceptable, not to mention face-saving, dispensation. On the surface, Yang's and Shen's novels seem to represent two very different worlds. In reality, however, they record different registers on the same scale of intellectual control. In Yang's *Washing in Public*, we witness the party at the height of its strength, at a time when its prestige and organizational power could easily force compliance even when it was not given willingly. Shen Rong scans a much-changed sociopolitical topography, one in which the party is increasingly obliged to broker its relationship with intellectuals, to curry favor with them, and to cajole them into malleable, mutually compromised pacts of cooperation. The nature of the difference between the two ages of socialist intellectual control and the process by which the earlier, coercive style of indoctrination was changed into self-imposed acquiescence has been dealt with at length and with great eloquence by the Hungarian writer Miklós Haraszti, author of *The Velvet Prison: Artists Under State Socialism*.[12]

COMPARATIVE SOCIALISM

Why give prominence to a Hungarian artist rather than cite a hallowed Chinese intellectual, a faddish opinion maker from the cultural diaspora, or some local expert in matters Chinese?

The answer is twofold: first, whereas up to the late 1980s there was increasing discussion among literary and cultural critics about the banefully complementary marriage of traditional Chinese authoritarianism to modern totalitarianism—something that was perhaps symptomatic of a Chinese penchant for "vertical linkages," *zongxiang lianxi*—little energy was devoted to looking westward at the socialist cultures of the Soviet Union and Europe. When it came to remarking on the outside world, it remained generally more fashionable among the Chinese intelligentsia to make comparisons between China and the acknowledged cultural and political superpower the United States or, more grudgingly, Japan. Chinese writers were wary of identifying with the former socialist bloc, even though they were nurtured after the 1920s by similar ideals and conditioned by like practices. With the events of 1989 and thereafter—the government repression of mass protests in cities throughout China, as well as the fall of the Berlin Wall and the collapse of communist governments in the West—the experience of the former socialist regimes, including those who struggled with them, has generally been interpreted by Chinese writers, exiled and home bound alike, in the light of the progressive teleology of the ideological endgame. In terms of academic work, however, there has been an increased interest in comparative socialism over the past years. In considering Chinese culture after the 1970s, the writings from the once fraternal socialist states, as well as works by authors who have lived under the strictures of official censorship, can be a valuable aid in understanding the predicament of urban elitist and popular culture in mainland China.

Second, whereas socialist culture is a unique construct, up to the 1990s there was little adequate study of socialist culture per se by Chinese writers.[13] In the 1980s, Chinese intellectuals and artists generally rode high on a wave of "cultural reassessment" or, to use the crude popular term, "culture mania," *wenhua re*. It was trendy to sift through the shards of the crumbling past and attempt to decipher from what one found some oracular message for the present.[14] Then the prognosis for China ranged from the gray and cautious optimism of the neophytes of post–neo-Confucianism, *xin ruxue*,[15] which in some cases informed the attitudes of authoritarian pragmatists, to the slash-and-burn approach of extreme iconoclasts who condemned the Chinese experience in toto. Certainly, reams of learned papers, comments, interviews, and articles were written by scholastic and cultural neo-authoritarians and conservatives across the board starting in the late 1980s. Many writers, however, kept safely within the boundaries of tradition or satisfied their intellectual yearnings by engaging in abstract philosophical discussion. Only rarely did they venture out to make timid intellectual forays in the minefield of communist culture itself.[16]

Only after 1989 were some Chinese writers forced to consider the devastating effects of socialism on the cultural life of the nation, but even then the process has been slow and reluctant. Indeed, it has always been easier to condemn the "Grand Tradition" of China's imperial past as a scapegoat for all the ills of the Sino-socialist present. In 1988, during the debate sparked by the polemic television documentary *River Elegy*, Heshang, discussed in the next chapter, two critics put their finger on the crucial weakness of the pointed "totalistic iconoclasm" of the series' authors. Their comments are relevant here:

> The nature of the Chinese polity is such that while intellectuals can flog our ancestors, they must be careful to circumnavigate the reef of direct criticism [of the status quo]. A new form of absurdity has grown out of our unnatural scholastic atmosphere. Owing to an insufficiently detailed study of [contemporary] reality, people use the massive construct of "culture" to provide a slapdash explanation of everything, much like our ancestors used the theory of *yin* and *yang* and the eight trigrams to describe the universe. Ironically, they [contemporary critics] attack traditional culture by employing the very methods of the culture that they so detest. . . . Meanwhile, we are entirely at a loss when confronted with the present reality, one that is calling for immediate attention. As always, people prefer to wallow in emotional outpourings, literary flights of fancy, and artistic inspiration rather than engage in exacting rational reflection.[17]

Of course, one cannot deny the considerable "strategic" value of the subterfuges employed by the "culturalists," *wenhuapai*, when dealing with contemporary intellectual and political problems. These graduates of the great school of Mao Zedong Thought were all too familiar with the boundless possibilities of "making the past serve the present" or "manipulating the past to attack the present."[18] While much has been and will be written on the use of this device—one that Miklós Haraszti says nurtures a "civilization between the lines"[19]—its overall effect has been to confuse some of the basic issues involved in an analysis of the cultural situation in China, indeed to divert attention from such an analysis in favor of more attractive and less hazardous culturalistic endeavors. During the 1980s and early 1990s, it was common to hear artists discuss among chosen Chinese and foreign friends their films, art, novels, essays, and academic studies in terms of the sly but clever way they had managed to slip a controversial line, sentiment, or point of view into an otherwise prolix and flabby work.

Far from agreeing with those who believed that "cultures that speak in forked tongues cannot long endure," Haraszti wrote:

> Communication between the lines already dominates our directed culture. This technique is not the specialty of the artist only. Bureaucrats, too, speak between the lines: they, too, apply self-censorship. Even the most loyal sub-

ject must wear bifocals to read between the lines: this is in fact the only way to decipher the real structure of our culture. . . .

The reader must not think that we detest the perversity of this hidden public life and that we participate in it because we are forced to. On the contrary, the technique of writing between the lines is, for us, identical with artistic technique. It is a part of our skill and a test of our professionalism. Even the prestige accorded to us by officialdom is partly predicated on our talent for talking between the lines. . . .

. . . Debates between the lines are an acceptable launching ground for trial balloons, a laboratory of consensus, a chamber for the expression of manageable new interests, an archive of weather reports. *The opinions expressed there are not alien to the state but are perhaps simply premature.*[20]

Generally, when compared with intellectuals in the Soviet Union or Eastern Europe, the Chinese (and here perhaps we should include Taiwan and the newly "liberated" Hong Kong as well) appear in a less than favorable light. In the 1980s, Bo Yang and Lung-kee Sun were particularly outspoken in regard to what they perceived of as being the "fatal flaws" of Chinese intellectuals, be they on the mainland or elsewhere.[21] Thus it became something of a commonplace that the Chinese intelligentsia had a more compliant attitude toward the day-to-day rule of totalitarianism/authoritarianism than did intellectuals in Eastern Europe (the cultural pedigree and role of gleeful "self-abasement" are described in chapter 10, "To Screw Foreigners Is Patriotic").

More than three decades ago, Benjamin Schwartz summed up what he regarded as being the general underpinnings of this view: "The ardent cravings for a sense of national dignity, the deep spiritual insecurity, the long tradition of authoritarianism, the orientation toward state service, the rejection of 'capitalist' values, etc., would all appear to have created preconditions [among intellectuals] for a complaisant attitude toward the Communist state."[22] Schwartz himself argued against accepting this view, yet it is one that is still endlessly proffered by Chinese writers and China specialists, despite past evidence and the testimony of recent events that such a simplistic analysis deserved serious reconsideration.[23]

This is not to say that mainland cultural commentators all failed to turn their attentions to socialist culture. From the mid- to late 1980s, the art critic Li Xianting (also known by the pen names Hu Cun and Li Jiatun),[24] literary critics like Zhu Dake, Liu Xiaobo, and Li Jie, and the journalist-historian Dai Qing[25] were among a small but highly public group of writers who touched on various aspects of this new form of civilization.[26] In the fields of political science and history, a number of writers have been involved in this enterprise while generally being careful to maintain their credentials as participants in mainstream intellectual discourse. In the late 1980s, fringe critics and rogue thinkers were few in number, or simply not vocal enough to be heard. But perhaps the desire to be heard, loud and often, forced some of the more original and perceptive minds to speak out in the "space between the lines." Nonetheless, faced with something of a dearth of indigenous critiques of China's socialist culture, it is beneficial to cast an eye westward for prescient analyses of the situation by China's European soul mates. While being sorely aware of the national, historical, and cultural differences between China and Eastern Europe's socialist experience, Miklós Haraszti's work is one of the most insightful, albeit irreverent and often tongue-in-cheek, guides to mainland China's post-1976 "new age" of culture.

THE VELVET PRISON

Haraszti is a poet, sociologist, and political activist. He was born in 1945 in Jerusalem but grew up in Hungary. Among other things, he studied Chinese at university where he majored in philosophy and has maintained an interest in developments in China. Expelled from the university for political activism, he worked for a year in a factory, and on the basis of those experiences he wrote *A Worker in a Worker's State*, for which he was arraigned in court on charges of subversion. It is significant that George Konrád, the man who wrote the foreword to Haraszti's *Velvet Prison*, is, with Ivan Szelényi, the author of *Intellectuals on the Road to Class Power*, an important study of intellectuals under state socialism. During 1989, Haraszti became involved with the democratic politics of a pluralistic Hungary.

The *Velvet Prison* is a samizdat volume in which the author affects the cynical tone of the victorious artist-bureaucrat as in turn he fixes his ironic gaze on establishment writers, young hopefuls, and dissidents. His aim lay, in the words of the Sinologist Simon Leys, in "charting the topography of a grim new world."[27]

Haraszti depicts a realm in which the crude, military style of Stalinist (for which we can also read Maoist) rule with its attendant purges, denunciations, and struggles has finally given way to a new dawn of "soft," civilian government. Technocrats reformulate the social contract, one in which, as we have noted earlier, consensus replaces coercion and complicity subverts criticism. Censorship is no longer the job of a ham-fisted apparat but a partnership involving artists, audiences, and commissars alike. It is "progressive censorship." This new dispensation has been described in various ways: the Czech writer Václav Havel spoke of it as "invisible violence,"[28] and Haraszti dubbed it "the velvet prison." It is a prison with an aesthetic all of its own; even (self-)repression has become a form of high art.

Liu Zaifu, a leading party literary critic in the 1980s, outlined some aspects of the Chinese version of this art in a lengthy analysis of the literature of the "new age" in 1986. At a major cultural conference Liu presented an overview of the developments in the decade following the end of the Cultural Revolution. He called on all Chinese to undergo a period of "national confession" to rid themselves of the stigmata of the Cultural Revolution, revealing what he thought would be the collective effect of such a confessional:

> Of course, when we talk about a "self-critical attitude" [zishen yishi, an expression that can also mean "self-censoring attitude"], we are aware that we are facing a new age. We engage in self-examination so as to be able to adjust ourselves more readily to modernization, and so we are all the more equipped to participate in it. This is not a form of abject self-negation but, rather, a positive act through which we will find value in the lessons of history and become all the more clear-headed as we stride toward the future. . . . Writers who deeply love their country will use their powerful skills to mobilize and encourage our people to join in the struggle, to advance, to create, to offer the light and warmth of their lives to the present great age. Our writers will bring to completion this glorious social task.[29]

In charting the course of state socialism, Haraszti provides us with a paradigm that can be applied to other party-controlled prison cultures. He notes that harsh and bloody methods are unavoidable in the early phase of establishing revolutionary discipline, at a time before people have been cowed into submission and opponents liquidated. Industry, agriculture, and even the arts are nationalized, and gradually the talented and ambitious, young and old become shareholders, if not functionaries, in the corporate monopoly of the state. If they balk at the new order, they are silenced, voluntarily or by force. Liberated from the irksome burdens of competition and no longer required to rely on innate talent or the popular fads exploited by the usurious culture brokers of a money economy, most artists and writers now vie to become company men. In the process, they relinquish their right to produce art with no social purpose or significance, "art for art's sake."

Paranoia on the part of the ruling elite during the lean years, or rather decades, of military rule means that life can be hard. Intellectuals and cultural figures are invariably set upon as negative examples, symbols of the corrupting ideologies of the past, and they must pay dearly for their newfound social privileges. But as the quixotic rule of a Stalin or Mao gives way to the quiet strength of collective leadership, technocrats in every field gradually replace the strident hard-liners and army veterans.

If he or she is to prosper, each artist must learn to be a cultural politician and executive in the streamlined corporate structure. Artists are jealous of the considerable fringe benefits accorded them—better-than-average incomes, fame at home, trips overseas, and, best of all, the sense of mission and importance allotted to them by the party. It may have taken some older Chinese artists a generation to come to grips with the peculiar "market forces" of socialist culture, but for the middle-aged and younger creators raised in the closed system, the ground rules are well established, and only the most suicidally irresponsible attempt to ignore them entirely.

Years of living as salaried company men and sharing in the political power denied their bourgeois brethren gradually deprives these socialist artists of the desire to return to the "retrogressive" individualistic ways of the past. When given the chance, they are at a loss as to what to do. So it was that during the precious months of so-called bourgeois liberalization,[30] in 1985–1986 under the *Pax* Hu Yaobang, established artists willingly squandered their freedom. Again, during the interregnum of Party General Secretary Zhao Ziyang in 1988 and early 1989, during what was later decried as a "high tide of bourgeois liberalization," few writers struck out for individuality. More often than not, those who did were already noted independent cultural figures. While experimenting with what for China were innovative themes, such as alienation, humanism, absurdity, and sex, state artists were ever careful to conform to the new, expanded state specifications.

Gradually, all manner of modernist sleight of hand could be permitted as the enlightened socialist state pursued an "open door" policy, be it in the guise of *glasnost* or economic "reform" agendas.[31] Although slow in dawning, Chinese leaders, too, realized that the medium was not the message, and since the 1980s, foreign artistic techniques, like so much non-Chinese hardware, have been imported to enhance socialist culture, as long, of course, as their "spirit is permanently detained at the customs gate."[32] Abstract art, pseudo-Punk poetry, film noir, and Taoist fiction all may gradually be tailored to serve the people. "The cacophony of well-known slogans is transformed into a jazz symphony."[33] After all, as Haraszti's state writer asks so pertinently, "Why shouldn't I utilize the style of Robbe-Grillet or Andy Warhol when our police use French tear gas and our citizens are registered on American computers?"[34] Indeed, during the popular revival of the Mao cult in the early 1990s, Chinese artists applied the Warhol technique to rework the Great Leader in a fashion that, although frowned on by the authorities, was a money spinner on the international market.[35]

In giving a delegation of Romanian ideologues and artists a "short introduction" to the literary scene in early 1989, Wang Meng, a prominent writer and the minister of culture since 1986, emphasized that social realism was no longer regarded as the sole creative principle in Chinese culture. Now modernism, romanticism, and various avant-garde techniques, he said, were permitted.[36] Once more, Haraszti provides the perfect exegesis of Wang's comments. He wrote about "parasitic innovation" as being the rubric of the civilian phase of socialist culture. In so doing, Haraszti provided a pen portrait of Wang Meng himself, one of the most deft literary raiders in China, a man whose significance in 1980s and 1990s culture is discussed at length in the following chapters. As Haraszti wrote,

> Our social base is too weak to induce a renaissance of autochthonous individualism. We select from the prepackaged expressions of individualism concocted in the West, and we do so from the vantage point of the state: this is our innovative method. We prune the chaotic outgrowth crowding the jungle of capitalism and carefully transplant selected cuttings to the greenhouse of socialism. As in industry, so too in art: we have no technology of our "own." Our colleges of art teach the methods of, and justification for, this aesthetic parasitism. Even our art criticism is now opening up to the West. This facilitates organized innovation. This is the rebirth of innovation, at the price, of course, of eliminating the demand for originality.[37]

THE DIALECTICS OF DISSENT

The evolution of progressive censorship under soft totalitarianism is, nonetheless, a process fraught with difficulties. A situation that may directly threaten the coalescence of state and artist can arise if the transition from "military" to "civilian" forms of rule is unduly long or unruly. As Haraszti notes in his work, in China "the *yin* and *yang* of hard and soft policies have alternated."[38] The end result of repeated political backsliding on the part of the state leads to disaffection among artists; the number of "nonintegrated" intellectuals increases in leaps and bounds with each extended period of repression. Again, our Hungarian guide comments presciently that "the new generation will get frustrated if their hopes are thwarted by Stalinist methods."[39] And he subsequently observes that

> any effort on the part of the state to spurn artists' attempts to collaborate can lead to real tension, even to the creation of cultural kamikazes—the dissident artists—although hardly any such artists are to be found in countries where the transition from Stalinism to de-Stalinization was swift and resolute. State artists feel threatened by dissidents who strive for the restoration of individualism.[40]

In the decade after the December 1978 Third Plenum of the Communist Party's Eleventh Central Committee, a meeting that marked the party's gradual turning away from militant socialism in favor of economic reform, Deng Xiaoping initiated or condoned the following six major cultural-political purges:

- March 1979, an antiliberalization campaign was launched with the announcement of the Four Basic Principles.[41] This was followed by the arrest of Wei Jingsheng and other democracy activists and a ban on nonofficial publications.
- January 1980, the party propaganda chief Hu Yaobang attacked the "negative social effects" of controversial artistic products like stories and dramas and called on artists to be more socially responsible.
- August 1981, a campaign against the screenplay writer Bai Hua and the malaise of bourgeois liberalization that continued into 1982 and affected many writers.
- October 1983, the antispiritual pollution campaign was begun to prevent the corrupting influences of the West from undermining party leadership and social cohesion.
- January 1987, the anti–bourgeois liberalization campaign was started after student demonstrations in late 1986 and the fall of Hu Yaobang.[42]
- June 1989, a cultural purge followed in the wake of the crushing of the student-led protest movement on 4 June. This purge continued in fits and starts into 1990 (see chapter 2, "An Iron Fist in a Velvet Glove").

Each of these movements witnessed the disaffection of numbers of artists and intellectuals. In the late 1980s — in particular after the 1987 and 1989 purges — there was an exponential increase in their number. In early 1989, with the Communist Party's economic austerity program and rumors of yet another ideological putsch on the way, it is significant that the poet Bei Dao first responded to the astrophysicist Fang Lizhi's 6 January call for a general amnesty for political prisoners by organizing a petition of thirty-three leading writers and intellectuals in Beijing.[43] The reaction to Fang's call among the campaign-weary intelligentsia of that city was enthusiastic.[44] Although one can interpret this with various optimistic glosses, again I would choose Haraszti's paradigm and suggest that rather than being merely a sign of increased intellectual independence on the part of the signatories, the petitions circulating through China in early 1989 were an indicator of the state's extreme incompetence in dealing with its own employees. The erratic purge-and-pacify policies of the 1980s that resulted from swings in political line and temper among the leadership inculcated a rebelliousness among some members of the intellectual world. Furthermore, the heavy-handed actions of the government following the 4 June Beijing massacre were a serious threat to the carefully balanced relationship between the state and the artist. Yet as Mao's supporters faded from the scene by a process of biological attrition, the wise counsels of leading apparatchiki suggested ways and means of repairing or containing the damage done. Indeed, as we will see from the later discussion of the 1989 party ruling on culture, the structure for internal dialogue had been in place for some time.

Even in the China of the late 1980s, however, there were those who were prepared to champion humanistic over party values, freedom of expression over the Four Basic Principles. One of these men was Fang Lizhi. The veteran playwright Wu Zuguang was another. Wu dared to take the party at its word and rejected the duty of self-censorship expected of all establishment intellectuals, as well as speaking out against the state censorship system.[45] Haraszti calls such figures "Naive Heroes,"[46] and one could then imagine that the path to the high-tech prison culture of China's future would be littered with their good intentions.

Truly aberrant dissident elements do appear as well, identified by Haraszti as "Maverick Artists." They are the real enemy, for they reject the very presuppositions of state culture and its lucrative rewards. Few of China's Maverick Artists were known overseas before 1989, although a number of the celebrated "misty," *menglong*, poets belonged to this group. For years they produced their own samizdat literature in preference to being published in official journals. Bei Dao was the most famous of these writers, and in Beijing on 2 April 1989, he led the remaining members of the *Today* literary group called in part to commemorate the Tiananmen incident of 1976 in a "postmodernist" gathering at the Central Drama Academy. But even then, their number was small and was being constantly eroded as the engineers of soft cultural options such as Hu Qili, then the cultural commissar in the Politburo,[47] and Wang Meng, the creative minister of culture,[48] worked hard at co-opting them. After 1989, they resurfaced to produce new irregular samizdat journals like *Contemporary Chinese Poetry* and survived on the outskirts of acceptability.[49]

The Maverick Artists are at their most dangerous and antisocial when they show themselves willing to sacrifice the privileges of the assimilated in order to retain their independence. Yet as Harazsti points out, by so doing they are doomed to eke out a meager existence as fringe dwellers in a state-owned cultural desert crowded with mirages. Haraszti, that rarest of creatures, a self-mocking dissident, included himself in their number.[50] At best they are ignored; at worst they may be imprisoned, jeered at all the while by fellow artists for their utopian idealism. An even more odious possibility arises when the state decides to breed or tolerate a small number of Maverick Artists for propaganda purposes.[51] Indeed, in the 1980s, battery-bred dissidents played a positive role in the Soviet bloc as international public relations personalities.

In the Chinese cultural world as it evolved from the 1980s, there was an innovative development in the history of the velvet prison as depicted by Haraszti. Hong Kong and Taiwanese cultural entrepreneurs who frequently traveled inland on cultural shopping trips had an increasing impact on elite mainland culture. Similarly, due to the opportunities provided by the international market for unofficial Chinese art and film, Maverick Artists were able to achieve a status, and an income, unknown to their brethren in other (now formerly) socialist nations. Due to the laxity of the state's policing of the arts and their own independent contact with the outside world, many of these artists have become a permanent, well-heeled subclass within China's cultural hierarchy. Some have been so successful (and here one thinks of *yuan*-rich artists like Wang Guangyi, Liu Wei, Liu Dahong, and Fang Lijun or filmmakers like Zhang Yuan and Wu Wenguang) that cultural novices who may have once been attracted to a career as state artists now become understudies in the dissident establishment or counterculture hierarchy.

One wonders how long it will be before China's leaders, too, widen the definition of social responsibility to embrace their own free-range Maverick Artists. After all, as Haraszti notes,

> [Dissidents] are nutrients, like broken blossoms in a garden. . . . We can utilise their aesthetic discoveries, just as we do the experiments of Western artists. We introduce their themes between the lines. We can create "valuable" and "organic" innovations from their unacceptable conceits. Thus do dissidents become the untraceable initiators of some of our legalised fashions, the unmentionable source of some of the "problems" that are solved by "rational debate." They make cultural politicians more sensitive and critics more clever; they lubricate social integration by their brave but self-annihilating acts. The more talented and flexible the state, the more pleasurably it can suck the dissidents' vital fluids into the organism of state culture.[52]

As I shall demonstrate in the following chapters, China's Maverick Artists have been cultivating their own gardens and helping the state farms of art in the process, not only by the provision of fodder but also in the experimental development of new hybrid cultural species.

CREATIVE GUIDELINES

Corporate or directed culture is by no means unique to socialist systems. In the West, Taiwan, and Japan, the publishing industry also acts as a regulating force on authors, as does the lucrative system of literary and art grants that are dispensed in such countries as Australia. But such simplistic comparisons—ones often made in criticism of writers like Haraszti—should not be allowed to detract from the importance of analyzing late-socialist culture. All corporations have their rules and regulations, their code of behavior and "hidden agenda." Haraszti writes: "We [that is, state artists] anticipate the next guideline (which we hope to shape ourselves), and this is not just wishful thinking. Today the consensus of state socialism is built out of the compromise of professionals, critics, planners, and artists."[53] In reformist China, a new element was added to the equation: that of global capitalism and the "socialist market economy."

Chinese writers anticipated new guidelines, ones that would see the end of the wasteful and punitive old-style campaigns of the Deng Xiaoping period, from the mid-1980s onward. Just such an official concoction finally appeared in February 1989, entitled "The Party Central Committee's Opinions on the Increased Enhancement of Art and Literature" (hereafter referred to as "Opinions") and printed in the *People's Daily* on 11 March.[54]

In the guise of a pseudolegal directive, this document was a milestone in the history of mainland arts insofar as it put an official imprimatur on the demilitarization of Chinese culture.[55] On 14 March, the *People's Daily* printed an editorial commentary on the document, pointing out its salient features.[56] The commentary remarked, for example, on a new managerial role for the Communist Party:

> This document clearly points out that the party is to take the role of political leadership and direction; it determines and modulates cultural policy, is in charge of ideological work, and is to ensure that culture develops in the correct direction. Leading party organs must take care to respect the peculiarities and [objective] laws of culture; it must minimize interference and involvement in debates concerning actual artistic works and scholastic questions. *Leaders must implement the party line and policies correctly, and they must be energetic in the pursuit and study of new means and ways by which culture can be directed under our present new historical circumstances,* and so forth.[57]

It was an ideal policy statement: so much of it was couched in such obfuscated language that it was open to a multiplicity of interpretations.[58] The following is a typical example of the type of catch-22 formulation germane to the document:

> All works of art—works that are not ideologically harmful, are artistically desirable and capable of giving people artistic pleasure and entertainment—are permissible as long as they do not contravene the constitution, the laws of the land, or the relevant interdictions of the state. [2:1]

Another classic example of reform-period doublethink came at the end of "Opinions":

> Our slogan remains: liberate thinking, seek truth from facts, unite as one, and look to the future. Those who are mired in ossified thinking as well as those who negate Marxism are an extreme minority. People should not denounce those who cannot ideologically keep up with the pace of reform as

ossified, nor should people label as bourgeois liberalization comments that are perhaps somewhat extreme. [5:2]

While it happily removed the party from the mire of day-to-day cultural control, the document emphasized the need for the leadership to engage actively in "the macromanipulation and guidance" of culture.[59] Certainly it was a progressive piece of writing in keeping with the civilian phase of socialist construction, rejecting once more the policy of "class struggle as the key link" and its concomitant narrow understanding of culture. In superficial terms, "Opinions" also looked a little different from Mao Zedong's "Yan'an Forum Talks on Art and Literature." Although the cultocrats who drafted the statement may have believed that "Opinions" could replace "Talks," in essence the two shared the same political lineage.[60] Whereas "Talks" emphasized "serving the workers, peasants, and soldiers," the updated formulation of the 1980s spoke of "serving the people and socialism,"[61] although Mao formulated his dogma during the anti-Japanese war and demanded that art and literature be used to "unite the people, educate the people, attack the enemy, and vanquish the enemy," the new peacetime statement said much the same thing without quite the panache of Maospeak.[62] The reformist equivalent of Mao's call can be found in item 2, section 1, of "Opinions":

[We must] exploit the varied capabilities of art and literature to arouse the national spirit, raise the quality of the broad masses, inspire people, beautify their spirit, and strive endlessly to satisfy the multifarious and multilayered cultural needs of the people, to edify, influence, educate, and excite the people for the sake of social progress. . . . We need warm paeans in favor of revolution, construction, and all beautiful things. At the same time we need [works that will] lash out at base and corrupt things. But their aim and underlying tone must be to enhance our national self-confidence and strengthen national cohesion, as well as being able to further socialist construction and the reform and open door policies.

At every turn of phrase, "Opinions" indulged in self-contradictory statements that we must presume involved a high level of complicity on the part of Wang Meng, the literary bureaucrat par excellence. Indeed, Haraszti describes the role of literary technocrats like Wang Meng in the following way:

The professional writer knows that the right to speak carries with it responsibility. His writing must be not only beautiful but also useful: his care with these two aspects is what makes him a writer. . . .
Long gone are the days when artists waited, in happy or frightened ignorance, for successive instructions concerning speedy fulfillment of the five-year plan! Today every artist is a minor politician of culture. We prepare

our innovations so as to bid competitively for the creation of an official aesthetic. In our eyes the state represents not a monolithic body of rules but rather a live network of lobbies. We play with it, we know how to use it, and we have allies and enemies at the controls. . . .

Progressive censorship does not demand from us a vision of the perfect society, or even evidence of ideological fealty, but rather proof of sincere participation. Its chief wish is that social unity be preserved. Its tolerance, although not unlimited, is considerable. Its scope is determined not by autocratic fiat but by the flexibility of minds that are willing to cooperate.[63]

In April 1989, the *People's Daily* commentator said much the same about the rights and duties of the state artist:

Cultural workers are engaged in a special type of intellectual activity and enjoy considerable freedom in what and how they write. The party no longer demands that culture be subordinated to politics; even less does it demand it fulfill temporary, concrete, or direct political tasks. Cultural workers, however, have a duty to appreciate the social significance of culture and to clarify their position vis-à-vis personal social responsibility.[64]

Again, this statement can fruitfully be compared with other comments by Haraszti on post-Stalinist art:

Post-Stalinist art shares a similar objective with Stalinist art: to strengthen social integration. The difference is that civilian or soft aesthetics are designed not for an audience newly incorporated into the socialist state but for a populace born into it. Socialization, not conquest, is the underlying assumption of the new aesthetic.

. . . Politically, the post-Stalinist artist is no longer expected to declare his allegiance. His loyalty is assumed. Under Stalinism, everyone was guilty until proven innocent. Today, it is just the reverse. We anticipate reforms, read between the lines, and criticize society as intimately as do members of the Politburo. If we seem to break with the strictures of Stalinist tradition, it is only to better effect its intentions. Still, every work of art must somehow prove that it neither opposes the primacy of state-planning nor harbors plans of its own against the existing order. Only constructive neutrality is required. . . .

In the post-Stalinist era, solipsistic art is not prohibited because the state demands that every work of art demonstrate overt political engagement. The prohibition is a prerequisite: the work of art must find a relationship with its social context. It must seek a place in directed culture. And frankly, doing so is not too difficult. As long as we do not directly criticize the bureaucracy [read the party], its attitudes, or its discourse, we are already constructive. The careful (and clever) artist himself chooses the aspect of his art that will resonate with the social context. An ostensibly ambiguous or aesthetically neutral work of art is as acceptable as one that is unabashedly progovernment. The mere possibility of constructive interpretation is enough to establish a link between the artist and the state. It then falls to the critics—those chroniclers of context—to baptize and inaugurate this linkage.[65]

Haraszti talks of state artists becoming board members in the corporation of the state, partaking of the wealth as shareholders in the cultural enterprise. "Opinions," interestingly enough, while generally affecting the shopworn diction of the military past—there is the usual talk of "the ranks of writers and artists," "raising high the banner of patriotism and socialism," and "tireless struggle"—was in keeping with the general economic rationalization of the times. In the document there is much ado about "establishing and perfecting the socialist cultural market and giving correct direction to mass consumption of cultural products." Behind this rhetoric were the realities of economic reform.

Again, Haraszti comments that while under capitalism, products can be divided into the categories of *unmarketable, nonprofitable,* and *blockbuster,* in post-Stalinist/Maoist socialism, culture is classified as *prohibited, tolerated,* and *supported.* During the 1980s, it gradually dawned on Chinese artists that if they could not produce popular works that would sell—something that become increasingly worrisome for "serious" writers—then they must rely on state support: a monthly stipend, publication in subsidized magazines, or even grants. Now that market forces played such a decisive role in the cultural production line, even some of the more liberal artists expressed outrage at the undermining of their traditional role as "engineers of human souls." While popular literature—variously *dazhong, tongsu, disu,* or *meisu wenxue* in mainland parlance—became profitable, serious writing, *chun* or *yansu wenxue,* found itself threatened, resulting in 1995 in a "call to arms" by self-proclaimed idealistic younger writers (see chapter 11, "Kowtowing to the Vulgar"). It could also be argued that the stance of the "angry young man of letters" who rails against the impotence of official culture and the sellout of serious writers is merely a pose that fits snugly into a certain market niche.

For a time the answer in Hungary, as Haraszti observed, was to force commercial culture to subsidize highbrow art.[66] In fact, during the 1980s, many mainland publishers did just that.[67] Under the political and economic entrepreneurial talents of Wu Tianming, the head of the Xi'an Film Studio in the late 1980s, that studio became the home of the "new wave" movie industry and was able to finance commercial flops like Chen Kaige's *The Teacher* and Tian Zhuangzhuang's *Horse Thief* on the back of popular cinema nasties. Similarly, in the mid-1990s, Tian Zhuangzhuang, having been elevated to a position of authority at the

Beijing Film Studio, attempted to do the same for younger directors. But there are limits to which the state would condone a return to undirected popular culture at any given time. Cultural campaigns, like the 1996 antispiritual pollution purge, or the ceaseless publishing rectifications—five in Beijing in a three-year period according to 1988 statistics published in the *Beijing Daily*, for example— were one way the state found to regulate the situation.[68] This strategy could, however, backfire when intellectual magazines were also banned on the basis that they "threatened stability," for it forced writers who were eager to be involved in some form of official discourse underground or into salons, something that could occasionally disturb the peace.[69] Indeed, after the Beijing massacre of 1989, officials in the party's Department of Propaganda told the editor of the prominent liberal journal *Reading* that one of the reasons his magazine was tolerated was because the authorities wanted to keep an eye on intellectual malcontents and his publication provided an ideal "window on the opposition."

THE VELVET BASTILLE

On 3–4 June 1989, the People's Liberation Army (PLA) crushed the mass protest movement in Beijing, and similar demonstrations were quelled in cities throughout the country. In the following months, the leading engineers of the Chinese velvet prison discussed in this chapter were toppled from power. Zhao Ziyang, Hu Qili, Yan Mingfu, Wang Meng, Liu Xinwu, and many others were removed from their posts, and a cultural purge was begun. Many of the writers mentioned here were, for a time, silenced, imprisoned or forced into exile or hiding.

The actions of China's rulers would certainly have been repugnant to writers like Miklós Haraszti, but as I hope to demonstrate, developments in mainland China after 4 June 1989 did not necessarily negate Haraszti's paradigm for soft culture. While during the early 1990s they lurched at times toward militant socialism in the realm of ideology, party leaders still preached reform and the economic and cultural pluralism to which it had given birth.

General indicators showed that work on the Chinese velvet prison continued apace in the 1990s, and the long-term prognosis was good. Chinese party leaders were tireless in their claims that China's "national peculiarities," its *guoqing* (discussed in chapter 10, "To Screw Foreigners Is Patriotic"), made the wholesale adoption of foreign socialism—and presumably its theatrical late-1980s denouement—impracticable. Some local intellectuals also reoriented themselves over time to critique globalization, liberal thought, and pro-Western attitudes. Given that in the 1990s the Communist Party of China remained determined to be different, before speculating about the future we would do well to consider what unique materials it had on hand to construct a "velvet prison with Chinese characteristics."[70]

The purges of the 1980s and particularly the cultural maelstrom of the early 1990s that will be outlined here further liberated artists from the embrace of the state and allowed them to move closer to the market. But it was a regulated market with a Janus mien and gimlet eyes set on both mutable party policy and the shifting whims of investors and consumers. In terms of literary output, the evidence suggested that many writers and artists remained snug in the self-imposed confines of progressive censorship.[71]

Many state artists were eager to take their rightful place once more on the ship of state, not as self-important navigators at the helm, but ranked in position along with party censors, salesmen, and accountants. How long would it be before the accountant once more made the censor's work impossible; how many artful dissidents were now hidden in their serried ranks? As they played the market and pursued politics, perhaps they were giving another meaning to the expression "velvet revolution."

CHAPTER TWO

An Iron Fist in a Velvet Glove

Deng Xiaoping advanced a new policy on the arts at the opening session of the Fourth Congress of Chinese Writers and Artists in October 1979. It was the first time that such a gathering had been convened since the Cultural Revolution. Many who had participated in the previous congress had not survived the intervening years. Deng addressed the meeting, and his statement was hailed as epoch making:

> We must persevere with Comrade Mao Zedong's policy to ensure that our literature and art serves the broad masses of the People. First and foremost, it must serve the workers, peasants, and soldiers. We must persevere with the policies of allowing a hundred flowers to blossom, abandon the old in favor of the new, use foreign things to serve China, and make the past serve the present. In terms of cultural creation, we advocate the free development of different styles and genres. In the realm of cultural theory, we advocate free debate between different points of view and academic schools.[1]

Although anointed by these words, the creators of the new age of mainland Chinese culture tried to take the arts in different directions. A decade later, when a battle over the fate of official culture developed in the wake of the 4 June Beijing massacre, Deng's name and words were invoked once more, this time to justify a cultural purge.[2] The new cultural bureaucrats who had come to power during the 1980s were driven from office. They were replaced in most cases by a group of old-style party ideologues and veteran propagandists who did their best to rein in the artistic license that had seen the growth of cultural diversity on an unparalleled scale in the history of the People's Republic of China.

Immediately after 4 June, a number of prominent writers found themselves the victims of official bans. A range of books were also interdicted in secret publishing circulars.[3] Distributed "internally" (that is, to a restricted audience of publishing organizations) throughout the country, the *Indexes of Banned Books and*

Periodicals[4] listed not only politically sensitive works by purged writers but also the titles of soft porn and books that had been published for the black market. Thus, a biography of the ousted party leader Zhao Ziyang and a philosophical tract by formerly lauded official writers like Li Zehou[5] were banned along with titles like AIDS *and Gay Men* and *Confessions of a Fallen Woman*. In the realm of bourgeois liberalism, ideological laxity and moral turpitude went hand in hand. Three volumes of the indexes were produced in rapid succession during the months following 4 June.[6]

More than books and journals, however, were affected by the purge. Some writers were detained by the police for involvement with (or "the instigation of," *shandong*, as the authorities described it) the student protests.[7] Others went into exile, and for a time there were rumors that a number of prominent novelists preferred to "put down their pens" rather than cooperate with the new leadership.

Despite the bans, it took time for the purge to have a direct impact on literary journals and book production. *Please Don't Treat Me Like a Human*, the Beijing comic writer Wang Shuo's most overt political satire, for example, was serialized in a leading Nanjing literary journal starting in August 1989, with the last installment appearing in December (see chapter 4, "The Apotheosis of the *Liumang*," for details).[8] And months passed before the cultural bureaucracy was cleared of liberals like Wang Meng, the man appointed to oversee the arts during Hu Yaobang's heyday in 1986.

The logic of the post–June 1989 purge demanded a ruthless campaign. Previous efforts to contain the unregulated arts world in 1983 and 1987 had failed, in particular because party leaders argued that cultural purges could endanger the economic reforms. In 1989, things were different. The authorities claimed that the mass protests had been sparked, among other things, by corrupting capitalist values. Liu Baiyu, a senior party novelist, summed up this view at a cultural forum in July 1989 organized by the party's Department of Propaganda:

> [Over the years] the revolutionary and progressive cultural tradition of the party has been negated. People have supported the wholesale adoption of Western bourgeois values, resulting in the takeover of the cultural sphere and the frenzied propagation of bourgeois liberalization. The People's spirit has been polluted by all of this, their souls sullied. . . . what began as an ideological transformation ultimately found expression in political action [that is, the student protests].[9]

Writer-officials like Liu Baiyu demanded a clean sweep of the arts. It soon became evident, however, that organizational and economic realities made this all but impossible. Furthermore, as we will see, the nature of Chinese factional politics, the inherent contradictions of the reform policies themselves, widespread ideological disaffection, and the sheer tactical difficulties of instituting such a purge frustrated at every turn the older bureaucrats and their younger opportunistic supporters.

In 1990, a number of exiled writers and critics declared that after 4 June, new literary developments and growth in the mainland were impossible[10] and that China had entered the equivalent of a cultural "ice age."[11] They were woefully out of touch.

OUT WITH THE NEW, IN WITH THE OLD

During the years of Wang Meng's reign as minister of culture (1986–1989), rigid pro-Maoist literary figures had suffered general derision and rejection at the hands of the ascendant litterateurs. Wang's "faction," *bang*—to use a convenient shorthand for an amorphous and ambitious crowd of mostly middle-aged writers—included figures like the novelists Liu Xinwu, Zhang Jie, Shen Rong, and Wang Anyi and critics like Liu Zaifu and Li Tuo. Older "leftist" writers (that is, devotees of the official socialist realist canon) enjoyed little of the media attention that was so readily lavished on these younger and more controversial figures. They also missed out on cultural junkets to the West and were not offered the kind of lucrative publishing contracts in Hong Kong and Taiwan that were given to ideologically more adventurous writers.

The aged poet Zang Kejia, a hack establishment worthy who had been staunchly opposed to new literary trends from the early 1980s onward, summed up the sentiment of this group during the earlier 1987 cultural purge:

> There is excessive praise for middle-aged and young writers on the literary scene at the moment. A situation exists in which the young are being used to oppress veteran writers. . . . Just look at them; they're intoxicated with themselves. They think that the more incomprehensible a work is, the better. All the classics and [socialist] realist works have been attacked as conservative and dated. Then one has these younger writers who are constantly flitting off overseas, and it is becoming increasingly difficult for older writers even to get a look in. It's even hard for us to get our work published. We hope that all workers in the arts will undertake a renewed study of Chairman Mao's "Yan'an Forum Talks on Art and Literature" and thereby further their ideological remolding and enhance their struggle against bourgeois liberalism.[12]

After 4 June, articles in the *People's Daily*, the party newspaper that articulated the new political line, supported the grievances of older comrades like Zang

Kejia. They claimed that whenever writers had raised their voices in opposition to the prevalent liberalism of the late 1980s, the party's then general secretary Zhao Ziyang had "repeatedly and insolently interfered with their protests, resulting in their being stifled, attacked, vilified, and slandered."[13] When the old school had a chance to take their revenge, they showed no hesitation.[14]

The 1988 television series *River Elegy*—the most widely watched and debated documentary ever produced on the mainland—was the first victim of the cultural purge. The multipart documentary series was the result of a combined effort involving academics, writers, and television directors and technicians. A six-hour-long meditation on the historical origins of the state of China in the 1980s, *River Elegy* introduced a mass audience to debates about politics, culture, and economic reform that had previously been restricted to intellectual circles. By juxtaposing images and statements, along with a dramatic narrative intoned like a party propaganda film, the producers created a work with a barely disguised subtext that equated Maoist-Stalinist political and economic orthodoxy with state Confucianism and traditional culture. The result of this admixture, the series' creators claimed, was a disastrous formula for the future of China. They suggested that the solution to the nation's problems was to abandon the traditional inland, earth-bound worldview (as symbolized in particular by the Great Wall and agrarian culture) for a revolutionary orientation linked to the sea, commerce, and contact with the outside world. The series was overtly polemic and unabashedly in favor of Zhao Ziyang.[15]

Following its first screening in June 1988, numerous laudatory articles were published in the mainland press,[16] and the narration was hurriedly produced in book form.[17] Some viewers wrote to China Central TV suggesting that the booklet be issued as reading material in political study sessions throughout the country.[18] But many viewers were outraged by the series. To question the value of the nation's most beloved symbols—the Great Wall and the Yellow River—and cast aspersions on Confucianism was, they claimed, tantamount to cultural nihilism. The debate surrounding *River Elegy* soon spilled over into Hong Kong and Taiwan and was also featured in the international Chinese press. In their dyspeptic attacks on the series, it became evident that, for the first time, traditionalists in favor of the five thousand years of Chinese cultural excellence in Taiwan and stalwart revolutionaries in the Communist Party shared the same ground as well as a common rhetoric.

After Zhao Ziyang's fall from grace in mid-1989, critics of *River Elegy* came to the fore again, claiming that their opposition to the series had been muzzled by the "bourgeois liberal press." The documentary was identified by propagandists as being a central feature of the corrupting "microclimate," *xiao qihou*, that had directly contributed to the nationwide unrest of 1989.[19] Zhao himself was criticized for having promoted the series and suggesting to foreign visitors that they watch it to gain a better understanding of China.[20]

The official denunciation of *River Elegy* was launched in mid-July 1989 when the *People's Daily* published a lengthy attack on the program that had reportedly been written in October 1988 but was subsequently suppressed by the series' supporters in the media.[21] This was followed in early August by the *Beijing Daily*, the leading newspaper of the capital, which was firmly in control of conservative forces, launching a column entitled "The Hundred Fallacies of *River Elegy*."[22]

River Elegy was attacked for "negating national traditions, disparaging the history of the Chinese revolution and socialist construction, propagating wholesale Westernization and playing a prominent role in confusing the thinking of the whole nation." Leading orthodox cultural figures claimed that works like *River Elegy* were proof positive that the cultural scene was a disaster area, *zhongzaiqu*, that had suffered the depredations of bourgeois liberalization. Along with the editors of pro-Maoist journals and research institutes in the capital, they now called for a new Yan'an-style cultural rectification.[23] The first such rectification begun in the early 1940s in the Communist-occupied base of Yan'an in Shaanxi Province, West China, had seen the purge of dissenting writers and the establishment of Maoist orthodoxy.[24]

River Elegy's opponents first criticized Zhao Ziyang's laissez-faire stance on culture, an approach that advocated "less intervention and less involvement," *shao ganyu, shao jieru,* in the arts.[25] What they wanted was firm leadership and for the party to reassert its control over all areas of culture. Soon afterward, the party's Department of Propaganda called for renewed ideological work and supported a rectification of the arts.[26]

Despite the exaggerated tone of these public pronouncements, the general style of the bureaucratic shakeup was one of "velvet terror." Wang Meng, for example, was not purged but "allowed to retire" from the Ministry of Culture in early September 1989. He remarked that his "soft landing," *ruan zhaolu,* had been facilitated by a request he had made in late 1988 to retire from politics and concentrate on writing (see "A Storm in a Rice Bowl" in chapter 11, "Kowtowing to the Vulgar," for further details). The new acting cultural minister was the poet-playwright He Jingzhi, a vice director of the Department of Propaganda whose reputation rested on his coauthorship of the 1940s Yan'an-period agitprop opera *The White-Haired Girl*. He was a "temporary" replacement who lasted in the job for more than two years.[27] Eventually, as the bureaucracy was re-formed, liberal policies were also denounced. In early 1990, the cultural "tolerance, generosity, laxity" promoted by Hu Yaobang came under attack,[28] as did the policy of the "two freedoms" (*liangge ziyou*: creative freedom and critical freedom), announced in late 1988.[29] As one critic now dared to write, linking cultural liberalism with American influence and counterrevolution,

> some years back, there were people both in and outside China who praised some of our comrades [that is, Hu Yaobang and Zhao Ziyang] to the skies. . . . But the more praise they got, the more enthusiastic our comrades became about being tolerant, lax, and eventually permissive. They allowed bad works to flood the market; then they felt that it was all right to abandon the true path of Marxism-Leninism and socialism and even acceptable to make fun of party and state leaders in public forums. That led to people giving speeches, pamphleteering, and engaging in counterrevolutionary instigation, the end result of which was the turmoil [of 1989] and the counterrevolutionary riot [of 3–4 June].
>
> . . . An individual can think and write whatever he wishes, but if he publishes his work and has an effect on others, in particular on young people, then that author will have to accept the strictures of the law and official regulations. There is no such thing as absolute freedom of speech. If you preach "tolerance, generosity, laxity" in contravention of these realities, you are guilty of ideological compromise and defeatism.[30]

In early 1990, the winners in the new literary dispensation attended the launching of the journal *Mainstay*, the major post–June 1989 vehicle for orthodox cultured opinion.[31] It subsequently published a full list of right-thinking literary figures, mostly men in their sixties and older who tried throughout the early 1990s to limit the artistic freedoms engendered by the economic reforms.[32]

THE BAODING CONFERENCE

In April 1990, the new cultural mini-czars[33] held a celebratory conference at Baoding in Hebei Province.[34] The meeting reaffirmed the orthodox message of an earlier gathering, the April 1987 Zhuozhou Arts Conference that had been convened by conservative forces after the fall of Hu Yaobang to fight against the tide of bourgeois liberalism.[35] In early 1990, it was revealed that Zhao Ziyang had frustrated the comrades at the 1987 conference, and now, with Zhao out of the way, the participants felt that it was high time they took a stand against the ideological decay rampant in the arts world.[36] Both meetings attacked cultural pluralism and affirmed the need to "cleanse" the art world of liberalization and encourage "keynote" (*zhu xuanlü*, politically correct) socialist culture. "Keynote culture" was first enunciated by the Film Bureau chief, Teng Jinxian, in early 1990 and became the watchword for official Chinese arts throughout the 1990s.[37]

According to He Jingzhi, "keynote culture" consisted of "cultural works that reflect socialism, give expression to communist ideals and the spirit of the socialist age, reveal the main contradictions in the socialist era, and depict the new socialist man and that can fill people with enthusiasm and create unity among the masses."[38]

Not everyone was adept at producing works that fulfilled all these requirements, and at the Baoding meeting it was noted, presumably with glee, that "some people have indeed stopped writing. . . . They need to go through a period of reflection and self-readjustment. As for the 'cultural elite,' they have never been interested in serving the People . . . and their absence is no loss to our socialist cultural enterprise."[39]

Thus, by mid-1990, a revamped Maoist cultural line officially held sway in China, and a loose coalition of conservatives was in charge of the nation's central arts bureaucracy as well as its chief propaganda and cultural organs. Their control extended to a number of newspapers and magazines. In the literary sphere, these publications included the specialist weeklies *Literary Gazette* and *China Culture News* and the journals *Works and Contention* and *Literary Theory and Criticism* and the new journal *Mainstay*.[40] The victors in the purge published a gloating editorial in the major national literary monthly, *People's Literature*—formerly a bastion of Wang Meng's influence edited by the novelist Liu Xinwu—in which they said, "We will no longer allow this forum for the literature of the People to be monopolized by a 'spiritual aristocracy'."[41] "Above all," the new editors continued,

> we treasure our younger readers. Today they are but buds bursting with the coming spring, but in the future they will blossom as the builders of a strong and prosperous modern nation. A basic standard by which to judge a responsible writer is to see if he or she can accept the sacred responsibility of nurturing the young with sunlight and dew, so that their souls can soar freely and they can become the inheritors of the socialist cause. Or are they trying to corrupt our young people with putrescent filth and convert them into creatures who will attempt to bury socialism?[42]

It soon became obvious, however, that such strict and, by 1990, risible, ideologically correct control was limited to this small number of publications. Considerable editorial diversity existed elsewhere. This was particularly evident in the provinces far from the control of Beijing's cultural bureaucracy. Major regional literary journals like *Zhongshan* (Nanjing), *Harvest* (Shanghai), *Huacheng* (Guangzhou), and *Literary Discussion* (Tianjin)[43] continued to flourish.

Nor was the politics of revenge marked with unalloyed success. The controversial Shanghai *Wenhui Monthly*, a popular magazine that had published many of the now-banned writers, was closed down in mid-1990 amid rumors of conservative pressure. Soon thereafter, however, many of its authors turned to a new weekly broadsheet, the *Wenhui Daily Enlarged Edition*,[44] and the *Wenhui Book Review*, which, for example, introduced the works of Milan Kundera and reported on cultural developments that were generally ignored in the Beijing cultural media. These papers became a staple for elite culture—and it is noteworthy that the bastion for this "liberalism" was the southern city of Shanghai—until the effects of the cultural purge in Beijing passed in 1992 and major new publishing ventures were started in the capital in 1993.

The reasons for the development of this anomalous situation were complex. The repeated insistence by party leaders that there would not be another mass movement or purge of culture like those seen in the past limited the extent to which any campaign could be anything more than a cosmetic, and administrative, readjustment. The burgeoning mass publication market and the reduction of state subsidies through the 1980s had also given publishers greater freedom to pursue popular tastes and trends rather than slavishly follow the directives of the leadership.

Apart from the political practicalities and limitations already discussed, the variety of cultural expression in China, the sheer mass of newspapers, journals, television and radio programs, music, and film made it increasingly difficult for the authorities to police culture as they once did. The cadre of censors was itself changing radically. Younger, better-educated, and more sophisticated editors were giving the old system a new face. In the previous chapter we explored Haraszti's view that self-censorship becomes an art form. From now on, we will also see that when state paranoia is reproduced in the psyche of the subject, "the state can look forward to a future in which the bureaucracies of supervision can be allowed to wither away, their function having been, in effect, privatized."[45]

LITERARY LIP SERVICE

As was to be expected during such a major political campaign as the 1989 purge, a volume of the leader-of-the-moment's pronouncements on culture was hurriedly produced. In late October 1989, *Deng Xiaoping on Art and Literature* appeared, and newspapers reported that local authorities and writers were eagerly studying it well into 1990.[46]

A far more serious task, however, was the need to reaffirm the party's traditional cultural canon. In 1989, a scholar by the name of Xia Zhongyi had published an article in *Literary Review* that questioned the importance and validity of Mao Zedong's May 1942 "Yan'an Forum Talks on Art and Literature." The "Talks" had been enshrined as holy writ and became the basis for party culture and post-1949 arts policy.[47] After the purge of Liu Zaifu, the editor in chief of *Literary Review*, the journal hastily published a series of attacks on Xia.[48] The basic tenor of these was expressed succinctly by Zhang Jiong, an orthodox party literary historian from the Chinese Academy of Social Sciences. Zhang said that Xia Zhongyi had "in reality wantonly misinterpreted and belittled Mao Zedong's cultural thought. He shows no respect for his forbears or for historical reality. Many of his arguments are made in the most arbitrary fashion, and they unabashedly reveal a shoddy style of scholarship completely lacking in serious intent."[49]

Other organs of the ruling faction engaged in a similarly one-sided "debate" in favor of Mao's cultural thought. They staunchly rebutted critiques of Mao that had appeared in the late 1980s, in particular that of the Shanghai commentator Li Jie published in early 1989. In his "On the Mao Zedong Phenomenon—Notes from a Survivor," Li wrote:

> It is a truism to say that you get the government you deserve. The collective stupidity of the Chinese meant that they got, and they deserved nothing more than to get, a ruler like Mao Zedong . . . .
>
> Mao was a very rare revolutionary leader. We can compare the significance of Mao Zedong in Chinese history to the importance of Hitler in world history. It is a creative thing. In a sense, modernism would not have come about without Hitler. Similarly, Mao created the conditions for both modernism and postmodernism in China.[50]

Silenced by the media purge begun in June 1989, and in some cases, under investigation on suspicion of counterrevolutionary activities, writers like Li Jie were unable to defend themselves or reply to the flood of invective that was now unleashed. Their critics praised the eternal importance of the "Yan'an Talks" and denounced in outraged tones all attempts that had been made throughout the 1980s to reevaluate the "Talks" or question the permanent relevance of Mao Zedong Thought to Chinese literature.[51] Jin Sheng, the author of some of the most colorful screeds against cultural liberalism, railed:

> Confronted with the kind of vituperative language [that is found in essays like Li Jie's reflections on Mao Zedong], it is impossible to understand how such things could appear in the pages of a socialist cultural journal run by the Communist Party of China. . . . [Well may people say,] "The Communist Party is subsidizing magazines that denounce the Communist Party." It is a situation that even the scheming politicians of bourgeois nations would find hard to comprehend. Yet this is just what has been going in our avowedly socialist cultural sphere! What a cruel irony! And how truly shocking![52]

After June 1989, the former mayor of Tianjin, Li Ruihuan, was appointed as the new cadre in the Politburo responsible for propaganda and the arts. Li replaced Hu Qili, the ousted cohort of both Hu Yaobang and Zhao Ziyang. He was a model worker, originally a carpenter, who had reportedly excelled as a moderate administrator before his promotion to work in Beijing. Although he was the ostensible ideological taskmaster in the Politburo, it soon became evident that Li Ruihuan was reluctant to pursue any radical policies. His approach to cultural issues first moderated and then undermined the extremist purge of culture that the organizations under his control, the Ministry of Culture and Department of Propaganda, advocated.

Li was quick to emphasize the need to oppose "ossification," *jianghua*, a code word for neo-Maoist ideological narrowness, while still ostensibly pursuing policies to stall bourgeois liberalization.[53] In late 1989, he concentrated his energies on the antipornography campaign that had been under way for some time and used it to play down the need for a widespread cultural purge.[54] Then, in early 1990, he turned his attention to promoting national culture, *hongyang minzu wenhua*. Rather than support the attacks that extremists were making on the contemporary arts, Li Ruihuan promoted a less overtly ideological approach and said it was his task to encourage an environment that would favor a new cultural flowering, *fanrong wenyi*.[55] As he remarked to a gathering of *People's Daily* journalists in late April 1990, "Ideological work has to be carried out in such a way that people can accept what you're saying. Only if they're willing to listen to you, will it have any effect. If people run away at the very sight of you, how can you achieve anything?"[56]

Li Ruihuan's strategy would have had the tacit support of his Politburo colleagues, and it effectively diverted the entire course of the anti–bourgeois liberalization movement.[57] However, it was the very same kind of balancing act that had led both Hu Yaobang and Zhao Ziyang to grief before him. In June 1990, the revived cultural mummies under He Jingzhi were further enlivened by the wave of conservative confidence generated by the April Baoding meeting, at which they had openly denounced the liberalism of the Wang Meng era. It was thus in a testy mood of suspicion that they decided to take Li Ruihuan to task for his moderation. In late June 1990, *China Culture*, a twice-weekly newspaper run by the Ministry of Culture, produced an issue whose first two pages were devoted to "Directives from the Center Regarding Ideological Questions." Dozens of quotations from speeches by Deng Xiaoping, Jiang Zemin, and Li Peng were reproduced, but Li Ruihuan, the man responsible for party ideology, was most prominent by his absence.[58] An accompanying editorial was also pointedly critical of the ideological confusion that Li Ruihuan's soft line was presumed to encourage:

> There are certain individuals who chose to ignore official decisions by the center, as well as speeches made by leading comrades who represent the

center. They anxiously await some so-called new direction, and when it does not come, they are not above chasing the wind or clutching at shadows. They try to fabricate one out of thin air. . . . They believe they can see a wisp of cloud on the horizon and speculate that this may presage a new storm [in their favor]. But all this merely serves to confuse and undermine the martial spirit. Such people pose a serious threat. It is such an atmosphere that creates ideological confusion, one that can all too readily be exploited by bourgeois liberal elements and political schemers.[59]

The confrontation between Li Ruihuan and his opponents continued in the party-controlled media well into 1991. What at the time seemed like a run-of-the-mill power struggle had, however, far more important consequences for mainland cultural life. The long-winded, elliptical, and often esoteric statements on culture that were churned out during 1989–1991 told another story, about the undoing of an entrenched style of official cultural control. The dialectics of contemporary culture in China—a realm caught between political requirements and economic realities, ideological strictures and public pressure—created the mayhem that cultural figures of every hue set out to manipulate and exploit to their own advantage during the 1990s. The party's main ideological foes were the imperatives that lay at the very heart of its own reform policies. Never before had dialectics so closely reflected the definition given to it by the Soviet philosopher Alexander Zinoviev: "Dialectics is a way of moving blindfold in an unknown empty space filled with imaginary obstacles; of moving without support and without resistance. And without an objective."[60]

THE LITERATURE OF POLEMICS AND SATIRE

As Zinoviev also noted in his classic work, *Homo Sovieticus*, the literature of denunciation is both an important cultural by-product of socialism and a peculiarly rich form of writing. "It is the only branch of human culture," he observed, "in which people can achieve some competence without training or literary ability . . . the denunciation is the most profound, comprehensive and sincere form of personal self-expression."[61] Some of the most colorful and entertaining writing of modern Chinese literature belongs to this genre. In the Cultural Revolution, denunciations in the form of secret depositions to the authorities, big-character posters, and defamatory articles and editorials were poured forth gratis or for a pittance and with a measure of revolutionary zeal. In comparison, the post-June output of the literature of indictment in China proved to be quite disappointing.

Although there was no dearth of people willing to write attacks on vanquished public figures, there were rumors that in keeping with the new economism of socialist culture, large sums of money had to be offered for quality screeds to be produced. Nonetheless, the major denunciations, *da pipan wenzhang*, published in official newspapers lacked the flair, passion, and rhetorical flights that had characterized the genre in the past. Marginally more interesting were the hefty "cut-and-paste" volumes like *Liu Xiaobo: The Man and His Machinations* published in 1989, followed by *The True Mien of China's Contemporary "Elite"* in 1990 and *The Machinations of the Exiled "Elite"* in mid-1991.[62] All these books were premised on the assumption that the writers, students, businessmen, and intellectuals lumped together and excoriated in their pages for their involvement with the 1989 protests constituted a viable threat to the People's Republic of China. Despite this, the editors of these works included for the reader's reference a large number of articles by the people being denounced. Many of these "negative teaching materials," *fanmian jiaocai*, as they were known, were actually balanced and rational critiques of the government and the party. The inclusion of this material allowed many readers to become acquainted with the ideas of writers who, before the purge, were known only in academic circles. Presumably, party propagandists were so anxious to vilify their enemies that they failed to consider that their readers might be more readily convinced by the impassioned arguments of the victims of the purge than by the shrill denunciations that prefaced them. This is not to discount the possibility, however, that disgruntled editors were exploiting the revolutionary zeal of the proto-Maoists to spread illicit political propaganda in the news media.

The spiteful yet entertaining essays of the deputy head of the party's Department of Propaganda, Xu Weicheng (a former Cultural Revolution–period propagandist who, because of the odium of the past, now hid behind the alias Yu Xinyan),[63] and Ouyang Shan, a veteran Yan'an-period literary figure—the only writer Mao spoke of positively in his "Yan'an Talks"—were significant contributions to the dying art of literary denunciation.[64] Both authors, for example, fulminated against the bourgeois machinations of the writers of *River Elegy*, the spread of ideological canker, and the dangers of free speech. With attention to rhetorical flourish at the expense of logic and a rich use of political jargon and vituperative, anachronistic cliché, the style of the essays was highly comic and possibly even worthy of being called "revolutionary camp." Xu Weicheng was particularly noteworthy for articles attacking the imprisoned dissident Wei Jingsheng as "China's Judas Iscariot," lambasting astrophysicist Fang Lizhi for cowardly finding shelter under a "foreign umbrella" (when he sought political asylum in the U.S. embassy in Beijing during the Beijing massacre), and comparing advocates of Western-style liberalism in China with AIDS sufferers in the West.[65] Produced in the time-honored style of mud-raking leftist writers of 1930s Shanghai, these slim volumes represented the most significant batch of polemic essays of the 1989 purge.

SCAPEGOATS AND "TOLERATED OPPOSITION"

A handful of scapegoats blamed for the cultural mayhem of the late 1980s were thus featured in the mass media. It was very much a case of naming the usual suspects. Liu Xiaobo, the official state "nihilist," won permanent fame for, among other things, being quoted as suggesting that China could benefit, as Hong Kong did, from a lengthy stint as a colony.[66] Liu Zaifu, the tedious establishment Marxist literary critic, was castigated ad nauseam for his obfuscating writings on the literary obvious,[67] and Wang Meng, the former minister, known for his slick and amusing essays on the cultural scene published under the pen name Yang Yu (literally "Sun Shower"), was repeatedly decried for his advocacy of cultural pluralism. Their main critics were Li Zhun—known in literary circles as "little Li Zhun," to distinguish him from the older novelist of the same name—an ideologue with the Propaganda Department, who energetically produced long, lackluster articles,[68] and Dong Xuewen, an academic hack from Peking University called the "He Xin of the literary sphere."[69] These writers eagerly filled the breach created by the banning or, in some cases, temporary silencing of many of China's leading critics and writers.

With a slew of major cultural journals and newspapers now under strict control, minor publications were able to take advantage of the situation. Whereas in the publishing boom of 1988, these "down-market" magazines often had difficulty attracting the nation's literary glitterati, after 1989 they provided a necessary forum for the frustrated writers doing as much as the official purge to "democratize" elite culture and force serious writers into the market. Smaller papers in Beijing and throughout the provinces also took up the slack and published essays and stories by a wide range of disaffected prominent writers and academics.

Faced with the satirical attacks of people like Xu Weicheng, opponents of political orthodoxy also resorted to the casual essay, a popular vehicle for literary debate since the apogee of the satirical essay, zawen, in the mid-1930s. The leading Guangzhou bimonthly Essays grew in size to support its new writers, many of whom had declined to cooperate with the Beijing authorities. Its pages now carried everything from hidden political comment in mock-classical poetry and prose works with pointed titles like "Musings on the Aftereffects of the 'Cultural Revolution'," to pungent essays and memoirs by such literary veterans as Xiao

Qian, Shi Zhicun, Duanmu Hongliang, and Ke Ling, men who had been active from before the Communist takeover in 1949.[70]

Even literary renegades were welcome in *Essays'* pages. For example, it ran pointed articles by the woman writer Dai Houying, a controversial figure since the publication of her early 1980s novel *Oh Humanity!* and a close associate of dissident figures like Wang Ruowang.[71] Dai had relinquished the editorship of *The Square*, an exiles' literary journal in the United States, to return home to Shanghai for family reasons in late 1990, and publication in journals like *Essays* revived her literary career on the mainland.[72] Wang Meng also used the journal as one of the outlets for the polished and often tongue-in-cheek articles that he began producing in prodigious quantities following his ouster. Even humorous anecdotes by the renowned artist Huang Yongyu, a man who went into voluntary exile in Hong Kong after his cartoon attacks on the Chinese Premier Li Peng in 1989—one famously featuring Li as a tortoise, *wangba*, or "bastard"— were regularly published in the early 1990s issues of *Essays*, complete with illustrations.[73] If the post 1989 literary witch-hunt had been pursued with the fervor of purges past, when even the vaguest hint of innuendo was taken to be a sign of counterrevolution, dozens if not hundreds of authors and editors would have been suppressed.

Moreover, if the purge meant that a "bamboo curtain" had descended around China, it had little effect in isolating mainland authors. If anything, the restrictions at home only encouraged increasing numbers of writers to search out opportunities for offshore publication. The Hong Kong and Taiwan media were not hampered by party committees and censorship regulations; furthermore, they offered payments in hard currency, an attractive prospect for writers who were feeling the effects of the inflationary spiral caused by the economic reforms.

In May 1990, shortly after her release from Qincheng, Beijing's maximum security jail for political prisoners, the journalist Dai Qing smuggled out to Hong Kong an account of her post–4 June confinement. "My Imprisonment," an irony-laden memoir that lambasted both the Beijing authorities and extremist dissidents, was immediately serialized in *Ming Pao*, a leading Hong Kong daily.[74] Thereafter, although Dai's work remained banned on the mainland, she continued to publish commentaries and essays in Hong Kong and Taiwan newspapers.[75] Similarly, the playwright Wu Zuguang—a man ordered to quit the party in August 1987 for his repeated criticism of official censorship[76]—sent out articles via friends to the British territory when they were rejected for publication in Beijing.[77] And Yang Xianyi, a renowned translator and an outspoken critic of the government's actions on 4 June, agreed to have a collection of his private doggerel poems, *dayou shi*—classical Chinese poems with a wicked political edge that he exchanged with friends—produced in Hong Kong.[78]

Less prominent writers and journalists who were not protected by their literary fame published their work outside China under pen names. Thus paradoxically, by forcing some of China's most controversial and talented writers to seek outlets in Hong Kong and Taiwan during and after the purge, the development of a cross-cultural dialogue in the "Chinese commonwealth" was given a considerable impetus.[79] The long-term effects of the increased contacts between artists marginalized by the purge and Hong Kong's and Taiwan's culture industries were felt well into the 1990s and are discussed in chapter 5, "The Graying of Chinese Culture," and chapter 7, "Packaged Dissent."

BETWEEN BUST AND BOOM

In December 1990, He Jingzhi, the acting minister of culture, produced a major policy paper on culture. Appearing under the modest title "Some Opinions Regarding the Creation of a Socialist Culture with Chinese Characteristics,"[80] it filled two crammed pages of type in Beijing's major cultural newspaper when it was eventually published for public delectation in early 1991. He was adamant that the cultural purge be pursued at all costs, and his followers produced a series of articles in his support.[81] The strident tone and hard line of this new wave of attacks were obviously aimed at the relatively moderate stance of Li Ruihuan, who had repeatedly emphasized that cultural enrichment (that is, noninterference in the arts) had to take precedence over political struggle.[82]

Shortly after He's statement was circulated, his ministerial predecessor, Wang Meng, was criticized for the first time by name in the official media for advocating cultural pluralism.[83] This was a major strategic error on the part of Wang's enemies, since party discipline decreed that no member of the party's Central Committee (at that time Wang was still a member) could be attacked in the press without prior Politburo agreement. It was the type of blunder, however, that Wang had been waiting for. He immediately sent a letter of protest to the party general secretary, Jiang Zemin, and declared that such attacks were a form of "culture clubbing," *da gunzi*, or unfair denunciation, the like of which had not been seen since the days of the Gang of Four and the Cultural Revolution.

The bickering in the cultural and propaganda world seemed on the verge of further escalation when, in an act of rare political reconciliation, Jiang Zemin invited forty leading cultural figures to party headquarters in Zhongnanhai for a roundtable discussion on 1 March 1991.[84] It was the first gathering of its kind since 4 June, and in an obvious gesture of cultural solidarity, it was held on the Lantern Festival, Yuanxiao jie, marking the Fifteenth Day of the First Lunar Month, *yuanyue shiwu*, after the Chinese New Year. Traditionally it was a time for families and friends to gather in harmony, reminisce about the past, and prepare for the future.

Wang Meng, a veteran writer and bureaucrat; Xia Yan, a man known for his relatively liberal views; and the woman novelist Shen Rong all were invited, along with the incumbent cultocrats and their ideological henchmen.[85] It was extraordinary that both the bureaucratic victors of the 1989 purge and their deposed opponents would be feted by the party leader in this fashion. While Jiang's invitation to tea was interpreted as yet another example of the authorities' reluctance to become embroiled in factional differences, it was also an indication that the party was neither willing nor able to support a purely repressive cultural line.

At the meeting Jiang attempted to strike a balance between the contending views of arts policy. His published remarks also revealed inherent contradictions in the party line, which called for maintaining strict ideological control while somehow encouraging a national cultural renaissance. The official report of the meeting summarized Jiang's remarks in a manner that admirably reflected the jargonistic doublethink of Chinese party leaders, a report couched in the language of schoolmarmish condescension. It is worth quoting at length:

> Much has been achieved in the year since the promulgation of Party Central's directive calling for the arts world to "grasp rectification while pursuing development." . . . He [that is, Jiang] hoped that cultural workers would persevere with the Four Basic Principles and oppose bourgeois liberalization, that they would persevere with the policies of serving the masses and socialism as well as pursuing the policy to allow a hundred flowers to bloom and different schools of thought to contend. It was necessary to respect and guarantee the creativity of individuals. Cultural workers must constantly be aware of the fact that they are the engineers of human souls, that the People are the mothers of cultural workers, and an effort must be made to serve spiritual nourishment to the People. He also said that in the theoretical realm, it was necessary to promote debate and contention in an atmosphere of equality. One must encourage comradely and well-intentioned criticism and self-criticism. It was important to use reason to convince people, to learn from others' strengths in overcoming one's own shortcomings, show mutual respect, learn from one another, and talk things over with one another so that everyone can advance together.[86]

Both Wang Meng and his ally Shen Rong took advantage of the occasion to make pointed comments on the inherent absurdity of the present cultural policies. Whereas Wang was more circumspect in his remarks, Shen was less restrained. She noted that life was not easy for China's writers. One moment the party demanded that they "rectify" themselves so as to keep up with new political priorities, and the next they were being admonished to help manufacture a new "boom" in cultural production.

"Now I don't have any idea where all this acrimony . . . comes from," she said, "or what kind of authoritative backing it might have, but I do know that it's all pretty scary." Shen went on to suggest rather sardonically that central party leaders should first fight it out among themselves and then issue documents telling writers just what was expected of them. She also observed that at the moment, writers felt as though they were wending their way through a minefield. Until Party Central could produce a coherent arts policy, Shen urged the party's Department of Propaganda to help clear away some of the land mines scattered over the cultural terrain instead of simply waiting for the explosion when someone puts a foot out of place.[87]

The opinions of the "other side" in the conversation with Jiang Zemin were best summed up by Wei Wei, an elderly army novelist. In a published version of his comments, Wei declared that corruption and bourgeois liberalization were "a pair of cancerous twins festering in the body politic" and that they threatened the very life of the party. The degenerate influence of the West was particularly baneful. "We can engage in as much trade with the imperialists as we want, but we should harbor no illusions. We must increase our strength one-hundred fold, in particular our spiritual resources, for if we let down our spiritual guard, then no number of tanks will be able to protect us."[88] He warned that in the past the party's calls to oppose liberalization had eventually been abandoned and many comrades who were determined to continue the struggle had been removed from office. "This is unjust," Wei Wei complained, and he appealed to party leaders that this time they must pursue the fight against cultural liberalization "to the very end." He further opined that despite the unfortunate setbacks that had occurred in Eastern Europe in 1989–1990, the future of socialism was bright. In conclusion, to express his overall optimism, he quoted a line from a poem written by Mao Zedong in 1960:

> On the ice-clad rock rising high and sheer
> A flower blooms sweet and fair.[89]

On the same day that the Lantern Festival meeting took place, the party and government organizations in charge of culture issued a major policy statement entitled "Opinions on Enhancing Cultural Creativity."[90] It was the first such document published since the Central Committee of the Communist Party had issued "Opinions on the Increased Enhancement of Art and Literature" in early 1989, discussed in the previous chapter.

Far from being simply a policy statement in favor of cultural stagnation, as was claimed by Bi Hua, a leading Hong Kong–based critic of mainland culture,[91] the new document appeared to be a compromise charter aimed at ensuring cultural containment and peace of mind for the dithering bureaucrats who had composed it. Although it abrogated certain elements of the early 1989 document, the new "Opinions" was hardly a clarion call to arms for the nation's Maoist recidivists. It indicated, above all, that when it came to culture, the party could speak only with a forked tongue.

The post–4 June purge had only a limited effect on overall productivity in the arts,[92] although as had been the case in earlier campaigns against cultural diversity, innovative and avant-garde artists were forced either to compromise themselves or to seek new outlets and backing for their work overseas. Not all writers, however, were anxious to exploit official confusion to their own ends. A few rogue individuals, like the Sichuan poet Zhou Lunyou, refused to cooperate with state culture in any way. A leading proponent of "not-not poetry," *feifei zhuyi*, in the 1980s, Zhou produced a manifesto entitled "A Stance of Rejection" in late December 1991. Even though choked with the romantic bombast of the misunderstood underground poet, Zhou's manifesto was a spirited rebuttal of the corrosive influence of literary capitulation that had marked the mainland cultural scene in the early 1990s. His call for artistic independence ended with the following appeal:

> In the name of history and reality, in the name of human decency, in the name of the absolute dignity and conscience of the poet, and in the name of pure art we declare:
> We will not cooperate with a phony value system—
>
> - Reject their magazines and payments.
> - Reject their critiques and acceptance.
> - Reject their publishers and their censors.
> - Reject their lecterns and "academic" meetings.
> - Reject their "writers' associations," "artists' associations," "poets' associations," for they all are sham artistic yamen that corrupt art and repress creativity.[93]

A few weeks later, Deng Xiaoping traveled to the south of China and, in a series of speeches, ushered in a new wave of economic reform throughout the country (see chapter 7, "Packaged Dissent"). The Chinese media hailed Deng's statements for encouraging "another grand advance along the road of the open door and reform." For both elite and official culture, however, it presaged a series of new and delicate negotiations that made statements like that of Zhou Lunyou appear touchingly naive.

CHAPTER THREE

Traveling Heavy

INTELLECTUAL BAGGAGE

He Xin, a scholar turned government adviser, had a positive assessment of the dramatic decline of independent intellectual activity in China that followed in the wake of the 4 June 1989 Beijing massacre. In early October that year, he wrote:

> The overall situation in China now is stable. The "independent" intellectuals have for all intents and purposes been obliterated. To a certain extent they brought it on themselves. . . .
>
> China is unquestionably entering a new phase politically. . . . However, some intellectuals will have to pay the price in this new era. In the Eastern tradition, the individual finds expression through the collective, while in the West, the collective finds its meaning in the individual. In this sense, it is worthwhile as long as one can achieve the development of the whole in exchange and regain control over the excessively inflated egos that have emerged in recent years. All this is possible now; not only is it necessary, it also in keeping with the spirit of the East.[1]

In regard to the events of 1989, He Xin went on to say that "in my personal opinion, the majority of Western politicians and intellectuals basically misread the situation this time around. This is because they have let themselves be misled by the emotionalism and hopes of a group of independent-style Chinese intellectuals and right-wing students."[2] Although one of the most insightful commentators on the intellectual scene on the mainland during the late 1980s, He was a bit too smug about the demise of China's independent intellectuals and a little too eager to take advantage of the vacuum left by their fall.

After 4 June, He Xin become a pro-stability media star, and in private he bragged about an imminent appointment to an important government position. But He Xin's meteoric rise to prominence as a sometime adviser to the Chinese leadership—he wrote policy papers for party and state leaders—was short-lived. His constant indulgence in media politics and embarrassing public exchanges with foreign writers all contributed to the gradual decline of his political fortunes. After 1992, critical of the new directions in economic policy that incorporated a shift away from state planning and favored a massive buildup of the private sector, He Xin became the Jeremiah of the reforms. By the mid-1990s, he was devoting his energies to trading in antiques, although he still occasionally sent memorials to Party Central.[3] For his trouble, He Xin had earned the lasting enmity of nearly all of China's leading cultural and intellectual figures. Obviously, this was not something that concerned him unduly.

Progovernment scholars like He Xin and the Communist Party's exiled critics were generally comfortable with the notion that the academics and writers who aligned themselves with the 1989 protest movement or condemned the government's violent crushing of it could be considered "liberal" or "independent" intellectuals, *ziyou zhishifenzi*. To accept this view and classify the whole range of dissident Chinese opinion both inside and outside China in these terms, however, tends to cloud the issues involving the Chinese intellectual diaspora more than clarify them. The majority of intellectual exiles who fled China in 1989–1990 and the many who were arrested, detained, or purged after June were not so much "independent" thinkers as persecuted inhabitants of a bureaucratic and intellectual "gray zone"; they were official and semiofficial intellectuals who, through their independent action, had lost the patronage of the state.[4]

THE WRITING DIASPORA

During the protest movement of 1989, hundreds of prominent intellectuals added their voices to the general clamor for clean government and political reform. Together with the students and citizens of Beijing, they offered the Communist Party a unique opportunity to win back the confidence of the nation and negotiate a new political and social contract. Tragically, but not surprisingly, that opportunity was forfeited. After the Beijing massacre, it soon became a truism to claim that the party had also lost irrevocably the support of the intelligentsia and brought its own legitimacy into serious question. As we will see in the following chapters, since the early 1990s, intellectual and cultural legitimacy in mainland China has been a contested realm, and under the umbrella of party rule a crucial realignment of power has been taking place.

In the months following the suppression of the protest movement, an intellectual and cultural diaspora developed on a scale not seen in the Chinese world since the Communist Party came to power on the mainland and the Nationalist

(KMT) government withdrew to Taiwan in 1949. After 4 June, a number of China's best-known writers and intellectual figures, as well as many of the prominent student leaders, fled the country, joining large communities of Chinese students and scholars who were already abroad, forming what the Harvard philosopher Tu Wei-ming presumed was a "cultural China," a global field of Chinese intellectual activity and debate.

At the time, the exiles won the sympathy and support of many foreign governments, the international media, the citizens of the countries in which they took refuge, and local Chinese communities. Some of them organized a new political party, the Federation for a Democratic China,[5] using donated funds, and in 1990, they began publishing a political and theoretical journal called *Democratic China* with backing from the Taiwan press. One of the new journal's editors was Su Xiaokang, the lead writer for the television series *River Elegy*. Other writers in exile set up an association of their own and launched two literary journals, one based in Oslo (the revived samizdat journal *Today*, which was later moved to Stockholm) and the other in San Francisco (*Square*, a short-lived publication initially edited by Dai Houying and then by the Guangzhou novelist Kong Jiesheng).[6]

Similarly, Chinese journalists in North America banded together and established a weekly newspaper, the *Press Freedom Herald*, which they hoped would be instrumental in breaking the news blockade imposed by the Communist authorities on the mainland after 4 June. Numerous other groups and publications inspired by the protest movement sprang up around the world. For a time, it even seemed possible that the vital intellectual and cultural life of the mainland of the 1980s, although dispersed, would now continue overseas.

The new exiles based their own political legitimacy on involvement in the 1989 movement. But when they arrived in the United States, they were greeted by groups of earlier exiles, scholars, and students. In particular, there were the dissidents who had organized the Chinese Democratic Alliance in the early 1980s.[7] The alliance had a more impressive pedigree than did the "instant dissidents" of 1989. Its members had not waited until 1989 to "discover" democracy in mass rallies, and long ago the Communist Party had labeled it a "counterrevolutionary" organization. Many people who traded energetically in the 1990s on their reputation as famous "dissidents" had, in fact, strenuously avoided all contact with the alliance before June 1989.

In the months following the massacre, the intellectual diaspora gradually lost the cachet and public profile it had enjoyed. Financial support also began to dry up. Supporters of the dissidents were not happy to see donated money being used to fund international junkets and seminars for self-important intellectuals and student activists. The Chinese press reported that the exiles had been quick to set up a hierarchy of privilege, a mirror image of that of the Communist Party they so vilified, one that dictated how expensive their hotel rooms not only could but, in some cases, *needed* to be. It was even claimed that intellectuals were divvying up donated funds according to the official bureaucratic ranking they had held on the mainland. Ironically, the party's scale of worth now provided the exiles with their own.

In some cases, overspending and personal indulgence were even defended. This was particularly true in the case of Wuer Kaixi, the flamboyant student leader who had been one of the focal points of media attention from the start of the student protests. Like his fellow students, Wuer had grown up not in a period of Stalinist oppression or even Maoist instability but in the China of the 1980s, an era in which economic carpetbaggerism and decadence flourished to a degree unprecedented in contemporary Chinese history.[8] This was reflected in the "me-generation" attitudes of many younger student stars. The denouement of this band of media freedom fighters readily brought to mind the corruption and demise of an earlier generation of Chinese rebels, those who established the Heavenly Kingdom, Taiping tianguo, in Nanjing in the mid-nineteenth century. Similarly, when considering the early and acrimonious antics of the exiles, one is reminded of Alexander Zinoviev's caustic observations on the *homo sovieticus* overseas:

> Do you know who's the main enemy of the Soviet émigré in the West? Another Soviet émigré who got here earlier. The West has to share out the same amount of attention and goods among an ever greater number of claimants. . . . In general, this emigration is a dictatorship of duds. . . . There is no common enemy. There are only personal enemies. The enemy is always the one who is closest to you and the immediate threat or hindrance to your well-being. . . . All the chances of being published or getting some kind of publicity had already been cornered by scoundrels like me who had arrived here earlier.[9]

Meanwhile, back in China the "regime," as it was now fashionable to call the government, remained disconcertingly stable. The political purge that had begun in June 1989 continued into 1991, although as was noted in the previous chapter, its focus was increasingly blurred by considerations of realpolitik and factional infighting. Flurries of new arrests, investigations, and dismissals became part of life in Beijing, and after 1990, mini-crackdowns were begun during the annual "anniversary season" of the 1989 protests dating from 15 April (the date the deposed party general secretary Hu Yaobang died in 1989, an event that sparked the protests) to 4 June. The small band of dissidents who remained active in the 1990s would use these occasions to make public protests in the hope of focusing international media attention on their plight.

Other public events also provided opportunities for dissident activity and re-sulted in regular official repression. This was evident, for example, during October 1990 when the Eleventh Asian Games concluded in Beijing and again in the summer of 1995 on the eve of the United Nations International Women's Conference, which was sponsored by the Chinese government. However, because the architects of this fitful terror concentrated almost exclusively on bureaucratic and factional enemies, as well as on a small quota of unrepentant "bad elements," they did not succeed in wiping out intellectual life—or even dissent—on the mainland. Publicly pinning its claim to legitimacy on economic performance, national traditions, and patriotic goals, the party weathered the chaos of 1989 and during the early 1990s confined debates about the future of the nation for many in mainland China at least within the parameters of its own agenda.

DEMOCRATIC CREDENTIALS

In October 1990, Lu Keng, a veteran Chinese journalist and U.S.-based political commentator, remarked in a review of the democracy activists, "It is plain for all to see that to a great extent the entire political fate of China will depend on this group of young people overseas."[10] Other observers were less gung-ho and readily acknowledged that factional struggles had quickly overwhelmed and at times even paralyzed the fledgling democracy movement in exile. For Lu Keng, a writer who spent much of his time reporting on developments in the Chinese democracy camp in North America for the Hong Kong–Taiwan press, these all were nothing more than teething problems, a mere question of overorganization that, given time, could be resolved. Such blind optimism remained popular for years in intellectual circles in Hong Kong and abroad.

Hu Ping, chairman of the Chinese Democratic Alliance and an activist with a history of prodemocracy agitation that went back to 1979, was more pessimistic about the future. Along with his close associate Xu Bangtai, a dissident from Shang-hai, Hu was also one of the most thoughtful of the international dissidents. He had written an impressive and important samizdat article entitled "On the Freedom of Speech" in 1979 in which he discussed the role of oppositionist forces in China. Ten years later, Wang Dan, one of the student leaders of the 1989 movement (eventual-ly exiled to the United States in 1998), produced his own work on the subject. Sadly, it was far inferior to Hu's earlier essay in terms of both content and style. That was not surprising, since Wang, like most of the younger activists of the late 1980s, was ignorant of Hu Ping's work and the activities of dissidents in the late 1970s.[11]

In Eastern Europe, middle-aged dissidents had provided the young not only with a tradition of opposition but also an important intellectual heritage. In

China, people like Liu Binyan, Wang Ruowang and Yan Jiaqi, men who reveled in their reputation as dissidents after 4 June, had previously been anxious not to compromise their working relationship with the Communist authorities and had therefore eschewed the works of dissidents like Wei Jingsheng, Liu Qing, Xu Wenli, and others who had spoken out in 1978–1979. In 1990, Yan Jiaqi, a government think-tank intellectual turned activist in 1989 and the first chairman of the newly founded Federation for a Democratic China, heaped praise on Hu Ping's work. Hu, however, made the bitter observation, "It's far too late now . . . if people had only recognized the value of it at the time, things might have been very different."[12]

Commenting on the newly arrived dissidents in late 1990, who were embroiled in petty feuds and struggles over both money and media attention, Hu Ping wrote: "There has hardly been any improvement in the level of agreement within the ranks of the democracy movement since they left the Square [in 1989]. What possible hope is there if this situation continues?"[13] Hu was one of the figures who was painfully aware of the difficulties of the situation and made many practical proposals to moderate the relationships among the rancorous oppositionist forces overseas who pursued the rivalries that had developed in Tiananmen.

The split between the recent and older exiles was not easily resolved. Factional strife, tale telling, and general backbiting were exacerbated by the amount of international media attention and money that was lavished on the exiled democracy activists during the early 1990s. One of the most contentious issues in the groups was the question of "credentials," or *zige*, a term with powerful connotations in Chinese. Could ten years of quiet but persistent activism both inside mainland China and out (as in the case of Hu Ping and his alliance) match six weeks of dramatic demonstrating and flight (as represented by the activists of the federation)? Some members of the federation dismissed the alliance for having failed to achieve anything significant during the 1980s. They argued that their years of editorializing and plotting were negligible in comparison with the media blitz and government repression of the 1989 movement that had internationalized China's political dilemmas. Another major point of difference between the two organizations was their relationship with the Communist Party of China. The alliance had been denounced as an antiparty, antisocialist, and anti-Chinese group in the service of imperialism. Meanwhile, some leaders of the federation, a number of whom had served in the Communist Party as erstwhile reformers, looked forward to the day when they could return to the mainland to continue their work as part of the ruling class.

Not all the divisions, however, fell neatly across the lines separating members of the two groups. According to reports published in the Hong Kong press, the intellectuals in exile in America also split into rival "academic" camps. There was talk of there being a "Chicago school " that consisted predominantly of literary theoreticians who wanted to pursue the May Fourth enlightenment tradition of utilizing "culture and science" to save the nation and preferred scholastic research to direct political involvement. Then there was the "Princeton school," whose members were more politically engagé.[14] Such groupings were highly fluid if not semifictitious, and key figures roamed between countries and cities with a dizzying frequency as if engaged in some elaborate guerrilla warfare strategy, enjoying the jet-setting celebrity of fashionable "small world" academics. Meanwhile, Chen Yizi, formerly a key figure in the Chinese government's reformist bureaucracy, struck out on his own and established the "Contemporary China Research Center," which elicited the support of leading China scholars and began producing a journal of international repute.[15]

Lu Keng, a journalist with an unhappy history with the communist government, had not ventured back to mainland China since 1987. He was particularly upbeat in his reports about the amount of popular support in China for the overseas activists after 4 June. Just after the Beijing massacre, many people in major urban centers, outraged by the callous actions of the government, had privately rejoiced at every fortunate escape by students and workers on the most wanted lists as police arrests increased. But as the situation stabilized and numbers of detainees were released from late 1989 on, things changed. By 1990, it was common to hear people in Beijing criticize the leading exiles for abandoning China or for failing to come back and take responsibility for their actions in inciting the protests, especially following the declaration of martial law. The people that I met during 1990–1991, from intellectuals to comrades in the street, were fairly unanimous in their opinion that the activists who fled in 1989 were living off a reputation based on their radicalism during the mass movement and the suffering of their erstwhile supporters in the capital following the government crackdown while many innocents or moderates had been detained, taking the burden of responsibility for the protests. As one writer, himself in exile, put it, media-hungry exiles like the former student leaders Chai Ling, Li Lu, and Shen Tong were now "eating steamed bread soaked in blood."[16] Whereas this may have been unfair, it was a widely held view among other Chinese exiles and among people on the mainland.

Prominent intellectuals and students had, by the very fact of their exile, suffered a serious blow to their credibility. This was particularly so, since it was widely perceived on the mainland that many of the key agitators of 1989 had sought refuge with former imperialist powers (that is, France, England, and the United States) and the KMT government in Taiwan. The mainland authorities were well aware of the jealous reaction of its people to reports of dissidents living off the fat of the land overseas, and the official media took delight in portraying them all as traitors to the nation.

In October 1990, for example, the *People's Daily* carried an attack on the writer Zu Wei who had visited Taiwan earlier in the year. He had marveled at the island's free press and wealth and was now denounced on the mainland for "shamelessly" fawning on the Taiwanese authorities and media. The report continued in a tone of disgust that when Liu Binyan and Yan Jiaqi visited the island, "they were quite willing to trade their pride in for slavishness, wagging their tails and rolling about on the ground for their new-found masters. . . . Although they all are playing different roles in this auction of integrity, their downfall follows the same pattern. . . . We can only thank them for revealing their true nature to our people."[17] Reports like this played in particular on the growing resentment of Taiwan's wealth among mainland citizens and a spreading belief that if the protests in China led to a political collapse, chaos and economic dislocation might well be the result, rather than democracy and prosperity.

Knowing full well that rabid attacks on the exiles would only elicit sympathy for their cause, the Chinese government by and large responded to the activities of the dissidents by ignoring them. When they did want to lambast an exiled activist, they would often utilize foreign media reports. These reports were supposed to be taken as factual and "objective" accounts and were presumably far more damaging than government rhetoric. If the protest movement of 1989 had been a public statement against corruption and the secret hierarchies that ruled China, the famous exiles readily gave the impression that they were little better than the system they opposed.

CHARGE IT!

Many of the activists and intellectuals simply found themselves lost in the West. Freed from the repressive environment of the state apparatus and faced with seemingly unlimited freedom, many of them indulged in an orgy of what in party jargon would be called "extreme individualism." Although chaotic, China in the 1980s remained an externally coercive society; little emphasis was placed on self-regulation or personal morality. The absence of these forms of suffocating socialization often resulted in anarchy when individuals traveled abroad.[18] Some student leaders, young people nurtured by a corrupt state and venal society, acted with such license in the West that although they had been the darlings of the international press, they suffered a spectacular loss of popularity, especially in the Chinese community. Others who had been taken up and groomed by image consultants and political lobbyists reinvented themselves and managed to remain favorites of the U.S. media. The most outstanding example of such a makeover was Li Lu. Although a minor student activist in 1989, by the mid-1990s Li had published an autobiography in English, was the subject of a feature-length "documentary," had graduated with a doctorate from Columbia University, and was promoted as the spokesman for the Chinese democracy movement and eventually started a high-risk hedge fund on Madison Avenue. In U.S. press reports, he did not shy from being compared with Nelson Mandela.[19]

A story from the Hong Kong press concerning the Second Congress of the Federation for a Democratic China held in San Francisco in late September 1990 is revealing in regard to the ground rules pursued by the exiles. It was reported that the leaders of the organization were in the habit of running up phone tabs in their hotels that exceeded the actual hotel bill itself. To prevent the misuse of public, that is, donated, funds for private long-distance and international calls, telephone cards were issued. The cards were to be handed in when delegates had finished their official business. It turned out, however, that Wuer Kaixi, the young ex–vice chairman of the federation, gave back his card but kept a record of the code number on it. An excess of U.S. $1,800 appeared on the federation's next phone bill. The responsible functionary decided that the situation could be dealt with in one of two ways: either make Wuer Kaixi cough up the money or renege on the phone bill. He decided not to pay.

This action was questioned at the October 1990 conference by a Chinese doctoral student in computer studies. He pointed out that a record of the unpaid bill would remain in the system for years to come and that it would damage the organization's credit rating in the future, not to mention causing offense to past and future donors of funds. After duly discussing the issue, the delegates decided that the federation's credit rating was more important than the $1,800, and action was promised. Nowhere in the report of the incident or of the attendant debate, however, were any doubts raised concerning the probity of misusing federation funds in this way. Nor did anyone question the implications of attempting to defraud the telephone company or the decision to pay the bill only after it had become an issue with the media and people realized it could limit future sources of income. While the end result of the delegates' deliberations was commendable, the naked pragmatism of their approach was also noteworthy.[20]

PERIODICAL FEVER

Sudden exile was certainly disconcerting. Yet in many ways it was easier for Chinese dissidents in 1989 than it had been for many European exiles in the past or, for that matter, Chinese exiles or displaced people uprooted by the political turmoil of the late 1940s.

The 1989 exiles did not have to cope with the trauma faced, say, by Czech, Hungarian, or even Soviet émigrés who had to create their own publishing world

and linguistic communities overseas. The Chinese exiles could negotiate contracts with the ready-made, and wealthy, publishing industries of Hong Kong and
Taiwan. Countries like the United States also had an extensive range of Chinese-
language media. Publishers in Hong Kong and Taiwan created special book series to accommodate the writings of exiled and jailed intellectuals, and major
newspapers and magazines started to run regular articles by and interviews with
the star dissidents (Chai Ling, for example, wrote a cloying essay-column on her
petit-bourgeois aspirations for a yuppie Hong Kong weekly). Royalty checks were
handsome, especially in the case of Taiwan where, unlike the mainland, writers
were paid highly for their work. However, the style of the mainlanders' writing—
a theoretical and narrative mode influenced by decades of exposure to the wood-
en language of party prose—often limited their audience appeal and hampered
their relationships with editors. Naturally, in Taiwan and Hong Kong where the
readership determined the economic well-being of publications, it was not always
economically viable to indulge the endless polemic ruminations of ex-Marxist intellectuals on obscure points of political theory and history. Some writers did work
out a formula to satisfy the demands of the new readership. As mainland China
and the Communist Party were increasingly demonized through the 1990s, particularly in the U.S. mass media, a few authors successfully concentrated on producing chilling accounts of past Communist atrocities and stories of the Chinese
gulag. Although these works were undeniably worthy, and valuable, their best-
seller status and shock value often obscured the fact that similar works had been
produced for decades but had enjoyed little public impact.

Since the mainlanders were also used to running their own organizations and
publishing projects, despite the media largesse they initially enjoyed, many of
them tended to look down on Hong Kong and Taiwan. To overcome the limitations of the "overseas Chinese" publishing scene, they established a number of
new journals. One of the new magazines, begun in October 1990, was the bimonthly *Twenty-First Century*,[21] under the auspices of the Institute of Chinese
Studies at the Chinese University of Hong Kong. Edited by Liu Qingfeng, an academic and wife of the mainland philosopher Jin Guantao, *Twenty-First Century*
argued in favor of Hong Kong as a major focus for Chinese intellectual debate.
With an editorial board that included leading intellectuals and prominent proponents of neo-Confucianism on the mainland, in Taiwan, Hong Kong, and the
United States, its publication announcement claimed for the journal a unique
role in the media world of Greater China:

> We have faith in two things. In the first place, we believe that intellectuals
> play a pivotal role in the long-term progress of a nation. Second, that Chi-
> nese intellectuals who are scattered throughout the world are essential to
> that progress. Hong Kong is ideally situated for the dissemination of infor-

mation, an understanding of the changing scene [in China], and the exchange of ideas.

We are convinced that Chinese intellectuals throughout the world are
both willing and able to establish a pluralistic culture that will look toward
the twenty-first century.[22]

The magazine was of such a scholarly bent that it could often be received by
readers in the mainland without official interference and after 1997 was openly sold
in select bookstores. *Twenty-First Century* was the first publication of its kind to provide an open forum for concerned Chinese readers and writers inside and outside
the mainland. Because of its increased availability and generally high quality, it became a major independent forum for intellectual and ideological debate from the
early 1990s, eclipsing earlier publications like *Chinese Intellectual*, which had appeared under the editorship of the Hunan dissident Liang Heng in the 1980s.[23]

Other new publications like *Democratic China*, the theoretical organ for the
Federation for a Democratic China mentioned earlier, were more overtly political. The first issues showed it generally to be of high quality, and it compared favorably with the New York–based *China Spring*, the monthly journal of the Chinese Democratic Alliance. Both publications, which were banned in China, also
provided an outlet for the discussion of current political issues that had been ignored or underrated by mainland intellectuals and dissidents in the past, a case
in point being the status of Tibet. While avoiding the limitations of established
nonmainland Chinese magazines, the dissident journals did, however, reflect the
factionalism and sectarianism of their mainland editors. Even leading Hong
Kong monthlies like *The Nineties Monthly*, *Open Magazine*, and *Cheng Ming*
showed the bias of their editors by favoring certain exiles over others. The editors
often pursued their local conflicts by pitting individuals or groups from the mainland against one another in their pages.[24]

CULTURAL "ETS"

Even in the relatively liberal late 1980s, there was a rush by writers and intellectuals to accept self-imposed exile. In 1988, the Shanghai critic Zhu Dake wrote
about the phenomenon, and his remarks, still relevant in the 1990s, were a fit
comment on both the exhilarating and degrading nature of that experience:

People fly off to distant parts, flee this impoverished land in search of a new
world, paradise.

It is the physical manifestation of a spiritual longing. This great migration gives form to a sense of national hopelessness; it's a new superstition

with the outside world as its totem. Postindustrial society appears as a ter-restrial refraction of some heavenly blueprint, enticing troubled souls to venture forth and enjoy.

Taken from another angle, these neighboring people will be devastated as they witness yellow-skinned ETs descending on every corner of the globe, in-vading their streets, pillaging their wealth, culture, and women. People as-sume the style of the exile, undertake a crusade of the weak, and cast a net of gentle terror over the world as a process of colonization in reverse unfolds. This is the ironic revenge of the descendants of Genghis Khan. . . .

[Exile] is certainly a moral process suffused with shame and pangs of conscience. The writer in exile must learn to be thick skinned and shame-less, to bow his head as he stands beneath the eaves of his patron's magna-nimity, to accept the downward gaze and ridicule of new divinities. People must first understand that they are the descendants of a fallen tribe—only then can they become citizens of the world.[25]

Cut off from the scene in China and confronted by the pluralistic confusion of foreign climes, some of the displaced cultural figures all too readily turned to-ward conservatism, preserving a threatened sense of identity with a panoply of tra-ditional attitudes, cronyism, festivals, dances, and performances or, as the 1990s progressed, a revived "leftist essentialism" combined with a subaltern attitude. National festivals and holidays also gave them and China's diplomatic represen-tatives an opportunity to reestablish contact on neutral cultural ground. While some members of the Chinese avant-garde in exile joined in the artistic life of their new homes, others reverted gradually to worshiping the fossilized culture against which they had originally rebelled with such passion. Su Xiaokang, for ex-ample, the main writer of the iconoclastic 1988 television series *River Elegy* and the editor of *Democratic China*, became far more receptive to "traditional" cul-ture when he went to Taiwan, the self-proclaimed bastion of Chinese values.[26]

Throughout the 1980s, the mainland intellectual world of which the present literati in exile were a part had been marked by a general fascination with the most up-to-date and fashionable theories of international academia. Scholars and critics vied with one another to parade the latest buzz words and state-of-the-art international theoretical paradigms, stunning their fellows with intellectual chic. Now in the West themselves, many felt they had to come to grips with the intel-lectual, political, and cultural traditions that formed the basis of Euro-American society. This academic "retooling" was to play a significant role in the cultural de-bate that flourished on the mainland from the mid-1990s.

It is important to remember, however, that these mostly were people whose in-tellectual aspirations were strongly rooted in the political heritage of utilitarianism and state Confucianism, a tradition in which the educated person's highest fulfillment was conceived in terms of servitude to the nation-state. All well and good perhaps in the Chinese cultural context, but observers and analysts were easily misled if they accepted the democratic-sounding rhetoric of dissidents and intellectuals without considering the context in which it was being used and the power play of which it was a part.

In the late 1980s and early 1990s, it was fashionable in Western academic circles to discuss the rise of civil society and the role that popular pressure groups had played in the transformation of European socialist states. This style of discourse also armed many Chinese exiles with a new vocabulary, just as Marxism-Leninism had given intellectuals and politicians a new language in the 1930s.[27] To speak in the latest jargon did not mean that the culture behind that language infiltrated Chinese political or social practice. So while the level of discussion among exiles (and eventually among writers *in situ* on the mainland) seemed to undergo a considerable upgrading in the early 1990s, the subtext of the debates in the long run may well prove to be little different from that of the past. The outpourings of this Chinese subaltern would, however, supposedly be quantifiable by the criteria of the international academic industry.

It was among the students and scholars who were overseas before 1989 rather than in the cadre of famous newly born dissidents — be they intellectuals, bureaucrats, or students — that perhaps a more profound change could be detected. Hu Ping and his group as well as Chinese graduate students in America, Europe, and elsewhere, were important in this context. Their years overseas, unencumbered by political stardom or media attention, had presumably enabled them to try and live the ideals that they hoped to see realized in the China of the future.

After having generally been ignored throughout the 1980s, one subject of intense debate among the exiles old and new was the relationship of "Communist culture" to Chinese tradition and intellectual life both at home and abroad. Gong Xiaoxia was a political activist in Guangzhou in the 1970s. As a doctoral scholar in the United States, she publicly engaged with many of the political issues raised by the 1989 protest movement. Like an increasing number of dissidents overseas, she recognized elements in the Chinese political equation that she felt made the situation very different from that of other socialist nations. Gong argued that the Cultural Revolution and the decade of reform that followed not only undermined the primacy of the party but also corrupted the society itself. Commenting on the difficulties of democratization in early 1990, she wrote:

> We are further away from democratization now than we were seventy years ago [at the time of the May Fourth movement] or even in the late Qing dynasty. . . . A basic condition for democracy is mutual respect, a respect for

the rights of others. . . . Forty years of Communist culture have eliminated the positive things that were introduced from the West and undermined the relatively humanistic values of traditional Chinese culture . . . what has grown in its place is a Communist culture in which suspicion and struggle are the norm. . . .

What type of society are we faced with today? One in which people have no respect for either themselves or others. There is no basic code of conduct or standard of right or wrong . . . no wonder people say China must experience anarchy before democracy can develop. Democracy requires not only order but a basic respect for order. . . .

What we can do is make a start with ourselves.[28]

A later exile from the mainland, the singer-songwriter Hou Te-chien (Hou Dejian), made a similar observation in late July 1990:

I believe the democracy movement overseas should concentrate on the Chinese students studying abroad, overseas Chinese, and foreigners. There is much that can be done, especially since the democratization of attitudes of international Chinese students will have a crucial impact on the future direction China takes. . . . More people have to have a sense of involvement, this is the key to the success of the international movement.[29]

INTELLECTUAL MAKEOVER

Among exiled intellectuals for a time there was also a considerable amount of critical reflection on the events of 1989. Yuan Zhiming was another of the writers of *River Elegy*, the television series that was branded by the government as part of a wave of "cultural nihilism" that contributed to the protests. In an article published in January 1990, Yuan questioned what would have happened in 1989 if the most famous Chinese public intellectuals—Fang Lizhi, Liu Binyan, Yan Jiaqi, Chen Yizi, and Su Xiaokang, had "courageously stood forward and led the movement." He continues his speculation in the tone of a guilty survivor:

If we had formulated some mature, rational and feasible plan of action and organized a democratic front incorporating the students and civilians, if we had worked harmoniously together to struggle for dialogue with the authorities, how would it have turned out? Of course, we may still have been vanquished, but at least we could say we had done everything in our power to prevent defeat.

. . . When the time came for real action, we [intellectuals] were struck impotent. Suddenly there was no sign of all that blustering heroism. Keeping ourselves clean, evading responsibility, knowing when to stop, and playing safe—that's what we're good at. We never wanted to be standard-bearers; we did our level best to keep out of it. But now? Why, we're all heroes! Forgive my caustic tone, but none of us, neither you nor me, and none of the intellectuals on the mainland, can avoid the shameful truth.[30]

Yuan Zhiming was by no means the only one to have engaged in soul-searching during the months after 4 June. An impressive reassessment of the activities of mainland intellectuals in the 1980s was made by the journalist Liu Binyan. Liu, formerly a pragmatic velvet prison dissident who finally admitted his complicity in the creation of the media mythology regarding Deng Xiaoping's enlightened attitudes, made a number of penetrating observations about the 1989 movement, its relationship with the Beijing spring of 1978–1979, and the role played by intellectuals in the 1980s. In particular, he castigated the moral failure of intellectuals like himself in the past, their abiding faith in wise rulers, and their inability to initiate independent protests. These were the very shortcomings for which Liu Binyan and others had previously been criticized by independent thinkers like Liu Xiaobo.[31] Contrition for his previous optimism regarding the viability of the communist government, however, led Liu throughout the 1990s to err on the other side of excess by repeatedly predicting the imminent collapse of the People's Republic.

Liu Binyan was at least more candid about the self-censorship that had tainted his reportage during the avowedly "liberal" years of the 1980s. The Yugoslav novelist Danilo Kiš wrote about the long-term effects of self-censorship in terms that very much describe Liu's transformation from the time he was purged from the party in 1987 and traveled to the United States in 1988:

Self-censorship is the negative pole of creative energy; it is distracting and irritating; sometimes, when it comes in contact with the positive pole, it produces a spark. When that happens, the writer, overcoming his fear, kills his [self-appointed censor] double, and in the violent collapse of years of prudence, shame, and humiliation the metaphors disintegrate, the circumlocutions crumble, and there remains only the raw language of action—the pamphlet. There is no more censor-double to discover what lies between the lines; everything is written black on white, down to the last atom of discontent.[32]

Much of Liu Binyan's post-1989 work also reflected the profound impact that Eastern European dissident thought had on him.[33] Yet it was one of the ironies of this period of self-castigation that developments in Eastern Europe in late 1989 and early 1990 actually strengthened the Chinese exiles' confidence in moral leaders. Václav Havel, the Czech playwright turned president, in particular provided a role model of the sage-king, *shengwang*, the intellectual ruler.

It was probably no coincidence that among the leaders of the community in exile, it was a trained philosopher (Hu Ping) and Liu Binyan, a writer who specialized in supporting the purportedly innocent victims of oppression against an unfeeling bureaucracy, who achieved public prominence. During the 1980s, Liu was dubbed "Clear-Sky Liu" (Liu Qingtian) in China, a reference to the prickly but loyal officials of the feudal past. After the massacre, it was fashionable for a time to compare him with Havel, although there was little in his writings or activities to warrant this.[34]

Among the Soviet exiles, acerbic critics like Alexander Zinoviev had emerged to deflate the heroic self-image that dissidents developed overseas. Other émigré writers like Edward Limonov and Vassily Aksyonov were equally biting in their fictional writings on exiles. The new Chinese community of exiles produced its own group of relentless commentators. One of these was Bei Ling (Huang Beiling), an underground socialite poet from Shanghai. Before leaving China in 1988, Bei Ling was one of the most active members of the unofficial literary scene in Beijing. After a period at Brown University in Providence, Rhode Island, Bei Ling moved to Boston to teach and write. Apart from editing the literary journal *Tendency*, he continued to pen occasional articles on literature and politics for the Chinese press in North America, Hong Kong, and Taiwan. In one of these essays, he commented on the games Chinese writers and intellectuals played abroad:

> It's funny how a man whose life has been inextricably entwined with politics [in exile] suddenly hides behind the label of writer and tries to keep his distance from things the moment he is actually required to become politically committed. Equally strange is the fact that a "leader of the democracy movement" who has an executive position in the Federation for a Democratic China will suddenly declare himself to be an intellectual who believes in liberalism. In my opinion, all this is self-indulgent posturing; it is also the reason that so little has come of the Chinese political opposition. . . .
>
> To have the best of both worlds and to show off your cleverness, that's the tradition of the Chinese literati. When a "democracy activist" in the role of a politician appears at some political occasion, he always makes a big noise about how he is really an independent intellectual, yet when wearing the hat of an intellectual at some scholastic or cultural function, he will launch enthusiastically into a disquisition on Chinese politics.[35]

Bei Ling was equally disturbed by the student leaders in exile. He noted that one report on Chai Ling's appearance in the West claimed that she was welcomed by the Chinese Democratic Federation as "a living goddess of democracy." He remarked sardonically, "We've just managed to get rid of one god, Mao Zedong, and now here we have the democracy activists creating a new goddess on our behalf."[36] In 1995, when the debate concerning the film *The Gate of Heavenly Peace*, a controversial documentary about the student protests, flared up, Chai Ling was once more cast by her supporters as the unassailable goddess of democracy. Again, independent critics like Ye Ren, the pen name of a U.S.-based scholar who had recently arrived from China, came to the fore to deflate the kewpie-doll demagogue (for details, see chapter 12, "Totalitarian Nostalgia").

QUICK FIXES . . .

In 1989 many student demonstrators had agitated for instant democracy. They believed that in their nebulous demands, the people could find the solution to all of China's problems. Yet while the nation's crises — economic, ecological, educational, social, population, political, and cultural — were easy enough to identify, few could decide what they meant by the vague term *democracy*. The intellectuals who supported the demonstrators also generally shared their sense of urgency and the need for radical action to remedy the situation. The rejection of tradition, however defined, and a desire for completely new "quick fix" solutions to intractable political and cultural problems would seem to have become endemic to Chinese intellectual life.[37]

The American-based Chinese scholar Lin Yü-sheng commented on the tendency among Chinese intellectuals toward "totalistic" solutions.[38] Whereas it would seem obvious that more subtle and complex methods would be required to deal with the convoluted realities of China, some groups preferred simply to seek new totalistic models in the West.[39] Reflecting on the twentieth-century Chinese intellectual tradition in 1989, Lin bewailed the fact that extreme antitraditionalism had such a wide appeal even seventy years after the May Fourth movement, when cultural iconoclasm had led to the complete negation of the past. The May Fourth movement was a shorthand for a period of patriotic and intellectual upheaval from 1917 to the late 1920s, during which writers and intellectuals led a nationwide popular attack on all traditional cultural values. "This is the tragedy of Chinese culture," Lin said. "The May Fourth method of 'using philosophy and culture to resolve problems' has been preserved to the present day and, in a manner of speaking, has even been immensely enhanced."[40]

It was partly dissatisfaction with the rate of reform in the late 1980s that led some intellectuals to take an extreme stance during the protest movement. This was typical of the "quick fix" or "totalistic" mentality, one that was characterized by a desire to make a clean break with the past, abandon the present system, and push for radical, systemic change. Xu Jilin, a Shanghai-based scholar and specialist in twentieth-century Chinese intellectual history, observed this phenomenon in the late 1980s and wrote that he feared that China's intellectuals were enmeshed in what he called the "vicious cycle of the May Fourth." His remarks, published in early 1989, applied perhaps with similar urgency to the dilemmas of Chinese intellectuals both inside and outside China in the 1990s. "The post-1979 intellectual enlightenment [in China]," Xu wrote, "seems to have repeated the pattern of the May Fourth movement."

> There are startling similarities between these two periods [the 1920s and the 1980s]: general anxiety over the backwardness of the nation and deep-felt anguish over the premature demise of democracy. As people in both periods looked beyond the superficial aspects of the current system to delve into Chinese traditional culture, they discovered many elements there antagonistic to modernization. The result in both cases was cultural reassessment. But as this reassessment was in itself inspired by a mood of political utilitarianism rather than being part of a quest for knowledge, all the cultural debates that resulted from it have invariably been tinged with an ideological hue and marked by a desire for immediate results. . . .
>
> Whenever the paradigms of social and cultural systems undergo a process of renewal or change, it is inevitable that there will be a period of disorientation. The West experienced such a phase in its own recent history. However, because the cultural transformation experienced by the West was by its very nature spontaneous and independent, it didn't lead to a chain reaction by means of which the entire social, political, and economic framework was destabilized. But in China's case, the cultural crisis is part and parcel of the dilemmas of the society as a whole. Cultural and moral models have lost their authority and are thus powerless to ameliorate the crisis.
>
> At this crucial juncture, people pin their hopes on the emergence of new, rational forces. But what they find instead is the appearance of countless disparate, irrational, and chaotic influences. Before rational elements have a chance to join into a coherent whole, the blind destructiveness of the chaotic forces may well push the society toward total collapse.[41]

Among the exiles, there certainly was an awareness of these dangers. As one scholar, trying to avoid the emotional extremism of so many of his fellows, said in mid-1990: "In the past we embraced Communism wholeheartedly; now we are prepared to abandon it lock, stock, and barrel. This is hardly a rational approach."[42]

...AND NO MOVEMENT

Another central feature of the pursuit of the "quick fix" was what could be dubbed a "movement mentality," *yundong yishi*, that was shared by many mainland Chinese. Like the Soviet Union, history in Communist Chinese society was delineated by party congresses, speeches, state plans, and anniversaries. But the Chinese calibrated party life according to a new timetable, one that was set by the political movement, the government-orchestrated purge. Thus, it was not uncommon to hear people measuring their lives according to the schedule of campaigns. Lives were spoken of as having improved "since the Cultural Revolution," or "after the Third Plenum." Hiccups in national progress were experienced "at the time of the antispiritual pollution campaign" or "during the movement against bourgeois liberalization." The first few years of the 1990s were spoken of as being "since the turmoil," or "after the shooting" (if the speaker remained in China), or again "since the democracy movement" (if the speaker was overseas). Then in early 1992, Deng Xiaoping's "tour of the south," *nanxun*, ushered in a "new wave of economic reform," and everything was different once more. People estimate that in the nearly five decades of the People's Republic, there has been a purge or political campaign of some description on an average of once every two years. Reviewing the 1980s, Liu Binyan concluded that the political metabolism of the nation ran according to a biennial rhythm. Therefore, he posited, something dramatic should have happened in 1991.[43] But that was a year of no particular significance, although from then up to 1997 time passed as if it were a deathwatch for Deng Xiaoping.

Movements, *yundong*, form more than just a time frame; until the mid-1990s they were the basis for political and public activity in China. As the then party general secretary Hu Yaobang said in 1982, "Communism is, first and foremost, a movement."[44] The abiding essence of Mao Zedong Thought was the political purge and counterpurge that would unfold during a movement. Purges provided people with an opportunity to settle old scores and restart stalled careers. Even during the liberal years of the 1980s, there were constant "civil movements": politeness campaigns, public hygiene drives, and so on, that took up the slack between the various political and more recently regular anticorruption campaigns. Over the years, movements became for the people of mainland China the most natural form of popular political expression, although the style of participation was rigidly limited and the process itself quite routine. It was a charade with a deadly significance, a form of mass theater that could have devastating consequences. One reason that the 1989 protest movement attracted the support of huge numbers of people who knew exactly how to march, write slogans, draw political cartoons, and make rousing speeches to the milling crowds was that it fulfilled the paradigm of the movement, the underlying schema of mainland Chinese political culture for decades. Aware of the likely outcome of popular defiance, they joined in the demonstrations enthusiastically to vent political frustrations and release pent-up emotion.[45]

During the 1989 movement, moderate activists like Wang Dan, Wang Chaohua, and Dai Qing cautioned against the confrontation encouraged by the extremism of government and demonstrators alike. They were foolhardy individuals who attempted to counsel the protesters that it was time to break free from the movement mentality. They were ignored at the time and dismissed for their lack of ardor after 1989. It was the emotional demagogues and political poseurs who achieved notoriety, be they pumped-up "intellectual leaders" like Yan Jiaqi or histrionic-prone agitators like Chai Ling and Li Lu.

Despite his generally myopic approach to politics, He Xin was also a perceptive observer of the abiding "movement mentality" of Chinese intellectuals. In 1988, he wrote:

> The Chinese seem to be at the same time both an aged and immature people.
>
> In terms of its history and culture, China is a senile nation, yet in terms of political wisdom and civilized behavior it is immature. . . .
>
> Immaturity expresses itself in one particular way: there always are those people who are all too willing to get emotionally carried away and become instigators. Some of them calculate that by so doing, they can gain personal advantage, become political activists, for example, and attain a prominent political position. It is a tragic fact that there always are spectators aplenty, people who are all too willing to get worked up. This is what has led to people's plunging into one "craze" after another—frenzied activities related to politics and ideology or some form of economic Great Leap Forward.
>
> The quintessential expression of this kind of frenzy is the "movement" [*yundong*], including movements that are not so called, and they have occurred time and again. For decades now, Chinese society has been caught up in a cycle of repeated movements.[46]

Liu Xiaobo, one of He Xin's bêtes noires, was one of the few participants in the 1989 movement who tried to encourage participants toward internal democratization. He was outspokenly critical of the antigovernment slogans and increasingly hate-filled rhetoric on Tiananmen Square. Another sober voice was that of the investigative journalist Dai Qing. After the students began a mass hunger strike in mid-May, she warned them that they had become pawns in an internal party struggle. Her efforts to mediate between the protesters and the government earned her the lasting enmity of both. After 4 June, she was detained by the police and investigated for being an "instigator of turmoil." In her memoir "My Imprisonment," published shortly after her release in May 1990, Dai reflected on the penchant the Chinese had for radical political change in the twentieth century. Her comments gave voice to what was probably a widespread if conservative view on the mainland. It was a view that regarded social chaos or disorder, *luan*, as being the greatest threat to the nation's prosperity and gradual political reform.

> I'm quite against "overthrowing" anything. My thinking on this subject was clarified by the late [historian] Li Shu.[47] When I interviewed him [in 1986], he said something that sent a wave of delight through me. "If at all possible it is best to avoid revolutions altogether." . . . The present debate [on politics] has pitted mass democracy and enlightened dictatorship [against each other]. If I must be classified, then I suppose I belong to the latter group . . . but my evaluation of China's present autocrats has certainly been no more flattering than that of the advocates of mass democracy. . . . However, I feel that revolution (that is, overthrowing [a system]) is far more fearful than maintaining the present political order, and the damage it would cause to China would be far greater.[48]

After the violent conclusion of the 1989 movement, many in exile attempted to keep the "movement mentality" alive. Fundamental change, the adoption of a more democratic outlook, and the acquisition of new political habits would take time and effort; movements alone offered the "quick fix" to which so many were still addicted.

HOLDING OUT AND HANGING ON

While reckless bravado remained the basis for official propaganda, in 1990 it was still difficult to evaluate the level of intellectual debate and civil disobedience in China, since the general environment was stifled by the post–4 June purge. It was easy then, indeed even fashionable, to say that the intellectual scene had been obliterated by the post-June clampdown and claim that any worthwhile new culture must come from overseas. It was an argument that was attractive, especially to the exiles, but the inability or unwillingness of the government to carry out a consistent, ideologically based purge led to a cautious revival of the intellectual scene after 1991.

Highlighting the ambivalence of the intellectuals' commitment to the democracy movement overseas was the fact that following the government relaxation in 1990–1991, there was increasing talk among some exiles about a return to China. Whereas in the Russian tradition, there may have been a place for the exiled writer or thinker to return in triumph, in China such a homecoming would rarely be welcomed. If a compromise with the authorities led to some form of reconciliation, it would be seen popularly as "pacification," *zhao'an*. This is a classical Chinese expression used to describe the subversion or co-opting of rebel leaders through promises of personal safety, an amnesty, some form of official recognition, or a government appointment. As Lee Yee, the editor in chief of *The Nineties Monthly*, one of the internationally most widely read Hong Kong journals until its demise in 1998, remarked in October 1990, many of the famous dissidents were actually "waiting for 'pacification' or even a change in the political climate on the mainland and were therefore unwilling to make an effort to study the language of their new home, or go to university . . . to begin to make a future for themselves."[49] Some dreamed of becoming a Chinese Václav Havel, Nelson Mandela, another Sun Yat-sen, or even a Lenin. Given the situation in China during the 1990s, however, the more relevant parallel was probably that of the Western-trained intellectuals and students who returned to the mainland in the 1950s. Most of this large group of talented returnees were employed by the new communist state, but they were subjected to the most demeaning forms of surveillance and lived under a cloud of suspicion throughout their careers.

The issue of rehabilitation, *pingfan*, was one of even more immediate relevance to exiles and remnant supporters of the movement on the mainland. When, how, and by whom the 4 June Beijing massacre and even the protest movement itself would be officially reevaluated and the victims rehabilitated were questions that people have been concerned with since the dawn of 4 June.[50] For years, people have scrutinized speeches and editorials in the official press for any hint of a change of tone when the events of 1989 were discussed. Similarly, the shifting terminology used by the leaders was studied with the art and intensity of veteran Kremlinologists, but since the issues touched on the lives of all Chinese, extraordinary passion was also involved. People soon noticed that from late 1989 on, there was a gradual shift in official descriptions of the movement. First it was dubbed the "turmoil that led to a counterrevolutionary rebellion" and then the "disturbance that occurred between spring and summer." The massacre itself underwent a euphemistic transformation from "quelling the counterrevolutionary riot" to the neutral "June Fourth incident." Any return to early descriptions was avidly noted and weighed up. Any leaders who had never referred to the incident at all were immediately pegged as future "reformers" or "pragmatists," and the hope for an eventual rehabilitation of the movement after the death of one or a number of the gerontocrats were pinned on them.[51]

The hope for an official rehabilitation of the activists and the movement of 1989 was one thing that, for a time, united Chinese intellectuals both on the mainland and overseas who shared a belief that an official overturning of the verdict, *fan'an*, on the major post–Cultural Revolution historical incident was crucial to social and political unity. This augured well for the Chinese Communist Party—after all, for people to believe that the party's evaluation of the events was still crucial and meaningful in the 1990s indicated that by default, there was a general acceptance of the party's preeminent political role and its right of tutelage.

Even as the 1989 protests were in full swing, Liu Xiaobo foresaw this development. In a pamphlet issued on Tiananmen Square, Liu warned demonstrators of the dangers of agitating for an official rehabilitation (that is, official approval of their patriotic protests) of their cause. He called rehabilitation "an abnormal and twisted phenomenon in (contemporary) Chinese history." He decried the "right to rehabilitate" as yet another form of political "privilege," a means by which the party maintained its own image and ensured the loyalty of its subjects. He argued that for the students to plead for rehabilitation was an acknowledgment of the government's role as the ultimate political and historical arbiter in China. "As long as the concept of rehabilitation exists," Liu wrote, "there is no chance for democracy and the rule of law in China."[52] Indeed, despite the hue and cry over the Communist Party's lack of authority, the general recognition among intellectuals of "rehabilitation" as a party prerogative amounted to a de facto recognition of its political legitimacy. This was a sobering indication of how little was achieved by the 1989 movement and its overblown rhetoric.

WRITTEN OUT OF HISTORY

Recalling Yuan Zhiming's comments in which he cautioned people against taking any notice of the intellectuals the next time there was a mass protest movement, one must question just how much of a role the self-styled independent intellectuals and activists, especially those now overseas, could really play in events in China.

One writer described in the bleakest of terms the short-range possibilities that intellectuals may have on the nation's political life. They bring to mind the fate that awaited patriotic students, businesspeople, and individuals who returned to mainland China after the Communist revolution in 1949:

> No matter what happens, the mutual disdain with which the exiles and the power holders regard each other cannot easily be overcome. There are only two likely scenarios in the near future. One is that there will be a dramatic change on the mainland and everything is turned on its head. In that case, the exiles will pack up and head home. But even then, they will no longer

be main players on the stage of history. Their return will be celebrated for a moment, and then their luster will fade and disappear.

The other possibility is that the party will make some necessary concessions, do something to salve popular resentment, thereby extending its lease on life. This won't involve forgiveness for the exiles, and people on the mainland will gradually forget about them. With the passing of time, the exiles will gradually be lost in the crowd and may well end their days in obscurity. Of course, they will be able to live out their lives in a free and democratic society; but it won't be theirs, for others have made the sacrifices that built it.[53]

CHAPTER FOUR

The Apotheosis of the *Liumang*

TERMINAL TURMOIL

In late April 1989, the Chinese government dubbed the student demonstrations that began after the death of Hu Yaobang on 15 April premeditated "turmoil," *dongluan*. The mass agitation that followed was supposedly aimed at destabilizing and overturning the nation's socialist system.[1] The causes of the turmoil were variously identified as the influence of Western intellectual and cultural trends in China during the 1980s—part of an alleged long-term U.S. strategy of encouraging "peaceful evolution" in socialist states—and the bourgeois liberalism promoted by such individuals as the astrophysicist Fang Lizhi, the literary critic Liu Xiaobo, and the writer Su Xiaokang and tolerated by party leaders like Hu Yaobang and Zhao Ziyang.[2]

This chapter is concerned with another form of turmoil, the responsibility for which cannot so easily be laid at the doorstep of malign foreign influences or outspoken, courageous individuals. It is what could be called *terminal turmoil*, a condition that developed in the wake of popular disaffection from Communist Party orthodoxy in the age of China's economic reform since the 1970s. Even though political authority in China had been constantly undermined, ideological fealty was still demanded from all. In the late 1980s, as life increasingly began to revolve around the market and not the study session, people were unsure as to how they should participate in social and political reality. Existence and illusion—or everyday life and political posturing—were often indistinguishable, and everyone had to learn how to act as a broker, negotiating a relationship between the two.

This existential malaise was accompanied by extraordinary psychological tensions. It could also be seen as the continuation and latest phase of the cultural uncertainty that has existed in China since the collapse of traditional orthodoxy in the late Qing and early republican periods nearly a century ago, the early decades of Communist rule having provided but a brief respite. It was a state of mind that became a regular feature of Chinese Communist culture in the late 1980s and 1990s, and as such it will not necessarily be coterminus with the end of formal Communist rule in China. It is part and parcel of the existential sociopolitical crisis that the Communist Party variously attempted to ignore, escape from, avert, and even co-opt. However, this particular form of *dongluan* could neither be quashed by military action nor eradicated by such unfortunate slogans as the 1990 party favorite: "Stability must crush all else."[3]

The fiction of Wang Shuo,[4] the Beijing writer who rose to prominence in 1987 and enjoyed nationwide celebrity as a novelist until 1992, reveals to us, perhaps better than any other body of writing, an internal perception of China's "terminal turmoil," depicting as he does in his numerous stories and novels the world of what I choose to call "*liumang* culture." As we will see, this rubric covers a range of creative artists and their audiences. It is also shorthand for certain urban attitudes that have been quintessentially expressed not in the tones of overt dissent but more often in the playful and ironic creations of popular culture. This is not to suggest, however, that Wang's importance should be seen only in terms of the dysfunction of official ideology with the growth of individual economic, social, and intellectual spheres. While many contemporary writers and artists have attempted to step around or ignore what they generally regard as being the corpse of the post-1942 party-directed art world that is Maoist culture, others found in the crumbling edifice of party culture fragments that could be appropriated for the creation of more vital work.[5]

Wang Shuo was not a doomsayer or a pessimist but a playful writer of serious intent who availed himself of the contemporary Chinese cultural order to depict a fictional world of great humor, perception, and release. In his work, we are dealing not only with entertainment fiction or coded political writing but also with a far more compelling form of art: a literature of escape and sublimation. This chapter attempts to trace the base elements of Wang's fictional formulas back to earlier literary and cultural sources, suggesting thereby certain "mythic" features of a body of writing that straddled both elite and popular cultural spheres in contemporary China.

FACES OF THE *LIUMANG*

In modern Chinese usage, *liumang* is a word with some of the most negative connotations in the language. In the following remarks, the expression is used loosely in an attempt to describe both a social phenomenon and its cultural refraction. The first scholar to have suggested that the significance of the word *liumang* may be seen in broader social and artistic terms is the Sinologist John Minford. Writing in 1985 about unofficial contemporary Chinese culture, he said:

> On this post-Mao wasteland a strange new indigenous culture is evolving, which could, perhaps a little provocatively, be called the culture of the *liumang* (an untranslatable term loosely meaning loafer, hoodlum, hobo, bum, punk).[6] The original *liumang* is to be seen cruising the inner city streets on his Flying Pigeon bicycle, looking (somewhat lethargically) for the action, reflective sunglasses flashing a sinister warning. *Liumang* in everyday speech is a harsh word. It is the word for antisocial behavior, a category of crime.
>
> But the *liumang* generation as I see it is a wider concept. Rapist, whore, black-marketeer, unemployed youth, alienated intellectual, frustrated artist or poet—the spectrum has its dark satanic end, its long middle band of relentless grey, and, shining at the other end, a patch of visionary light. It is an embryonic alternative culture.[7]

Whereas Minford noted that "*liumang* culture" was "similar in certain striking ways to that of the 1960s in the US and Europe"—something noted at virtually the same time by the Chinese critic He Xin (see the section "Superfluous People, Knights-Errant, and *Liumang*" in this chapter)—the focus of my comments is the indigenous aspects of the phenomenon.

The term *liumang* has a venerable pedigree in modern Chinese urban life, appearing as early as a century ago when it was first used to describe the rootless rowdies and petty criminals who plagued the growing port city of Shanghai,[8] and a rich underworld culture developed there in the first half of the twentieth century.[9] This definition was expanded to include people guilty of a large range of sexual misdemeanors, giving the term its most common range of meanings today.[10] In legal terms "a *liumang* crime" denoted anything from premarital sex to gang rape. To "play the *liumang*," *shua liumang*, is used in everyday speech to describe overt sexual suggestions or harassment of a woman by a man.[11]

The unsettling relevance and even appeal of the unruly *liumang* was recognized in the early years of the republic. Ah Q, Lu Xun's fictional Chinese everyman, is an obvious example. In the early 1920s, Zhou Zuoren, Lu Xun's brother, declared in a famous essay that "two demons live within me. . . . One is a gentleman, the other a *liumang*."[12] He went on to describe the clash between the ill-mannered, carousing, and unfettered *liumang* (a cultural id?) and the gentleman, *shenshi*, who, Zhou says, would "teach me how to present myself to young ladies, how to speak properly." The Jekyll and Hyde aspects of Zhou's character tormented him: he found that whenever he went from simply mouthing pleasantries to putting on the affected airs of the gentleman, his *liumang* alter ego would reassert itself.[13] Torn by these two demons, Zhou was unwilling to abandon either one. "I love the attitude of the gentleman and the spirit of the *liumang*," he wrote. In this essay, Zhou seemed to posit that the spirit of the *liumang* and the attitude of the gentleman were struggling for supremacy in the Chinese soul. He concluded by expressing the hope that each would eventually be able to accommodate the other, to arrive at some constitutional arrangement in which they both could hold sway. It would be better still if the *liumang* were female, he argued, then she could marry the gentleman and give birth to "an ideal prince" fit to be head of state.[14]

More recently, politically engagé writers have observed that the *liumang* nature was not limited to outrageous novelists, disrespectful critics, or street brawlers. They saw the *liumang* persona as incorporating an ominous political dimension. In his defense at his 1991 trial, the Beijing political activist Chen Ziming (who stood accused as one of the instigators of the 1989 protests) pointed out that one of the elements of the "new thinking" advocated by Wang Juntao and himself before June 1989 was for the social elite to "accept the moral duty of rebuilding the cultural superstructure and opposing the tide of *liumang* and *pizi* [riffraff] culture as well as vulgarization."[15] Disdain for the "vulgar masses" and warnings against the inroads of popular culture, *tongsu* or *dazhong wenhua*, on "serious" and committed culture, *yansu wenhua*, have been the theme of much debate in China since the early 1980s (for more on this, see chapter 11, "Kowtowing to the Vulgar"). In early 1989, the *Economic Weekly*, a Beijing paper run by Wang and Chen, published an article that commented on the *liumang* dimensions of politics. It pinpointed a social and political malaise that the author argued was far more serious than that created by social misfits, cultural rowdies, and excons and one hinted at in some of Wang Shuo's 1980s fiction. The article could also be read as an attack on the salient *liumang* nature of Communist Party rule.

> Feudalism is particularly to blame [for immoral business dealings], for such nefarious activities are one of the specialties of the *liumang*, the rootless and the dregs of society. I'm afraid they have a lot more to do with the proletariat than the bourgeoisie.
>
> The lumpen or *liumang* proletariat despises labor; it is nonproductive and parasitical. Its members do not create wealth for the society, they only consume and destroy. . . .
>
> In the age of reform, they have appeared once more in the guise of the most unscrupulous [entrepreneurs], utterly without conscience and contemptuous of the law. They take what they can and squander what they get. Unlike the bourgeoisie, who reinvest their profits and expand production, the *liumang* proletariat eats and spends until there is nothing left. They are wasteful and extravagant in the extreme and live as if there were no tomorrow.

This social stratum is adventurous, vengeful, opportunistic, and destructive.

This *liumang* mentality has already insinuated its way into some party and state organs, companies, and industries. Creaming off a percentage of whatever passes through their hands, they take every advantage of their position to eat and drink for free, exploit every bit of power they have, and use whatever resources are available to them—be it land, means of transportation, even official seals—for their personal benefit. . . .

. . . Acting as though their workplace is a piece of turf in some mafia network, doing whatever they please, and ignoring all laws and principles, these things are all part and parcel of the *liumang* mentality.[16]

A similar thesis was enunciated by the U.S.-based historian Ying-shih Yü who believed that twentieth-century Chinese history has seen the "fringe elements" *bianyuan renwu* of society, the thugs, *liumang*, and so on[17] displace intellectuals on the center stage of social and political life.[18] He equated these dregs with the "new class" spoken of by the Yugoslav dissident Milovan Djilas.[19] According to this interpretation, the playful and irreverent *liumang*, the dispossessed masses, were merely waiting in the wings for power, their frivolous attitude a disguise for more ominous political intentions.[20] In response to this argument, Wang Yi, a historian with the Chinese Academy of Social Sciences, rejected Yü's sympathetic vision of the traditional intellectual, preferring instead to cast the literati as the handmaidens of the true *liumang* of Chinese history, the power holders, a relationship that he described as being the inevitable consequence of what he called "the *liumang* emperor phenomenon."[21] Wang argued that the rise of the *liumang* and the subordination of intellectuals are abiding elements of Chinese history and hardly just an aberration of the twentieth century.[22] Similarly, in his history of beggars in China, published in 1990, the scholar Qu Yanbin noted the pervasive element of the "*liumang* mentality," *liumang yishi*, in the traditional beggar counterculture and its relationship with politics.[23] Also in the early 1990s, a number of other writers produced lengthy histories of the *liumang* in Chinese society to cash in on the popular interest in Wang Shuo's fiction and the *liumang*.[24]

The *liumang*-type characters that appear in Wang Shuo's fiction certainly developed an appreciation of the world of realpolitik, and they knew just how factional power holders acted when they were on top. Indeed, much of Wang's political satire revolves around the abuse of power by unprincipled individuals or groups. For example, in Wang's 1989 story "An Attitude," the narrator Fang Yan is arraigned in court for practicing literature without a license. One of the judges asks him how he would handle things if he were put in charge of the cultural world:

Of course, it'd be a case of letting those who submit to me prosper and those who cross me perish. Forget all that rubbish about literary forms and ideological content; none of that stuff matters. I'll support my *gemen'r* [buddies or mates] come what may; even if I was forced to purge them, I'd make sure to let them down gently. As for anyone I don't get on with or who doesn't respect me, I'd show them no mercy whatsoever.[25]

THE ENTERPRISING AUTHOR

Wang Shuo was born in 1958 and came to prominence in the mid-1980s with the publication of an impressive number of short stories that ranged from comic tales to detective fiction and love stories. By the late 1980s, he had become one of the most popular urban writers in China with a particularly large following among teenagers and readers in their twenties, especially Beijing youth, although his fans also included "intellectuals" and members of the Red Guard generation. Although he was not the subject of as much public critical attention before 1988 as other writers were, one indication of his appeal was that a number of his stories were adapted for the screen; 1988 was even dubbed the "Wang Shuo year" of Chinese film, with no fewer than four of his stories being made into feature films.[26] Of these—*fleurs de mal* as one writer dubbed them,[27] *The Operators* by Mi Jiashan of the Emei Film Studio in Sichuan and *Samsara* by Huang Jianxin of the Xi'an Film Studio best reflected the bizarre spirit of the works on which they were based.[28] In 1988, *The Operators* was arguably the most outstanding satire to be produced for the Chinese screen since Huang Jianxin's mordantly witty *Black Cannon Incident* of 1985. Huang's own *Samsara* took a dark look at the world of the entrepreneur, adding to the original story an apocalyptic view of the future (at the end, the protagonist of the film jumps off a building).[29]

In 1989, Zuo Shula, a Beijing film critic born in 1954, published a Chinese-style "new journalism" biographical essay on Wang. Zuo, who spent days interviewing and socializing with Wang, tried, in his cheeky portrait, to capture the mood of what may be called the other Cultural Revolution generation. They were not the idealistic Red Guards, but their younger brothers and sisters who witnessed it all but grew up not disillusioned but dismissive, young people who had never believed the strident rhetoric. It was a generation to which both Zuo and Wang belonged. This younger generation, people who were now in their thirties, either were born at the inception of the Cultural Revolution or were still in primary school at the time. They spent their childhood in a world that was both chaotic and mendacious; they came of age in the materialistic 1980s, enjoying the consumer culture of the reform age with few of the ideological, intellectual, or emotional qualms experienced by the older generations. Indeed, Wang's popularity among readers in their twenties and early thirties genuinely mystified and distressed their elders (even those in the Red Guard generation), many of whom initially responded to the Wang Shuo craze by dismissing the author as a literary "lightweight" or a mere purveyor of the much-maligned genre of "popular fiction."

A few samples from Zuo's essay may help convey something of the flavor of the whole work:

> Wang Shuo—Manchu Bannerman—is nothing much to look at. When the "historically unprecedented" Cultural Revolution broke out in 1966, he was in his second year of primary school. As Mao said, in those days every man was a law unto himself. Everything and everybody except for the Red Sun had been overthrown. . . .
>
> Given this state of affairs, it didn't take much effort for little Wang Shuo to learn that his father, a military officer who'd boasted about fighting the Japs in the war, had actually worked for them as a policeman.
>
> As the Cultural Revolution took hold, so did the tendency among the kids of Beijing to become delinquents. . . . Young toughs set out from their home turf, creating havoc, and looking for thrills. The boys and girls of Beijing from twelve to twenty lived for kicks and sex. In 1969, when the senior high school kids all were banished to the countryside, the city settled down a little.
>
> "The prairie fires cannot burn all the grass; when the spring winds blow it is reborn." Wang Shuo's generation grew up in the 1970s, and there was nothing the older kids could do that they couldn't do even better. They let loose with a vengeance and took the town over again, though not on the same scale as the Red Guards.[30]

During the Cultural Revolution, Wang was jailed twice, once for getting involved in a gang fight, the second time for grabbing a policeman's cap when Tiananmen Square was being cleared during the first Tiananmen incident of 5 April 1976. After he graduated from middle school in the same year, his father made him join the People's Liberation Army as a sailor. He was stationed at Qingdao with the North Sea Fleet and soon found the hierarchy and corruption in the navy to be oppressive. He rebelled by spending most of his time womanizing and lazing about on the beach. As Zuo records:

> He . . . became a sailor of leisure. He took no notice of rules and regulations. A serviceman who doesn't have the slightest interest in joining the party or getting a commission and doesn't break the law can get away with a hell of a lot. At worst he'd be booted out. So what was there to be scared

of? . . . "Let our thinking break free of all restraints, the Internationale will be realized!" was Wang Shuo's theme song.[31]

In 1978, Wang published his first story in *People's Liberation Army Literature and Art*.[32] It impressed the editors so much that he was even given a job with the magazine. Apart from rejecting manuscripts by the two then prominent literary figures, Yao Xueyin and Wang Yaping,[33] Wang says he left no mark on the journal. With the beginning of the reform era, he joined some childhood friends in Beijing and started a smuggling operation in the south, thereby launching a new career as a PLA profiteer.[34] In early 1979, he returned to his base in a mood of patriotic self-sacrifice when the Sino-Vietnamese conflict broke out, only to find that he was neither needed nor wanted at the front. Demobilized in 1980, he worked for a pharmaceutical company in Beijing for three years, spending most of his time lolling about the office, going to films, and chasing women. He got involved in illegal trade again, was caught and fined by the police, became a professional bagman (like the hero in the film *Samsara*), and even toyed with the idea of buying a car and becoming a taxi driver when that became a profitable new career option in the early 1980s. Wang finally decided to go straight, but after spending all his savings, he started living off his women friends, first a Youth League party secretary and then a flight attendant. His affair with the latter became the basis of his unexceptional 1984 story "The Flight Stewardess,"[35] which marked his true literary debut. While he was still living with the stewardess, Wang started an affair with a dancer. He moved in with her, and they eventually got married and had a daughter.[36] They separated in 1993 at around the time Wang gave up writing fiction and launched a new career as a filmmaker.

In 1986, Wang Shuo began publishing fiction regularly. The novelist's own vision of himself is summed up in remarks he made to Zuo Shula:

I know just what I'm capable of. If you think I should be doing something for others, serving the People or whatnot, well, quite frankly, I reckon about the only thing I could manage to do in that department is to polish their shoes. I've got no other talents. I've lived this long and apart from my mouth, which has been overexercised, everything else is underdeveloped. I can't just go out and lie to people, can I? (After all, I've tried and it doesn't work.) It's no fun, either—you need to know just as much as you do to write fiction, and it doesn't have the same status. . . . Anyway, writing isn't entirely the same as prostitution, something you can get away with if you're shameless enough. Even now, I wouldn't say I'm a master of the technique of fiction writing. Buggered if I know all the ins and outs of it. And if you want me to natter on about intellectual content, philosophy, the grand sweep . . . well, just give me a break.[37]

Although Wang's rebellious spirit and the absurdist political dimension of his writing may have been chiefly informed by the iconoclasm of the Cultural Revolution, his independence as an individual and an artist had much more to do with the reforms of the 1980s. Whereas older establishment figures actually had to make an effort to "engage in life," *shenru shenghuo*, to use the dated party formula, by going on planned research trips for their new novels, Wang Shuo just lived. Not an official state artist on a fixed wage, he made a living from his writing and enjoyed an unfettered existence, spending his spare time engaging in various business activities and playing mahjong with his friends. Up to the early 1990s, Wang Shuo and his circle of friends belonged to the category labeled by the state as "socially idle people."[38] Wang characterized the reasons for his virtually unique status in the Chinese cultural world of the late 1980s in remarks he made to a journalist concerning the types of characters he preferred writing about. The journalist observed that

> Wang Shuo is lucky to be a member of the least restricted social group [in China]: the financially independent unemployed. They are not what is usually understood by the term *entrepreneur*; they have no grand ambitions as far as work or lifestyle goes; financially well-off, they can't be induced by material benefits or hurt by their withdrawal. In relative terms, their souls are untormented, and although they are careful not to break the law, they can do just about whatever they want.[39]

Less charitable commentators declared that Wang's favorite characters were nothing less than "potential criminals."[40]

LIUMANG, PIZI, AND WANZHU

Zuo Shula quotes a young literary theoretician who said that Wang "enjoys — even positively delights in — depicting the *liumang* lifestyle."[41] Zuo himself discusses Wang's relationship with his father, a representative of the older generation, in the terms of a *liumang*-esque exchange:

> Wang Shuo's parents subscribed to the theory "spare the rod and spoil the child." Every time he acted up, his father beat the shit out of him. This went on until the old boy was physically too feeble to get away with it. Apart from toughening Wang Shuo's hide, the beatings only succeeded in making him hate his old man. And given his father's dubious past, it was only natural that Wang Shuo's rebellion began at home. . . .
>   "You're nothing but a hooligan [*liumang*]!" his father shouted.
>   "Chairman Mao teaches us to distinguish between big and small prob-

lems," Wang Shuo retorted. "So-and-so's father was penalized for hooliganism, and still they let him have a position in the leadership. My case is insignificant compared with his."

"You've got a real attitude problem, young man."

"Everyone makes mistakes. I'm just like you: a good person who's made mistakes."

The father exploded. "Get the hell out of here!"

"Where to?" the son responded, not fazed in the slightest. "I wouldn't stay here if I had anywhere else to go. I'm a 'blossom of the Motherland,' and it's your patriotic duty to nurture me. Part of the wages and the apartment you get from the state are intended for me."[42]

Much of the dialogue in Wang's story "The Operators" was taken from such exchanges.[43]

Whereas 1980s Chinese literature saw a general trend to displace the inhumanly perfect protagonists of the pre-1978 era with normal, if sometimes ill-adjusted, law-abiding people, Wang Shuo's fiction went a step further, finding its heroes in the underbelly of urban society, among "potential criminals," the idle and chronically unemployable. Increasing numbers of *liumang*-type characters had made an appearance in Chinese literature in the late 1970s,[44] yet Wang's consistently understanding and sympathetic, as well as highly popular, portrayal of such figures became, according to one critic, "a means for overturning the extreme value judgments [of China]. Life can no longer be understood in terms of black and white or good and bad. With Wang Shuo we enter a state of confusion."[45] It was a state that critics found unsettling because it found expression in the realm, diction, and style of an irrepressible, and not particularly pleasant, group:

> They're bored and frustrated, creating their own diversions. They don't give a damn whether normal people sympathize with them or view them with distaste. They do nothing and treat those who go about their business earnestly with ridicule and derision. In practical terms, they are the "dregs" rejected by society; their activities show them to be blatantly out of step with or in opposition to the normal order and the moral precepts of the society. Their psychological makeup determines that they are completely incompatible with the environment, and when the rest of us look down on them with disgust and displeasure, they respond with an even more dismissive stance.[46]

In his comic fiction, not only did Wang Shuo reject the heroic models of post–Cultural Revolution literature—intellectuals, students, rustic (as opposed to revolutionary) peasants, and sentimental or heroic soldiers—he also went against accepted moral standards.[47] Much of his writing represented an anarchic "unofficial" world, one that Wang colored with the rich and sardonic patois of Beijing. For a time, Wang Shuo was considered to be primarily a contemporary writer of "common person" fiction, *pingmin xiaoshuo*, yet at every turn he threatened and at times defiled the existing (or, rather, revived and expanded the post–Cultural Revolution) official canon. His promoters even claimed for his comic writings the status of "new Beijing fiction";[48] others decried it as "*liumang* literature" that was beneath contempt.[49]

Both his fans and his detractors were drawn to compare Wang with Lao She, an earlier Manchu novelist renowned for his poignant stories and his genius in representing the fatalistic and humorous temper of the Old Peking before 1949. Lao She, a celebrated People's artist, was also a key figure in party literary history, and his works were interpreted to be ideologically acceptable (with, perhaps, the exception of a problematic anti-Communist political sci-fi satire *Cat City* [Maocheng ji] written in the 1940s). In the early 1980s, a number of Beijing-based writers vied to be crowned with the mantle of Lao She's successor.[50] That Wang could even be considered in the running rankled the self-appointed upholders of literary morality as well as the champions of critical realism. One irate critic decried Wang's writing as nothing less than an assault on cultural orthodoxy: "First and foremost, his [fiction] is a reaction against Mr Lao She. Lao She also wrote about prostitutes, but he did so from a critical high ground. One can only conclude that Lao She was a great man, Wang Shuo a nothing."[51]

The story "Hot and Cold, Measure for Measure,"[52] later made into one of the four 1988 Wang Shuo films, describes the career of Zhang Ming, a personable and humorous ex–labor reform con who makes a living as a blackmailer (he impersonates a policeman and extorts money from rich Hong Kong travelers who pick up the women for whom Zhang and his friends pimp). Wu Di, an innocent but adventurous university student, finds herself attracted to Zhang and his unfettered lifestyle and eventually falls in love with him. She enters his world, becomes a prostitute, and, still in love with him though despairing at the realization he may never have loved her at all, kills herself when they are finally detained by the police. Zhang is sent back to jail. After his release, and at the end of the story, he takes up with another girl who is strikingly similar to Wu Di.

A critique of the story written by Chen Yishui of the Municipal Institute for Labor Reform in Jinan, Shandong Province, perhaps best summed up the general reaction among more "responsible" readers to Wang's work and is typical of the tone of many attacks on Wang in the early 1990s:

> This is a work that describes in dulcet tones the pleasures of a licentious,
> treacherous, and boorish criminal world. It's as if the author is standing on
> a grassy knoll in the middle of a swamp, appealing affectionately to his

young readers to gather around and hear his tale. But I despair for these young readers; I fear that they will sink into the mire and be unable to extricate themselves. . . .

The writer's literary talent is undeniable. He cunningly sucks his readers, especially younger ones, into the thick of this tale of felony and vice. It's an excellent textbook on a host of subjects ranging from how to seduce young girls to ways of concealing a crime. The first half of the story in which the man is the protagonist glorifies the seduction of women, unrestrained hooliganism, fraud, and crime. When a woman takes center stage in the second half, cock-teasing and egotistical hedonism are championed. These two halves make a whole in which the bleached bones of the dissolute relations between young men and women, of an unbridled and "free" lifestyle, are laid bare. It's hard to believe that these sorts of things are happening in China in the mid-1980s. Even if they are, they are surely rare and isolated phenomena. We must ask ourselves, what possible benefit is it to anyone to exaggerate such unrepresentative, foul and smutty things and parade them in public? . . .

If this isn't a primer for sexual crime, what is it?[53]

Wang Shuo and his opus represented a phenomenon that not only horrified the Jinan Municipal Institute for Labor Reform—hardly an organization one would think could claim the moral high ground—but frightened "decent" society in general: the rise to social prominence of the *liumang*, a term that, as we have seen, covered everything from hooligans to alienated youth, individualists, and unscrupulous entrepreneurs. While the reform policies encouraged private business initiative, both party reformists and their opponents were often appalled by the sorts of people who took the lead.

Many of the stories Wang Shuo published up to the end of 1991, when he took a break from his career as a fiction writer, were populated with what critics have called *pizi, wanzhu*, or just plain *liumang*.

Pizi is another difficult term to translate. It is often rendered as "ruffian" or "riffraff," though in contemporary usage it often implies a kind of cunning and intelligence; in certain contexts, the expression *smart-ass* is a suitable rendering. When commenting on two of the four films based on Wang Shuo's stories, Song Chong, the former head of the Beijing Film Studio (relieved of his post after June 1989) said that they were representative of "*pizi* culture." He was quoted as having remarked that: "[these films] are written by a *pizi* for *pizi*; *pizi* read them to read about *pizi*; and in the end it has given birth to a whole new class of *pizi*."[54] The *pizi* in this context can be taken to mean a type of garrulous, wisecracking *liumang*. Echoing a refrain from He Xin (see the following section), the film critic Zhong Chengxiang, the most energetic critic of bourgeois liberalization in the post–4 June film world, spoke of the "hippy irreverence" of the films. "I am of the opinion that this 'hippy irreverence'[55] is inimical to ideological cohesion and the encouragement of ideals. It has the side effect of [encouraging] laxity and dissolution."[56]

Wanzhu is a Beijing term that Wang Shuo employed to characterize the protagonists of the novella *The Operators*. In Beijing dialect, the word *wan* (or *wan'r*, pronounced *wa'r*, literally "to play" or "fool around") has the meaning of "to do" or "to work." It often conveys a slightly self-deprecating or flippant tone, as in the expression used by glib litterateurs, *wan'r wenxue*, "to play at writing literature." Apart from this more obvious use, it also appears in a variety of phrases such as *wan'r bu zhuan* (can't handle or deal with),[57] *wan'r huahuo* (play dirty), *wan'r yinde* (screw someone), *wan'r wan* (to be wiped out or finished), and even *wan'r qu* (get lost).[58] It is known for its use in a classical Confucian expression: *wan ren sang de, wan wu sang zhi*, "to toy with people undermines morality; to play with curios undermines rectitude."[59] In the 1980s, the expression gained an ever wider currency and was used by many young people as a substitute for the vulgar verb *gao* (meaning a number of things from "to do," "carry out" to "screw"). *Gao* was popularized by Mao Zedong, for whom it was a dialect verb common in his Hunan argot. His use of it led to the creation of such bizarre political slogans as *gao geming* (make revolution) and *ba jingji gaoshangqu* (get the economy going). The somewhat supercilious *wan'r* had none of the gung-ho enthusiasm of *gao*, and it became an ideal vehicle for the expression of the glib irreverence that increasingly typified youth culture in the early 1990s.[60]

The *wanzhu* was "a master of *wan'r* (fooling around)." Wang Shuo's "The Operators" is an episodic tale of the antics of a group of three self-employed *wanzhu* who set up the "Three T Company." They sell their services as "social stuntmen." As their own promotional line puts it, they are proxies who "get people out of difficulty, help people amuse themselves, and take the place of people in trouble." Thus the name "Three T," *santi* in Chinese, literally "the three substitutes."[61] Their services include sending out one of their number to fill in for a man who can't make a date with a young woman. The stand-in keeps the girl in question occupied with blather about the meaning of life, touching on Nietzschean philosophy, Freud, and existentialism—hot topics that dominated the conversations of affected young Beijing pseuds, the object of much of Wang Shuo's satire, in the late 1980s. After taking on the task of entertaining the neglected girl, Yang Zhong, the "Three T Company" worker, eventually exhausts himself and is in turn subjected to a mock-Freudian analysis. She asks, "I'm sure you really want to marry your mother?" The dumbfounded Yang Zhong then weathers a typical Wang Shuo-esque rant:

> Now I'm not saying that you and your mother are married. That would be outrageous. No one can marry their own mother, that's incest. What I'm saying is that you'd like to be married to your mother but you can't be-

cause of your father unless your father was castrated, though that would-n't really solve matters because of ethical considerations, so you agonize over it, and you can't fall for anyone else and only want to marry your mother but you can't because of your father; how come I'm talking in cir-cles? Anyway, I don't know, but that's just the way it is, and in foreign books of quotations they say that the person you end up looking for as a partner is really your mother.[62]

But despite desultory efforts to make a living at such nonsensical body dou-bling in the late 1980s and suffering the consequences, the *wanzhu* were essen-tially little more than windy Chinese slackers. The spirit of *wanzhu* complacen-cy is perhaps best summed up in an outburst that Yu Guan, the company manager, makes after being hectored by Zhao Yaoshun,[63] a self-important and condescending middle-aged intellectual who has just told him that he should take a more positive attitude toward life and society. Yu Guan responds:

> We can put up with all types of inconvenience and still feel perfectly at ease. That's because we know there's no such thing as perfection in this world. Things are the same wherever you go. We ask nothing of other peo-ple; even if our lives are unsatisfactory, we don't go around blaming others. Anyway, no one else can be blamed; not that we feel that we've been badly done by or that we should despise the world. If you make it, you can influ-ence the whole world; if you're poor, then just take care of yourself.[64] Since we won't get anywhere, we'd rather just live out our days in peace.[65]

If this is a declaration of disaffection, it was also a statement of disinterested-ness. Often the stance of the *wanzhu* is somewhat more positive, although not in any way constructive. At one point, Yu Guan advises a friend, "That's the idea, enjoy life to the full, that'll really piss everyone off mightily."[66] A critic writing in late 1989 saw the *wanzhu* as representing a threat to the society, but in his com-ments it is easy to see why such characters were popular, especially with disaf-fected urban youth:

> The *wanzhu* of his [Wang Shuo's] pen despise all that is noble; for them [nobility] is nothing but a cloak of hypocrisy. They don't believe in any-thing, since for them beliefs are nothing more than lies concocted to fool people. They're fed up with all the talk of ideals and consider ideals fit only for cretins and simpletons. They are in open rebellion against the social order and moral standards, for they think that order and morality are but a smokescreen masking a vile and ridiculous farce.[67]

A more positive appraisal of Wang's *wanzhu* was made by the critic Dai Jin-hua, who wrote in early 1989 that in the context of the economic and social

changes of 1988, Wang's heroes represented a type of "new person," *xinren*. Dai
even went so far as to call them "contemporary heroes." She makes the point that
Wang's works did not reject the society out of hand but offered the reader a means
of coming to grips with a society in which ideological systems and values were in
a state of extreme flux. Readers could finally enjoy, Dai claimed, a modern literature in which they could find "release, satisfaction, and consolation."[68] At the
time, this was a valid point and similar to observations made by Liu Qing, a
Shanghai scholar of youth culture. Liu had called the "antiheroes" of "The Operators" "pseudo-*pizi*," a group of characters caught between real low-life hooligans and socially acceptable hypocrites, which Wang Shuo employed in his fiction as sardonic yet understanding observers to reflect and comment on
contemporary society.[69] Certainly, Wang Shuo popularized elements of Beijing's
underclass, but it was an underclass that had been digested by the party's army-
brat elite to which he belonged. At one time, the party appropriated the voice of
the peasantry and dispossessed proletariat. In the late 1980s, popular writers like
Wang Shuo commercialized the language of Old Peking and its lower classes
and claimed it for themselves.

In the film version of "The Operators,"[70] the director Mi Jiashan symbolized
the social "chaos" or ideological and economic turmoil of the late 1980s in a fashion show staged at the end of a prize-giving ceremony organized by the Three-T
Company. As one reviewer described the episode:

> Various pairs of opposites from throughout Chinese history are thrown to-
> gether on stage: an imperial plenipotentiary with a near-naked female
> weight lifter; a landlord and a poor peasant; the Red and White armies; the-
> PLA and Chiang Kai-shek bandits; a Red Guard and a Capitalist Roader . . .
> all disco dancing on the same stage. It is a historically important collage, a
> miniaturization of Chinese society itself, one in which numerous ideologies
> are trapped discoing on the same stage. . . .
>   . . . On one hand Wang Shuo is engaged in an unprecedented satiriza-
> tion of tradition; on the other he has declared at seminars that "there's noth-
> ing particularly wrong with tradition." This is a typical reflection of how two
> different ideologies are disco dancing in the heads of a generation of Chi-
> nese thinkers. . . . After much reflection there's only one solution: just
> dance on![71]

The literary critic Huang Ziping claimed that he popularized the term *wan* in
reference to literature in the 1980s.[72] Be that as it may, by the end of the decade
the expression was being used to cover nearly any activity, from dabbling in philosophy to speculating on the stock market. It had become fashionable to *wan*,

but as the Shanghai literary critic Zhu Dake observed: "In a kingdom where all belief has been lost who, after all, is playing with whom?"[73]

In 1989, Wang Shuo published a sequel to "The Operators." The new story, "An Attitude," was an extraordinary satire of the Chinese literary world, in particular the Beijing literary scene in the late 1980s.[74] The same group of friends, *gemen'r*, as appeared in "The Operators" once more find themselves at loose ends. Being a *liumang* is too much like hard work, they argue, so they decide to do the next best thing and really slack off: they become writers.

The story contains a parody of a writer discussing literature with a group of literary groupies. Wang's hero Fang Yan is kidnapped and forced to address a gathering of university students. In his lecture, Fang reveals his view of what he means by "playing at literature," *wan wenxue*. His remarks lead to a confrontation, and the values championed by the self-important university students definitely come off second best. Fang makes the point that literature is nothing more than a "wank" (here a rather free translation for the word *wan*):

> "Personally, I'm in favor of literature serving the Workers, Peasants, and Soldiers."
>
> The audience hisses.
>
> "That's to say I'm in favor of fooling around with literature for the sake of Workers, Peasants, and Soldiers."
>
> Peals of laughter mixed with whistles.
>
> "There's nothing people in the older generation like me can do about it. . . ."
>
> Laughter.
>
> "We're fixated on being concerned for the Nation and the People. We've never seen ourselves as individuals. If it wasn't for the attraction of being able to aspire to some lofty purpose or other, life'd hold no interest at all. It'd be a bore, everything is a bore!"
>
> The audience laughs.
>
> "It's been like this my whole life. You can't expect an eighty-year-old to change. Would it even be possible? I'm too old; might as well drop dead and be done with it."
>
> Applause.[75]

But the audience is full of fashionably serious and idealistic young people—a favorite target of Wang Shuo's satire.[76]

> A girl stood up and asked loudly, her face bright red: "But do we have to *wan* literature?" She sat down again quickly, disappearing in the mass of people.
>
> "Do you have to *wan*? You can't do anything but *wan*." I replied.

"Well, we're not going to." A pack of sweet, innocent girls in the front row chorused, "No way."

"So what *do* you *wan?*"

"Nothing; we'll head for the hills at the first hint of *wan.*"

"Spend all your time hiding at home then?"

"We study Western modernism." One daring girl spoke up. . . .

"You're still *wan*, it's just that you're doing it for yourself and your own mob."

"All right, if that's how you want it, we do *wan*, and we like it. But we don't want your type of *wan*. The way we *wan*, we can come up with philosophical insight."

"Whatever you say, you're free to do what you want. But since we're all into *wan*, why not do it for the majority of people?"

"We like to *wan* with the elite."77

"But normal people need you much more than the elite does. They're in a pitiful position; if we don't *wan* for them, no one else will. As for the elite, they've always got ways to occupy themselves; if all else fails, they can always get their kicks out of reading foreign books."78

The author's barbs were not meant only for students, even if college kids and intellectuals were constant targets in his stories.79 After making a string of disparaging comments about the intellectual elite, Fang Yan imitates Deng Xiaoping's style of speech and proclaims: "I have repeatedly said with all sincerity and concern that under no circumstances should we ever forget the masses, 99 percent of the population. So long as the 800 million peasants and 3 million PLA men are at peace, the empire will be stable."80

The students start heckling, and Fang Yan launches into an attack on them. He finishes his argument by angrily shouting: " 'Don't any of you try pulling any shit on me—I'm a *liumang*, and I'm not scared of anyone!' "81

The elements of political satire here—the mimicking of the avuncular utterances of cultural and party leaders, the slight against the elite followed by an attack on the pompous insincerity of the "party elder" (Fang Yan), and the final explosion and admission—are obvious. It was this spirit of controlled confusion in Wang Shuo's comic writing that reflected the absurdities of a China in which the hidebound ethos of party rule was spinning out of kilter with the freewheeling economic realities of the society at large. While various groups, political conservatives, radicals, and elitists argued their positions in the public media—and attempted to influence party policy—Wang Shuo's fictional world fed off the absurdities of contemporary China to win him a mass following. In the process, he conflated the realms of serious and popular literature in a fashion that was to become a prevalent style in the 1990s, so much so that even nonparty writers and critics who presumed themselves to be the embodiment of an idealized literati tradition blamed Wang for the degradation of Chinese culture (see chapter 11, "Kowtowing to the Vulgar").

In 1990, Wang was most frequently criticized for his playfulness in regard to the sacrosanct realm of literature. His critics charged that his approach was in direct conflict with the premises of socialist culture. In an article pointing out the dangers of the philosophy of *wan*, Jin Sheng, mentioned earlier, a leading orthodox critic who rose to prominence after June 1989, quoted from Wang's story "An Attitude."[82] Others darkly hinted that writers like Wang were guilty of a socially irresponsible "hippy approach" in their writing,[83] and yet another outraged writer in Shanghai published a critique that read in part:

> In [Wang Shuo's novel] *Living Dangerously* and "An Attitude," profanity becomes the be-all and end-all. Fang Yan and his pals act as though they are living for profanity alone. In fact, they are the slaves of blasphemy . . . not only has profanity devoured Fang Yan, Yu Guan, and the others; it has overwhelmed all ideals and even Wang Shuo himself, a man who once showed promise as a talented novelist.[84]

Although Wang Shuo published only one story in 1990, it is not hard to imagine his response to these fulminations. Again we can refer to Zuo Shula's observations on the writer, in which he said the following about the generational conflict in China:

> Wang Shuo doesn't care what other people might say about him. To be quite honest, which of those leaders, famous men, or "scholars," including the people of his father's generation, have led completely blameless lives? You can't help laughing at all that crap they feed you about how "we 1950s people are so uncomplicated, so serious."[85]

SUPERFLUOUS PEOPLE, KNIGHTS-ERRANT, AND THE *LIUMANG*

On one level, the *liumang*, *wanzhu* and *pizi* of Wang Shuo's fiction represented the spirit of the alienated, semicriminal fringe of Beijing youth culture and Chinese urban life in general. Nonetheless, it was a street culture that had been reformulated by a writer who came from a privileged army background, a subaltern translated into literary and cultural trope by a canny writer for an avid audience. Offshore critics at times interpreted Wang's loutish heroes variously as Chinese

Gen-Xers, or slackers, but the *liumang* society contained a wider spectrum of meaning and significance that included important strains from premodern Chinese popular culture.

The debate about what could be termed *"liumang* culture" in China first came into the open in the mid-1980s. While the Sinologist translator John Minford was reflecting on the positive significance of the *liumang* in mid-1985 (see the section "Faces of the *Liumang*" in this chapter), the critic He Xin perceived an unsettling skein connecting certain disparate social, cultural, and political phenomena. The approach He took in those early vitriolic essays, the first of which was published under the title "Absurdity and Superfluous People in Contemporary Literature" in 1985, is highly suggestive in terms of our considerations of *"liumang* culture" as well as being indicative of the increasing official wariness of urban social trends reflected in literature.

> When approaching deconstruction, collapse, or transformation, virtually every culture produces different anticultural elements. Chinese history is no exception. For example, there were the wandering scholars and knights-errant of the Warring States period [before the fifth century B.C.] who used their writings to confound authority or who broke taboos with their fighting. There were the wanton literati of the Wei-Jin period, represented by the totally uninhibited Sages of the Bamboo Grove [third century A.D.] . . . It is in such antisocial attitudes that we can see common elements between the superfluous man [of nineteenth-century Russian fiction] and the outsider (or hippies). Thus certain contemporary literary trends lead us to reflect deeply on their real significance.[86]

Equating antisocial elements of traditional China and the modern West when commenting on the 1985 short story "Variations Without a Theme" by the Beijing writer Xu Xing,[87] He Xin wrote:

> In fact, the "hippies" that appeared in the West in the 1970s were also a kind of "superfluous people." In historical terms, whenever traditional values break down or when a culture goes through a period of crisis, an attitude surfaces that casts doubt on, satirizes, and calls for a reevaluation of basic values, culture, and even life itself. "Superfluous people" evince just such a temper. China has had these types since ancient times; there's nothing new or different about them today. For example, there was the obfuscating [philosopher] Zhuangzi, as well as Liezi and Yang Zhu, and of course the disciples of Liu Ling, the man who took the world for the inside of his pants and life for a bout of drinking.[88] There's also the Mad Monk Master Ji who defamed the Buddha and swore at the patriarchs,[89] and the like. All of them

share the same cynical "hippy" spirit. Nietzsche summed up the intellectual crisis of the Western value system in one sentence: "God is dead!"[90]

It is of no small interest to note at this juncture that in his 1989 autobiography, *Solitude and Challenge,* He Xin revealed that in his youth he fell in with members of Beijing's underground secret societies and became something of a *liumang* himself.[91] Some would argue that his juvenile dalliances with these louts stood him in good stead for the future. His support for the government after 4 June (see chapter 3, "Traveling Heavy") and his eagerness to see his ideological enemies and intellectual rivals routed earned for him the reputation of being little more than a "political *liumang*."

In early 1986, the literary critic Liu Xiaobo (later to become one of He Xin's nemeses) made his first foray into the field of contemporary culture by publishing an article that may be construed as a response to He Xin's attack on "superfluous people" and "hippy art."[92] Liu made a spirited defense of three experimental writers popular in 1985—Xu Xing, Chen Cun, and Liu Suola. He praised them for "ridiculing the sacred, the lofty, and commonly valued standards and traditional attitudes." Liu asked:

> Who are the protagonists [in the three stories by Xu, Chen, and Liu]? Are they models of decadence and cynicism? Are they the descendants of the "superfluous people" and "derelicts" that appear so often in Chinese and Western nineteenth- and twentieth-century literature? Are they a contemporary Chinese mutant form of the "absurdists," "Dadaists," "black humorists," and "beat generation" of modern and contemporary Western literature? It would seem that they contain elements of all these.[93]

Liu also concurred that there was something of the "hippy" in the protagonists of these stories, and he approved of it. Like He Xin, Liu Xiaobo saw traditional "individualists" like Zhuangzi, Tao Yuanming, and the Seven Sages of the Bamboo Grove as being related to these modern spokespeople for irreverence.[94] Whereas He Xin had disapproved, Liu Xiaobo was overwhelmingly enthusiastic. In 1990, these three novelists were to be grouped together again by another critic, along with three other Beijing writers who had risen to prominence in the late 1980s—Ma Jian, Liu Yiran,[95] and Wang Shuo—to be denounced as "rebellious aristocrats" whose works displayed a "*liumang* mentality."[96] The connection between the earlier novelists like Xu Xing and Wang Shuo was recognized by filmmakers as well, and Mi Jiashan included material from Xu's "Variations Without a Theme"—the subject of He Xin's original critique—in his screen version of "The Operators."[97] Xu's story was narrated by a youth who worked as a waiter in a major hotel. Despite this camouflage, it exuded an existential angst. A story with far stronger links to the *liumang* subculture was Kai Fangyi's "Each Take a Turn." Produced in early 1987 by a real waiter working in a joint-venture hotel in the capital, it was written mostly in the argot of Beijing.[98]

While there may be no direct, easily identified connection between the 1980s and 1990s cultural *liumang*, the knight-errant, and the unconventional figures of tradition, a reading of Chinese literature and criticism reveals a generic relationship.[99] It is one that some writers—of whom He Xin is only the most prominent—warned the authorities was of crucial importance in understanding and coping with the attitude of China's urban youth.

Knights-errant—*youxia*, *xiake*, or *xiashi*—wandering chivalrous fighters for justice and sometimes simply self-righteous toughs, formed a special and usually admired group in traditional China. They often were Buddhist or Taoist mendicants who in turn were inspired by the values of the knight-errant or fantastic adventures described by Tang dynasty (seventh century) narrative *chuanqi* or *haoxia* tales.[100] They represented for many the free and unfettered spirit of the individual. The ideals of the knight-errant are generally enunciated as altruism, justice, individual freedom, personal loyalty, courage, truthfulness and mutual faith, honor and fame, generosity, and contempt for wealth.[101] The range of qualities of the knight-errant from positive through to negative is not unlike those said to be possessed by the modern urban *liumang*, as discussed in this chapter. In contemporary China, the *liumang* were a different order of displaced persons, not necessarily the rural or urban dispossessed or vagrants.

The traditional popularity of the exploits of knight-errant heroes had been kept alive, albeit in a subdued form, in party literature since the 1950s. Qu Bo's 1957 novel *Tracks in the Snowy Forest*—on which both the 1960s Hong Kong martial arts film *Treasure Island*[102] and the Beijing Revolutionary Model Opera *Taking Tiger Mountain by Strategy* were based—depicted, for example, a more wholesome, revolutionary group of heroes. Traditional popular knight-errant culture underwent a revival on the mainland in the 1980s, fostered initially by the introduction of kungfu (*wuxia* and *wuda*) literature, films, and television series from Hong Kong. Martial arts genres had continued to develop in both Hong Kong and Taiwan since the 1950s, and it was this refined and modernized version of an ancient subculture that was now reimported to the mainland.

After 1980, increasing numbers of mainland filmmakers and TV directors attempted to emulate Hong Kong kungfu movies with films like *The Mysterious Great Buddha*.[103] The mainland even produced its own answer to Hong Kong's Bruce Lee in the person of Li Lianjie, later known as Jet Lee, the martial arts champion who starred in the 1982 box-office hit *Shaolin Temple*.[104] Also during the 1980s, the modern master of martial arts fiction, Jin Yong, a Hong Kong–based tycoon journalist,[105] became the most popular writer on the mainland and arguably the most widely read living Chinese novelist.[106]

This newborn popularity of martial arts culture can be seen in relation to a complex of social issues on the mainland. It was in part a popular response to the official negation of Cultural Revolution ideology, a corollary to the spiritual confusion that ensued and an expression of the longing for a sense of cultural continuity (one that was based in popular traditions, rather than on elitist or Confucian/Communist models).[107] Although the object of serious study, if not reverence, in Hong Kong and Taiwan since the 1970s, it was not until the late 1980s that scholars and critics on the mainland began to investigate the importance of kungfu culture in contemporary Chinese life and the reasons for its overwhelmingly popular following. In early 1989, for example, Wang Zheng, a reporter writing in the *People's Daily*, pondered the question of why so many top-ranking intellectuals, not to mention average readers, were devotees of modern kungfu fiction:

> Some Chinese intellectuals complain that "life is a bore." . . . It seems that today, when people should be thanking their lucky stars that life is "peaceful and uneventful," there's a feeling that people don't have any way of expressing themselves to the extent of their abilities. Meanwhile, Chinese intellectuals remain bound by the traditional sense of mission and social responsibility; thus they are itching to do something with their lives. . . . In the great dramas of kungfu novels, they can find a passionate release, even if the actual fighting is fairly meaningless. . . . The heroes of these novels do not have to worry about distinguishing good from bad, nor do they care one whit for convention, propriety, or the law; they do what they feel like, have no regrets and no complaints. Although they endure incredible hardships, in the end poetic justice is always theirs. This clearly gives intellectuals who are totally powerless to extricate themselves from the Way of the Golden Mean a certain kind of spiritual comfort.[108]

Wang argued that readers were excited by the personal possibilities with which the reforms presented them but were frustrated by their impotence in the face of the actual economic maelstrom in which they lived. "They are burdened by heavy workloads," he wrote, "undernourished and weighed down by endless household chores." They did not dare go against prevailing conventions, attempt to leave their mark on the world, or create any excitement in their lives. Only in kungfu fiction could they find an escape, "a momentary reprieve in the chivalrous personalities of heroes who were willing to fight to the death to protect their integrity."[109] Here Wang Zheng makes a perceptive observation concerning the seemingly paradoxical nature of contemporary Chinese life: "Perhaps there's some advanced genetic factor in our cultural makeup: the scholars [descendants] of the Yellow Emperor may be living in a preindustrial society, yet strangely enough, they experience the same sense of indifference and isolation as the inhabitants of the postindustrial world."[110]

Wang went on to suggest that readers were able to overcome the sense of desperate isolation they felt by relating to the figure of the martial arts hero "bearing his sword through the vast wilderness, don't-ask-me-where-I'm-from-or-where-I'm-going, silently and proudly living with the unlimited solitude and loneliness [of his existence]."[111] Whereas in the past, Wang comments, the Chinese intellectual could abandon the world for the life of a recluse in the mountains; today he has no alternative but to search for an escape in books.[112] People had argued for decades that the true spirit of the knight-errant had been in decline since the end of the Qing dynasty. Tan Sitong, a late-Qing thinker and activist, was an early martyr to the cause of political reform. He was often depicted in both popular and official culture as a young chivalrous hero.[113]

Chen Pingyuan, a mainland literary historian, observed that the martial spirit of intellectuals in late-nineteenth-century China had disappeared by the time of the early republic, the knight-errant tradition becoming more of a literary artifact than a living reality. He remarked that in the late 1980s, university students combined their study of existentialism with a passion for kungfu novels.[114] (It is not surprising, therefore, that this kind of martial arts bravado was reflected in some of the slogans, songs, and poses of the 1989 popular protests.) Claims that even the hooligans were not as raffish as they used to be, however, were not new. Writing in 1924, Zhou Zuoren noted, "Today when all past values have been forgotten, even the ruffians are decadent. They've turned into those *liumang* whom you see getting up to their tricks on the wharves in the treaty ports. The ruffians of the past seem, in retrospect, as distant as the supernatural beings or yoga masters you find in old books.[115]

It was perhaps no coincidence, then, that Wei Xiaobao, the "hero" of Jin Yong's last novel *The Deer and the Cauldron*, was not a martial hero but a quick-witted comic *liumang* whose antics repulsed even the purists among Jin's readers.[116] Wei's personality also had a generic similarity to some of Wang Shuo's loutish characters. As the appeal of *liumang* culture spread on the mainland in the 1990s and the term *liumang* was used popularly even by irreverent yet basically strait-laced figures in both publishing and music (people like the Shanghai editor and writer He Ping and the Beijing rock singer He Yong come to mind), it was not uncommon to hear individuals refer to themselves as the modern-day Wei Xiaobao.

In his comic fiction, Wang Shuo created a world that at times could be best understood as inhabited by modern or posttraditional knights-errant. His heroes are not chivalric, sexless killing machines bent on upholding a personal code of

honor. They are the fast-talking—sometimes foul-mouthed[117]—streetwise, womanizing youths who use their wits to negotiate a path through the turbulent and
chaotic world of the reforms. One major group of Wang's characters reappeared
in stories and novels either under the same names or similar personae. Based on
a coterie of his own friends, many of whom also were writers, they are bound by
gemen'r, or "mateship," relations familiar to readers of the martial arts literature of
the past.[118] Their weapons, however, are of a different order: relentless repartee
and caustic cynicism replace the glinting sword of the swashbuckling hero.[119]
During all-night sessions of mahjong or over endless beers in a muggy haze of cigarette smoke, they spar with one another in a competitive "rave," *kan*.[120] As Shi
Ba, the protagonist of Wang's novella *Flotsam*, says, "Everyone calls me a living
Foolish Old Man, and sure I talk my way through [*kan*] the mountains with my
mouth day by day without respite."[121]

The knight-errant might delight in killing for personal satisfaction or honor,
but the *liumang* gets his thrills by cutting someone to the quick.[122] The archaic
(and nonchaotic) hierarchy and code of honor of the *xiake* figure only on a verbal plane and have little practical relevance. In a world of disintegration in which
normalizing standards of good and evil have ceased to operate, the *liumang* hero
is a trickster who plays tricks on others and who is subjected to them himself.[123]
Their foes are not as obvious as the scheming enemies of martial arts fiction; they
are often merely gray bureaucrats or hapless dupes. Wang's characters fight
valiantly, nonetheless, if not fairly, whenever they are confronted by conventional society. Although they do not always score a decisive victory—the *liumang* does
not presume there is such a thing—they never need to recognize defeat.

Wang Shuo's characters are not members of the intellectual or political elite
who inhabit so many of the works of other modern mainland Chinese writers, although some of his heroes obviously come from relatively privileged cadre families.[124] Nor do they belong to the fictionalized peasantry of the "native soil" genre
or to the angst-ridden urbanites of late-1980s "new realism"; even less are they the
soldiers and workers that crowd the remnant products of socialist realist literature.
Elements of commonality between Wang Shuo's late-1980s heroes could be
found in "*liumang* music,"[125] a genre that was very different from the more earnest
"message rock 'n' roll" of Cui Jian. Wang even took a potshot at Cui's famous 1987
song "Nothing to My Name" in a scene in his first novel, *Living Dangerously*.

> "I want to give you my hope
>   I want to help make you free. . ."

> The song playing over the restaurant's speakers was like a covert whisper.
>   "Great lyrics!" this guy behind us said to his girlfriend. "Gives me goose
> bumps just listening to it. '. . . make you free.' Like, how majestic. What else

could you possibly offer, eh? Take me, for example, what more could I give you, except maybe my democratic rights and every penny I earn."

"If that's asking too much, just forget it," the girl responded. "Give them to someone who cares."

"Wow, tough chick." The guy mumbled to himself. "He must be desperate."

We looked at each other and chuckled silently, heads bowed.[126]

In 1991, one trend in nonofficial art led a leading Beijing critic to dub some younger painters as *popi*, or *liumang* artists,[127] and for some years a number of "floating artists," *mangliu yishujia*, in the capital pursued a lifestyle and affected an attitude that seemed like a parody of that of the *liumang* characters we have been discussing here (see "Big Business" in chapter 8, "Artful Marketing").[128] Wang Shuo's readers enjoyed a kind of vicarious delight in the adventures of his *liumang* rowdies in a manner not all that dissimilar to the satisfaction that Wang Zheng noted among devotees of martial arts fiction in 1989.[129] By the mid-1990s, however, with the rise of the highly paid *liumang* artist and rock performer, it was sometimes difficult to tell whether art was imitating life or whether life was but an insipid copy of art.

THE MARRIAGE OF *LIUMANG* AND *GEMEN'R*

One of the central values of the *liumang*, as of the knight-errant, was that of mateship, the bonding of friends and associates that behooved a person to stick up for his allies, or *gemen'r* in contemporary Beijing parlance. Written as either *ge'rmen* or *gemen'r*, the term has a long history in the Chinese capital.

In his *Dictionary of Beijing Argot*, Xu Shirong differentiates between *ge'rmen*, which denotes "a relationship between elder and younger brother," and *gemen'r*, which he defines as: "(1) The same as *ge'rmen*, (2) a mode of address among young people . . . , (3) an expression used by disreputable persons to express affinity for one another."[130] Another source defines *ge'rmen* as "[a term used among] men of a similar age who have a relatively close relationship or who are in the same line of work."[131]

In 1980s and 1990s Beijing, the word *gemen'r* could even mean "you" or "I/me." It even gave birth to a female equivalent, *jiemen'r*. *Gemen'rbang*, or *gemen'r* factions or gangs (as well as *jiemen'rbang*), were unofficial groupings that cut through the official or public hierarchy and acted as an alternative form of social stratification. There was even an expression—"*gemen'r* solidarity" *gemen'r yiqi*—that described such loyalty. Officially, *gemen'r* solidarity was decried as "the reflection of feudal, clannish thinking and the small production [in other words, peasant] mentality; it is the remnant of retrograde and effete traditions."[132] And in the same *Dictionary of Spiritual Civilization* from which this citation is taken, it says that "to emphasize *gemen'r* solidarity in a socialist society, to favor the supremacy of personal relationships regardless of general standards of right and wrong, to think only of the personal well-being of one's *gemen'r* . . . leads all too easily to actions that are detrimental to the society and others . . . *gemen'r* solidarity should be replaced by healthy comradely affection."[133]

Gemen'r is a word that was formerly the sole province of the toughs of the city; but it enjoyed a new lease on life with the social upheavals that saw the destruction of Beijing society in the 1950s and 1960s. The Cultural Revolution introduced the language and attitude of the deracinated underclasses to the children of the party bureaucrats who had flooded into Beijing in the 1950s. The young revolutionary rebels were encouraged by Mao Zedong in the mid-1960s to bring down a party structure that he found inimical to him and his thought. Over the years since then, the underclasses, still marginal and oftentimes dispossessed — in particular, in the poorer southern suburbs of the old city — had their culture and language further appropriated by the children of army cadres, people like Wang Shuo and the film director Jiang Wen, or the offspring of the cultural elite like Wu Huan, the son of the playwright Wu Zuguang.[134] The term *gemen'r* is part of the body of language that found its way into the mass media via these and other cultural writers[135] who actively fashioned elements of "Old Peking" into marketable cultural styles. This was typical of the history of cant words that first gained currency in popular slang, entering the colloquial language eventually to be validated by literary or media usage.[136]

In 1987, before Wang Shuo's fiction had popularized the term in the national media, Li You, a reportage writer (an author of a kind of literary journalism) and self-styled "Pekingologist," discussed the term *gemen'r* at some length in his monthly column on contemporary life in the capital. Li said that although using *guanxi* or connections was now an accepted way of life, in Beijing there was an added dimension to *guanxi* relationships, a reliance on *gemen'r*. *Gemen'r* were involved in nearly all social transactions, from buying products that were in short supply to getting children into kindergarten or obtaining medical treatment.[137] In the age of disorder, knights-errant, *liumang*, and individualists came together in Wang Shuo's fictional world to provide a mythology for the subculture of the young (and even not so young). In the realm of everyday social reality, *gemen'r* were, as Li You observed, "a necessary complement" to a system in which political control was overwrought and the market economy was underdeveloped.

As the party and state were increasingly perceived as being morally bankrupt and the workplace as merely a microcosm of the state, it was often felt that only strong *gemen'r* relationships could inspire people to acts of heroism or even basic decency, thereby helping the individual maintain workable social relationships. That is not to say, however, that the *gemen'r* spirit did not have a dark side. This violent mien of the *gemen'r* is particularly evident in the depiction of the heroes of Mount Liangshan in the classical novel *The Water Margin*. The literary historian C. T. Hsia disparaged the "gang morality," sadism, and misogyny of the novel, and a similar critique has been central to W. J. F. Jenner's discussion of the *haohan*, or "good bloke" tradition of Chinese culture and its modern parallels,[138] including the brutish, modern incarnation of the *haohan* in memoirs like Lao Gui's *Bloody Sunset*.[139] Zhang Yimou's 1988 film *Red Sorghum*, much praised for its earthy exuberance and tragic power, is also a striking contemporary example of the pitiless, heroic priapism of the *gemen'r*, making the film on one level an artfully crafted paean to peasant cronyism.

When *liumang* get together in *gemen'r* gangs, antisocial behavior is a natural corollary. One of the most telling descriptions of the mind-set of *liumang* mateship can be found in Wang Shuo's 1988 novel, *Living Dangerously*. Described by the editors of the journal in which it appeared as a study of "a group of hippies . . . whose antics and irreverence conceal frustration and confusion,"[140] *Living Dangerously* is a teasing and intriguing "murder" mystery in which both life and death are pursued for "kicks."[141] At one point, the protagonist describes a nostalgic scene from his youth that encapsulates much of the spirit of the knight-errant/*liumang* hybrid of contemporary China:

> Our favorite game when we were kids was one in which a few of us would play murderers and the rest would be official troops. The killers got a couple of minutes to hide before the authorities started hunting them down. Even though the troops had the right to torture their captives, everyone wanted to be one of the murderers. That's because when they were on the run, they could make fools of the others, and even when they got caught, they could put on a big act of being unrepentant and unyielding. It gave them the greatest opportunity of showing off and being creative. We all turned the killers into the good guys [*haohan*].[142]

These *liumang* have moved out of the ghettos of Chinese urban culture; they have declared their presence without rancor, fear, or inferiority; they live in their own world confident that they or people like them will survive all comers. In a world inhabited by the *liumang*, the freedom and self-determination generated by the new economic order does not necessarily establish a new moral order. Indications are that the *liumang* provide the economic chaos with a glib, sophists' rationale. Social reality and ideological illusion compete to rule in a topsy-turvy world in which the possibility of retribution is no great threat and victory always belongs to the operators. The cynical truth of this is illustrated in many episodes in Wang Shuo's 1988–1989 connected stories "The Operators" and "An Attitude." In "An Attitude," for example, one of the "writers" remarks to a Taiwan compatriot that nothing that happens in China can worry him or his friends: "Even if the Gang of Four came back, it wouldn't faze us one bit."[143]

In another scene set in the story's *liumang* literary salon, the *gemen'r* pack gangs up on an unsuspecting human rights activist in what was an obvious reference to the events of early 1989. A scruffy young man in jeans appears at the club: "probably a decadent poet and masturbator," the narrator Fang Yan thinks to himself. The fellow is holding a petition calling for the protection of human rights in China, and he has come to solicit signatures. This is a not-so-subtle reference to the petition for the release of Wei Jingsheng launched by Chen Jun and Bei Dao in early 1989. The piece of paper "looked like someone had pissed on it and then dried it in a dank room: it stank."

The *liumang* authors refuse to sign. "We've got more than enough human rights," one of them blurts out. "Any more and we wouldn't know what to do with 'em." Another breaks in with the observation: "You're one of that mob who's pushing for 'total Westernization' aren't you? . . . well, you just go back and tell your bosses . . . you can forget about trying to forge a path for China. We're not going anywhere!" One of the others ends the encounter angrily with the words: "Who do you think you are, anyway? Just because you dump on the Communist Party, you reckon you're a hero. Let me tell you, things have changed. No matter what happens your lot's not going to end up being in charge."[144]

The gang of writers send the petitioner packing amid a hail of abuse. As he flees, one of them remarks: "It's really true [what they say]: when the nation is in crisis, all types of evil creatures come out of the woodwork and all manner of phony Dragon Emperors stalk the land."[145]

NO MAN'S LAND, MODERN CHINESE PICARESQUE

In 1924, Zhou Zuoren stated that it was a source of great regret that apart from the author of *The Water Margin,* no Chinese writer had really attempted to create a "literature of *liumang* life," a "picaresque literature" to use Zhou's English phrase.[146] Picaresque novels are stories of rogues who serve a number of masters. The adventures of the *pícaro,* or rogue—Zhou Zuoren accepted "picaroon" as a suitable translation for *liumang*—are used to satirize the society of the time.[147] The novel *No Man's Land,* or *Please Don't Treat Me Like a Human,* published in late 1989,[148] was Wang Shuo's most political and pointed farce. It was also replete with strong picaresque elements.

No Man's Land lacks a first-person narrator, generally regarded as a central feature of the picaresque novel, yet stylistically it shares a number of elements with the genre: Like the picaresque novel, it has an episodic plot, whose openness allows the writer to project a chaotic sense of the world and give voice to "the fantastic, the improbable, and even the weird."[149] Like traditional works of the picaresque, it too follows closely the fate of its hero, "a relative innocent [Tang Yuanbao] developing into a picaro because the world he meets is roguish."[150] And unlike more modern works of black humor or philosophical absurdity in which a central impetus is to reveal that there are no final answers to the human condition, "in the picaresque world, the chaos is radical; it extends to the very roots of life."[151] It is this last point that is of particular relevance in reading a novel so powerfully infused with the fin-de-siècle ambience of China in the late 1980s as *No Man's Land*.

The editorial note in *Zhongshan*, the Nanjing literary bimonthly that serialized this extraordinary story over the six months after the Beijing massacre, claimed that *No Man's Land* was "an experiment by the author, and not just another clever depiction of 'hippies'." "Rather," the editors wrote, "it is a story that is completely off-the-wall. The writer employs wildly exaggerated urban language to lampoon and censure the evils both of traditional culture and contemporary society."[152]

It is impossible to review all the themes and ideas of such a complex novel as *No Man's Land* in this short précis. First and foremost, the story should be seen in the light of broader contemporary cultural issues. In particular, the novel was written against the backdrop of a continued debate concerning the Chinese "national character" that after the late 1980s was a central feature of the "cultural fever" that engulfed the reading public and informed discussions about the direction of the country's economic and political transformation. It was a debate that concerned what could be called the tradition of self-loathing or self-hate in modern Chinese culture (see chapter 10, "To Screw Foreigners Is Patriotic").

No Man's Land was first mentioned as a novel within a story. In "An Attitude," the narrator Fang Yan announces to a clutch of fawning foreigners that his next literary work would be called *Don't Treat Me Like a Human*.[153] The explanation of the title that Fang Yan gives is that in the book, "one person pleads with his fellow Chinese: whatever you do, don't treat me like a human being. If you treat me like a person, it'll be the end of me and I'll share everyone else's faults. Then our nation's problems will never be solved."[154] In a number of Wang's earlier stories, there are hints that some characters feel completely dehumanized[155] or they sense a need to undergo a complete transformation,[156] but in *No Man's Land*, self-destruction and reconstruction become a motivating force, a national imperative, one that is realized through a mordant and deeply unsettling tale.

Set in a comic dystopia, *No Man's Land* is about a group of *gemen'r* who are not unlike the "heroes" encountered in Wang's earlier stories "The Operators" and "An Attitude." This time around, however, they are *liumang* with political power, and they bring to mind Ying-shih Yü's dire view that twentieth-century Chinese politics had witnessed the rise and domination of the louts. The story opens with the group discussing, in all seriousness, ways in which they can avenge the recent loss of face China has suffered owing to a defeat at an international sports competition in Sapporo, Japan. The first scene describes a meeting of the self-appointed Central Competition Committee (Zhongsaiwei), a group of *gemen'r* who soon show that theirs is a farcical mixture of the Central Advisory Commission of party elders (Zhongguwei), the Politburo of the Communist Party itself, local party committee dullards, and a chaotic Chinese company board of directors. One of the committee members says: "The only talent bequeathed to us by our ancestors, apart from knowing how to eat, is an ability to fight."[157] Only by beating up on someone else, says another of the group, "can we overcome the frustrations of the past century."[158] The device of using a competition to prove national strength and restore wounded pride recalls numerous stories from martial arts fiction, film, and television series about late-Qing and early-Republican heroes defeating foreign boxers or karate masters with mysterious Chinese kungfu and fancy footwork.[159] In *No Man's Land*, however, the purpose of the Central Competition Committee is to find a Chinese everyman who will not only redeem national pride but also be willing to be sacrificed for the greater glory of his country.

Following an exhaustive search for local talent, the committee selects Tang Yuanbao, a crooked pedicab driver, a *liumang* or *pizi*, who coincidentally turns out to be adept in what is supposedly the most powerful form of Chinese kungfu, *damengquan*, literally "great dream boxing." We soon discover that Tang has learned the art of "dreaming on" from his father, a centenarian, who also happens to be the last living Boxer rebel from the turn of the century.

Yuanbao's rigorous training program starts with a physical checkup and an oath taking. He is enlisted to join the "organization," *zuzhi*, a term that generally denotes the Communist Party. After this induction, Yuanbao says in a take-off of party hyperbole, "From now on I'm no longer human . . . I'm not an ordinary person."[160] Thereupon he is universally hailed as China's number one he-man, a *nanzihan*.

The novel is replete with elements of political farce. Sometimes the mocking of party culture and biting references to the Beijing literary scene and Chinese history come so thick and fast that it is nearly impossible to disentangle them all. One particularly pointed incident occurs, for example, when the Central Competition Committee decides that Yuanbao needs to undergo political indoctrination. Their hopes are frustrated when they discover there are no study groups left

in the city—this is a reference to the decay of the Maoist-style study sessions during the 1980s. Finally, a covert underground party cell—the last group of bona
fide Communists to be found—is discovered, and Yuanbao is duly sent along. But
as the cell members discuss the corruption of the bureaucracy, the need for workers' rights, and another revolution, it becomes evident that they are not Communists at all but Trotskyites. The episode concludes with their all being dragged off
by men in white coats who claim that the politicos are actually lunatics who have
escaped from an asylum.[161] Wang peppers the surreal narrative with other half-ex-
plained incidents, like one involving student demonstrations and a "massacre" in
which protesters are mowed down by tanks that shoot water and flowers.[162]

Another one of the story's main themes is the eventual castration of the hero.
This happens when the leadership learns that changes in the competition rules
mean that only women can go to Sapporo. Having been declared to be the nation's number one he-man, Yuanbao is now put under the knife, a cruel irony for
a fellow who, through his victory at an international competition, was supposed
to bear witness to the virility of his motherland. Readers of the novel would have
immediately appreciated the reference to popular self-mocking critiques of
China as an emasculated land full of impotent individuals.[163]

In the meantime, Yuanbao's father, Tang Guotao, is arrested and questioned
by the police on suspicion of betraying the Boxer movement and for complicity
in plotting the collapse of the Qing dynasty itself.[164] The father's interrogation
runs as a subtheme through the novel, and Wang Shuo loses no opportunity to
parody the style of police questioning that he had previously employed in his detective fiction.[165] The whole episode—the interrogation and confession of Tang
Guotao—can be taken as a satire on the party's abuse of history and the purges of
political leaders such as Peng Dehuai, Liu Shaoqi, Lin Biao, the Gang of Four,
and more recently Zhao Ziyang himself. Following the ouster of these party leaders, the ills of the nation were blamed on them, often to the point of absurdity.[166]
Similarly, Tang Yuanbao's father is found guilty not only of his betrayal of the
Boxer movement but also of an "undeniable responsibility for the various social
disorders, evils, and general corruption" in contemporary China. He is pilloried
by his judges for being "the cause of all chaos, troubles, and misfortune . . . he is
more dangerous than typhoons, earthquakes, fires, floods, air disasters, train
crashes, car accidents, sunken ships, inflation, 'back door-ism,' [and] excessive
eating and drinking by bureaucrats all added together. He is public enemy number one." Accordingly, the old man is sentenced to life imprisonment. His only
response to the list of accusations leveled against him is a simple question: "What
are you people going to do when the Communists finally get back in power?"[167]

The climax of the novel is the martial arts competition in Sapporo. Athletes
from all over the world gather to participate in the championships for "the art

of endurance," *renshu*. It is a contest that will determine which nation can tolerate the most humiliation and pain. The athletes are subjected to tests that include being bound (Tang Yuanbao allows himself to be compressed into a smaller and tighter shape than any of the others); being ridden piggyback by a burly heavyweight and expected "to run like a horse, crawl like a dog, and bleat like a sheep" (Tang goes one better than his rivals by drinking the piss of his rider and then giving the thumbs' up); having long needles stuck under their fingernails and in their chests (while some of the others succumb to the pain, Tang smiles broadly and encourages his torturer, concerned that his tormentor may weaken before he does); standing on a hotplate (a veritable *teppanyaki* for the sole—Tang saunters around ignoring the heat); being submerged in water as the temperature is lowered to the freezing point; and a self-humiliation trial consisting of hitting one's own face (Tang beats himself until he is "as purple as an eggplant, his skin so swollen that it was as thin and translucent as paper"). China's champion not only perseveres through all of these tortures, but he also delights in the pain, even thrives on it while, one by one, the other competitors fall by the wayside.

Finally, Tang Yuanbao elects to perform his own trial of endurance, the ultimate feat of self-inflicted denigration. He takes a sharp blade, cuts around the skin at his neck and pulls off his face. The message is unmistakable, only an athlete from China can come out a winner even if he loses his face.

Yuanbao is acclaimed the undisputed world champion and receives his award in an Olympic-style ceremony. The Chinese flag is raised aloft to the accompaniment of the national anthem. The ceremony is broadcast live to China, and the nation celebrates ecstatically. The final scene of the novel depicts a city over which the massive mushroom cloud of an atomic explosion appears, with the cloud casting an increasingly large shadow over the landscape.[168] The moment that Tang's redemptive action wins the international endurance title for China, a national apocalypse unfolds.

Wang Shuo had experimented successfully with distinctive Beijing dialogue and slang in his earlier novel *Living Dangerously*, in which he employed long passages of unpunctuated dialogue and interior monologues, and in the story "An Attitude," in which he repeatedly used triple idioms or clichés, *chengyu*, for impact. Although official party discourse has been manipulated to considerable effect by other writers since the mid-1980s,[169] and by Wang himself in "The Operators" and "An Attitude," in *No Man's Land* he parodied party language to an unprecedented degree. One example will have to suffice here. The inhabitants of Tang Yuanbao's neighborhood of Tanzi Alley present a formal "letter of appreciation," *ganxiexin*, to the party leader who had saved them from the depredations of the faux party leadership represented by the Competition Committee. The letter is choked in the logorrhea of Chinese political and commercial language, but Tang Yuanbao's mother starts reading as if it were a tearful incantation:

> You have righted the wrong and crushed the bad in one fell swoop. Respected wise dear teacher leader helmsman pathfinder vanguard pioneer designer bright light torch devil-deflecting mirror dog-beating stick dad mum granddad grandma old ancestor primal ape Supreme Deity Jade Emperor Guanyin Bodhisattva commander in chief:
>
> > You who are busy with ten thousand weighty matters each day, long-suffering one bad habits die hard and overworked to the point of illness done too often can be habit-forming shouldering heavy responsibilities speeding through the skies powerful and unconstrained staving off disaster and helping the poor dispelling the evil and ousting the heterodox, you who eliminate rheumatism cold sweats strengthen the *yang* and invigorate the spleen the brain who are good for the liver stomach pain relieving and cough repressing, and able to cure constipation.
> >
> > You personally yourself in propria persona have come deigned lowered yourself honored us with your presence to investigate look over police search patrol pay a visit to ask about express solicitude and come to our alley. For our alley this is the most magnanimous expression of concern a massive encouragement a great impetus a considerable relief formidable expression of trust and care a great honor and really a nice thing to do. We are little people knaves the black-haired scum your children grandchildren tufts of grass little dogs and cats a gang of *liumang* the cretinous crowds the great masses the hundred surnames and we feel oh-so-lucky extremely moved exceedingly uneasy terribly embarrassed so very pleased boundingly enthusiastic very very overwhelmed by our good fortune grateful as all get out tears o'erfill our eyes our hearts swell like the seas and we're utterly and thoroughly lost for words. Ten thousand words a million songs endless mountains and seas ceaseless groans and grumbles mumbles and whispers expressions and phrases all combine into one sentiment that rends the very skies an hysterical sound cracking through the universe circling the rafters for three days deafening reverberating through heaven and earth moving all who hear it mysterious and beautiful beyond compare making people drunk pissed completely out of it so they don't know the taste of meat for three days for it is the overriding chord of the age: longlife longlife longlonglife longlife longlife longlonglife!

Yuanbao's mother faints dead away from exhaustion, and the recitation is taken up by first one and then another neighbor. They are eventually cut short by the leading cadre, who grunts that he's heard more than enough of this type of panegyric before. Even if all the inhabitants of the alley expired singing his praises, it still wouldn't be enough to impress him.[170]

WANG SHUO AGONISTES

During the post–4 June cultural purge, the most pointed attacks on Wang Shuo centered on the films based on his stories.[171] As I have noted, although his fiction, in particular "The Operators" and "An Attitude," was criticized, Wang was not subjected to any concentrated denunciation. In private, commentators speculated that it was because the revanchist authorities dismissed Wang as a mere writer of popular fiction, not "serious literature." Others reasoned that since the novelist was not embroiled in the acrimonious literary factional squabbles that determined the direction of cultural purges, no one in the post-1989 bureaucracy had any scores to settle with him. And there were always wags who were convinced that one could never underestimate the stupidity of the authorities; they argued that the ideological watchdogs simply did not understand provocative novels like *No Man's Land*.

In June 1991, Wang Shuo followed a series of shorter works with another novel, *I'm Your Dad*, a sophisticated domestic comedy.[172] Ma Linsheng, a divorcé who works in a bookshop, agonizes over his role as the father of an increasingly rebellious teenage son, Ma Rui. One minute Linsheng plays the blustering tyrant who wants to force his son, a youth with a ready response to every sign of parental authority, to learn the hypocritical ways of the world,[173] and the next he is at pains to be on an equal footing with the boy, practice in-house democracy, and be a *gemen'r*, or "buddy."[174] But Linsheng's efforts lead to hubris, and the relationship with his son sours. Ma Linsheng's sense of self-worth and respect are gradually undermined by the imposed equality, and the a-hierarchical arrangement collapses.[175] *I'm Your Dad* is bitingly cruel and lovingly indulgent in turns. As the tale progresses, Wang Shuo reveals an antiauthoritarianism and cynicism that is as extreme as anything in his earlier work, yet in an instant this gives way to sardonic understanding, compromise, and helplessness as father and son face the immutable pattern of their life together. Apart from being an entertaining and deeply perceptive study of the psychology of power and family relationships, *I'm Your Dad* was also widely appreciated as a masterful meditation on the dilemmas of urban mainland China, with numerous political asides and jokes thrown in for good measure.[176]

Ma Linsheng both succeeds and fails as a father; more important, the novel—remarkably interpreted by one editor as "an educational work"[177]—questioned the nature of social roles and responsibilities. Whereas the father never really does learn that he has turned into the opposite of the type of person he had wanted to be, his son, Ma Rui, understands everything "and, having understood, was horrified." Finally, the boy in all his adolescent wisdom says, "Look dad, you're my dad, and I'm your son, and nothing else is going to work. So from now on let's neither of us force the other to be something he's not, okay?"[178]

Wang Shuo did not deny that Ma Rui's approach to the complexities of a rancorous father-son relationship mirrored his own view of the testy accommodation arrived at between the Communist Party and its subjects in the early 1990s.

Wang, however, did not encourage any particular interpretation of his fiction. He said of his writing that he had tried to find a middle ground between pure art and popular culture. "If you happen to discover anything profound in what I do, that's your business (whether there was anything of depth in the first place is another matter). If the profundity evades you, at least I can promise you a good time."[179] One publishing house was so confident of Wang's cachet as a writer with mass appeal that in mid-1992 they produced a four-volume *The Works of Wang Shuo*, in what some people suggested was a mock imitation of the four volumes of *The Selected Works of Mao Zedong*.[180] *The Works* were also the subject of an unprecedented commercial promotional campaign, which included the distribution of a glossy color poster of Wang Shuo, the *liumang* storyteller turned multimedia personality.

Under the regime of sham Chinese socialism, the time was right for the *liumang* to take his place as a model worker in the new order. As we shall see in chapter 5, "The Graying of Chinese Culture," and chapter 7, "Packaged Dissent," the new 1992 push to put economics in command, engineered by Deng Xiaoping, the grand architect of reform, helped further domesticate Wang Shuo's satirical style. As the spirit of commercialized socialism spread in the 1990s, the language of Wang Shuo, itself a refined artistic articulation of nonmainstream social and cultural forces, gave many people a means with which to deal with the schizophrenic realities of the nation.

For many writers and intellectuals, Wang Shuo had shown a way that promised not only survival (physical, intellectual, and emotional) but also a measure of prosperity. Wang's own career path was a paradigm for the new socialist artist, the 1990s entrepreneur writer; and in his novels, Wang had provided a diction and attitude that, even if they did not ensure victory, would guarantee success. The knight-errant was never the hero of quixotic rebellion; similarly, the socialized *liumang*, the survivor, was a vehicle for moral absolution and escape. In 1990s China, the intelligentsia, a group that had survived against all odds—the fall of the Qing dynasty, the chaos of the republic, and the depredations of the People's Republic—increasingly overcame their reluctance and jumped on the Wang Shuo band wagon.

It has been the aim of this chapter to show that Wang Shuo's fictional world offers a unique perspective on the changing face of Chinese urban elite and popular culture. Looking beyond the superficial humor and limited political subversiveness of Wang's stories, as well as the more simplistic and obvious issues of youth alienation and emotional confusion, I have tried to identify persistent elements of popular cultural myth and demonstrate how they are refracted in the work of one of China's most versatile contemporary writers.

The Shanghai literary critic Zhu Dake made his own assessment of the role of the playful vagabonds of Chinese culture, both past and present. He was particularly critical of his contemporaries, and we can read in his comments—originally aimed at Ma Yuan, a writer of Tibeto-magic realism—a criticism of the early Wang Shuo. In his 1988 essay, "A Heartless Literature," Zhu wrote:

> The playful vagabond belongs to a grand tradition. . . . The tradition attempts to hypothesize an alternative, spurious goal outside the usual utilitarian ones in order to distract people's attention from their anxieties. The achievement of this false goal gives the impression that complex desires have been fulfilled in a fashion impossible in the real world.
>
> Game playing may be a pseudophilosophy of life, but it has inspired countless artists with a desire to really live. Zhuangzi, Tao Yuanming, Liu Ling, Ruan Ji, Ji Kang, Su Shi, Xu Wei, Zhu Da. . . . These names represent a playful spirit that has always excited people: they play games, [and] their strategy is to present a false self to the world while preserving their real selves. This tradition tells us: the real game players are those who play false games.[181]

The sodality of the world of the *liumang* benefited from the traditional gemütlichkeit of the *gemen'r*. For a time, the gang of friends represented in Wang Shuo's comic works seemed to have come to life in the Seahorse Club, which was active in the late 1980s and mentioned in the story "An Attitude." At times it was difficult to distinguish between Wang's fictional creations and his circle of writer–business partners.[182]

As time passed, however, success and new ventures led the members of the club in different directions. In the wider world of Beijing society, the old rules that governed *gemen'r* also underwent a transformation, one that accelerated after 1992. As entrepreneurialism became a socioeconomic norm, even the *liumang* found themselves gainful employment. Sodality was replaced, to a great extent, by an attitude encapsulated in the Beijing slang expression *sha ci*. *Sha ci*, literally "to kill the closest," gained currency during the mid-1990s. It was used to denote a trend among money-hungry men and women in the Chinese capital. Whereas in the past, premodern brother-sister (*xiongdi/jiemei* or *gemen'r/jiemen'r*) relations acted as the viable alternative to the rigid and inefficient state structure, as the market economy flourished, the very connections that had once provided a crucial safety net for the individual now offered a convenient launching pad for the entrepreneurial. To *sha ci* was to take advantage of those close at hand, one's confidants and friends, to get a foot in the door of the marketplace and steal a march on the competition. If in the process, a former comrade-in-arms, a childhood friend, or long-term associate had to be sacrificed for the sake of a business deal, then so be it. After all, perhaps in the future an opportunity would present itself for them to *sha huilai*, "kill in return."

CHAPTER FIVE

The Graying of Chinese Culture

RED + YELLOW = GRAY

After 1989, propagandists once more had begun promoting the reds of revolution while economic reformers were, above all, attracted by the glitter of gold, yet the true color of ideological and cultural dysfunction in 1990s China was gray. The pall cast over the nation was an indication of the contradictory nature of the reform philosophy: the party legitimized its continued monopoly of power in terms of Marxism-Leninism and Mao Zedong Thought while doggedly pursuing economic reforms that allowed for personal initiative, the accumulation of wealth, and the birth of destabilizing social phenomena that increasingly militated against orthodox party control. The resulting anomie was both abstract (reflected in absurdly contradictory policy statements carried ad nauseam in the mass media) and concrete. Most of all, in organizational terms this anomie was reflected by the tensions among factions in the party bureaucracy. There was constant "horse trading" among fluid factional groups over policy and personnel changes. The cultural world was both pawn and player in this continuous process of negotiation.

June 1989 supposedly marked the end of liberal cultural policies and a return to tighter ideological control. After a purge of the cultural sphere aimed, as is usual with such campaigns, at ousting bureaucratic enemies, the Ministry of Culture and the Propaganda Department in Beijing, as well as leading cultural organs (various associations and publications), came under the sway of ideologues in favor of a more traditional Marxist-Leninist approach. Organizational power in the main cultural organizations was ostensibly subjected to stricter ideological control, and major policy statements by these ministries were generally "hardline." However, the official policy to carry out "rectification," *zhengdun*, at the same time as encouraging cultural "prosperity," *fanrong*, allowed for considerable (and confusing) leeway. These policies and the factional interests that informed them made it possible for the "shadow ministry" of the purged Wang Meng and his friends to keep functioning, and they developed a sphere of influence outside the narrow realm of sanctioned official state culture. Wang and his fellows became a considerable annoyance and threat to the doctrinaire cultural incumbents (see chapter 2, "An Iron Fist in a Velvet Glove" as to how this situation developed and for the impact it had on mainstream culture).

The year 1990 ended with the *Beijing Youth News*, the leading Beijing youth paper run under the auspices of the Municipal Communist Youth League, concluding its discussion of the values of the young (the so-called third and fourth generations of the People's Republic, people in their teens to early thirties). In a final article, members of the "second generation" (those in their forties) were trumpeted as saying, "We are definitely not gray."[1]

In fact, throughout 1991, the color gray seemed the basic tone of mainland Chinese culture. As the year drew to an end, there was increasing internal discussion about the need to carry out a campaign not to sweep away "yellow" or pornographic culture, something that had been a feature of party policy—and impotence—since 1989,[2] but to purge the nation of "gray culture"—to *sao hui*, as it was put—and "gray sentiment,"[3] to carry out a movement to eliminate the insidious influence of the gray—the doubtful, ironic, lackadaisical, and cynical elements of society—that had become endemic to Chinese life.

In the 1970s, it was common for analysts of Eastern European countries to talk of the "gray zones" of life that individuals negotiated between the "red structures" of officialdom and the "black domains" of illegality. Writers spoke of a "gray belt" of activities "that the law [did] not specifically forbid but that [were] in fact prohibited by the authorities."[4] But in early 1990s' China, what did it mean to be "gray"? It certainly was not a phenomenon limited to the gray-rinse set who ruled the country—men who were obviously dyeing their hair in order to maintain an appearance of youthful vigor—although much of the gray sentiment that suffused the society emanated from the wayward political and economic policies of the gerontocrats in Party Central during the 1980s. It was, rather, a syndrome that combined hopelessness, uncertainty, and ennui with irony, sarcasm, and a large dose of fatalism. It was a mood that enveloped both the individual and an ambience that suffused the urban world. It was a zeitgeist that was noticeably prevalent in youth culture. It was the temper, in particular, of the capital, Beijing.

The year 1991 saw a further development of the complex and often contradictory relationship between official and popular or mass culture. It was an uneasy coexistence, one characterized more by constant compromise rather than simply a mutual antagonism or entrenched opposition. In 1991, like 1990, the heavily subsidized state culture extolled the party's major propaganda line. Meanwhile, disparate and often unexpected elements or responses appeared in the media—

films, television series, books, and songs—that were understood in one way by the authorities while the society at large made its own interpretations that often did not accord with those of the party. This chapter attempts to trace, with concrete examples, the developing rift between the avowed state culture and mass cultural consumption. This process had been unfolding for many years, yet the early 1990s marked a new and intriguing phase, and as we will see, although there were times when a "dialogue" among the various forms of culture was nearly impossible, there also were clear signs that there was great, if not even increasing, room for cultural negotiation and manipulation in China.

The year 1991 started out with a number of important events that, among others, this chapter will review in an attempt to delineate the contours of the cultural landscape of 1990s China. These events included the surprise success of the 1990 television soap opera *Aspirations* and efforts by the authorities to co-opt the show in January 1991. Another was the popularity of the hagiographic biopic (biography) *Jiao Yulu*, a film about a selfless model cadre, and the subsequent debate about Jiao and the Taiwan singer/essayist San Mao carried out in the pages of a leading Beijing youth newspaper. The January 1991 release of the sometimes-controversial rock singer Cui Jian's second album *Resolution*, the restaging of the Cultural Revolution Model Opera *The Red Lantern* on 9 January as part of the official celebrations to mark the bicentenary of the advent of opera in the capital,[5] and the appearance of the writer Ke Yunlu's new *qigong* novel, *The New Age*, were other developments that reveal some of the directions of cultural change.

ASPIRATIONS,
A MORALITY PLAY FOR UNITY AND STABILITY

Aspirations, also known as *Yearnings*, is generally regarded as Chinese television's first major successful soap opera.[6] The fifty-part series was first screened on local stations in 1990 and then broadcast nationally on China Central Television starting in December. Its overwhelming popularity took the party leadership by surprise, and there was a scramble to heap praise on it.[7]

The story revolves around the relationship between two families: the Lius, a sturdy tribe of workers, and the Wangs, a clan of "intellectuals" (or, rather, state functionaries masquerading as members of the intelligentsia). As a history of life that traces the relationship of the families since the Cultural Revolution, *Aspirations* chronicles how the saintly woman worker Liu Huifang takes pity on Wang Husheng, the politically abused son of a purged cadre/intellectual. Despite the objections of Huifang's mother and the long-standing relationship between Huifang and Song Dacheng (a model worker), Liu and Wang marry and have a son. Meanwhile, Husheng's sister, Wang Yaru, has secretly given birth to a child of her own with her lover, Luo Gang, who is forced to abandon the baby girl when he is arrested as a counterrevolutionary. By a quirk of fate, this girl, Xiaofang, ends up as the adopted daughter of Liu Huifang. Huifang's doting on the child and Wang Yaru's opposition to the Wang family's having anything to do with the "great unwashed" masses (that is, the Lius) eventually leads to the collapse of the marriage of Liu Huifang and Wang Husheng. With the end of the Cultural Revolution in 1976, Wang the Elder (Husheng and Yaru's cadre father) is rehabilitated and reunited with his family. The battle of wills between the Wangs and the Lius continues, however, and ever-new elements of antagonism and conflict are introduced by the economic reforms of the 1980s. Throughout the drama, Liu Huifang is depicted as a paragon of virtue, sacrifice, and self-denial, and Song Dacheng, her former beau, although married to Huifang's erstwhile best friend (Xu Yuejuan), is devoted to her. Huifang sacrifices everything for her adopted daughter, Xiaofang, hoping to provide the child with the education that she had denied herself.[8] Yaru, who repeatedly attempts to frustrate Liu's efforts on behalf of Xiaofang, discovers in the end that she has been maliciously persecuting a young girl who is none other than her own long-lost and lamented daughter.

This soap opera created something of a China in miniature: it depicted a world of frustration, half-truths, goodness abused, betrayal, social hierarchy, and selfishness masquerading as self-sacrifice. The clash between the two families, though focused on a child, involved a range of highly emotive issues concerning privilege, education, class background, and the sense of self-worth. It displayed the abiding tensions between the haves and have-nots, and the masses and the cadres (here thinly disguised as intellectuals) in Chinese society. According to the *Aspirations*' view of the world, women enjoy power only as the surrogates for men; fulfillment is achieved by manipulating others and deceiving oneself.[9] In keeping with the standard soap opera formula, *Aspirations* concentrates on marriage, children, sex (an ogre that peeps out fitfully from a mesh of symbolic references), and, most important of all, power and betrayal. Members of the older generation (Mother Liu and Wang Yaru) vie with each other for control and ultimately end up destroying the lives of the young (Liu Huifang and Wang Husheng; Song Dacheng and Xu Yuejuan). This then leads the younger generation to use their own children in the struggle for empowerment, compromise, and autonomy, both among themselves and vis-à-vis their elders.

Above all, the world of *Aspirations* is one in which everything is done in the name of the children, the next generation. "Save the children!" the famous last line of Lu Xun's story "Diary of a Madman," was a clarion call of the May Fourth period in the 1920s, not to mention its use as a slogan in the youth-oriented 1989 protest movement. Similarly, this soap of the early 1990s hinges its drama on the fate of the foundling Xiaofang. Absent, however, in this convoluted TV-epic is even a hint of the idealism of the May Fourth. In the world of the Lius and the Wangs, superficial concern for children is but a thin guise for the parental will to power. Zheng Wanlong, one of the creators of the series, said the story was "about everyday things, cabbage and bean curd, bean curd and cabbage."[10] Yet it is a bitter dish that could satisfy only the most maudlin. It appears that no one in the series, except for Song Dacheng and Xu Yuejuan, ever really wants to have sex, and when they do, it is solely for the sake of procreation. In *Aspirations*, children are an ideal human resource that can be tirelessly exploited. The show's success, like that of so many soap operas, both Chinese and foreign, relies on the mesmerizing qualities of a tortured yet appealing tale depicted in the prurient tones of schlock TV. As Sandra Tsing Loh, the columnist for *Buzz*, wrote concerning the phenomenally successful U.S. television series *Baywatch*:

> What's really at the heart of *Baywatch* turns out to be good old-fashioned storytelling—*old* old-fashioned. We're talking Ancient Greece when actors donned huge masks and clogs and yelled at thousands of drunken revellers on a hill with not-so-keen attention spans. *Baywatch* plot turns have that same yelled quality, because now the village is global. Stories need to hold their shape all the way out to Outer Mongolia.[11]

In early January, 1991, Li Ruihuan, the standing member of the party's Political Bureau in charge of culture and ideology, finally formulated an official response to *Aspirations*. Li had been the leading figure in the promotion of "velvet ideology" from late 1989. He rarely mentioned the "struggle against bourgeois liberalization" in his public statements and, as we have seen earlier, clashed a number of times with hard-line figures in the *People's Daily*[12] and the Ministry of Culture (for details of this struggle, see chapter 2).

At an official Party Central reception for the cast and crew of *Aspirations* in party headquarters at Zhongnanhai, Li Ruihuan observed that it was important to analyze why the show had been such a hit: "We must do some earnest research and reach a few conclusions, and try and work out some of the reasons" for its success, he said.[13] Li went on to praise the series for promoting what he called "socialist ethics and morals" and expressed a hope that other television productions could be used to inculcate "subliminally," *buzhi bujue, qianyi mohua*, positive values in Chinese television viewers. Li Ruihuan said that he found in the personal relations depicted on screen "a new model of relationships that is sincere, honest, equal, mutually supportive, united, friendly, and harmonious," nothing less than a modern interpretation of positive, traditional Chinese communality. Thus, Li admitted that, by reaffirming the core values of Chinese civilization, the series was an ideal format for a creative denunciation and rejection of the "national nihilism" and the homegrown values that had supposedly plagued the nation since the 1980s.[14]

While Li Ruihuan tried to put a positive ideological gloss—dare we even say a "socialist human face"?—on the series, the creators of *Aspirations* were more honest about what they thought they had achieved. The novelist Zheng Wanlong—one of six people involved with the series' concept and script—rejected the suggestion that it was an "ethical moral tale," especially since, he observed, the ethics and the morals of China in the 1990s were "Communist morals." "All we did," Zheng claimed, "was to depict some traditional morals." His cowriter, the novelist Wang Shuo, was even more brash about the ideological incorrectness of their approach, observing: "When we set about writing up the story, we were quite explicit that it should contain no [idealistic] motivation: if you've got any good ideas, then keep them well away from us; we only wanted to express the most traditional values."[15] Dubious sentiments perhaps, but after all, Wang Shuo had been identified by one critic in mid-1989 as a writer who had used his literature to create "a kingdom of gray."[16]

The central themes for the series were formulated over a two-day period in early 1989 by an original group of four, including Wang Shuo and Zheng Wanlong. They were joined by Chen Changben, a vice minister of culture.[17] Wang Shuo was quite clear about how they could create a popular story: "Make somebody as good as is possible and then let them be done over really badly. It's easy for people to sympathize with their fate; then you have a show."[18]

Some critics, far from finding in the series the positive traditional and socialist values posited by Li Ruihuan, saw *Aspirations* as a display case of many of the most deviant aspects of the Chinese national character.[19] The saintly woman icon Liu Huifang came in for particularly harsh comment from one writer, Wang Wenying. Ultimately, Wang complained, Liu's selflessness "leaves her with only one protection: endurance and compliance. She converts all of life's difficulties into a form of personal agony, repressing and punishing herself in the process. . . . It might be all right for an individual, but if this is to be taken as a national cultural spirit, then surely it's a cause for concern."[20] Despite these remarks, Liu Huifang was an early 1990s icon, and she soon appeared in TV ads, adding her luster to the lure of various luxury consumer items.

The series was a godsend to Chinese semioticians and others, and it was interpreted in a number of intriguing ways. Jin Zhaojun, a prominent music critic, credited the popularity of the series to its use of a traditional morality play to reinstate the broad masses as the heroes of popular culture. He pointed out that the show recast the history of the Cultural Revolution to beautify the past, glorify moral perfectionism, and rationalize the psychological alienation felt by low-income earners since the advent of the disruptive economic reforms.[21] A similar point was made by the literary scholar Chen Sihe when speaking at a forum organized on the series by the Shanghai Academy of Social Sciences in 1991. Chen remarked that the central reason for the series' popularity was that it gave expression to mass dissatisfaction about the social and financial inequalities that were developing throughout the society.[22] But the Shanghai-based philosopher Zhu Xueqin saw the series as compensating for the egregious failure of the "elite culture," *jingying wenhua*, to address social realities and problems over the past decade. He also noted that programs like *Aspirations* put further pressure on Chinese intellectuals, a class that was widely perceived as being incapable of providing cultural leadership or coherence to the nation in this time of need.[23] Zhu's fears about the cultural impotence of the intelligentsia were to deepen over the next few years and make him a central combatant in the polemic debate over the "War of Resistance" launched in 1995 (see chapter 11, "Kowtowing to the Vulgar"). A commentator for the *Beijing Youth News*, a paper aimed at middle-school students, summed up the popularity of the series: "The loss of morals and the aspiration for morality have come together to create the unique psychological context of society today."[24]

These interpretations were far more in keeping with the egalitarian sentiment of average Chinese urbanites, so strongly expressed in the anticorruption slogans of the 1989 protest movement, than with Li Ruihuan's more opportunistic and upbeat view of the series. To see *Aspirations* in the light of a traditional and even Maoist moral context brings us closer, perhaps, to understanding how wide the gap between the official and the popular realm of culture in China had become.

Although Shanghai audiences had avidly watched *Aspirations*, it did not have the same popular impact as it did in Beijing. The intelligentsia in particular were sorely aware of the show's anti-intellectual bent and the implied criticism of the "Shanghai style," as expressed in the person of Wang Husheng, whose name literally means "Wang born-in-Shanghai," the ungrateful and self-centered husband of Liu Huifang. The difference in responses to the series among both the general public and the intelligentsia in Beijing and Shanghai was typical of the post-1989 gulf between the two cities. Beijing generally showed itself to be more conservative, yet intellectually and culturally opportunistic, whereas Shanghai commentators were more measured when responding to the things that excited people in the north.

In some cases, when independent critics in Shanghai were too overt in their analysis of the deeper significance of the series, official pressure was applied to silence them. Xu Jilin, a prominent intellectual historian at the East China Chemical Industry Academy, and Zhu Xueqin, the scholar mentioned earlier, were particularly outspoken in their criticisms of the show at a forum organized by the *Wenhui Daily*, the leading newspaper in Shanghai. Xu maintained that the series reflected the "collective unconsciousness" of a culture still entangled in the mindless roots of millennia of Confucian thinking. He said the program was antimodernist and espoused values that even figures in the May Fourth period would have found hopelessly antiquated. "It's nothing particularly worth worrying about," he reflected, "but it will be very bad news if a whole slew of shows like this are made."[25] The editors of the *Wenhui Daily* were reportedly criticized by leaders of the Propaganda Department for publishing such comments.

Meanwhile, more ideologically steadfast cultural bureaucrats than Li Ruihuan saw in the popularity of the series an opportunity to denounce bourgeois liberalism and even elements of the government's reform policies. Malaqinfu, the postpurge head of the Chinese Writers' Association, availed himself of the debate surrounding *Aspirations* to attack the commercialized morals of the 1980s which, he claimed, were characterized by selfishness and estrangement. As a result, he said, "Cultural works now praise individuals who set themselves up in opposition to the society. They concentrate on depicting ugliness, evil, alienation, and nihilism . . . the very things that the masses abhor." Malaqinfu interpreted the self-denial of Liu Huifang and Song Dacheng—as well as the lifelong unhappiness that resulted from their indulgent martyrdom—to be an affirmation of socialist collective values.[26]

Another, distinctly bleak, view of the masses' relationship with the educated was reflected in the woman director Li Shaohong's powerful 1991 tale of peasant violence, *Bloody Morning*, a film based on Gabriel Marcia Marquez's *A Chronicle of a Death Foretold*.[27] Though one of the finest works of China's innovative cinema produced in the first years after the 1989 purge, Li's film was prevented from being screened overseas and criticized for its derogatory view of the masses.[28] The film was criticized by many viewers for portraying a negative image of the peasantry. Whereas the public may well have profited from a debate about the issues raised by *Bloody Morning*, ideological restrictions made it impossible. Through a combination of official repression and public sentiment, this well-crafted and confronting film was virtually hounded from the public arena.

For all its emotive energy and depiction of the dark realities of Chinese relationships, viewers found in *Aspirations* a confirmation of the centrality of "interpersonal sentiment," *renqing*, the skein of *guanxi* that binds people to one another, for better or worse. In terms of traditional Chinese popular culture, the real significance of *Aspirations* is that given the unnerving confusion of the commercialization of society in the early 1990s, it only served to reinforce the traits of fatalism, *ting tian you ming*, reconciliation with one's status, *an fen*, and forbearance, *rennai*, that had conspired to stifle the individual in the past.[29] It was just the type of binding moral nexus that despite its feudalistic overtones, the party, anxious for unity and stability at any cost, encouraged, and one that was not particularly unsuited to the conservative project of international "third-wave neo-Confucians" and the supporters of "Asian values" either.

It was only as the 1990s progressed that the dictatorship of "interpersonal sentiment" was seen as a major stumbling block in the future development of China, and particularly the Chinese economy. "A ghost, an ancient spirit hovers over the land of China," a leading reporter wrote in 1993. "It is 'face' [*mianzi*], something that can neither be seen nor touched. The debt of 'interpersonal sentiment' that everyone carries in their hearts is stifling our very economic well-being."[30] On an entirely different level, the success of *Aspirations* was a victory for one of the most representative paradigms of American popular culture. With this medium, the message of peaceful evolution—the primacy of economics over politics, consumption in place of contention—continued to insinuate itself into the living rooms of hundreds of millions of mainland TV viewers.[31] It was a development that increasingly served the needs of the Communist authorities while also preparing China's artistic soil for the germination of global culture. Popular culture became the opiate of the consumer, and as it was transmogrified by stylistic improvements inspired by the Hong Kong, Taiwan, and international media, it converted areas of contestation into spheres of co-option.

VALE SAN MAO, *VIVE* JIAO YULU

After June 1989, Lei Feng, the red samaritan People's Liberation Army soldier martyred by a rogue telegraph pole in 1962, was duly trotted out to reeducate and inspire the recalcitrant youth and ill-behaved citizens of China. Above all, the party's revolutionary successors were exhorted to learn from what was blithely called Lei Feng's "screw spirit," *luosiding jingshen*, immortalized in the peasant-soldier's famous line: "I'll be a bolt in whatever part of the machinery of state the party wants to screw me."[32] But having been promoted too many times to have much impact the "learn from Comrade Lei Feng" campaign soon wore thin. Popular attitudes toward the repeated, virtually annual, efforts to get the nation to emulate the soldier, a glum do-gooder, were summed up in the popular saying: "Lei Feng comes every year in March then leaves again in April."[33] In early 1990, Li Ruihuan turned instead to the promotion of Jiao Yulu, a model self-sacrificing party secretary who died from cancer and overwork in Henan in 1964.

While the promotion of Lei Feng enjoined the whole society to be selfless and live austerely, Jiao Yulu was supposedly an embodiment of Communist values that party cadres, already awash in the world of economic reform and corruption, could emulate.[34] He was also an icon aimed at reconciling the masses with the party by convincing them that there are—or at least were—good and incorruptible cadres. On the political plane, Li Ruihuan used Jiao Yulu as part of his over-all strategy to mollify the masses who were unimpressed by the attempted return to "poverty politics" symbolized by the frugal Lei Feng, the role model preferred by more extremist propagandists.

As part of the campaign to promote the ideal selfless cadre, a biopic based on Jiao's later career was made by Sichuan's Emei Film Studio and released in February 1991.[35] More than 420 prints of the movie were distributed during its initial release, reportedly a record for a Chinese film.[36] It starred Li Xuejian, whose box-office appeal was assured by his popular portrayal of the ingratiating and impotent Song Dacheng in Aspirations (although he was also known in theater circles for an early stage role as Lin Biao).

Jiao Yulu related how, in December 1962, at the height of the "three years of natural disasters" (an official code expression for mass famine and economic dislocation) resulting from the Great Leap Forward, Jiao Yulu was sent as the new party secretary to Lankao County in Henan. In this job, Jiao worked tirelessly to improve agricultural productivity and prevent the local population from abandoning the area to go begging for food elsewhere. Eventually Jiao falls ill and is hospitalized with cancer, to which he eventually succumbs. The film unabashedly skirts the fact that it was Maoist policies that led to Lankao's parlous straits in the first place, emphasizing instead Jiao's role as the good party man who worked unstintingly to address local problems. In terms of cinematic technique, the director craftily updated the revolutionary realist style of filmmaking typical of the socialist martyr biopic with long opening and closing sequences that were obviously inspired by Chen Kaige and Zhang Yimou's Yellow Earth.

Jiao's moral probity and self-righteousness apparently appealed to audiences throughout the country (or at least to those who organized corvée audiences to watch the film), and the film was a marked box-office success. Jiao's charismatic appeal was not essentially all that different from that of the goddess Liu Huifang in Aspirations. Both were extravagantly self-sacrificing, "good" people who found fulfillment (and moral uplift) in constantly giving to others in a spirit of abnegation. Liu Huifang destroys her marriage and family for the sake of the foundling Xiaofang; Jiao Yulu punishes his family and ultimately works himself to death for the party and the People. The indulgent flagellations of both figures appealed strongly to the abiding idealism and moral perfectionism of contemporary Chinese culture (something that will be discussed further in chapter 12, "Totalitarian Nostalgia"). As noted earlier, there was also a strong strain of moral idealism in the student movement of 1989, with its stress on self-sacrifice, martyrdom, and service to the "People of China," or at least superficially so, since behind such high-minded sloganeering among the student leaders often lurked an egregious egotism and inflated sense of self.[37] Such moral absolutism has remained a powerful and constant force in Chinese life, one that has been repeatedly reinforced by party propaganda. It could be argued that although the gap between the party's moralistic propaganda (official rhetoric) and its often mendacious practice may have led to a general disaffection from contemporary political leaders, it has not necessarily undermined the power of party symbolism. Furthermore, there is no clear line of demarcation between the mass culture suffused with ideological traits that serve narrow-minded and authoritarian rule and more traditional and staid forms of party propaganda. In the early 1990s, many viewers could find succor and edification in works like *Jiao Yulu* while remaining anxious to reject crude propagandistic overtures made to them in the form of ideological campaigns, study sessions, or droning exhortations to toe the official line.

As in the case of other propaganda initiatives in the age of ideological dysfunction, Jiao Yulu was subject to a form of inversion: for some he was an abstract icon of goodness, a mythical figure representing party ideals in an age when symbol and reality shared little or no common ground. No one could reconcile the contradiction of the market reforms based on the profit motive and selfishness with the nonreligious charitable and selfless spirit of dated party martyrs. Yet the battle for the "soul of China," to use a handy cliché, was clearly reflected in such cultural events as the success of the film *Jiao Yulu*.

During 1991, the contrast between social reality (or mass psychology) and party propaganda was brought into stark relief during a debate involving Jiao Yulu and conducted in the pages of the *Beijing Youth News*. In the early 1990s, the *Beijing Youth News*, which was run under the umbrella of the Beijing Municipal Communist Party Youth League, was published twice weekly. Although a fairly lackluster minor publication during the 1980s, it had benefited from the gradual influx of young editors, journalists, and art editors who had been educated at universities and colleges at the height of the 1980s liberalization. Many of them were able to combine a nose for newsworthy topics and stories with an energetic political stance that, while patriotic, was not mired in the ideological sludge favored by their elders.[38] This team of relatively young (mostly in their twenties and thirties) journalists and designers used the paper as a forum to attract a range of writers, including fringe academics, music critics, and trendy columnists. Its layout—an unstinting use of large news photographs and clever captions and headlines—along with a tone that steered a steady course between the rank sensationalism of the gutter press and the buttoned-up drudgery of "serious" party papers set it apart. In late 1991, the editors decided to cash in on the nationwide fad for weekend papers engendered by increased leisure time among urban dwellers by launching a weekend edition as well. It subsequently became a top-selling daily newspaper. Because of its pedigree as a publication of the Municipal Youth League, many middle schools also obliged their students to subscribe to it.[39] Up to the renewed cultural purge of 1996 when the head of the paper was ousted, the *Beijing Youth News* was one of the most sophisticated ideological publications produced in the mainland.

Starting in early April 1991, the paper ran a series of articles on the issue of self-sacrifice that revolved around two juxtaposed quotations. The first was related to the cadre-martyr Jiao Yulu, and the other was a quotation from the popular Taiwan writer and celebrity San Mao, who had committed suicide in Taipei on 4 January 1991. (Her death was a major news story not only in Hong Kong and Taiwan but also on the mainland where her work had become popular during the 1980s, in particular among teenagers and people in their early twenties.)[40]

The quotations were published under the headline: "Two Famous Lines, One About Jiao Yulu and the Other from San Mao—Which Would You Choose?"

In his heart he had a place for all the People, but no room for himself. (Jiao Yulu)

If you give everything to others, you will discover you've spent your life abusing one person: yourself. (San Mao)[41]

San Mao, the nom de plume of Chen Ping, was born in 1943.[42] She grew up in Taiwan and studied in Spain and at the Goethe Institute. After a checkered career working and teaching in America, the Canary Islands, and Spain, she married a Spaniard and went to live with him in the Sahara for two years. After her husband's death in 1979, San Mao returned to live in Taiwan, although she continued to travel widely and wrote prodigious amounts of mellifluous prose as well as a number of hit songs. In 1986 she was named one of Taiwan's "ten best-selling authors." Popular in Hong Kong and Taiwan as a model of the acquisitive and modern petit-bourgeois romantic from the mid-1970s, San Mao's influence belatedly spread to mainland China in the late 1980s. Her self-absorbed image and cutesy, egotistical prose appealed strongly to the adolescent-at-heart readers of the mainland, who were experiencing the type of consumer revolution that had helped make San Mao so popular in Hong Kong and Taiwan more than a decade earlier. Her suicide in a Taipei hospital in early 1991 sent shock waves throughout the Chinese cultural world.

The aim of the *Beijing Youth News* discussion was to contrast the selfless community spirit of the party hero who died for the People with the self-interested egotism of a bourgeois writer who killed herself for no socially significant reason.[43] Not surprisingly, throughout its reports on the popular responses to this orchestrated "debate," the *Beijing Youth News* gave greater weight to student and reader opinions that favored Jiao Yulu's party spirit. Many of the published letters extolled Jiao's admirable personality and deeds; they generally observed that his spirit of sacrifice was even more relevant to the China of the 1990s when the prof-it motive and consumerism had become the chief motivating forces in everyday life. Not all the praise was unqualified, however, and one anonymous respondent spoke with the candor usually reserved for private conversations: "Jiao Yulu real-ly was a good man, but he's not a suitable role model for my generation: he made life such a chore."[44]

Another comment that the paper's editors claimed "reflected the opinion of a considerable number of middle-school students" was "Nowadays, everyone — from the state to the individual — talks about pragmatism. It's the most basic and natural thing. First and foremost, you have to look out for yourself; only then can you think about helping other people."[45] Another student speaking at a seminar organized by a middle school to discuss the two quotations said that once he had a job and a settled family life, he would be delighted to help others just as Jiao Yulu did. This was the same student who had interrupted the discussion to sug-gest they break up early so they would not miss the early evening screening of the cartoon series *Teenage Mutant Ninja Turtles* on TV.[46] The report published on this student seminar in the *Beijing Youth News* concluded: "The education that middle-school students get today might allow them to appreciate and support Jiao Yulu; the realities of life, however, force them to make other personal choices."[47]

A correspondent from the Beijing Academy of Commerce pointed out that it was impossible to expect San Mao to be a "female Jiao Yulu." It was granted that the world would be a better place if everyone were like Jiao, but life was far more complicated than that: "How can you ask us to make such a simplistic choice when we are faced by such complex realities?"[48]

Over the following weeks, the paper continued to publish selected readers' re-sponses to the question "Which would you choose?" Analyzing the hundreds of letters that were received (few of which were presumably fit to print)[49] Zhang Qian, a commentator from the Beijing Youth Political College, an institution closely aligned with the party Youth League, noticed a disturbing trend: "The ma-jority of young people who are in favor of Jiao Yulu rationalize their choice in gen-eral 'humanist' terms. They evaluate him from various angles: 'love,' 'conscience,' and 'self-fulfillment.' They do not base [their decisions] on the social or political effectiveness [of Jiao as a role model]." Translating this statement into clearer, "bourgeois liberalist" terms, it was evident that even those readers who opted for Jiao Yulu had made their choice on the basis of such concepts as "abstract human value" or "humanist" considerations, both of which were anathema to official class-based party propaganda.[50] That is, the correspondents were, quite literally making the right choice for the wrong reason.

Rather than berate their readers for ideological irresponsibility, however, the editors of the paper concluded that all they could hope to achieve through the

Jiao Yulu–San Mao debate was to "show [adolescent readers] an alternative and tell them that there was a higher plane on which they could live and express more sublime ideals."[51] Zhang Qian also found that while many students were happy to see more Jiao Yulu–like people appear in their midst, they were not interested in emulating his actions themselves. Zhang admitted that many of the young people participating in the discussion had reached their adolescence before June 1989, a time when various "new intellectual trends" (read "corrupting bourgeois ideas") held sway. Even so, he did shy away from admitting a more sobering fact: that the way young people were thinking about themselves and the society in early 1990s China was also a product of the market-oriented economic reforms and the intellectual open door of the past decade.[52]

In summation, the editors of the Beijing Youth News found that many of young people simply failed to see the relevance of Jiao Yulu as a viable role model. "He made life too much of a 'chore.' If you can't protect and respect yourself, if you don't attempt to develop and perfect yourself but choose to squander your efforts in selflessly giving to others, then you're wasting your energies. Or to put it more crudely, your life'll be a failure."[53] One teacher, however, observed that the discussion had at least one positive outcome. Because of the public nature of the debate, the school where he worked had enjoyed a period of relative openness and honesty. At first, only a few people dared to say out loud what they thought, but in the end, despite extreme differences of opinion, both sides were willing to speak their minds.[54]

Thus, in the early 1990s marketplace of ideological influence, the style of propagandistic cajoling itself had to take on a new face. "Of course," the concluding editorial opinion of the Beijing Youth News stated, "you are free to achieve your ideals according to your preferred lifestyle, but at least you should recognize the validity of Jiao Yulu's approach. Such recognition is the first positive step."[55]

Soft-sell propaganda also had its rewards, and in mid-1991 the Beijing Youth News was given a Youth League journalism award for the purported success of its Jiao Yulu–San Mao debate.

LIFE, BE OUT OF IT

The color gray continued as a theme in the Chinese capital during the summer months of 1991. As we saw in the Jiao Yulu–San Mao debate, some young people found that the party paragon repulsed them because he had made his life into such a chore, lei. The same theme of life as a chore or a bore, lei or fan, reappeared in early May in the guise of T-shirts, or "cultural [T-] shirts," wenhua shan, as they were called by the media,[56] which carried silk-screened statements and illustrations. In the words of one right-thinking critic of the phenomenon, "The [T-shirts carry] gloomy, negative and cynical messages that do one thing, and one thing only: they encourage a mood of decadence."[57]

The "cultural T-shirts" that first appeared in Beijing in early May were the brainchild of Kong Yongqian, a Beijing entrepreneur-artist. Soon they spread throughout the country. (For a detailed history and discussion of the shirts, see chapter 6, "Consuming T-shirts in Beijing.")

Two of the hottest-selling and most memorable shirts carried the legends: "I'm pissed, leave me alone," *fanzhe ne, bie li wo,* and "Life's a bore," *zhen lei.* Another was covered in stylized ration coupons and tickets with the line "Making ends meet," *lajia daikou,* running over the top. Another showed a row of monkeys covering their ears, eyes, and mouths with their hands, under which ran the comment "Keeping out of harm's way," *buhui lai shi'r.* Many others had similarly ironic messages, most of which, given the charged political atmosphere of Beijing in 1991—a time when China was still something of an international pariah due to 1989 and when an extended economic downturn had thrown the future of the reforms into doubt—could be construed as pointed satire referring to June 4 and its oppressive aftermath. Initially praised by the official media in July 1991, a note of outrage about the shirts was sounded by a writer in the *Economic Daily,* a leading Beijing newspaper, who asked:

> Are the messages [on the T-shirts] beautiful and uplifting? Do they help foster the social ambience we need? . . . What if all Chinese were to wear [a T-shirt reading] "I'm pissed, leave me alone" (though that's quite impossible)? *What a terrifying image we would present to the rest of the world. We can best do without this type of gray humor, if only for the sake of the image of the reform and open door policies.*[58]

By this time, Kong Yongqian, the man behind the concept, had been detained by the police, questioned, and "reeducated," and the companies and individuals involved in producing and marketing the shirts were fined and punished. Meanwhile, the *Beijing Youth News,* playing its role as the party paper packaged for the querulous teens of today, took up the theme of life being a chore and a bore — one of the most popular legends borne by the predominantly young T-shirt wearers over the summer—in another discussion it sponsored in late October entitled "Reflections Inspired by the Words 'Chore' and 'Bore'."[59] In his comments on the relevance of this discussion, an editor of the paper said that according to municipal Youth League statistics, more than half the city's middle-school students were confronted by problems that they lumped together in a zone of "gray sentiment," and their attitudes toward life reflected a "gray sense of humor." It was observed that the popularity of the character-emblazoned T-shirts of the summer was merely the latest expression of a general perplexity that the discussion aimed at airing publicly.

The response from readers to this new discussion was overwhelming. Within eight weeks the paper had received more than two thousand essays on the subject,[60] some of which were published.[61] As one commented:

> Think back to [the revolutionary martyrs] Liu Hulan and Lei Feng, who were also our age. You wouldn't have caught them saying life's a chore or a bore. . . . It is not that our world is too small or that our spiritual space is not large enough—we are letting ourselves get bogged down in concrete details. No wonder everything is a chore and a bore. To put it quite frankly, there's a spiritual vacuum; [people have a] lack of faith in life.[62]

It was a refrain that was all too familiar from the past (not to mention other climes). In the first years after the Cultural Revolution, the early 1980s, such sentiments had been voiced during a discussion on youthful despair resulting from the middle-school student Pan Xiao's letter on "why the road of life is getting narrower and narrower," sponsored by the *China Youth News*.[63] The need for revived moral and cultural standards was also a key element in He Xin's cultural critiques from 1985 onward. The same concern was also at the heart of the party's program aimed at the reeducation of the nation's youth after June 4 1989.

Another student correspondent, from Hubei Province, in the "bore and chore" debate identified the crux of the matter in a stark and uncompromising fashion:

> Maybe we are different from our parents: we don't get so worked up by screaming a few slogans that our eyes fill with tears. And it should hardly come as a surprise that we don't get any flush of self-fulfillment by secretly cleaning up a classroom . . . it's just that we expect more. It's time for us to think about everything we wear—from head to toe; to think about what we want to eat, and how we want to play; to be concerned with things, from what we say to what we think . . . that means the pressure is greater too, so we thirst for some avenue of release.[64]

A final discussion among teachers, Youth League secretaries, propagandists, and selected students was organized by the paper and published on 27 December 1991. The discussants did their best to emphasize the social nature of the graying phenomenon: all young people go through a period of uncertainty in their adolescence and early twenties as they face new and complex pressures and responsibilities. Their conclusion was couched in the trite paternalism that had proved so futile in influencing popular attitudes in the past: "Only those who realize that their youth is a period of struggle, only those who appreciate that they are fighting for grand human ideals and the fate of the nation will understand that they must have no truck with such words as *bore* and *chore*."⁶⁵

Zhu Xun, the assistant director of the Primary and Middle School Telephone Hotline Center in Beijing, said that people of all ages experienced ennui; the crucial thing was to turn such negative emotions into a source of positive inspiration. It is noteworthy, however, that following the media purge of 1989 the more universal sources of angst in the society—fears for the future political stability of the nation, anxiety about economic reform and its adverse impact, environmental concerns, and so on—could no longer be addressed directly in such public forums. Orchestrated discussions like that concerning San Mao and Jiao Yulu, and the later readers' debate on life as a chore and a bore were a shrewd attempt to confront ideological issues among youth openly while guiding people away from politically treacherous attitudes. In private, however, Chinese young people in the major urban centers spoke in a way that indicated that they could not be so easily manipulated.⁶⁶

SELLING SOCIALISM AND IDEOLOGY IN A CONSUMER'S MARKET

As the currency of party propaganda became increasingly devalued, more refined forms for packaging, presenting, and selling the party line were developed. The ham-fisted methods of propaganda, though hardly abandoned, increasingly gave way to the soft sell. We have seen the tactics employed by one newspaper, the *Beijing Youth News*, in dealing with knotty questions encountered on the front line of ideological work among minors. A similar range of methods were developed by other propagandists. And not all were old and Mao-suited cadres; many of them were now young (or younger) ambitious apparatchiki who kept in touch by pager services and fax machines. They enjoyed large state budgets and a relatively free hand to hawk the superiority of socialism and the official versions of Chinese culture and history to the average comrade in the street.

Some of these updated ideological tactics were awkward and comic; others were more successful. These propagandists—though they were now often called "PR people" in keeping with the mood of modernization—recognized the changing realities of Chinese society and were anxious to maintain a place in an increasingly diverse cultural market. This meant that to compete effectively for the hearts and minds of consumers, they had to commodify actively party ideology, its slogans, icons, policies, and mode of language (for more on this, see chapter 9, "CCP™ & Adcult PRC).

Younger editors, writers, television production crews, and propagandists also played a more ambivalent role in the media. Many approached the task of making pro-party TV specials or writing screeds in favor of some political line with a sophisticated cynicism: they greedily accepted official largesse (the pay for this sort of work increased in direct proportion to the decline in public interest) while sometimes sneaking subversive messages into their work. But when the bottom line was top dollar, subversion became little more than a piquant marketing ploy that also served to salve the conscience of the guilty toady. Others spared themselves such refinements and simply churned out mind-numbing humbug, laughing all the way to the People's Bank. It was not outside the realm of possibility that a few of them sincerely believed in what they were doing.

Following the dismemberment of the Soviet Union, the Chinese Communist Party was anxious to keep its customers, formerly known as "the broad masses of the People," satisfied in a material sense, allowing the growth of a variegated (the word *pluralistic* was eschewed for its negative, bourgeois associations) and relatively vital commercial culture. Pop and rock music, the booming video market, and large segments of the publishing and leisure industry came under the sway of refined party control. Even though China remained politically repressive, relative economic freedom and certain fiscal imperatives in the cultural sphere allowed for a liberalism that invigorated the autonomous social sphere and increasingly entangled individuals in the crossover realm between official and commercial as well as nonofficial culture.

While there had been a marked tendency to update the style of party propaganda since the early 1980s, post–June 1989 developments revealed increasingly complex responses to the more diversified cultural pressures. In the 1990s, party culture now eagerly decked itself out in commercial garb: its songs, celebrations, and publications attempted to emulate, manipulate, and co-opt images borrowed from the consumer market.

Karaoke bars, clubs, and even home karaoke units had been popular for some years—Wang Shuo and his writer friends in the Seahorse Club opened up their own karaoke bar on Dongsi Shitiao in central Beijing in August 1990, in the early days of the bar boom.[67] According to 1991 statistics, more than 80 percent of the most popular six hundred songs used in the bars originated outside the mainland (mostly from Taiwan and Hong Kong) and were, to quote one report, "unhealthy or insufficiently healthy, and some contained serious political errors."[68] Despite disputes over the content of the songs, 1991 was named the year of the "karaoke craze," *kala* OK *re*, with 107 new bars opened in the Chinese capital during the first half of the year alone.[69] Karaoke provided a perfect outlet for the narcissistic element of DIY culture: a small stage, a mechanical orchestra, and a video screen showing a music-television rendition of the song, or in more salubrious estab-

lishments, a large screen reflecting the singer's image as the "work of art" was created and appreciated as instant-replay reverie. It was the ultimate in state-imposed
and self-orchestrated solipsism.[70]

In late 1989, the new party general secretary, Jiang Zemin, had attempted to
ride a wave of choral enthusiasm when he led the nation in singing "Without the
Chinese Communist Party, There Would Be No New China," but it was not until
mid-1991 that the party's Central Department of Propaganda launched a strategy
of packaging classic revolutionary ditties for karaoke customers. The resultant first
batch of "Everybody Sing Along: China Karaoke Song Treasury" was available on
tape, video, CD, and in printed form in late May 1991 christened by none other
than Li Ruihuan, the Politburo's cultural chief. The songs, which numbered one
thousand when the final release was made later in the year, were selected with an
eye to combating the negative influences of the foreign products that monopolized the market.[71] The threat of popular music from Hong Kong and Taiwan had
been recognized for nearly a decade, and in the early 1980s, Teresa Teng (Deng
Lijun) cassettes were confiscated and burned in an attempt to deter people from
nonmainland music. It was not until the early 1990s, however, that steps were finally taken to fight back the saccharine wave of offshore love songs, not with bans
and reeducation, but with the party's own top of the pops. Here again was an example of the party's new style of ideological engagement with the enemy, one that
took the form of a competitive blitzkrieg in the marketplace rather than the droning and ineffective campaigns organized around political study sessions.

Gu Xiaoming, a professor of history at Fudan University in Shanghai, neatly
summed up the inherent contradiction in the party's new approach to these issues
at a forum on publishing in mid-1990. He said that official publishing policy repeatedly failed to reconcile the economic necessity of letting market trends have
their way with the pressing ideological need to "guide the market," *yindao shichang*, at every turn.[72] In the case of the new party karaoke favorites, there was little indication of how competitive the official golden oldies were or whether internal directives had been issued to ensure that every karaoke establishment kept
them in constant supply. Yet there was no doubt that the state weighed in with
heavy support for the package: for a time, a song from the "Treasury" was screened
on TV every night and taught to viewers.[73]

Karaoke bars were not the only battlefront in the commodified war of the ideologues. During the celebrations of the seventieth anniversary of the founding of
the Communist Party on 1 July 1991, various commercial tricks were used to help
promote the cause. Sang Ye, a noted Chinese journalist-writer living in Australia
who was back in China collecting material for a new project,[74] remarked on an
advertising billboard outside a privately run music store at Dongsi in central Beijing on 1 July that took ironic advantage of the revived Chairman Mao cult: "The

sun rises and sets, but then it rises again. Buy a karaoke cassette of 'Sing a Song for the Party' and we'll give you a picture of Chairman Mao for free. The more you buy, the more you'll get."[75]

The marketplace was now seen as being in the minds of the consumers; the fight against "peaceful evolution" was no longer something that could only be confronted or defeated in elitist debates and politics classes. The party's attempts to engineer a new, popular "corporate identity" (or CI *xingxiang*, as it was called in the Chinese neologism) was part of a struggle not only for the hearts and minds of the masses but also for their purse strings. Historical validity and the political status quo were all well and good, but under the regime of reform and the awesome specter of the dwindling communist world, economic viability and constant images of prosperity—in the streets and shops as well as on television—also were crucial to the party's continued claim to legitimacy.

Also on 1 July, Sang Ye noticed that a musical instrument store was trying to drum up business by organizing its own amateur musicians to stand outside and play the party anthem "Without the Chinese Communist Party, There Would Be No New China." The players were sporting sashes that read: "Enthusiastic Service, Sure to Please," leading one observer of the scene to comment that he could not tell whether they were selling the party or using the party to hawk their goods.[76] A young pedicab driver had stopped to listen and then sang a parody version of the song:

> There would be no New China without the Communist Party
> Without a New China, there'd be no orchestra music
> Without orchestras, there'd be no music shops
> Without music shops, no one would pay us
> Without any pay, we could never keep our wives happy . . .

The youth was wearing one of the recently fashionable cultural T-shirts which read, in a takeoff of a famous Cultural Revolution quotation: "I'm not afraid of hardship, or afraid of dying, and I'm not afraid of you."[77]

The party propaganda machine had been anxious to exploit the mass wave of nostalgia for the great dead men of the revolutionary past that had swelled up in the late 1980s. Historical epics made for the screen and numerous publications, as well as the re-release of old socialist black-and-white film classics, aided the official push to strengthen the legitimacy of present policies by harking back to past glories.[78] Minicults involving various party leaders had flourished sporadically from the 1980s (especially as they provided an excuse for the hometown authorities of such leaders to invest state funds in local hagiographic projects), but in 1989 a new Chairman Mao cult developed that peaked in the period up to late 1993, the occasion of the Great Leader's centenary.[79] Even though the party sought to promote the great revolutionaries of the past to confirm its present authority, the masses' responses often had little to do with the official line. In popular culture, the defunct leaders were often treated as revived deities, figures bereft of immediate political and historical significance that embodied traditional rather than political charismatic elements. In his 1990s reincarnation, Mao Zedong was the laconic and brilliant thinker and strategist; Zhou Enlai was the loyal minister who sacrificed his health and ultimately his life for the People; Jiang Qing was the fickle and crazed "white-boned demon"; and Lin Biao was recast as an evil, opium-smoking, military genius. They all were joined by a host of other revolutionaries who had made twentieth-century Chinese history. Compared with the gray bureaucrats of the 1990s, people like Jiang Zemin, Li Peng, Zhu Rongji, and Qiao Shi—men who rose to power through murky bureaucratic infighting—the older leaders were real saints (or devils) who continued to loom large in the popular imagination.

Through books, comics, films, and television, the "dead revolutionary males" (DReMs, to sinicize a politically correct formulation from the West) originally promoted in the late 1970s now finally found a niche in the traditional pantheon alongside such figures as the martial heroes Zhuge Liang, Guan Gong, and Liu Bei. In 1990–1991, a popular interlude in a major celebration held by a prosperous work unit or company in the capital or on television might be to welcome some of the stage or screen actors who play the DReMs—Mao, Zhou, Lin, or Jiang—to do a skit for the audience based on some historical incident.[80] Launching into their patter in heavy local accents and done up in a modern version of opera masks, *lianpu*—Mao with his brushed-back hair and mole, Lin bald and myopic, Zhou bushy-browed and face drawn—they would act as comics or compères, talking heads who added a touch of class to an evening's entertainment.

Perhaps this phenomenon could even be interpreted as a kind of "camp transition" during which a former style of politics that had "lost its power to dominate cultural meanings, becomes available, in the present, for definition according to contemporary codes of taste."[81] Andrew Ross, from whom this quotation is taken, noted that objects become camp "precisely because of their historical association with a power that is now in decline," differing from the "graceless sincerity" of kitsch: icons still revered "because they intend serious support for a culture that still holds real power in defining the shape of . . . tastes."[82] These leaders were now stylized and examples of "instant character," figures whose very theatricality expressed "a state of continual incandescence."[83] While publicly content to see the party greats receiving such attention, in private some more sober-minded cadres were dismayed that formerly sacrosanct figures had been reclaimed by the masses in such an irreverent manner.

In the party's venture into the commercial world, television remained the key outlet for up-market propaganda. Although serious book series and journals were aimed more at middle-school and university students and other social elites,[84] it was the nightly bombardment of the general public with television images that was a major focus for the propagandists. The popular 1988 television documentary *River Elegy*, discussed earlier, was followed in August 1990 by an official made-for-TV riposte, *On the Road: A Century of Marxism*. This four-part series was first screened amid considerable fanfare on Central Television and was followed by the publication of the bombastic narration in the pages of the *Guangming Daily*, one of the nation's leading newspapers. *On the Road* was produced by the party's own Department of Propaganda, advised by Deng Liqun, who was one of the most active Maoists in the land and a man trained in the art of the cultural purge back in Yan'an in the early 1940s and who remained active throughout the 1990s as the party's leading critic of incipient liberalization.

Each of the four half-hour episodes in the series extolled one of the party's Four Basic Principles (that is, adhere doggedly to socialism, to the People's dictatorship, to the party leadership, and to Marxism-Leninism and Mao Zedong Thought). The tone of the show was set by the theme song that began each episode. The opening credits would roll as the popular pop-rock singer Liu Huan boomed out:

> You are a seed of fire, igniting this slumbering land; (the screen shows an image of Karl Marx)
>
> You are a prophecy, describing the path for all human ideals; (cut to a picture of Lenin)
>
> You are a banner, fluttering in the wind ready to face all on-coming storms; (images of Mao)
>
> You spoke a truth, you are a banner, having fallen and risen, you emerged victorious. (Deng Xiaoping shown bobbing up and down in the water as he does the breast stroke)

In addition to these four patron saints of Deng's China, *On the Road* heaped praise on other leaders like the aged Chen Yun, a supporter of the planned economy, and Wang Zhen, an incoherent and incontinent ex–army leader extolled for opening up the barren northeast wilds for agriculture, a feat he accomplished with an army of forced labor. And on the subject of the party's track record, the narrative—most of it written by formerly "liberal" intellectuals like Qin Xiaoying—waxed eloquent.[85] The series also depicted the four decades of Communist rule as almost an unmitigated triumph. "Our party," the narrator intoned, "can cope with success, but even more important, it is a party that can weather defeat." The disasters of the late 1950s and the Cultural Revolution were thus blithely passed over. The narrators reserved a special dig at the West when discussing the future fate of socialist China. As footage of the collapse of Communism in Eastern Europe in late 1989 appeared on the screen, the commentary deftly summed up the mood of bravado that characterized so much post-1989 propaganda by the new generation (see also chapter 10, "To Screw Foreigners Is Patriotic"):

As the 20th Century draws to a close, socialism is faced with a serious test. Western politicians see a bloodless victory coming in 1999, and have gone so far as to predict that socialism will be "routed." But aren't they being a little premature . . . ? After all, socialism has always marched resolutely forward amidst all of their curses![86]

In 1991, a number of other series in a similar mold appeared, including the State Education Commission–sponsored *Song for the Holy Land,* a multiepisode paean for reform screened in November.[87] Another series, *Looking Along the Great Wall,* also was broadcast late in the year. Written by the leading party/army reportage writers Liu Yazhou and Qian Gang and made by the military division of Central TV with Japanese financial backing, the series used the Great Wall as a focus for its exaggerated and dramatic paean to Mother China and rebutted the disparaging abuse this grand national icon had suffered at the hands of the makers of *River Elegy.* It was widely acclaimed for its sophisticated and subtle approach to propagating the patriotic party line on traditional Chinese culture and the modern world.[88] Another multiepisode feel-good production, this time one about the glorious history of the martyrs of the People's Army, was *Soul of the Nation,* which, like a number of these series, was soon available in book form and on video at Xinhua Bookstores and film outlets.[89]

Not all the TV documentaries of this period, however, were so relentlessly progovernment. The eight-hour documentary *Tiananmen* was a far more complex and critical series about contemporary China. Made over a three-year period for Central Television by the young TV directors Shi Jian and Chen Jue, members of one of the first semi-independent media workshops in Beijing, it presented enough of a layered and ambiguous view of China from the late 1980s that it was not broadcast on the mainland. And a surreptitious screening at the International Film Festival in Hong Kong in early 1992 led to punitive bans being placed on the feral directors for some time. One quotation from the narration for the last episode, "Remembering Things Past" (Wangshi) gives the flavor of this extraordinary production. After a series of interviews about the Great Leap Forward and Cultural Revolution intercut with footage taken at Tiananmen Square, the narrator concludes the series with the following words:

Life has chosen us to shoulder the burden of the present. We continue our travels, regardless of what life has given or withheld.

What forgetfulness has resigned us to, memory forces us to accept.

Now at this moment as you face life square on, as you continue your struggle, what is it that keeps you going? As life goes on, as the months and days pass. As time itself passes, utterly impartial. . . .

Perhaps you will hear the events of a distant past; they may recount some tale of hope, long borne, and now clearly calling out to be heeded. For life needs to be heard; the months and days need to be heard. Time itself needs to be heard, in all its detail. . . .

Today goes on, every moment so very real.

Our present travails will also be recalled, and reflected upon

Today, too, is life, a witness. . .

Even when dressed up with the glitz of television, party culture was still not all that popular, so inducements often had to be found to keep viewers watching. Again, taking the lead from commercial TV, game shows and newspaper competitions were introduced that tested the skills of participants in memorizing party trivia: there were now history bees that concentrated on the minutiae of the inexorable rise to power of the Communists and their ever victorious rule; competitions on government environmental policy, requiring contestants to identify passages from state leaders' speeches on the subject; and "fill in the blanks" contests on TV series like *On the Road* to gauge whether the audience had managed to stay awake for the whole show. Prizes were in the inimitable style of late-Qing kitsch and monotonously pedestrian. They were generally of the order of gifts familiar to most "foreign friends" of China—chunky cloisonné vases, black-framed landscapes made from cork or wire, and a range of dreary mass-produced neo-trad bric-a-brac, although by the mid-1980s white goods also made a debut.

Considering their proximity to Hong Kong, it is not surprising that in southern cities like Guangzhou, the commercialization of politics developed much faster than in the north. For instance, in 1990 when a new law on the national flag was promulgated, municipal leaders organized a solemn flag-raising ceremony that was telecast provincewide. As the five-stars-on-red of the Chinese flag was hoisted up the flagpole, a seductive female voice announced: "Today's ceremony was generously sponsored by the following factories."[90]

KONG-TAI AND ZHONGYANG

Commercialization in China in the early 1990s had a side very different from these crude party promotions, one that was most directly expressed in the increasingly sophisticated and powerful images used in television advertising. TV commercials were first broadcast in Shanghai in 1979, and they were developed in the early 1980s with the introduction of a daily eighty-minute advertising program on Central TV.[91] Many of these ads were crude and risible "factory announcements" that lauded the merits of products like cement mixers and forklifts. From this point, they were gradually transmogrified into slavish imitations of Hong Kong, Taiwanese, and Japanese models, and after the late 1980s, these slicker local productions competed with the imported ads.[92] The world presented in such advertising was one nearly entirely divorced from the ideological landscape constructed by the party. This TV realm shared the universal vocabulary (and stilted syntax) of international consumerism: the nuclear (in China's case, parents and one child) or extended family presented as enjoying the liberating graces of shiny, new, and mostly superfluous products. During the early 1990s, this vision of the consumer's paradise, rather than the state religion of Marxism-Leninism and Mao Thought, became the true opiate of the masses.

Cars, cigarettes, water heaters, dishwashers, a cornucopia of Chinese medicines, shampoo, home karaoke units, PCs, CD-ROMs, and so on were only some of the products promoted for use and display by the well-dressed petit-bourgeois family living in its bright and cheerful apartment. Their consumption frenzy, however, supposedly took place after hours; for if official state news and propaganda were to be believed, the same families would be spending their daylight hours engaged in constructing socialism, fighting against peaceful evolution, and on the lookout for the pernicious sprouts of bourgeois liberalization. It is noteworthy that about this same time—from 1991 on—it was fashionable in Beijing and other Chinese cities to redecorate one's apartment. While the outside world and the work unit remained in many ways unchanged, people with the economic wherewithal were anxious to transform their immediate environment, translating their visions of individual comfort and bourgeois life into their personal living space, their apartments. In the villages and townships of richer provinces like Guangdong in the far south, or Zhejiang near Shanghai, large Hong Kong–style peasant villas were constructed. These were often two- or three-story cement boxes with blue-tinted windows, balconies, and tiled exteriors and fitted out with a mixture of modern Southeast Asian mod-con luxury and trimmed in proletarian excess. In Beijing, such grandeur was enjoyed by rich businesspeople, well-endowed cadres, and media personalities and artists with access to foreign markets who moved to the estate and villa developments that mushroomed on the outskirts of the city.

The obvious dissonance between the state-sanctioned worldview and the fantasies of advertising culture did not go entirely unnoticed by Chinese propagandists. Although in the early 1990s, there was scant awareness of the power of advertising in foisting a new consciousness and ideology on audiences in China inimical to state orthodoxy, one Department of Propaganda worker is said to have pointed out to the leaders that consumer advertising was a direct threat to the

party's long-term ideological work. As this all-too-obvious observation contradict-
ed the overriding policy of economic reform and the imperatives to mire the
masses in consumerism, however, no particular efforts were made to look into the
matter: advertising was generally a gray zone where even the most daring propagandists did not, for the time being at least, wish to venture. There also was little
evidence at this time that nonofficial observers and critics were taking the problem seriously. Academics and writers armed with the weaponry of new Marxist or
postmodern criticism initially preferred to devote their energies to rummaging
around for po-mo or wannabe po-mo elements in Chinese literature and art than
to face the dilemmas of a massive burgeoning commercial culture in their large-
ly premodern society.93 When commercialization became a fashionable topic
after 1992, most critics embraced it with unseemly haste (see chapter 11, "Kowtowing to the Vulgar").

It was the remodeling of urban life through commercial culture and its ramifications on the hinterland that was vaunted as the spearhead of "peaceful evolution" in China in the early 1990s. The beacons of the future, it was frequently argued, were not necessarily the rhetoric-rich thinkers or politicians of the West (or
their Chinese admirers, who were seen as such a threat by party authorities) but
the crass and glib consumer models of Hong Kong and Taiwan, which had already digested the essence of global culture. And one of the major elements of
both elite and popular culture over the years—in the case of the elite particularly since June 1989—was the reorientation of the Chinese worldview to include
Hong Kong and Taiwan as cultural (and here the word is used in its broadest
sense) centers.

Since the early 1980s, there had been a gradual decentralization in the popular imagination in mainland China. No longer was Beijing, often referred to simply as the "Center," Zhongyang,94 regarded as the sole normative source of national significance and the chief arbiter of social, political, and cultural values.
Instead, the stentorian tones of Central People's Broadcasting were replaced by a
mellower register closer to that used in Taiwan's official media, and the rebirth of
local radio and the concomitant development of regional television allowed the
diverse peoples and cultures of the mainland a public voice and style of their own
once more. The Beijing "fashion sense"—drab and poorly tailored revolutionary
cotton and synthetic clothes, and the baggy PLA-style uniform popularized by the
Red Guards—gave way to new paragons of couture from the south.

The political charisma of Beijing had been in a steady decline since the fall of
Lin Biao in 1971, and this devolution of influence continued during the 1980s
until, after the student protests of 1989, it was transformed into something of a
negative charisma. The voice of the Center was less a clarion call to the future
than a nagging reminder of the past. In terms of mass culture, the Center, the

focus of sociopolitical meaning, the body of symbols and associations that propped up a sense of identity, place, and significance in the Chinese world, now expanded to include Taiwan and Hong Kong (Kong-Tai, or Gang-Tai, in popular Chinese shorthand). The great accommodation that was to mark the 1990s and that will continue to do so in the next century was well under way.

The evolution of this "Chinese commonwealth," or Greater China, had begun in the late 1970s with the introduction of nonmainland Chinese films and continued with the clash between official disapproval and popular desire for Canto Pop in the early 1980s. After numerous official bans and confiscations of cassette tapes, the works of massively popular singers like Taiwan's Teresa Teng (Deng Lijun, 1953–1995)—who first came to prominence on the mainland with the controversial (denounced variously as "traitorous" and "pornographic") nostalgic ode "When Will You Return"[95]—finally gained the upper hand. Teresa's sudden demise in Thailand in 1995 elicited a deeply felt moment of unified Chinese cultural mourning[96] and led many of Beijing's leading rock 'n' rollers to pay their respects in song.

In the cassette tape "A Tribute to Teresa Teng: A Rocking Farewell," groups like Black Panther, Tang Dynasty, 1989, and Again sang their condolences. A note that accompanied the cassette read:

> Over a decade ago, Teresa Teng's lucid and sweet voice softened the hearts of many music lovers. In our midst there lives a group of young and courageous musicians. Before they knew anything about John Lennon or Bob Dylan, they had their first encounters with Teresa. Although they eventually chose another style of music to express themselves, many people still enjoy Teresa Teng.[97]

The incursions from the south had begun with music, film theme songs, and films and continued with films and a boom in literature,[98] as well as the "cartoon classics" of Cai Zhizhong[99] from "Tai-Kong," as Hong Kong and Taiwan were spoken of in mainland officialese.[100] Fashions, hairstyles, consumer items, interior decorating, lifestyles, cuisine, and even mainstream language, *putonghua*,[101] increasingly emulated the south. In terms of mass culture,[102] Hong Kong and Taiwan had been trendsetters for some time, so much so that when executives at Shanghai TV were planning their 1992 Spring Festival Extravaganza—the major television event of the year—they dispatched writers to the Zhuhai Special Economic Zone in Guangdong where they could pick up Hong Kong television, and for three days they studied the programs of the neighboring territory to garner ideas for their own TV special.

As a way station, Guangzhou itself had also risen in prominence. Imitating Hong Kong (the local Cantonese long ago abandoned the strident revolutionary style of officialese for the softer, slicker enunciation of the British territory), Guangzhou in the early 1990s was claimed by some to be the second most influential mainland city after Beijing, and it had gone further in its efforts to sweep away feudal remnants and introduce democratic elements into its social life.[103] After the further wave of economic reforms initiated by Deng Xiaoping in 1992, of which more will be said later, Shanghai began working hard to catch up as the nation's leading city. Whether the mercantile practices of these cities would have any long-term democratizing effects remained, however, a matter for speculation.

The tensions between center and periphery further increased after 1989, with much attention being given to the changing attitudes of Chinese intellectuals toward this issue.[104] Activists who found themselves becalmed in the West after 4 June were courted by sympathetic Hong Kong and Taiwan media organizations, and they sought to manipulate the situation in their favor (see chapter 3, "Traveling Heavy"). Many of those who remained on the mainland, despite the initial severity of the cultural and ideological purge waged by the authorities, continued to publish essays and books through the U.S. dollar–paying publishing outlets of southeast China.[105] In 1991, the two leading Taiwan daily newspaper organizations even made a concerted effort to "land on the mainland," *zai dalu denglu,* as party critics of this cultural incursion reportedly identified it.

In early May 1991, Ya Hsüan, the editor of the Taiwan daily *United Daily News* arts supplement, and two of his colleagues invited nine mainland writers to a talkfest in Guangzhou. Most of the writers—whose number included Wu Zuguang, Bai Hua, Liu Xinwu, Wang Zengqi, Cong Weixi, Li Rui, Shu Ting, and Li Hangyu—were controversial figures or connected with the purged literary faction of the former minister of culture, Wang Meng. They discussed the larger realm of Chinese letters and cultural contacts across the straits. The published comments of a number of the participants indicate there was little concern that the rabidly hard line being pursued by the Ministry of Culture and the party Propaganda Department would have any substantial effect on the future development of Chinese culture as a whole, for indeed the writers present liked to think of themselves as representing the best of contemporary letters.[106]

In mid-1991, Ch'en Kuo-hsiang, deputy editor of the *China Times,* a leading Taiwan daily, traveled extensively in the mainland, meeting leading cultural and intellectual figures, journalists, academics, economists, and independent commentators in a bid to solicit contributions to a new international weekly magazine, the *China Times Weekly.* The magazine, designed as a Chinese-language *Newsweek,* was launched in the first week of 1992, its early issues featuring articles by mainland writers and critics along with works by Taiwan-, Hong Kong-, and overseas-based writers, creating yet another general forum for the Chinese intellectual and journalistic commonwealth. Although the *China Times Weekly* flourished for only a few years, it was the most ambitious of such ventures, attempting to remain above sectarian politics so it could gradually gain a foothold on the mainland on behalf of the large media conglomerate that ran it.

Similar magazines based in Hong Kong were published fortnightly or monthly. Nearly all, with the exception of the *Ming Pao Monthly* and the highbrow bimonthly *Twenty-First Century*, had fallen afoul of the Communist authorities in the 1980s and been banned on the mainland as "reactionary publications." That the editors of the *China Times Weekly* could travel in the mainland commissioning articles by a range of controversial writers and critics in Beijing, Shanghai, and other cities was significant in itself. In part, this opportunity was made possible by mainland attempts to court the Taiwan media as the island moved more rapidly in the direction of cultural and political independence.

By the mid-1990s, however, competition in the print media marketplace was considerable, and mainland organizations had begun to imitate the glossy commercial style of Hong Kong and Taiwan publications in their search for a stable market niche. Also in 1992, with the backing of *Ming Pao* Publishers in Hong Kong, Dong Xiuyu, the editor in chief of Joint Publishing, one of the mainland's veteran liberal party publishing organizations, attempted to set up a news journal of its own, *Life Weekly*.[107] This glossy product weathered numerous editorial storms and finally began regular publication in 1996. A sister journal to *Reading*, the influential highbrow monthly that Joint Publishing had been producing since the late 1970s, *Life Weekly* aimed to be the Beijing-based "journal of record" of China's changing urban landscape at the turn of the century.

On the mainland, the importance of the united front with Taiwan was such that surprising latitude was allowed in regard to compatriots from across the straits. This was particularly evident, for example, in the area of rock music. The paramount Beijing rock singer Cui Jian, a trumpeter/singer who had risen to prominence in the late 1980s, was regularly banned from performing in Beijing, yet when the Taiwan rocker Chao Ch'uan visited the capital in 1991, the officially supported concert he gave in late June was a sellout success,[108] as were the T-shirts that were produced for the occasion which bore the title of one of his best-known songs: "I May Be Ugly, but I'm Tender."[109]

Similar care was shown at the time in dealing with Taiwan journalists. One Beijing dissident released from jail in 1991 was reportedly cautioned not to have any contact with foreign reporters, although, his minders indicated, Taiwan journalists were OK. This situation changed as relations across the straits became more strained during 1995, and especially as the first democratic presidential election on Taiwan approached in March 1996.

COMPRADORES OF ELITE CULTURE

One of the correspondents in the Jiao Yulu–San Mao discussion about self-sacrifice quoted a line from the Taiwan rock singer Lo Tayu (Luo Dayou): "I'll give you the spring and leave the winter for myself."[110]

In his iconoclastic youth in the late 1970s and early 1980s, Lo was famous in Taipei for dressing in black, sporting long hair, and wearing dark glasses, even at night. Although to the jaded Western gaze it was an image that smacked of tired rock cliché, Lo presented a striking pose to a prim and proper society that was in many ways a clone of early 1960s U.S. culture. The lyrics of some of his songs mocked the KMT authorities as well as fusty Confucian values, but it was as a romantic singer that Lo became known on the mainland in 1983. Eventually, small Lo Tayu fan clubs sprouted up in Beijing and Shanghai.[111] Having moved to Hong Kong in 1988, Lo released in early 1991 a song that directly addressed his concerns for the future of the territory, now his adopted home. The porous nature of the audiovisual world of greater China was demonstrated by the fact that within a short time, a copy of the MTV of this pointedly satirical song, "Queen's Road East,"[112] was circulating among middle-school students in Beijing.

The video clip of "Queen's Road East" showed Lo and his collaborator, Lin Hsi, dressed in Mao suits and dark glasses marching and singing in the streets of Hong Kong's Central District as a group of Red Guards struck revolutionary poses in time with the music or stood in line waving bouquets of flowers to welcome the comrades from the north.[113] Some of the more choice lyrics, written by Lin, ran as follows:

> There's this royal friend of mine, you find her on our coins
> She just never ages, and they all call her the Queen
> Every time I go out shopping, she comes along with me
> Though her face doesn't show it, she's always a big hit
>
> Our bosom friends go far away with only a "bye-bye"
> We'll have to rely on great comrades to try out their new ideas.[114]

In China, more than in many societies, there was until the early 1990s a fairly clear divide between "high" or elite and "mass" or popular culture. Evidence of the former was to be found in serious literary journals, samizdat poetry collections, and the official book and periodical literature, the academies (of art and music), and innovative films. Nonofficial culture championed the serious, the elite, and the values of the intelligentsia. Mass culture, which covered the products of state-funded industries and Kong-Tai imports, was the province of the tabloids, mass-circulation monthlies, cartoon books, pop music, martial arts films and literature, and so on. Even when they enjoyed the fruits of mass culture, the members of the elite, regardless of their ideological persuasions, tended to do so only furtively or with an eye to appropriating it for their own agendas. This situation changed radically after 1989, in particular after 1992 when nonofficial elites and some members of state culture found (an unacknowledged) common ground in opposing mass culture, whether it be homegrown or imported (see chapter 11, "Kowtowing to the Vulgar").

In China, as elsewhere, rock 'n' roll tended to be one of the first cultural forms that seemed to cut across the boundaries of high- and lowbrow. With the appeal of the Wang Shuo style of pop hooliganism, the music of mainland rockers was interpreted by disaffected intellectuals and critics as being part of a larger, subversive mood of deconstruction that would help undermine party rule, or at least create greater possibilities for "discursive space" in the urban landscape.[115]

Cui Jian and his work had occupied the borderlands of permissibility for some years. Despite on-off interdictions on his performing in Beijing since 1987, there were times when he verged on the acceptable. In late 1988, for example, he was the subject of a medium-length article in the *People's Daily* that praised his appeal to Chinese youth.[116] It was at a time when Cui blindfolded himself with a red scarf and sang at a concert with noted PLA vocalists to help boost *People's Daily* subscriptions. Later, he represented China at the Eurovision Song Contest, and he was touted by Wang Meng during a visit to New Zealand in late March 1989 as an example of the mainland's cultural liberalism.

Cui's rock may have still had a subversive edge in the late 1980s, but the way to the future was perhaps indicated by the recording and marketing of "prison songs," *qiuge*, by the Shanghai songster Zhang Heng in 1988. These songs, which spoke of the suffering of jailbirds and labor-reform inmates, were in the venerable tradition of popular Chinese protest songs and poetry; however, they were promoted in keeping with the instant traditions of 1980s money-making. Cassettes of the songs sold so well that the official media began speculating what their popularity signified and hinting that they were a valuable form of release for pent-up mass frustrations.[117] Presumably raucous *liumang* songs like "The Official Banquet Song," "Don't Push," and "In-House Entrepreneur" of 1988–1989 were similarly therapeutic.[118]

Entrepreneurial state organizations took a significant step toward domesticating such new musical trends in 1989. The Beijing Time-Efficiency Travel Company reportedly set up its own rock 'n' roll groups to entertain foreign travelers as well as satisfy local musical tastes.[119] As Miklós Haraszti observed: "The more talented and flexible the state, the more pleasurably it can suck the dissidents' vital fluids into the organism of state culture."[120]

While 1990 saw an unprecedented level of activity among mainland rock groups, more hidebound critics found unsettling the social impact of the new music. At the Baoding "Seminar on Cultural Thought" in mid-April 1990, Qu Wei of the Shanghai Philharmonic Orchestra named pop music as an ever present threat to the nation. "The bourgeoisie of the West," he warned, "use pop songs to propagate their view of life and their value system. We should never underestimate [the danger] of this. Our foreign enemies have not for an instant forgotten that music can change the way people think."[121] The subtext of Qu's argument, one that had been voiced by critics since the early 1980s in regard to Kong-Tai pop, was that the mass popularity of such music threatened the cultural supremacy of mainland musicians and the academic industry.

Despite these concerns, in 1991, there were also moments during which Cui Jian achieved new heights of official toleration or even acceptability; and these came hot on the heels of his attempts to ingratiate himself with the authorities in 1990 when he performed benefit concerts for the Eleventh Asian Games being held in Beijing.[122] The games were part of an intense public relations exercise by the Chinese authorities to repair its image, so badly damaged by the events of 1989. In January 1991, for example, Cui released a new album, *Resolution*.[123] In March he traveled to Hong Kong. Throughout the year, despite reported bans in Beijing, he appeared regularly at small rock gatherings and occasionally played the trumpet, as well as performing in the provinces. Similarly, tours of the United States and Hong Kong and concerts around China indicated that Cui and his fellows had not been driven as far underground as was often portrayed, by both the non-Chinese media and themselves.

During 1991, *Resolution* was available in official outlets along with modish black-and-white public relations posters of the singer wearing a large and colorful corsage in the shape of a five-pointed star, a reference to the flag of the People's Republic.[124] Even the inclusion of a number of older Cui favorites failed to disguise the fact that the energy and imagination of his earlier work were missing. The new album was reported to be far from a commercial hit either on the mainland or overseas in the Pacific pop market. Marginally more successful was Cui's teaming up with Zhang Yuan, a graduate of the Beijing Film Academy and a member of the "sixth generation" of mainland filmmakers (see chapter 7, "Packaged Dissent"), to make music-television versions of three songs from his new tape.[125] Although the video clips were not broadcast in Beijing, they were reportedly aired in some provinces and on Hong Kong and Taiwan television. These were, however, by no means the first mainland music television ads, the mainland-based Taiwan singer Hou Te-chien having produced a series of clips in early 1989.[126] It was the dissemination of music television tapes in the provinces of China in 1991 that expanded the impact of rock and the youth and commercial culture of which it was a part. Nonetheless, the real victory for video music was not in the realm of rock but in the popularity of karaoke, which experienced a boom during the early 1990s, as we observed earlier.

Mainland Chinese rock 'n' roll, or pop 'n' roll as it could be more aptly described, gradually became a permanent fixture of the Beijing cultural scene. Even while the excessive propagation of rock was supposedly forbidden in the Chinese-language media in 1990–1991, the capital's bands were so much part and parcel of the expat ghetto-*cum*-tourist scene that they were featured in the weekend edition of the *China Daily* in late 1991.[127] Meanwhile, the music and its accompanying subculture of dress, hairdos, and lifestyles took on a life of their own. The conundrum for purveyors of this mildly heretical version of fashion rock was a difficult and delicate one: either strike a pose with your image, lyrics, and attitude that show you refuse to be co-opted or tolerated and thereby cut yourself off from performance venues, an audience, and a chance to compete with other groups; or work to cultivate a vagueness or even polished imitation image and enjoy official toleration with all the privileges that it could bring. Some individuals pursued a credo perhaps best summed up in the words of a song by the Polish group "Dezerter":

> I am but a crumb in the dragon's mouth
> I want to become a bit which will poison its entire organism.[128]

By the early 1990s, however, it was by no means clear whether Cui Jian and the clone bands that were proliferating in the capital were such crumbs or merely pearls with which the dragon toyed. As the flag bearer of mainland rock, Cui often argued that he had taken on the role to negotiate performing space for the rock scene as a whole, and there was little doubt that in the gray zone of cultural tolerance and coexistence, Cui did have a seminal impact. Yet the repeated and irregular official interdictions against his work only served to give Cui a seemingly endless lease on artistic life, and license. The quality of his later work and the corpus of his music probably would have condemned him to a short-lived career in a normal cultural market, but the unsteady politics of mainland repression lent him a long-term validity and the appeal reserved for a veteran campaigner.

In the early 1990s, Cui was a man who was always willing to do a turn for the foreign media, and this was one of the reasons that made some officials feel dyspeptic.[129] Although he was approaching middle age, his success and image condemned him to mime a condition of permanent alienation and youth rebellion. Younger rockers thought it was time for the King of Chinese rock to grow up and to make room for them. Not all that long ago in a reply to a question as to what he thought of Lo Tayu, Cui Jian had remarked, "A bit old." Following the mainland "year of rock 'n' roll" in 1990, a common refrain heard in Beijing was: "It's time to exterminate *qiangbi* [literally "execute by firing squad"] Cui Jian." And there were younger groups and musicians among middle-school students who were only too anxious to see the back of him. "I'm from the Third World. Where I come from there is a mass of Cui Jian fans who only sing his songs. . . . But I don't think there's any fixed concept of what rock 'n' roll should be. Everyone has his own interpretation." So said Wang Haizhou, a high school student who in 1991 had been playing a keyboard for four years and was hopeful of starting his own one-man electronic band. He had also written some of his own songs. The lyrics to one of them went as follows:

> I keep trying to ring up idealism
> But the line is always busy
> Before the next defeat, don't you need
> To save up a bit of dignity.[130]

At the beginning of the decade, mainland rock 'n' roll was a small but not insignificant part of urban youth culture. Its gradual development, guided as much by political pressures as by the practiced hand of Kong-Tai music producers and distributors, was one of the new trends in niche marketing in the cultural scene, and it was also something of a barometer of how officialdom dealt with forces beyond its control—even if these were inadvertently fostered by the party's own economic and united front policies. It was part of the larger imperative felt in China to produce local and, at the same time, modern and internationally recognized cultural products that could be subsumed under the rubric of "Chinese characteristics." The forms of rock, be they purely musical or more a matter of lifestyle choices, ranged from the innovative, rebellious, and threatening to the domesticated and dweebish. As it was with the case of most cultural imports, the localized version could be used to explain a number of contradictory phenomena. Indeed, it could be argued that by tolerating Beijing-style rock 'n' roll, the party (or factions within it) ensured that one of the most potentially subversive and commercial forms of Western culture could be safely engorged by the Chinese soy-sauce vat of assimilation.

Erratic political repression forced people like Cui to look for contacts and contracts overseas. They needed funding, an appreciative or at least a receptive audience, a distribution outlet for their work, and the protective coating of offshore recognition that came with it. Furthermore, the commercial complications of contracts entered into with Hong Kong and Taiwan capitalists were often easier to deal with than the suffocating and high-maintenance relationships developed in the borderlands of official and nonofficial culture on the mainland.

In April 1991, Cui Jian visited Hong Kong, where he participated in a discussion organized by a TV station on "The Future of Rock 'n' Roll on the Two Sides of the Straits."[131] Cui had already got bad local press for his superficial and negative observations on Hong Kong music and his flippant dismissal of the local cultural life—he might have been a struggling nonofficial Beijing rocker, but he rejected the territory in the style typical of an elitist mainland artist for being nothing more than a "cultural desert."[132] When he took part in the discussion, he clashed with the singer/songwriter Hou Te-chien, who participated by phone from Taipei. Hou had been sent back to Taiwan in mid-1990 for his outspoken critique of the Communist government. During his years on the mainland (he arrived there in 1983), Hou had maintained that music could play a positive and independent political role in China, and in the discussion he emphasized its significance as a mouthpiece for the frustrations of youth. Cui, a crafty negotiator in the bourse of mainland cultural politics, skirted the issue and spoke instead of the individual dimension of his work.[133] Later, Cui remarked that the "conflict" between him and Hou had been greatly exaggerated by the media.[134]

While Cui's street cred and market appeal in Hong Kong and Taiwan waned in 1991, other mainland music makers were packaged by nonmainland companies and entrepreneurs and launched in the Asia-Pacific market. This included albums by Panther, Chang Kuan, and Ai Jing, as well as *Black Moon—The Other Side of China*, a collection of mainland rock produced by Chen Zhe in Hong Kong.[135] Despite stricter cultural control after June 1989 and the uncertain fate of rock music up to 1992, contacts with the Hong Kong and Taiwan music industry went from strength to strength. In a number of cases, contracts with Hong Kong and Taiwan music producers ensured that groups or individuals could make a living from offshore earnings. These shifts in Beijing rock paralleled developments in the realms of misty poetry, art, and new-wave films in the late 1980s.

Despite his clash with Hou Te-chien in Hong Kong in 1991, Cui Jian continued to strike the pose of the struggling oracular rock icon on his home turf. In late December 1995, former associates in Hong Kong found his obfuscation so impenetrable as to make communication all but impossible. In the public media, he would sometimes play dumb, or at other times, when it suited him, he would give a convincing performance as the disaffected artist. In an interview with the BBC screened in late March 1996, for example, Cui talked about the difficulties he encountered trying to play in Beijing and the obstacles to performing outside the city—although out-of-town gigs were not that uncommon. The BBC crew just happened to be on hand when the organizers of a show in south China got in touch with Cui to tell him they had been forced by the Public Security Bureau to cancel his appearance. In the ensuing interview with the British journalists, Cui commented that people said rock 'n' roll helped bring down the Soviet Union, so it could be important to China's future. It was a set piece with all the elements of a made-for-TV news item. Like the part-time dissidents of the late

1980s, intellectuals who cultivated official tolerance while presenting themselves to the Kong-Tai and Western media as oppressed people of conscience, Cui also was a master at negotiating space for survival.

Regardless of all this showmanship, the rock scene in Beijing was, perhaps, still a hive of covert oppositionism. By mid-1995, however, a glitzy media package on the scene was being beamed throughout the region by satellite on a weekly basis via Hong Kong VTV's *Out-of-It China*, Feichang Zhongguo, a regular program on mainland music presented from Beijing by Rose Luo (Luo Qi). A designer-bohemian figure who affected the dumb/drugged style of cool, Rose had an image in keeping with the international MTV black-clad grunge bimbo à la early Courtney Love. She—Rose, not Courtney—spoke in broken Chinese, with West Coast–accented English thrown in for good measure. Her adviser on the show was Wang Di, a noted Beijing singer turned rock impresario, and the slick patter that marked the program was East-by-Southeast-Asia export quality at every turn. This mainland show was a sister production of *The Tide*, Da chaoliu, a regular show on Kong-Tai and Pacific pop presented by the campy Taiwan-Chinese David Wang (Wang Dawei), who also babbled in designer Trans-Pacific English.

The story of the irresistible rise of music video culture since the debut of the MTV channel in 1981 is a familiar one. When it was first beamed into Eastern Europe, Russia, and various Asian countries, including China in the early 1990s, MTV celebrated the fact that although it fed off the rebellious image of rock 'n' roll and its by-now venerable antiestablishment ethos, it was also the flickering embodiment of contemporary consumer capitalism. The antagonism between rebellion and co-option had been central to rock from the 1950s, but as John Heileman wrote in the inaugural issue of the *Modern Review* in 1991: "By embracing such conflicts rather than worrying about them, MTV has become the global archetype of institutionalised counter-culture."[136]

Heileman went on to observe:

Combining conventional commercials with promotional shorts for various record company assets, MTV is the first television channel in history to show nothing but adverts. Never has the central fallacy of the mass media been so clearly exposed: television has nothing to do with delivering programmes to you; it exists to deliver you to consumer goods companies.[137]

In 1991, reporters noted with regret that all of Shanghai's 1989 ten top of the pops were from Hong Kong. The following year, seven of ten, including the first three places, were occupied by Kong-Tai singers. One reporter said: "Conceptually and musically, [mainland] music seems obsolete. It is incapable of engaging the psychological changes of our youth and equally unable to satisfy their musical needs."[138] This writer opined that it was necessary to accept rock so as to strengthen local popular music, for failing to do so would only further weaken mainland music, "causing it to fall far behind in its ability to keep up with increasingly refined popular listening tastes, so much so that it will very quickly lose its place in the market to Canto Pop." The article concluded with the warning that if Chinese rock is not encouraged, then when Euro-American rock 'n' roll finally floods into China the local industry will be swamped. "The Beatles [*sic*] once said 'Give Peace a Chance'," so, he appealed, "How about giving rock 'n' roll a chance?"

By the mid-1990s, it appeared that commercial rock had a fighting chance. Streetside stalls and state music shops sold cassettes and CDs of mainland rock 'n' roll music by groups that often subsisted on contracts made with Taiwanese and Hong Kong record companies or by performing outside Beijing (*zou xue* in mainland parlance, or "moonlighting").[139] A sign of the times was the debut, in late 1995, of the fashion shop Heavy Metal Heaven, Jinshu tiantang, on Xidan in central Beijing. HMH, one of a number of such stores, catered to heavy metal groups, fans, and fashion victims given to decking themselves out in leather and chains for gigs at the hot nightspots like Poachers' Inn in Sanlitun, NASA with its Russian dancing girls, or Hot Spot, a disco in the 3581 Military Compound staffed by tall, demobilized PLA soldiers dressed in black and carrying small electric truncheons.[140] While the goods at Heavy Metal Heaven were faux Western, the carrying bags emblazoned with the word "nonmainstream," *fei zhuliu* were in chic Taiwan style, although covered in lines from Chairman Mao that had been popularized as quotation songs in the Cultural Revolution. The marriage of metal rebellion and revolutionary romanticism packaged as Taiwan trendiness was a winning combination:

> Dig deep the bunkers
> Store widely the grain
> Don't be a hegemon.
> Prepare for war;
> Prepare for famine,
> All for the People.

Or as another of the quotations-for-crooning went: "The world is yours, but it is also ours. But in the final analysis, it is yours. You are young and full of energy, like the sun at eight or nine o'clock in the morning. The hope of the future rests with you."[141]

This second quotation had truly ironical connotations, given the fact that probably the only young people who sang quotation songs like this were Heavy Metalists. Real life was even more ironic, for Mao had originally addressed the remark to the young Li Peng and his classmates who were studying in Moscow.

The dilemmas of mainland rock were part of what could be construed as the compradorization of the Chinese avant-garde. For many artists to survive in the maelstrom of political control and economic chaos, they had to ferret out every source of funding they could. This led to the rapid evolution of the limited alternative-cultural market of the 1980s, one that had formerly been the target of co-option by the state. Faced with an often intemperate, although not entirely hostile or oppressive, official line, innovative artists anxious to pursue their creative careers made a decent living, and achieved a measure of recognition while being drawn gradually into commercial relationships with the outside world, whether it be in the form of foreign buyers or Hong Kong or Taiwan interests (publishers, record companies, galleries, film critics, and so on). This phenomenon was formulaic enough when seen from the angle of the commodification and internationalization of culture. The specific nature of mainland arts politics, however, lent the process a tantalizing twist.

Since June 1989, the creative slack of the avant-garde had been taken up by Hong Kong and Taiwan.[142] Cultural compradores appeared in every field. Film was one of the most obvious examples, with internationally marketable directors like Chen Kaige and Zhang Yimou making films to suit the palate of art-house film audiences with foreign (mostly Hong Kong and Taiwan) financing.[143] Gruesome tales and pseudoprofundities abounded in the mainland cinescape—bizarre murders, tales of peasant atavism, Taoist mysticism, and stories of the Wisdom of the East— and the promoters of export films were ready to exploit these local resources to the full. This was all too obvious in the oeuvre of Zhang Yimou and Chen Kaige during the early 1990s. Similarly, as we have noted, the rock and MTV video scene were also prime examples of "cultural integration" (if we wish to put a positive new-world-order gloss on it), and the "avant-garde/modernist/postmodern" mainland art world was also penetrated by adventure-capital art dealers from Hong Kong and Taiwan who produced a range of art journals used to promote local artists. Meanwhile, as we observed earlier, magazines like the *China Times Weekly* promised to attract the attention of mainland writers who found themselves at loose ends.

The mainland authorities preached cultural diversity (plurality but not pluralism), although they still were fearful of the uncontrolled development of popular culture that could act as a fifth column for Western "peaceful evolutionists" determined to use Hollywood and rock to promote foreign values and undermine Chinese socialism. They allowed semiofficial journals and the publication of a range of literature that was strikingly out of step with their "keynote" socialist message (for details, see chapter 2, "An Iron Fist in a Velvet Glove"). There were constant exhortations to support the Maoist-inspired official cultural canon, while in reality local publishers, overseas influences, and popular and intellectual tastes had created, or were creating, a number of parallel canons. Wary that overt cultural repression would send the wrong political messages to overseas governments (including that of Taiwan) and businesses, thereby possibly affecting investments, and bound up in labyrinthine infighting, the authorities were often prepared to suffer divergent art forms. Thus, outside the red market of official culture and the black market specializing in overtly illicit dissident work, there was also an intriguing gray marketplace enjoyed by the cultural elite.

Cultural incursion, however, was a multilaned highway. Whereas 1991 started out with Lo Tayu's lighthearted message of political gloom regarding the future of Hong Kong, it finished with a sophisticated and humorous music-television version of "My 1997" by Ai Jing, a female vocalist from Shenyang. In the tones of a Chinese Suzanne Vega, the twenty-two-year-old Ai Jing tells of the rites of artistic passage from her hometown in the northeast via Beijing, where she had a stint "in the East Song and Dance Ensemble led by the famous Wang Kun," to the Bund in Shanghai, eventually ending up in Guangzhou in the south. Caught there, she laments that her boyfriend, a Hong Kong resident and the producer of her album, could freely travel to the mainland, whereas she was not allowed to return the compliment. The lyrics perhaps reflected the wishes of other northern consumers as they surveyed the market and the pleasures of the south:

> Roll on 1997,
> Then I'll be able to go to Hong Kong!
> Roll on 1997,
> Let me stand in Hung-hom Stadium!
> Roll on 1997,
> I can go with him to a midnight show!
> Come on, I want to find out
> What's so fragrant about the Fragrant Harbor . . .
> Roll on 1997,
> Hurry up and give me a big red stamp.

At the end of one rendition of this song in Beijing, the singer added in a low voice: "Don't worry, only six more years to go."[144] In November 1991, Zhang Yuan completed a slick five-minute video clip of Ai's song that was played on Hong Kong television when the singer's first album was released there. And with a record-producer/boyfriend in the territory, it was not long before Ai Jing made her way across the border to become part of the Asia-Pacific pop circuit.

A TRADITION OF CRISIS MANAGEMENT

Premodern popular culture also continued to flourish on the mainland after 1989, benefiting greatly from the official policy to "enhance national culture" mentioned earlier that was part of a series of strategies initiated to counter the subversive influence of Western ideas. The emphasis on Chinese exclusivity, *guo-qing*, and the values of the past were, however, no longer so easily adapted to the narrow concerns of party propaganda. The gray ambience created by political uncertainty, social unrest, and economic confusion only served to enhance the dark, retrogressive, and often malevolent aspects of revived traditions.

The fin-de-siècle ambience of mainland cultural life was no better reflected than in the rich body of literature of crisis, doom, and fatalism being published. An earlier wave of crisis writings had reached a peak in 1988–1989. Many of those works concentrated on environmental degradation and overpopulation and the social, economic, and political obstacles to China's modernization.[145] A number of prominent works of this genre were banned or subjected to criticism. In 1990, new, equally disturbing, books appeared, and one of them, *Who'll Take up the Contract?* by the reportage writers Jia Lusheng and Su Ya, was denounced and withdrawn from circulation.[146] Even though alarmist works that fed the popular sense of impending doom—including a very popular study of Nostradamus by Ōjima Tsutomu translated from the Japanese—were given short shrift by official reviewers,[147] studies of China's numerous crises written in more measured tones, although not necessarily more upbeat, continued to be published. Noteworthy examples of such work were the annual *State of the Nation Report* and Hu Angang's *China on the Path to the Twenty-First Century*.[148]

A small but by no means insignificant body of writing that continued after the "culture fever" discussions of the 1980s also appeared. There was, for example, Yuan Hongbing's *Winds in the Wilderness*, an impassioned attack on the weakness of the national character, discussed at length in chapter 10, "To Screw Foreigners Is Patriotic," and *The Chinese: Escaping the Dead End* by Shi Zhongwen, which examines the impact of the market reforms on the fabric of society.[149] New editions of and commentaries on the *Book of Changes*, the perennial Chinese guide to an uncertain future, were numerous, and little serious attempt was made either to stop or criticize their publication.[150] Meanwhile, a fascination among intellectuals with Zen Buddhism[151] and the continuing popularity of *qigong* (a complex of Taoist practices)[152]—including the star status of the young miracle-worker "adept" Zhang Baosheng[153]—were part and parcel of a Chinese new-age, self-salvation mentality that was becoming more and more popular. Although the end of the century loomed large in people's minds, a more immediate concern was that as the paternalistic state divested itself of its social burdens, self-reliance would be the only way to deal with the resulting upheavals.

Another facet of "crisis publishing" was the popularity of both modern and traditional handbooks on strategies for surviving in chaotic times, some of which were pointedly humorous in their approach to China's dilemmas. One of the best-selling works of this genre was Li Zongwu's *The Science of the Thick and the*

Black. A study of how to advance oneself in the world—be it in government service or the private sphere—by cultivating a thick skin and a dark heart, *The Science of the Thick and the Black* was written in the early republican era, the 1910s, and was later hailed as a Chinese equivalent to Machiavelli's *The Prince*. Li Zongwu (d. 1944) summed up his philosophy of the "thick and black" as follows:

> We all are born with a face, and to be thick-skinned is its prerogative. God also gives us all a heart, and it can be as black as pitch. . . . All things dear to man can come from being thick-skinned and black-hearted: fame and wealth, palaces, wives, concubines, clothes, chariots, and horses. How wondrous indeed is the Creator! What riches there are of which man can avail himself! To fail to do so would be the greatest of all follies. . . .
>
> Herein I have revealed the secret of the ages. To achieve a thickness of skin that is formless and a blackness of heart that is colorless is to have perfected the Science of the Thick and the Black.[154]

Although it was popular in Hong Kong and Taiwan in the late 1970s, Li's satirical classic was first reprinted on the mainland only in early 1989. After that and despite the publishing purge after 4 June, a sequel appeared, and in 1991, a biography of the creator of this "science" was greeted with enthusiasm by readers who frequented urban bookstalls.[155] The availability and relevance of the book were of concern to critics, with some voicing outrage that Li's deeply cynical philosophy was now being touted so openly in socialist China.[156] It was noted—not without irony, however—that the Central Party School, the training ground for the nation's political commissars, was the leading publisher of *The Science of the Thick and the Black*, and by early 1993, a reported 400,000 copies of the book had been sold by the school alone.[157] Other publishers were quick to take advantage of the commercial cachet of the "thick and black" phenomenon and in turn produced volumes offering "thick and black" guides to everything from love, moneymaking, and salesmanship to making friends and influencing people and public speaking.[158] One young rake imitating Li's writing style even wrote an *Anti-Science of the Thick and the Black* on the mainland and had it published in Hong Kong.[159] Not that the rediscovery of Li Zongwu was limited to China. Capitalizing on the fascination with East Asian writings and "Asian values" as applied to business and management, Chiu-ning Chu produced in England a volume entitled *Thick Face Black Heart: Thriving and Succeeding in Everyday Life and Work Using the Ancient Wisdom of the East*.[160] Meanwhile, on the mainland, a cartoon version of Li Zongwu's book appeared in imitation of Cai Zhizhong's best-selling cartoon classics for the masses.[161] But Chinese works on manipulating the status quo were not the only thing on the entrepreneurial market. C. Northcote Parkinson's *Parkinson's Law, or the Pur-*

suit of Progress had been available in translation since 1982, and Lawrence J. Peter's *The Peter Principle* appeared in 1988. To add to this rich range of Chinese and Western comic writings on politics and society, in 1992 the scripts of *Yes, Minister* and *Yes, Prime Minister*, the biting satires of British political life, were published in Shanghai.[162]

The most noteworthy of the traditional works on how to survive and prosper by playing one's cards right reprinted after 1989, however, was *Caigen tan*, or *The Roots of Wisdom*.[163] Compiled by Hong Yingming of the Wanli Reign period of the late-Ming dynasty (sixteenth century), an age of uncertainty during which many scholar-literati chose eremitic escape over practical involvement with the world,[164] *The Roots of Wisdom* was a volume of Confucian, Taoist, and Buddhist aphorisms designed to help the reader navigate a path of safety through chaos, corruption, and confusion. It had been unavailable on the mainland for decades until, in the early 1990s, it was realized that this collection of traditional survivor's wisdom could be of service both in support of the party status quo and in providing readers with ways and means of negotiating their way around it as well as the treacherous waters of economic reform. As the editors of the *Beijing Youth News* noted at a forum on the book in late 1991, Chinese society was going through a period of complex and confusing social change; foreign self-help books from Dale Carnegie to works on social intercourse and body language had risen and fallen in popularity: now it was time for a homegrown product like *The Roots of Wisdom* to storm the market.[165] As the paper's editors commented, "*The Roots of Wisdom* emphasizes two things: 'forbearance' [*ren*] and 'suffering' [*ku*], but at the same time it is replete with an understanding of the dialectics of life; it helps readers develop a subjective worldview that is healthy and provides them with wide horizons."[166]

During the *Beijing Youth News* discussion, a number of speakers emphasized how the Japanese had used the philosophy of moral pragmatism expounded in *The Roots of Wisdom* to serve their economic modernization. As one speaker remarked, "You have to admire the Japanese for one thing, they can bring dead things back to life and dress the ancients in modern garb and make the mummies dance."[167] Another said that in the years following the "political storm" of 1989, people had tired of fashionable Western currents of thought that had no foundation in Chinese culture and were now increasingly turning to the resources of tradition.[168] Whereas the *Beijing Youth News* had nothing but praise for the book, another critic writing for an orthodox publisher's magazine earlier in the year decried *The Roots of Wisdom* for its didactic and retrogressive stodginess.[169] Once again, conservative party propagandists were warning about the recidivist nature of a popular phenomenon created by the party's reform policies, and a "progressive" party propaganda outfit like the *Beijing Youth News* responded by using reports on *The Roots of Wisdom* craze to boost its own profile as a "cutting-edge" populist publication while at the same time maintaining a studied objective stance that did not betray what was still basically a conservative agenda.

Other aspects of traditional culture revamped to suit the contingencies of contemporary China also flourished in various forms. On the back cover of the January 1991 issue of the major Beijing literary journal *October*, there was an advertisement for a new novel serialized in its pages. It was for Ke Yunlu's *The New Age*, a sequel to his best-selling 1989 novel *The Great Qigong Masters.*[170]

That earlier novel followed the researches of Ouyang Jue ("Ouyang the Enlightened"), a young scholar besotted with *qigong*, Chinese yoga. Ouyang's spiritual odyssey in that book, what he called a search for "universalistic thinking," touched on nearly every aspect of the "Wisdom of the East": the hexagrams of the *Book of Changes*, Laozi, Zhuangzi, geomancy, acupuncture, Chinese herbal medicine, and Zen (Chan) Buddhism, with discussions of UFOs, astral projection, and the pyramids thrown in for good measure.[171] In his 1991 book *The New Age*, Ke Yunlu promised novel interpretations of the *Tao Te Ching*, the *Book of Changes*, the Bible, and the Buddhist canon. "*The New Age* is a work of science and philosophy in the form of a novel," the advertisement in *October* solemnly declared, "combining these with religion and fiction."[172] Subsequently, the magazine's editors reportedly received numerous complaints from readers outraged that a serious literary journal would propagate feudal superstition by publishing such a book. This charge and the substance of Ke's barely coherent esoteric mishmash were sufficient to prevent temporarily the sale of the second half of the book. Huacheng Publishers in Guangzhou were reportedly quick to take advantage of the hard line in Beijing and bought the rights to the book. *The New Age* did appear eventually in mid-1992, but it was published by the University Press of Inner Mongolia.[173] This was another example of a common trend in Chinese culture in the 1990s: although the rule of ideology won the day in the center, the laws of the market were victorious in the highly competitive periphery.

AT MIDDLE AGE, THE PEOPLE'S REPUBLIC GOES GRAY

Once more the *Beijing Youth News* comes to our aid in making some general observations on the state of mainland culture in the early 1990s. In a discussion about male role models, the paper asked, "Who would you choose, the good or the strong, Song Dacheng or Blake Carrington [of the U.S. soap opera *Dynasty*, broadcast in China in late 1991]?" The authorities were said to have allowed the screening of *Dynasty* on prime-time television to allow Chinese audiences an insight into the decadent lifestyles of the rich and famous bourgeoisie of the West. If anything, it gave viewers a taste for much more and provided a series of tacky role models for emulation. Coming as it did just one year after the extraordinary success of the homegrown morality soap *Aspirations,* the positive response to the very different moral universe of *Dynasty* was a surprise to propagandists and media figures in general. In a survey of opinions about the series published in late November 1991, one writer commented: "A decade ago, the whole society was easily caught up with one particular fad, the scope for thought was concomitantly narrow. Now there are endlessly shifting fashions, appearing and fading, sparking people's imagination from every possible angle."[174]

A philosophy student from Beijing Normal University said that if Blake Carrington and Song Dacheng were the only two choices open to her, then she preferred to remain a spinster.

The essence of the debate was not that different from the dispute over the quotations from San Mao and Jiao Yulu that had been conducted by the *Beijing Youth News* earlier in 1991. For many viewers, Blake Carrington had the charisma of a successful man, an image that was in tune with the rags-to-riches economic mood of China. Song Dacheng, on the other hand, remained the model of avowed party values, the embodiment of all that was selfless, sacrificing, and pliant. He was, in other words, out of date. Blake Carrington represented romance and adventure; Song Dacheng, although more reliable, was drab and unexciting. It was unfortunate that the paper's editors had decided in the first place that the choice of role models should be limited to these two obnoxious characters. Things would have been very different, perhaps, if the competition had been between the real, and not just the nominal, role models in the two TV series: Liu Huifang and Alexis Carrington Dolby Dexter.

An official internal report on the T-shirt craze of the summer months of 1991 concluded with a statement that is perhaps a fitting summation of this survey of the "graying of Chinese culture":

> The "gray culture shirts" have come and gone. Although this phenomenon has disappeared, it does not mean that the "gray sentiments" harbored by certain individuals have vanished. Who knows, next year they may discover some new medium for expression. The whole incident has been a lesson to us all: how can people be fired with the spirit of the past and regain that former level of enthusiasm? It is a question that must be asked, for we still have such a long way to go.[175]

Indeed, "they" did find a new medium for expression as early as 1992. In February, Beijing Television screened the twenty-six-part sitcom *The Editors,* a collaborative project involving the novelist Wang Shuo, the screenwriter Feng Xiaogang, and others.[176] The series revolved around the relationships and misadventures of a group of editors in the magazine *Guide to Life*. It was the most pointed social and political satire to have appeared on Chinese television, and it was produced by the same people who had created *Aspirations*. Much of the language and many of the incidents in *The Editors* were suffused with the creeping "gray ambience" of contemporary Beijing culture. The wisecracking leads played by the comic actors Ge You and Lü Liping lampooned party culture and soon were urban heroes. Not surprisingly, the show was an instant hit in Beijing and Shanghai, and the scripts were published in two volumes in February 1992 to cash in on the series' popularity.[177]

Representing another medium of expression was Yang Ping, one of the news-seeking editors of the *Beijing Youth News*. Young and fervently patriotic; up-to-date but with a massive chip on his shoulder; disparaging of the intellectual elite but himself filled with the afflatus that came with a sense of educated superiority, Yang was one of the most active editors and writers for that newspaper during the first half of the 1990s. One of his main interests was cultural criticism. His success in this area—he was a key figure in organizing the debates published in the *Beijing Youth News* discussed in this chapter—led to his involvement with the founding and editing of *Strategy and Management* in 1993 (discussed in chapter 10, "To Screw Foreigners Is Patriotic"). Yang was also the type of youthful party writer who worked hard at bridging the gap between official ideology and the restive youth culture described in this chapter. In the summer of 1993, he wrote a critique of what he called "China's hippies and yuppies." Remarking on the rebellious youth culture of the late 1980s and early 1990s, he lauded their achievement:

> Cui Jian's rock smashed the cage confining the souls of numerous people. His music became the banner for a generation in search of the essence of life and who were opposed to mainstream culture;
>
> Wang Shuo's fiction gave the youth of the late 1980s an intellectual armory with which to satirize and reject traditional civilization;
>
> The popular cultural T-shirts gave expression to the self-congratulation of numerous low-income earners who refused to give in to mundane practicality. . . .
>
> Regardless of how willful and unrestrained they may have been, deep down the hippies were idealists. They may have had no concern for the nation or family, but the sincerity of their pursuit of life was never in doubt.

This was a radical reinterpretation by a committed young patriotic propagandist of the "decadent" culture of youth. While Chinese hippies were spared the usual excoriation in his article, Yang Ping was merciless in his denunciation of a new group that had appeared in the urban landscape: the Chinese yuppie, *yapishi*. "All they are concerned about," Yang Ping fulminated, "is their own survival; their immediate happiness is paramount. All they think about is money; all they crave is comfort. [China's] hippies [*xipishi*] may have laid claim to being vulgar people, *suren*, but it is the yuppies who really are a tribe of vile individualists."[178]

CHAPTER SIX

Consuming T-shirts in Beijing

DRIP-DRY CULTURE

In early May 1991, a form of commercial performance art appeared in the streets of Beijing. The artwork consisted of T-shirts, or "cultural shirts," *wenhua shan*, as they were dubbed by the media, bearing humorous, ironic, and, some claimed, political silk-screened statements and illustrations that were sold at street stalls and in shops throughout the city. From the outset, these shirts, not unlike the "attitude T-shirts" in other countries,[1] were a runaway popular success. They were a unique reflection of the temper of the times, resulting in numerous imitations. Some people even claimed that the "cultural shirts" gave rise to a "T-shirt culture" in their own right.[2]

A detailed history of the appearance and transformation of "T-shirt culture" in Beijing enables us to investigate the way in which both politics and commercial pressures coincided to transform aberrant nonofficial culture in China in the early 1990s. In particular, it is possible to observe the manner in which compromise and negotiation have had an impact on developing and limiting cultural expression in ways that do not fit neatly into dichotomies related to such rubrics as "dissident culture," "oppositionist forces," or the "political underground."

The cultural T-shirts were the creation of Kong Yongqian, a Beijing entrepreneur-artist, and over the summer months of 1991 their message spread throughout the country. In late June, Kong was detained by the police for questioning, and his colleagues were put under investigation. The authorities told the designer that the shirts constituted the most serious political incident that had occurred in the capital since 4 June 1989, yet after a few days he was released, with no charges pending. Nonetheless, an official ban led to the confiscation and destruction of thousands of Kong's shirts, although there was little the authorities could do about the shirts that had already been sold, and people persisted in wearing them through the hot summer months. Attempts were subsequently made to manufacture a competing line in progovernment propaganda clothes, and other artists anxious to cash in on the craze produced various imitation lines in topwear. These upbeat shirts, along with others bearing unambiguous, positive messages, appeared again in the summer months of both 1992 and 1993 and were common thereafter.

Although at the time it was not generally known that Kong Yongqian was the mastermind behind this exhibitionist Chinese ACT-UP prank,[3] the artist did leave one telltale signature on a number of his designs: the romanized name "Kong Long," an equivalent of the Chinese word for "dinosaur." The first part of the word, *kong*, was homophonous with Kong's surname, the family name of the Confucius clan;[4] the second element *long*, dragon, referred to the year that Chen Mei, a graduate of the Central Art Academy and Kong's partner in the venture, was born. Kong also signed a number of shirts with the initials KLR, short for Kong Laore (homophonous with the expressions "always fashionable Kong" or "Kong always gets into trouble"), a play on the name Kong Laoer, Kong Family Son Number Two, a pejorative name for Confucius, the second son in his family.

Both of Kong Yongqian's parents were from Sichuan, but he was born in Beijing in 1962 and, apart from short periods in the countryside, had lived there all his life. His fascination with writing on clothing began at an early age. Even in primary school during the Cultural Revolution, Kong was obsessed with showing how, as an intellectual's child and therefore the object of proletarian disdain, he was more frugal and unassuming than his worker-peasant classmates. One thing he did to emphasize his "Lei Feng spirit" of frugality was to draw patches all over his clothes with a fountain pen. From then on, he developed the habit of drawing and writing on his clothes, a practice that was aided in the 1980s by the ready availability of felt-tipped markers. Later, when Kong traveled out of Beijing on business, instead of searching out stickers with the place-names of the cities he visited to put on his luggage, he wrote the names of the places he had been on his clothing. Every year, he would draw or paint designs on T-shirts for his own use. These were always popular with friends, and in 1990, he decided to use white T-shirts as a canvas for his public art.

Apart from periods at schools in Shunyi County outside the capital where his parents were sent during the Cultural Revolution, Kong attended primary and middle school in Xinjiekou, Beijing, from 1969 to 1976. Upon leaving middle school, he studied at the Beijing Municipal School of Art and Design (1977–1981). After his graduation, he spent a short period in a state-allocated position as a designer in Beijing Number Four Jade Carving Factory before arranging a transfer to the Oriental Song and Dance Ensemble, where he spent nearly two years as a set designer. He then went to work for the Beijing Television Station, where he had a number of jobs as a designer, cameraman, and production assistant. Kong also had a number of other casual jobs[5] after going to work for the *China Envi-*

ronment News, where he was an arts editor and photographic journalist for seven years, from May 1984 to May 1991.[6]

SIGNS OF SATIRE

The T-shirts of Kong Yongqian had their greatest impact in Beijing, a city where sardonic humor and straight-faced irony that often verged on gallows humor were appreciated perhaps more than anywhere else in China. Above all, the people of the capital enjoy the clever use of language and apothegms, and Kong's shirts were aimed specifically at playing up to the idiosyncratic wit of the city. It is just such humor that particularly riled China's po-faced party rulers. To be understood, the legends on the T-shirts he designed should be seen in the context of a wider tradition of humor and political joking in China in general and in Beijing in particular.

Comic rhyming folk sayings, *minyao*, "jingles," or rhyming sayings, *shunkou-liu'r*, and proverbs or popular sayings, *yanyu*, have been common in China since the late 1970s. Naturally, such forms of mass verbal culture can be found earlier in the use and comic abuse of Mao quotations during the Cultural Revolution, a period when political humor was not unknown in the otherwise dour landscape of China.[7] Comic folk sayings have traditionally had a political and often sarcastic dimension. As early as the reign of Emperor Wu of the Han more than two thousand years ago, there was a bureau attached to the court, the Yuefu, whose duty it was to collect folk songs and ballads (*min'ge*, including *minyao* and *geyao*, hereafter referred to as "rhyming sayings") for both ritualistic and political purposes, a means by which the rulers could gauge popular sentiment.

By the late 1980s, rhyming sayings increasingly reflected dissatisfaction with the party and the corruption engendered by its reform policies and monopoly on power. One preliminary analysis of contemporary sarcastic rhyming sayings was published in Hunan shortly before 4 June.[8] The author of the essay noted that in China, politics and sudden shifts in economic policy were having an unprecedented impact on the lives of the average citizen and that the new rhyming sayings most accurately reflected mass opinion. While the writer offered scant analysis of the popular sayings, he did take the opportunity to list a few humorous quips that had probably not previously appeared in print on the mainland. For example, one of the most common rhymes related to the new rich of 1988 went as follows:

> I travel in a Benz taxi, have a foreign squeeze, smoke devil's cigarettes, drink whisky, wear the latest fashions, make money hand over fist.
> I've caught AIDS; I enjoy the sauna, go bowling, and play video games.

My aim is to be an entrepreneur; what do I care if I'm kicked out of my state job?[9]

When writing about the failures of economic reform in the Hong Kong press in late 1988 and early 1989, even the conservative critic He Xin used a number of satirical popular sayings to emphasize his point and presumably to catch the attention of those in power in a fashion that no amount of sophistry or balanced arguments could equal.[10] One of the sayings he quoted was related to the sudden price increases of mid-1988 which contributed directly to the political unrest of 1989: "[There are] ten hundred million Chinese, and nine hundred million are doing deals. They are united as one to cheat Party Central. But the center isn't scared; they just force all the prices up."[11] Since political jokes were becoming rampant by the early 1990s, it was all but impossible for the authorities to ignore them any more or to overlook the underlying causes of their currency. In early 1992, one writer called for a concerted effort to collect these rhyming and satirical sayings so the authorities could get a better idea of what various social strata were really thinking.[12] A typical example of a quip that summed up popular frustration with the economic reforms was included in a 1993 compendium of satirical rhymes published in northeast China:

The coast gets rich
Hawkers make a mint
State workers suffer
Teachers go poor
And bureaucrats get drunk.[13]

Another good example of a post-1989 saying was a play on homophones that described the sorry fate of China's party rulers since 1976:

The congee [Zhou Enlai] goes and the pig [Zhu De] dies
With the pig dead, it will have no hair [Mao Zedong]
Without hair, draw [Hua Guofeng] one instead
If that's no good, paste [Hu Yaobang] one together
If it doesn't look right, take a picture [Zhao Ziyang]
If the picture doesn't come out, then do as best you can [Jiang Zemin].[14]

From the late 1980s, jokes with explicit sexual overtones implicating leading comrades both living and dead were even more popular.

As Gregor Benton pointed out in an essay on political humor in China, however,

political jokes are revolutions only metaphorically. They are moral victories, not material ones. To be sure, officials whose pride is wounded will smart for a while and may lash out at those responsible for the hurt. But the more cynical and far-sighted among them know that political jokes and the other small freedoms that irritate some zealots are a useful means of dissipating tensions and of keeping people happy, and that it would be foolish to deal with them too harshly. . . . To permit jokes against the state is . . . a clever insurance against more serious challenges to the system.[15]

Kong Yongqian was certainly mindful of both the power and the limitations of his anarchic T-shirts. Despite popular, media, and official interpretations of the shirts, Kong was adamant that he was not interested in being politically provocative. He wanted the messages of his shirts (both those that were sold and others he planned to produce) to garner a wider appeal and achieve a significance that went beyond the limited concerns of political debate in China. He also was interested in using nonofficial colloquial language to communicate sentiments that many people shared but were unable to give voice to in public and, in the process, to make money out of the project.

The 1989 protest movement and subsequent events did, however, have a direct influence on Kong's decision to design the T-shirts. As a reporter for the *China Environment News*, he had enjoyed reasonably good access to the movement and the epicenter of student activities on Tiananmen Square. He remained very much a bystander. Although excited by the initial enthusiasm of the protesters—both students and others—he was repelled by what he regarded as the narrow, "traditional," and "feudal" nature of many of the slogans employed by the participants.[16] He also noted the array of T-shirts that were produced by student protesters, in particular those at arts and theater colleges in the capital, and that were widely worn during the movement.[17] Kong himself got one of the T-shirts that appeared shortly before 4 June that featured the Goddess of Democracy.[18] He also remarked that while standing on the Monument to the People's Heroes in the center of Tiananmen on the night of 3 June and the morning of 4 June, he wished he had been wearing a T-shirt so that all the people there could have signed their names on it.[19]

Following the protest movement and deeply aware that most contemporary mainland avant-garde art was divorced from the society as a whole, Kong Yongqian became interested in finding his own way of using art to influence public opinion in a nonacademic, nonelitist fashion. For a time he was involved in attempts to set up a popular, nongovernment environmental organization, but he soon abandoned them, dejected by the fact that the project had been hijacked by narrow sectarian and personal interests. He envisaged that designs on T-shirts could have a mass impact in a way that none of his other activities in the realm of art or journalism ever could. The shirts were aimed at amusing and unsettling people who had fallen into an emotional torpor after 1989; they were supposed to be a means for creating a mood of public excitement, to rekindle for a moment the easygoing carnival atmosphere of the street protests; perhaps, he reasoned, they would even make people think about their predicament.[20] Kong wanted not only to bring the power of art and the artist into the marketplace, but he hoped also to "empower" the consumer by creating a streetwise product. It was an attempt to confound elite culture—written culture, academic art, and political language—by using the nub of contemporary Chinese life, the marketplace. The shirts would exploit the traditional focal point of the educated elite, the written word, and by utilizing unconventional typefaces and calligraphy to carry colloquial messages, they would also be an unspoken protest against both official parole and advertising patter.

PRÊT-À-PORTER

The mainland marketplace was certainly ready for the T-shirts. Since the advent of the reform policies, China had seen the gradual development of a market economy. A whole strata of self-sufficient entrepreneurs had appeared, from people who hawked clothes in streetside stalls to others who ran private restaurants, hair salons, and a variety of small businesses. Everyone, as a common saying went, was getting into business, *quan min jie shang*. Amid this moneymaking mania, street culture had also made an appearance. It was characterized by a number of things: highly popular private bookstalls in the major cities that specialized in publications devoted to sex, violence, scandal, and spiritualism; movie theaters screening Hong Kong and Taiwan kungfu movies; shops catering to high school students that specialized in gifts and cards for boy- and girlfriends, not to mention the perennially popular video-game parlors that dotted the cities. All these aspects of a burgeoning petit-bourgeois consumer culture peacefully coexisted with official party ideology and its slogans exhorting people to be mindful of the five pay attentions, four beauties, and three loves, to support campaigns on family planning, road safety, and public hygiene and, above all, to adhere to socialism.

T-shirts had occupied a place in the Chinese market for many years before Kong started producing his silk screens. The expression *wenhua shan*, "cultural T-shirt," adopted by the Chinese media in mid-1991 to describe Kong's shirts, had been in general use in the Chinese rag trade for more than a decade. According to one source, loose, round-necked T-shirts generally favored by the elderly had been called *wenhua shan* or *laotou shan*, literally "old men's shirts," for years.[21] Another commentator remarked that T-shirts carrying patriotic messages had been worn by China's Vietnam War veterans in the early 1980s,[22] while yet another said that slogan T-shirts had appeared on the mainland as far back as the 1950s bearing legends like "Oppose the U.S., Support Korea, and Protect the Motherland" and "Oppose Revisionism, Prevent Revisionism."[23] The first politically ironic T-shirt that I know of appeared as early as 1988 when Ah Xian (Liu Jixian), an unemployed Beijing artist who later moved to Australia, produced a top with a picture of the party martyr Lei Feng on it with the same image in red silhouette on the back, an unspoken reference to the shadowy presence of party propaganda. Nor had 4 June eclipsed "message" T-shirts. In 1990, it was possible to find shirts at Beijing stalls sporting the image of the supposedly banned rock/pop singer Cui Jian.[24]

When Kong first contemplated designing T-shirts, state-run enterprises were generally producing simple, unadorned white cotton tops. Co-op enterprises, on the other hand, had been making shirts with pirated commercial logos for years. The brand names Adidas and Nike were particularly popular. Also starting in 1990, the Taiwanese Challenger Company had set up a factory to produce T-shirts that were initially sold at outlets like the Beijing Friendship Store, a shop that encouraged hard currency sales. Most of the shirts that sold for 15 *yuan* carried pictures of Western cartoon characters, tacky images of Beijing tourist spots like the Great Wall and the Summer Palace, and a range of opera masks aimed at both the tourist and local markets.[25] Large quantities of T-shirts from Guangdong, which featured luxury consumer goods like sports cars and motorbikes, were sold on the Beijing market in the early summer of 1991. Hong Kong film and pop stars like Leon Lai, Anita Mui, and Andy Lau (Li Ming, Mei Yanfang, and Liu Dehua) also were popular. Of a generally higher quality than the local product—at the time, producers in Beijing still lacked the technical ability to put high-definition images on clothing—they were also very pricey, retailing for as much as 37 *yuan* each.

Among the many things that motivated him to produce the shirts, Kong said he was particularly interested in providing an inexpensive local product that reflected northern—that is, Beijing—sentiments and did not simply rehash the nostrums of Hong Kong and Taiwan teeny-bopper culture. During his questioning, he told the police that he did not see why the market for shirts, especially those exploiting Chinese images, should be controlled by outsiders. His interrogators were, he says, unimpressed by this avowed "patriotic sentiment." As we have already noted, in the early 1990s, faced with the expansion of commercial culture, many Beijing, or northern, writers, designers, artists, musicians, and others were reacting to the incursions of "southern"—that is, southeast China (Guangdong, Fujian, Hong Kong, Taiwan)—culture in their work.

Kong Yongqian's plans to create the T-shirts finally crystallized in September 1990 when he came across the *Shōgakukan Dictionary of New Chinese Words* in the apartment of a friend who worked as a Japanese-language translator for Chinese Central TV. Edited by a group of China specialists and translators and published in Tokyo in 1985,[26] the dictionary contained both then-new expressions as well as many common and bizarre mainland political terms. Each entry consisted of an explanation in Japanese and an English translation. The compilers also provided numerous charts and graphics illustrating a range of subjects like the scale of cadre wages, street signs, a table outlining the structure of government administration, and a picture detailing the parts of a bicycle. No current mainland dictionaries listed such a range of both popular and official expressions.[27] Gathered together in one volume, this body of language struck Kong as both fantastic and absurd, especially as so many expressions were becoming increasingly outmoded and quaint as the economic reforms made a mockery of dated official rhetoric. He was drawn in particular to the entries listing numbered political slogans like "the Four Bigs," *sida*, "the Four Great Freedoms," *si daziyou*, and "the Four Pests," *sihai*.[28] But after the first rush of enthusiasm for this catalog of mostly passé expressions, Kong realized that many of the lists were incomplete and, after copying down reams of words at his friend's place, he started keeping notes of expressions he thought could or should be put together. The dictionary did, however, have a seminal influence on his project, and his famous T-shirt "Making ends meet," *lajia daikou*, was inspired by an entry that described ration coupons.[29] Another aspect of the dictionary that impressed Kong was the banality of much of the vocabulary listed and the condescending paternalism of many expressions. Among other things, he wanted to do a series of about ten T-shirts that reproduced either entire sections of the dictionary or long lists of the risible political terms that had been stockpiled in the Chinese collective memory since the rise of the Communists to power.

The same week he discovered the Japanese book, Kong Yongqian read the U.S.-based academic Lung-kee Sun's The *"Deep Structure" of Chinese Culture*, a complex and tortured analysis of the Chinese national character.[30] This impassioned work gave Kong a focus to his scattered reflections on the Chinese condition. Before reading Sun, he thought of himself as being a typical product of the ideological hodgepodge of 1980s mainland China, in particular of the "cultural frenzy" that had developed since the middle of the decade when faddish Western and Chinese cultural theories had created crazes among the urban elite for everything from Freudian psychoanalysis to Taoist metaphysics. He saw himself as being someone with wide-ranging interests who was drifting in intellectual confusion. Among other things, Sun's book led directly to the design of a number of T-shirts that used concepts lifted from the scholar's work but framed in highly colloquial language. For example, Kong created a shirt with the picture of a dog sit-ting up and begging that had a legend running down one side: "Real honest, real frugal, real down-to-earth, really know my place, real obedient, really well behaved."[31] This was inspired by Sun's observations on obedience, or *tinghua*.[32] Two other T-shirts—"Never provoked anyone or upset anyone," *cong mei zhaoguo shei, ye mei reguo shei*, and "Say what people want to hear," *duo shuo haohua*—also were influenced by Sun's comments on the Chinese predilection for learning to accept one's lot and (pretend) to be submissive to authority.[33] Kong even planned one shirt devoted to the word "heart/mind," *xin*, something Sun discusses at great length, but the official ban on the shirts forestalled its production.[34]

A third source of inspiration for the T-shirts was the fiction of Wang Shuo. Like many other readers in Beijing, Kong had been familiar with Wang's stories for some years, and in mid-1990, along with other fans, he enthusiastically devoured the first collection of Wang Shuo's comic stories.[35] As we pointed out earlier, the language in much of Wang Shuo's satirical fiction was a parody or inversion of official party language, New China Newspeak, Xinhua wenti, the flat or wooden parole of bureaucrats and political sloganeering. More than any other contemporary Chinese writer, Wang made Beijing streetwise irreverence into an art form, and a commercial one at that. The effect of Wang's success on other writers, artists, and the populace at large was immeasurable. As the writer Wang Meng commented in a review of Wang Shuo's popularity in early 1993: "What he does is place all forms of language on the same plane of discourse, regardless of whether it be the language of earnest discussion or badinage, whether it be the elegant or vulgar, sad or happy. . . . Although you can't accuse him of using language to incite counterrevolution or to instigate people to engage in serious criminal acts, Wang Shuo can be said to manipulate language in every other way at his disposal"[36] (for a discussion of the nexus between Wang Meng and Wang Shuo, see chapter 11, "Kowtowing to the Vulgar").

Wang Shuo's comic genius had reached something of an apogee with the publication in 1989 of his novel *No Man's Land*. Kong was so impressed by that book that even after he was under a police order to cease producing his T-shirts, he made a private run of shirts for friends that carried the text of the "letter of appreciation" to be found at the end of the novel (and in translation in chapter 4, "The Apotheosis of the *Liumang*"). Indeed, Kong's very first shirt, an example of his future style made up to interest potential investors, bore the simple Beijing expression "real profound" or "deep," *te shenchen*. As a satirical or tongue-in-cheek saying, "real profound" had been current for some years, but it was not until the publication of Wang Shuo's 1988 story "The Operators" and its sequel "An Attitude"—in which the protagonists decide to set up their own literary journal called *Real Profound*—that the term was enshrined in satirical parlance.[37]

The irony of its fate as a slogan was that although the T-shirt design impressed his prospective investors, Kong eventually decided that the expression was too lackluster to appear on his clothes. One Wang Shuo–ified term that did make it into a silk-screen print, however, was the word *shi'r* (thing, matter, event, hassle, trouble), and Kong created the transiently famous legend "Some things become something only when you make something of them. Then they can be a real thing."[38] Kong's T-shirts featured other words that were common in Wang's writings like *fan* (annoyed or pissed)—as in *fanzhe ne, bie li wo*—and *te* (very, extremely, absolutely),[39] as in the T-shirt he produced that was covered in Beijing slang expressions.

Other less specific sources for the shirts were sayings and slang expressions Kong collected by listening to everyday Beijing speech, along with his own reflections on everyday life, including his relationship with others (for example, with his then girlfriend Chen Mei) and thoughts about the society as a whole.[40]

As we have noted, like many other Chinese artists, writers, and intellectuals in their late twenties and early thirties, Kong had been deeply influenced by the melee of "cultural frenzy" that had erupted on the mainland during the 1980s. Part of the fever included public discussion of Chinese and Western culture, including the hoary debate concerning the contents and significance of the "Chinese national character," *guominxing*, whose nature, some argued, militated against China's ever becoming a modern, democratic society. To a certain extent, Kong hoped that some of the legends on his T-shirts would be part of the continuing popular questioning of Chineseness (many controversial elements of which were discussed in the works of authors like Lung-kee Sun), and Kong's long-term plan for the shirts included an ironic reinterpretation of a number of elements of traditional Chinese culture that were held dear by Han exclusivists: Chinese medicine, martial arts, *qigong*, food, and so on. Although he did design two shirts using woodblock prints from traditional books on medicine and meditation,[41] they were only a sample of what he wanted to do. When he attempted to explain to the police interrogators in early July his interest in reflecting the debates about the national character and traditional culture in his shirts, their reaction was sheer incredulity. One of the interrogators said that Kong might think he was engaged in enhancing national culture, *hongyang minzu wenhua*—an official expression that could be used to cover virtually any public or private interest in China's past—but he was very sadly mistaken if he thought his T-shirts had anything to do with the glorification of the Chinese nation.[42]

But Kong's aims were not only enmeshed with national identity discourse. One of his favorite books was *How to Win Friends and Influence People*, the self-promotion classic by Dale Carnegie that had developed a mass following in entrepreneurial China in the 1980s.

A SELLOUT

Kong had collected most of the terms and expressions he wanted to use on the shirts during September 1990, spending many hours in conversation with friends discussing his ideas and collecting amusing sayings and phrases for possible inclusion in future designs. He literally talked—or *kan*, to use the Beijing slang expression—the shirts into existence. At this juncture, he sent the final lists of legends for the shirts by express mail to a former colleague who now worked as a photographer for Xinhua Books in the Shenzhen Special Economic Zone to have them set in Hong Kong, where there was a larger, more "modern" range of typefaces. The finished product, much of it done in a style not previously seen in Beijing, was then sent back to the northern capital, also by express mail.

After months of preparation and the arduous search for backers, Chen Mei, Kong's girlfriend, who had recently graduated from the Central Art Academy, helped find the money to produce the shirts. Chen's father introduced Kong to a group willing to invest in the project. In late March 1991, the artist signed a contract to produce the T-shirts with Li Hongao and Lian Jianxin, two cadres in the management committee of the Number Three Retired Cadres' Recuperation Facility for Military Personnel of Shijingshan District in the western suburbs of Beijing.[43] The agreement would be in effect for one year starting on 1 April; profits were to be split sixty/forty.[44] Kong was to provide the expertise for the business while Li and Lian came up with the capital and premises. Production began at the Zhenxing Arts and Crafts Factory,[45] a subsidiary of the Recuperation Facility. Even though others who had heard of the project were certain it would be politically risky, Li and Lian were determined to gamble on the plan in an effort to expand their business. In the spring of 1991, Kong quit his job with the *China Environment News* to devote himself full time to the new venture.

In early June, the Recuperation Facility provided 20,000 *yuan* for the purchase of 2,300 white, round-necked T-shirts at 2.9 to 3.5 *yuan* each, plus other materials. Once printed, the shirts were sold for a wholesale price of 5 to 5.5 *yuan*. The success of the shirts was immediate and immense. By mid-June, Kong's designs were being printed in five different locales; there were more than fifty street-stall outlets; and numerous state-run and collective (co-op) clothing stores also were selling them. Soon there were plans to expand the enterprise and set up a clothing factory so that production could be regularized.[47] The demand for the shirts continued to skyrocket, and Kong soon found himself under pressure to come up with one to two new designs every day. In the following weeks, he created some 57 of his own designs and sparked a summer fashion craze which, according to official sources, saw the appearance of more than 130 different types of cultural T-shirt in the space of little over a month.[48]

Within weeks of the first appearance of Kong Yongqian's T-shirts, businesses operating in the rapaciously entrepreneurial environment of Beijing were energetically imitating his style. Soon stall owners were hawking T-shirts carrying their own designs and captions, and some were even said to be making prints to order.[49] The imitation shirts included, among other things, Mao quotations, produced in an attempt to cash in on the nongovernment revival of the Mao cult.[50] One particularly popular T-shirt simply read, "I'm bored" or "Life's a bore," *zhen lei,* an expression taken from Kong's "Beijing Slang" design, and a sentiment already much discussed in the media in 1991 (see the discussion of the San Mao and Jiao Yulu debate in chapter 5).[51] As it was in the days before China's new copyright law was being enforced, many of the imitators tried appealing to middle-school and university students by using cartoons from the Taiwan artist Cai Zhizhong's adaptations of the classics, such as Cai's images of Confucius bearing sayings like "To tell you the truth, I'm uneducated too" or "Do you have a diploma?"[52] Another imaginative line was positively Dorothy Parkeresque. It read: "Too scared to hang myself; don't have a knife to commit harakiri; would take poison if I had any; and would jump off a building if I could find a way. But I'm still living."[53] Other shirts featured overtly political statements. One, for example, bore the words "bloody incident," *xuean,* a none-too-subtle reference to the 4 June Beijing massacre; another simply read "informer," *mitan.* These, and a number of other shirts, infuriated the police, who concluded that they all were manufactured by Kong. In keeping with the paranoid logic of Chinese officialdom that saw conspiracies and plots everywhere, they also thought that Kong's project was being surreptitiously supported by malcontents and inimical foreign forces.[54]

Kong, on the other hand, saw his work as a vehicle for a number of things, none of which were so overtly political. Primarily, for both commercial and artistic reasons, he wanted the sayings and pictures on the shirts to appeal to a wide range of people. He hoped various sections of the population could see the shirts as a way to make some kind of personalized statement while not having actually to verbalize their thoughts directly. This act of consumption-display would allow people to engage in a voiceless exchange, a silent dialogue between like-minded individuals free from the complications and restrictions of any extraneous *guanxi* (entwining interpersonal relationships) or censorship. The shirts would also provide people with an opportunity to release pent-up emotions and frustrations, regardless of whether they were personal, social, or political. It was this dimension of the T-shirt craze—that of a popular, unspoken conspiracy of self-expression writ large in satirical and ironic terms—that the authorities may well have found particularly unsettling.

Kong had hoped that his clothes would inspire people to rebel against the conformity of the printed Chinese character that had been so strictly limited by official sanction, convention, and technology in the past and to use "uncalligraphic," that is, nonelitist, styles of writing to create their own messages and pictures for T-shirts.[55] Similarly, an aspect of the popularity of the shirts in Beijing could be linked to the general interest that the people of that city have in *kan renao*, or "enjoying a spectacle." The protests of 1989 had been an ideal expression of this passion,[56] and the T-shirts provided the first chance since 4 June for locals to enjoy harmless street disruption.

The T-shirts were, however, primarily a popular consumer item. By wearing them and walking around in public, people could express their shopper's individuality as well as participate in a lighthearted attempt to ameliorate the stultifying, confused, and highly confrontational social ambience of Chinese urban life in the early 1990s. The shirts made it possible for consumers to be circumscribed rebels; they gave individuals an opportunity to express themselves through a safe and collective medium. For his part, Kong was reacting against the tradition of academic art and elite culture in which he had been educated. The designing and production of the T-shirts was a venture aimed at helping him achieve a modicum of economic independence as well as a sense of cultural satisfaction. Seen in the context of China's economic transformation, Kong was also involved in "commodifying" elements of Chinese written culture, political discourse, and street humor in a style that was peculiar to Beijing but one that had a wider, even trans-Chinese, appeal.

One stall owner in Haidian, the university district of Beijing, said that at the height of the popularity of "cultural T-shirts" in May and June 1991, he was selling 150 shirts a day at an average of 5 to 6 *yuan* apiece. The most popular were two of Kong's designs: "I'm pissed, leave me alone," *fanzhe ne, bie li wo*, and "Making ends meet," *lajia daikou*, plus a pirated shirt inspired by Kong's "Beijing slang" *Beijing tuhua* shirt: "Life's a bore," *zhen lei*.[57] These three designs accounted for around one-third of all sales. They also were the most expensive, selling for 10 *yuan* each.[58] Another article, reporting on the state of shirt sales before the enterprise fell foul of the authorities, claimed that stalls in the main shopping districts of Beijing sold at least two hundred shirts a day.[59] They were particularly popular with lower-class workers, hawkers, and young people, it was said. But Kong noted that university students were fairly slow to respond to the fad, as were the intelligentsia; not surprising, since neither group was particularly renowned for its street savvy. Even when the "educated classes" did belatedly catch on to the trend, they saw the shirts as being a minor cultural diversion with little real significance. Many individuals of a conservative bent of mind—and they were not necessarily party hacks but often members of various Beijing elites—were shocked and disturbed by the flippancy of the messages that the shirts sported.

It is interesting to note here that even the street-stall entrepreneurs were initially hesitant to sell the shirts. This was possibly due to a fear of the political repercussions of hawking a product that engaged directly with the written language, formerly the strict province of official regulation. Small-business people and entrepreneurs had, after all, been heavily implicated in the events of 1989 and were still under considerable government pressure in the early 1990s. Added to this was the fact that stall hawkers in the capital were generally fairly conservative, following market trends that indicated popular taste rather than attempting to predict or influence them. They did not, according to Kong, initiate fashion trends themselves. Like so many others, they were caught unprepared by the enthusiastic public response to the shirts.

T-SHIRT CITY

The initial official reaction to Kong Yongqian's T-shirts was surprisingly encouraging. Throughout June 1991, the leading official newspapers, like the *Beijing Youth News* and *Wenhui Daily* in Shanghai, ran approving articles on the shirts that were by then roaming the streets of the capital and even turning up in far-flung provincial towns and cities. The thirty-minute economics program on China Central Television (CCTV), the economic news station of Beijing TV, as well as a number of newspapers and magazines, were even planning to invite Kong Yongqian to talk about his designs and overnight business success.[60]

One newspaper went so far as to carry a front-page story including pictures of both the T-shirts and Kong Yongqian. Written by Tang Chenglin, a former colleague of Kong's at the *China Environment News*, the article was probably the longest positive report on the shirts published in the mainland Chinese press. It appeared on 2 July, just as the official ban on the shirts was being policed. Oddly enough, even though Tang's article was accompanied by a picture of Kong at home wearing one of the shirts, he did not mention the artist's role in the appearance of the "culture T-shirts," and, according to Kong, Tang did not learn about it until the article went to press.[61]

Tang did include a few streetside reactions to the shirts in his report:

- "Monkey," the nickname of a stall owner at the Dongsi Market, one of Beijing's busiest spots, was selling more than three hundred T-shirts a day. Most of them sported pictures of movie stars and beautiful women drawn with a calligraphy brush. The reporter asked a number of young men and women why they were attracted to these images. The answer was the same: although none of them could really tell who the pictures were of, they liked the informality of the designs and composition.[62]

- At the night market in Xidan, the reporter witnessed a young couple purchasing a T-shirt with the words "Nothing to My Name," *yi wu suoyou*, the title of a well-known early song by Cui Jian written in art lettering. The 1987 song went, in part,

> It's ages now I've been asking you:
> When will you come away with me?
> But all you ever do is laugh at me, 'cause
> I've got nothing to my name.
>
> I want to give you my hope
> I want to help make you free
> But all you ever do is laugh at me, 'cause
> I've got nothing to my name.[63]

The young man liked the T-shirt version because it "showed a sense of ambition: you might not have anything at the moment, but that meant you could make a future for yourself." The girl was attracted to the colors of the shirt, black words on a blue background. She felt they expressed a certain vitality and appeared "modern."[64]

The journalist-writer Sang Ye, who wrote about the shirts for the Hong Kong press, was free to report more radical popular responses. While discussing the shirts with a stall owner in late June, Sang said he heard someone say, "They won't let us demonstrate or stick up big-character posters, but they can't stop us from saying what we want on our own clothes." The stall owner was quick to disassociate himself from this remark: "That's not why I'm selling them, pal. Feel free to buy them if you want. You can think what ever you want about what they say, be as reactionary as you want, but don't blame it on me!"[65] Sang called the appearance of the shirts a new style of political movement, a *yundong*—a true "consumer revolution" perhaps—that featured "voiceless slogans" on display in the streets. Another article published in the Hong Kong press called the shirts "a Democracy Wall on the chest."[66] Kong Yongqian's police interrogators later told him that they regarded many of the legends on his shirts as being "slogans."[67] While giving expression to the individual, the shirts actually reflected a group or mass consciousness. Like the colorful and varied street protests of 1989, it was self-expression that achieved its aims in the safety of the collective.[68]

An interpretation of the shirts, typical of the Hong Kong and Taiwan press response to the phenomenon, noted that although the authorities were anxious to prevent any popular antigovernment protests as the second anniversary of the 4 June Beijing massacre drew near, the masses had other plans. One report argued that the T-shirts, a product of China's unique political culture, appeared just as the anniversary was approaching and were a response to it. Others noted that the shirts were in circulation in the weeks leading up to the seventieth anniversary of the founding of the Communist Party on 1 July 1991, a major event scheduled to be celebrated on a grand scale by party leaders who were still feeling unsettled two years after the events of spring 1989 and were anxious to reaffirm the party's history and preeminent role in China's past, present, and future salvation. Some of the shirts, particularly a few carrying quotations from Mao Zedong, could certainly be regarded as political broadsides. Take, for example, the shirt that bore the title of Mao's famous 1930 article on local rebellions: "A Spark Can Start a Prairie Fire,"[69] or another with the line from Mao's garrulous 1965 anti-Soviet poem: "Don't fart! [that is, "don't give me any bullshit!"] See how the world is changing around you."[70] Another, more creative, use of a Mao quotation was "I'm not afraid of hardship, or afraid of dying, and I'm not afraid of you," *yi bupa ku, er bupa si, ye bupa ni*, the last phrase having been added to the original 1969 quotation written to commemorate the army martyr Wang Jie.[71] Then there was Kong's own comical rewriting of a line from the good soldier and red samaritan Lei Feng's diary: "Revolutionary soldiers are but bricks / moved around according to the party's wish."[72]

At the time of his interrogation in July 1991, the police told Kong that according to their estimates, one in ten students in Beijing was wearing his shirts. Perhaps just as, if not more, disturbing were reports that Hong Kong and Taiwan businesspeople in the capital had complained to the authorities that some of their workers went to the office in T-shirts with the strange legends on them. The police reasoned that this might adversely affect investor confidence.[73] There was even a popular rumor that Chen Xitong, the mayor of Beijing, had noticed members of his staff wearing the shirts and was outraged.

GET OFF MY BACK!

According to official sources, the first warnings about the T-shirts and their "negative social impact" (a blanket expression used to describe any public or private work or act of which the authorities disapproved) were made by the Xidan Industry and Commerce Office and the Xidan District Management Committee, which sent a joint report on the subject to the Beijing Municipal Committee in late June.[74]

On 29 June 1991, the Beijing Municipal Industrial and Commercial Administration Bureau moved to close the gaping loophole that had allowed the T-shirts to appear in the first place, by issuing a "Circular Strictly Prohibiting the Manufacture and Sale of Products Carrying Unhealthy Images and Legends."

The circular declared that the shirts were "harmful to socialist morality and/or have a negative influence." Among other things, the circular appealed to "the masses of consumers to boycott such products [as the T-shirts], by refusing to buy, wear, or use them."[75] A further "Circular Concerning the Decision on the Case of the Illegal Manufacture and Sale of 'Cultural T-shirts' " was made at around the same time, and it was on the basis of this ruling that Kong Yongqian was eventually fined.[76]

On 2 July, the Beijing Municipal Committee, the Public Security Bureau (PSB), and the Bureau of Industry and Commerce acting in concert began to purge the T-shirts from the marketplace. The Thirteenth Department of the PSB immediately detained Kong Yongqian at his apartment for questioning in relation to charges of speculation, profiteering, and illegal trading. At the same time, the T-shirt production lines at Kong's parents' home at Sanbulao Alley near Xinjie-kou, Fengtai, and at Shijingshan were closed down. The equipment for producing the silk-screen T-shirts and designs was also confiscated.[77] Kong was questioned for three days by police from the Seventh and Thirteenth Departments as well as by officers of the Special Trades Section of the Municipal PSB.[78] This was the second time he had been detained for questioning, the first interrogation having been conducted by the local police, *pian'rjing*, on 18 June.[79]

Kong Yongqian believed that the authorities were distressed by both the extraordinary popularity of the shirts and the repeated reports in the foreign media and nonmainland (Hong Kong and Taiwan) Chinese-language press that interpreted his work as being political in intent. During the questioning, Kong's interrogators asked him whether he knew that the foreign media regarded the shirts as a form of political protest. The police were particularly interested in finding out who was really behind the T-shirts: had Kong been working at someone else's behest, and was he aware of the grave political consequences of what he had been doing?[80] It took three days of nonstop questioning and months of subsequent surveillance to convince them that Kong was a rogue individual and not part of some elaborate political plot with sinister international connections.

And when it came to the interpretation of individual T-shirts, Kong and his interrogators repeatedly found themselves at loggerheads. In the first place, the police were convinced that a number of the shirts were a pointed affront aimed at the authorities. One shirt with the image of a howling dog under which was the legend "Natural Mien," *ziran bense*, caused considerable offense. The police took the dog to be a vicious wolf and the message of the shirt to be a warning that people should beware of evil. Presumably, Kong remarked, they saw themselves mirrored in the features of the snarling canine. Another highly questionable picture was that of an eagle with the words "If you don't like what you see, don't look," *bukan ladao*, underneath it. The authorities regarded this as being provocative, despite Kong's explanation that he had meant it to be an ironic comment aimed at buyers of the T-shirts: if you don't like what you see, you don't have to buy. Regardless of Kong's protests, many people who had bought the shirt had taken it to be a comment on the government following 4 June and were delighted to be able to take a potshot at the authorities by wearing it.[81]

Then there was the T-shirt bearing the four lines: "Behave yourself; keep your mouth shut; just play safe; easy does it," *zuo laoshi ren / shuo laoshi hua / ban laoshi shi / laolao shishi*. Its mantric style was highly reminiscent of Lin Biao's instructional incantation directed at the revolutionary masses during the early phase of the Cultural Revolution — "read Chairman Mao's works; do what the chairman tells you; and become a good soldier of the chairman," *du Mao zhuxide shu, ting Mao zhuxide hua, zhao Mao zhuxide zhishi banshi, zuo Mao zhuxide hao zhanshi*. But the police wanted to know just why the word for "person," *ren*, in the first line was printed at a disturbing angle reminiscent of a Cultural Revolution big-character poster denunciation of a party leader. Again, why had Kong chosen such a sly-looking fox as the image for the T-shirt with the legend "Tonight we meet for the first time," *jinwan women xiangshi*?[82] The designer argued that it was meant as a comical and comely image that would amuse young women. Another was a silhouette of a man in tails talking with a woman with the caption "Keeping it clean" or "chaste embrace," *zuohuai buluan*, which incensed the police, as they regarded the implication of the words as being obscene.[83]

The design "Making ends meet," *lajia daikou*, featured an oversized pocket on the front of the T-shirt with the following documents in it: a monthly bus pass, grain rations, cloth rations, cooking oil rations, meal tickets, employment ID card, student ID, marriage license, urban residence permit, household register, resident's coupon booklet, bicycle registration, secret bank account, exit/entry permit, letter of introduction, and a name card.[84] Kong had realized that the excessive interest shown in this particular shirt by the police during his first interrogation meant that he would be questioned again about it. The journalist Sang Ye even speculated that the appearance of "Making ends meet" may well have sparked the harsh official reaction to the shirts in July.[85]

Kong's interrogators were particularly critical of him for including grain rations and a household register, *hukouben*, in his checklist of daily necessities and documents. They told him that they felt the shirt derided the administrative mechanisms used by the state to maintain social stability, that for them the shirt was a blatant expression of the artist's deep-seated antagonism toward the government and the economic status quo.[86] Kong recalls the tenor of their remarks as follows: "You're resentful of the government's long-term policies, aren't you? You can't hide the way you feel. . . . Why do you despise the socialist system so much?

We want to know what's made you think like this, and we can assure you we have all the time in the world in which to find out."[87]

He responded by telling them that his original idea was to cover a T-shirt in pockets with some form of ID or coupon sticking out of each one, but his friends (in particular, although he did not say this to the police, Zhou Bin, a quick-witted Beijing man who worked in the advertising department of the *China Environment News*) had persuaded him to make just one large pocket. As for the contents of the pouch, he explained, there were many items in it that had little contemporary relevance (like grain coupons which were increasingly rare in the early 1990s and had in some cases become collectors' items) and had been included only for nostalgic reasons. Others, like the household register, were there because they were a simple and unavoidable fact of everyday life. Furthermore, Kong argued, why should the PSB be so upset by the inclusion of a household register, since most of the contact between the average Chinese and police was regulated by such registers and, without them, a lot of policemen and women would find themselves out of a job?[88]

"Making ends meet" was a particularly popular design with buyers, as it treated with indulgent irony some of the most irksome elements of the daily grind in urban China. The shirt also must have made an impression on Wang Shuo, whose works were among Kong's original inspirations, because he included a reference to it in "Ad People," a thirty-part television series, whose scripts were published in early 1993.[89]

Next came the shirt "A total failure: I'd like to be a smuggler but don't have the nerve / wanna be a bureaucrat but ain't sly enough / if I slack off at work I'll be canned / wanna start a stall but don't have the cash."[90] Kong recalls the police interpreted it in the following way: "We've been liberated all these years, and here you are acting as though we haven't achieved anything. What the hell do you want to do, eh? Rob a bank, become a smuggler? What's going on in that head of yours?" Kong then explained that what he meant by "A total failure" was that for a person to wear the shirt was a statement that he had not engaged in any of the socially negative or illegal deeds described on it. That's why he was "a total failure." The police explanation of the shirt, Kong responded, was as narrow and rigid as the original official reactions to Cui Jian's early rock songs which had so unsettled the authorities in the late 1980s.[91]

Finally, after questioning him about "I'm pissed, leave me alone," the investigators raised the issue of the shirt that read "Some things become something only when you make something of them. Then they can be a real thing." This line had often been taken to be a sardonic reference to the government's violent overreaction to the protests of 1989. By this stage in the interrogation process, however, the police were running out of steam, and they simply said to Kong: "What you're saying is that the less notice you take of something, then the less important it is? Well, we disagree. So you just think about it."

Much of the final interrogation session consisted of the artist and the police haggling over their entirely different interpretations of each of the shirts. At times the police became hysterical—reminiscent, Kong said, of the rabid style of questioning common during the Cultural Revolution.[92] Although Kong's reasons for creating the shirts were complex and multifarious, the investigating officers were incapable of believing that a person without hidden political grievances or an agenda could be the mastermind of the disturbing craze. At best, they thought him a simpleton.[93] For his part, Kong treated the police like anybody else who was interested in the shirts, explaining them with a confusing mixture of clarity and straight-faced doublethink.

Kong was finally instructed to write a detailed history of the T-shirts for the record and include an explanation of what he had hoped to achieve by designing them. The police also demanded that he admit that the T-shirts were an example of bourgeois liberalization.[94] If he failed to comply, it was suggested, he could look forward to a stint in jail. Kong responded that since he was now both unemployed and penniless, he didn't care if they locked him up, that then the state could take care of him. The interrogators were visibly disappointed by his attitude and decided to release him on the condition that he told the others involved in the T-shirt operation (Chen Mei, Bai Xincheng, and Bai Xinhua) to come in for questioning.[95] A few days later the police appeared at his apartment and confiscated the *Shōgakukan Dictionary of New Chinese Words*.[96]

FROM RICHES TO RAGS

On 3 July, the three government offices involved in the case held a joint meeting to decide on the necessary measures to sweep the remaining shirts out of the marketplace, and for the rest of the month, clothing stalls and shops throughout the capital were raided in implementation of a ban on selling thirty-four of the T-shirt designs, mostly Kong's. In mid-July, the authorities in Tianjin, Taiyuan in Shanxi Province, and a number of other cities also prohibited T-shirts that demonstrated explicit "gray sentiments."

For example, alerted to the dangers of the "walking protests" by the Beijing authorities and media in July, the Municipal Government of Xi'an deployed forces to crush the fad throughout Shaanxi. Local officials warned against the dangers of the shirts and called "for measures to be taken to prevent the dissemination of unhealthy ideological tendencies." Six municipal offices under the auspices of the local Department of Propaganda launched an offensive, including confiscations of shirts, the reeducation of manufacturers, and a range of penalties for those involved in the shirt trade. In one joint raid on 31 July that involved the combined forces of the Department of Commerce and Industry, the Tax Office, and the local police, sixteen stalls were investigated and 1,074 T-shirts were removed. By 5 August, raids throughout Xi'an had led to the confiscation of 2,285 of the offending items of clothing.[97]

Kong Yongqian's July detention was followed by occasional police harassment and informal questioning. Only after months of uncertainty was a final decision on the case made. On 17 January 1992, Kong received an official notification from the Bureau of Industry and Commerce of Shijingshan District, Beijing, dated 5 November 1991.[98] It stated that the bureau had carried out an official investigation into the T-shirts produced and marketed by Kong and Chen Mei from 6 July to 6 September. The investigation concluded that Kong, in cooperation with the Number Three Retired Cadres' Recuperation Facility, was responsible for creating more than thirty silk screens for the manufacture of 6,345 T-shirts featuring such "unhealthy designs and legends" as "I'm pissed, leave me alone" and "Keeping it clean," of which 566 were sold. Furthermore, from 20 April to the end of June, Kong and Chen had printed 13,816 T-shirts at Kong's home at Xinjiekou, during which time contractual arrangements were entered into with the Beijing Municipal Knitwear Company and the Beijing Municipal Textile Science Research Institute for the production and sale of 3,800 shirts. A total of 23,961 T-shirts were produced "without any of the regular formalities having been completed." According to Kong's own reckoning, he manufactured more than 40,000 T-shirts of which an unknown number were destroyed by the authorities.[99]

The bureau concluded that the T-shirt incident was the work of certain individuals and profiteers who had "willfully disrupted the marketplace." If they had found Kong to have been involved in a premeditated plot to undermine the "unity and stability" of the society—a serious political charge—the case would have been handed over to the police. In keeping with the new "offender pays" policies of the Chinese bureaucracy, however, Kong Yongqian was notified that all profits from the venture, as well as the means of production, had been confiscated and a fine of 20,000 *yuan* imposed on him and his coworkers. This fine was duly paid on 17 January 1992, the singer Cui Jian giving Kong a loan of 3,000 *yuan*.[100]

As is so often the case with such governmental bans, black market interest in the T-shirts was considerable. Over the summer of 1991, the surreptitious printing and sale of "cultural T-shirts" continued, and prices for contraband shirts rocketed. In one case, a young fellow would part with one of Kong's T-shirts only in exchange for a top bearing a picture of Madonna plus U.S. $10 in cash.[101] According to internal reports, the ban served only to advertise the existence of the shirts and stimulated an increased demand among consumers for them.[102]

COLOR ME GRAY

As for the official media, by early July the tenor of comments in the Beijing press had changed radically, with the tone of mild approval and uncertainty that had been common the previous month suddenly hardening into one of outrage and warning. Apart from the extraordinary popularity of the shirts themselves, Kong reasoned that a major contributing factor in this official about-face were foreign media reports, in particular in the Chinese-language press and on the BBC and Voice of America, which interpreted the shirts as a form of political protest marking the anniversary of the 4 June Beijing massacre.

Published at the behest of the authorities, the following stern comment made by a critic writing for the *Economic Daily* was a typical example of official disapproval:

> Are the messages [on the T-shirts] beautiful and uplifting? Do they help foster the social ambience we need? Of course, there are those who will opine that they are humorous, at most playfully self-deprecating, funny, and a matter of individual expression. But what if all Chinese were to wear [a T-shirt reading] "I'm pissed, leave me alone" (though that's quite impossible)? *What a terrifying image we would present to the rest of the world. We can best do without this type of gray humor, if only for the sake of the image of the reform and open door policies.*[103]

The article appealed to the authorities to make those designing and selling the T-shirts "accept their social responsibilities," that is, pay for their crime. It is noteworthy that on the way to his place of detention, a young policeman had shown Kong Yongqian the work site for the Western Overpass Construction Project around Xibianmen, a major new engineering project in the capital, and as he watched the builder's laborers at work, the officer said to him: how would anything get done in China if everyone wore your T-shirt saying "I'm pissed, leave me alone"?[104] Also, during his detention, Kong Yongqian was asked: If every young person in the capital wore one of these shirts, "what would become of the place?" And as the interrogator struck Kong's head and face with his fan (it was the height of summer), he said: "Before you know it, people will be demonstrating in the streets again."[105] Attempts by the designer to explain that the shirt "I'm pissed, leave me alone" was inspired by a lover's quarrel were ignored. Despite their official displeasure, at the end of his interrogation, some of the police asked Kong on the sly to give them some of these shirts. Then later, a man working for the Ministry of State Security, China's KGB, who was preparing to travel to France asked Kong to give him six of his most typical shirt designs.[106]

In mid-July, the *Beijing Youth News*, which had originally printed an article praising the shirts, carried an essay by a commentator on the unsettling "anticultural" aspects of the shirts. The article claimed that the shirts were the latest in a tradition of antisocial behavior that had links to the Dadaists and hippies in the West and Wang Shuo's fiction, especially his 1989 novel *No Man's Land*, in China. Just as the conservative cultural critic He Xin had attacked the "hippy culture" of certain writers in 1985 (see chapter 4, "The Apotheosis of the *Liumang*"), this commentator remarked that China was too poor and backward to afford the luxury of this type of irrational "anticulturalism" and "youthful nihilism," these "diseases of twentieth-century man." Although he reluctantly admitted that the creators of the "cultural T-shirts" were perhaps interested in transforming Chinese culture, the method they had chosen was irrational and impracticable. In the West, "anticultural" and "antiestablishment" attitudes were a luxury that young people could afford. But the youth of China, the writer in the *Beijing Youth News* pointed out, had to face up to reality, accept their responsibilities, and grow out of their habit of finding release through such self-indulgent emotionalism.[107]

As one critic remarked after official action was taken against the shirts, "They carry gloomy, negative, and cynical messages that do one thing, and one thing only: encourage a sense of decadence."[108] Other news organizations in the capital lagged behind in propagating the official view. The China News Agency, the official overseas Chinese news service, was a case in point, publishing a positive review of the shirts as late as on 10 July.[109] As was increasingly common on mainland China, the ideological line taken in Beijing was not necessarily immediately followed in the provinces. Around this time, the Shanghai daily *New People's Evening News* published a report on the T-shirt craze in the capital, approving of the way in which many of the shirts like "I'm pissed, leave me alone" gave people a chance to express their individualism.[110] Since the tenor of propaganda in Shanghai was in certain respects at loggerheads with the Beijing municipal authorities and their high-level supporters during the early months of 1991, it is interesting to speculate whether this late pro-T-shirt article was a riposte to the hard line being taken in the north (for more on this see chapter 7, "Packaged Dissent"). Again, in Harbin, northeast China, one newspaper still praised the shirts as late as 17 July.[111]

By September, however, an official line on the corrosive ideological nature of the shirts had been formulated and implemented nationwide. It had been decided that the shirts represented, in short, "gray sentiments," *huise qingxu*, or, as one internal analysis of the phenomenon called them, "gray culture T-shirts."[112] The previous chapter dealt at length with the subject of "the graying of Chinese culture" and the nature of "gray sentiments" in urban China and their perceived threat. Such sentiments were now represented in the official media as being "a syndrome that combined hopelessness, uncertainty, and ennui with irony, sarcasm, and a large dose of fatalism. It is a mood that enveloped both the individual and an ambience that suffused the urban world. It is a zeitgeist that is notice-ably prevalent in youth culture."[113]

The perceived threat of gray thoughts and attitudes was by no means new. As early as 1959, official critics were on the lookout for young people who had "a gray outlook on life," one that reflected a dangerously ambivalent attitude toward party rule.[114] In the early 1990s, grayness was increasingly identified as a long-term canker in the Chinese body politic.[115]

During his interrogation, the police asked Kong Yongqian whether he thought the sentiments expressed in his T-shirts were, indeed, "gray."[116] Kong fudged the an-swer, but the question helped him surmise that this question in itself indicated that the municipal authorities had decided that the shirts were not to be treated as a po-litical threat, in which case they would have been ideologically "black," and instead were to be regarded merely as an example of wayward and negative thinking. His shirts were therefore seen by the authorities as constituting an act of youthful folly rather than being a premeditated attack on socialism. The new official line on "gray sentiments" was transmitted both internally[117] and in the popular media, with one pointed article attacking the insidious malaise of incipient youth disgruntlement appearing, for example, in the *Southern Daily*, the main Guangzhou newspaper.[118]

In early October 1991, another article in the Beijing press criticized the legends on Kong's shirts, commenting with unconcealed relief that the weather was now too cold for people to wear them anymore. It called on manufacturers to produce only clothing that reflected China's true national spirit and sense of optimism. It was accompanied by a photograph of a young couple wearing T-shirts that read "We're broke," *meiqian*, standing in front of a bookstall near the Imperial Palace Museum in Shenyang, Liaoning Province. The caption read "Being Trendy: . . . are T-shirts with such odd legends really all that cool, that stylish, and with it?" The writer said that the sentiments conveyed by the shirts (having referred to shirts that had been produced by Kong) were socially detrimental:

> Negativity and complaint, together with the expression of abnormal senti-ments are of no benefit whatsoever and are even positively harmful to both our [socialist] enterprise and daily life itself. This is reason enough for our young people to stir themselves, look reality squarely in the face, shoulder their historical burden, and work and study with their feet planted firmly on the ground.[119]

As we saw in the preceding chapter, the *Beijing Youth News*—anxious as al-ways to avail itself of popular issues to boost its profile and sales—in late October started a discussion, "Reflections Inspired by the Words 'Chore' and 'Bore'," which attempted to confront the threat of "gray sentiments" and a "gray sense of humor" as evinced by Kong's T-shirts.

SHIRTS *SANS* ATTITUDE

With Kong's guerrilla operation out of the running, others were quick to exploit the popularity of т-shirts for their own ends. In August 1991, Wang Youshen, an arts editor at the *Beijing Youth News* and an active member of the semi-underground art scene, produced т-shirt designs for a charity concert held for the flood-stricken regions of east China. The concert was cosponsored by the *Beijing Youth News*, and one of the shirts produced for the occasion read: "We're all in the same boat," *fengyu tongzhou*.[120] Wang also created a series of shirts using images from the newspaper, including a news picture of a highly animated Li Ruihuan, the "liberal" Politburo leader in charge of ideology, and a scene in a new stock exchange. During the summer of 1992, Wang also designed a т-shirt to promote the newspaper and another to advertise an art exhibition he organized in July of that year.[121] In 1993, he produced a shirt for friends that had on it a page from *The Stratagems of Sunzi*, and in 1994 he took the initiative to use т-shirts, shopping bags, and a range of products to help create a new "corporate identity," CI *xingxiang*, for the *Beijing Youth News*.[122]

Satire and Humor, the *People's Daily* comic supplement, took a dig at the shirts in October 1991 when it published a cartoon of an old peasant addressing a youngster holding a brush captioned: "Listen, my child, we don't want to write 'life's a bore,' but this. . . ." as he points at the freshly written line on his own т-shirt: "Socialism is good!"[123] As we pointed out earlier, in 1991 lines from Mao's poems and quotations had made a fleeting appearance on some shirts. Again, in the summer months of 1992, a number of Mao т-shirts appeared in stalls in Beijing and the provinces, an indication that local entrepreneurs had been alerted to the commercial possibilities of the т-shirt and used it to cash in on the post-1989 Mao fad. In 1992, the shirts included many portraits of Mao (either as a young man or in his prime) and lines rehashed from the Cultural Revolution like: "I love studying Chairman Mao's works."[124] People presumably wore such shirts as a comic inversion of what was formerly holy writ. The same summer, in keeping with the new high tide of reform initiated by Deng Xiaoping's tour of the south (see chapter 7, "Packaged Dissent"), т-shirts bearing pro-Deng sayings also appeared in Beijing. Examples of their none-too-subtle slogans include "The People Support You, Comrade Xiaoping!" and "Comrade Xiaoping is leading us along the road of Socialism to make China a strong nation."[125] The Ministry of Textile Industries reportedly set up a Cultural т-shirt Research Association,[126] not to study Kong's work, but to formulate ways to exploit the т-shirt fashion to help promote Chinese textile products.

In a roundup of the Beijing cultural phenomena of 1992, one writer pointed out other new developments in the т-shirt market. After the bans on "cultural т-shirts" in 1991, the writer states, people had become far more streetwise. Forget the line "Leave me alone, I'm pissed," the commentator says, nowadays the T-shirt was the latest arena for advertising. They had become mini, moving billboards used variously for the promotion of films, TV shows, newspapers, and magazines as well as prominent business executives. The ironic protest T-shirts of the Kong Yongqian year had become the inspiration for "promo-culture shirts."[127] This was very much part and parcel of the frenzied commercialization of Chinese culture—official, fringe, and even dissident—in general, a socialist velvet prison with consumer characteristics. By 1996, Beijing Keystone Printing was advertising its services to foreign investors in China, encouraging them to put their "corporate logo on T-shirts." Keystone's publicity line was as simple as it was eloquent: "It's not just a shirt. . . . *It's good advertising.*"[128]

Liu Yajun, one of Kong Yongqian's former colleagues at the *China Environment News*, was also anxious to exploit the possibilities indicated by Kong's initial success. Liu, himself an aspiring artist who found his way to the *Beijing Youth News* where he worked with Wang Youshen, was quick to cash in on the immense popularity of the early 1992 TV sitcom *The Editors.* He quickly produced a T-shirt with an image of Yu Deli (played by Hou Yuehua, son of the comic dialogue, *xiangsheng,* star Hou Baolin), the greasy entrepreneurial advertising man in the editorial department featured in the TV series, along with the quotation: "Money may not be omnipotent, but without it you're as good as impotent."[129] Inspired directly by Kong's shirts and mindful of the trouble that the designer had found himself in, Liu said in an interview with me in May 1993 that he did not need official permission to produce his anodyne fashions, what he called "Liu Yajun's Humorous Cartoon Shirts."[130] He suggested that the impunity with which he produced these new designs was a sure sign that the political atmosphere in the capital had changed by mid-1992.[131] He created twenty asinine cartoon shirts in 1992 and continued the series with mild commercial success in 1993. But the fad, and the spirit, that had made the original T-shirts so popular had passed, as had the general urban ambience, and mass commercialization and pop entertainment increasingly absorbed the popular imagination and forced quirky experiments like Kong Yongqian's T-shirts into the straitjacket of bland consumer culture.

The wider acceptance of Kong's shirts was not always so felicitous. Zhou Guoqiang (aka Aqu Qiangba), one of Kong's old friends and an enthusiastic admirer of the "culture T-shirt" escapade, was a computer enthusiast and a leading labor activist. He also created a number of T-shirts, pointedly called *wenhua shan,* which carried workers' rights slogans. Zhou was detained and sentenced to three years of reeducation through labor in a Heilongjiang prison camp in September 1994 for printing the seditious clothes.[132] Political exploitation of the shirts was not unique to the mainland. Overseas dissident groups and writers were quick to read their own messages into the humble culture shirt. In its inimitable fashion, the U.S.-based dissident journal *Democratic China* saw the shirts as having political associations with their own cause. "The reason that the Communist authorities could not tolerate the shirts," an article on popular culture claimed in late 1992, "was that they reminded the 'unruly masses' of the democratic slogans they had previously written on banners and signs."[133]

Indeed, the trouble with political T-shirts and undershirts continued in August 1992 when China Post issued a 5 *yuan* RMB stamp to commemorate the Twenty-Fifth Olympiad. It featured six runners, three of whom were sporting running tops with numbers on them. A somewhat esoteric interpretation claimed that looking from the right-hand side, the first and second runners' shirts read 89 (the first runner is 17, 1 + 7 = 8, the second runner is 9), and the third runner on the left hand of the stamp was number 64 (or 6.4, *liu si*, the shortened form of "4 June"). The supposed scandal surrounding the stamp was widely reported in the Hong Kong and Taiwanese press, with claims being made that this had led to its withdrawal from circulation.[134]

In early 1993, there was a class reunion for the 1982 graduates of the Beijing Film Academy (the so-called fifth generation of Chinese filmmakers), including such luminaries as Zhang Yimou, Tian Zhuangzhuang, Chen Kaige, and Wu Ziniu. All present received a "cultural T-shirt," the front of which read "Ten long years, let's not talk about it!" *shinian le, bie ti ta la!* This was a comic rewriting of a line from the Cultural Revolution–period Model Beijing Opera "Taking Tiger Mountain by Strategy," in which Hunter Chang says "It's been eight long years [since all this began], let's not talk about it!"[135] On the back of the shirt were the words "First gathering in ten years," *shinian shouju.*[136]

T-shirts were also pressed into service for China's bid for the Olympic Games in 2000. On 14 April 1993, the *Beijing Evening News* reported that a competition for T-shirt designs was being held from 10 April to 15 June to see who could come up with the best design for an Olympic Games bid shirt. The logo to be used was "Everyone's Hoping for the Olympics," *zhongpan Aoyun.*[137] By May, a number of pro-Olympic designs were being sold at stalls throughout Beijing, as were shorts with matching Olympic Games propaganda on them. Meanwhile, various rakes pointed out that the Chinese promotional tag "*zhongpan Aoyun*" was homophonous with the line "Everyone's Hoping for an Australian Olympics." Again in the spring of 1996, a new message T-shirt appeared in such far-flung spots as the former imperial summer resort of Chengde, Beijing, and Shanghai, and it was subsequently banned. The sleeves consisted of a British flag and a flag of the People's Republic, and in the center of the shirt was a billboard painter painting over the Union Jack. The message was about the return of the former British crown colony of Hong Kong to mainland China scheduled for 1 July 1997. In July 1996, the Chinese government forbade all forms of nonofficial commercial exploitation of the upcoming takeover. But it did not restrain itself from issuing commemorative coins, belt buckles, fridge magnets, and other memorabilia of the event, which went on sale one year ahead of time.

Meanwhile, in Hong Kong the patriotic "Red Capitalist" David Tang picked up on the T-shirt fad for his own ends. In 1995, a line of message T-shirts was sold at Tang's retro-Shanghai Pedder Street store, Shanghai Tang, in central Hong Kong. Some carried innocuous macho-literati clichés like: "[I'm like] a heron in crowd of chickens," or "One mountain isn't big enough for two tigers," as well as more patriotic sentiments like "You can't have a foot in both camps at once."[138] Other T-shirts featured the paintings of some of the "avant-garde" mainland artists that Tang had been instrumental in promoting since 1993, as well as embroidered T-shirts that carried the Hong Kong Special Administrative Region symbol and red stars that signified the resumption of mainland suzerainty over the territory.

By this time, it seemed that just about everybody was using T-shirts for one purpose or another, and references to Kong's work continued to appear. In his 1992 novel *Hearsay*, Liu Xinwu, a prominent Beijing writer and ally of Wang Meng mentioned previously, depicted an unruly and ideologically incorrect middle-school student. As a badge of his bad attitude, the boy wears a version of Kong's "Making ends meet."[139] Liu, an official liberal who had risen to fame from the late 1970s as a writer of pedagogical fiction, thus located Kong's work in the realm of juvenile misbehavior. In early 1993, in the third episode of the CCTV series *There's No Denying It's Love*, written by Wang Shuo and others, Gao Qiang, the taxi driver protagonist played by Xie Yuan, is accused of indulging in "gray sentiments." In the seventh episode, one of the characters "quotes" Kong's T-shirt: "Nothing will ever happen to me," *buhui lai shi'r.* Again, in the third episode of *Ad People*, written by Wang Shuo, Su Lei, and Wei Ren, the line "you can't fool me," *wo yan'rli roubude shazi*, appears,[140] reminiscent of Kong's shirt of an owl that had a similar line underneath it (*gemen'r jiemen'r yanli wo burou shazi*). In the third episode of the popular 1993 TV series *A Beijing Man in New York* (see chapter 10, "To Screw Foreigners Is Patriotic"), the protagonist Wang Qiming returns to his apartment after a day of abasement in the wilds of Manhattan, and when confronted by his wife, he growls: "I'm pissed, leave me alone." Even obscure literary debate drew on lines from Kong's shirts, as in the example of an essay on "metaphysics" by the novelist and editor Han Shaogong in the January 1994 issue of *Reading*, which began: "Some things are just like that popular saying 'the more you make of something the more of a thing it becomes."[141]

READING GAOL

Long after the furor over the original shirts had died down, Kong Yongqian was still bewailing the fact that he had not found an analysis that reflected the complex motivation he had in designing the T-shirts or their import—questions that even he had difficulty in answering clearly. I discovered that while traveling through China in May and June 1992, when I asked critics, journalists, artists, and academics in a number of major cities what they made of the shirts, though they were quick to admit they were significant and that they recognized Kong's "signature style," they were at a loss to explain it. There was, however, one notable attempt by a Beijing writer to assign Kong a place in the hierarchy of contemporary nonofficial Chinese culture.

In 1992, an art critic, Li Xianting, a former editor of the *China Art News* and a leading exponent, analyst, and promoter of new art movements on the mainland, published an article in the Hong Kong journal *Twenty-First Century*. In it he interpreted the post-1989 cultural mood as being one reflected best in the works of a particular group of artists. "Their attitude and language," he declared, "share a surprising number of traits; they are characterized by ennui, a roguish humor, and ironic realism."[142] In the same essay, Kong is mentioned a number of times.[143] Here was an artist/designer who availed himself of the language and images of the elite culture to create a place for irony and self-reflection in the marketplace (shades of Jenny Holzer and Barbara Kruger). Attacked for "anticulturalism," as was the Beijing novelist Wang Shuo, Kong's T-shirts gave "voice" to the images and ambience we find in the artists Liu Xiaodong,[144] Fang Lijun, Liu Wei, and others whose paintings were represented by Li Xianting under the rubrics of "cynical realism" and "political pop" (see chapter 8, "Artful Marketing").[145]

In his article, Li also talked about the tendency toward "deconstruction" in the work of Chinese artists in the early 1990s. The pop art products of painters like Wang Guangyi who combined Coca-Cola ads with Cultural Revolution posters and Yu Youhan and his ilk with their imitation Warhol portraits of Mao were regarded as being central to the trend among middle-aged and younger artists to "deconstruct" or at least "dissipate," *xiaojie*, official culture. Again, Kong Yongqian was mentioned in this context, and Li concluded his article by claiming that Kong's T-shirts "gave the most accurate and powerful expression to the universal mood of Chinese society today—ennui and roguish humor."[146]

One of Kong's T-shirts, "Beijing slang," even featured the Chinese word for "deconstruction," *jiegou*, split between the two upper corners of the design. Kong had read some elementary works on the subject of deconstruction as well as writings on semiotics when these theories were at the height of fashion in China in the late 1980s. Before he began printing the shirts, he discussed his plans with the

Shaanxi poet Daozi, who had moved to Beijing. The poet, a friend of Li Xianting, told Kong that the shirts were a project of deconstruction in their own right, although Daozi failed to offer Kong any particular theoretical underpinnings of his belief. Daozi, like Li Xianting, used the concept in a basically utilitarian fashion: these were critics facing the daily realities of political power who were not so much interested in theoretical niceties as in deploying anything that appeared to "deconstruct," that is, subvert, party ideology and a status quo that condemned them to a marginal position. Kong, himself an artistic utilitarian who was ready to plunder any faddish expression for his shirts, was quick to exploit this recent intellectual fad.[147]

Perhaps it is necessary here to enter a caveat in regard to the supposedly new generation of irreverent cultural subversives that Li Xianting wrote about. In the 1990s, the views of critics like Li gained considerable currency in China and overseas as tolerated dissent on the mainland itself was commercialized. A disparate range of cultural phenomena, including Kong's T-shirts, Wang Shuo's fiction, Cui Jian's rock music, and the works of a number of artists were claimed to represent a significant, and mutually complementary, trend in Beijing's nonofficial culture. Li Xianting, himself very much the product of the "critical realist" tradition of Chinese modernism, saw in the work of these younger artists a further undermining of party rule, in particular through a subversion of its linguistic, artistic, and cultural codes. However, I would caution against claiming too much for supposedly antiestablishment works that are best seen as part of complex process of cultural reorganization that is far from being subversive, alternative, or even threatening to the structures of power, criticism, or production among China's urban elites.

Since language, or public parole, and reality had for many decades enjoyed at best only an accidental relationship in China, there was no great difficulty for a creative artist to engage in an ironic inversion of language. The novelist Wang Shuo was a master of this technique in the late 1980s, as we observed earlier. To a considerable extent, Kong Yongqian's T-shirts had a similar effect of highlighting the absurdities of both language and the reality it supposedly represented, playfully working with signs—literally Chinese characters—and meaning as part of an attempt to reveal what was hidden or perhaps felt behind the facade of words. It was not, however, so easy to claim a "hard-core deconstructionist"[148] pedigree for the shirts. Although Kong engaged enthusiastically and whimsically with Chinese "logocentrism," he did not see it as some sort of satanic influence to be exorcised or unraveled in an act of confrontational performance art but, rather, as a core element of the Chinese culture that should by rights be open to imaginative and lighthearted subversion. Some of Kong's shirts certainly indulged in "soft-core deconstruction" insofar as they undertook a kind of social unmasking, showing their creator's "alertness to conundrums, logical contradictions, enigmas, and ironic reversals."[149] But they went, and aimed to go, no further.

Kong was by no means the first contemporary Chinese artist whose work reflected a fascination with language and art in his work. Even before the Cultural Revolution, the Hunan artist Huang Yongyu had combined ink sketches with aphoristic sayings that delighted in the follies of the human condition.[150] And since the mid-1980s, a number of academic artists had been undermining the sacerdotal authority of the Chinese written language. In 1985, for example, Gu Wenda made various uses of Chinese characters, both real and invented, in a series of paintings executed in Hangzhou. In 1986–1987, Wu Shanzhuan created "Red Humor," an installation that featured Cultural Revolution–like big-character posters and slogans covering the walls, floor, and ceiling of a room.[151] Wu's attack on academic art as well as the institution of the art gallery as a place of exhibition, especially in his performance art at the "1989 Modern Art Exhibition" in Beijing, reflected his continued interest in challenging the artistic status quo.[152] Kong Yongqian recalled that at the time of the 1989 exhibition, he had commented to friends that, given the commercialization of Chinese life and culture, the China Art Gallery should have been turned into a massive free market where entrepreneurs from all over the country could set up their stalls and sell their wares. In 1991, his T-shirts were the first successful attempt to bring certain academic artistic concerns into the streets of China's cities since the public demonstrations of the "Stars" artist's group in the late 1970s. Whereas the "Stars' " art and Kong's T-shirts were certainly victims of political fiat, it was market socialism that had a far greater and deadening impact on alternative cultures as the 1990s proceeded.

Since the initial onslaughts on Chinese written characters in the mid-1980s, the Beijing–New York artist Xu Bing's *A Book from the Sky*, with its nonsense images, has found international recognition as a major "play" on the written Chinese word. The beautifully crafted woodblock noncharacters reverently displayed in clothbound volumes tended to remystify the very subject that people claimed they had set out to subvert. Inspired partially by Kong's T-shirts, Wang Hua, Xu Bing's former partner, designed a range of clothes covered in passages from *A Book from the Sky*, which she started hawking in 1991.[153] Other lesser works that also manipulated the Chinese written and printed word were produced by artists, including Wang Guangyi in Wuhan and Wang Youshen in Beijing, as well as many others.

Liu Xiaobo, the reprobate philosopher who became a born-again popular culturist in 1991–1992 after he was released from his first stint in jail, was the only other prominent critic to have commented on Kong's shirts at length. He included a series of questions on the "cultural T-shirts" in an amateurish Taiwan-funded survey of popular culture that he carried out in Beijing in 1992, the results of which were published by the *China Times Weekly* in March 1993.[154] Despite

the expense and trouble taken to complete the survey, its rather slapdash method-
ology (for example, the idiosyncratic sampling of the Beijing population, with the
range of vague questions posed to informants as well as the lack of any controls)
made it a problematic endeavor at best.

In the case of the T-shirts, informants were simply asked: "Have you seen people wearing cultural T-shirts? (That is, the *laotou shan* with writing on them that
have been popular over the last two years.)" To this 69.1 percent answered yes.
This was followed by, "If you have seen or heard of these shirts, what do you think
of them?" The response was that 41.4 percent couldn't care less; 16.8 percent
thought they were boring; 15.6 percent felt them to be individualistic and interesting; and so on.[155] There was no indication in the questionnaire which of the
340 kinds of "cultural T-shirts" that appeared in the summer of 1991 were being
referred to or whether the pro-Mao, pro-Deng, and advertisement T-shirts more
common since then were also included.

Liu's concluding comments on the shirts were more representative of views
held by mainstream mainland intellectuals and even the authorities:

> "Cultural T-shirts" definitely helped people find an outlet for the sense of op-
> pression they had felt after 4 June. The reasons for their popularity were, in
> many ways, like that of [the television sitcom] *The Editors*. People no longer
> express their opposition directly or engage in confrontation. They show their
> dissatisfaction by making jokes and engaging in badinage [*tiaokan*]. It is a
> type of "barbed cynicism," "a critical indifference," a prankster mentality
> that treats all that is "holy," "sublime," all "sense of mission" and "duty" with
> contempt. It is the way mass psychology articulates itself.[156]

In conclusion, Liu gave two examples of the shirts ("I'm pissed, leave me
alone!" and "Making ends meet") and remarked that their creator, Kong
Yongqian, was questioned by the police, had his entrepreneur's license canceled,
and was "forced to flee to Australia."[157] Although Kong was questioned by the police, he never had a license (it was held by the clothing factories that produced
the shirts), and was certainly not forced to leave China, as Liu well knew. (Liu
first met Kong in November 1991 and again on a number of occasions in April and
May 1992. During these meetings Kong told Liu about the shirts and his questioning by the police). Whereas Kong did not flee China, it was rumored in Beijing that a number of people had applied for refugee status in Europe, claiming
that they were responsible for the T-shirt craze of 1991 and had been politically
persecuted as a result.

When he saw Liu's survey in March 1993, Kong Yongqian simply observed that
Liu's analysis of the T-shirts was "essentially the same as that of the Public Security Bureau and the party media."[158]

CLOSED SHOP

Following his release in early July 1991, Kong Yongqian made a living doing piece-meal work as an artist. This included printing a run of shirts for the Goethe In-stitute in Beijing, designing a record cover for Cui Jian, taking a bit part in Zhang Yuan's film *Beijing Bastards* (see the next chapter),[159] and making a few comic T-shirts for friends. One of these limited-circulation shirts featured the "letter of gratitude" from Wang Shuo's novel *No Man's Land*, quoted in chapter 4, "The Apotheosis of a *Liumang*," and another, "Salvation Is at Hand," *huitou shi an*, which consisted of a fictitious speech given by a party boss to a worker who want-ed to quit his job and go into private business. Another one-off shirt made for friends read "I simply must fart," *wo zong biebuzhu pi*.

In July 1992, Kong traveled to Australia where, among other things, he helped design a shirt featuring an image taken from a late 1960s Mao Zedong carpet with a local artist (Simon Barney) for an exhibition of the journalist Sang Ye's Cultural Revolution memorabilia at the Powerhouse Museum in Sydney. In May 1993, he returned to Beijing for two weeks to collect material for a mixed-media installation designed with me and included in the "Mao Goes Pop: China Post-1989" exhibition at the Museum of Contemporary Art, Sydney, which opened on 1 June 1993. Kong returned to Beijing to work on new projects in June 1994.

In retrospect, Kong ruminated that it was probably fortunate that his shirts were banned and destroyed in 1991. As a result, he did not have to endure the ig-nominy of official tolerance and gradual acceptance. In midsummer 1993, the Shanghai *Liberation Daily* published a comment on "cultural T-shirts" and their continued popularity in China's urban centers. The article concluded that as a phenomenon and a healthy expression of individuality, the shirts should be ap-preciated, even encouraged when necessary, but certainly not dismissed.[160] In 1994, the appraisal of the shirts in the media was even more positive, and one re-port stated that with the recent popularity of T-shirts bearing logos like "Show a little love," *fengxian aixin*, the shirts had become a healthy medium for the ex-pression of mass sentiment and for social pacification.[161] The original fad for Kong's shirts had, indeed, given the expression "cultural T-shirt" a kind of mass currency. In the 1994 *Dictionary of New Chinese Words and Expressions*, the ex-pression *wenhua shan* was given three entries: "cultural T-shirt," "cultural T-shirt craze," and "cultural T-shirt person."[162] In none of the entries, however, was any reference made to Kong or the problematic nature of the shirts. While these words had entered mainstream language, both the artist and his original enter-prise were effectively written, if not out of history, then at least out of official lex-icography. Although Kong Yongqian had not been able to cash in on the fashion he started, he certainly showed everybody else the political and commercial possibilities of the humble T-shirt.

"People in Beijing are using new ways to package themselves," wrote a commentator remarking on how advertising had replaced satire on T-shirts in 1994. "The stage during which people expressed themselves by wearing slogans that said what they were thinking is now nothing more than a minor episode in a particular historical epoch."[163] By the mid-1990s, the expensive imported or pirate brand-name T-shirt increasingly replaced the whimsy of the cultural shirts. The age of the *T xu* (the Mandarin version of *T suet*, the Hong Kong Cantonese term), had truly arrived. In the space of only three years, the mainland word *wenhua shan* had become too corny and old-fashioned to express the slick, high-quality flavor of the brand product favored by Beijing consumers.[164]

Since consumption was the byword of urban life in China, it was only a matter of time before, in some wave of manufactured nostalgia, revivalist, or retro fashion Kong's T-shirts would be repackaged and marketed once more. Perhaps this time even the party could underwrite the enterprise. All that would have to be done to dull the edge of the questionable message T-shirts would be to place Kong's ironic sayings within the embrace of quotation marks.[165]

CHAPTER SEVEN

Packaged Dissent

DENG XIAOPING'S PROGRESS

Given the events of early June 1989 and the purge that followed in their wake, it would have been reasonable to expect that China was entering an extended period of cultural isolation and revanchism. The imperatives of economic reform, international pressure, and internal party dissension, however, soon brought an end to the overt cultural repression ushered in by the Beijing massacre, even if political purges continued in fits and starts.

After a period of economic and social retrenchment from 1989 to late 1991, Deng Xiaoping, the grand architect, *zong shejishi*, of reform as he was now called, traveled to south China in early 1992 on a tour of inspection. The trip was lauded in the media as an epoch-marking *nanxun*, a classical term meaning "imperial progress to the south." It was an expression that was used to depict the grand tours the Qing dynasty emperors Kangxi and Qianlong had made of the southern Yangzi-region provinces of the empire and had regularly been employed to describe Chairman Mao's trips out of the capital.

Deng's trip lasted from 18 January to 21 February and took him to Guangdong Province and the Special Economic Zones that abutted Hong Kong and Macao. The speeches he made at the time initiated a new wave of change, another leap in China's move toward the market. He damned cautious party purists who argued that many elements of economic reform were intrinsically capitalist in nature, by saying that endless wrangling over such issues was pointless and wasteful. Deng remarked, for example, that the stock market was something China had to experiment with. If it, and a host of other new economic measures, turned out to be harmful to the socialist enterprise, then they could be abandoned at some point in the future. The key, he claimed, was to dare to experiment. Hailed as a "new movement to liberate thinking" that went even further than the party's campaign to move away from strict Maoism in the late 1970s,[1] Deng's speeches encouraged people to throw ideological caution to the wind in the pursuit of economic well-being. Every aspect of life was affected by the intensification of the resultant push toward what was generally celebrated as "primitive capitalism," and despite recurrent purges and proto-Maoist mumblings among ideologues, the cultural sphere reflected the new trends that were changing the nation.

The ideas that Deng expressed in both casual and formal talks during the tour had been mooted over the previous years. After the collapse of the Soviet Union in 1991, Chinese leaders repeatedly commented that the only way for socialist China to avoid a similar fate was through increasing economic prosperity. The bottom line was the party line. As a preamble to Deng's 1992 statement, during 1991 the Shanghai press — used in the past by leaders to float ideas that were out of kilter with the mainstream orthodoxy of the north — published a number of authoritative articles on the need for party leaders to be more adventurous in introducing supposedly capitalist ideas.[2] They called for a greater "liberation of thought," a rejection of ideological strictures.

Deng Xiaoping's political deus ex machina for reform was greeted in the official Chinese media with the type of cloying romantic hyperbole that had been lavished on Mao in his heyday, although in 1990s China it read more like a Wang Shuo–esque spoof. As the journalist Chen Xitian wrote in the lead report on Deng's visit to the Special Economic Zone (SEZ) of Shenzhen, entitled "The Breeze Blows from the East and the Vista Is of Spring":

> An early spring has arrived in the south of China.
>
> Shenzhen in January. The flowers and trees are bursting forth with the message of the season.
>
> As we embark on a new year, the heroic stature of Shenzhen will allow it to make yet another grand advance on the road of the open door and reform.
>
> Deng Xiaoping, the grand architect of the open door and reform policies, the dearly beloved comrade of all the peoples of China, has visited Shenzhen!
>
> Comrade Xiaoping has come at a crucial juncture in the history of our nation's socialist modernization. His presence here is the greatest possible expression of solicitude and support for the SEZ. It offers both extraordinary encouragement and a great impetus to the people of Shenzhen.[3]

The response to Deng's activities by the cultural bureaucracy that had entrenched itself following 1989 was far less enthusiastic. Deng pointedly remarked that while rightist thought (that is, bourgeois liberalization) was still a cause for concern, "leftism," that is, Maoist ideology, remained the great danger to Chinese political life. His comments sparked attacks on leading cultural Maoists, and gatherings of liberal intellectuals of a kind that had not been seen for nearly three years were organized in Beijing. Such meetings were followed by the publication of books that took direct inspiration from Deng's remarks and attacked political and cultural conservatives.[4] Even the hardy party Propaganda Department curmudgeon Xu Weicheng (Yu Xinyan) was reportedly cowed, although not completely silenced.[5] Others, like the trenchant Maoist Deng Liqun, were circumspect for a time but soon started petitioning Party Central on the need to maintain ideological rectitude.

Strapped by limited funds and suffering from a serious image problem, the cultural authorities—a nationwide network of bureaucracies that ostensibly administered every aspect of cultural activity and life—were, by 1992, in retreat. The declining influence of these ideologically narrow figures—"leftists," "post-Maoists," "conservatives," call them what you will—was summed up in a saying common among Beijing writers: "Their rule doesn't extend beyond the Third Ring Road [of the capital]; all they have is a few guns; they control only a couple of journals and newspapers; and they can rely only on the support of a handful of officials."

The underground—nonofficial musicians, artists, filmmakers, writers, and thinkers—went more public to sign contracts with Hong Kong and Taiwan companies. Whereas those who really threatened the status quo—labor activists and outspoken individuals of conscience—were harassed and imprisoned by the authorities, the more sophisticated artistic rowdies were grudgingly tolerated. As the official cultural world stagnated, the alternative cultural sphere developed its own power hierarchies and protocols that could adjust to the party's fickle policy shifts.

The Abandoned Capital

In 1993, perhaps no incident illustrated so concisely the state of Chinese culture and the cynical relationship among "manufacturers," cultural products, consumers, and official arts watchdogs following Deng's southern tour than the fate of Jia Pingwa's novel *The Abandoned Capital*. The appearance of this book also provided Chinese critics and intellectuals with an opportunity to make themselves heard again in the public arena after a lengthy hiatus.[6]

Published in Beijing at the start of the year, *The Abandoned Capital*, or *Necropolis*, was a soft porn work of fiction by Jia Pingwa, a popular and, until then, well-regarded writer of highbrow novels from Shaanxi Province, northwest China. Even before it appeared, there was talk of *The Abandoned Capital's* being the most salacious Chinese sex story since the famous late-Ming *Jinping-mei* (sixteenth century). Others claimed that it could be compared with the greatest work of Chinese fiction, and it was hailed as "a modern-day *The Story of the Stone.*" Scandal merged with envy when after a bidding war the successful publisher, Beijing Publishing House, one of the most prestigious groups in the capital, leaked a story to the media that Jia Pingwa had been paid one million *yuan* for the rights to the book.

The novel, a roman à clef, chronicles the adventures of Zhuang Zhidie, a licentious writer and literary star who lives in a provincial city, a down-at-the-heels former capital that still basks in its former glory. Zhuang's literary fame brings him attention and, eventually, leads to his downfall. The story limns a landscape of malevolent and brooding corruption, a dystopic nightmare that reflects the plangent fate of an ancient culture. The women that Zhuang works his way through during the unfolding tale are for the most part pathetic and fawning creatures, crudely depicted sex objects whose bodily fluids act as the connective glue of the plot. Written in a style imitative of traditional fiction and full of "quickie" sex scenes, the novel was provided with an extra dimension of titillation by the author, who expunged numerous passages from the text, presumably because they were too sexually explicit to be printed. After each lacuna in the text, Jia Pingwa teasingly adds a note to the effect that "Here the writer deleted 563 words." It was supposedly his way of hinting that the elided material was deemed too hot for the censors/publisher/reader to handle.

One short excerpt from the novel should be enough to communicate the attractions of this particular literary device:

Zhuang Zhidie's mother, who shared the tiny flat, was asleep.

His wife quickly slipped out of her clothes.

"But you're not wearing any underclothes, not even a bra!" exclaimed Zhuang Zhidie.

"All the easier for you to get on with the job," she replied.

He pushed her into the imitation leather seat, lifted her legs up and apart, and set to work kissing her nether regions.

❏ ❏ ❏❏ ❏ ❏   *(here the author has expunged 42 characters).*

Her squirming only served to excite further Zhuang's passion. His tongue and mouth worked busily.

Suddenly he felt an itch on his back. He had his wife scratch it for him.

"It's a mosquito. What's a mosquito doing inside in the middle of the day?" she wondered. She scratched away and then exclaimed,

"What do you think you're biting? Whaaaatttt, whoaaaaa. . . ."

She abandoned her scratching as her eyes stared heavenward, her body going quite stiff. Zhuang Zhidie felt a wave of warm liquid come streaming forth.

❏ ❏ ❏❏ ❏ ❏   *(here the author has expunged 333 characters).*

Zhuang stood up and looked at her with a smirk on his face. She asked,

"What's it taste like?"

"You try it," Zhuang responded as his mouth met hers. As he straight-ened up, he cried in pain and fell onto her body.

"What's wrong?" she asked.

"My foot still hurts."

"So you can't really use all your strength."

"I'm fine," he responded, and with that he started up again.

"Let me do some of the work this time," she said.

She stood up and let him sit down.

❏ ❏ ❏❏ ❏ ❏   *(here the author has expunged 25 characters)*.

"Don't cry out, the old woman will hear us."

I don't care, she said, and she cried out regardless. He stuffed a hand-kerchief into her mouth, which she bit on hard.

❏ ❏ ❏❏ ❏ ❏   *(here the author has expunged 18 characters)*.

"Hurry up and get dressed," Zhuang Zhidie said.[7]

Jia himself claimed that the deleted material appeared in the original draft and was cut out only after both he and the publisher weighed the possible conse-quences of allowing his lurid depictions.[8] While the lacunae-littered text begged speculation as to whether Jia had really ever bothered to write the deep-throat porn so coyly censored in the published version, one reviewer decided to use Jia's strategy of absence to critical effect. Of the hundreds of comments published dur-ing *The Abandoned Capital* controversy of 1993–1994, one of the most amusing was penned by the journalist and raconteur He Dong, the brother of the conser-vative critic He Xin mentioned in previous chapters. In an obvious reference to Jia Pingwa's lowly background, He Dong reminded his readers that Chairman Mao had repeatedly warned the Chinese that the reeducation of the peasantry was a pressing task. He finished his review of the novel with the following line: "And here the writer has deleted three characters," followed by three empty boxes. These were blanks that could easily filled in by Beijing readers who knew just what He Dong was trying to say: *Cao ni ma*! or "Get fucked!"

Sex aside, although few critics or readers seemed to be able to ignore this as-pect of the novel, *The Abandoned Capital* was a masterful depiction of the ambi-ence of late-twentieth-century China. It was in the tradition of the literature of self-loathing written by Chinese elitist intellectuals since the latter half of the nineteenth century (see chapter 10, "To Screw Foreigners Is Patriotic"). One of the volumes of criticism published in late 1993 devoted to the debate of this and other aspects of the book was edited by Xiao Xialin, a young critic, with the help of Tian Zhenying, the editor of Jia's novel. Xiao's book collected a range of re-sponses to the book from published and interview sources. Many of the articles selected gave voice to the outrage, concern, and distress that many people felt in regard to the novel's success; others were full of praise for the book and expressed delight that such a prurient work—one that also had a profound message for readers regarding the degraded state of life in contemporary China—had finally been published.

Xiao, who was soon to become one of the most outspoken critics of contemporary cultural life (see chapter 11, "Kowtowing to the Vulgar"), praised *The Abandoned Capital* as presenting fin-de-siècle Chinese readers with a microcosm of life in the form of a fin-de-siècle novel.[9] He wrote the following in the introduction to his book *Who Does The Abandoned Capital Abandon?*

> The range of opinions about *The Abandoned Capital* make us confront the image of a place that, in this present age of transformation, can be claimed to be nothing less than an "abandoned capital society." Ours is the world of the abandoned capital. Everywhere you look, the basic values of civilization—justice, truth, ideals, and the sublime—are in a state of alienation. Morality itself has nothing more than a utilitarian value. All we dream of now and hope for in the future are money and sex. The unprincipled process of moneymaking and sexual gratification has gravely undermined the pillars of civilized society.[10]

Xiao continued in this vein and declared that marriage, elite intellectual culture, religion, politics, and business all were part of the "abandoned capital." "What is it, this abandoned capital?" Xiao asks. "The portrait of contemporary society; everything from the collective to the individual. This is the homeland in which we dwell; this is the significance of our existence." Xiao predicted that since the book so powerfully revealed the dark side of Chinese life, its publication would usher in a period of national reflection.[11] While he might have hoped to steal a march on the process by publishing a commercially profitable volume of critiques, Xiao's book registered little more than a blip in best-seller lists. The success of Jia Pingwa's novel, however, did excite in many would-be mass market authors a hope that they might be the next to cash in on a new craze for works of long fiction.

The introductory essay of the other volume of critiques of *The Abandoned Capital*, Duo Wei's *The Flavor of The Abandoned Capital*, expressed a far less benign view of both Jia Pingwa and his work. Li Shulei, a professor of literature, wrote that the novel proved that although Jia may have been determined to reveal his soul to his readers through the novel, all that he had really succeeded in doing was to prove that he had no soul at all! Li went on to castigate the novel for being an insincere commercial ploy that documented Jia Pingwa's fall from the status of a writer of serious literature to that of a mere hack who was willing to churn out sensational potboilers for an eager and ill-lettered public.[12] The unintended irony of this critique was that unlike Li Shulei, Xiao Xialin—the man who would soon make a name for himself as a self-appointed defender of literary morals—had found in *The Abandoned Capital* a work of deep spirituality and significance.

Not surprisingly, in the still ostensibly sexually repressive atmosphere of mainland China, *The Abandoned Capital* was an immediate sensation. It not only held out the promise of pornography, but it also lambasted its protagonists, who themselves were writers and intellectuals. They were members of the intelligentsia, people who had been popular targets for derision since the days of Mao when the educated were under constant suspicion of being politically unreliable. As Jia remarked on his choice of subject matter, "I picked the literati as my main characters because I'm most familiar with them; they're a tragic class of people on the road to extinction. The thing is, if the elite of our country have degenerated to that extent [as depicted in his novel], you can just imagine the rest."[13] That the book was written by an author with impeccable credentials affirmed by years of publishing "pure" or highbrow fiction made the book's appearance even more controversial. If anything, *The Abandoned Capital* was taken by some critics to be yet another sign that serious writers were now prepared to "kowtow to the vulgar," *meisu*, for the sake of fame and gain (see chapter 11, "Kowtowing to the Vulgar").

The publication of *The Abandoned Capital* was also an indication of how lenient, or slack, the authorities had become. In terms of crass popular culture, at least, the situation was even more freewheeling than it had been at the height of bourgeois liberalism in the late 1980s. The tardy official response to the public furor created by the book was also symptomatic of the relationship between the dysfunctional political ideology of the past (Marxism-Leninism and Mao Thought) and the commercial realities of the present.

It was only in late 1993 that leaders of the Communist Party's Department of Propaganda belatedly took action against *The Abandoned Capital*. Claiming that the department had received numerous letters from worried teachers and parents, who complained that adolescents were being corrupted by the novel, a ban was finally declared. The publishers were ordered to surrender the profits they had made from the best-seller, presumably quite a hefty sum if reports that more than half a million copies of the book had been sold during the months of its heyday are to be believed (and that is not including sales of various pirated editions), and unsold copies of the novel were confiscated.[14]

Although controversial literature could appear—even if only to be eventually banned—political correctness, Chinese-style, was still far from dead. After all, officially the best-selling book for 1993 was the lugubrious third volume of *The Selected Works of Deng Xiaoping*. This is hardly surprising, since it was required reading in nationwide political study sessions. Apart from the release of this book, there were other signs that the scene was being prepared for Deng's demise. In

1994, Deng's ninetieth year, an officially orchestrated "Deng Xiaoping craze" swept the nation with the publication of dictionaries on Deng thought, the appearance of a new and enlarged edition of the three volumes of the great architect's selected works, as well as seminars and study sessions on the subject.[15] Around this time, 18K gold–plated badges bearing Deng's portrait were minted in preparation for the not-too-distant day when he "would go to meet Marx."[16] And in late 1996, the screening on CCTV of a multiepisode hagiography of the leader marked the apogee of his life in propaganda.

Other big sellers in the book stores in 1993, however, were perhaps more indicative of the wider preferences of China's urban readers. These included investment guides with titles like *Futures and the Market,* a slew of computer books like *A Complete DOS Handbook,* and similar reference works. Although 1993 was the year of the centenary of Mao's birth and despite the popular revival of the Mao cult in 1990, books related to Mao Zedong that had sold solidly in 1991–1992 only fared well in the heavy-industrial city of Wuhan in 1993.[17]

The publishing industry, like the Chinese media in general, had grown quickly since the early 1990s. According to reports, a new newspaper was produced at the rate of one every one and a half days in China during 1993, bringing the total number of dailies and weeklies to two thousand by early 1994.[18] In particular, papers with commercial and lifestyle news were on the increase. This was not surprising given the economic developments in China that emphasized the consumer and the investor over all else.

Liang Heng, the assistant director of the Chinese News and Publishing Administration, the body in charge of publishing, commented on the new directions in publishing. Whereas in the past, party organs had established news organizations with state funds to disseminate official propaganda, he said, now many groups were finding independent financial backing to launch new papers and, in the process, were "vampirizing" existing state media resources in the hope of making money.[19] In 1996, as part of an ideological purge aimed at reining in the media, many of the papers that had flourished since 1993 were taken over by newly created media conglomerates that were created in the hope of both exploiting the information revolution and regulating it if and when it got out of hand.

Because of the political and economic pressures that overwhelmed them after 4 June 1989, Chinese intellectuals generally resigned themselves to a period of relative inactivity and observation. The enlivening atmosphere of debate that had been common in the late 1980s cooled during the purges that followed the massacre. From 1992 to 1993, however, many intellectuals and writers began to take a more active role in the public discussion of issues like the significance of *The Abandoned Capital.* Of course, this is not to say that groups and individuals who were more interested in political power and influence had been silent in the interim. A number of shadowy figures moved into the public arena after 1989, anxious to take advantage of the conservative backlash to act as government or would-be government advisers. Another, perhaps more widespread, form of engagement, however, was to be found in the marketplace, and many intellectuals, as well as *soi-disant* "democracy activists" or dissidents, tried their hand at business ventures, which included everything from tourism and real estate speculation to publishing and the electronic media.

As in other periods of national cultural upheaval and change (the 1920s, early 1930s, late 1940s, mid-1980s), magazines and journals were, in 1990s China, a major vehicle for the expression of divergent opinions. Starting in early 1993, new journals also acted as a focal point for intellectual debates, factions, and fashions. It was time to *la shantou*, literally "to occupy a mountaintop"; it was a common term used to describe the efforts of an individual or group to secure a notional position in opposition to others from which they could make forays into the cultural and political realms. In contemporary Chinese usage—in the past *la shantou* referred to the forming of factions and engagement in warfare, such as in the case of Red Guard groups during the Cultural Revolution—the expression denoted a fortress mentality. It described a clique that took up a certain intellectual/political stance, often merely for strategic purposes, and manipulated the media (a journal, newspaper, or TV show) to propagate a view, posture, or range of opinion to launch offensives against its enemies or rivals. In the highly competitive realm of 1990s journal publication, only the most hidebound official rags, however, maintained even the semblance of any coherent ideological line. Other semi-independent journals—independent only to a limited extent, for all of them still came under the direction of the party's Department of Propaganda and Publication Administration and were thus ultimately subject to censorship—enjoyed considerably greater latitude.

A number of major, new journals appeared during the early 1990s. They included *Orient, Frontiers, Excellence, Chinese Culture,* and *Strategy and Management.* These publications were, for the most part, semi-independent and, in some cases, indirectly funded by wealthy individuals, arms of the government, or groups in the south. As a form of political insurance, some set aside honorary editorial positions for official fossils or foreign dignitaries.[20] The writers and activists who clustered around these journals formed loose coalitions and, in some cases, attempted to develop agendas that would be taken up by government or future leaders. Other magazines, particularly those specializing in contemporary art (for example, *Art News,* established in late 1993) were funded with outside money and became vehicles for the promotion of China's nonofficial arts scene overseas. Via the medium of glossy full-color printing and designer graphics, the works published and their authors enjoyed a higher status and kudos locally.

BANKABLE DISSENT

Since the early 1980s, China had produced a small body of material that could be called "bankable dissent": nonofficial or semi-illicit works, be they in the fields of art, literature, music, or film, that, owing to the repressive state control, could accrue a certain market value—and street cred—regardless of (even, in some cases, despite) their artistic merits.

In the past, the authorities—a byzantine jumble of bureaucracies mired in a dated ideology that had always been a few plenums away from catching up with the society's rapid social and economic realities— had generally responded to cultural provocation with bans and political purges. For those attacked—the rock musicians and producers of politically explicit artwork and risqué literature—reputations were made and inflated on the basis of a modicum of talent and a large dose of official displeasure. A government ban, after all, would attract international media attention and the Kong-Tai press, and during the 1980s a number of mediocre artists achieved recognition on the basis of such notoriety.

But the Chinese avant-garde had entered the doldrums in the late 1980s when increasing official tolerance threatened to leave entrepreneurial cultural dissidents with nothing new to say and no particular harassment of which to complain. As Zhu Dake wrote at the time: "The image of the pained soul evaporates the moment the red glare dims. Only actors hard on the trail of fame and fortune can still strike the pose of the rebel."[21] But all that changed on 4 June 1989.

Although initially the ensuing cultural purge was vicious, as we noted in the preceding chapters, after 1990 the state and party authorities became enmeshed in and hampered by their own ideological schizophrenia, administrative laxity, realpolitik, and simple incompetence. Economic reform forced them to encourage ever more investment from Hong Kong, Taiwan, and foreign sources while they attempted to maintain control over official culture. Up to 1996, the government had become wary of further large-scale political crackdowns: a bad press could scare wary investors away or disaffect dollars-rich Taiwan and Hong Kong compatriots. Purges were not necessarily good politics. Even the sloganizing of the mid-1990s reflected the anodyne nature of ideology. Rather than the Sturm and Drang of campaigns past and the colorful catch phrases that accompanied them, after late 1995, Party General Secretary Jiang Zemin started a bland movement to "talk up politics," *jiang zhengzhi*. This was interpreted as a plan to devise some form of "political macrocontrol program" along the lines of the late 1990s economic blueprint that would forestall further ideological dystrophia.[22] Of concern was the threat of the Taiwan experience, in which open politics and a free press had contributed to the push for complete democratization and even independence on the island. The policy of "talking politics" led in 1996–1997 to criticisms of spiritual pollution and renewed attempts to limit cultural autonomy and regulate the cultural market.[23]

During 1996, films and books were once more banned; new rules governing censorship were introduced; and there were threats to close down leading intellectual journals and calls for the reeducation of errant editors. The propaganda organs also urged a general rejection of corrupting "Western" influences on culture, lifestyles, attitudes, and social values. It was all part of the classic strategy of demonizing the Western Other in order to repress political and cultural opponents on the home front. It was always easier, and politically safer, to blame the canker of U.S. cultural values, for example, than to confront the systemic problems behind the deleterious social impact of economic reform. Since 1976, the Communist Party had instigated similar cultural purges approximately once every two years, but in general, they had had little effect other than educating both the bureaucracy and cultural workers in ways to negotiate a more sophisticated accommodation with each other.[24] By late 1997, however, the tide was turning once more. More ambitious reforms of the state sector, downsizing and corporatization went hand in hand with a more benign relationship with the United States and a loosening up in 1998 of the publishing and cultural spheres.

The prefects of anticommunist culture, be they overseas or in the Chinese realms of Kong-Tai, deemed certain "struggling artists" to be worthy and, by contrast with the status quo, revered. But praise and support for such people often were prefaced on a contempt for the official cultural world rather than on a true regard for the artists and their place in their local context. Beginning in the late 1980s, the need for an imaginative placement of China's alternative artists within the narrative framework of more familiar cultures, Western or socialist (Eastern European and Soviet), became a paradigmatic element of discussions of mainland culture, both off- and onshore.

Toward the end of 1993, in the main hotels of Beijing, you could pick up the latest issue of *China Guide*, a glossy coffee-table journal produced by editors and writers in Beijing and Hong Kong. Scattered among the more ponderous pieces on the Chinese economy, GATT (General Agreement on Tariffs and Trade) and U.S.-China relations, there were lengthy illustration-laden articles on the young director Zhang Yuan's banned underground movie, *Beijing Bastards*; Wu Wenguang's epic-length documentary on the Cultural Revolution, *1966*; the rock group Pressure Points; and a report on a major Chinese avant-garde (that is, nonofficial) art exhibition held in Berlin.[25]

Long gone, it would seem, were the days when illicit movies and unofficial art would simply slip into the maw of state censorship, never to be seen or heard of

again. Officially engineered memory holes were now spaces gravid with possibility, and a range of commercially minded artists were ready to take advantage of
the situation.

China Guide was very much a product of the chaotic cultural scene of the
mainland in the 1990s, a place where the true test of success was not necessarily
official recognition but, rather, market value and potential. You could get away
with just about anything, as people in Beijing never tired of saying, if you only
paid attention to *baozhuang*, "packaging," or *daban*, "cosmetic appearance." If
you know how to *chaozuo*, "beat up," a cultural product, you were in the money.
In the case of *China Guide*, the surface sheen was made possible by offshore
funding (Hong Kong/Taiwan); the style was Chumpy (international Chinese up-
wardly mobile you-name-it); and the content was a mixture of po-faced economic palaver with naughty-boy art supplying a slightly illicit edge to the product.

Although Zhang Yuan's *Beijing Bastards* did win a smattering of awards in Europe and Japan, on the mainland all he got was official censure, something that,
in 1994, temporarily added to his filmmaking prospects and his credentials as a
leading nonstate filmmaker. It is worth pausing to consider the career of this film
and its maker and the ways in which it aids in our investigation of 1990s nonofficial Chinese culture.

Zhang Yuan was a provincial artist, born in Nanjing in 1961. He had gone to
Beijing to study film and was frustrated by what he saw as the affected posturing
and international critical success of his cinematic elders, the stars of the "fifth
generation" of filmmakers like Zhang Yimou and Chen Kaige, who had risen to
prominence during the 1980s.[26] Zhang Yuan was one of the new generation of
cultural young bloods who were not prepared to wait in the wings to achieve
recognition by working their way through the treacherous, state-funded cultural hierarchy. Systemic change and the nature of generational conflicts, as well
as new paths to fame, wealth, and social mobility, had transformed the inner dynamics of the cultural scene through the 1980s, and in the 1990s the further
commodification of culture had an impact on both established and aspiring
artists. Institutional culture was less forthcoming with patronage than it had
been in the late 1980s. Under the aegis of cultocrats like Wang Meng and the
filmmaker Wu Tianming, head of the Xi'an Film Studio for a time, writers and
directors had limited access to official cultural outlets; after the early 1990s, opportunities were scarce.

Zhang, who had quit his state-allocated job at the PLA 1 August Film Studio
shortly after graduating from the Beijing Film Academy, struck on a formula for
success. It was a formula that has been employed by many others in many other
climes before him. Here he was, an independent Chinese filmmaker with something of a cinematic track record (*Mother*, Mama, his earlier documentary, had

enjoyed some controversy, and he had had some success making music videos), who had produced a new film, *Beijing Bastards*. It was a movie with enough "attitude" to make him a hot item outside China and to establish him as a prominent alternative artist within the country. The authorities could not abide the fact that the film had been made in disregard of the official cultural system. Apart from overt bans, however, they were unwilling or—without recourse to brute police or army force—unable to crush independents like Zhang. Despite all their bureaucratic decrees and strictures, the apparat was witness to the constant parasitical use and exploitation of state resources (personnel, equipment, venues) by younger artists like Zhang.

For international film organizers, films like those made by Zhang Yuan, or Wu Wenguang (director of the 1990 *Bumming in Beijing: The Last Dreamers*, the 1993 droning epic 1966, and a later sequel to *Bumming* made in Europe)[27] filled an important art-market niche. They represented harassed, independent, underground filmmakers from the demonized "last totalitarian empire" (Cuba, North Korea, and Vietnam could barely even begin to compete with the sheer magnitude of China, the recent horrors of 4 June, and the annual media-enhanced suppression of dissidents). If mainstream culture was the preserve of the state (a highly dubious assertion, as has been demonstrated in earlier chapters), then these "independent" figures represented something "authentic." Even if nonmainland critics and connoisseurs were dubious of some nonofficial films—*Beijing Bastards*, for example, was hardly an unalloyed success on the film circuit—people overseas justified their support for it, or works like it; to do so was arguably a way of championing greater creative space in China. Such an argument was not without a certainly validity. Nonetheless, one could also contend that the manner in which these "creative spaces" were fashioned in China from the 1980s onward by a highly ambitious elite would have an important impact on just how open and free things might be in the future. Also, in these new "creative spaces," there were indications of how oppositional forces, suppressed voices, and dissident views outside the bounds of nonofficial art would be regarded and dealt with.

Despite the momentary setback that Zhang Yuan suffered in 1994 when the authorities tried to ban his filmmaking altogether, he was soon back on the international circuit. First there was his cut-and-paste documentary *Square* in 1995, and then in 1996, he made *Sons*,[28] a dipsomaniacal tale of a dysfunctional theatrical family, beer, and *Erguotou* (a popular rot-gut Beijing rice wine) abuse. The film's cottage-industry style and indulgent recording of rowdy bouts of drunkenness were enough to win Zhang an award for best director and the jury prize at the Rotterdam Film Festival. While planning a new film, he used a Rockefeller Foundation grant to travel in the United States over the summer of 1996 while people back in Beijing weathered the tempests of the new cultural purge.

Some observers claimed that independent filmmaking flourished in China during the first half of the 1990s for a number of reasons. First, there was an ideological resistance in the system to crushing the new filmmakers. Corrupt officials were also willing, for bribes, to ignore people who flouted the rules. Furthermore, as nonofficial films achieved an international status, their directors were sheathed in a cloak of media protection. This last point in particular is of interest in our inquiry. The symbiotic relationship between dissidents and the foreign media, the former providing grist to the mill of manufactured international opinion, had developed over many years. Moreover, nonofficial cultural figures in China fit neatly into the formulaic categories first developed as a result of Western media relations with dissidents in Eastern Europe and the Soviet Union.

Since the early 1980s, some Chinese artists and poets had indeed benefited from the spotlight of international media attention. The "Stars," the independent Beijing artists' collective of the late 1970s and early 1980s, was one of the first groups to be so protected. As I have commented elsewhere:

Following the arrests of leading democracy activists and the closure of many of Beijing's unofficial journals [in the late 1970s], the salon featuring the "Stars" took on a new appearance. The involvement of foreigners, in particular diplomats, students and reporters, became a central feature of the young people's cultural scene, and it set a pattern and tone for years to come. Foreign interest in and support for the young artists, writers and activists was for any number of reasons: the desire to have direct contact with Chinese who were acting outside the limits of government control, the attraction of surreptitious exchanges with "dissidents," the titillation of tasting "forbidden fruit" for those who took Chinese lovers. . . .

. . . In the years since, foreign art patrons, be they reporters, diplomats, "experts" working for the Chinese, or students and Sinologists, have become an invariable part of the human landscape of Beijing. The positive aspect of their role is undeniable. In a country whose mainstream culture is still primarily directed by State fiat—even when the State is hiding behind the chimera of pluralism—the unemployed, unrecognised and often talented artists and writers who inhabit the outskirts of officialdom must find an alternate route to recognition, livelihood and fame. In comparison to the average citizen, the foreigner is blessed with luxurious living conditions and a prodigious salary, and this relative wealth encrusted with the patina of foreign exoticism allows many of them to assume the role of instant connoisseur and culture expert. They hold parties in their spacious flats, at which sleek young Chinese men and women, many dressed in fashions imported from Guangzhou, disport with foreign friends. In many cases it's an oriental incarnation of the "pet primitive" psychology Tom

Wolfe described so tellingly in *The Painted Word*. In fact, the *fin-de-siècle* ambience of the Beijing scene in the past few years is caught better in works like Wolfe's "These Radical Chic Evenings" than anything written about China to date.[29]

The foreign salon, the *yang shalong*, played an inestimable role in helping nonofficial mainland culture go international in the 1980s. Film festival organizers and critics overseas (Hong Kong, Taiwan, and Japan also were instrumental, as were individuals and organizations in many Western countries) often felt themselves to be not only expressing artistic discrimination by their support but also exercising a morally worthy function by promoting these nascent artists. This happened, for example, in the case of theater festival organizers who introduced internationally the work of the independent Beijing playwright Mou Sen, another example of a talent-challenged individual from a politically deprived background given aid and succor by an indulgent world in the mid-1990s. The support he received helped launch an international career, one that was reinforced by his appearance in the films made by his friend, Wu Wenguang. There are those who celebrated this internationalization of Chinese avant-garde art, the collapse of boundaries, and the cross-cultural movement of bodies.[30] However, perhaps amid the laudable moves toward an artistic global dialogue in the late twentieth century, we also have witnessed a reconfiguration of the presumed bourgeois civilizing duties of an earlier age. A century after the zenith of Western empires, some international cultural brokers appeared to have the "courage" to shoulder once more the "white man's burden."

The line of reasoning pursued by both indigenous cultural figures and their supporters, one that praxis seemed to support, was that international recognition would force the mainland authorities to tolerate innovative cultural figures and thereby contribute to a future liberalization of cultural production in general. International support also gave Zhang Yuan and his fellows a bargaining position within China, not to mention opportunities for financial backing for new ventures. Judging, however, from the works of these nonofficial cultural producers up to 1996, the year when the central government began to reassert cultural control over them, they had royally squandered their cultural capital. They had also indulged cynically in the very freedoms and basic latitudes of self-expression of which earlier generations of mainland artists had, for nearly four decades, been deprived and persecuted for attempting to secure.

Trading on their international success, many of the independents played their Western supporters and mainland opponents against each other to create an alternative system of countercultural hierarchy that, although less restricted and paternalistic than the official culture, represented a kind of baneful orthodoxy and fit neatly into the chain of production and consumption for global festival culture.

In the 1980s, successful filmmakers like Chen Kaige, an artist who gradually abandoned the artistic and cultural sincerity of his powerful early films for a more polished art-house exoticism, provided a role model for his juniors on how to exploit the systems and renege on the cultural promise of the early, open-minded post–Cultural Revolution era in favor of a designer veneer. In the 1990s, directors like Zhang Yuan and Wu Wenguang showed their contemporaries and successors the way to navigate the treacherous political and artistic waters of late socialist China. A new generation was finding their own solutions to similar problems. They had rebelled against a generation who had developed means and ways of reaching an accommodation with mainland and international culture and ended up acting in much the same way.

In 1995, Tony Rayns, a prominent Western cinéaste who had been an advocate for Chinese film since the early 1980s, wrote in the London journal *Index on Censorship* that "the more people who see films like *Beijing Bastards* and [He Jianjun's 1994] *Postman*, the more valuable the films become as bargaining chips in the struggle for a genuine freedom of expression in China."[31] Given, however, the type of cultural expression evinced by filmmakers and others during the extraordinarily freewheeling early 1990s, the meaning of "genuine freedom of expression" had complex political and cultural implications.

FORMULAS FOR SUCCESS

Certainly, Zhang Yuan suffered from erratic official censure and persecution. By all rights, he should have been free to pursue his artistic vision, regardless of what it was, without suffering such unwarranted state intervention and constant harassment. But his success was the result of intricate cultural factors that cannot be understood simply in terms of dissident or nonofficial culture. Zhang was one of many mainland artists who over the years discovered a successful formula for the production of marketable alternative cultural material.

In the case of *Beijing Bastards*, the "formula" worked roughly in the following way:

1. The film was completed in 1992 without official backing, financing, or permission.
2. Some of the budget came from Hong Kong, and postproduction work was done in France, allowing the project fiscal independence from the state.
3. Zhang Yuan himself had often been promoted in the mainland media (for example, in the *Beijing Youth News*) as a "sixth-generation" director, that is, a member of a younger group that was one up from the somewhat tired, middle-aged, and overexposed "fifth generation" represented by Chen

Kaige, Zhang Yimou, and Tian Zhuangzhuang. The need among nonmainland journalists and festival organizers to discover "new blood" thus added
to his marketability.

4. Zhang had a banned docudrama to his credit—*Mother* (1990)—which had
   been financed by China's Handicapped Association and was about mentally
   handicapped children.[32]

5. He had also directed a number of music videos, one of considerable quality
   (Ai Jing's *My 1997*, see chapter 5, "The Graying of Chinese Culture"), and a
   few other mediocre clips that featured the rock prince Cui Jian, who also
   happened to be the producer and star of *Bastards*.

6. *Beijing Bastards* itself tried to be on the cutting edge of Chinese grunge.
   It bore all the trademarks of the underground: It dwelt on the ill-kempt and
   ill-mannered boys and babes of the Beijing rock scene and their attendant
   hangers-on. It contained sex (a clumsy rape), larceny, endless swearing in
   Beijing *patois*, and dimly lit rock parties featuring Cui Jian, as well as hot-
   look bands like Dreaming.[33] The atmosphere was dull, gray, and gloomy:
   very post-/pre-holocaust Beijing. The disjunctive tale centered on the surreptitious underground scene; it was a story of dysfunction and disaffection in an
   age of economic excess. All in all, it was a winning combination, even if the
   actual film was vacuous and technically inept to a fault.

7. The final step in the formula was crucial. Once the film was made, all that
   Zhang needed in order to secure success was an official ban. And lo and
   behold! in late 1993 the authorities came through. Outraged by the international success of *Bastards*, the powers that be banned Zhang from working on his next project, a film version of the novelist Liu Zhenyun's short
   story "Chicken Feathers." Overnight, a cinematic nonevent was turned into
   a mini cause célèbre.

8. The Hong Kong and Taiwan press played their part on cue by claiming for
   Zhang and his fellows the status of cultural hero-underdogs of the year.

But this was one of the secrets of the success of cultural entrepreneurs like Zhang
Yuan: they had little need to produce a class product, for its provenance and official displeasure alone could induce investors—be they nonmainland critics, film
festivals, or producers—to support a director who was conceived of as a quixotic
figure in a milieu of cultural repression. Zhang was one of a number of artists
whose very existence presumably acted as a cultural barometer indicating that a
civil society à la the former Eastern Europe nations was developing on the mainland. Although the work of people like Zhang Yuan was a bit too "cottage industry," some supporters reasoned that backing work that represented China's cultural avant-garde was akin to investing in a futures market.

Zhang Yuan and his fellow directors were often viewed sympathetically by those both in- and outside China who argued that the variety offered by nonofficial artists, regardless of their actual accomplishments, was better than the staple diet of commercial or official culture. But this was a sympathy premised on a willful disregard of the history of cultural censorship and manipulation on the mainland, a sympathy that absolved itself of a need to consider the marketplace and the acuity of promoters.

In 1996, Zhang was busy at work on *East Palace, West Palace* (Donggong xigong), the first film with an overt gay theme made in Beijing. Scorned by my gay friends in the capital as voyeuristic (s)exploitation of a highly sensitive issue involving a generally repressed and victimized minority, Zhang's work, with unswerving entrepreneurship, had hit on an issue sure to appeal to the international art-house world and its attendant critics.[34] The double-edged irony is complete when one considers that such an important and much-abused topic in Chinese urban life was being depicted partly for its sensational value by a director who had an established record of overcoming his filmic deficiencies by pursuing the controversial.

Although Zhang Yuan enjoyed an international career, back on the mainland, some film critics, journalists, and others who had apprised themselves of the panoply of Western po-mo thinking—as well as postcolonialism—were actively questioning the success of directors like Zhang Yuan and Wu Wenguang. These directors were seen as having made films that "satisfied the Western gaze,"[35] that played into the hands of Western cultural hegemons who, consciously or not, were colonizing elite Chinese culture by pursuing a project of binary-oppositional mythmaking. By praising nonofficial artists, it was argued, the West was reenacting its old colonial ploy of "Othering," *tazhehua*, the Chinese, maintaining hegemonic Western discourse within the field of "China," and further engaging in power politics by using dissident cultural figures as pawns. If one can bother wading through the verbiage of such analyses, it was evident that there was no small measure of truth in this view. One could, however, take things one (or many) step(s) further and also consider the role of the homebred postcolonial critics themselves.

A number of these figures were among the avant-garde of enthusiastic supporters of nonofficial/mainstream film and art up to the early 1990s. Once these alternative cultural products were accepted internationally, however, the local critics' role as intermediaries and gatekeepers was superseded. In their place, overseas festival organizers/critics (be they ethnically Chinese or not) became the key intermediaries who could broker the talent directly. New strategies of cultural politics inevitably developed. In some cases, the deployment of po-mo theories on the mainland had a layered emotive edge that was now wrapped up in and warped by an academic jargon that made the discussion of the issues impenetrable to nonspecialist readers. In the residual authoritarian environment of China, critics could play cultural politics while avoiding official censure (party hacks had difficulty with the new vocabulary, too). As they pursued their own ideological agenda, establishing themselves as independent cultural critics, they effectively cut themselves off from intelligent and interested readers of all social strata.

Not that things have been easy for Chinese critics over the last two decades. Many of the most controversial cultural works, especially the films of the 1990s, were not readily available for general exhibition, so those who could comment on them with a measure of authority were a privileged minority. Most of these critics were based in Beijing and had access to videotapes of films by directors like Zhang Yuan, Wu Wenguang, and Wang Xiaoshuai.[36] For the filmmakers, this limited exposure meant they were effectively isolated from any open and informed public discussion of their work. Sympathetic younger journalists and cultural critics might go to closed screenings or home previews of the films, but those who were not part of this elite cultural milieu or who lived in other cities knew of the films by reputation alone. Lacking a constructive critical environment, it was little wonder that distorting and self-serving reviews in both the mainland and nonmainland media had such an impact on the younger directors.[37] It was easy, therefore, for irate mainland po-moists to denounce Othering Westerners and easier still for them to maintain their own position of indigenous authenticity and critical luxury knowing full well that they could play both sides with relative impunity. They also knew that the party's own hegemony was a major contributing factor to the maintenance of popular Chinese views of a demonized Western cultural hegemonic discourse. The tensions between the Western Other and the variously mediated cultural Self thus constantly produced a type of critical friction that served to shore up the authority of the "independent commentators" as savant critic-patriots.

For its part, the entertainment, youth, and intellectual press of the mainland made constant mention of banned films and their directors, thereby reinforcing the public recognition of the filmmakers. Thus, critics like Lin Xudong, Ding Dong, Xie Yong, and Dai Jinhua[38] who referred to nonofficial cinematic works in the public media were able themselves to claim an authorial position as critics and partake of the mysterious charisma of the illicit films that it had been their privilege to see and was now their right to critique. It was difficult for non-scene writers, or non-Beijing-based thinkers, to challenge their authoritative opinions, not only because access to the films was so limited, but also because few independent or pro-independent critics and writers would want to lambast works that expanded the horizons for more diverse cultural production in the future. To do so would be tantamount to aiding and abetting cultural repression.[39] As was so often the case in the nonofficial realm of mainland culture, a tactical response to cultural control served simultaneously as a strategy for self-validation.

ALTERNATING ALTERNATIVES

It would be naive to think of the nonofficial artist as somehow being outside or merely the victim of the process of packaging and hype, *baozhuang chaozuo*. Many of them, whether filmmakers, artists, or writers, were knowingly enmeshed in a complex skein of relationships. It could certainly be argued that they were forced into this passive position by the state corporate system in China, international audiences, critics (or the demon "global culture"), and Kong-Tai middle-people and that their skills at maneuvering among the contending forces working to dominate artistic creation and marketing were a canny response to the relative helplessness of their situation. But to do so is to presume that some sort of unadulterated artistic or cultural state existed, a supposed period of "innocence," before mainland China's reentry into the linear narrative of Westernizing modernity and historical progress in the 1970s.

Developments in the mainland underground and alternative cultural spheres also were closely monitored by the large exile Chinese community. Many "prodigal cultural dissidents" made a tentative return to the mainland in 1993. The returnees and visitors included the artist-poet Yan Li (based in New York), the peripatetic poets Yang Lian (Amherst, Berlin, London, and other ports of call), Bei Ling (Boston), Meng Lang (Brown University in Providence, Rhode Island), and artists like Cai Guo Qiang (Tokyo, New York, and Quanzhou), Xu Bing (New York and Beijing), Huang Rui (Tokyo), and Ai Weiwei (New York and Beijing), to name but a few members of the artistic diaspora. A number of them jetted back on short "cultural shopping tours," shuttling oppositionists gathering information for their future writing or artwork. Some returned to assess the possibilities of establishing migratory careers. The ideal was to be able to occupy a loft in a suitably up-market overseas city while maintaining a pied-à-terre in Beijing or Shanghai. As the 1990s progressed, the annual "return" trip to the mainland became a ritual reality-cum-authenticity check.

Having said all this, it also is important to remember that many mainstream and fringe cultural figures on the mainland were also doing their best to navigate a course through the treacherous waters of contemporary Chinese life so as to express themselves through their art with a measure of sincerity. There were filmmakers, songwriters, artists, and writers who wanted to use their talents to communicate with the larger community while also avoiding political persecution, that is, individuals straining to be financially successful while maintaining their artistic independence. Unless wealthy enough from overseas sales—and here one thinks of artists like Fang Lijun, Liu Wei, Wang Guangyi, and Feng Mengbo—to stay above the fray, they had little choice but to live double (or multiple) lives. The majority, however, gradually gave in to forces—political and social, cultural and economic, official and international—that increasingly shaped their work. Clever operators like Zhang Yuan or Wu Wenguang could educate their fellows in how to straddle the systems (official and offshore), but some prickly individuals rebelled against the co-option of oppositionist solidarity, people who tried to develop a modus vivendi for basic survival and, if possible, prosperity. One such arrant figure was He Yong, a Beijing "punk" rocker.[40] In his early 1990s song "Garbage Dump," He spoke with the anger of a young, urban nihilist. It featured such lines as "We eat our conscience and shit out ideology" and ended with the shout "Tear it down, tear it down." In 1994, He made a music video of the song with friends in Beijing that was screened on Asia-wide satellite TV. It was available on He Yong's debut tape, released in Hong Kong in 1994, and sold also on the mainland. But "Garbage Dump" was only one register in He Yong's musical scale, and a nostalgic ballad, "Bell and Drum Towers," which spoke of the decay of his childhood neighborhood in the north of the old city of Beijing, became a local hit and was even screened on Central Television in 1994.[41] He Yong had a long history of cooperation with and estrangement from both Cui Jian and Zhang Yuan. He wanted to achieve recognition as an alternative artist, but at the same time he was anxious to avoid the confines of being labeled a dissident rebel. Similarly, he needed the support of the alternative cultural structures of the capital and the backup of the Hong Kong recording and marketing business, but he refused to give up his testy individuality. Like many others in the nonofficial world, he wanted it both ways: recognition both locally and overseas but complete freedom from constricting typecasting. He therefore had to devote much of his time and energy to negotiating relationships with official cultural structures, the alternative arts scene, and offshore music promoters.

In this discussion of packaged dissent, I have argued against simply accepting a scale of cultural authenticity or veracity that is measured against the yardstick of official displeasure that a work or artist incurs. As I pointed out earlier, some of the most significant mainland literature appeared not in unofficial or exile journals but in state-funded publications. Similarly, in the art world, although many of the most talented younger artists were touted internationally as being representatives of a subversive new wave, they were developing locally a strong and vital commercial art scene with their own publications and outlets, about which more will be said in the following chapter. To quote Arthur C. Danto, "You cannot politically defy the institutions when all you really wanted was to be clasped to their bosoms and hope in time to be cherished under the very framework of values you are thinking of overcoming." As Danto goes on to say: "That would be co-optation, revolution only in the sense of a circulation of élites rather than the extirpation of the very impulses of élitism."[42]

The persecution of artistic works by enforcing bans and instituting police harassment provides only one scale for evaluating nonofficial Chinese culture in the 1990s. As this chapter has attempted to show, it is a scale decided by a complex system of political, and personal, economics. The work of the artist that is destroyed, or the value of the cultural dissident who is jailed, may be less valid in market terms because it/he/she cannot circulate in the global network built up for such works. In an environment in which the hierarchy of punishments determines surplus value, enforced invisibility is the ultimate violence against the individual, whereas those who can maintain a public profile become the international face of contemporary Chinese culture.

PHOTO INSERT

FIGURE ONE

T-shirt designs by Kong Yongqian. Clockwise: "Listen up everyone, they can't fool me" (night owl); "Nothing will ever happen to me" (four monkeys); "Natural Mien" (wolf/dog); "If you don't like what you see, don't look" (bald eagle). (Photograph by Lois Conner.)

FIGURE TWO

T-shirt designs by Kong Yongqian. Left to right: "A total failure"; "Making ends meet" (pocket). (Photograph by Lois Conner.)

FIGURE THREE

T-shirt design by Kong Yongqian. "What should I do: stick with my office job or start up a street stall?" (Photograph by Lois Conner.)

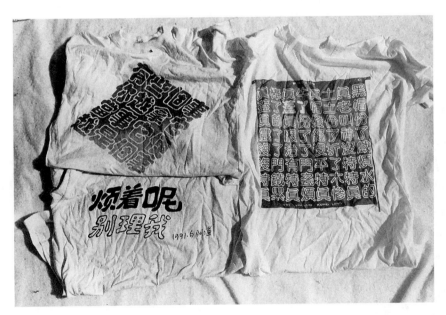

FIGURE FOUR

T-shirt designs by Kong Yongqian. Clockwise: "Beijing slang"; "I'm pissed, leave me alone"; "Some things only become something when you make something of them." (Photograph by Lois Conner.)

— —孩子，咱不写"真累"，写这……

FIGURE FIVE

"Listen, my child, we don't want to write 'Life's a bore,' but this: 'Socialism is good!'" (Cartoon in the "Satire and Humor Supplement," *People's Daily*, 20 October 1991.)

FIGURE SIX

T-shirt designs. Left to right: "There's a real difference between having money and having none"—Liu Yajun cartoon; "I might be ugly but I'm tender"—Chao Ch'uan. (Photograph by Lois Conner.)

FIGURE SEVEN

T-shirt designs. Left to right: "Parting shot" (Cui Jian song title) (designer unknown); "It wasn't even genuine booze"—Liu Yajun humorous cartoon (1993). (Photograph by Lois Conner.)

FIGURE EIGHT

"The Honeymoon" (or "Spring Fills the Courtyard"), oil on canvas, Liu Dahong (1991). (Courtesy of Schoeni Art Gallery Ltd., Hong Kong.)

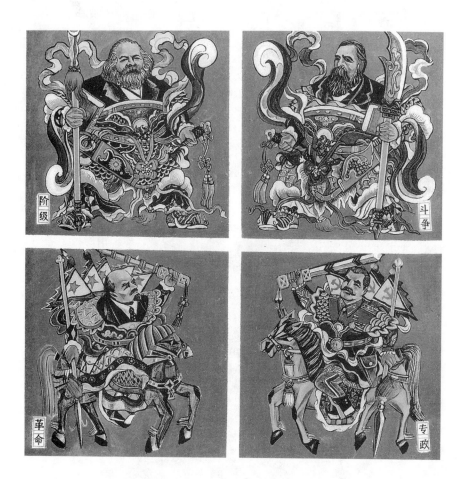

FIGURE NINE

"Door Gods/Guards," oil on canvas, Liu Dahong (1991). (Courtesy of Schoeni Art Gallery Ltd., Hong Kong.)

FIGURE TEN

"The Meeting," oil on board, Liu Dahong (1991). (Courtesy of Schoeni Art Gallery Ltd., Hong Kong.)

FIGURE ELEVEN

"Flying Dragon in the Heavens," Cai Guo Qiang, preflight kite (1997). (Louisiana Museum of Modern Art, Humlebaek, Denmark. Reproduced with permission.)

FIGURE TWELVE

"MB@Game!" Feng Mengbo, digital logo (1996). (Courtesy of the artist.)

FIGURE THIRTEEN

"Red Flag" sedan advertisement, China Number One Automobile Corporation. Reverse side of an Air China boarding pass, 1998.

FIGURE FOURTEEN

"The East Is Red No. 1." Advertisment for a Beijing Aerospace Dawn Food & Beverage, Inc., health drink. (Courtesy of Sang Ye.)

FIGURE FIFTEEN

"Yang Gensi." Part of the Goldlion Company's advertising campaign featuring army and party martyrs on the reverse side of the Goldlion® logo Dongdaqiao intersection, Beijing, 1998.

FIGURE SIXTEEN

"Hand-in-Hand, Progressing Together, Let Us Let Your Brand Name Radiate Over China. China Can Say YES to Your Brand!" (Advertasia Street Furniture Ltd. Company, Wangfujing, Beijing, 1998.)

FIGURE SEVENTEEN

"Xueliang Glasses." The brand name of an optometrists' chain store that is a reference to Mao Zedong's line: "The people's eyes are as bright as snow [xueliang]" (that is, they can see reality clearly). Shop hoarding, Dongsi, Beijing, 1998.

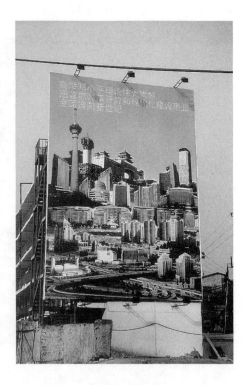

FIGURE EIGHTEEN

"Raise high the Great Banner of Deng Xiaoping Theory and push the enterprise of the Open Door and Reform, as well as of modernization, in our capital city into the twenty-first century!" Propaganda poster, Dongdan intersection construction site, Beijing, 1998.

FIGURE NINETEEN

"As the Sun Rises, the Waves on the River Glisten Brighter Than Fire." Promotional poster for a 1998 documentary film directed by Zhuge Hongyun. (Courtesy of Sang Ye.)

FIGURE TWENTY

May Fourth Avenue. The picture beneath the street sign bears the legend "Be a civilized citizen, construct a civilized city." Shatan'r, Beijing, 1998.

FIGURE TWENTY-ONE

"The Power of the Powerless." Cui Jian album promotional poster. Dongsi, Beijing, 1998.

FIGURE TWENTY-TWO (FOLLOWING PAGE)

"A Study in Perspective: 1995, 1996, 1997," Ai Weiwei, three photographs (1997). (Courtesy of the artist.)

Artful Marketing

SIX ESSAYS ON ART

Four of the essays that appear here in a slightly modified form were originally written for the catalogs of various art exhibitions. One was for the first show of work by Liu Dahong, a Shanghai-based artist, in Hong Kong in 1992; the second was for the first major exhibition of unofficial mainland art held in the British territory in 1993; the third was for a collection of contemporary Taiwanese art that toured Australia in 1995; and the fourth was for a 1997 installation by Cai Guo Qiang in Denmark.[1] The fifth essay, on the computer-artist Feng Mengbo, originally appeared in an issue of *Art Asia Pacific* devoted to Chinese art in 1997, and "Big Business" was written for a 1998 art show that did not eventuate.

BIG BUSINESS

In late September 1979, a symbolic act of artistic defiance marked the first exhibition of the "Stars," the seminal group of nonofficial artists in Beijing. Refused a venue for their disorderly array of work—paintings, woodcuts, sculpture, and collages—the artists set themselves up *en plein air* in the small public park next to the China Art Gallery. This act of cultural disobedience immediately aroused the ire of the authorities, and the artists were soon moved on by the police. Nonetheless, that open-air display marked out a new realm for nonofficial culture on mainland China, one that has had profound resonances for the history of similar art over the past two decades.

By displaying their work in that bleak park, the "Stars" had occupied a space that paralleled the temple of high proletarian art, the China Art Gallery. That building loomed at the intersection of two of the city's busiest streets. Completed in 1960, the gallery joined the "Ten Grand Edifices" constructed in Beijing to celebrate the first decade of the People's Republic, an eclectic series of architectural behemoths that gave concrete expression to the early life of socialist China. In the art gallery, an ill-digested European neoclassicism was married to flimsy socialist chinoiserie via the intermediary of Soviet monumental art deco. For two decades, it was home to the evanescent whims of Maoist agitprop; in the late 1970s it was still the national locus for the exhibition and dissemination of official art. The incident involving the "Stars," however, marked the bifurcation of canonical state art and the alternative or parallel visual arts cultures that had been developing surreptitiously since the early 1970s.

Ejected unceremoniously from the embrace of the state, the "Stars" arranged their works as if setting up a street stall, and the foreign media eagerly recorded the incident. Stalls, *tan'r*, hawking all manner of produce and manufacture from the nascent private sector mushroomed throughout the capital as a modicum of individual enterprise was permitted under the new open door and reform policies recently initiated by the Communist Party. Now the "Stars," in an unwitting parody of the new commercialism, exposed for public scrutiny their previously covert artistic creation to a curious, bemused, and, in many cases, befuddled audience. It was an act with dual significance. On the one hand, it cast the artists in the role of street peddlers, and on the other, it unabashedly stationed nonofficial art on the doorstep of the orthodox cultural world.

In the years since those events, nonofficial art has continued in its ambivalent role. With one eye trained on the marketplace and the other on official orthodoxy, it has achieved the status of a cultural barometer that with its ebb and flow has recorded the covert artistic vitality of the nation. It is in the oscillation between Caesar and Mammon that much contemporary mainland art has been able to flourish. . . .

A decade later, in February 1989, the China Art Gallery hosted a retrospective exhibition of post-1978 art. The show delineated a history of alternative art that located its origins in the work of the "Stars" and their contemporaries. No curbside artistic flea market this, however; the "1989 Modern Art Exhibition" was a very public celebration of the diversity of post–Cultural Revolution artistic life. With the nation now awash in what was dubbed a "tide of commodification," *shangpin dachao*, the crude political repression of the late 1970s had been transmogrified in a fashion that was in keeping with the exigencies of economic reform.

After years of playing hide-and-seek with the authorities, many artists found themselves caught between the Scylla of politics and the Charybdis of commercialization. As a reflection of this fraught relationship, Wu Shanzhuan, a graduate of the Zhejiang Arts Academy, created a performance art piece for the 1989 exhibition called "Big Business." The report on his work published in *Fine Arts in China*, the leading semiofficial organ for parallel art in Beijing, described it in the following way:

> On the morning of 5 February [1989], Wu Shanzhuan took up the position assigned to his work in the exhibition hall on the first floor [of the China Art Gallery] and sold prawns. Many people crowded around to buy. After approximately half an hour, two men in plain clothes ordered him to stop, tore up his sign, and forced Wu to go with them. Shortly after this, Wu reappeared in the hall and wrote on a blackboard: "Closed temporarily for stocktaking."

The authorities fined the artist 20 *yuan* for illicit trading. Wu's own statement on his work makes his stance on the business at hand perfectly clear:

> Anyone can make a name for himself doing business. Anyone can make himself rich.
>
> Selling prawns in the China Art Gallery was a protest against the gallery itself, that law court at which works of art are put on trial. Art, like an innocent, sacrificial lamb, is subjected to a quasi-legal process by the authority of the gallery. Artists, as eyewitnesses, are forced to give evidence. It is a waste of good space.
>
> Selling prawns at the China Art Gallery was a protest against art theorists. Works of art that start out as signifying nothing suffer, by the power of the theorists, the tragedy of being made to signify everything. The artist as producer of the "goods" is forced to go around hawking his wares. It's a waste of good money.
>
> On the morning of 5 February, 1989, the China Art Gallery became the black market it has always been; art theory, the profiteer it really is.
>
> It's big business. You've got something, but you can't go out and sell it directly; or you want something, but you can't just go and buy it. There's a middleman/woman with his/her black briefcase who intercedes to maintain our mythic tradition.[2]

By the time that Wu Shanzhuan wrote this, the China Art Gallery itself had changed. Falling prey to the economic rationalism that swept the cultural scene in the late 1980s, it was now host to the most unlikely shows, including the "1989 Modern Art Exhibition."

In the early 1990s, Wu became an export commodity in his own right, and his installations adorned museums and galleries at various locales throughout Europe. Perhaps the most telling of his post-China work, one created much in the vein of "Big Business," was the installation "Showing China from Its Best Sides" designed with his partner Inga Thórsdóttir. Created in collaboration with a number of Chinese corporations, it was featured in the exhibition "Des de el País del

Centre: avantguardes artistíques xineses" at the Barcelona Centre d'Art Santa
Mónica, June-September 1995. It consisted of all manner of neotrad product
from China and momentarily turned the Spanish exhibition space into a kind of
Chinatown emporium. Wu had moved from gustatory crustacea to autooriental-
ist kitsch.

For those who remained at home, however, as economic atavism consumed
the country, the relationship between official and alternative, mainstream and
marginal cultures continued their metempsychosis. In 1995, many nonofficial
artistic hopefuls, young men and women anxious to achieve the local and international recognition that had launched so many brilliant careers since the late
1970s, actively courted official displeasure as part of their presale publicity. Although in the past, this strategy had worked wonders for many artists, filmmakers,
and writers of middling talent, it was no longer necessarily effective.

For the first half of the 1990s, the disheveled grounds of the former imperial
pleasance, the Garden of Perfect Brightness (Yuan Ming Yuan) in the northwest-
ern suburbs of Beijing, and the makeshift villages that had sprung up there
around the old Fuyuan Gate became home to a motley crowd of deracinated
artists and cultural wannabes.[3] Known raffishly as the "West Village," the Yuan
Ming Yuan Artists' Village in Haidian was the launching pad for a number of
artistic careers (the internationally celebrated painter Fang Lijun once had a studio there). It was also an ideal vantage point from which to observe the city's art
scene. In early 1995, shortly before the police cordoned off the area and dispersed
the artists, the journalist Sang Ye interviewed one of the local painters:

> Some people realize that the only way to make a future for themselves is to
> act up. But it's a career option that doesn't suit everyone. Like, I know this
> guy . . . [who] was really hoping to create some kind of disturbance so he
> could be picked up by the authorities. Once he set up a stall opposite the
> China Art Gallery to exhibit his "black paintings." He wanted to confront
> the government, but nowadays the authorities are as cunning as you are.
> When Old Ma [Desheng] and the "Stars" were detained for putting on
> their exhibition, it was really explosive. Now here you have this wannabe
> lining up his works along a wall in an alley, and the authorities simply ig-
> nore him. They didn't want to give the kid a break. They didn't allow him
> a chance to stir up any trouble or a make a name for himself. How would it
> feel to be treated like that? The guy simply overplayed his hand.[4]

Will Whitey Like It?

The first "Stars" exhibition had only hinted at the type of cultural displacement
that was to develop in China in the late 1970s. The "Stars" were also the avant-

garde in the "foreign salons" that appeared initially in Beijing and then in provincial cities throughout the 1980s (see chapter 7, "Packaged Dissent"). As new talent was displayed and discovered, the relationship between the artists and the connoisseurs at the soirées appeared increasingly like an oriental version of the "Apache Dance," that choreographed duet common in World War I Paris clip joints described so tellingly by Tom Wolfe in *The Painted Word*:

> The artist . . . like the female in the act, stamping her feet, yelling defiance one moment, feigning indifference the next, resisting the advances of her pursuer with absolute contempt . . . more thrashing about . . . more rake-a-cheek fury . . . more yelling and carrying on . . . until finally with one last mighty and marvelous ambiguous shriek—*pain! ecstasy!*—she submits. . . . Paff paff paff paff paff. . . . How you do it, my boy! . . . and the house lights rise and Everyone, *tout le monde*, applauds.[5]

Nor did the salon culture escape the notice of local critics. Li Xianting, a leading supporter-*cum*-curator of the nonofficial art world since the 1970s, was wary of the impact of the amateur collectors:

> Foreigners who are given to collecting, or studying, Chinese modern art are, in many cases, inclined to pay undue attention to "unofficial" artists who do not belong to state-run art organizations. Their judgment, however, is suspect, for they tend to be attracted to anything that is "unofficial," and they are surrounded by a group boasting that they are China's artistic avant-garde, although they may be far from that.[6]

The display of alternative art increasingly gravitated from the furtive and surreal gatherings organized in the apartments of prosperous expats in the 1980s to the galleries, museums, and exhibition spaces of the international scene in the 1990s. Li Xianting himself, though cashiered from state employ, flourished as an independent critic and curator on the international scene. Following the events of 1989, when popular demonstrations against the government were suppressed in Beijing and other cities, nonofficial culture enjoyed a burgeoning reputation for representing an artistic view somehow more authentic and essential than the cultural products touted by officialdom or the commercial mass media.

National elites, be they economic or cultural, have gradually seceded from their own countries. Involved in transnational or global ventures and more often in transit than *in situ*, they need not be mired in the limiting realities of nation-states. Much of the contemporary art that has been displayed internationally since the mid-1980s has not been exhibited in China proper. In many cases, these are works that as yet have no place in the realm of state culture and circulate instead through the galleries of the West and affluent Asia.

To an extent in the 1990s, mainland nonofficial artists have been constituted as a diaspora (the po-mo carry-all category that, along with subalterns and cultural hybridity, is the label *du jour* for any significant Other), and they have achieved exposure in a stereotypical postmodern environment, one of dispersion, in which the periphery masquerades as center and the globe-trotting disenfranchised always travel with a return-trip ticket. Their works find a home in the international museum without walls, validated not only by overseas curatorial fiat but also by the state art against which they are juxtaposed. For without the impotent interdictions and papal bulls of the official mainland overculture, how viable would any of the alternative work of the "counterculture" really be? Just as in the case of Chinese rock 'n' roll, experimental fiction, antiestablishment poetry, and covert cinema, art, too, gains much of its visibility only when set against the gloomy backdrop manufactured by the state.

The art of the Chinese avant-garde is thus exhibited in a geopolitical and temporal utopos (nonplace), whose shifting borders are marked by the categories invented to package them (political pop, cynical realism, or what have you) and the charismatic names of international art sites: London, Paris, Berlin, Barcelona, Venice, Copenhagen, Hong Kong, Sydney, San Francisco, New York, or São Paolo. Traveling along a particular political and cultural trajectory determined in the late 1970s, these mainland artists move nearly exclusively in the realm of hyperreality, one of a Chinese culture conjured up in the catalogs and reviews of the international cognoscenti, the avant-garde of cultural appreciation. Those canny enough to learn how to play the international art system (or lucky enough to be picked up by the right dealer) find grudging approval among foreign observers and colleagues who applaud the fact that they, too, have insinuated themselves into the mechanism of fame and have broken through into the big time.

A few of their number, like the installation artists Xu Bing and Cai Guo Qiang who are ostensibly resident in New York, or the Beijing-based multimedia artist Feng Mengbo, rarely touch the ground at all. Theirs is a peripatetic mode, one that has embraced cybersphere as they fax, phone, and e-mail plans for their latest installations to venues around the world. Deprived of loci in China, they have become members of that country's self-funding cultural caravan. Their currency ensures for their overseas investor-supporters safe *entrée* into the world of edgy, up-and coming oriental culture. Other artists, as yet still earthbound, would rely on the realm of Sino-Cyberia in their search for exposure or await discovery and display at one of the chic eatery-galleries of Beijing. In recent years, expat mainland activists have also taken to organizing regional exhibitions (in the United States, Singapore, and Australia, for example) so that through their good works they, too, can be admitted into the company of the critics and the collectors.

The face of dissent has changed in the 1990s, in keeping with the age of the pager and website. As the artist who spoke to Sang Ye put it when commenting on one bohemian colleague:

> Just take a look at this joker's name card. He's damned well put "homeless artist" on it. Homeless, my ass. He's even included an address and phone number! He's scared people won't be able to find him, that he might miss out on making a deal. Even the homeless are printing name cards these days. It's fucked.

By the mid-1990s, the orbit of many artists took them far away from the well-worn paths of the pet primitives; they were moving upmarket, and they honed their skills accordingly. Again, as Sang Ye's interlocutor put it,

> Of course, no one ever pretended he wasn't interested in making a buck. Everyone here wants to cut a deal. There's only two types of people in this world: those who want to be famous and those who want to make a fortune. . . . Doing deals has become a science, and people around here are real pros. They've got the whole game down pat. They've turned alternative art into their own form of planned economy. They've set their sights on fame and gain, doing the squeeze and slipping out overseas.

Further on, he says:

> Whenever you've got a good supply of foreigners, it means you've got major access to the latest market info and the art world. The downside is that once they're here, they won't leave, always in your face, trying to promote you, and fucking around with your head. What's any of that got to do with being an "independent artist"? It's bullshit.[7]

In the mid-1980s an anxious cry was heard among Chinese artists, be they film-makers or painters. They despaired of official recognition and fixed instead their professional eye on the international market. The cry was "Will whitey like it?" *laowai hui xihuan ma?*[8] The inchoate sense of frustration with the local scene that had developed in the 1970s coalesced into a new cultural formula that was in keeping with the general national economic push to, as Chinese sports people of the time put it, "break free of Asia and go international," *chongchu Yazhou, zou xiang shijie*. Foreigners, *laowai*—an ambivalent term of arrogant and grudging respect for Westerners, "whitey"—were a key to the long march overseas. Their appreciation, or at least connivance in support of the nonofficial arts, became a central feature of the cultural impetus of the mainland, just as international investors had increased commerce with local manufacturers. Artists who had originally been more intent to *épater le parti* were becoming more interested in pandering to *la bourgeoisie internationale*.

With one eye on the market and the other on prevailing party policies, the constant self-questioning of artists—one that was by no means always restricted to existential dilemmas and often an anxious reflection, "But have I been noticed yet?"—led to an unprecedented richness and variety in avant-garde works. In the 1990s, cultural authenticity and taste increasingly became the arena in which individual worth and strength were finding expression. The frustration of popular political will in 1989, however, though providing the impetus for many artists' careers, also fed directly into the narrow, often xenophobic, and pseudo-nationalist cultural hype that marked the decade. Now it was commonplace for well-traveled, trend-setting artists to deny the value of Western culture, belittle Euro-America's appreciation (not to mention acquisition) of their own work, bewail the blight of global culture, and scoff at the West's failure to understand the ineffable profundity of the contemporary Chinese artistic œuvre. In the 1990s, "Will whitey like it?" was married inexorably to the assertive and appropriate rejoinder, "Anyway, whitey just can't understand us!" *fanzheng, laowai bu dong!*

In the late nineteenth century, Chinese literati-artists increasingly argued that the essence of their art was beyond the ken of the West. They repeated the dismissive comments made by earlier literati critics that for all the technical achievements of Western representational painting, "the result is not worthy of enjoyment by the connoisseur" and that true "lovers of antiquity" shunned Westernized styles of art.9

Nearly a century later, artistic styles and genres—be they neoliterati painting, post–socialist realist oils, avant-garde installations, or ephemeral performance pieces—reflected the diversity of mainland Chinese cultural expression. For all the international recognition that artists across the spectrum achieved, however, it was acceptance in China, at the center of cultural hierarchy and worth, that many artists still craved. No matter how much whitey may invest in one's work, in the end they really just don't get it.

REFORMIST BAROQUE

More than any other painter in the China of the early 1990s, Liu Dahong was the artist laureate of reform.

The economic marvels and social dislocations, the political upheavals and cultural confusion of China's reform age have been so widely commented on as to be clichéd. And it is just these clichés, the widespread state of disquiet and instability, the tantalizing decadence and enthralling disarray of contemporary urban China, that Liu Dahong's art both reflects and revels in.

Liu's work should not be condemned to the narrow category of dissident art. Here we find none of the stark messages of 1970s critical realism or the confused exuberance of the early 1980s or even the angst and ennui of the early 1990s. Not for him the mannered deconstructions or the furtive postmodernist poses that fashion dictates. Liu Dahong's dystopia offers a world fit for travel, leisure, and dwelling. Chinese literati art created an ephemeral vision pulsating with *qi*, but the rural idyll and eremitic fantasies of the past have been stamped out and Liu presents a grotesque urban reality that in turn amuses and horrifies. Fleetingness, decay, and ruins; fortune, chance, adventure; as well as corruption, lasciviousness, and indulgence are the topos of Liu's artistic landscape.

It may not be meaningful to claim a postmodern status for Liu's work (although the very vagueness and uncertainty of the term have lent it a near universal cachet), yet there are certain familiar po-mo elements to be found in it: the location of "strange, eclectic, violent, timeless worlds in the present," a making fun of the past while keeping it alive, a search for new ways to present the unpresentable, thereby breaking down the barriers that keep the profane separated from the everyday.[10]

There is pastiche and parody aplenty in Liu's work as well. Certainly, others have had their way with the image of Chairman Mao; for example, the Mao on a red grid by Wang Guangyi, Wang Youshen's *Portrait Series*, and Yu Youhan's *Whitney Houston with the Chairman*, not to mention the *Chairmen Mao Series* of the New York–based artist Zhang Hongtu. In those works Mao, has, above all, a market value. But in Liu Dahong's work, the chairman has found another role in the afterlife. His image has been digested and mixed with traditional subject matter (in *Mao for all Seasons*, for instance). Elsewhere Mao is found lecturing the pantheon of Chinese revolutionary martyrs and heroes while striking a pose familiar to us from pictures dating from the 1942 "Yan'an Forum Talks on Art and Literature" that have determined the party line on culture ever since.

Liu Dahong's artful marriage of peasant and religious kitsch — motifs from mass-produced New Year's paintings, *nianhua*, or Tibetan tankas — with a contemporary political argot results in a range of works from the decoratively flippant Marx-Engels-Lenin-Stalin guardian demons (*Door Guards/Gods*), the *Revolutionary Opera Hexagrams*, and the comic plenum of *The Meeting*, to the repulsively funny caricature of *Harmony* in which the revolutionary effulgence of Mao-as-boddhisattva beats down on a hapless Tibet. The party has trumpeted Mao Zedong Thought for its successful combination of the universal truth of Marxism-Leninism with the particular realities of China; Liu Dahong reformulates this victory and invites a limp and lackluster revolutionary tradition to find a place in the continuing stream of Chinese cultural becoming.

The works that play with political themes invite a knowing complicity on the part of a mainland Chinese audience. When these works—mostly unexhibit/-ed-itable, unprint/-ed-able in China[11]—are unveiled to the offshore market (Hong Kong, Taiwan, and farther afield), perhaps another mechanism is at work, one of chic voyeurism.

But here are there not also elements of the Baroque? The Baroque sensibility of seventeenth-century Europe was one of instability, political disturbance, and moral crisis. It was an epoch of dislocation and alienation, whose inhabitants perceived themselves to be "modern."[12] Liu's work has certainly been influenced by Bosch and Brueghel—and there is much of the Gothic both in China and on the canvas—but Liu's paintings are the product of an age of unprecedented prosperity, even ostentation. Nowhere else in early 1990s Chinese artistic culture do we find such a rich, entertaining, and unsettling portrait of the state of the state.

Liu himself is a product of a colonial environment, the seaside resort city of Qingdao, in Shandong Province, formerly a German possession. He created an exuberant and kaleidoscopic overview of that city in his 1987 work *Summertime*.

After he left art school in the late 1980s, Liu settled in Shanghai, a city that for decades trailed clouds of colonial glory through a grimy revolutionary makeover, a city of pretension and fallen grace. It is within the ambit of Shanghai, yesteryear's adventurer's paradise and China's most intriguing entrepreneurial port, that Liu Dahong weaves his painterly tales. Many of his most extraordinary works exude the atmosphere of that metropolis, the "Great Terrible City" that Lin Yutang described in his "Hymn to Shanghai" written in the 1930s:

> Shanghai is terrible, very terrible. Shanghai is terrible in her strange mixture of Eastern and Western vulgarity, in her superficial refinements, in her naked and unmasked worship of Mammon, in her emptiness, commonness, and bad taste.... She is terrible in her greatness as well as in her weakness, terrible in her monstrosities, perversities, and inanities, terrible in her joys and follies, and in her tears, bitterness, and degradation.[13]

A 1989 series of Shanghai vignettes—including *Grandmother* and *Grandfather*—with its mannerist figures and tactile ambience, succinctly bespeaks the inviting congestion of the wooden houses in the alleys of the city. Other paintings like *Late Spring*, *Good Times*, and *The Mid-Autumn Festival* unfurl dimensions both magical and monstrous, colonial and contemporary, debauched and delightful. In short, it is a world of reformist Baroque.

In November 1992, Liu's first one-man show, "Liu Da Hong: Paintings 1986–92," was held at the China Club in Hong Kong. With this successful debut, Liu turned his attention to depicting another energetic Chinese colonial enclave, Hong Kong.

EXPLOIT, EXPORT, EXPROPRIATE

It is both a cruel and happy fate to be an artist in reformist China.

Cruel because chances for exhibiting one's work are slight, recognition rare and distorting, and there is little or no chance of having an impact on society at any level. One is engaged in a solipsistic project, auto-orientalizing, and forced to curry favor with the Occidental Other. Cruel, too, that cultural repression is not what it used to be. An erratic toleration has replaced pervasive totalitarianism; a laissez-faire realpolitik has been instituted for the rebellious who act within reason. Dissident and diverse art thus become another jewel in the crown of Chinese socialism.

Happy, too, is this fate. Repression gives life and creation a thrill missing in other systems. Whereas it may be true of postindustrial cultures that everything is interesting while nothing has any meaning (*pace* Philip Roth), in China few things are of any interest, yet some achieve a modicum of meaning. Significance is occasionally significant. The art markets of Hong Kong, Taiwan, and the West cautiously welcome the perennial avant-garde of mainland China with its alluring sheen of the illicit underground. Success in the international marketplace brings reward, the like of which many younger official artists can only dream: a measure of hard-currency wealth, exhibitions, and private (not officially controlled and supervised) trips overseas, and even a grudging, if jealous, acceptance among one's fellows.

Although many have said that the cultural and political scene in China was reaching a point of unprecedented liberalization in 1988–1989, there is much evidence to show that it was, in reality, nearing bankruptcy and that the tumultuous events of mid-1989 offered a kind of redemption.

The economic, political, and social chaos of the preceding months and years led me to comment in late 1988:

> What perspective is possible now that the China Art Gallery [in central Beijing], the proletarian palace of socialist art, makes its halls available to virtually any self-styled avant-garde artist who can afford the rental fee? The end result of reform may well be the creation of a new avant-garde art-to-order: dissent on tap. Works of striking individuality continue to appear in both Beijing and the provinces. However, the government's erratic and hedonistic economic policies tend to encourage a soul-destroying cynicism in artists of lesser genius.[14]

A number of powerful artists have been active in Beijing since 1989. Among these are Liu Wei, Fang Lijun, and Liu Xiaodong. Along with some other painters, writers (notably Wang Shuo) and certain members of the entertainment industry, they belong to or are at least fringe dwellers in the world of the *liumang*, the lout, hooligan, rogue, or pícaro. They are part of

> what may be called the other Cultural Revolution generation. They were not the idealistic Red Guards, but their younger brothers and sisters who witnessed it all but grew up not disillusioned but dismissive, young people who had never believed the strident rhetoric. . . . They spent their child-hood in a world that was both chaotic and mendacious; they came of age in the materialistic 1980s, enjoying the consumer culture of the reform age with few of the ideological, intellectual, or emotional qualms experienced by the older generations (see chapter 4, "The Apotheosis of the *Liumang*").

In the early 1990s, Fang Lijun and Liu Wei, both graduates of the Central Art Academy, were noted for a carefree lifestyle that was the envy of their fellows. Their work, particularly the bizarre portraits done by Liu Wei, illustrated the world of the *liumang*. The artists exhibited together[15] and were excluded from one semiofficial show in 1991,[16] presumably for not conforming to the image of the well-behaved academy graduate. Liu Xiaodong, a provincial who made good in the capital and, though not necessarily a pícaro by nature, peopled his canvas-es with the cool, *ku*, *liumang* denizens of late-1980s and early-1990s Beijing. Fang Lijun summed up his personal philosophical outlook as follows:

> Only a stupid bastard would allow himself to be cheated time and time again. We would rather be called hopeless, bored, dangerous, rogues and confused than be cheated again. Don't try any of your old tricks on us, for all dogma will be thoroughly questioned, negated and thrown into the rub-bish bin.[17]

It is not an attitude calculated to please the authorities or the critics. Baude-laire remarked that "the chief task of genius is precisely to invent a stereotype." Wang Shuo's depiction in fiction of the *liumang*, or wisecracking young opera-tor, created just such a stereotype. Other works in the genre of *"liumang* art" were included in the exhibition "China's New Art, Post-1989" under the rubric of "cyn-ical realism."[18] Representative artists included Wang Jingsong, Song Yonghong, Yu Hong, and Shen Xiaotong, many of whom were provincials active in Beijing from the late 1980s. Theirs was a cynicism that was often tempered by a large mea-sure of self-conscious irony and humor.

The economic marvels of reformist China, however, have also taken their toll on the semiofficial art scene. Previously I spoke of the "soul-destroying cynicism" that has grown in tandem with the ideological collapse and the economic boom of the 1980s. It is a cynicism that differs in many respects from the existential con-dition shared by the earlier-mentioned artists during the early 1990s era of "high-

Dengist irony" (that is, the irony born of hard-line political posturing, on one hand, and economic utilitarianism, on the other). Mocking society and politics can have a considerable, enlivening impact, yet when such an artistic stance is grounded in a derision of self-respect and integrity, it ends up feeding on and betraying the newfound dignity of the individual that has been the bedrock of China's fledgling post-Maoist culture. The glib cynicism of the 1990s seizes on and exploits any market trend; one minute it masquerades as modernist, the next po-mo, and then again as postcolonial. Often hard to distinguish from the more profound and self-aware questioning of rogue artists, it is a creative attitude that is unredeemed by humor and bloated with a sense of its own importance. It is a cynicism that is cynical even about itself.

In April 1989, the China Art Gallery hosted the "Modern Art Exhibition," a grand gathering of China's then-new art, an art that was simultaneously nascent and senile. Nascent in that it represented so many trends of international culture freshly introduced (or reintroduced) to mainland China and yet senile because even the most up-to-date "isms" and foreign fads flooded the scene on a wave of consumerist popularity, impressing artists and viewers for a while with their aura of international street cred and then falling out of fashion. To a certain extent, the "Modern Art Exhibition" was a museumlike display of flash-frozen styles, innovations that seemed to lead nowhere, tired-out artistic trends of academic rather than artistic interest.[19]

The local intelligentsia and commentators have seen cynicism in the arts as symptomatic of the unsettling "postideological" age of 1990s reformist China; overseas observers and buyers have often interpreted it in the formulaic language of Soviet and Eastern European dissent; and all the while, artists and writers have been engaged in the unsentimental project of adorning themselves and their works with it. But the cynicism—one that can be both positive when self-reflective as well as destructive of the creative impulse, as we already have observed—that runs as a thread through so much of the most interesting literature, music, and art from China today should not simply be seen as a product of a post-Mao ideological malaise. It is more a mood that is the product of the long-term marginalization of elite culture.

The basic tenor of twentieth-century Chinese intellectual life has been determined by a belief among intellectuals (the self-description enjoyed by writers, artists, and thinkers) that they can and should play a preeminent role in the transformation and modernization not only of China but of the Chinese national character as well. Often ignoring their own inadequacies as autochthonous individuals, they have generally evinced a cocky eagerness to reform, educate, and lead. More often than not, they have been ignored by the society at large. They have readily equated modernity with superiority and a lack of the same as being a mark of the inferior. Their neophilia, the need to be modern, new, and up-to-date, became a protean impulse, and any ideology or cultural form that promised to satisfy this need was embraced. As the guardians of the traditional ways, their predecessors—the literati—were seen as having failed egregiously to maintain China's cultural vitality. Throughout the century, however, intellectuals have been regularly shunted to the sidelines or enlisted only to embellish or justify the status of the rulers.

In the late 1980s, the society's liberal atmosphere made the mannered poses of the suffering artist often appear shallow and unconvincing, even when they were genuine. Then, with the unfolding of the events of 1989, moral renewal seemed possible. The student protests, the popular enthusiasm for radical change, and the international media attention followed by the massacre and its attendant state repression literally overnight validated a cultural mood of angst. And herein lay the root cause of the painful dilemma of mainland intellectuals and cultural figures in the late 1980s. They had increasingly come to enjoy a social prominence and sense of self-esteem unknown in any other period of party rule. At the same time, they were forced to bear witness to a national economic transformation that once more obviated their role in the society. Their frustrations due to this heightened sense of impotence—public profile without a concomitant political or social impact—in no small part contributed to the rebellion among the intelligentsia in 1988–1989. The political and economic crises that led to the protest movement in Beijing and cities throughout China between April and June 1989, seemed to offer cultural figures a chance finally to play a decisive role in public life. But like so many others, they misjudged the situation and their own importance. To be cynical about the party's hypocritical economic policies was easy, whereas to reject its self-righteous cruelty and dated ideology after the events of Tiananmen Square was an act of self-affirmation and measured daring. But the horror of 4 June and its aftermath gradually gave way to further economic and cultural laxity, and many of the works gathered in the exhibition "China's New Art, Post-1989" reflect the emotional and ideological confusion that artists experienced as a result. Again we are faced with both a spectrum of cynicism and a scale of angst. At one end of this spectrum there was heartfelt sincerity and depth, at the other, a shallow and callous wish to manipulate and exploit.

The 1989 "Modern Art Exhibition" and the 4 June Beijing massacre may also be taken as convenient markers for the end of the artistic-historical narrative in mainland China. That narrative—the story of the new enlightenment and cultural development since the late 1970s marked by discoveries, innovations, efforts to catch up with East Asia and the West, and new perceptions, many of which were all too eagerly culled from overseas—had run its course. It is a narrative in which "making art was understood to be carrying forward the history of discovery and making new breakthroughs."[20] From 1989 onward, however, as many mainland critics and artists have commented, that earlier narrative cohesion has unraveled.

Innovation and variation inspired by both foreign models and native traditions continued in the 1990s, but a growing cultural pluralism and the marginalization of overt political ideology in the society left creative artists in all areas increasingly unsure of not only their impact but also their relevance. The avant-garde of the nineteenth century was a reaction to the commodification of art, and the commodification of the avant-garde in China was a major factor in the rise of the spirit of cynicism (be it the ironic disinterestedness of artists like Liu Wei or the calculated poses of others) in culture. It is a cynicism that toyed with the tropes of life on the mainland while fixing a steely gaze on the international art market.

The 4 June massacre and the repression that unfolded in its wake did not close China off from the world again. Factions in the government were soon forced into an uneasy compromise, and it was the resultant stalemate in the early 1990s that made even the most world-weary cynicism a near comic platitude. Even though totalitarian governments are generally noted for having a low tolerance for satire, after late 1990 political satire of a type rarely seen in mainland China flourished. In early 1992, just as Deng Xiaoping was making his tour of the south, satire and the widespread attitude of cynicism even made it onto television with the screening of the sitcom *The Editors*. The series won a government award; the language of the Beijing *liumang* found a nationwide audience; and the more hip organs of the party media even promoted it.[21] It is doubtful whether the style of flippant cynicism seen in all the arts of mainland China in the early 1990s would have been similarly welcomed during earlier periods of official "liberalization" such as in 1986 or 1988–1989. Now even the orthodox no longer know what orthodoxy means. While 4 June provided independent artists with an opportunity for transcendence, the marked failure of totalitarian government to be its ruthless self stole that moment away. China has joined the world, and the works in "China's New Art, Post-1989," as well as the cultural mechanisms that made the exhibition possible in the first place, reveal how this was taking place.

Many of the efforts of mainland Chinese artists are, to use a buzz expression of the 1980s, directed at "going international," *zou xiang shijie*. It is the kind of cultural trajectory that shares something with the program of late-nineteenth-century Japanese thinkers who wanted to "slough off Asia," *datsu a*,[22] in the bid to become a modern "civilized" nation. The difference is that whereas the Japanese wanted to identify themselves with the West, Chinese concerns today are more with "breaking out of Asia," *chongchu Yazhou*, to prove themselves on the world stage while still championing their "Chineseness." Going global, however, will not necessarily presage becoming globalized. An oft-repeated claim of the 1989 student agitators and the popular responses to it was that the massive, peaceful prodemocratic demonstrations staged on and around Tiananmen Square proved that the Chinese people had finally come of age. They had caught the world's attention through the spectacle of presumed innocent political frenzy. Beijing occupied, for the allotted fifteen minutes, the center stage of electronic media fame. Momentarily, China was part of the narrative of international contemporary life, comprehensible because the crude and universal (dare we say Hollywood?) paradigm was applied to harsh and contradictory realities: the young pitted against the old, the people against the power holders, dissidents against ideologues, free spirits against an ossified status quo. The outline of the story was so familiar as to be tedious; only the names had been changed to confuse the guileless.

International interest in the types of Chinese art represented in this exhibition has led to some significant reactions in the local scene. There are those who, while applauding the efforts of contemporary artists to produce export-quality goods, have cautioned against the pitfalls of international recognition. Fearful that overseas buyers and critics will lavish wealth and fame on the undeserving, or corrupt the deserving, they have been at pains to create and manipulate an art market on their own terms. From the early 1990s on, there was a concerted effort being made by a group of (generally) younger critics, in particular Lü Peng from Sichuan (although he later abandoned art in favor of real estate), to create a "market awareness" for the "new" art in mainland China itself and an attempt to keep the art at home by buying it up. It was seen by some to be like an investment in the future, and the local critic-entrepreneurs encouraged state enterprises and entrepreneurs to get in on the ground floor.

There also are sincere patriotic reasons for developing the local art market. China's history as a colonized and subjugated nation was repeatedly subjected to cultural ransacking. Now, rather than see the overseas market replace the colonial powers of the past and carry off the spoils of unofficial art, local critics were justifiably desirous of mounting a counteroffensive. In this context, the nonofficial Guangzhou Art Biennial, first held in October 1992, was perhaps the most significant development.[23] The exhibition mostly featured regional artists from Hubei and Sichuan, yet it was attended by art critics, writers, and others from China's major cities. In his opening address at the biennial, Lü Peng, the energetic critic behind the exhibition, stated: "We are writing the history of Chinese art in the 1990s. This biennial is but the first page in that history. In our enterprise, industrialists, artists, and creators all are equally important."[24]

Among other things, the organizers of this "art fair," as it was dubbed (bringing to mind the biannual Guangzhou Trade Fair), claimed it would help Chinese cultural products "compete in the international art market in a regulated fashion." Whether this meant that local prices were competitive with those offered by offshore buyers and that the artist would pocket as much as he or she would have done in a direct foreign sale was not made clear. Since the Communist Party officially enshrined the "socialist market economy" in its political program in October 1992, one could only speculate: How long will it be before the authorities finally abandon the role of censor and don the guise of promoter, championing the avant-garde as but one more pulchritudinous and profitable blossom among the hundred flowers of sanctioned Chinese culture? There were just such tendencies in the cultural sphere in the late 1980s, and as orthodox Maoist cultocrats made way for young apparatchiki through the 1990s, great possibilities for the future began to open up.

While recognizing the endeavors and cultural significance of mainland critics and the ways in which their concerns reflected the ambitions and frustrations of intellectuals generally, one must not discount the practical dimensions of their role as the "gatekeepers" of aesthetic taste and the arbiters of new cultural canons. By creating a market for the product at home, the critics were affirming their own role as connoisseurs and conduits to fame. They were coming out of the closet of dissent and announcing their presence as middlemen who could guide and inform the taste of the collector-as-investor.[25] Again, in these efforts, we witness a disparate group of disenfranchised intellectuals attempting to regain a position of prestige and influence. Their efforts were strenuous and genuine enough, though it may well be that radical market reforms and political exigencies will ultimately relegate them to the sidelines, just as radical revolutionary change did after 1949.

An editorial in the early 1992 issue of the Sichuan-based journal *Art & Market* cautioned collectors in Hong Kong, Taiwan, and elsewhere to avoid the manifold pitfalls of the fledgling mainland market by keeping in close contact with informed art historians, theoreticians, and critics.[26] Previously content with their role as mentors and discoverers of the young, it appeared that some critics were now anxious to become the insider traders/compradors of the art scene. One of their number even went so far as to suggest that artists should adopt a scale of payment for the reviews of critics to be calculated at so many *yuan* per thousand words. The payout would vary depending on the extent of the critic's international fame and theoretical influence. "Criticism is the love a critic presents to the artist," opined Peng De, "a love that must be repaid by the artist in kind." That's right, the artist or his or her agent should pay for the privilege of critical approbation. To this end, Peng divided mainland critics into five classes and suggested that those in the highest category (people with an international reputation, who published theoretical works of influence, had an academic or official title, and were over sixty years of age) should be paid 1,000 *yuan* per thousand words.[27] In the international context, these are market conditions that are all too familiar. Of course, their suggested imposition in the realm of the unofficial art market in China leads one to speculate just how honest a critic's investment in an artist may be.

The change in the Chinese cultural landscape was sudden and extreme. Erratic government policies concerning arts publications and exhibitions — constant bans, censorship, and irregular attempts at co-option — made regular comment and analysis of art trends uneven at best. Unlike other art markets, the covert actions of Chinese artists and critics active outside or on the rim of official culture since mid-1989 have allowed them an added cachet that has made them more marketable. Given this confusing topography, it may not be hard to create an atmosphere of critical acceptance for undiscovered talent; but what happens when people indulge in "discovery for discovery's sake" or become enmeshed in what Robert Hughes calls "the slide of art criticism into promotion"?[28]

"China's New Art, Post-1989" provided a selection of the most noteworthy products of an extraordinary range of mainland Chinese artists (a number of whom had literally "broken out of Asia" and were living overseas). The exhibition allowed viewers a chance to see works by many of China's leading younger, semi-official artists. There were pieces from the fallen "Stars"; the political parodies of painters like Liu Dahong and Wang Guangyi; the disturbed urban peoplescapes of Liu Wei, Fang Lijun, Liu Xiaodong, and others; and a range of abstract, conceptual, and installation art. The fact that the "1989 Modern Art Exhibition" was held in Beijing at all was significant. The value (and tragedy) of the 1993 show, "China's New Art, Post-1989," comes not only from the works but also from the fact that it was possible only outside China. But even though the Guangzhou Biennial promised much, it was still a regional exhibition showcasing a limited number of artists and styles. "China's New Art, Post-1989," on the other hand, covered a much larger territory both physically and creatively. Only major changes in the structure of the official cultural bureaucracy in Beijing would have made such a display possible there. Now that Hong Kong and Taiwan were becoming integrated with southeast China as an economic region, it is significant that a commonwealth of cultural exchange also was possible. This exhibition was part of that commonwealth.

After the early 1980s, the barriers in China between elite and mass culture became blurred in many areas (film, literature, television, advertising, music), but change was more glacial in the art world, particularly in the art born of the academy. There should be no doubt that most of the works in "China's New Art, Post-1989" were created by artists trained in the elite art academies. Many of them were waiting in the wings to return to its embrace or find a niche in the academically endorsed artscape of the West. If their work appeared daring, innovative, and dissenting in the context of mainland China, in the non-Chinese context the question remains: Have the artists here moved only marginally away from the status of the "primitive pet" who can enjoy the largesse of patrons while maintaining a status as the exotic or dissident Other?

Many artists in the exhibition glibly manipulated political images and themes, most conspicuously that of Mao Zedong, whose renewed popularity in China dates from the late 1980s, reaching a zenith in 1991–1992. Elsewhere I have commented on this phenomenon in terms of "camp transition," one that occurs when a former style of politics that "has lost its power to dominate culture meanings becomes available, in the present, for definition according to contemporary codes of taste."[29] A number of artists here have taken to playful misrepresentations and rehearsals of the chairman. They include Wang Guangyi, Liu Dahong, Yu Youhan, Wang Ziwei, and Liu Wei. The avant-garde cannibalized Chinese political culture as it developed a new artistic vocabulary after 1976, just as party promotional culture was to countercannibalize the avant-garde after the late 1980s (see chapter 9, "CCP™ & Adcult PRC").

It is not surprising, however, that much of the cultural iconoclasm that plays with Chinese political symbols tempers its irony with a disturbing measure of validation: by turning orthodoxy on its head, the heterodox engage in an act of self-affirmation while staking a claim in a future regime that can incorporate them. On this most sublime level, Mao has become a consumer item.

Mao and other passé icons of the militant phase of Chinese socialism could now safely be reinvented for popular and elite delectation. In 1980s America, Madonna shocked and delighted her audiences with provocative evocations of Catholic symbols, ones that were both culturally powerful and commercially exploitable. Political parody in China worked in a similar fashion. Things might have been different—and dangerous—if Deng Xiaoping was the figure being given the Warhol treatment here.[30]

And it is in the dialectic of commodification and consumption that much of the art in "China's New Art, Post-1989" fulfilled its promise of "newness." The artists represented were exploiting or commodifying images of their world—political, social, cultural, and emotional—and this offshore export exhibition in turn attempted to position their works in international structures of display and consumption.

TAIWAN, CHINA'S OTHER

Taiwan is a disturbing presence. While politically and economically an autonomous entity, culturally the Precious Island is caught in a web of belonging and becoming with the mainland and Hong Kong. For the mainland, in particular, Taiwan is the other China. It is China's Other.

Up to the late 1970s, the mental geography of people on Taiwan and the mainland had created a barrier along the Taiwan Straits that was as culturally impregnable as it was ideologically. For Taiwanese, the mainland was a hell on earth, and the masses there lived, as the propagandist would have it, in "deep water and scorching fire," *shuishen huore*, under the rule of an insane and inhuman government. The rich heritage of the national past was denied them while Taiwan became the repository of all that was truly Chinese. For mainlanders, Taiwan barely registered at all, except as an ideological bogey. It was, effectively, a terra incognita.

During the 1980s, that barrier gradually changed into a semipermeable membrane, and a process of culture/style/notional osmosis has been under way ever since. The Taiwanese cultural solvent most often passes through and, in many cases, is modified by Hong Kong. The process is gradually drawing the two very different cultural concentrates into a state of equilibrium.

With contact came recognition, and from recognition followed prejudice and platitudes.

The most common mainland response to any sign of Taiwanese confidence is "So you've got more money than we do, big deal!" *nimen Taiwanren bu jiushi you jige qian ma?* The Taiwan reaction is equally stereotypical: "So what if you're bigger than we are?" *nimen bu jiushi juede ni da ma?*

Such remarks betray formalistic elements of tension between Taiwan and the mainland—one stable and prosperous, the other restive and inequitable—but the relationship is now far more complex and nuanced.

The commercial culture of Taiwan—including advertising in both the electronic and print media—has had an incalculable impact on the mainland. Taiwan has filtered and digested the global culture of Euro-America and Japan for "Chinese" delectation and, like Hong Kong, has developed a form of product presentation and placement that appeals directly to mainland consumers.

Yet the island provides much more that this. For the mainland arts world, it is a source of offshore funding and predigested cultural information, as well as being a site for exhibition and publication. It often provides an interested audience and, in some cases, a launching pad to the West, and the El Dorado of the First World.

Decades of militant Communism and political infighting have forced nearly everyone on the mainland into a pact with the devil. Despite its own melancholy past, Taiwan has not been burdened with the direct weight of China's oppressively venerable history. As the beneficiary of decades of Americanization, the island is seen as being both worldly wise but also more naive than the mainland.

Its people are generally ignorant of the language, symbols, icons, and fads of Chinese socialism. Attempts have been made to absorb mainland tropes in Taiwanese popular culture, as in the case of the music of Lo Tayu whose 1988 song "Comrade Lover," for example, contains lines like "You're as beautiful as a slogan." The Taiwanese have remained, nonetheless, ideological innocents, and mainlanders deride them for it; all the time secretly jealous that they themselves are forever deprived the luxury of a relatively untroubled history and the attitudes it has instilled. Unsullied by the horror and violence of Maoism, Taiwan points to a future of pure materialism, narrow social and national goals, and pragmatism. It is a prospect that both delights and unsettles people on the mainland. . . .

. . . Music and film were the first areas in which Taiwan revealed itself to the citizens of the People's Republic.

In the early 1980s, easy-listening love songs by Taiwan stars like Teresa Teng found their way to continental China. After decades of stentorian political anthems, these mellow tunes communicated a world that was both romantic and tacky, human and humdrum. It was just what sentiment-starved audiences on the mainland craved. The authorities tried in vain to ban the music on the grounds that it corrupted public morals and was detrimental to the ideological well-being of the people. Cheap, modern technology in the form of cassette players confounded the interdictions, and singers like Teng unwittingly launched a revolution in musical styles. Her songs also introduced a realm of bourgeois fantasy that helped pave the way for the boom in mainland commercial tastes from the late 1980s. The success of Fei Hsiang, a Taiwan singer of mixed (part American) parentage, is also noteworthy. Fei enjoyed a meteoric fame on the mainland in the late 1980s, the Eurasian teen idol's popularity with the young transgressing against accepted mainland Han views of monoethnicity.

The Taiwan folk/pop singer Hou Te-chien, one of the island's media stars, defected secretly to the mainland in 1983. For the Taiwanese authorities, it was an act of high treason; for Hou, it was a journey of self-discovery (see chapter 3, "Traveling Heavy").

Hou's most famous song, "Descendants of the Dragon," is a brooding but patriotic folk anthem that had made him rich on Taiwan and soon gave him star status on the mainland. At the time, it was the best-selling pop song ever marketed in China. Shortly after arriving in Beijing, Hou appeared on television. Here was a famous singer who addressed his audiences without a script. His casual and familiar manner flew in the face of the mechanical, stilted mode of mainland performers. For his audience, Hou was the embodiment of modern, international music, and yet he possessed a "Westernized" personality that remained reassuringly Chinese. Official support for this famous returned "Taiwan compatriot" gave Hou a unique cultural freedom, and he used it to promote a personal style that epitomized the impact of middle-of-the-road Taiwan culture on the mainland.

Hou was also the first to make music videos in China, producing a few rough clips with the Guangzhou director Sun Zhou in 1989. He became involved in the 1989 protest movement and acted for a time as godfather to the nascent mainland rock 'n' roll scene. An outspoken and independent critic of the authorities, he was forcibly "repatriated" to Taiwan in 1990 where he subsequently languished in relative obscurity, pursuing his passion for *feng shui*.

Hou's old associates and friends in the Taiwan and Hong Kong music business turned their own sights on the mainland in the early 1990s, both for its potential as a market and as a source of export-quality talent. Soon, offshore companies had up-and-coming mainland rockers and pop singers under contract and were producing slick music videos to promote them.

It is a process tried and true: a viable mainland product could be massaged with Taiwan/Hong Kong know-how and packaged for sale abroad. Success in the marketplace validates and reinforces the formula. The relationship that such exchanges foster is thus cultural, as well as commercial and contractual. While mainland dissident and nonofficial culture (be it intellectual or artistic) continues to annoy the Communist Party, Taiwan investors have helped it find a much-needed outlet. . . .

. . . In the late 1970s, Taiwan films gave mainlanders access to a lowbrow aesthetic expressed in their own language and cultural idiom. Most of the films screened on the mainland were mindless light comedies and saccharine love stories that dwelled on the trials and tribulations of the island's Westernized bourgeoisie. Yet as in the case of the music of Teresa Teng, the world depicted in these films was strangely inspirational: it showed a receptive audience that a modern, self-centered, and materialistic Chinese society was possible and revealed, for better or worse, what it might look like. It was just what the me-generation mainlanders of the 1980s wanted.

In the realm of art-house cinema, Taiwanese films had other lessons to teach. The "new wave" of mainland movies surged in the late 1980s with filmmakers like Chen Kaige, Zhang Yimou, and Tian Zhuangzhuang achieving international recognition. Around the same time, they discovered the work of Taiwanese directors like Hou Hsiao-hsien.

The mainlanders, regardless of their ostensible artistic agenda, were imbued with the rhetoric and vision of the Mao era and confident that they were the representatives of a new and independent voice in Chinese culture. They felt their work was epic in both nature and significance.

The films of artists like Hou Hsiao-hsien encouraged the mainland directors to turn occasionally their gaze away from the grand sweep of history and to instill in their films a more human dimension.

Bloated with their sense of cultural afflatus, the mainland directors were unsettled—and at times inspired—by the artistic vision of Hou, whose interest in the commonplace, ordinary people and the dross of daily life, his concern with memory and the past, was something they had repeatedly overlooked, or failed to appreciate.

The same is true in the field of literature. Pulp love stories and martial arts fiction from Kong-Tai were popular with the general reader, and highbrow fiction set on the mainland before 1949 inspired a range of mainland writers (as well as film- and television-makers) to explore the realities of contemporary China at a temporal remove. . . .

. . . Taiwan is something of a "missing link" for the mainland. In many areas, the significance of Taiwanese culture has been that it has built on and developed the values of the New Culture and May Fourth movements of the 1920s. Forced to eschew the radical leftism and utopianism that grew up in 1930s China (and that eventually won out on the mainland), the "Taiwan style" is more personal and intimate, more at home with the grand tradition of China while still engaged with the problems of modernity and Westernization. It allows space for the individual, as well as idiosyncrasy and irrelevance. While these things also concern mainland cultural figures, they are rarely of cultural usefulness to them per se. Ultimately, they are nugatory, little more than minor distractions from major ideological debates, power struggles, and factional strife.

But culture is not confined to these individuals, and perhaps the "yuppie" style of Taiwan will lead the way for the small enclaves of cultivated wealth that are gradually appearing on the mainland. There are the Ming-dynasty and Sino-Japanese–style tea shops, such as the Purple Wisteria Stove (Tzu-t'eng-lu), and Pekingese eateries like Ching Chao-yin in Taipei, which exudes an ambience and maintains a culinary quality that is still rare in north China.[31] Books using handmade paper and traditional printing are produced and reach a sizable audience of avid, well-educated readers. The classics of the West and culture of Europe and America can be appreciated with relative equanimity by the educated of Taiwan, many of whom have studied or traveled overseas. The 1990s has seen the first efforts of Taiwanese entrepreneurs to export (or is it re-port?) this elite insouciance to the mainland.

While Taiwan has prized itself for being a stronghold, oasis, and even a fortress of Chinese culture, maintaining and developing a tradition lost to the mainland for political reasons, it has also undergone a form of cultural ossification and kitsch conversion that have made it possible for Taiwanese artists and writers to play in a field of juxtaposition and irony in a manner not so readily available to their fellows on the mainland. The latter still live in a more stark ideological sphere, and their playfulness has tended to concentrate on subverting a body of political symbols rather than attempting to examine the nature of subversion itself. Since so few on the mainland are conversant with the legacy of anything other than the Maoist past, this is hardly surprising.

Although Hong Kong is a fundamental model and its influence is pervasive in the south of China, particularly in the neighboring Cantonese-speaking province of Guangdong, the Taiwan style has a more diverse impact. Of course, there is the larger Fujian, or *Minnan*, dialect region of Taiwan and Fujian Province and the general impact of Taiwan capital along the coast, but it is the power of Taiwan as a Mandarin-speaking, central cultural entity that gives it the greater prestige.

Taiwan encountered and became absorbed into the network of cultural globalization before the mainland did. As such, Taiwan-Chinese (*guoyu*, "the national language," as it is called on the island, as opposed to Taiwanese, *Minnanhua*, or *putonghua*, "the standard language," on the mainland) has developed a modern, fashionable and even postmodern vocabulary. It is a language that moves freely through the osmotic shield of the Taiwan Straits, at times enhancing and then obstructing exchange.

Thus, the import of Taiwan, like that of Hong Kong, is not merely financial. It is also an influence of modes and possibilities, providing glimpses of alternatives and otherness. . . .

DRACO VOLANS EST IN COELO

Perhaps more so than most other great ancient civilizations, China is notably lacking in the monumental evidence of its historical and cultural longevity.[32] Myth and symbol more than physical artifacts make up so much of what is often presented as proof of its thousands of years of continuous civilization.

Of course, the depredations of civil unrest, internecine strife, and willful vandalism have done much to demolish the remains of the rich array of Chinese achievement. The fragile nature of Chinese buildings, too, many of them constructed in perishable wood and tile, has meant that few ancient structures or even their foundations have survived. Most of the renowned palaces, temples, and houses are of recent provenance, at best the work of the energetic builders or rebuilders of the last great dynasties, the Ming and Qing.

Surveying the legacy of the Chinese past, it is easy to be drawn to consider those famous lines of Shelley's "Ozymandias," the poet's meditation on the fallen grandeur of Ramses II of Egypt:

> And on the pedestal, these words appear:
> My name is Ozymandias, King of Kings,
> Look on my Works, ye Mighty, and despair!
> Nothing beside remains. Round the decay
> Of that colossal Wreck, boundless and bare
> The lone and level sands stretch far away.

It is on a level stretch of sand surrounding the remains of another ancient civilization that Cai Guo Qiang has so often sought a place for his own monumental, tantalizing, and wisely transient work.

Cai Guo Qiang has been making his artistic presence felt outside China for some years, having migrated to Japan in 1986. He left the mainland at a crucial juncture in the contemporary cultural history of that nation. The post–Cultural Revolution thaw, the political and economic uncertainties of those years, and the genuine curiosity that Chinese artists had in the rest of the world allowed for a kind of openness and innovative naïveté that made the decade of the 1980s one of the most exciting and important since the blossoming of urban culture in Shanghai in the 1930s. It was a time when there was a tense, but vital, conversation with and about Western art and thought in China; it was also a period of enlivening spiritual upheaval and confusion.

Cai, like many others, had come to his maturity in a country wracked by political terror and cultural nihilism. The driving energy and need that many of his generation felt somehow to fill the vacuum created during their youthful years allowed them to venture deeply in the revived cultural landscape of China.

During the early 1980s, Cai, like a number of other artists and poets of the day, abandoned the urban environment of Maoist-Han China that had nurtured them and went traveling in the near-to-foreign western borderlands of the People's Republic, Xinjiang, and Tibet. As an artist, Cai was imbued with the spirit of adventurous playfulness that marked some of the most talented individuals of that age on the mainland, and he was fortunate to leave before being caught up in the deadening zeitgeist that has seen that spirit transformed into a cynical caricature of itself. It is that cynicism, as well as a narrow pomposity, that has come more readily to mark nonofficial mainland culture in the 1990s.

Born and raised in the ancient mercantile city of Quanzhou on the coast of Fujian Province, over the past decade Cai Guo Qiang has often chosen to trade on the history and mystery of his homeland. His cultural visitations around the world—and he has alighted in many lands, in Europe, Asia, America, and Australia—have been as frequent as they have been inventive. Over the years, his work has drawn inspiration from a number of sources: geomancy, traditional medicine, history, myth, and philosophy. In particular, Cai has used medicine, *yao*, and gunpowder, *huoyao* (literally "fire medicine") to create and investigate his artistic vision.

Cai's work is often transcultural as well as being culturally transgressive, and not only global, but often intergalactic. Starting in 1989 he has created a series of ambitious works entitled "Project for Extraterrestrials."[33]

Among these ET-oriented projects, the artist designed an evanescent addition to the Great Wall of China by igniting a line of gunpowder ten thousand meters in length in the desert at the Jiayu Guan, the gate at the western extremity of the present wall. The flaming extension shot heavenward for just one hundred seconds.[34] Unbeknownst to Cai, this spectacle for spacemen contained a double irony. For modern myth would have us believe that the Great Wall is the only man-made structure that is visible from the moon. Like so many tales related to that pseudoserpentine crenellation, this is a fiction.

The wall itself has a history of but a few centuries, and what is extant today dates mostly from the Ming dynasty.[35] In recent decades, much of what is presented as the age-old wall is a latter-day theme park version, reconstructed as a political symbol and a lucrative attraction for the tourist trade. Furthermore, according to NASA, from approximately six hundred miles above the earth, the Great Wall is invisible, as are other more recent engineering feats like the Suez Canal, the railroads across the Great Salt Lake of Utah, and interstate highways.[36] Cai's fiery elongation of the Great Wall therefore added illusion to myth by creating a momentary extension to an assumed structure for the delectation of presumed extraterrestrials. Even though the real wall remains invisible from the moon, the flash of that one-hundred-second postwall may well travel far into the future, visible in intergalactic space for centuries to come.

The artist's provocative manifestations have not been restricted to celestial observers alone. In 1995, as part of the centenary celebrations of the Venice Biennial, Cai Guo Qiang loaded a junk that had been brought from Quanzhou—his hometown and the port from which the Italian Marco Polo had set out on his return voyage to Europe—with Chinese medicines. He then piloted the boat from Piazza San Marco down the Grand Canal to the Palazzo Giustiniani. Thus, to use the title of this work, he "brought to Venice what Marco Polo forgot." In Cai's explanation of the cargo, he said that the herbal medicine was representative of the Eastern worldview, so different from commonplace Oriental manufactures, that Marco had been unable to bring back with him to Venice.

In the present installation, "Draco Volans Est in Coelo," Cai Guo Qiang delivers another multilayered message from the Orient, one borne aloft by a pyrotechnical dragon kite. Again, the artist in his transgressive role as shaman/showman evokes a work, in this case the dragon, a creation that bears in its fragile structure layers of meaning as both ritual object and mass spectacle.

The Chinese dragon, *long*, is born of a zoological miscegenation. It has the head of a camel, the horns of a stag, the eyes of a rabbit (or devil), and the ears of a cow (or ox). These are joined by the neck of a snake to the belly of a sea monster. It is covered with the scales of a carp and has the claws of an eagle and the pads of a tiger. Along its back are eighty-one scales. It has whiskers on either side of its mouth and a beard on its chin, and it carries in its mouth a pearl, the symbol of wisdom. Furthermore, the dragon can change size at will and, in an instant, can shrink as small as a silkworm or become so gargantuan that its form fills the skies.

By alighting on the dragon for this installation, Cai Guo Qiang has chosen one of the stereotypical and ubiquitous motifs of chinoiserie. Cai uses it to revisit both the cultural clichés of China and the apprehensive and exoticized perceptions of that country among Europeans. It is in the dragon cliché that East and West can confront each other, in a mood of formulated recognition and formulaic self-assertion.

Although the dragon has a venerable history in China—dragonlike creatures, the *kui*, festooned ancient bronzes—its rise to the status of imperial emblem was gradual. From the time of the Tang dynasty (seventh century), it was employed by the imperial house, and in the following dynasty (the Song, tenth to thirteenth centuries) it became the crest of the imperial house, a five-clawed dragon being reserved for the use of the emperor and his family and a four-clawed creature being a common decoration on the robes of lesser officials. In the middle of the nineteenth century, in need of an identifying national symbol as it reluctantly entered the world of international politics, the Manchu-Qing government chose the Dragon Banner. This Yellow Dragon Flag of the Great Qing Empire, Da Qing huanglong qi, as it was called, was first hoisted by Chinese diplomatic missions in the West in early 1862, at the start of the reign of the Tongzhi emperor.

Thus, something that had been the mark of imperial power became, in the age of the nation-state when the invention of individual national identities were de rigueur, emblematic of China as a country. As the rule of the Qing dynasty faltered, revolutionary patriots set on the overthrow of the imperial house rejected the dragon and its symbolism; it was regarded as being symptomatic of a dated and reactionary tradition.

After the Revolution of 1911, which saw the fall of imperial rule, the dragon was abrogated by nationalists as they formulated a new sense of self-identity. Yet as the century progressed, this ancient icon was gradually reclaimed as a mark of the country's nascent nation-building temper. Eschewed as a remnant of the feudal past on mainland China during the height of Maoism, it has been only in the last decade or so that the dragon has been embraced once more as being emblematic of the Han people, as well as a commercial icon with a high-recognition factor for tourists.

During the 1980s, the Taiwanese singer/songwriter Hou Te-chien's "Heirs of the Dragon" became something of an unofficial Chinese anthem on mainland China, Taiwan, and Hong Kong. Although a moving ballad that was even used by the student protesters in Tiananmen Square in 1989, "Heirs" had originally been written after the U.S. abandonment of the Republic of China in 1978 to express a profound frustration with the traditions that the song appeared, at least superficially, to romanticize. His lyrics describe a sense that many Chinese have had of growing up not secure in the reassuring embrace of the dragon but, rather, constricted by this snakelike totem and oppressed by its mighty claws. As part of the song goes:

In the ancient East there is a dragon;
China is its name.
In the ancient East there lives a people,
The dragon's heirs every one.
Under the mighty claws of this mighty dragon I grew up
And its heir I have become.
Like it or not—
Once and forever, an heir of the dragon.

The Taiwan-based essayist and cultural critic Bo Yang once remarked: "I really don't know why the Chinese people have chosen this grim, hideous figure of the dragon to symbolise our nation! In fact, the dragon can only symbolise the hardships of our people! Whenever anyone mentions 'Heirs of the Dragon,' my hair stands on end."[37]

In the late 1980s, when there was a mood in China of self-questioning, the authors of the nationally popular television series *River Elegy* identified the dragon as a malevolent and threatening force in the country's cultural landscape. As they said in the series:

Some say there is an element in Chinese culture that tolerates evil; others say the fatal weaknesses of the Chinese national character are worldly wisdom, fatalism and a docile acceptance of suffering. This is no accident. . . . Water is the lifeblood of agriculture, and it is the dragon king who rules over water. For this reason, this nation both loves and hates the dragon, worships him and curses him. It is a complex combination of emotions, as twisted as the form of the dragon itself . . .

You could say that [the dragon] is the symbol of our nation. But has anyone ever considered why the Chinese adore this terrifying monster?[38]

As the Chinese economy has boomed in the 1990s, so too have the aspirations to make good the nationalist hopes of the past. Once more the dragon has been transmogrified into a proud national icon.

The threat of the Chinese dragon has figured in the European mind for more than a century. There has been a lingering fear of what will happen "when the dragon wakes." In recent years the English author David Wingrove exploited this line of thought in his best-selling, multivolume epic *Chung Kuo*.[39] In this sci-fi tale Wingrove depicts a future in which the Chinese Han have overwhelmed the world and rewritten the history of humankind to blot out the existence of Western civilization. According to their account, the Roman Empire was extinguished in the first century A.D. by General Ban Chao of the Eastern Han dynasty, and that defeat led to an unbroken Han hegemony for more than two millennia.

Wingrove's novel chronicles the attempts by a group of Hung Mao (literally "Red Hairs," an old pejorative Chinese expression for the Dutch subsequently used to denote Westerners in general), the Dispersionists, to break free of the stagnant rule of the Han, led by the Seven, the ruling Council of Chung Kuo. Through armed rebellion, they attempt to rediscover their hidden history and build a new European culture, not on an earth colonized by the Han, but in the stars. The emblem of the Han ruling house of the Seven is the Yuelong, or Moon Dragon, a dark and ghastly insignia of power and deadening stasis that consists of seven dragons arranged to form a great wheel, their snouts meeting at the hub of the wheel, their lithe bodies forming the spokes, and their tails, the rim.

In his recent work, Cai Guo Qiang has been playing, even dwelling, on the image of the Oriental Dragon as shibboleth of the Western imagination. The dragon has become something of a self-fulfilling augury of change, threat, and difference, and Cai is relentless in his investigation of its looming presence. In late 1996, he exhibited an installation at the Guggenheim Gallery in SoHo, New York, called "Cry Dragon/Cry Wolf: The Ark of Genghis Khan."[40] His work consisted of a huge log raft that appeared to be held aloft by inflated sheepskins of the type used in fording rivers by the Mongols, rulers of the Yuan dynasty (thirteenth century) that once held sway over much of Asia and parts of Europe. The ark was seemingly powered by Toyota car motors running at full throttle, the unambiguous symbol of the Asian economic rise and technological thrust into Euro-America. The contraption was named the Ark of Genghis Khan, a menacing marriage of the biblical Noah's far more benign boat with the mechanism of relentless expansion represented by the Golden Hordes.

In the work Cai designed for the opening of the AsiaPacific Triennial held in Brisbane, Australia (September 1996–January 1997), the artist chose a more beneficent combination, melding the Chinese dragon with the Rainbow Serpent of Aboriginal legend. Sadly, Cai's pyrotechnic masterstroke, designed to explode magnificently along the Brisbane River, was thwarted by an accident on the eve of its ignition when a stray explosion in the warehouse where the installation was being stored destroyed it. At the best of times, the fugitive evanescence of Cai's work points tellingly at the transience of art, its creator, and its audience. In this case, however, the unwitnessed and premature detonation of his work fulfilled the artist's design in a most unexpected manner.

That experience has by no means daunted Cai in his search for ways to confront the deep-seated expectations of cultural difference. In "Draco Volans Est in Coelo" Cai Guo Qiang releases his dragon over the Øresund between Denmark and Sweden. But what is the particular dragon he has chosen? The Chinese genus of *long* incorporates many species: "the Celestial Dragon *tianlong*, which protects and supports the mansions of the gods, the Spiritual Dragon *shenlong*, which produces wind and rain to benefit mankind; the Dragon of Hidden Trea-sures *fucanglong*, which mounts guard over the wealth concealed from the mor-tal eye; the Winged Dragon *yinglong*; the Horned Dragon *qiulong*; the Coiling Dragon *panlong*, which inhabits the waters; and the Yellow Dragon *huanglong*, which emerged from the River Luo to present the elements of writing to the leg-endary Emperor Fu Xi."[41]

This is a conundrum that spectators must resolve for themselves as they con-template Cai Guo Qiang's fiery dragon in flight in the winter sky of northern Eu-rope. As we recall the line from the *Book of Changes* from which this work takes its name, "draco volans est in coelo," *fei long zai tian*, or "flying dragon in the sky," it would be good also to remember the reading for the last line of the hexagram Qian "The Creative," the locus classicus of Cai's work. It says, again in Latin translation, "draco transgressus est, est quod poeniteat," *kang long you hui*, or "the arrogant dragon will have cause to repent."

The ancient oracle warns against titanic aspirations that exceed one's true abil-ities, the perverse pursuit of which make it inevitable that a precipitous collapse will surely follow.[42] And it is at such a moment, at the point of soaring majesty, that Cai Guo Qiang's flying dragon, having achieved its own epiphany, explodes, self-immolates, and falls to earth.

"MB@GAME!"—A BEIJING SCREENSAVER

Opposite the Australian embassy in Beijing, there is a row of nondescript resi-dential high-rise buildings. They are indistinguishable from the hundreds of functional cement blocks of flats that litter the landscape of reformist-era urban China. The embassy, which is situated on Dongzhimenwai Road, is itself an un-carved block of another kind and of another age. An ominous low-lying super-ter-ranean bunker, it is both office and home to the Australian diplomats in the city. On the thirteenth floor of Dongwai Tower Block No. 24 that stands opposite the entrance to the embassy you can find the artist, Feng Mengbo, and his writer wife, Han Xiaozheng. Childhood sweethearts, they now occupy a small flat crammed with the remains of Mengbo's earlier career as an oil painter, and the technical clutter—VDT, laser printer, scanner, external drive, CD-ROM recorder—of his pres-ent métier as one of China's first computer artists.

A cardinal principle of Chairman Mao's cultural politics was the promotion of "revolutionary romanticism." He admonished artists to combine a politically pro-gressive attitude and socialist realism with a heightened style of heroic romanti-cism. It was that kind of unabashed cultural imperative that, during the decade of the Cultural Revolution (1966–1976) produced, among other things, a batch of revolutionary Beijing operas that combined a conservative cultural form of opera with semiorchestral music, Western-style stage sets and costumes, and modern, revolutionary themes. For many older people today, the music of the operas is little less than "the threnody of the [Chinese] holocaust," for it was these sounds that were the Muzak wallpaper of the violent purges and campaigns of that tumultuous time. For the children of the Cultural Revolution, however—and Feng Mengbo was born at the inception of that movement—the operas and the bizarre culture they represented were imbibed along with their mother's milk. What for their parents and grandparents were the shrill sounds of terror are for Feng and many of his fellows the surroundsound of nostalgia and childhood innocence.

Feng studied design at the Beijing School of Arts and Crafts before going on to the printmaking department of the Central Academy of Fine Arts, from which he graduated in 1991. He came of age in the video game era of China's 1980s reforms, and his first major works reflected his childhood obsessions. During the early 1990s he produced a series of works called *The Video Endgame Series*. Sated on the mindless repetition of video arcade inanities, Feng put his pleasure where his work was. He covered numerous canvases with the digital bric-a-brac of the video screen, reproducing in loving and blurry detail the effects of the small stage of the VDT on huge painted surfaces.[43]

Among the pictures in *Video Endgame Series*, "Long March," featured a Chinese figure, a blue-uniformed revolutionary sporting a Red Guard armband. This pugnacious street fighter often used as his weapons—variously as hand grenades, bullets, or nonspecific projectiles—crushed Coca-Cola cans, the symbol of another form of aggressive and romanticized revolution. Fuzzy maps of China, the young Chairman Mao, and heroes from revolutionary operas appeared in the series juxtaposed against, and sometimes in conflict with, the lurking denizens of the international video game universe: muscular ninjas, mysterious assassins, and dinosaurs.[44]

Another series of paintings in a similar vein was *Taxi! Taxi!—Mao Zedong I-III* (Lao Mao dadi) which the artist explained in the following way:

> In 1990, when I was still at the academy, I suddenly realized that the way Mao Zedong waved his hand at the army [of Red Guards] gathered in Tiananmen Square during the Cultural Revolution was very similar to the way people wave to hail a taxi. So I copied the image of Mao waving and put a common yellow taxicab in front of him—the kind you see everywhere in Beijing today.[45]

These paintings, playing as they did on the collation of high revolutionary icons with the hallmarks of late consumer socialism, were part of the popular deconstructive temper of the late 1980s and the early 1990s. Many commentators offered explanations of this wave of "political pop," as it was dubbed, that empha-sized its subversive subtext. I, however, regard the clever "sight gags" of this genre of art as less prescient than posed, not so much culturally liberating as commer-cially and politically strategic. By the mid-1990s, Feng Mengbo himself had moved on, abandoning the perspective of a video game voyeur staring passively at the screen, for that of the interactive surfer enmeshed in the digital world itself.

My Private Album, a family photographic album completed in 1996, was the artist's first interactive CD-ROM. It was the third work Feng produced with that title, evidence of his fixated pursuit of the topic. The first was a set of engravings; the second in 1991–1992 was the installation "Air Dry," consisting of handmade paper and netting. Begun in the autumn of 1995, Mengbo originally envisaged compiling "Air Dry" as a slide collection that would narrate the history of his fam-ily. In the spring of 1996, the quest for an uninterrupted recitation of his family history gave way to an interactive CD-ROM gallery of pictures. As he explained in his essay introduction to the disk:

> I wanted to give my audience greater freedom to manipulate my work. Be-cause mine is the story of a Chinese family, I felt that an interactive disk would help me break free of the constrictions of a linear narrative and bring the work closer to reproducing the palimpsest nature of memory itself.
>
> The three generations of my family crowd together in picture after pic-ture and stare out at me. Their gaze weighs on me. Birth, old age, infirmi-ty, and death all are reflected here. It is a space we all share. Humankind shares it with nature, its flourishing and decay, its alternating seasons. We don't crave startling changes. Perhaps all we ever wait for is the fresh green of another spring, or the first snowfall of another winter.[46]

This new work did indeed reflect the artist's loving obsession with his family. Long eschewed by many nonofficial Chinese artists, the family made an appear-ance more readily in their work in recent years. One recalls especially the can-vases of the Sichuan painter Zhang Xiaogang and the photographic gallery pic-tures of Wang Jingsong. Mengbo's own work is both more personal and naive. As he remarked,

> I am tired of art that strains to be new and different. I also despise those who pursue aestheticism. All of that affected posing pales into insignificance in the face of life itself.
>
> My art is concerned with the commonplace lives of ordinary people. I'm fascinated by the fact that despite all its travails, humankind battles on for survival, struggles to maintain its basic dignity, ever hopeful and often hu-morous. I've always been partial to works that express a spirit of optimism. For this I am grateful to my father. I remember that when I was a young boy,

we were so poor that to save money my father made me a bed. It was not only utilitarian, for he didn't neglect to shape it with beautiful lines. I also remember how carefully he carved out a five-pointed red star for me, knowing how much I loved that symbol, and how my whole family got involved in ever-so-carefully painting it for me.[47]

Produced under his own cyber rubric "MB@Game!" since mid-1996 *My Private Album* has been exhibited at the Fruitmarket Gallery in Edinburgh; the New Gallery in Graz, Austria; the Aaltonen Museum of Art, Turke, Finland; and at Art Focus in Jerusalem. Despite his protestations against "art that strains to be new and different," one of the primary reasons that *My Private Album* has led to such widespread interest is the very fact that an artist from mainland China, a presumably technically backward and politically repressive country, has produced such a hi-tech example of personalized artistic whimsy. If the Seagull Camera, revolutionary cultural paraphernalia, sepia-tinted photos of Old China, and quaint scenes of Old Peking in Feng's CD-ROM tour were replaced, say, by snaps taken from the family in *Muriel's Wedding* or were pictures of the dysfunctional Westie characters depicted in *Idiot Box*, one could hardly imagine the techie artist being feted in Euro-America and Israel.

Starting in late 1996, Mengbo returned to the yellow taxis, the *huangchong* (literally "locusts"), that had featured in *Taxi! Taxi! — Mao Zedong*. This time, the ubiquitous Beijing taxi appears as the central character in a new CD-ROM saga, that of the peripatetic meandering of a cab around the city of Beijing. In this new project Feng teamed up with a three-dimensional designer who helped him create the taxi truck protagonist of the story, and an Italian businessman friend, a long-term resident in Beijing, who provided much of the digital video footage that Feng used in his taxi tales.[48]

The novelty of computer-generated art in China and the exoticism of mainland Chinese computer artists overseas have doubtlessly been factors in Mengbo's international success. Revolutionary Chinese imagery has featured in the work of nonmainland designers for years, in particular in the work of Hong Kong designers and artists like the avant-garde theater group Zuni Icosahedron and the creative team working for the "Red Capitalist" David Tang who runs the Pedder Street Shanghai Tang fashion and accessories boutique. Mainland artists have generally been slow to utilize computers to meld the commercial with the Communist. For people in Hong Kong, that endgame became, in 1997, something of an end in itself. As with so much cyber alterity and video expression, however, one is left wondering whether the mediocre is the message. As yet another hip artist carves up a slab of stale revolutionary signifiers for more commercial pastiche art, you might cast a knowing wink at the surface wit and clever juxtaposition, but even the most elaborately worked digital braincandy often has only as much staying power as run-of-the-mill transient video images. They rarely deserve more than fifteen nanoseconds of frame.

Mengbo is not the only Beijing artist who has moved his work into the realm of cyberspace. While Jiao Yingqi, a lecturer in the Chinese Central Academy of Industrial Design, has also been making computer-generated art in recent times, the graphic artist Wang Wangwang has been using a Macintosh to create slick calendars and magazines since 1993. Wang's calendar "Remember Mao Zedong, Be Grateful to Deng Xiaoping 1994–1995" combined computer cut-and-paste images of Mao Zedong and Deng Xiaoping to great effect.[49] And although Feng Mengbo uses the Internet to find useful software and e-mail his friends, a clutch of Japanese art enthusiasts in Beijing have set up a webzine devoted to Chinese nonofficial culture. The zine is called "New Cyber-Chinatown," and it is edited and designed by a Japanese group calling themselves the Beijing Freeks. Led by Nochi Jun'ichi and Nishikawa Iku, their magazine has been on-line via the Japanese art home page of Rengeiza since late 1996.[50]

In their computer-cluttered flat in Dongwai Tower Block No. 24, Feng Mengbo and Xiaozheng carved out their own version of virtual reality. The solipsistic realm of the artist's world is summed up eloquently in the opening credits to *My Private Album*, which shows the Metro Goldwyn Mayer Trade Mark emblem, the roaring lion's head wreathed in the slogan "Ars gratia artis," replaced by Mengbo's own braying image. The couple have little to do with the society around them. Feng's art is displayed internationally and marketed mostly through his Hong Kong agent, the ubiquitous Johnson Chang. Even though Mengbo has achieved a reputation as one of mainland China's leading computer artists overseas, at home hardly anyone has heard of, let alone seen, his work. In 1996–1997, the fashion for the Internet in China was such that the common traditional greeting "Have you eaten?" was, among the monied few at least, supplanted for a time by a new line of greeting, "Are you wired?"[51] Feng Mengbo has been wired for some time; all he needs now is to get connected to planet China.

CHAPTER NINE

CCP™ & Adcult PRC

This chapter offers a perspective on mainland Chinese popular culture—both official and mass market—by focusing on certain aspects of the evolution and manipulation of contemporary advertising. In particular, it discusses some of the issues arising from the intersection of advertising and avant-garde/popular culture, on the one hand, and politics and propaganda (or representational pedagogy), on the other.

Against the background of advertising culture in contemporary mainland China, I venture some observations on the impact that commercial culture has had on the ways in which the Chinese Communist Party is promoted and promotes itself in the public media. The pervasive influence of the "Kong-Tai style" has been of immense importance to advertising and pop culture since the late 1970s and the ways that it, as well as the nontraditional (that is, nonsocialist) styles of promotion, have influenced party propaganda. Of particular interest is the role that the homegrown "avant-garde" that developed from the 1980s to the early 1990s has played in the party's evolving a commercial mien.

China's official (that is, state-funded) propaganda and entertainment have, for some years, developed a style of "corporate advertising." Much studied in relation to the U.S. mass media, corporate advertising promotes legitimation in a number of ways, including through the appropriation of the meaning of national and cultural traditions and the manipulation of what have been termed "paleosymbolic scenes" (the private and subjective meaning of scenes represented in terms of and linked to the public ideological context).[1]

The party has moved to present itself not simply as the ruling political party, *zhizheng dang*, an expression used to sheathe the apparatus of rule in a cloak of constitutional formality, but also as the final or ultimate historical choice of the Chinese people. Moreover, its multifaceted propaganda/public relations organizations increasingly represent it through a statist-corporate voice that offers basic definitions of group morality and ethics, consensus, coherence, and community in ways more familiar to us from international corporate advertising practice than Maoist hyperpropaganda. Not only does the party manipulate routine public pronouncements and orchestrate news reporting to achieve this end; it pursues its goals also through a range of national media entertainments and promotions. It realizes this through the party's Propaganda Department, the government instrumentalities devoted to public enlightenment like the Ministries of Culture and Television and Broadcasting (subsumed in 1998 by a new Ministry of Information Industries), as well as a myriad of subordinate organizations: party newspapers, Central TV, Central People's Radio, and so on. At other times, the party's messages are conveyed through nonparty organs and allied mass media that are directed at one level or another by in-house party committees. Such committees function as both surrogates for party authority and representatives if not mediators for nonparty interests. As a result, they are enmeshed in a complex of relationships that range from the purely propagandistic-ideological to the corporate-promotional.

THE VELVET PRISON OF CONSUMPTION

During the 1980s, the avowed official ideology—what the authorities presumably out of habit rather than sincere belief still call "Marxism-Leninism Mao Zedong Thought"—expanded to embrace a burgeoning realm of market culture. Issues related to consumerism, that aspect of social life influenced in numerous subtle ways by the economic reforms of the 1980s and 1990s, became part of public discussion as well as intellectual and dissident debate.

As early as the mid-1980s, the Beijing novelist Liu Xinwu had observed the inroads made on the mainland political psyche by the predominantly imported commercial ethos of Hong Kong and Japan. In "Zooming in on May 19," a controversial work of literary journalism published in 1985, Liu discussed the impact of a soccer riot that occurred in the Chinese capital on 19 May 1985, after the visiting Hong Kong team trounced the home side. The rioters, mostly young men, vented their spleen by overturning and trashing a number of foreigners' vehicles, identifiable by their special license plates. In one passage of his story, Liu reflects on international wire service news reports that compared the soccer hooligans with the anti–foreign Boxer rebels active in Beijing at the turn of the century.

> From what he could remember, Hua Zhiming [the protagonist of Liu's semifictional account] said it didn't seem like they were picking on cars with foreigners or Hong Kong people. He and the others were not, after all, the same as the Boxers who had appeared in Beijing eighty-five years earlier. Now *they* were xenophobes. Remember their oath?

Heavenly spirits, earthly wraiths
We beg all masters to answer our call:
First, Tripitaka and Pigsy,
Second, Sandy and Monkey,
Third, Erlang show your might,
Fourth, Ma Chao and Huang Hansheng,
Fifth, our ancestor Mad Monk Ji,
Sixth, Liu Shuqing the knight-errant,
Seventh, Flying Dart Huang Santai,
Eighth, Leng Yubing of the past dynasty,
Ninth, the Doctor Hua Tuo to cure all ills,
Tenth, Pagoda Bearer Devaraja, and the Three Princes Jintuo,
    Mutuo, and Nata
to lead 100,000 heavenly troops. . .

This chant is proof that in their own unlettered fashion, the Boxers wanted to invoke the force of every symbol in traditional Chinese culture. Hua and his fellow rioters, however, had no leaders, plan of action, organization, or aim. They were simply a mob incited by football fever. If they were to have a chant, it probably would have gone something like this:

Heavenly spirits, earthly wraiths
We all want to have a good time,
Let's evoke Xi Xiulan, Zhang Mingmin,
Wang Mingquan, Xu Xiaoming;[2]
Let's watch [the HK TV series] "Huo Yuanjia"
and "Love Binds the Rivers and Mountains"
We want jeans,
We want discos and Washi Cosmetics,
We want Sharp, Toshiba, and Hitachi electrical appliances,
We want Suzuki, Yamaha, plus Seiko and Citizen. . .

They are the most ardent consumers of popular Hong Kong culture and Japanese products. The real reason they targeted foreigners and Hong Kong people during the incident was that they disliked the way these people enjoyed special privileges in Beijing and flaunt their superiority. What the mob was expressing was a long-repressed resentment and jealousy.[3]

One of the central features of consumer culture is that through it shoppers are differentiated and treated as individuals via a so-called commodity self; identities and consumer profiles are melded and desires stimulated and directed by the guiding hand of advertisers. The design, promotion, and sale of consumer items, from the most mundane to the luxury, however, generally contain encoded messages that are aimed at appealing to a certain market niche or to buyers with a specific "economic profile." Whereas this aspect of marketing is readily seen in a highly negative light as manipulative, in the environment of mainland China in the 1980s and 1990s, to be "targeted" favorably by advertisers was a new, and generally welcome, experience. It was in marked contrast to the previous ways in which people were targeted—in political campaigns or when subjected to investigation. People had a sense that in the marketplace, there was room for the "expression of the individual" and a kind of "consumer empowerment" that had been virtually unknown in the past.

It was a period in which the individual, increasingly freed from subservience and fealty to the party-state, discovered the heady delights of individuated identity, of feeling special because he or she was being appealed to through advertising rather than simply propagated at by the state. Instead of living in a constant state of tension created by revolutionary agitprop, the consumer comes to live "inside a perpetual marketing event," to be a permanent participant in what has been called the "advertised life."[4] Advertising proffered a materialist "liberation," yet its promise seemed to lead to another form of subjugation and passivity just as beguiling as the utopian dialectical materialism of high Maoism. As Jiwei Ci observed in his study of the Chinese revolutionary market:

> Without asceticism, without altruism, without collectivism, hedonism knows no bounds except those imposed by reality, and these bounds do not dampen hedonism but only sour it. . . . China's utopian project, which had begun as ideologically sweetened asceticism, ended as disenchanted hedonism. What is worse, those at the anticlimactic end of this failed journey could not find even the comfort that comes from the confident certainty of a noble beginning and the strength therein to begin anew.[5]

The consumption of goods in an environment of abundance, even relative abundance, signaled radical change on the mainland. Yet it accorded with the government's argument on the issue of human rights that group economic rights (access to employment, housing, food, and so on) should receive priority over the sovereign rights of the individual (freedom of speech and association).

To be sure, the economic makeover of China may presage the much-touted growth of civil society, but arguably this will be one in which the individual is construed more as a self-centered consumer than a sovereign citizen. Advertising culture generally presents an image of itself in a realm of supposed liberal pluralism and harmonious consensus. But what happens when corporate competition feeds into patterns established by party-ordained ideological conditioning?

While differences—regional, linguistic, and ethnic—have been accommodated by advertising culture, party pedagogical advertising has continued to pursue its goals of presenting a narrative of Chinese history and the primacy of the party in that history, for the purpose of the direction and containment of the public. Collective voices, memories of resistance, as well as the histories of subordinate groups that were or are at variance with the party's narrative, are most often effectively excluded from the public realm, or so channeled and prescribed as to be little more than marginal.

During the 1980s, the issue of individualism—the philosophical and political importance of the autonomous self—enjoyed only a short period of relatively open contention.[6] Debates about unique human value, the status of abstract individuality, and the nature of imposed party constructions of the self cauterized the intellectual world and provoked government bans and denunciations from 1983 onward. After that brief flourishing of discussion and dissent, energies once devoted to the market of ideas were redirected into the stock market, and the rising tide of commercialization allowed for the reification of the individual in the public sphere not in terms of autonomy but, rather, as the subject of advertising propaganda—a matrix of stimulated desires embodied in the molded persona of the shopper.

The growth of modern consumer culture in mainland China seems to have occurred on two levels simultaneously. Apart from the impetus to satisfy the actual needs of shoppers, superfluous choices and symbolic shopping came to occupy a central position in mainstream culture. As we will see later, the party also enjoyed a purchase on the realm of hyperreality, its own symbols becoming part of the metacultural landscape of the flourishing commodity culture. Because of the cultural isolation engendered by censorship, even much of the imported advertising employed a symbolic language in tune with China's political landscape and removed from its "indigenous" Euro-American context.

The images, clothing, lifestyle, and language of the advertised life were in marked contrast to the sodden official ideology that still filled the media, but that is not to say that the creators of these ads were averse to using party- or state-sanctioned culture if it helped push a product. Indeed, a melding of old socialist icons with new commercial practices became possible in just this environment. By employing the tropes of nostalgia, state enterprises attempted to cast themselves as representatives of both national and consumer interests. An example of this style of agitprop appeared in early 1997 when the Number One Motor Factory, now a joint venture invested with a new lease on life by foreign capital, launched a national competition for an advertising slogan to introduce the remodeled "Audi–Chrysler–Red Flag" car. The original "Red Flag," Hongqi, a triumphant product of the command economy, was a gas-guzzling state limo that ferried high-level cadres around the cities of China from study session to plenum in the heyday of

Maoism. The advertisement took up nearly half a page in the weekend edition of the *Beijing Youth News* in early 1997:

> All Chinese celebrated the birth of the original "Red Flag" limousine. All Chinese have been proud of the brilliant glories of the "Red Flag."
>
> Today, we are appealing to every Chinese to take up their pens and celebrate the great leap of a new generation of "Red Flag" cars. . .
>
> **Cheer us on! Step on the gas!!!**
>
> "Red Flag" is a product that really belongs to the Chinese people.
>
> In 1958, designers at the Number One Automobile Manufacturing Plant combined their extraordinary talents to create the first generation of Chinese luxury limousine, the "Red Flag." They wrote the first page in the history of China's automotive industry.
>
> As the paramount make of Chinese vehicle, the "Red Flag" is not merely a legend in motoring history. It crystallizes the ceaseless faith, the tireless struggles, and the fiery emotion of the whole country over a period of dozens of years and a number of generations. It symbolizes the eternal glories of the wisdom and the spirit of the Chinese nation.
>
> The "Red Flag" is a National Car of the latest international standard. . . .
>
> We are determined to create a new slogan for the "Red Flag" that will resonate everywhere. We want to raise high the bright red banner of Chinese-manufactured cars, the banner of our national industry. We need a slogan from every warm-blooded Chinese. If you want to make your contribution to the resurgence of the national automotive industry, then pick up your pen and participate in our advertising slogan campaign!![7]

Other commercial efforts were more sophisticated and less directly redolent of party iconography. The success of the economic reforms was making a range of commodities and services available to successful individuals and groups that enabled them to go "lifestyle shopping."[8] These imagined and constructed "lifestyles," as well as the promise of satisfaction piqued by advertising, were commonly an amalgam of worlds represented in the electronic and print media, including everything from TV advertising and market-oriented party propaganda to popular U.S. and Latin American soap operas, music TV culture beamed in on VTV, B-grade movies from Hong Kong and Taiwan, and the published tales of self-made comrades overseas.

The imperative toward self-transformation has a venerable history in China that predates the new trends of lifestyle consumerism. Moral self-correction was, for example, a central feature of both Confucian and Buddhist thought. Since the late-nineteenth century, writers had observed that there was a pressing need for the Chinese as individuals and a nation to undergo transformation or reform, *gaizao* or *gaige*. Remolding the physical self or the body had been seen by many thinkers and political activists as part of the process of revolution and becoming "modern." Mao Zedong, among others, was an advocate from an early age of physical training and self-strengthening. In the 1990s, conspicuous consumption rather than mere physical prowess or political reform was taken as the fast track to renewal. The reshaping or accessorizing of the external self, along with a commercialization of the spirit, was now touted as a way of enhancing China's unique spiritual civilization, *jingshen wenming*. This was very much in contrast to the Cultural Revolution–period epiphany in which individuals experienced "revolution exploding in the depths of the soul," *linghun shenchu baofa geming*, or the imperatives of the early-reformist era to create the new socialist person, *shehuizhuyi xinren*, who was morally, intellectually, and physically, *de zhi ti*, oriented toward the party's program.

THE KONG-TAI STYLE

The pervasive influence of the "Kong-Tai style" has been of immense importance in this cultural amalgam. The expression itself is a shorthand for the introduction into China of Hong Kong and Taiwan advertising and pop culture from the late 1970s onward. But the commercial impact of Kong-Tai should not be seen simply as part and parcel of an overall influx of capital, the conversion of China into an avaricious consumer society, and the vulgarization of social mores. The process of cultural osmosis that has existed since the late 1970s is complex and multifaceted, and Kong-Tai has in many ways provided the mainland with the means for bridging the gaps with both its own past and its possible future. After the Communist takeover of 1949, Kong-Tai culture initially survived in isolated offshore centers, which increasingly from the 1960s and 1970s onward were transformed into wealthy consumer societies. Hong Kong and Taiwan developed the popular written and performance culture that had once been a feature of mainland urban life, particularly of Shanghai and Beijing during the Republican period. The literary ambience created by the novelist Zhang Ailing (whose works enjoyed a popular revival on the mainland in the 1990s) and the music of 1940s Shanghai, to give only two obvious examples, became essential elements of Kong-Tai culture in the 1950s and have gone through a number of revivals. Commercial styles of film, music, essay writing, and journalism flourished in these offshore Chinese centers and have provided indigenous forms of modern pop culture that infiltrated the mainland as early as the late 1970s when the first Kong-Tai films were screened inland.

In the 1980s, the Kong-Tai style, with its evocation of hip, modernized Shanghai decadence, worldly petit-bourgeois patina, and consumer sheen profoundly influenced the face of mainland culture. Writers on the mainland have generally had only a marginal interest in it, rarely taking it seriously even when debates in elite culture were sparked by issues related to commercialization. Mainland critics have generally been blinded by their own linguistic bias, chauvinistic prejudice, or lack of resources to appreciate the transformative significance of these formerly peripheral worlds.[9] The situation has been quite different, of course, in regard to elitist mainland attitudes toward the intelligentsia-based or "highbrow" culture of Kong-Tai.[10]

Many of the early advertisements for consumer items were imported from or inspired by Kong-Tai and Japan, the leading entrepôt cultures for the mainland. The influence of Kong-Tai in mainland advertising has been truly profound. The early ads in China, beginning in 1979, were clumsy, often little more than risible announcements for nonconsumer industrial products and manufactures like cement mixers and bulldozers.[11] But in the 1980s, as ideological justifications for the new commercial culture were found, advertising producers and outlets proliferated. Zhong Xingzuo, the novelist Ah Cheng's brother, established a major television advertising production company in Beijing, the Xingzuo Ad Workshop, which produced innovative clone ads in the style of Kong-Tai and Japan but with local color.[12] Similar companies, many of which were spawned by state-run film and television organizations, flourished in southern cities like Guangzhou. Due to ease of access, these ad agencies came more directly under the sway of Hong Kong archetypes and thereby set the standards of quality and innovation for inland provinces and the north.[13]

Kong-Tai had become cultural trendsetters because they were perceived as being modern, integrated urban environments, their communications more developed and their consumer cultures more sophisticated than those of the out-of-touch northern capital of Beijing. In reaction, in 1993 the government attempted to ban viewers using satellite dishes (guo, literally "wok") to watch Kong-Tai TV programing. Even in Beijing and Shanghai, however, people failed to take down their dishes, and many organizations argued that it was professionally necessary to keep the flow of info-tainment from stations like Star TV or VTV so that local programers and writers could enrich their own work.[14] Cable television, with its numbing tides of B- and C-grade movies and soft programing, was more readily accessible in the major urban centers, though satellite TV boomed in the boondocks and, throughout the early and mid-1990s, allowed audiences to feel that they were part of a virtual global village even while they imbued narrowly defined nationalist ideology (this was particularly evident, for instance, with the broadcasting of the 1996 Atlanta Olympics).

The consumer age also led to a new style of campaign, not a repetition of the theatrical political movements of the past, yundong, but ever new waves of media-generated and media-enhanced frenzies and crazes (*re, xianxiang*, and *chao*, as they are variously called). These crazes included the rise and fall of a broad spectrum of ready-made fashions, from the reconsumption of Chairman Mao that began in the late 1980s, to the Hula Hoop fever of 1992,[15] as well as the media-fired cultural debates of 1993–1996, discussed in chapter 11, "Kowtowing to the Vulgar." Manufacturing *re* (literally "fevers") became the focus of many publicists, be they official (the party, for example, attempted to engender a "fever for the study of Deng Xiaoping's works" in 1993 and new "patriotic fevers" at various times) or private. The style of these party-PR campaigns was imitative of Kong-Tai commercial culture, and much of the language used for the promotions, whether it be in the political or the cultural realm, was taken from the Kong-Tai media.

The Kong-Tai style has also had a major impact on the public face of the party. This is obvious in regard to the updated political paraphernalia of congresses and meetings, the new style of political slogans (now cannily recycled as "public service announcements"), and banners, as well as language, in every realm of the media and the Chinese Internet.[16]

PARTY INC.

In the 1980s, officially orchestrated national moments included or were encapsulated in entertainment specials like the annual Spring Festival Entertainment Extravaganza (Chunjie lianhuan wanhui), which was first broadcast in 1978 and became a direct national linkup telecast in 1983. This tele-event includes artists from throughout the country (and politically vetted nonmainland compatriots) and came to provide a yearly sense of occasion and the affirmation of shared values. Its successful production was a major political task for television stations everywhere in China. Whereas in the past, in the period of high-Maoism, party congresses and plenary sessions marked the significant media moments, during the reform era state-decreed holiday celebrations like 1 May (International Labor Day) and 1 October (National Day) and various "politico-tainment" occasions have been imbued with a greater significance and nationwide ramifications. Starting on 1 July 1997, Hong Kong Day also joined this list of calendarial entertainment celebrations that have over the years signaled the regulated and directed passage of national time.[17]

Soap operas with a message like the TV series *Aspirations*, discussed in chapter 5, "The Graying of Chinese Culture," and other series with redeeming themes about good cadres and the incorruptibility of the party, were developed in the 1980s and 1990s. They were originally modeled on party morality plays, theater productions, and feature films, gradually absorbing styles of characterization and dramatization from popular Kong-Tai, Japanese, Latin American, and U.S. series that were screened in China.

It was not until the 1990s that, for want of better terminology, "politico-tainment" or "partimercials" appeared. Party culture, even when packaged for television ratings, was not necessarily all that popular, and since it was in competition with more commercial (and in many cases foreign) programs, inducements had to be found to keep viewers watching. Taking the lead from the "opposition," quiz shows and newspaper competitions were introduced that tested the skills of participants in memorizing, for example, official party history, not to mention facts and figures related to the SAR-to be, the Special Administrative Region of Hong Kong.[18]

The conscious development of party and state "institutional advertising," *gongguan guanggao*, and "public service announcements," *gongyi guanggao*, as they were now called,[19] has been a gradual process, but awareness of these modified forms of propaganda has been heightened by the general evolution of commercial culture. This is particularly evident in the pages of journals like *Modern Advertising*, a magazine published by the Chinese Advertising Association in Beijing since 1994, and *Chinese Advertising*, a journal produced out of Shanghai since the early 1980s. With the establishment of Spiritual Civilization Propaganda Offices at the provincial and municipal level, the use of a new, commercial standard in state propaganda became evident.[20] When in 1996, the party launched its latest "spiritual civilization" offensive, which featured moralizing slogans exhorting people throughout the country to comply with road rules and to speak politely, huge computer-enhanced images, neon slogan boards, and advertising displays were erected throughout Beijing and provincial cities to help deliver the message.

Similarly, the creation of "corporate identities" for venerable state institutions developed apace after the mid-1980s and became something of a fad in 1993. The influence of the Kong-Tai mercantile environment was, again, fundamental. Since many state bodies like the Bank of China and China Travel, and publishing organizations like Joint Publishers, Commercial Press, and Chung-hwa Books, as well as various other state or pseudoprivate groups, engaged in business in Hong Kong, they were the first to construct a corporate facade, which was then introduced to their head and branch offices on the mainland.[21]

In journalism, the influence of the commercial style was also increasingly noticeable in the most successful of the party-affiliated press, such as the *Beijing Youth News*, the newspaper of the Beijing Municipal Communist Youth League discussed in chapter 5, "The Graying of Chinese Culture." Founded in 1949, it resumed publication after the Cultural Revolution–induced hiatus in July 1981. The editor, Cui Enqing, a protégé of Hu Yaobang, was one of a group of editors and propagandists whose number included figures like Wang Ruoshui at the *People's Daily* and Qin Benli of the Shanghai *World Economic Herald*, both active (though subsequently purged) in the 1980s. Their reformist style marked a sea change in party agitprop. Cui's paper, in particular, set a course that broke free of the invidious relationship between party-controlled papers and readers, encapsulated in the derogatory line "official papers are run by officials and subscribed to and read only by officials," *guanbao guan ban guan ding guan kan*. The nontraditional layout of the paper, the typographical fonts (often imitative of Kong-Tai models), the design of the pages, and provocative headlines immediately alerted readers—primarily adolescents and young adults—to the fact that this was not a run-of-the-mill propaganda organ.[22] The language of the reports was also in marked contrast to the hackneyed style of official rhetoric, and a form of easy-to-digest verbal fast food, *wenhua kuaican*, was introduced that constantly ingested the latest expressions and news gimmicks common in the Kong-Tai media and in the street culture of Beijing. These innovations paid off. During the first half of the 1990s, the *Beijing Youth News* became the most popular daily in the Chinese capital.[23] Between 1990 and 1992, the paper's income jumped 2,500 percent; in 1993, the paper grew another 300 percent.[24]

The government's push for more realistic reporting, for both political and social reasons, also created a tougher documentary style in newspapers like the *Beijing Youth News*. Whether covering stories like natural disasters (floods and so on), housing problems, or social issues, a "hard copy" style of journalism became standard in its pages. There were still numerous limitations in reporting on political or politics-related issues, however. Nonetheless, a corps of journalists, editors, and designers now existed in the mainland media who constantly negotiated a working relationship between the esoteric communications favored by traditional staid propagandists, as against a more newsworthy style of partial disclosure and pseudohonesty that fit in with the modernized urban style of contemporary mainland life.

At the other end of the spectrum, in relation to avant-garde culture, Kong-Tai has also played an inestimable role in promoting, financing, and exporting new and originally controversial cultural products from the mainland, as I have noted throughout this book.

AVANT-GARDE POP AND PROPAGANDA

The nascent avant-garde culture of the 1980s and early 1990s employed subversive strategies and engaged in an insurgent reworking of traditional party symbols, language, or histories. In this process, many of the artists functioned in parallel to official culture. If not working for state institutions, at least they often fed off their funding and structures while advancing their own agendas. Some of the cultural products of these artists were in turn cannibalized in the 1990s by party propagandists, especially younger media workers (some of whom also play a double role as nonofficial artists), to serve, expand, and diversify the interests of entrenched power elites, including themselves. In the continued, often fractious, negotiation between state and nonstate state culture, this mutual cannibalization led to the creation of a relatively more vital audiovisual pedagogical culture.

This can be observed with pop art, especially "political pop," *zhengzhi bopu*, as it was termed by the Beijing art critic/freelance curator Li Xianting in 1991. Pop art was one of the most common and commercially successful styles favored by the late-1980s and early-1990s artistic avant-garde.[25] Prominent artists included Wang Guangyi, who combined Cultural Revolution posters with Coca-Cola and Maxwell House advertising imagery; Yu Youhan, who juxtaposed, among other things, Chairman Mao with Whitney Houston; and Liu Dahong, the master of China's "reformist baroque." But for all the refreshing novelty and irreverence of early Chinese pop, its subsequent economic and political trajectory paralleled the rise of commercial art in other climes. Indeed, in 1997, Li Xianting laid claim to another style of flash, postpop consumer painting that he dubbed "gaudy art," *yansu yishu*, pictures that limned the face of China's newly rich, men and women who themselves were coming to appreciate the irony of the admiring mockery of the avant-garde.[26]

In one of the Shanghai artist Liu Dahong's early-1990s socialist comic works, *Spring Fills the Courtyard*, Mao Zedong was pictured in Yan'an lecturing a hall full of China's real and fictitious party heroes and martyrs. The figures include Lei Feng, a number of Beijing Revolutionary Opera characters, the model agricultural Dazhai Brigade Leader Chen Yonggui, as well as Yang Kaihui and Jiang Qing (Mao's second and fourth wives, respectively). Liu even insinuated a portrait of himself into the absurdist gathering.[27]

Even this type of send-up of party history through art has been purloined by more straitlaced artists who have used Liu's pop style to update party iconography. The Eighth National Art Exhibition in 1995, for instance, contained a number of works that were obviously inspired by Liu's Bosch-pop humor. In one of these, a work entitled *Group Photograph of the Age*, the PLA artists Tang Zhigang and Lei Yan collect party martyrs for a joint photograph at an old-style studio with the line "The People's Photograph Shop Commemorates Those Who Serve the People." Yet in this army painting, although the style is mock-playful, there is no irony evident or, presumably, intended.[28]

The appropriation of "pop" art for party purposes has been paralleled in the field of photography. The realist photography that signaled a break from traditional posed propaganda pictures first appeared among the "Stars" group in the late 1970s and is now regularly featured in the official media and state-sponsored exhibitions. One member of that avant-garde group went on to become a leading photographer and editor for the official media. She was Wang Miao, a friend of the unofficial poets Bei Dao and Gu Cheng (d. 1993), who became the head of the mainland-run *China Travel* magazine in Hong Kong in the 1980s. Similarly, in the mid-1990s, practitioners of the "new documentary photography," *xin jishi sheying*, acclaimed by writers like the sometime-unofficial poet Daozi as part of a postcolonial avant-garde, often had their works accepted in the mainstream and arts media.[29]

Of course, one could interpret the rise of such artists in the 1980s as part of an unintentional Trojan-horse strategy signifying an avant-garde infiltration of sanctioned state culture. One could just as easily argue that the position of such figures in the apparat has also served a dual (or multiple) purpose. As the years passed and the threatening innovations of the avant-garde became part of new artistic standards, these artists participated, either intentionally or by default, in the creation of a more inclusive official culture. All these photographers and painters have acted as a conduit for Kong-Tai–foreign styles introduced into the mainstream media. Those artistic milieus, increasingly accepted by educational institutions and mass media outlets, have in turn been adopted by many party propagandists to serve their own ends.

This can be seen, too, in film. With the rise of "new wave" films starting in the mid-1980s, the body of party symbolism, mythology, and style was used by artists for the independent and ironic investigations of cultural norms. This led to the creation of works like Huang Jianxin's *The Black Cannon Incident* (1985) and Chen Kaige's *Yellow Earth* (1986). The Yan'an mythology, as well as the Anti-Japanese War (depicted in works like Wu Ziniu's *One and Eight* and Zhang Yimou's *Red Sorghum*) were recast in ways that played a significant role in the repackaging and commercialization of twentieth-century Chinese history along the general lines determined by a party-defined nostalgia. These filmic reprises of party culture, albeit originally seditious if not tongue-in-cheek, have over the years aided and abetted in the reformulation and rebirth of party culture as part of mainstream Chinese culture, both on the mainland and in the Sino-Kong-Tai world, as well as farther afield throughout "Greater China."

Entertainment culture in the service of the party has played a role also in the decontextualization of history and historical incidents. Because the background and detailed content of events are blurred, it becomes unclear just how any one incident should be historically situated. This style of "fuzzy logic" is consistently used with the aim of rendering the party of today innocent of culpability for the past.

THE DIALECTICS OF AVANT AND DERRIÈRE

The great divide between high and low art remains, literally, academic. For decades, elements of high art have been feeding the wellsprings of advertising culture, as James Twitchell eloquently demonstrated in his study of the subject.[30] Meanwhile, lowbrow or vernacular culture has often availed itself of gimmicks, techniques, motifs, subject matter, and styles from high modernism. That avant-garde Chinese culture has similarly fed party adcult comes, therefore, as no great surprise. We are reminded of an observation made by Arthur C. Danto, a philosopher of art, in an essay entitled "Bad Aesthetic Times":

> An awful lot of what was introduced in a kind of anti-establishment spirit has — such is the irony of things — found its way into the highest precincts of contemporary high art, as if co-operation were irresistible, and the art world, like the commercial world, feeds and flourishes on what was intended to call it in question and overthrow it.[31]

The various efforts of mainland Chinese avant-gardes of the 1970s and 1980s (their "disturbatory art," to use Danto's expression) appeared initially aesthetically unsettling and "bad" to those nurtured in the tradition of the party's artistic canon. During the 1990s, however, as we have observed, the techniques and poses of the avant-garde were well on the way to becoming part of accepted standards, and they were also used as the means for teaching and communicating good aesthetics in educational institutions and the media by younger state employees, thereby aiding in the creation of an alternative or at least dilated canon of taste.

One is inevitably tempted to ponder future possibilities. When, for example, revivals of mainland Chinese 1970s–1990s modernism and postmodernism are manufactured in the future, will the canonized avant-garde appear as dreary and pedagogical in comparison with the revitalized and commodified mainstream (official and commercial) culture as modernism so often does today in Euro-America when it is juxtaposed with the more vibrant vernacular arts like graffiti, caricature, comics, and advertising? Similarly, after the first wave of avant-gardist inversions of communist symbolism in 1976 and the subsequent retakes of these inversions by commerce and partycult from the late 1980s onward, can't we also expect to see nonofficial artists and writers further plunder the new advertising culture for their work, to indulge themselves in party-based bricolage? If so, party artists — or avant-gardists working for the party on contract — may well respond with counterbricolage.

To keep abreast of the demands of the market — the international arts and film circuit, advertisers' needs, party initiatives — the avant-garde must perforce attempt ever new innovations of the stock of Chinese-based sign systems and

values. These are sign systems that have been formulated and articulated by the
authorities for nearly half a century, and the further appropriation of them by
the avant-gardists may give birth to the type of "second-degree kitsch" that is so
common in postindustrial societies, one that is "self-referential — a sort of
kitsch-kitsch. . . . It capitalizes on an acquired taste for tackiness. It is a popularization of camp sensibility, a perspective wherein appreciation of the 'ugly'
conveys to the spectator an aura of refined decadence, an ironic enjoyment
from a position of enlightened superiority."[32] Presumably, the avant-garde will
also compose anthologies of previous avant-garde strategies, thereby enabling
them to be recirculated into mainstream political and commodity culture and
create a nostalgic revival of post-totalitarian tropes that have been colonized by
the corporate-totalitarian state.

FROM SLOGANS TO JINGLES

By the 1990s, the marriage of propaganda and mainstream advertising was pro-
ceeding according to its own rules and conventions. In Shanghai, for example,
the boomtown of the post-1992 high tide of economic reform, some wily advertisers formulated methods for remaining politically correct while waiting for an influx of nonparty corporate advertising dollars.

   In early 1995, the Charisma Advertising Agency (Shanghai Fengcai guanggao
gongsi), a small local concern, featured party slogans on all its lit advertising displays along Changshu Road just outside the Hilton Hotel in the Jing'an District.
The displays, put up on 1 October 1994 to commemorate the forty-fifth anniversary of the People's Republic, carried small and discreet messages like "Long Live
Marxism-Leninism, Mao Zedong Thought!" and made it clear by featuring the
company's name and telephone number that, for a price, the slogans could be replaced with commercial ads by any interested party or, rather, company. The
Shanghai Charisma Advertising Agency was run by Shen Xuejiang, a captain in
the local PLA Cultural Department and an award-winning artist himself (specializing in nudes). Over the summer of 1995, his propaganda signs were, indeed, displaced by more profitable messages.[33] Just as the "attention engineers" devoted to
the creation of consumer culture in America were born of the Christian tradition,
so commercial propagandists of China like Shen Xuejiang were steeped in Communist propaganda techniques.[34]

   "The East Is Red" (Dongfang Hong), the Maoist theme song that for a time re-
placed the national anthem as the song of the state (as well as being the name of
China's first satellite), was used as a commercial name in Hong Kong for decades.
In the late 1990s, the Beijing Aerospace Dawn Food & Beverage Company, Inc.,

marketed its own "The East Is Red No. 1" health drink, "produced with the skill and knowhow of 'China's aeronautical scientists' and using 'saccharomycetes' that have orbited the earth for 15 days." A truly space-age drop.

Sometimes the commercial sector has treated party icons as considerably less than sacrosanct, but in ways that were anything but hostile. Indeed, this commercialization of party icons has played on the fact that many people feel comfortable with the images—and this sense of familiarity, driven home through the new commercialization, indirectly becomes a reinforcement of politico-cultural legitimacy.

For example, the 1997–1998 Goldlion (Jinlilai) Company's advertising campaign in Beijing featured small, circular billboards along the length of Chaoyangmenwai Street—from the Ministry of Foreign Affairs at Chaoyangmen to Dongdaqiao. On each of the red billboards—the color of the Goldlion Sock and Fashion brand is white lettering on a red background, reminiscent of the Cultural Revolution color scheme used for political slogans—the trademarked brand name "Goldlion" was displayed on one side, and on the verso was a picture of one of the heroes or martyrs from the official pantheon of revolutionary saints, including those mentioned in these pages, like Lei Feng, Kong Fansen, and Lai Ning, as well as many others. These "revolutionary ads" sat comfortably with the McDonald's and KFC outlets that clustered around the Dongdaqiao intersection.

Not even patriotic palaver escaped the machinations of adcult PRC. In early 1998, on Wangfujing, the busiest shopping street in Beijing, the Advertasia Street Furniture, Ltd., Company had covered a bus shelter with a promo for itself that bore a legend in English, reading "China Can Say YES to Your Brand!" (this was a play on the title of the 1996 anti-U.S. best-selling book *China Can Say No!*) and a sentence in Chinese: "Hand in Hand, Progressing Together, Let Us Let Your Brand Name Radiate Over China," *xieshou gongjin, rang ninde pinpai shanyao Zhongguo dadi*. This was followed by contact phone and fax numbers.

As we saw in chapter 6, "Consuming T-shirts in Beijing," lines from Chairman Mao's poetry and hoary quotations had been appearing on clothes since 1991. Although the use of dead leaders' pictures in product promotion was forbidden, as the 1990s progressed, Mao quotations appeared in TV ads and on billboards more and more frequently.

One insecticide, for example, was advertised with the slogan "Away with all pests!" *yao saochu yiqie hairenchong, quan wu di*! a line from an anti-imperialist poem that Mao wrote in 1963.[35] Similarly, the TV commercial voice-over promoting one make of vacuum cleaner warned viewers that "dust won't disappear of its own accord," *huichen buhui ziji paodiao*, a phrase taken from Mao, who famously declared that reactionaries would have to be swept away because like dust, they would not disappear automatically.[36] And in 1995–1996, the Great Leader's immediately recognizable calligraphic inscription for the expression "the People," *renmin*, was used by the Haicheng Pager Company in advertisments around Beijing that read "Haicheng Pagers, wholeheartedly serving the People."[37]

Meanwhile, in the south, the Zhang Xiaoquan Knife and Scissor Store on East Nanjing Road in Shanghai promoted its wares with a 1956 quotation from Mao, "Zhang Xiaoquan knives and scissors should not be abandoned even after ten thousand years!"[38]

CORPORATE COMMUNISM

The infiltration by Kong-Tai and international commercial culture and the co-opting of elements of the avant-garde have had a profound influence on the appearance of the mainland Chinese media. It is necessary, of course, to consider whether these developments are merely cosmetic. Has the commercialization of official culture fundamentally altered the nature of information exchange and the power structures of control and propaganda?

It is obvious that the mainland media and popular or mass culture have been transformed since the advent of the reform era and that there has clearly been an accelerated shift away from the staple saturation indoctrination and campaign-based propaganda of the past. That does not necessarily mean, however, that there has been a concomitant fundamental change in the polity. Rather, I would suggest that through broad-based appeals to national symbols and patriotic indoctrination—usually delivered via a mass medium that has appropriated elements of avant-garde art and global advertising styles—the ideological promotion of the party continues to stake a competitive claim on the public's attention and continues to shape psychocultural norms.[39] It also appears evident that the development of advertising propaganda in China perpetuates ideological practices in which the public is repeatedly invoked but also sequestered and repressed within the sphere of the mass media. As John Heileman wrote in regard to the introduction of commercialism in eastern Europe after 1989: "For now, the commercial is not an enemy of that community, but a defining characteristic of its aspirations." [40] In China, such commercialism includes promotional positioning, or at least posturing, by the Communist Party. In a culture of appearances like that of the mainland, one in which so much of what is articulated is by the authorities, culture is surface *sans* substance, such promotional tactics encapsulate a unique environment of commodified socialism.

It is often considered that commodity culture and the market have undermined the primacy of party rule in China. This is supposedly a process that has been accelerated by the opening up of greater public spaces and discursive realms, realms supposedly replete with possibilities for subversion, rebellion, and empowerment, as well as being the result of international political and economic pressures and the tripartite dialogue within the Chinese world—Sino-Kong-Tai. It is argued that the party's control has thus been weakened, or at least diversified, and its ideology gradually undermined to the point of becoming little more than window dressing disguising a basic nationalistic political and economic agenda (although in the late 1990s, some also argued that the party's agenda favored globalization and national capitulation). While these views may be valid insofar as they go, the party as an organization has also benefited greatly from many of these various pressures, including advertising culture. The party retains its role of domination, and through competition in the marketplace, its sign system has been enriched and enhanced.

A consequence of the new politics of advertising culture is that through a melding of the commercial and the political, the text and subtext of mass culture, the party in its multifarious forms has continued to create a particular version of social and political reality that subverts others. It has used (or, rather, enjoyed the political dividends of, since the party is not necessarily a conscious actor in this process) a seeming "democracy of images" to reinforce its own primacy.[41] It backs up its image as a responsible ruling government with a range of rhetorical and representational devices that prey on popular culture, language, and images—just as it did, for example, during the Yan'an period. Party adcult actively limits the spheres it attempts to appropriate, helps transform them into commercial or media clichés, and therefore desensitizes the public to their power. Whereas people as viewers, consumers, and citizens may to an extent become critical agents of these very clichés and repetitions, jaded by the info-blitz and content to indulge in private irony and covert rebellion, this does not necessarily free them from the enmeshing power of the images and the narratives behind them.

The party is not the monolithic source of signs and significance that it once presumed to be. By entering the marketplace of images, it has certainly witnessed a devaluation of its ideological currency, but that has not in the long run necessarily resulted in hyperinflation or sign bankruptcy. One reason is that because of the nature of party domination in China and its still relatively strict control of the mass media, the party is able to isolate itself from the wholesale ransacking of its sign system (language, symbols, and so on) by an advertising culture. Not surprisingly, however, in certain areas the party style appears ludicrous and old-fashioned, and in others a modern corporate identity is articulated with varying degrees of success (and that depends on which segment of the society one is discussing). Party PR workers—and that is how they have described themselves since mid-1998 when the party's Department of Propaganda changed its English name to the CCP Publicity Department—have absorbed elements of corporate culture and promotional strategies that are reflected in the marked shifts of its public presentation. Nonetheless, they are aware that once you abandon the language of cliché, trouble and confusion can ensue.

Generational changes have meant that the party's media outlets, as well as the media in general, are run by worldly younger men and women, people trained in the post-Mao educational environment who are more in touch than their predecessors with the social realities of the country. As I noted, some of those "propagandists" (the word has a quaint air when once considers the role of these individuals) also are active participants in nonofficial cultural activities. Through this new corps of media personnel, the overall party view of history, nationhood, and identity has to an extent been successfully refashioned and has become part of the basic range of signs, the paleosymbolism, that propagandist advertisers appeal to even when they do not directly represent them or even place any store in them. As Mihajlo Mihajlov observed in regard to Soviet propaganda in the past, "those very myths and fictions themselves become instruments of power even when the subjects cease to believe in them." [42]

Even this cursory review of the relationship between segments of the state-funded arts and propaganda industries and facets of the Chinese avant-garde reveals a dynamic symbiosis between the public realm and nonofficial culture. The tropes of new wave films, TV miniseries, political sloganizing, "T-shirt culture," and pop art, to name the areas touched on both here and earlier, provide intriguing evidence that just as the avant-garde has made a parasitical use of the party's wealth of symbols, so too "Party Inc." plunders the avant-garde in return. Both sides—if one can speak in terms of such a crude dichotomy—have a voracious appetite for the consumption of each other. The mutual cannibalization is continuous and beneficial to all parties concerned. It is a process that reveals that both the party and the elements of the avant-garde, those who are not directly politically rebellious, have evolved a piecemeal modus vivendi with the overall commodification of culture that is often strikingly innovative and reassuringly "modern."

By studying the way in which party culture has engaged with its nonofficial opponents and advertising culture, we can observe that many of the possibilities of critical public cultures in China have themselves been subverted. The growth of public spaces has not necessarily led to popular or avant-garde cultures becoming vehicles for the representation or debate of what are presumed to be public truths. Again, it has been argued here that appropriation works both ways. When basic power structures remain intact, the second round of appropriation by the party is one that offers interesting clues to the nature of the development of official ideological culture in mainland China over the past twenty years.

James Twitchell observed the consanguineous relationship of religion and consumption, remarking that advertising "is the gospel of redemption in the fallen world of capitalism," the "Vulgate of the secular belief in the redemption of commerce."[43] Here I would argue that adcult is also offering a measure of redemption and a prolonged life to Chinese Communist Party hegemony—a hegemony that in the realm of political/cultural symbols and practice may well outlive the party itself.

CHAPTER TEN

To Screw Foreigners Is Patriotic

THE THRUST AND PARRY OF CULTURAL NATIONALISM

In *A Beijing Man in New York*, China's most popular 1993 television series, the protagonist Wang Qiming, a man on his way to making a fortune after a train of failures and betrayals, gets himself a local American prostitute.[1] She is white, blond, and buxom. Wang decides to take out his frustrations on the hired help. While thrusting himself onto the prostrate sex worker, Wang showers her with dollar bills. As the money swirls around the bed, Wang demands that she cry out repeatedly: "I love you, I love you."

According to one review, this was a particularly popular scene with mainland audiences, especially with some members of the Chinese intelligentsia.[2] It was also the type of encounter that has a certain paradigmatic significance. It could be argued that by having his way with an American whore while buying her endearments with a shower of greenbacks, Wang Qiming was making an eloquent statement (and inversion) of the century-old Chinese-foreign dilemma.[3]

A Beijing Man in New York was broadcast at a time when both the Chinese authorities and segments of the population were becoming irate about their (perceived) position in the new world order and the attitude of the United States toward China.[4] To an extent, the series was a reprisal of the Boxer mentality, but one bereft of any belief system. It also represented, perhaps, the coming of age of Chinese narcissism and bespoke a desire for revenge for all the real and perceived slights of the past century.[5]

In their representation of China as a nation ruthlessly violated by Western imperialism after the Opium Wars, many literati as well as twentieth-century intellectuals pointed out that the Qing Empire's military and spiritual weakness had made it an easy prey to aggressive foreigners. Questions of racial and political impotence have been central to Chinese thought and debates ever since.[6] Reformist and revolutionary movements in China over the past century were born of a passion for national independence and strength. Most of the contending groups in China have, despite ideological clashes and heated debates,[7] essentially pursued similar nationalistic goals.[8] A number of issues central to the political struggles of the late Qing, particularly those that unfolded during the two reform periods (the Hundred Days reform of 1898 and the Qing reforms of 1901–1907), which revolved around questions like the need for political change, limiting central power, and new economic policies, have been the object of interest since the late 1980s.[9] Some mainland academics also argued that the overwhelming popularity in the mid-1990s of lengthy fictional works like the novel *Zeng Guofan*, about the late-Qing politician and military commander of the same name (the book went through nine reprints after publication and sold more than 150,000 copies),[10] stemmed from a mass yearning for a new strongman to lead China.[11] Others maintained that the renewed popularity of Zeng—a man excoriated by Communist historians in the past—came about because intellectuals, students, and others were searching for role models who could teach them how to express their own political aspirations.[12] To an extent, the revenant Chairman Mao cult of the early 1990s (discussed in chapter 12, "Totalitarian Nostalgia") was also a reflection of these popular sentiments.

The end of the cold war witnessed the revival throughout the world of national aspirations and interests, so developments in China certainly did not occur in isolation. The rapid decay of Maoist ideological beliefs and the need for continued stability in the Chinese Communist Party led to an increased reliance on nationalism as a unifying ideology. During the 1980s, the party emphasized its role as the paramount patriotic force in the nation, and it mobilized nationalistic symbols and mythology to shore up its position. These efforts were, of course, contested a number of times by workers and students en masse, as in the case of the Beijing anti Hong Kong/foreign soccer riot of May 1985 (discussed in another context in chapter 9, "CCP™ & Adcult PRC")[13] and the anti-Japanese demonstrations of the same year (aimed against what many perceived as being national economic capitulationism). In many ways, both manifestations were a precursor to the student movements of 1986 and 1989. By the 1990s, however, the situation had changed.[14] Patriotic sentiment was no longer the sole province of the party and its propagandists. Just as commercialization created a new and avaricious social contract, so too in the 1990s did nationalism increasingly became the basis for a consensus beyond the bounds of official culture. It was a consensus that for a time, at least, benefited the party (or, as noted earlier, should we talk simply of "the power holders"?). Both economic realities and national priorities required a strong central state and thus tended naturally to give an ideologically weakened Communist Party a renewed role in the broader contest for the nation.

Since 1989 there was undoubtedly an erosion of the authority of the party-state, yet it could also be argued that since then, attempts were made to reformulate and

broaden the basis of national authority as the ambit of what constituted "patriotic" expanded. This was particularly evident in the party's strenuous efforts at carrying out patriotic indoctrination and "state-of-the-nation education," *guoqing
jiaoyu*,[15] aimed particularly at workers and the young.[16] This movement was
launched by the party's general secretary, Jiang Zemin, after the Tiananmen
protests[17] and was pursued in various forms[18] before reaching something of a bureaucratic climax in late 1994 with the publication of the party's "Outline for the
Implementation of the Policy on Patriotic Education."[19] That document
summed up the aims of patriotic education as being "the invigoration of the spirit of the nation, the enhancement of national cohesion, the establishment of national self-respect and pride, as well as the strengthening and development of the
broadest possible patriotic united front."[20]

As is usual in the case of the announcement of such central party initiatives,
propagandists and educators responded to the document enthusiastically and
published the usual range of iterative laudatory speeches.[21] In particular, it was
pointed out that the main beneficiaries of the new push for patriotic education
were to be China's 175 million young people and adolescents, "the main force for
the construction of a modernized socialist nation in the twenty-first century."[22]
Enterprising businesspeople from Hainan and Beijing, however, reacted in a
manner more in keeping with present Chinese economic realities by announcing that in cooperation with a Beijing film and television company, they were
planning a patriotic theme park in the capital. "China's Journey over the Last
Century" was scheduled for completion by 1999. To be built in the style of modern edu-tainment displays, it would feature a century of Chinese patriotism illustrated by themes organized around the number one hundred. Thus, there would
be one hundred heroes representing patriots over the last century, one hundred
major patriotic incidents, one hundred patriotic achievements, one hundred patriotic battles, and one hundred artistic expressions of patriotism[23] that would be
arranged in a theme park environment that was itself a China in miniature.[24]

After 1989, a period of relative political stability and intellectual stagnation
combined with economic frenzy to create the possibility for a rough-and-ready
confluence of forces and interests under the umbrella of patriotism. Although
many prominent dissidents were banned from returning to the mainland and others were periodically persecuted in China—especially when their activities
among workers threatened the status quo—there were also those who could travel freely and become involved in various business ventures. One could speculate
that it was only a matter of time before some aberrant exiles would indeed be welcomed back into the fold as "patriotic overseas Chinese."

In the broader context of Chinese society, since 1989 there had been numerous indications of a growing disenchantment with the West and its allies. People

were sorely aware that the post-1989 transformation in Eastern Europe and Russia was not as rapid or as positive as first expected. As in many other parts of the world, there was a general belief that the West, its values, and systems had not made that much difference to post-Communist countries and, in fact, constituted an imposition of "Western" universalist capitalist values. For those who supported the 1989 student movement, there was the added realization that if China had successfully undergone a major political upheaval at that time, the nation may well have been faced with the disorder that now dogged Russia's rulers.

Coupled with this was the underlying sentiment that the world (that is, the West) owed China something. Past humiliations were often used as an excuse to demand better treatment from the industrially developed nations. This was obvious, for example, in official responses to the question of China's human rights abuses, in particular with the publication of the white paper *Human Rights in China* in 1991.[25] The popular Mao cult that flourished in the early 1990s also had a perceptible antiforeign edge to it. Mao ruled a China that was effectively closed off from the West, and he instilled in the nation a sense of pride and self-worth, something people felt they had lost as the result of Deng Xiaoping's open door and reform policies. Even though Deng was admired for what he had done for the economy, Mao was revered for, among other things, keeping the superpowers, the United States and the Soviet Union, at bay.[26]

The demand for better treatment from the international community came to the fore during China's Olympic bid in 1993 when the mainland media called on the rest of the world to "give China a chance," *gei Zhongguo yige jihui.* The internal propaganda campaign for a Beijing Olympics emphasized the primacy of a unique Chinese national spirit and the ability of the people to "move mountains and drain the oceans" in their quest to create a perfect homeland, *jiayuan,* a paradise on earth.[27] The eventual failure of the Chinese bid was deemed to have been orchestrated by Western bullies, and the Olympic Committee's decision to give the 2000 Olympics to Sydney was seen as an affront to Chinese national sentiment (not to mention a lost business opportunity).[28]

While nationalist sentiment was being repackaged and flourished, the clampdown on oppositionist opinion in the media after 1989 meant that few divergent voices had an outlet in any wide-based public forum. Mass opinion was thus formed either by the salacious tabloid press and electronic media or by classified publications and news sources that reinforced accepted party dogma and political-cultural stereotypes. Although intellectuals regrouped and produced a number of significant publications after 1992 (some of which were banned in 1996), the diversification of the Chinese media and the wholesale commercialization of the nonpropaganda media—not to mention constant threats of closure by the authorities—meant that their impact was marginal at best. Without public intellectuals or open debate, few of the more extreme opinions that did appear—for example, those of Yuan Hongbing in his 1990 *Winds in the Wilderness* (discussed later), Wang Shan in his 1994 book *China Through the Third Eye*,[29] or Song Qiong and others' 1996 anti-American best-seller *China, Just Say No!*[30]—were challenged except, ironically, by pro-party propagandists.

At the same time, as the older comrades and their dated politics faded from the scene, a major generational and ideological shift was becoming irreversible. Until the early 1990s, narrow sectarian fundamentalists—people like the veteran propagandists Hu Qiaomu (now deceased), Deng Liqun, and Xu Weicheng (now defunct), as well as figures like Wang Zhen (now deceased)—favored some form of ideological constraint on the unbridled passions of national aspiration and economic power. But the Maoist worldview that gave China some kind of vision had been dismantled and lacked committed younger advocates.[31] In general, what remained was a crude pre–World War I positivism that was revised in the late 1970s and further enhanced by the international media's mythmaking and hype regarding the economic and cultural rise of "East Asia." There was now a near universal faith in science, material wealth, capitalism, and national strength. It was a faith tempered by neither the moderating influences of traditional culture nor, for all the talk about China's burgeoning middle class, any modern bourgeois angst. Nationalistic and ultrapatriotic sentiments could now be found across the political spectrum, and we can speculate that many of the individuals and groups who held such views had a following in the broader society. This chapter will attempt to reflect the range of expression that such sentiments took in the first half of the 1990s.

ORIENTAL ORIENTALISM

It's a state of mind / It's peace of mind / If you don't mind / Orientalism.
It's East and West / Forget the rest / So can you guess? / Orientalism.[32]

Much of the more serious cultural/nationalist debate that took place in the mainland Chinese media in the early 1990s appeared in the pages of a number of established and new journals and papers based mostly in Beijing. These included *Reading*, the oldest "liberal" monthly founded in the late 1970s, which had weathered the extraordinary ideological upheavals of the reform period; the two main organs of Chinese-style "national studies," *guoxue*,[33] *Chinese Culture* and *Scholar*;[34] *Orient*, the joint effort of a coalition of cultural conservatives and "liberals" (closed down in late 1996); *China Reader's Weekly*; *Studies*; *Strategy and Management*, a publication edited by younger conservatives with rumored People's Liberation Army backing and diverse business interests; and *Frontiers*, since 1997 a key forum for debate published in Hainan.[35] The last four publications came to prominence after the 1993 surge in the Chinese print media mentioned in chapter 7, "Packaged Dissent."

Articles and dialogues published in the more easily labeled "liberal" journals like *Reading, Orient,* and *Frontiers* generally skirted the issues of one-party rule and authoritarianism/totalitarianism or discussed them only in the oblique, eso-teric code common to the media of a censorious political environment. Nonethe-less, their editors, working under considerable constraints and constant pressure from party organs, maintained a forum for rational and informed debate that was unique in post-1949 Chinese history. The articles they published on the question of nationalism often argued for a balanced approach that provided a much-need-ed antidote to populist as well as utilitarian extremism.[36] *Strategy and Manage-ment* was more direct in its approach to the issues of nationalism and political power. This is not to say, however, that it was prepared to take issue editorially with the problem of authoritarianism; *on the contrary*, the general tenor of many articles in its pages on the subject of nationalism[37] was that the single-party state you have is better than the multiparty freewheeling chaos you do not. Its editors and many of its writers were troubled by the lack of morals, spiritual vacuity, and cultural lawlessness in contemporary China.

In the first issue of *Strategy and Management*, Wang Xiaodong, one of the journal's editors writing under the pen name Shi Zhong, took issue with Samuel P. Huntington's much-publicized, though academically risible, 1993 essay "The Clash of Civilizations." Wang rebuffed Huntington's notion that future world conflicts would be primarily cultural in nature, dividing as he did the world into the West, a Muslim cultural bloc, and a Confucian cultural sphere.[38] Wang de-nied that China could meaningfully be classified as a Confucian nation/civiliza-tion and asserted that the Chinese had no desire to Confucianize the rest of the world. He noted that Western values and civilization were generally welcomed by the Chinese, apart from instances in which their transmission involved econom-ic or other forms of imperialism. Any future conflicts, he went on to state, would depend primarily on questions of economic competition. Ideological, cultural, and other clashes, Wang claimed, are and would remain little more than a guise for conflicts of national interest.[39] He argued that China would come into con-flict with other powers because of its present economic strength and potential, factors that made it appear to be a threat to the United States. As support for his viewpoint, he quoted Mahathir bin Mohamad, the prime minister of Malaysia, who commented that following the collapse of the Soviet Union and the emer-gence of one superpower, small countries had no choice but either to be obedi-ent to that power or to resist it.[40]

Wang noted that during the past decade, Chinese intellectuals generally sought foreign nostrums as a solution to the nation's dilemmas. According to these intellectuals, the greatest obstacle to progress was a vaguely defined collection of "national traditions." But Wang questions: What happens if the Chinese come to perceive that there are active exterior obstacles to their efforts "to garner from the outside"? Such obstacles might take the form of trade or migration restrictions. In his argument in favor of developing "economic nationalism," Wang also quoted from *Yellow Peril*, a popular 1991 samizdat novel by Bao Mi (Wang Lixiong) which presented an apocalyptic view of China's future.[41] The novel is about a cataclysmic war that results from both an economic-*cum*-political struggle for resources in south China and international conflicts.[42] *Yellow Peril* depicted a disastrous scenario for China's future and was banned from publication on the mainland, although it was read widely either on computer disk or in printout form.

Gateway to Doomsday, a more positive futuristic novel—called in Chinese a "prophetic novel"—by the prominent playwright Qiao Liang, was published in mid-1995. Printed by the leading army Kunlun Publishing House in Beijing, Qiao's novel did not have to make the underground rounds.[43] Set mainly in Hong Kong, *Doomsday* tells of a couple, a Chinese army computer genius and his Sino-Russian lover, who conspire to save the world from the formidable threat of war, terrorists, and a deadly "apocalypse" computer virus so virulent that it infects the world's computers "like AIDS," with, of course, the exception of China which has surrounded itself with an electronic *cordon sanitaire*.[44] The Eurasian beauty, Chan, who constantly lubricates her talents with Bloody Marys, has the power to foretell the future and thereby helps her Chinese lover, Li Han, guide events to a positive outcome. Interestingly, Chan's clairvoyance is manifested only when she has sex. It would appear that in this instance at least, screwing a foreigner was good for everyone concerned.[45]

The novel is set on the cusp of the millennium, at a time when the world has been freed from territorial imperialism only to be overwhelmed by economic colonialism. China, once a victim of foreign aggression, is now a leading economic giant that symbolizes hope for the rest of humankind.[46] Among other things, *Doomsday* features an astronaut who is circling the globe as the new age dawns and who signs off his last broadcasts in 1999 with the words: "Good night America . . . good morning to the East. Good morning Asia."[47]

Fictional scenarios aside, other writers for *Strategy and Management* like Xiao Gongqin, the Shanghai-based historian who came to prominence in the late 1980s as a supporter of "new authoritarianism," were more restrained than Wang Xiaodong and not as imaginatively confident as Qiao Liang. In the early 1990s, Xiao repeatedly issued warnings about the dangers of weakened central govern-

ontrol. He pointed out that local mafias, corrupt police, and economic car-
ers would soon have China in a stranglehold and that Beijing would be incapable of imposing its will. Xiao saw no solution to the nation's problems in Western paradigms or in any political alternatives other than firm party rule. He also
wrote about the positive role that nationalism could play during the present period of "ideological transformation."[48]

Wang Hui, another critic of Huntington and the editor of *Reading* (since
1996), commented in *Strategy and Management* that the cultural reductionism
of Huntington's argument and the critical tendencies of Orientalism, introduced
into China in the early 1990s, were conflated by Chinese intellectuals and added
fuel to the debates on nationalism. Wang was also a prescient critic of the commercialization of nationalist debate in China and utopian views of globalization.[49] One of the most important issues raised by writers like Wang Hui was that
Western theories, including much postmodernist theorizing, although challenging and relatively subversive in the context of academia in the West, could readily be used to advance or consolidate cultural conservatism in the Chinese environment.[50] Or as the Shanghai academic and cultural critic Xu Jilin remarked,
postmodernism could become yet another "subterfuge in the cultural cold war"
with the West.[51]

In early 1995, the London-based academic Zhao Yiheng (Henry Zhao) published a lengthy critique of how Western "post studies," *houxue*, had contributed
to the development of a new conservatism among mainland intellectuals.[52]
Through the 1990s, there was an expanding literature on a plethora of Sino-post-
modernisms (poststructuralism, postcolonialism, and so on), and as critics like
Zhao noted, such theoretical strategies were more often than not used to validate
the transformative power of mass commercial culture (see the following chapter)
and negate the independent and critical role of the informed intellectual as if it
were some dated post-Enlightenment artifact.

Since the 1920s, independent or liberal intellectuals, *ziyou zhishifenzi*, had
been the bane of political authoritarians, be they Communist or Nationalist. The
small and cautious group of nonaligned thinkers and writers who came to public
prominence during the 1980s were routed in 1989, as He Xin gleefully observed
(see the opening section of chapter 3, "Traveling Heavy"), and in the 1990s, the
independent thinker was recast by mainland disciples of po-mo as the vanguard
of a cultural and ideological cargo cult of the West, the agents of moribund Enlightenment values, liberalism, and a bourgeois social conscience who had written themselves out of history.

In private, some writers claimed that the hue and cry over theory in the 1990s,
of which China was a part, was a far more complex battle for intellectual and ideo-

logical supremacy (*zhengduo huayuquan* is the common formulation in Chinese, literally "the struggle for discursive authority") launched by up-and-coming younger academics. At the same time, theoretical approaches like postcolonialism could be used to affirm the value of local and nativist cultural elements (*bentuhua*, or "sinicization") and to reject "Western" thought (sociocultural as well as political) as being colonizing, imperialist, and unsuited to Chinese realities.

Many of the more active and public younger intellectuals were interested in applying à la mode theory to issues of national sovereignty and cultural integrity.[53] By redefining intellectual debate in terms of "Chineseness," these mainland disciples of po-mo[54] could give conservative and nationalistic discourse a cloak of fashionable and modern (what, after all, was more "modern" than the latest Euro-American theories?) respectability. In late 1995, their cause was aided by proponents of traditional "national studies," philology, Confucian philosophy, and so on, who opined that Western-trained and Anglo-America–based intellectuals were out of touch with Chinese realities. They were accused of indulging in "pidgin academics," *yangjingbang xuefeng*, and thus were irrelevant to the discussions of mainland cultural development.[55]

Given the cultural maelstrom on the mainland, it was little wonder then that the works of Edward W. Said (in particular, *Orientalism*, 1978, and *Culture and Imperialism*, 1993) were so well received. Said's writings on Orientalism and the imperialist West's creation and control of Middle Eastern and Asian Others were prominent in intellectual debates dating from mid-1993. In the January 1994 issue of *Reading*, scholars at a roundtable discussion of the issue averred that the analysis of Orientalism was pursued only by marginalized Western and minority intellectuals who were trying to validate their own friable cultural positions in mainstream academia. Sun Jin, a scholar of theology and associate professor at the Lu Xun Literary Academy in Beijing, expressed what, at the time, seemed to be a fairly widely held view: when China becomes a truly strong nation, niggardly theoretical and intellectual questions like Orientalism, postmodernist discourse, and the talk of a global center and periphery will be easily dealt with. Then, and only then, Sun argued, would China enter into an equal dialogue with the world. Indeed, by that time, one may presume that the Chinese term for Orientalism, *dongfangzhuyi*, will have acquired a very new meaning, that of "the ideology of Oriental supremacy."[56]

Evidence of just such an approach appeared in the official journal *Liaowang* in late 1995. The author of the piece was Zhang Kuan, a U.S.-trained scholar of German studies who had written influential articles on Said's work for the mainland press.[57] He posited the formulation of a self-defining Orientalism to combat the "Orientalizing West":

Modern Western humanities and social sciences have been replete with colonialist discourse; indeed, it has also deeply influenced modern scholarship within China itself. This is evident in the way in which we constantly accept what the West touts as moral standards. We follow the requirements and signals of Westerners in expounding on all kinds of specific Chinese problems.

For some time, we have lacked the courage to challenge and check Western hegemonic and colonial discourse. Thus, one of the reasons we seem so passive when carrying out concrete negotiations with Western countries over issues like human rights, or intellectual property rights in the market economy, is that we have not come up with a mode of exposition that completely casts off Western hegemonic discourse.

During the present age of reform and the open door, in a period in which the formation of a Chinese socialist market economy is enmeshing us in international practice, the questions of preserving and upholding our own subjectivity in cultural terms and reinforcing identification with our own culture so as to enable victory in future international conflicts rightly deserve serious consideration by all responsible Chinese intellectuals.[58]

Having cast off the collectivism of their predecessors, they did not wish to be forced into a patriotic straitjacket by market nationalism. For independent Chinese intellectuals, the issue of whether they were individuals or part of the "responsible" "we" that Zhang Kuan talks about was also a matter worthy of serious consideration.[59] Zhang was taken to task by academics, both inside and outside China, for his blithe and politically self-serving statements. It was evident to many that yet again in the history of cultural and political debate in China, the Occidental Other, this time po-mo theory, was being framed in an internal elitist dialogue concerned with particularized Chinese problems, in the process currying favor with the power holders and the mass publishing market.

As Xiaomei Chen commented in her discussion of the "Occidentalist" habits of China's cultural elite:

> The West is also used as a powerful image against the official conservative Other by the official radical Self, who, ironically, as recent history has proven, allied itself with the conservative Other in its suppression of the Chinese people. Here we see the full implication of the problematic and paradoxical function of an Occidental Other in contemporary Chinese society.[60]

When observing the vitriol and mental acrobatics that is part of the use of po-mo in China, another insightful comment by Chen comes to mind:

> One can perhaps even argue that modern Chinese history, and China's problematic and paradoxical relationship with a Western Other, can be

seen as a highly theatrical event, in which the Chinese people play the roles of the Occidental Others. . . . The Chinese actors and actresses assume Occidental voices, wear Occidental costumes, while speaking, all the time, for the political interests of the Oriental Self.[61]

The po-mo-esque dimension of this theatricality surfaced as early as the 1970s when, for example, Roland Barthes commented in abstract delight on the far-from-sanguine anti–Lin Biao, anti-Confucius campaign, the *pi-Lin pi-Kong* movement, of which he said:

> In Chinese, Pilin-Pikong tinkles like a happy bell, and the campaign expresses itself in newly invented games: a cartoon, a poem, a skit by children, during which suddenly, between two dances, a little girl, all made-up, strikes down the ghost of Lin Piao; the political Text (but only that) causes these tiny "happenings."[62]

Such slick and obtuse observations were but a precursor to much that was written by some 1990s disciples of po-mo as the Text of China. Whether regarded as revolutionary, reformist, reactionary, or what-have-you, it has been read, misread, reread, or, when it hinders the progress of imposed theoretical constructs, simply left unread.

It was evident from the debates surrounding Sino-po-mo in the mid-1990s that a number of mainland intellectuals—many of whom had a self-image that could be summed up with a range of adjectives from disaffected, marginal, oppressed, and self-pitying to haughty and careerist—were using po-mo or traditionalist critiques to create a "discursive space" in the highly competitive intellectual marketplace of China. These writers staked out their authenticity as genuinely engaged intellectuals uncorrupted by Western experience, as opposed to the "pseudoforeign," *jia yangguizi*, but racially Chinese academics holed up in Euro-America. Thus, in their early stages (from the late 1980s to the mid-1990s), many of the debates concerning major new intellectual issues were reduced to the level of power play, personal attack, and mean-spirited denunciation. It appeared to be a woeful rehearsal of the politicized history of intellectual discussion that had begun in the twilight years of the Qing dynasty, a century earlier.

SELF-HATE AND SELF-APPROBATION

The religion of the Chinese today is cheating, deceit, blackmail and theft, eating, drinking, whoring, gambling and smoking. . . . We think any honest, humble gentleman a fool and regard any good person who works hard and demands little in return as an idiot. Crooks are our sages; thieves and swindlers our supermen . . . there are no greater cynics than the Chinese people.[63]

Many Chinese intellectuals pride themselves on being the harshest and most perceptive critics of themselves. There is a powerful, if hard-to-define, tradition of self-loathing in modern Chinese history. Its roots can perhaps be traced back to the late-Ming dynasty (sixteenth and seventeenth centuries) when some literati used the language of Buddhism and Confucian thought to engage in introspection and self-reflection.[64] This impulse to self-criticism surfaced again in the mid-nineteenth century, but now, given the context of China's confrontation with the Western imperial powers, it was a critique aimed at determining blame for the Qing dynasty's weakness and corruption. For more than a century, there has been a vigorous trend in both popular and intellectual circles to denounce the Chinese and China. In 1897, Tan Sitong, a young political reformist who was later martyred for his activities, saw the fate of the country in Buddhist terms:

> A calamitous destiny is now unfolding in China. It has been brought about by the evils committed by generations of tyrannical rulers, and also by the karmic deeds of the people during incalculable cycles of transmigration. When I look at China, I know that a great disaster is at hand.[65]

Similar sentiments were reflected in the writings and comments of a number of prominent essayists, journalists, and academics throughout the century (the names Li Zongwu, Xuan Yongguang, Lu Xun, Li Ao, Bo Yang, Lung-kee Sun, Long Yingtai, Liu Xiaobo, Li Jie, and Xiao Xialin come readily to mind),[66] and it is common to hear similar remarks whenever politics, the economy, culture, or the future of the nation are discussed in private. Self-contempt was also a useful weapon in the armory of an intellectual elite, whose writings often show an unseemly pleasure in condemning the nation and their fellow countrymen and women for what are often their own defects. This is, of course, hardly surprising given the fact that many members of the twentieth-century Chinese educated classes perceived the nation's cultural and intellectual tradition as being essentially a history of themselves writ large.

For many people there was, however, an abiding sense that China had somehow fallen from grace, that the glories of the longest continuing civilization (summed up in the popular mind by the phrase "five thousand years of culture," *wuqiannian wenhua*) were buried in the past and could in no way help China cope with its position in the modern world. The legacy of this baneful history was felt to have been exposed when the Qing court was confronted with the military and economic might of Western nations. The complexities and wealth of the written language and its culture have been seen by such critics to be nothing so much as a barrier to communication with the rest of the world. The political and social legacy of some two millennia was often characterized by the words *feudal* or *Confucian*, and was deemed a deadening weight and forming a "deep structure" that stymied change, was repressive, and was conducive ultimately to neither social nor political harmony.

According to this view, every element of Chinese reality only added to the crisis that was endemic to Chinese civilization and was so profound that widespread economic development would not necessarily be able to alleviate it. The list of problems facing the nation was long and harrowing:

> The population is catastrophically large. The political system (cosmetic Marxist-Leninist socialism with the characteristics of a corrupt police state) hinders the development of a mature society that can live rationally with the wealth as well as the problems that the economic reforms are creating. Environmental issues are of such a magnitude that they may well condemn future generations to congenital illness and poverty. An arbitrary legal system relying on government whim and personal connections is coupled with an erratic police mechanism that combines elements of Maoist draconianism with both traditional and modern methods of legalized coercion. The media lack independence and either serve party fiat or fritter away their energies on consumerist and cultural trivia; journalists devoted to the higher calling of pursuing truth and justice in their work are persecuted and hounded into silence. The carpetbagger, get-rich-quick mentality of both private entrepreneurs and large numbers of state cadres is self-centered, shortsighted, and unprincipled. This murky soup of a society is overseen by a party leadership that is ridden with nepotism and that rules according to the precepts of clan elders (a "Chinese mafia," as some Chinese have dubbed it). It directs the life of the nation through a bureaucracy of such size and labyrinthine structure that it is little better than an administrative "black hole." The educational tradition sanctifies learning by rote, and these pedagogical ills have been aggravated by a utilitarian approach to knowledge. In the wider society, there is a general lack of sympathy for the disadvantaged and poor coupled with malicious jealousy of the successful; an interest in the new that is satisfied by buying up foreign technology and gadgets; and a fascination with strong rulers. A pseudo emperor cult exists, although the state lacks a system of succession that can ensure stability. This self-critique is topped off with laments about the Chinese populace's complacency about the depth and seriousness of the crises facing the country.[67]

The modern tradition of self-loathing is widespread and powerful. Born of a deep-felt anxiety over material backwardness, military weakness, and political inadequacy, those tormented by this self-contempt recognize the role of the colonial powers in China's crisis but have generally tended to look internally or to history for the origins of the nation's troubles. The horrors of the past, especially those of the Cultural Revolution, are somehow justified and extolled by some authors who evince a pride in the callous violence to which so many were driven.[68] Under Mao, moral/political supremacy was seen as an answer to China's dilemma and the key to ensuring that the nation "made its contribution to the world." Following the success of the reforms, however, material strength, coupled with the innate and abiding moral power of the Chinese world, is believed by many to be the only way to overcome the nation's various inadequacies.

Nonetheless, some intellectuals and individuals feel that without systemic change and political reform, not to mention national moral reconstruction, no amount of wealth and power will make China a "modern" or internationally responsible nation. Starting in the late 1980s, articles and books dealing with the powerful sense of impending national crisis and written by people ostensibly concerned with the mood of nihilism born of a rejection of the party-state repeatedly claimed that unless something was done, the Chinese might finally be "expelled from the human race," or *kaichu qiuji.*[69]

While satisfying a need to explain China's woeful modern history, self-loathing also tends to reaffirm a prevalent sense of national uniqueness and moral superiority. Shame, weakness, and aggrieved sentiments traced to national humiliation are used regularly by propagandists and politicians to inculcate patriotic ire. Nor are views on the differences between China and the Western Other always macho or self-assertive. Wang Shuo, that master of irony, chortled about the superiority of the Chinese tradition of self-destruction. A writer who has delighted in excoriating (and lovingly allowed his characters to indulge in) Chinese foibles, in 1988 Wang made joyful national nihilism into something of a hip youth fashion, validating as a national achievement the type of all-pervasive corruption that He Xin denounces. Wang claimed that the Chinese know how to abuse themselves better than anyone else. In a book-length interview published in 1992, he remarked in a tone of smug abnegation: "Generally speaking, foreigners are pretty naive. . . . They're materially extremely wealthy, but impoverished in the realm of spiritual culture. They've just caught on to smoking dope, and that's such an artificial form of stimulation! We Chinese know how to get our kicks out of self-annihilation."[70]

According to this view, one that entails a kind of celebratory cultural determinism, not only has China failed to inherit and utilize the past creatively, but it also remains different from every other nation in that it has greater problems, a more complex burden of tradition, and a more vile populace. In all this, there is a creeping sense of schadenfreude. When analyzing the German situation in 1950, Hannah Arendt summed up this attitude in terms of another nation traumatized by recent totalitarianism. Her comments adumbrate an attitude readily found among the urban elite of mainland China since the 1970s:

> *Schadenfreude*, malicious joy in ruination. It is as though the Germans, denied the power to rule the world, had fallen in love with impotence as such, and now find a positive pleasure in contemplating international tensions and the unavoidable mistakes that occur in the business of governing, regardless of the possible consequences for themselves.[71]

Many of these aspects of self-loathing were also reflected in *River Elegy*, the 1988 didactic documentary series discussed earlier. The series offered a sweeping overview of the nation's history, symbols, and contemporary ills. Later denounced by the authorities, the series' reflections on China infuriated conservatives and nationalists throughout the Chinese commonwealth. The debate surrounding it provided the first public occasion when ideological opponents on the mainland and in Taiwan shared a reaction traced to a sense of wounded national pride. One of the key elements of the series was that it equated older civilizations (China, Egypt, Africa, and South America) with decadence, noncompetitive economies, and backwardness. This rhetorical device was aimed, on one level at least, at provoking the viewer into a patriotic response and feelings of outrage that the "Chinese tradition," along with past party policies, had combined to reduce China to its present (1988) status.[72]

In short, one of the recurrent themes of *River Elegy* was the frustration and hopelessness that its intellectual-journalist writers felt over the failure of their country to become a powerful, modern trading nation. The series' critique of the traditional polity and its ideology, along with its oblique references to the present regime, could be construed as an indictment of both the past and present systems' inability to turn China into an international power.[73] Although it also contained a subversive critique of the dominant ideology of the party, *River Elegy* with its self-important didactic narration read by a voice trained for Communist propaganda did, on a deeper level, uphold and validate the type of monolithic approach to reality that it claimed superficially to undermine. It is not surprising, therefore, that key figures in the series' production turned to less enlightened projects in the 1990s.

A number of the writers behind the series, including Su Xiaokang and Jin Guantao, have moved in different directions since leaving China in 1989; Xia Jun, the CCTV director of *River Elegy*, weathered the storms of the post-Tiananmen purge in Beijing. He subsequently teamed up with the reportage writer Mai Tianshu to produce two acclaimed peasant-based television documentaries. *The Peasants* and *The East* were multiepisode documentaries made in northwest China and produced in 1992 and 1993, respectively.[74] Filmed in southern Shanxi, one of the most ancient agrarian cultural centers of China (the "Hedong"—"East of the Yellow River"—area in southwest Shanxi), *The East* depicts a Chinese rural world marked by its cultural integrity. It is a premodern civilization not disrupted or atomized by social upheavals, political uncertainty, or chaotic modernization. Commentators on the series deployed a few expressions from the po-mo lexicon to observe that after watching *The East*, it was evident that in the 1990s the "peripheral world" of China should succor the spiritually depleted "center" of mainstream culture.

In *The East* Mai Tianshu, the writer of the series' narration, called for a rejection of theories introduced from the West (he hints but does not specify that Marxism-Leninism is included in this blanket condemnation of foreign thought).[75] One commentator noted that the significance of a work like *The East* was that it underlined

> the most significant stage in the spiritual evolution of Chinese intellectuals in the closing years of this century: they have abandoned the fleeting perspective of pseudo-Western tourists gazing from a distance at their own land and instead now look thoughtfully to "Mother Earth"; they have gone through a baptism, enthusiastically accepting the fads of Western thought, and have now resolutely returned to their native soil, the land that has nurtured our Chinese culture. They have set aside romanticism and passion in favor of practicality and rationalism; they have turned from cultural criticism to cultural construction and conservatism.[76]

The world that *The East* revealed, however, was hardly a pastoral idyll suffused with cultural value and abiding lessons for contemporary urban dwellers. Behind its veneer of folksy curiosity, the series affirmed some of the most backward-looking and premodern aspects of the Chinese rural world, including male domination, semifeudal social hierarchies, and educational inequalities. Both series presented a cloying portrayal of peasant culture and traditional values that were grounded in some of the most hidebound aspects of "national essence" discourse. Of course, such native-soil conservatism was hardly unique to these television documentaries. For years, the "new wave" directors of the 1980s like Zhang Yimou,[77] Chen Kaige, and Tian Zhuangzhuang had been creating works that contain undeniable elements of rural nostalgia (and voyeurism, now also called "oriental orientalism"). Their own complex brand of cinematic chauvinism (one informed by both the tradition of self-hate and national narcissism) fit in neatly with a film industry originating in nationalist aspirations in the 1920s and 1930s.[78]

Elements of self-hate and moral disgust, as well as the more commonly reported aspects of protest and rebellion, were crucial to the student-led demonstrations of 1989. For large numbers of intellectuals and students, the protest movement offered an opportunity for the educated elite to move back onto the center stage of Chinese history after decades of persecution and ignominy. For their part, many Beijing citizens supported the protests in the belief that the peaceful demonstrations showed, despite the rampant commercialization of the 1980s, that the Chinese still had a strong moral sense, were willing to stand up for questions of principle and, with a concerted effort, could overcome the negative legacies of both the imperial and socialist past. As the students so rightly claimed, the movement had a powerful patriotic and redemptive message, one that played a key role in mobilizing mass support.[79] With the failure of that movement and the continued stability (and evolution) of party rule, it is not surprising that an entrenched pattern of political activism in twentieth-century China has reappeared once more, one in which political advocacy and frustrated extremism are transformed into egregious nationalism.[80]

The 4 June Massacre of 1989 led for a time to an affirmation of the key elements of national self-hate. It told a tale of innocent youth slaughtered by an unresponsive gerontocracy that ruled over a nation that was corrupt, chaotic, and, above all, not "modern." The chance for a national redemption had been lost and, with it, the moral force and legitimacy of the rulers.

Before the upheavals of 1989, there was a vocal pro-Western lobby in China. Although some of their number went into exile after 4 June, many people who were previously politically engaged and remained on the mainland tried to take personal advantage of China's impressive economic performance, reasoning that money-making was now not only a viable modus vivendi but also as a revolutionary act that would presage true reform. In late 1993, a number of intellectuals in Shanghai launched a discussion on the "loss of the humanist spirit" in China.[81] They lamented the fact that the commercialization and de-politicization of culture had marginalized serious artistic issues and, as we noted earlier, that postmodernism was being sinicized by mainland intellectuals and writers who in many cases used it as a theoretical validation of their political disengagement, reticence, and moral neutrality in regard to the state.[82] (For more on this issue, see the following chapter.)

The widespread interest in the 1980s among the reading public in the faddish Western theories like psychoanalysis, existentialism, structuralism, and deconstruction had now dwindled. It was argued that in 1989 intellectuals had suffered a new displacement in terms of social position and prestige and that in the 1990s those who did not become involved in "abstract debates" (*qingtan*, or "idle talk") about theory were busy themselves either hawking their talents in the marketplace or attempting to exercise a more overt political influence as "thinking strategists" for present or prospective power holders.[83] As we will see in chapter 11, "Kowtowing to the Vulgar," critics and writers who decried the flaccid morals of mainstream ideology and were disturbed by the pluralistic commercialism encouraged by former mentors like Wang Meng spoke out in 1993 in favor of a new moral perfectionism, their outrage blossoming in 1995 into a denunciation of "capitulationism to the commercial."

In the early 1990s, with the nation's increased economic growth, there was a new twist in the tradition of self-loathing. People observed that China continued to advance economically without embarking on a drastic reform of the political or social system, and the debate about the "humanist spirit" was part of a cautious attempt by some thoughtful intellectuals to air these concerns in public. Many believed that the acquisition and maintenance of wealth would gradually transform the "national character," or at least obviate the need for any major shift in the public perception of it. Consumerism as the ultimate revolutionary action was now seen to be able to play a redemptive role in national life, for it allowed people to remake themselves, not through some abstract national project, but through the self-centered power of possession.

Whereas there was a strong spirit of self-reflection in the 1980s, economic success in the 1990s coupled with restrictions on intellectual debate and political repression encouraged more a mood of braggadocio. The national spirit that was being publicly reformulated in the 1990s was not necessarily based on mature reflection or open discussion but, rather, on a cocky, even vengeful, and perhaps purblind self-assurance that appealed to the mass market.

The faith in Chinese exclusivity was reflected even in that particularly Westernized art form: Chinese rock 'n' roll. Cui Jian, the godfather of the Chinese rock scene, claimed that northern, Beijing-based rock was completely different from Hong Kong and Taiwan imports. In an interview published in late 1993, he averred that northern Chinese could produce a robust, positive, and socially progressive type of music that was quite different from the negative and decadent rock of the West.[84] Other song writers like Hou Muren, and Kong Yongqian, the designer of the "cultural T-shirts" of 1991, pursued their work not because they wanted so much to overthrow the status quo but because they desired to enrich the cultural sphere of China and make their nation more competitive with the rest of the world, including other areas of the Chinese commonwealth. The authorities may have viewed their cultural products as potentially divisive and dangerous, but in the larger realm of China they were patriots. Others who dared to go further emerged as super-patriots.

YUAN HONGBING PISSING IN THE WIND

The race that dwells on continental East Asia once shone with a brilliance bestowed by the sun. Now it has its back to the icy wall of history, driven there by the forces of Fate. We must now show whether or not we are an inferior race, for Fate is pissing in our very faces.[85]

In 1990s China, radical views did not necessarily issue from pro-Maoist ideologues or conservatives. One firebrand was Yuan Hongbing, formerly a lecturer in law at Peking University and a labor organizer, whose involvement with a "peace charter" reportedly modeled on the Czechoslovak "Charter 77"[86] and detention in February 1994 put him in the front ranks of China's small public dissident movement.[87] From the evidence of his published writings, however, one would have thought that Yuan's philosophy was more akin to new-age Nietzscheism than liberalism.[88]

Yuan was one of the organizers of the controversial book *The Tide of History* in 1992, noted for its anticonservative, reformist tone. That book appeared shortly after Deng Xiaoping's tour of the south in January–February 1992 which marked a new stage of the economic reform.[89] Although *The Tide of History* fit in with the orthodoxy of the day—Deng's anti-ideological and pro-radical reform agenda—Yuan displayed a robust nationalism even in some of his published comments against a revival of Maoist-style "leftism." He declared that the changes overtaking China in the reform era were but a prelude to a great transformation that would also give birth to an "innovative cultural movement" and that would witness "the rebirth of the China Spirit," *Zhonghua jingshen*.[90] Yuan described the cultural movement in the following way (mixed metaphors and all):

> The leftist current of thought must be thoroughly purged, [for] if it is not, the China Spirit will not be able to break free of a millennia-long intellectual hell; it will not be able to pierce the clouds of feudal thought and embrace the sunlight of modernism that shines in the azure skies. It is imperative to cast aside the attitude of national defeatism, [for] if we fail to do so, the China Spirit will not be smelted into an iron will, and it will be as lifeless as the fallen leaves of history.
>
> . . . The renaissance of the China Spirit will be as a chiming of the morning bell of the Pacific age.
>
> All glory belongs to Great China [*weidade Zhonghua*]. The future belongs to the modernized China spirit—in the name of the new century![91]

Yuan's highly colorful and emotive sentiments had been decocted in an earlier volume entitled *Winds in the Wilderness*. This book appeared in mid-1990 and is perhaps more revealing not only of his own mind-set but also that of some of his coevals.[92] Some readers saw it as a philosophical tract of considerable individuality, and in the repressive intellectual atmosphere of post-Tiananmen China, *Winds in the Wilderness* gained a considerable following among university students. Official critics, however, declared it to be a "carefully concocted work of political propaganda," a "challenge to materialism mounted by subjective idealism."[93] It was banned for its egregious bourgeois liberalist tendencies.[94]

In the book, Yuan propounds what he calls "new heroism," a cause that is primarily concerned with the "fate of the race" and the role of strong man as national hero and savior.[95] Like Nietzsche (a philosopher whose high standing among Chinese intellectuals has a long history), Yuan spoke of the need for madness and irrationality.[96] He condemned all individual attempts to achieve freedom, whether it be to engage in politics or to flee China in search of a new life, as a betrayal of the race. He condemned, in particular, those who sought a solution to China's problems in the West. Indulging in what could be called "Sinofascism,"[97] Yuan proposed that the answer to the political, social, and cultural "ugliness" of the Chinese was purification through fire and blood, nothing less than total warfare: "even if this means that our blue skies darken with the color of blood that will not fade for a thousand years." One is reminded here of the sentiments of the 1920s futurist-turned-fascist Filippo Tommaso Marinetti, who wrote:

> War is beautiful because it initiates the dreamt-of metalization of the human body. War is beautiful because it enriches a flowering meadow with fiery orchids of machine guns. War is beautiful because it combines gunfire, the cannonades, the cease-fire, the scents, and the stench of putrefaction into a symphony.[98]

According to Yuan's particular vision, the first step toward national renewal is a "totalitarian style." "Only with totalitarianism will it be possible to fuse the weak, ignorant, and selfish individuals of the race into a powerful whole." The race needs strong, idealistic, dignified, and free men to achieve this end. In his own formulation of the neoauthoritarian/conservatism debate that had developed in China since the late 1980s,[99] Yuan observed that the "freedom fighter" must be crowned by a "democracy" that he would then manipulate to break the nexus between totalitarian rule and authoritarianism. This hero must put the welfare of the race above all other concerns, Yuan says, including those of the family.[100] Indeed, an appeal to race was a convenient way of coping with the complex legacies of cultural superiority, political exclusivity, and self-loathing that we have already described. By emphasizing race, the question of common humanity was also happily circumvented, as were the knotty problems of political, social, and personal morality and ethics that are germane to it.[101]

Yuan Hongbing's *Winds in the Wilderness* shared much with other tracts that were inward looking and rejected the outside world apart from the economic benefits that can be reaped from a relationship with it. As Yuan remarked when making a case against the West: "Scientific rationalism has said all it can within the context of Western civilization."[102]

While couched in excessively purple prose, few of the ideas Yuan expresses in this book were particularly new, or Chinese. Nor were Yuan's views of male primacy and racial strength unrelated to earlier trends among the priapic proponents of the avant-garde in the early 1980s.[103] The well-known "misty" poet Yang Lian's "Nuoerlang" cycle of poems, for example, although set in Tibet, gave voice to Han male dominance, and something of Yang's tone was reflected in the early 1990s writings of another poet, Zhou Lunyou, who in 1992 decried "leisure literature" and called for a "red writing" that was robust, unyielding, and muscular.[104] Similarly, some of the writers discussed in chapter 11, "Kowtowing to the Vulgar," like Zhang Chengzhi, belonged at least in the same school of over-the-top prose as Yuan Hongbing.

A BEIJING BASTARD IN NEW YORK

"By the way, fuck you!"[105]

In 1993, the portrayal of the national spirit was overshadowed by a television drama that brought into focus many of the questions that have been discussed here. The show was *A Beijing Man in New York*, referred to at the beginning of this chapter.[106]

A Beijing Man in New York depicted essentially a "spermatic journey," that is, an archetypal trip undertaken by a hero to a foreign land. Through his travails, the hero overcomes adversity, obtains fortune, and sires offspring by ravishing conquered beauties, leaving in his wake a legacy of riches and empire.[107]

Wang Qiming, the protagonist of the 1993 series, gave birth not to a lineage, as do the heroes of other travel-and-conquest epics, but to wealth, the legitimate product of his labors in New York. Material wealth was the means whereby the perceived cultural malaise and social impotence of China—as embodied by the character Wang, a disheveled Beijing artiste played by Jiang Wen, China's most popular male lead—are mollified.[108] For Wang money = wealth = potency = self-validation = continuity through bloodlines or capital investments. The series enthralled audiences because it was pregnant with possibility. The popularity of the show also was significant given the fact that television is the most widespread and powerful form of mass communication in China.[109]

Produced by Zheng Xiaolong and Feng Xiaogang, the makers of earlier Beijing Television Arts Center[110] successes like *Aspirations* in 1991 and *The Editors* in 1992, *A Beijing Man in New York* was the first mainland television series filmed entirely on location overseas.[111] It was also the first show of its type that attempted to reflect the fate of recent mainland immigrants to the West,[112] being based on Glen Cao's (Cao Guilin) popular book of the same name,[113] a work that had created a frenzy of interest when it was first serialized and broadcast on radio in 1991.[114] Cao's "novel" was only one of a number of books in a genre of mainland writing hailed as "new immigrant literature" following its appearance in the late 1980s.[115] It constituted a widely read genre that, over the years, tended to confirm many popular stereotypes of the West as being a realm lacking the "human senti-ment," *renqingwei'r*, that theoretically suffused Chinese life with a warmth, close-ness, and compassion unknown to any other peoples. The West, pitiless to immi-grants from Asia, was excessively materialistic, exploitative, and essentially racist, not to mention imperialistic vis-à-vis the Chinese.[116] The general tone of these works, in particular Cao's book, also fortuitously fulfilled some of the needs of post-1989 propaganda—as well as satisfying popular curiosity and prurience. They depicted the horrors of Western capitalism at the same time as they affirmed the positive dimensions (rags to riches) of the market economy that China was pursuing with such single-mindedness.[117]

Official and semiofficial reviews of the series generally concentrated on aspects of Sino-American differences, emphasizing that the work "focused on conflicts be-tween Chinese and Western culture, psychology and values," and that by watch-ing the show, "Chinese TV viewers could better understand American society and help those who entertain a rosy American dream to be more realistic."[118] China's physical poverty, wrote one commentator in *Reading*, would continue to spawn in-dividuals like Wang Qiming, but equally, the spiritual vacuity of New York would force more people to search for spiritual value, like Wang's antagonist David Mc-Carthy, a character who ends up going to China to teach English![119] Zha Xiduo (Zha Jianying), a critic who wrote for both the mainland and Hong Kong press, commented that the unifying theme of the series could be summed up in one line: "Screw you America," *Meiguo, wo cao ni daye!*[120] Here America was not a place renowned for democracy or its culture; rather, it was an El Dorado that held out a promise of material wealth and worldly success. Acquisition thus become a unify-ing goal, a shared aim of the diaspora, and the dissolvent of ideological differ-ences.[121] And despite a few vocal exceptions, audiences—bureaucrats, the "reading masses," and intellectuals—were at one in their praise of the show. It goes without saying that people approached the series and similar works with different percep-tions and variously found satisfaction or explication of entrenched attitudes.

The hero of the show, Wang Qiming, is forced to give up his avowedly whole-some Chinese values to be successful in America.[122] Yet his success reveals how those native values have informed his actions and helped him maintain a superior-ity and humanity clearly lacking in the "foreign," that is, American, characters in the story. Despite the vicissitudes of New York's dog-eat-dog commercial environ-ment, Wang retains elements of what is quintessentially Chinese—expressed in both negative and positive elements of his personality. Xu Jilin, the Shanghai scholar, summed up a large segment of querulous intellectual opinion when he wrote that Wang was in fact the television embodiment of Wang Shuo's "ruffians" or "smart-asses," the *pizi*.[123] Xu also opined that the intentional misrepresentation of the United States validated a view of reformist China that was becoming common among the Chinese themselves: the world created by a competitive market economy, whose model is to be found in the United States, is one in which there are no ground rules, no morality or rectitude, a place where the strong devour the weak.

Xu further argued that the Chinese version of the competitive spirit had less to do with a new commercial attitude than with the traditional *"pizi* mentality . . . that has always been a parasite on the underbelly of the society, present in the midst of the traveling knights, vagabonds, *liumang*, and the lumpen proletariat."[124] Like many critics before him, Xu pointed out that it was this type of "alternative culture" that invariably surfaces in periods of moral confusion, overwhelms society, and subverts mainstream culture itself.[125] While wiping out the remnants of outdated social practice, Xu says, the *"pizi* culture" prevented the development of a new social contract. It was a cultural cancer that confounded immorality with morality and order with lawlessness, giving birth thereby to a world of bullies in which everyone boasts: "I'm a *liumang* and nothing scares me."[126]

AVANT-GARDE NATIONALISTS

The East Computer Virus, *Dongfang bingdu*: As "The East Is Red," the Maoist national anthem, sounds up, a message appears on the computer screen: "Don't Kill Me, I'm Patriotic!"[127]

As the children of the Cultural Revolution and the reform era come into power and money, they are finding a new sense of self-importance and worth. Some of them are resentful of the real and imagined slights that they and their nation have suffered in the past, and their desire for strength and revenge is increasingly reflected in contemporary Chinese culture. Unofficial culture has reached or is reaching an uncomfortable accommodation with the economic, if not always the political, realities of the mainland. As its practitioners negotiate a relationship with both the state in all its complex manifestations and capital (often, but not always, the same thing), national pride and achievement act as a glue that further seals the pact. The patriotic consensus, aptly manipulated by diverse party organs, acts as a crucial element in the coherence of the otherwise fragmented Chinese world; timely exploitation of it in the public realm can also lead to political and commercial rewards.

These sentiments are also found among the most technically avant-garde members of the society, the *diannao chong*, or "computer bugs," a blanket term for computer hackers, pirates, rip-off merchants, as well as nerds-on-the-make with Chinese characteristics. That is what they are called in "Thieves' Alley" in Beijing. Thieves' Alley is in Zhongguancun, China's "Silicon Valley," part of the university district in the northwest suburbs of the capital. Colloquially, people refer to the area as "Electronics Street," Dianzi yitiao jie, but for the pros, the pirates, and the hackers, it is "Thieves' Alley," Pianzi yitiao jie. There is only one word's difference in Chinese, but it denotes the gaping gulf between the official line and socialist cyberspace, the virtual and the real.

Thieves' Alley was one of the homes of the massive Chinese pirating industry, and in early 1995, the journalist Sang Ye conducted an interview there with one of the masters of the trade. The computer bug that Sang Ye spoke to was said to be one of the Chinese capital's "Four Heavenly Kings of Hacking,"[128] and he had an attitude and ego that went with the title.

Trained in computing at Qinghua University, China's M.I.T., this Sino-CompuBug was one of the younger generation. He was in his early twenties; dressed in gray suit pants, Adidas shoes, and a bomber jacket—the uniform of the young business toughs of Beijing—he looked like just another typical, twenty-something Westernized Asian businessman. But the CompuBug was no nerd: he did not wear glasses, and he sported a crew cut favored by the I-mean-business young men of north China. A handsome man with a biting tongue and ready wit, he was always at the ready to take a call on his mobile phone.

The image was urbane enough, but the minute the CompuBug opened his mouth, out came the voice of the brash, in-your-face China that will be increasingly prominent in the future. It bespoke a resentment nurtured over years of childhood deprivation, a grinding poverty born of Mao Zedong's lunatic revolutionary policies and the isolation of the country from the West. He also harbored the pent-up fury of a bright generation of people inhabiting a massive nation tirelessly proud of its "five-thousand-year culture" and brought low in recent centuries by technological backwardness, social corruption, politically induced decay, and imperialist aggression. His message was unmistakable and unapologetic: We're here. We're mean. Get used to it.

His comments on the pressing issue of intellectual property rights reflected a spirit shared by many mainlanders in the increasingly anti-American mood of the mid-1990s as China's entry into the General Agreement on Tariffs and Trade (GATT) and the unsettling specter of globalization loomed:

> The way I see it, pirating software is no big deal. The four Little Dragons of Asia [Hong Kong, Taiwan, South Korea, and Singapore] created the wealth and prosperity they enjoy today by pirating. You tell me, what have those little shits in Hong Kong ever discovered? Zilch. They're a pack of pseudo-

foreign devils who started out as tailors and cobblers. Their genius for computers all comes from being able to pirate stuff. . . .

Foreign devils [Americans] are just plain unreasonable. To be honest,
they've been getting away with ripping off the Chinese for ages. What's all
this stuff about intellectual property? Whose ancestors got it all going in the
first place? I don't think there's any cut-and-dried answers, but just ask yourself, what's the basic element of computing? Binary notation. . . . That's the
theory of *yin-yang*. Everything in the universe is made up of *yin* and *yang*.
The Chinese discovered that first. Not only we get the idea first, we are the
first to apply it. . . .

Let's forget the hardware aspect of all of this. But what about electricity
and magnetic fields? Who discovered magnetism? Pardon me, it was us! . . .
Then what are you supposed to do with your data? How do you record it?
You need hard copy, after all. Well, it's obvious, you need paper to print a
hard copy and without Bi Sheng [the legendary Chinese inventor of paper],
those foreigners would still be writing on parchment. Can you cut parchment into A4 size and print on it? I don't think so! So when it comes down
to it, these fucking foreigners simply haven't got a clue. They can't face up
to the fact that they owe *us* for copyright infringement. So what the shit are
they making such a stink about? When we were advanced, they were free to
rip us off left, right, and center. Now they've just managed to move ahead of
us a little, and they won't let us have a fair go. As soon as they struck it rich,
they began lording it over everyone else. Isn't that right? Well, I'm going to
go right on copying whatever comes my way.[129]

For decades, Chinese education and propaganda have emphasized the role of
history in the fate of the Chinese nation-state. While many Chinese disciples of
postmodernism and postcolonialism were busy talking themselves out of a role as
the social and intellectual critics of the heritage of traditional and Communist mental habits, the ideology of progress, national wealth, and power continued to inform
public opinion. History and its supposedly inexorable workings determine for China a triumphant march toward a strong and modern future in which all the progressivist dreams of the past century—and the promise of Chinese civilization— will
supposedly be realized. Whereas Marxism-Leninism and Mao Thought have been
abandoned in all but name, the role of history in China's future remains steadfast.

In the late 1950s, China's utopian hopes were to surpass Britain and America
in a few decades. During the Cultural Revolution, China became the center of
world revolution and the most "progressive" force on the international scene.[130]
Now it is the Asia-Pacific century that beckons and beguiles.[131] The new mythology of East Asian material strength and spiritual worth touted equally by region-

al propagandists and the Western media has fed into the century-old Chinese dreams of national revival and supremacy. Whatever the economic and political realities of that future may be, it is important to be aware that the cultural attitudes and awareness that form the basis of Chinese attitudes across the political spectrum have been shaped by defunct party propaganda and express deeply frustrated and compelling nationalistic aspirations. This was evident in the official mainland media from the late 1980s and increasingly in the mass media, nonofficial intellectual, and cultural circles. It will also be evident in the future, regardless of the political direction the country happens to take, although in the 1990s, mature and moderate voices also expressed skepticism of a kind not previously aired publicly in the People's Republic.[132]

It is fitting to end a chapter entitled "To Screw Foreigners Is Patriotic"—itself a quotation from an interview with a Chinese prostitute working the Gold Coast of Australia—with a poem by a Chinese litterateur who has taken up residence in the Antipodes.

Ouyang Yu's poem "Sex Notice" was penned in English and published in a 1996 anthology of new, multicultural Australian writing.

I have come to this country for 90 days
90 days without a fuck

I've seen your dirty books dirty videos
and dirty, dirty mags

I want your women I want your girls
I want whoever is willing

Your sun is cold your moon is hot
your suburb is too too dead
and your city is arty your money thirsty
your life farty and lousy

so instead of boring me let me bore you
with a brand new China-made flute

to play you a tune of starved love
for five thousand years

to flood you with the fresh cum
of the Yellow River and the Yangtse
so if you want to come and be my love
call me at six six six plus triple sex.[133]

CHAPTER ELEVEN

Kowtowing to the Vulgar

"IRONIES"

Irony and cynicism were fad words in early 1990s Chinese culture. As we have repeatedly seen in this book, young(er) artists, be they painters, writers, or filmmakers, placed notional airquotes around just about everything that had once stood for convention in the socialist state. Playful rehearsals of the politics of their elders were not only a liberating act of circumscribed rebellion; they could also turn a profit. Airquotes, the telltale cipher of ironical derision, or at least their metaphorical equivalent, enjoyed a heyday as a powerfully subversive marker. As the years passed, however, the distinction between raised-eyebrow, knowing-wink irony and straight up-and-down officialese became increasingly blurred, often to the point of the two becoming mutually indistinguishable.

As older propagandists retired or simply tired of the dizzying shifts in party line, their role was taken up by younger writers, editors, and journalists, people who had internalized reformist doublethink during the 1980s. These men and women were examples of the new Sino-socialist person. They could appreciate irony as much as the next comrade, and they used it in both the official and the commercial media, weaving it into their work and lives as a basic riff. Thus, when irony itself was commodified and used "to grease the wheels of commerce, not . . . to resist its insidious effects,"[1] the complex cultural significance of market-oriented dissent revealed itself in a range of ways. Irony and its manifold incarnations played out its role as yet another ingredient in cultural stir-fry, *wenhua chaozuo*.

In her classic 1960s essay "On Camp," Susan Sontag observed that at its rebellious best, "camp puts everything in quotation marks." In "Notes on Camp," a 1992 reprisal of Sontag by Suzanne Moore, camp was found ultimately to be "about recuperation rather than revolution."[2] As Moore remarked on the 1990s fashion for camp culture in Euro-America, "Irony conquers all and tells us less than zero in the process." Irony was also a good way of selling indifferent art.

In the China of the 1990s, political and cultural desuetude, coupled with the sheer absurdities of the socialist marketplace, for all intents and purposes institutionalized irony in both elite and mass media culture. Kong Yongqian's irreverent T-shirts were banned, but the ideas that informed his early success came to be reworked and commercialized by others. Nonofficial artists hawked works of political pop, in particular quizzical representations of Chairman Mao and chinoiserie, in the international art world, but in China as the advertising culture consumed signs and signifiers of all descriptions in its maw, the pop seemed flat. Underground filmmakers like Zhang Yuan turned the ironic into a career choice, striking the pose of the oppressed artist while weaving a creative path between officialdom and the international art-house cinema circuit. Wang Shuo, the brilliant progenitor of the contemporary fictional *liumang*, became a paragon for many nonsubsidized writers as he himself fell by the wayside and was banned in 1996–1997. Wang had helped turn television and film writing into an enterprise while his parodies of party language and popularization of the *liumang* style became all but clichéd. The ultimate irony for Wang was that the kind of intellectuals and writers he had excoriated in his 1980s fiction took him, in the 1990s, as a role model in their search for popularity and cultural meaning, and he himself claimed he had, by default, joined the intellectual caste.

"Irony is the rhetorical necessity of the age, the critical accessory no one should leave home without. It has also replaced patriotism as the last refuge of scoundrels, for it means never having to say you really mean it."[3] In 1990s China, irony had become itself a "meme," a self-replicating cultural organism, a virus that infected the mainland body politic. Although neither as virulent nor as widespread as a pandemic, irony played a role in immunizing the culture against other spiritual pollutants and, in the continued repressive state of market socialism, acted as a validation for the artful dodgers of nonofficial culture. It made everyone who toyed with it a cynic, and as Oscar Wilde observed a century ago, the cynic is a person who knows the price of everything but the value of nothing.

Official culture itself existed in a skein of ironic relationships. Extreme commercialization and economic success had certainly shored up the rule of the Communist Party and convinced many that only by maintaining "stability and unity," *anding tuanjie*, could the nation, or at least the marketplace, prosper.[4] The advertising culture that had grown up both to service and to mold the urban petit-bourgeoisie also provided propagandists with new ways to insinuate their message into the fabric of modern life. Advertisers also plundered the tropes and images of party history to promote their products, thereby reinforcing a Communist culture that had once shunned commodities and preached revolutionary asceticism. The cultural avant-garde that had grown in the 1980s, though still officially disavowed, also provided inspiration for state artists (see chapter 9, "CCP™ & Adcult

PRC"). This "circularity and reciprocal interaction between popular and official discourse" was one of the central elements of late-twentieth-century Chinese culture, as it had been some one hundred years earlier.[5]

Kong-Tai investors were not only interested in financing pop and alternative culture. Capital was also available for patriotic theme parks, film projects, and exhibitions. In particular, Hong Kong businesspeople were investing in an accommodation with the Beijing authorities, and in the process they became an integral part of the cosmetic reconstruction of the face of Chinese socialism. Party culture was thus enmeshed in a dynamic of being both the colonizer of imported and avant-garde popular culture and also being colonized by it.

DISPIRITED HUMANISTS

In 1992, Deng Xiaoping's call for a new wave of reform presaged rapid commercialization and the spread of the ironic temper within elite culture. Writers and critics—some silenced by incarceration, others cautious about being too forthright regarding their concerns—gradually moved into the public arena. In articles carried in elite journals and papers, the popular press, and mass-market magazines, they engaged in a series of interconnected discussions on the directions of Chinese culture, the role of the intelligentsia, the individual artist, and the independent critic. They also debated the impact of commodification on culture and the place of mainstream ideology, as well as postmodernism and postcolonialism, in mainland life. These debates rearticulated concerns that, in one form or another, had exercised the minds of Chinese thinkers for more than a century. They also revealed the development of strategies among the cultural elite for dealing with complex social and political realities on the cusp of the new millennium.

What was particularly galling for some writers and critics was that after a short period of influence in the late 1970s and 1980s, serious literature and the realm of elitist criticism had been overwhelmed by commercial concerns. State funding in its multifarious forms was dwindling, and limited government resources were concentrated on official cultural projects and channeled through existing state institutions that had generally been purged of the alternative elites that had flourished under Wang Meng in the late 1980s. This meant that artists who were not willing to toe the official line or who were neither adept at feeding parasitically off the body politic nor able to produce work that was commercially viable had little chance of surviving. As yet, there were no independent foundations that would invest in fringe or elite culture, although by the middle of the decade entrepreneurs and companies were more active in supporting local cultural activities and even alternative cultural forms. This is why, as we have seen, offshore capital came to play such an important role in the development of nonofficial culture on the mainland in the early 1990s. For those writers whose work appealed neither to the authorities nor to outside investors, however, it was the marketplace that now determined their fate.

In mid-1993, a group of Shanghai intellectuals led by the literary historian Wang Xiaoming initiated a public discussion on what they called "the loss of the humanistic spirit."[6] Among other things, leading thinkers and writers debated how they should respond to the extreme commercialization of the society. What, if any, were the abiding moral and intellectual values of the past? How should the concerned individual act in the face of the combined autocracy of politics and capital? They lamented the lack of a deep-seated intellectual skepticism and an independently critical spirit in the intelligentsia; they questioned whether the tradition of liberalism in twentieth-century China was dead or in its death throes. This group, it was argued, was paralyzed by an inability to articulate any "ultimate concerns," *zhongji guanhuai,* and literary criticism itself seemed flaccid and cast adrift from any moral or aesthetic underpinnings, its course set by the prevailing winds of fashion and squalls of political necessity. It was as though even the basic questions that the Chinese asked about their predicament had to be imported from outside. Or as one editorial comment on the debate put it: "Problems exist on the mainland, but the questions are asked overseas; the phenomena are in China, but the explanations are given elsewhere."[7]

The plethora of articles published on the "humanistic spirit" expressed a sense among many publicly active intellectuals that if none of the (revived) scholastic standards and traditions of the past could withstand economic imperatives, then thinkers and independent commentators as a whole would be shunted aside by the market just as previously they had been marginalized by politics. To the scholars who generated the debate, a central concern was that intellectuals generally felt that tradition left them with only two choices: either to become strategists for the power holders and officials or to choose escape by engaging in arcane scholastic pursuits. Two of the broader issues that surfaced during the debate were the question of the impact of the deconstruction of all values in the present mainland environment, and the role that traditional Chinese cultural studies, *guoxue,* could play in contemporary life. Zhang Yiwu, known as the "postmaster," *houzhu,* of Peking University, for example, argued against the mythic status given to the "humanistic spirit" posited by a group of critics. Taking the po-mo high ground (an altitude from which conservatives were also fond of launching their assaults), he commented that the intellectuals engaged in the debate were a class of passé individuals who found themselves without a meaningful social or political role. Their very involvement in the humanist debate, he claimed, was an effort to create a discursive environment that would in turn lay itself open to colonization by "othering" Western intellectual traditions.[8]

The discussions continued for over two years, and at its height, the debate saw the publication of a new article on the issue on the average of every five days.[9] The often rancorous exchanges that took place, however, marked the collapse of the broad consensus among writers on major intellectual topics that had developed in the wake of 4 June.

Over the years, writers and intellectuals had learned, to their grief, that involvement in highbrow culture—in particular, the culture of criticism that encouraged the role of individual conscience, confronted tradition (both socialist and presocialist), and rejected literary cronyism—could be politically very risky. The cultural purges of the 1980s may have achieved little in narrow political terms, but they had repeatedly stunted the numerous sprouts of autonomous culture. As a result of these regular attacks, as well as the grinding administrative sanctions that the authorities placed on specific people and works, artists and intellectuals throughout the country had gradually evolved various nonthreatening alternative cultures. In the 1990s, popular or commercial culture seemed to many writers, from po-moists to traditional-style humanists, to be the most efficacious as well as safest way to promote cultural revolution in China.

Pop culture was politically and commercially legitimate. Its supporters claimed that it undermined the authoritarian sway of the party, that indigenous forms of pop had an added appeal of being suited to the rearticulation of traditional values for mass consumption. China pop, it was reasoned, could be both indigenous and modern, and strong enough to stave off the inroads of foreign or global (that is, American) cultural incursion.

As we have seen in previous chapters, irreverent cultural figures who turned the values of the socialist world on their head had indeed acted as a powerful corrosive on ideological constraints in the late 1980s and early 1990s. According to one school of thought, anything that undermined party domination and reaffirmed the writer/critic in their position as the arbiters of cultural value, was to be encouraged. Deconstruction or dissolution, *jiegou* and *xiaojie*, were the two pop-intellectual terms used to describe the subversive solvent that would presumably corrode the bindings of party ideology. The cynical realism and political pop, *wanshi xianshizhuyi* and *zhengzhi bopu* (see the section "Export, Exploit, Expropriate" in chapter 8), that sprang up in the avant-garde art world were regarded as politically effective, not to mention commercially attractive, ways of achieving these ends. For others, however, the high-art plundering of political culture for pecuniary ends corrupted the very spirit of the critical and self-questioning dimension of 1980s culture and did little to undermine the abiding hegemony of the Communist Party.[10]

As the marketplace for entertainment grew, playing the ironic and evasive wise guy became a role that many individuals, writers, intellectuals, and readers were ready to assume. It was not only a means for frustrating the imperatives of party ideology; it also provided an excuse for avoiding the complex political and cultural choices that faced them.[11] To stake a claim as a member of the "vulgar masses," *suren*—or at least for the champions of Sino-po-mo to claim that you were in a constant "dialogue with the vulgar," *shisu*—allowed you to reject the panoply of intellectual posturing (both sincere and hypocritical) common among writers and the endless disquisitions on personal ideals, choice, and integrity.

Writing in *Orient*, a leading forum for the discussion, the critic Wang Lixiong (and author of *Yellow Peril*) said of the intellectual adepts who prospered in the early 1990s,

> They might not talk like louts, but theirs is a realm of utter spiritual degradation. They are without integrity; they crave depravity; they are shameless and thick-skinned. They are always ready to sell out their principles, and they will take risks only if there's the chance of making a profit. They regard all that is sacred with disdain and despise all ideals.[12]

Regardless of Wang Lixiong's sense of revulsion, many writers now finally felt free to cast aside the traditional role of the intellectual and also to reject the hypocrisy of faux idealism. For people who had been segregated from and excoriated by the masses for so long under Maoism, it was a welcome relief to revel in the corruption and ethical confusion of the reform era. The cultural hooligan was the ideal vehicle for rationalizing this new betrayal of principle. The *liumang* was a mirror alternative to the straitlaced party cadre, but both followed the ebb and flow of prevailing fashion or policy, and both fed off the threat of their doppelgänger.

As critiques of the "loutification" of culture proliferated during 1994, the broader discussion concerning "humanism," social commitment, and moral perfectionism itself became a media mini-sensation. In the summer of that year, Zhang Chengzhi, a Beijing-based Muslim novelist and a prominent former Red Guard,[13] wrote an impassioned attack on the greed, vanity, and lack of patriotic backbone among contemporary Chinese intellectuals and writers. Zhang's screed was reprinted in the Shanghai *Wenhui Daily*, one of the main forums for the "humanist spirit" debate. What until then had been a relatively even-tempered discussion about the impact of commercialization became a media talking point, and correspondents of the *Wenhui Daily* engaged in a heated exchange for some weeks.[14] In the process, the print media discovered that sensational novels like *The Abandoned Capital* were not the only artistic hot spots. New cultural debates and literary causes célèbres could also be exploited to sell newspapers and books.[15]

A STORM IN A RICE BOWL

In the media frenzy that developed around the issue of the "humanistic spirit," Zhang Chengzhi was only one of the major cultural figures ready to enter the fray. Another was the writer and former bureaucrat Wang Meng. Wang's stance was diametrically opposed to that of Zhang, and in the ensuing print media skirmishes a kind of megalomaniac rivalry developed between opposing camps who took as their advocates Wang Meng on one side and Zhang Chengzhi on the other.

Wang Meng had been one of the most public and outspoken of the writers who came to prominence after the Cultural Revolution. Throughout the 1980s, he had addressed through his fiction and essays a broad readership, in particular young students and urban readers, thereby assuming the role of a liberal moral guide and cultural mentor. He used the essay, the feuilleton, in tussles with ideological foes at the same time as he acted as a literary therapist for readers confronted by the cultural maelstrom of that era. As the minister of culture from 1986 to 1989, his career was intertwined with the greater openness and artistic adventurism of that period. Before discussing his controversial role in the debates of the mid-1990s, however, it is necessary to say something of his early career, in particular the years after his ouster from the party-state bureaucracy and his rise as a semi-independent cultural broker.

Born in Beijing in 1934, Wang Meng was denounced in 1957 as a rightist, that is, a "reactionary and counterrevolutionary," for having made a mildly satirical dig at bureaucracy in a work of fiction entitled "The New Boy at the Organization Department."[16] He was sent into internal exile in Xinjiang, not returning to Beijing until the late 1970s. In 1978, Wang was officially exonerated along with tens of thousands of other intellectuals and writers. He went back to writing fiction and, by the early 1980s, was one of China's leading official novelists. His works were noted for their crafty, innovative use of literary devices, positive (that is, pro-party) and pro-reform satire, and relative depth. His political and literary acumen led him to be appointed minister of culture in 1986 during a high tide of cultural liberalization under Party General Secretary Hu Yaobang. A dexterous bureaucrat, Wang weathered various ideological storms and purges, particularly the "anti–bourgeois liberalization" campaign of early 1987, and survived in his post until September 1989.

During the late 1980s, while continuing his work as a bureaucrat and novelist, Wang also wrote a series of essays under the pen name Yang Yu ("Sun Shower"),[17] in which he touched on such knotty issues as cultural diversity and pluralism. He was, however, always careful to champion the prevailing, albeit "liberal," official line of the time. In one essay published in April 1988, he prefigured issues that were raised during the "humanist spirit" debate of 1993–1995, asking rhetorically: "Has our culture entered a period of weightlessness? Have we lost our goals, lost all gravitational pull?. . . Surely, the end result may be that we will lose the distinction between art and nonart, lose art itself, and therewith that very thing that makes the artist."[18] As the minister of culture, he oversaw and, to some extent, helped engineer the most lively and diverse—some would even say confused—period of cultural flowering that mainland China had experienced since 1949. It was an achievement, however, that came at some cost. As we related in earlier chapters, during those years pro-Maoist literary figures suffered general derision from the cliquish litterateurs gathered around Wang. They enjoyed little of the media attention lavished on more popular and better-selling authors; were generally included in only those official delegations sent to visit unfashionable foreign countries—mostly fraternal Eastern bloc or African nations, and North Korea; and were never able to cash in on sales in Hong Kong and Taiwan enjoyed by more talented and ideologically less burdened writers. As described in chapter 2, "An Iron Fist in a Velvet Glove," after 4 June these writer-bureaucrats had a chance to redress this perceived imbalance, and they did so with ill-concealed glee.

After the Beijing massacre, Wang was conspicuous for being one government minister who pointedly failed to pay his personal respects to the PLA martial law troops who occupied Beijing in early June 1989. Recognizing that his position was untenable in the post–4 June political climate, Wang asked to be relieved of his office later in the year. The ostensible reason for this request was failing health and a long-cherished desire to devote himself to creative writing. In early September 1989, the authorities allowed him to retire with a minimum of fuss, that is, without actually making him a victim of the general political purge that was in full swing at the time. Thereafter, he was able to enjoy his retirement undisturbed, indulging his passions for writing and mahjong in unequal measure. This situation may have had something to do with the efforts on Wang Meng's behalf by Hu Qiaomu, a leading orthodox ideologue who, it would appear, was fearful that an extreme cultural purge after 4 June could get out of hand. Hu was rumored to have appealed for lenient treatment for the three leading pro-party cultural figures who were thought to have been crucial to shaping the intellectual climate of China in the 1980s, men who could have easily been denounced now for bourgeois liberalization. They were Wang Meng, the philosopher Li Zehou, and the literary critic Liu Zaifu.[19]

Wang certainly became more active creatively after 1989, producing, among other things, new fictional works, including the novel A Season for Love and numerous essays. However, with the gradual relaxation in the political atmosphere in mid-1990 after the Politburo member Li Ruihuan's castigation of the Ministry of Culture for extremism, Wang attracted increasing political attention and support. As a result of the serious and continuing rifts in the party leadership on how to deal with culture and the arts, Wang Meng managed to negotiate an intriguing position for himself and a number of other writers. So many of his former colleagues and factional cronies rallied around his banner that during the early 1990s they formed, by default, something of a "shadow ministry of culture" in Beijing, which maintained a web of connections with leading provincial literary journals and groupings throughout the country and carried out its own war of resistance against the proponents of what was now derisively termed "red fundamentalism," *yuan hongzhizhuyi*.

The "leftist" bureaucracy attacks on Wang's faction began in earnest only in 1990, and his laissez-faire cultural policies were repeatedly denounced by the old new leaders well into 1991. The novelist Liu Xinwu, a long-standing friend and associate of Wang, was, for example, vilified at length in the *Literary Gazette* in May 1990,[20] and the new editors of *People's Literature*, a literary monthly previously run by Liu, raised a hue and cry about "no longer allowing this forum for the People's Literature to be monopolized by a 'spiritual aristocracy'." (For more on this, see chapter 2, "An Iron Fist in a Velvet Glove.") Despite these assaults, the first direct criticism of Wang by name did not appear in the media until January 1991. In an article sponsored by people in the new Ministry of Culture and the party's Propaganda Department, Wang was denounced for "doubting and negating Marxism while advocating pluralism in literature."[21] It was a clumsy miscalculation since, as a member of the party's Central Committee, Wang was theoretically immune to denunciation in the press without the prior consent of the Politburo. He reportedly wrote a letter of complaint to Party General Secretary Jiang Zemin in which he played on fears that extremist denunciations of the former cultural bureaucracy might signal to both China and the rest of the world that the excesses of the Cultural Revolution might revisit the nation and undermine the economic reform policies of the government.

As pointed out in "An Iron Fist in a Velvet Glove," central party leaders led by Jiang Zemin attempted to mollify both groups at a meeting in early 1991. Rigid ideologues took advantage of the occasion to express their concern that the post–4 June cultural purge would be allowed to peter out, as had been the case so many times before, while Wang Meng and his supporters called for the leaders to be more forthright on cultural issues. The upshot of the party's indecision led to an intensification of the conflict between the literary and cultural factions.

Members of the "Wang Meng gang," *Wang Meng bang*, a loose coalition of like-minded writer-editor bureaucrats, were quick to take advantage of the changing atmosphere. The woman novelist Zhang Jie, a close associate of Wang's, was the first to come to his defense in public. Her short story "Everyday Life," published in the Guangzhou literary journal *Huacheng* in April 1991, told of the daily grind of a grumpy man in the capital around the time of the Asian Games in the autumn of 1990. For the Beijing authorities, the games were an important occasion to show off the city and Chinese socialism to maximum advantage; their success was also a crucial step in the People's Republic bid to host the 2000 Olympics. In one passage Zhang used a comic "attack" on Wang Meng to slur Panpan, the wide-eyed and bloated panda mascot of the games, and to pay Wang an oblique, seemingly backhanded, compliment:

> . . . there, smack in the middle of the intersection stood a statue of "Panpan," an imitation of the Disney character Mickey Mouse. It was a slapdash job that didn't look like anything in particular, full-on postmodernism.
>
> Everyone said that Wang Meng, the former minister of culture who left office in 1989, had promoted the noxious mood of modernism. He [the protagonist] believed it, too. Every time he saw "artistic products" like Panpan that corrupted the rich and glorious cultural legacy of China, he felt that fellow Wang had been let off the hook far too easily.[22]

Despite such coded sideswipes, the next direct confrontation between the factions took place in the establishment literary media of Beijing in late 1991. The antagonism between the purged Wang and his successors broke out into the open when the *Literary Gazette,* China's leading official propaganda-arts weekly now run by trenchant political ideologues, published a "reader's letter" on 14 September signed Shen Ping.[23] Masquerading as a missive from a concerned reader, the letter condemned in no uncertain terms a story that Wang Meng had published in early 1989 entitled "Tough Porridge."[24] That story was a none-too-subtle satire of ossified habits and the stifling authority of the paterfamilias. Designed to lampoon conservative party cadres and castigate them for their entrenched undemocratic mind-set, "Tough Porridge" related its comic message by dissecting the unchanging breakfast menu of one family.

In the letter to the *Literary Gazette,* Shen Ping alleged that Wang's simple tale contained a subtext that blatantly "mocked reform." Furthermore, the letter claimed, Wang had used the story to launch a brazen assault on Deng Xiaoping and other political elders. This second accusation touched on a particularly sensitive issue. The mass criticisms during the 1989 protests of China's old leaders for being out of touch with the society and too set in their ways to lead the nation had directly contributed to the violent backlash in early June that year.[25] Shen Ping also claimed that Wang had purposely published his story at a time of serious social chaos, thereby taking advantage of the prevailing ideological confusion to agitate for wholesale privatization and the undermining of the socialist system.

The correspondent went on to quote a well-known Taiwanese anti-Communist publication which had reprinted the story with an editorial comment that "it ["Tough Porridge"] implicitly satirizes and vilifies the Communist system led by Deng Xiaoping." Given the control of the media on the mainland, the publication of this quotation itself was extraordinary. Since the Taiwan magazine referred to would have been available only to select and supposedly politically trustworthy readers, the implication was that Shen Ping had a special "background" or was, indeed, a party ideologue. Shen's letter further noted with a tone of concern that Wang's story had recently been given a literary award in the Fourth Tianjin Hundred Flowers Literature Competition, the details of which were made public in the July issue of *Fiction Monthly*. Shen Ping questioned the probity of the judges in giving a prize to such a dubious work of fiction.[26]

The publication of this defamatory letter was, without a doubt, a calculated response to Wang's waxing influence by the editors of the *Literary Gazette* and their factional supporters in the Ministry of Culture.[27] It was widely rumored in Beijing that the letter was actually written by Yan Zhaozhu, the establishment critic who had first denounced Wang by name in the press in early 1991, at the behest of Zheng Bonong, editor in chief of the *Literary Gazette*.[28] Zheng was himself part of the loose coalition of "leftist" cultural figures and bureaucrats who had come into power following June 1989. His coevals included figures in the Ministry of Culture (run until October 1992 by He Jingzhi, the acting minister), the All-China Artists' and Writers' Association (under the direction of Zhao Xun), the Writers' Association (under Malaqinfu), the party's Department of Propaganda (led by Wang Renzhi, Xu Weicheng, and others), and heads of the major media organizations in Beijing (including Ai Zhisheng and various figures in control of a range of newspapers, journals, television, and radio). By early 1991, many of these people were coming under increasing pressure from individuals in the Politburo and government, as well as the public, to be more flexible. Some were concerned that they might be removed from office in a counterpurge (and indeed, they were threatened with this in the aftermath of Deng Xiaoping's tour of the south).

Wang's response to the epistolary denunciation in *Literary Gazette* was as crafty as it was swift. He arrived back in Beijing from Singapore—his first trip overseas after 4 June 1989—on 12 September 1991. Shen Ping's letter was published two days later. On 15 September, Wang sent off a note to the editors of the *Literary Gazette* demanding that they explain why they had printed a letter that was an egregious political calumny. He also told them he would make an official complaint to the Central Committee and that he had no choice but to take legal action against the magazine and advise the media of the situation.[29] At that point, Wang engaged Zhang Sizhi, a leading senior Beijing lawyer, who had been both Jiang Qing's and the activist Wang Juntao's defense counsel, and another lawyer to draw up an indictment against the *Literary Gazette*, dated 1 October.[30] The suit was rejected by the Intermediate Court of the Beijing Municipality later in the month on the grounds that Shen Ping's letter constituted "legitimate criticism" and, as such was not actionable.[31] Given his involvement with contemporary Chinese legal practice and fiat, Wang was not particularly surprised by this outcome. He reasoned, however, that the publicity and kudos he earned from the exercise had been cheap at the price: the whole affair had cost him only 300 *yuan* in lawyers' fees.

Not satisfied with having made this a public and embarrassing case for the authorities or of availing himself of a legal means to repel what was obviously a studied political assault, Wang continued his counteroffensive by writing satirical articles for the press on the subject of rice gruel. These included an essay published in mid-November in the *Farmer's Daily* entitled "I Love Gruel"[32] and another in the December 1991 issue of *Reading*, "Talking About This Bowl of Porridge," which praised the virtues of both having your gruel and eating it.[33] He also allowed details of the case to be leaked to the Chinese and the overseas media; thus, numerous copies of his letter of complaint and the indictment he composed soon found their way into the hands of interested parties—both Chinese and foreign— in the capital.[34]

Although the party's Department of Propaganda was said to have ordered a media blackout on the incident, this ban had only a limited effect, yet another example of its unsteady influence in public affairs. *Wenhui Reader's Weekly*, a regional Shanghai weekly with a national readership, for instance, ran a front-page news item concerning Wang's litigation against *Literary Gazette* in late October 1991, thereby confirming rumors that had already spread through the provinces.[35] During a late-1991 trip to Australia, Wang verified stories that his adversaries had attempted to start a minicampaign against him but said that it had been quashed by the "timely and resolute action" of the Politburo. Nonetheless, attacks on the story and its author did not end with Shen Ping's testy letter. Other magazines under the control of, or allied with, the Ministry of Culture pursued the criticisms of Wang until the end of the year, although the tone of these later articles was increasingly mild, even perfunctory.[36] And just in case readers were wondering what all the fuss was about, *Literature and Contention*, a leading Beijing-based conservative magazine that had served the literary purge since 1989, reprinted in December Wang's original story in full, along with a copy of Shen Ping's letter.[37] This act was in itself in sharp contrast to the traditional style of party literary denunciations which featured fiery attacks on authors and their works in the media but never actually provided readers with the offensive originals. Now the public had the wherewithal to judge the matter for themselves.

A keen and sensitive observer of the shifting sands of Chinese politics who was at the time a member of the Central Committee and constrained by party discipline, Wang chose just the right moment to pursue this course of action, one that might well have proved dangerous at any other time. He was also wily enough not to push his luck after the lawsuit was rejected by the courts. After all, he had made his point; his opponents had been shamed; and the sallies against him had gradually decreased. Wang had stepped down from his moral high horse adroitly, dismounting just before his counterattack turned into a major incident that could offend even the more enlightened authorities, on whose patronage writers like himself relied. The anti–bourgeois liberalization campaign was still formally in force, and to flaunt one's literary independence for the sake of self-aggrandizement and a partial factional victory could have proved to be counterproductive.

The change in Wang's attitude can be gauged by comparing his initial response to the Shen Ping letter, "Some Facts About 'Tough Porridge',"[38] and the later essay published in the December issue of *Reading* mentioned earlier. The former was written in a tone of outrage, whereas the latter was a somewhat more conciliatory and evenhanded comment. But Wang outmaneuvered his detractors and did score one last point. In January 1992, he took another unprecedented step for a former minister and member of the party's Central Committee by publishing a book containing most of the relevant public documents surrounding the porridge kafuffle in Hong Kong.[39] Following the *Literary Gazette* incident, many of Wang's colleagues, friends, and supporters in the literary world also penned essays about rice congee in what amounted to a literary guerrilla counterattack on the conservatives. Even though none of them mentioned the criticism of Wang as such, informed readers would have been only too aware that it was this controversy that had inspired the sudden flood of porridge literature. Even Wang's overseas supporters rallied to the cause: Timothy Tung (Dong Dingshan), a New York–based writer and regular contributor to *Reading* who usually reported on the publishing scene in Manhattan, wrote an article in Wang's defense.[40] In October 1992, Wang also revealed that the Huacheng Publishers in Guangzhou were to produce a volume of these gruel-related essays.[41] This was the first time that such a literary protest had been staged—and published in book form—since the outspoken playwright Wu Zuguang was forced to resign from the party in 1987.[42] After his unceremonious ouster resulting from his criticisms of party censorship, Wu had edited a volume devoted to the theme of wine and forgetfulness entitled *Collected Essays on Alleviating Sorrows*. The title was a reference to the ways that traditional literati found to ignore official slights on their character.[43] Many of the people whose essays on wine appeared in Wu Zuguang's 1988 book also wrote about porridge in 1991–1992.

In late 1991, Zhang Jie, presumably outraged by the continued mudslinging aimed at Wang and the implied threat it posed to his allies, published another story in which she came to his defense. It was an absurdist tale entitled *On*

Heat.[44] This novella-length story describes an equine research association and the heavy-handed plots of its leaders to maintain their grip on power, including in a subplot the salacious details of their personal lives.[45] It is only too easy to read the story as a thinly disguised lambasting of the Writers' Association, the avowedly nongovernment organization headed by Malaqinfu that oversaw the work of state-funded writers. Many people took the story for just what it was, and the relevant office of the Department of Propaganda ordered a detailed analysis of the work in preparation for a full-scale denunciation. The Hong Kong press also reported that the department, which acted as the party's central censorship watchdog, had ordered the publishers of the story at the Nanjing *Zhongshan* literary journal to investigate the "ideological thrust" of Zhang's work.[46] Despite these moves, however, the cultural authorities appeared to be reluctant to condemn the novel in the press, probably because they knew that to do so would only bring it to the attention of a wider readership and inadvertently help people decode the mischievous intent of Zhang's roman à clef. Meanwhile, Zhang Jie herself continued to support Wang publicly. While attending a book launching held at the Italian embassy in Beijing in early 1992, for example, she pointedly remarked that Italian culture was healthy and normal because it could digest all types of things, even foods like Wang's tough porridge. She reportedly went on to say that a country that had troubles with its digestion or that rejected some types of food outright for being unacceptable to the body politic was a nation threatened by senescence.[47]

Meanwhile, in January 1992, Wang took his campaign of annoyance one step further by publishing in Shanghai eight letters from various prominent writers that he had received over the years. His introduction to the selected letters was dated September 1991, the month that he had been attacked for "Tough Porridge." In it he said: "Despite the fact that bad blood may mar relations between literary people, I still feel our arts scene is brimming with hope."[48] Among what was otherwise a fairly innocuous collection was one particular letter dated 8 April 1989 and signed by Malaqinfu, the man who, as party secretary of the Writers' Association, had energetically applied himself to the task of purging Wang's followers after 4 June. In this groveling letter—one written when Wang was still very much in power as minister of culture—Malaqinfu lavished praise on Wang before getting down to the real aim of his writing: to make a plea for an official position in the ministry. The appeal read in part: "Although I am fifty-eight years old . . . I beg you to consider the following: if you think I can still make a contribution, please find me a job. I will then be able to work humbly, prudently, and energetically under your guidance for a few more years."[49] In recognition of the fact that Malaqinfu was the lawful owner of the copyright of the letter, Wang instructed his editors to pay Malaqinfu a publication fee so as to avoid any legal complications. Other writers immediately took advantage of Wang's lead to have a dig at the now-be-leaguered Malaqinfu.[50]

In August and September 1992, Wang went on to publish in Shanghai a series of articles on problems related to the general issue of culture that were highly reminiscent of the style of his earlier controversial "Sun Shower" essays.[51] And in early September, he was featured prominently at a forum on "post–new era" (that is, post-1976) literature at Peking University. At that meeting he claimed a status for what he now styled "thin gruel literature," *xizhou wenxue*, that he declared was equal in import to the popular "literature of *badinage*," *tiaokan wenxue*, created by Wang Shuo. Both kinds of writing, Wang argued, represented the present pop-ularity of humorous and upbeat fiction. The literary critic He Xilai, an employee of the Chinese Academy of Social Sciences, took advantage of this supposedly academic gathering to defend Wang against the attacks of the "leftists" who claimed they had found a hidden political subtext in "Tough Porridge."[52]

In the 1990s, Wang remained the most skillful official cultural figure in China. Through his practiced political maneuvering, he not only played a key role in containing what could have been a devastating cultural purge in 1989–1990, but his literary career also continued to prosper. The contretemps surrounding the short story "Tough Porridge" revealed how the conflicting interests of the cultural bureaucracy turned a literary witch-hunt into a media spectacle. Instead of suf-fering the provocations of the Beijing cultocrats, or ignoring them, Wang chose to accept the challenge. It was a clever gambit deftly handled, and the "negative pub-licity" that he was given acted as a public boost to his moral and literary status.

This storm in Wang's rice bowl—intriguing though it may have been—was, from beginning to end, little more than an example of factional infighting. As with similar strife in the political and economic arenas, the sorties, skirmishes, routs, and victories of the parties involved were, for the most part, played out pub-licly in excruciating detail. Fascinating (and convenient) though this may be for students of contemporary official and elite Chinese culture, it had little to do with the main sphere of innovation: popular culture, an area in which Wang Meng now became embroiled. As economic priorities finally encroached on the realm of official, state-funded arts, a number of Hong Kong commentators remarked that the controversy surrounding "Tough Porridge" may have been the last exam-ple of a traditional party-style literary incident, *shijian*, of its type, one involving factions of arts bureaucrats, in mainland cultural politics.

As things developed in the mid-1990s, the major literary mudslinging was no longer limited to the realm of state-sponsored culture. Wang, however, was to fig-ure prominently in an imbroglio with new and younger opponents to his extraor-dinary versatility. In particular, in 1994, "upstart critics" like Wang Binbin and Xiao Xialin (see the section "Kowtowing to the Vulgar" in this chapter) raised their voices of opposition, not against official, state-sanctioned culture, but against Wang Meng and others who wanted to see Chinese culture move away from its ideological legacy as quickly as possible.

SHUNNING THE SUBLIME

After his resignation from the bureaucracy in 1989, Wang Meng survived the cultural ambush set by official opponents against his story "Tough Porridge." His deft handling of that political morass only endeared him further to his readers, many of whom, despite the cynicism of the early 1990s, evinced a residual idealism and faith in the avowedly enlightened values of reformist writers like Wang.

Then in early 1993, Wang published an essay in *Reading* entitled "Shunning the Sublime," and perceptions of him underwent a radical transformation.[53] The essay was in the carefully honed and persuasive style to which readers of Wang's literary and cultural criticisms had grown accustomed from the 1980s. He praised the growth of a kind of cultural pluralism in contemporary China that rejected the hypocritical moral perfectionism of the past. He argued that it was a sign of positive social and cultural progress that writers now felt emboldened to mock all forms of idealism and absolutism. Just as he had supported economic reform and cultural diversity as minister of culture in the 1980s, in the 1990s Wang Meng praised the market economy and cultural pluralism. It was the market, he argued, that was crucial to bringing an end to China's weighty authoritarian traditions. In particular, he singled out the fiction of Wang Shuo, generally known as "the literature of *badinage*," for praise. Wang Shuo's writing, he declared, depicted a world in which idealism, that farrago of political hypermythology that had brought the Chinese to so much grief in the past, had been lambasted and rejected. Contrary to the claims of many of his critics, Wang Meng averred, the louts, the *liumang*, of Wang Shuo's fictional world were not themselves guilty of defiling sacred ideals or social goodness. Rather, it was life itself, the recent history of China, that had been polluted by the so-called sacred and good. Of course, this was a coy way of saying that the ideology and utilitarian morality of the Communist Party itself were the root causes of the social degradation that critics were anxious to blame on contemporary commercial culture.[54]

Then in late 1994, Wang Meng continued his assault on authoritarian thought by moving from his critique of the "sublime" to offering an opinion on the "humanist spirit" discussion. Writing this time for *Orient*, he remarked that people had suggested that the economic reforms had led to a decay of social values, widespread avariciousness, and a general loss of the humanistic spirit in China. Such claims, he said, begged the question: what kind of specter had enlivened Chinese

society before the reforms? If anything, Wang declared, it was the destructive spirit of revolutionary radicalism, political denunciation, and sloganeering. What, he
asked, did any of this have to do with "humanism"? How could people mourn the
loss of a humanistic spirit that they had never even possessed? He concluded that
the clutch of intellectuals who were beating their breasts and decrying the lack of
"ultimate concerns" would be well advised to face this uncomfortable truth.
"Let's first have a little dose of reality; there will be time enough for talk of the ultimate in the future."[55] It was a view generally shared by Wang's allies like Chen
Jiangong, Liu Xinwu, and other writers mentioned in the earlier section of this
chapter "A Storm in a Rice Bowl."[56]

The reaction among many critics to these two essays was one of righteous indignation. Unlike in the past when Wang's chief foes had been entrenched
Maoist cultocrats, this time critical voices were raised among younger writers,
many of whom had previously been his supporters. To these critics, Wang Meng
seemed overly fixated on opposing the extremism of a dated ideology and residual party hegemony. Where he saw in the cultural market a solution to many of
China's long-standing woes, others perceived a dangerous new form of autocracy
and were wary of the effects of international capital on the mainland culture industry. For them the socioeconomic impact of the reforms had worked in tandem
with the authoritarian power structure that had rearticulated itself in terms of a
faux plurality.[57] As one commentator put it: "In their enthusiasm for popular culture and materialism, figures [like Wang Meng] have blurred the standards of
right and wrong and lost any critical edge. Pluralism has become a cloak that con-
ceals mediocrity; it is an excuse to a indulge in a carefree existence."[58]

Yet as Wang observed in comments made to a Hong Kong journalist about
these indignant reactions, "The search for standard-bearers, or the habit of wanting oneself to become a standard-bearer in the literary world, is still deeply entrenched." He said that people were used to a simple cultural logic—one conditioned by a vestigial nineteenth-century romanticism and revolutionary idealism:
Wang Meng was an author of serious literature who occupied a respected position in the Chinese world of letters, and people looked to him to declare war on
darkness; people hoped that he would hold the torch of illumination aloft and set
the whole world alight. But then Wang had affirmed the value of a *pizi* author
whose works were full of swear words. Hadn't he betrayed the People's wishes? In
his defense, Wang argued that only when writers were finally allowed to enjoy
true individualism, regardless of where that individualism might take them creatively (he did enter a caveat against illicit depictions of sex), would China have
some hope of developing a more liberal, even democratic, atmosphere, one in
which the life of the spirit might have some hope of flourishing.[59] Like so many
advocates of the market, he failed to appreciate the fact that giving people what

they want through entertainment culture often leads to a censorship over whatever *they* don't want to hear or know about, something that serves the interests of both government and business.

There was, however, another dimension to Wang Meng's stance, something endemic to the literary infighting of the politicized sphere of mainland culture. Among establishment litterateurs—even those who regarded themselves as reluctant fringe dwellers—there was a tireless enthusiasm for factional politics, one that subverted all forms of public discussion and debate, mutating it into rhetorical material to be deployed in the larger culture wars. The issues raised by independent critics included such things as the ideological nature and impact of a commodification of culture that was being championed by an avowedly totalitarian government; the evolution of a range of cultural and social values determined by markets within both mainland China and the larger Sino-Kong-Tai sphere; the role of controversial critics and writers as arbiters of artistic standards and taste; and the ways in which nonofficial mass culture and unaligned pop culture was being used in commercial and ideological struggles as it had been in China since the 1930s. Wang Meng, himself a victim of the overpoliticization of literary debate, had, with the publication of his essays, chosen to simplify the complex issues in the "humanist spirit" discussion and treat his rhetorical opponents merely as though they were sympathetic to the regnant official line.

HORSES FOR COURSES

The most pointed responses to Wang Meng's celebration of popular culture came not from his peers, whether or not they were ideological enemies, but from younger writers and critics in both the provinces and Beijing itself.

In late 1994, Wang Binbin, a young army critic based in Nanjing, took Wang Meng to task for being what he called "too clever by half," *guoyu congming*. In a satirical essay published in *Cultural Debate*, a journal devoted to literary criticism published in the northeast and favored by nonofficial writers, Binbin lambasted Wang Meng for his glib approval of commercial culture and his simplistic anti-idealist stance.[60] He pointed out that Wang Meng's approval of Wang Shuo was to a considerable extent a form of self-affirmation. In fact, he argued, Wang Meng's remarks about Wang Shuo were more of a self-description of how he had been "shunning the sublime" in his own recent literary outpourings than an accurate appraisal of Wang Shuo's fiction and its significance in contemporary Chinese culture.

Neither Wang Shuo nor Wang Meng, however, were purveyors of Mills & Boon– or Harlequin–style romances, cheap thrillers, or airport books. Wang

Shuo, in particular, had shown writers suckled by the state that commercial fiction could be a viable alternative to being on the official payroll. As an entrepreneurial author, he had been a major success. But now he was being blamed again for the degradation not of the masses as a whole—a criticism made of his work by a slew of conservative critics in the late 1980s and early 1990s—but for the corruption of other writers. Wang Shuo had unequivocally rejected the cherished myth of writer as seer and hero in Chinese letters. He was one of the first mainland writers to state simply that "writing is a profession, and one should treat it as one."[61] During the media debate about humanism and the sublime, he had been reproached for having the temerity to tell the literary elite that they were not necessarily the conscience of the society or the voice of the people. He gleefully remarked that their role in the grand narrative of Chinese history was highly overrated and that their existence was not necessarily relevant to the political and economic realities of the day.[62]

According to Wang Shuo, Wang Meng had been courting him since the late 1980s as both a writer-*cum*-cultural icon and a factional ally.[63] During the early years of his fame, Wang Shuo politely avoided cooperating with the Wang network and preferred to maintain his independence. Having consistently failed to draw the reluctant novelist into the embrace of his reformist sodality in the past, in the mid-1990s Wang Meng chose to use his literary authority not only to add his imprimatur to Wang Shuo's success but also, through his support of the younger novelist, to affirm the strategic approach to contemporary cultural issues shared by many of Wang Meng's ilk, that commercialization was to be embraced as it undermined party control and, by association, the sway of their foes in the arts bureaucracy.[64]

Wang Meng was himself a member, even the notional leader, of the very elite that Wang Shuo had outraged in the 1980s. His support for the younger novelist in 1993–1994 was seen by his critics as the result of his personal moral disarmament, something partially attributable to his fall from political grace but also due to the massive commercial success of Wang Shuo's style of writing, not to mention the best-selling prurient outpourings of serious-minded literary colleagues like Jia Pingwa. The debate that now centered on Wang Meng's stand in favor of commercialism over all else revealed, however, that the former culture minister was far from dispassionate in his view of the rising tide of commercialization and was quick to take umbrage when his authoritative role as cultural arbiter was called into question by younger critics like Wang Binbin. To an extent, Wang Meng had been using Wang Shuo as a feint, and Binbin had identified the strategy and called his bluff. The results were a rancorous public brawl that continued in Chinese newspapers and journals for some years.[65]

Wang Meng's response to Wang Binbin was swift and scathing. In mid-January 1995, he published a satirical essay in the mass-circulation Shanghai paper

New People's Evening News in which he said that Binbin was nothing more than a "black colt," *heiju*, in other words, an upstart. "Black colt" was also a coded diminutive for the expression "dark horse," *heima*, that is, someone who appeared unexpectedly and was not welcome. Some ten years earlier, Wang Meng had used the term to describe the irascible young critic Liu Xiaobo, a doctoral student who had rocketed to prominence in 1986 for his blanket condemnation of post–Cultural Revolution literature, in particular the style of velvet prison culture championed by Wang Meng and his supporters. Liu, who had praised an earlier generation of novelists for "shunning the sublime" in 1985, reserved his most pointed barbs for the "Beijing gang," *Beijing bang*, which prospered under the patronage of Wang Meng. In 1988, he wrote about the stifling patriarchy established by leading literary figures like Wang and cliquish critics like Li Tuo (known in Beijing as *"Tuoye"* or "Master Tuo"):

> The famous in China are much taken with acting as benefactors of others; they caress and suckle the unknown. They employ a kind of tenderness which is almost feminine, to possess, co-opt, and finally asphyxiate you. This is one of the peculiarities of Chinese culture. . . . Some people do indeed have the talent to excel, but shying away from the dangers of going it alone, they instead search out a discoverer. They look for support and security so that they can sleep easy at night; they fling themselves into the bosom of some grand authority or other and doze off in their warm embrace.[66]

Liu's critical ostentation made him many enemies and, at the time, Wang Meng dismissed him as a transient figure who would fade from the scene as abruptly as he had appeared.[67] Far from disappearing, however, Liu Xiaobo continued his career as an erratic and prescient critic of the Chinese cultural scene and became increasingly embroiled in politics. As a pivotal figure in the government repression of the 1989 protest movement (he was denounced as a "black hand" behind the protests), Liu was jailed and, even after his release in 1991, was banned from publishing in China.[68] Deprived of employment and the right to publish under his own name, Liu had effectively been silenced.[69]

Wang Meng's splenetic attack on Wang Binbin in early 1995 revealed a smoldering resentment over the criticisms he had been subjected to by younger writers like Liu. For those who remembered Liu Xiaobo as the "dark horse" of a decade ago, the reference in Wang's essay was clear; for others the murky metaphor was effective enough to bind Wang Binbin to a nameless extremist from the past. Wang Meng was also playing factional politics in the realm of orthodox culture. He was signaling that the upstart Wang Binbin in 1994 was like the Liu Xiaobo of 1985, a dangerous anarchist and possible nihilist. By making this association, Wang Meng was indicating that Wang Binbin, a second-rate gadfly, a mere colt compared with the stallionlike stature of Liu Xiaobo, was another wannabe critic who would stop at nothing to achieve fame.

Wang Meng concluded his essay on Wang Binbin with the observation that although Binbin had finally been awarded a higher academic degree in literature, albeit "with the greatest of difficulty," he had been repeatedly frustrated in his attempts to get anything published. The result of this was that he suffered from "an excessive amount of repressed libido" that had led him to write essays critical of the older writer.[70]

KOWTOWING TO THE VULGAR

As early as the late 1980s, some literary critics fretted that the post-1976 arts scene had entered a period of "cultural stagnation."[71] Was it something à la Brezhnev? Or simply a premature visitation by fin-de-siècle ennui? Writers and critics of all persuasions bewailed the fact that serious literature in mainland China had lost the privileged position it had enjoyed in the past. The inference was that they were also mourning their own precipitous fall from the status as "engineers of the human soul"—even though in the heyday of literary power up to the early 1980s, they had been engineers who worked primarily to realize the utopian designs of the grand architects of socialism. Now that they were obliged to search for artistic inspiration in themselves rather than in the carefully arranged dialectic and state-funded scenarios of "life," many found little more than tedium, passivity, and creative desuetude.[72] In the long term, frustration and impotence—mental states felt even more sorely by intellectuals in general[73]—seemed like they might have damaging consequences for the state as well.[74]

In the mid-1990s, the success of novels like *The Abandoned Capital*, the television series *A Beijing Man in New York*, and the rise to media stardom of the novelist Wang Shuo led critics to despair of the direction of elite culture once more. Writers formerly regarded as champions of serious literature, people like Jia Pingwa, were now derided for *meisu*, "kowtowing to the vulgar," or "pandering to the masses." In the realm of media debate, the rise of *meisu* was seen as a corollary to the loss of the humanistic spirit, and it soon became one of the most contentious expressions in the vocabulary of mainland culture.

Meisu has had a long history in Chinese, although in the late 1980s it became a common translation for the word "kitsch." The Hunan novelist Han Shaogong (the editor of *Frontiers* in the 1990s) used *meisu* for kitsch when introducing Milan Kundera's notion of the word as it appeared in *The Unbearable Lightness of Being*:

> The feeling induced by kitsch must be a kind the multitudes can share. Kitsch may not, therefore, depend on an unusual situation; it must derive

from the basic images people have engraved in their memories: the un-grateful daughter, the neglected father, children running on the grass, the motherland betrayed, first love.

Kitsch causes two tears to flow in quick succession. The first tear says: How nice to see children running on the grass!

The second tear says: How nice to be moved, together with all mankind, by children running on the grass!

It is the second tear that makes kitsch kitsch.

The brotherhood of man on earth will be possible only on a base of kitsch.

And no one knows this better than politicians. Whenever a camera is in the offing, they immediately run to the nearest child, lift it in the air, kiss it on the cheek. Kitsch is the aesthetic ideal of all politicians and all political parties and movements.

Those of us who live in a society where various political tendencies exist side by side and competing influences cancel or limit one another can manage more or less to escape the kitsch inquisition: the individual can pre-serve his individuality; the artist can create unusual works. But whenever a single political movement corners power, we find ourselves in the realm of *totalitarian kitsch.*

In Chinese, both elements of the expression *meisu—mei* and *su—*had a complex provenance. *Su* is a word with a particularly distasteful pedigree. It connotes all that is vulgar, common, unrefined, ill lettered, knavelike, and vile. To be "vulgar" is to be beyond the pale of what is cultured and literate. Most of the expressions in which the term *su* is used carry a negative gloss. *Sushang* are current, ephemeral fashions, indulged in by *suren,* "vulgar individuals," for the sake of appealing to *suqing,* "commonplace emotions," that are in the final analysis *su buke nai,* "unbearably crude," and represent nothing so much as a propensity for *meisu,* "kowtowing to the vulgar." To be a *suren,* "a vulgar indi-vidual," is, as the pre-Qin philosopher Xunzi put it, to be "a person without learning, without a sense of righteousness; to be someone who delights merely in wealth."[75]

As we observed in earlier chapters, for some writers like Wang Shuo, to play at being a "vulgar person" meant avoiding membership in the self-appointed intel-ligentsia and not being bound by the overweening desire to be didactic. To be a *vulgarisateur* was to be a realist in a mendacious world; at least irreverent "street louts" were not fettered by the hypocrisy of the chattering classes. Wang Shuo's fiction—one of his last published novellas was entitled *You're Not One of the Vul-*

gar Masses[76]—helped popularize the expression "vulgar person" among the young and also made it a watchword among elite intellectuals.

The burgeoning of mass-market popular culture led to despair among writers who had only recently regained their faith in the tradition of the Chinese literati-scholars, the political and cultural mandarins of the past, and an abiding belief in the romantic socialist dogma of the artist as prophet. Having borne witness to the decay of the socialist cultural welfare state during the past decade, they now saw their own influence waning. They felt that the writers who profited from the tide of commercialization were prostituting their talents and betraying the cause of a revived literati culture.

Seen in terms of cultural capital, of course, in the 1990s mainland urban elitist artists witnessed their stocks fall dramatically compared with the 1980s. Rabid commercialization left many without the wherewithal to appeal to a wider audience. Even cultural repression—the banning of a book, play, or film—no longer assured the artist of popular support or sympathy; people were simply too busy with their own depoliticized lives and finding cultural succor in a myriad of new diversions like pirated VCD films, karaoke bars, the popular press, and pulp fiction to care about the arcane machinations of literary coteries. They felt betrayed by an ideological environment that prized an idealism constructed out of empty and dated slogans, and they were threatened by a market that was just as fickle as any political movement. They were also disgruntled with the liberal writers and intellectuals who had been intimately involved with China's move away from the cultural authoritarianism of the past for being incapable of formulating new social or cultural ideals. To an extent, these disaffected writers were antagonistic toward the relative pluralism that made it possible for them to express their own heterodox opinions. They excoriated the economic reforms for creating freedoms that, in the long run, had the effect of marginalizing them.

Complaints about the vulgar tastes of the masses, their eagerness to pay for the cultural products of nonstate writers like the Kong-Tai novelists Jin Yong, Qiong Yao, San Mao, or Yi Shu, and the pressure this put on "serious literature" generated on the mainland had been common in the literary press in the mid-1980s. Objections to the flood of the popular were made not only by pro-state writers and the entrenched cultural bureaucracy but also by the cultural reformers and proponents of the avant-garde who rejected the state yet did not want their work or their social role to be subsumed by the mechanisms of the market. By the late 1980s and during the early 1990s, popular culture—in particular, television, film, music, and literature—became a realm where, as we saw in earlier chapters, the arts elite, both party and nonparty, struggled to establish primacy.

The opponents of the vulgarization that swept China in the mid-1980s were of the opinion that cultural strength depended somehow on its purity or the assumed unsullied motives of its leading proponents. It was a conceit that also neatly conflated the mythologies of socialist asceticism and Confucian moralism. In the 1990s, these writers felt it was their duty to fight for the "soul of China." Similar rhetorical battles had been joined by numerous writers and critics over the past century. The cultural campaigns waged in the name of "China's soul," however, had invariably had the effect of polarizing the arts scene and feeding into the ideological needs of the power holders.

In their published cris de coeur, these writers preyed on fears that had beggared mainland culture and public debate for decades. They tried to evoke the paranoia instilled in readers' minds by decades of Communist Party cultural witch-hunts and use it against a demonized cultural "enemy." Theirs was a militant romantic spirit—dare we even impose on it the old sobriquet of "revolutionary romanticism"? They were, to quote Miklós Haraszti once more, people who were "too deeply imbued with the tradition of commitment to be able to renounce easily socialist aesthetics' most fundamental axiom: the idea of *art as service*. . . . They . . . want their art to play . . . an active social role in shaping the consciousness of the culture of the nation."[77]

Liang Xiaosheng, a novelist and a former Red Guard whose literary fame peaked during the 1980s, was one of a number of prominent writers who vociferously opposed the rising tide of commercialization and singled out Wang Shuo for criticism. In mid-1995, Liang expressed his concerns in the following way: "[Today] the mature kowtows to the vulgarity of the superficial; thoughtfulness kowtows to the vulgarity of fashion; cultural standards kowtow to the vulgarity of the marketplace; and cultural responsibility and duty kowtow to the 'theories' of irreverence that are championed by street louts."[78]

THE WAR OF RESISTANCE

At the same time that Liang voiced his disapproval, the Huayi Publishing House, the same company that only three years earlier had produced the best-selling four-volume opus of Wang Shuo's fiction (see chapter 4, "The Apotheosis of the *Liumang*"), released the first two books in the *Refusal to Capitulate Collection*, Dikang touxiang shuxi. The books took issue with everything that Wang Shuo and the commercialized style of elite culture that he was supposed to represent stood for.

The *Refusal to Capitulate Collection* was the work of the literary critic and editor Xiao Xialin, a writer who had first come to public attention during the controversy surrounding Jia Pingwa's 1993 novel, *The Abandoned Capital*. Xia was a young (in his late twenties) literature graduate from Qufu, the hometown of Confucius in rural Shandong Province. As an editor at the *China Reader's Press*, a popular publishing weekly produced by the *Guangming Daily*, one of the nation's leading newspapers, Xiao was in an ideal position to publicize his particular view of Chinese letters. He used the *China Reader's Press* to create a popular and controversial forum for literary debate, in particular giving full rein to the opinions of critics like Wang Binbin, the army writer who had locked horns with Wang Meng in 1994.

In conversation with me in December 1995, Xiao said that in the early 1990s he had been shocked and outraged by what he called the unprincipled stand of writers like Wang Meng, his former cultural preceptor. Wang, he argued, was a traitor to his readers for having "sold out" or "capitulated," *touxiang*, to the market.[79] Xiao stated that he had put out the *Refusal to Capitulate Collection* as a statement of opposition to the widespread selling out to cultural commercialization that had infected China since 1992.

The title of the book series was inspired by the writings of Zhang Chengzhi, the novelist and polemicist mentioned earlier. Although born in Beijing, Zhang was ethnically of Hui-Muslim origin, and so as a child, he had been given the name of Said.[80] After a career as a Red Guard—he is generally identified as the student who created the term in 1966[81]—he spent years in the grasslands in the northwest of China, rising to prominence in the early 1980s as a writer of romantic, salt-of-the-earth fiction. It was Zhang's hyperbolic style and prose that gave Xiao Xialin his inspiration for the book series. As Zhang wrote in his typically inflammatory style: "Today we need a literature that will serve in the war of resistance. We must point out the dangers, reveal the crisis. We need a literature of self-respect and honor—even if it means that they [Wang Shuo et al.] are going to make fun of us using their Beijing slang." It is a fascinating statement coming as it does from a prominent former Red Guard, given that the Beijing Cultural Revolution warriors themselves championed a near *liumang*-esque style.[82]

Each volume in the series carried an introductory essay by Xiao Xialin entitled "Some Mourn While Others Celebrate."[83] Composed in a 1990s doggerel version of Cultural Revolution denunciatory prose, the essay was not merely a ploy to curry favor with cultural conservatives. Rather, Xiao was evoking the charisma of a rhetorical style that, despite the devaluation it had experienced since the 1980s, could still elicit a response from readers young and old, readers for whom the language of urgency, moral uplift, and idealism had been mediated for decades by party propaganda.

Just as the extremist student leader Chai Ling and her fellow demagogues had formulated their protests against the authorities in 1989 in mock-revolutionary rhetoric (see the section "The Rhetoric of Denunciation" in chapter 12), so now some six years later a prominent young editor was calling for a return to idealism and a rejection of commercialization by invoking the power of the only language that carried any vestige of authority, New China Newspeak. As Xiao wrote:

In the early 1990s, at the very moment when we needed cultural heroes, literary storm troopers, and a collective of conscience to undertake the difficult task of constructing a Great Wall of the Spirit, we have witnessed Wang Shuo launch his "revolution of the louts."[84] It is a revolution born at a time of national spiritual crisis. What astounds us is that there has been no concerted literary opposition to this "revolution." On the contrary, it has been received with great enthusiasm.

Wang Shuo has moved to the center stage of the literary world amid approbation; he has become a role model for writers. Moreover, China's writers have vied to join in his "revolution of louts." They have aligned themselves with Wang Shuo and endorsed the "loutishness" that now floods the nation.

In a virtuoso display of intellectual acrobatics, Xiao went on to claim that writers who were following the Wang Shuo model were responsible for having turned China into a nation of *liumang*, "collectively converting the people into louts." Among other things, they were guilty of perverting the purity and dignity of the Han (Chinese) language and of "undermining the spiritual achievements of the decade of reform." In a twist on the debates about cultural values in the 1990s, Xiao said that China's humanistic spirit had once more come under threat and faced extinction.

The louts' movement is symbolic of a historical turning point for contemporary Chinese writers. It has inspired the vast majority of Chinese writers to abandon their agreement with and understanding of the "modern." They have betrayed the ideals and enthusiasm they had in the 1980s. They are kowtowing to the vulgar and have capitulated to the public.[85]

With great fanfare, China's writers now promote the "anything goes" attitude of postmodernism. They regard Wang Shuo as being the hero of the day, the model for their deliverance. A new age has dawned, one in which Chinese writers are abandoning their efforts to save the world. Instead, they are engaging in so-called self-salvation and diversion. It is an age in which conscience is abandoned and brazen shamelessness is touted as glorious.[86]

Wang Shuo described his work and its relevance in a very different manner. Writing for *People's Literature* in early 1989, Wang said:

What I write is realist [fiction]. None of the crass elements in my writing are there just for the sake of attracting readers. They're there because society has given birth to such things. Perhaps they should be called "popular elements." I'm particularly interested in the social stratum that [enjoys] this popular lifestyle. It's one full of violence and sex, mockery and shamelessness. All I've done [in my fiction] is to have teased it out.[87]

Confronted by the national celebrity of Wang Shuo, Xiao Xialin observed that "ideals, beliefs, art, and conscience are no longer the spiritual mainstay of Chinese writers." This was an extraordinary statement in that it assumed that the majority of mainland Chinese writers—most of whom had drawn a state salary for much of their working lives—had generally been inspired by these laudable qualities in the first place. It was a breathtaking assertion given the fact that from 1949 (at least) until the late 1970s, the vast corpus of mainland cultural outpourings was the manifestation of political fiat, complicity, terror, and pressure. In the late 1970s, other forces had certainly come into play, but Xiao would probably have had a hard time proving statistically that works suffused with "ideals, beliefs, art, and conscience" were in the majority.

The relationship between the Beijing cultural avant-garde and its practitioners in the provinces was already a highly complex one. Many provincials aspired to the recognition, both local and international, that had been enjoyed by Beijing-based cultural and intellectual figures since the late 1970s. Many relocated themselves to the capital in search of fame and fortune (witness, for example, the careers of various nonestablishment filmmakers, writers, and artists during the 1980s and 1990s). Others who would travel to Beijing, or *jin Jing* (an expression dating from the imperial era that was still in currency), regarded the city as being decadent and effeminate. Writers like Zhou Lunyou (the Sichuan poet whose appeal for "red writing" was noted in the previous chapter) who were based in the southwest, and Li Jie, the acerbic Shanghai literary critic who will be discussed in the following chapter, were generally scornful of the limp-wristed Beijing style and rejected its temptations. Likewise, Xiao Xialin, Wang Binbin, and Zhang Chengzhi also eschewed the Beijing style. It was perhaps no coincidence that the flippant and irreverent manner they excoriated was the product of Wang Shuo, a part Manchu whose work has mined a vein first uncovered by the republican-period Manchu novelist, Lao She. Beginning in the late nineteenth century, many Han patriots blamed the world-weary Manchu canker for infecting the virulent political and cultural body of China. The Manchu temper, as much as the political venality of the Manchu–Qing dynasty, was indicted for polluting the racial spirit of the Han and was cited as the source of many of the nation's ills over the past 150 years.[88] Indeed, the Manchu ambience has often been characterized as being representative of the feminine, decadent, self-indulgent, sybaritic dimension of late-imperial Chinese culture.

Well might Zhang Chengzhi, Xiao Xialin, and others accuse the Wang Shuos of China of being collaborators. "Their aim in writing," Xiao fulminated, "is entirely for the sake of moneygrubbing commercialism and to indulge the pipe dreams of the middle class." Contemporary writers, Xiao continued, were nothing more than "wholesalers who trade in the Chinese written language."[89] By claiming the moral high ground, Xiao and Zhang cast themselves as independent critics of conscience who were absolved of complicity with either the party system or the marketplace. And this, despite the fact that their own publishing ventures and propagandistic stance exploited the state system, fed off popular fears and intellectual concerns and appealed to a constituency that had been manufactured over the decades by party propagandists' tireless warnings about the dangers of bourgeois values and nonpolitical culture. In their 1995 call to arms, they appealed to some ideal, prelapsarian moment before commercialization, blithely ignoring the ideological realities of the past when other "market forces" had predominated.

The contributors to the *Refusal to Capitulate Collection* were themselves involved in a canny commercial strategy. As the editor of the *China Reader's Press's* opinion page, Xiao Xialin promoted literary debate and focused on issues that he felt not only were important but also would appeal to a wide readership. He then availed himself of his position at a leading Beijing publisher and his connections with prominent critics (many of whom he featured in his newspaper) to edit a series of books aimed at turning a profit on a literary controversy that had a pointed political edge. Meanwhile, the editors of Huayi Publishers recognized the appeal of Xiao's views among university students and readers disaffected from an elite culture that seemed to have lost direction and produced the series amid considerable fanfare.

Neither side in this phony war, however, was willing to confront the authorities directly. For the opponents of commercial culture, it was easier to blame writers like Wang Shuo and Wang Meng for social decay and cultural bankruptcy than to question the mendacious policies of the Communist Party itself. Bred in an atmosphere of political hype and grandstanding, it was effortless for someone like Zhang Chengzhi to indulge in mock heroic sentiment: "I've been thinking. After the war of civilizations, they should at least find in the rubble of the defeated a few bodies of intellectuals who fought to the death. I despise surrender. In particular, in this war of civilizations, I loathe intellectuals who have made a vocation out of capitulation."[90]

Wang Shuo's response to these attacks came in late August 1995, during an interview given to a reporter from the *Beijing Youth Daily*. He remarked that the first two volumes of Xiao Xialin's series *Refusal to Capitulate Collection* were not unlike edited books of big-character posters produced in the Cultural Revolution.

"I don't understand where all this anger is coming from. Is it simply cultural posturing, or do they really believe all that stuff?" he queried. Wang went on to say, "nor do I see any evidence that Zhang Chengzhi has rejected the vulgar enticements of the world: he joined the army just so he could get an apartment, and he's got himself published in Japanese so he can be a best-selling author."

Wang pointed out that China in the 1990s had, in fact, nurtured two types of "louts," *liumang*. The first was the "relatively deep and meaningful lout" like Zhang Chengzhi, and the other was the "laissez-faire louts" that he represented.[91] Not satisfied with lambasting Zhang, Wang Shuo went on to observe that some of the best Chinese literature had been produced under dubious commercial circumstances. He cited the case of Lu Xun, the 1930s literary demigod, who published much of his work with the support of the Japanese bookstore owner Uchiyama Kenzō in Shanghai. Referring to critics of Lu Xun who claimed that Uchiyama was an agent for the Japanese secret police and that Lu Xun was thus inadvertently guilty of collaboration, Wang Shuo said that matters of principle were never all that clear-cut.[92]

It was this last flippant remark and the slur on the sacrosanct reputation of Lu Xun that finally gave the authorities an excuse to take action. During the debate about the "humanist spirit" and the initial controversy over "kowtowing to the vulgar," party propagandists had played only a marginal role. Throughout 1995, however, a new wave of cultural repression had been swelling in Beijing and Shanghai, and Wang Shuo, a writer who had weathered virtually unscathed the vicissitudes of the late 1980s and early 1990s, was one of its first victims. He tried to defend himself by making a jocular self-criticism in print, but it was to no avail. By mid-1996, an official ban had been placed on his work, and as a renewed campaign to "construct spiritual civilization" began in the second half of the year, he simply disappeared from view. In early 1997, rather than simply kowtow to the authorities, he decided to try his luck for a while in the United States, not returning until later in the year.

CATS' CLAWS AND SHARKS' APPETITES

Author A. was an established literary figure, yet he'd never been a best-seller. It bothered him. He made numerous contacts, and with the help of extravagant banquets and expensive gifts, he was able to make the acquaintance of a famous critic, J. The critic, himself feeling indebted to the generosity of A., made a promise: "It's a disgrace the way you've been ignored, so unjust! I'm going to write something to promote your work. Now, the strengths of your writing are that . . ."

A. didn't wait for the critic to finish. He waved his hand anxiously: "No need, really, no need at all for any of that. All I ask is that you write an attack on me. That's right, vilify me in print. Years of experience have proved to me that anyone you attack inevitably becomes a nationwide celebrity and even internationally famous. For your part, you can garner the appreciation and reward from another quarter. Thus, we can help each other!"[93]

Wang Meng would have been well advised to remember this satirical sketch, "Helping Each Other Out," that he wrote in the late 1980s. His bellicose criticism of Wang Binbin and, by association, Xiao Xialin afforded those writers a kind of media exposure that was, in the 1990s, usually reserved for pop culture stars.

The economic realities of contemporary Chinese culture added a new edge to the ideological debate. By the 1990s, there was a critical free market that functioned beyond state parameters. During the 1980s, literary and artistic commentators had been castigated and harassed for expressing unorthodox views; magazines were censured and restructured; and people were warned off for being unconventional. In the 1990s, however, established nonofficial critics had outlets in both the leading semi-independent journals[94] and the nonmainland Chinese press. Their successes provided a model for the young; and critical success, not for a work but for a critic, was often based on an alacrity in choosing a subject to either praise or condemn, or perhaps just a theoretical paradigm to promote. Just as infamy brought fame and fortune to authors, the strategically minded critic could make a career out of timely outspokenness.

In the past, the Communist Party's ideological firebrands like Chen Boda (a man who began his rise to prominence in Yan'an during the denunciation of the essayist Wang Shiwei) or Yao Wenyuan (a Shanghai literary critic in the late 1950s who achieved national fame and political favor for a denunciation that acted as a prelude to the Cultural Revolution), to mention but two obvious examples, had built reputations on the basis of what was then called "big criticisms," *da pipan*. In the 1990s, official hired hands had generally fallen into disrepute, as we saw in the case of post-1989 conservative writers Xu Weicheng, Cheng Daixi, and Dong Xuewen in chapter 2, "An Iron Fist in a Velvet Prison." The up-and-coming younger critics had to tread a narrow and treacherous line as they progressed toward fame, influence, and success. On one hand, they had to avoid being too rabid lest they be regarded as comical yelping pups spawned by the older, defunct Maoist watchdogs. On the other hand, they could ill afford to commence a thoroughgoing criticism of the authoritarian environment that had given birth to the range of cultural phenomena that they claimed to despise. To do so would have been nothing less than political suicide. Although nurtured by an official ideology that championed moral perfectionism, they were constrained to manipulate the market to gain an audience. That is, they attempted to achieve a legitimate standing in both realms so as to maintain a public profile while remaining politically correct.

Thus, even though there was room in mainland culture for the clamorous rhetoric of Xiao Xialin and Zhang Chengzhi, or the obnoxious hype of the authors of books like *China, Just Say No!* and the numerous clone volumes of patriotic pulp that appeared in 1996–1997, not to mention the convoluted posturing of savvy po-moists and finger-wagging theoreticians, the voice of the liberal skeptic was all too easily overwhelmed, or censored.

Many of the conditions in 1989 that had made it possible for the rise of cultural figures who acted as a social conscience in the public realm had been restrained or had disappeared. Censorship had led to the decline of reportage, or "faction," the genre that in the late 1980s had produced the popular works of investigative journalism by writers like Liu Binyan, Su Xiaokang, Dai Qing, and Zhao Yu. Similarly, artists had gradually learned how to combine political acuity and market sense to produce works that earned them enough notoriety to advance their careers but not so much that they were banned. Other nonofficial artists were trading on the international market and were not directly involved with the local critical climate. Furthermore, far from there being a cultural downturn in the 1990s, the publishing industry had burgeoned and the number of writers had grown. There was more culture than ever before. As it has been argued throughout this book, however, the voracious appetites both of the cultural industry and consumers did not necessarily mean that artists were enjoying an unconditional freedom to create.

The extremist opponents of the vulgar appeared not to be interested that the drive for success and profit in contemporary Chinese letters probably imposed a measure of order and regulation on a scene of unprecedented chaos. They appealed instead to readers and intellectuals to reject the commercial, and they did so by employing the language and style of the totalitarian past. They relied on outrage and militant hyperbole to elicit a sympathetic response from readers and to increase public awareness of the supposed threat to Chinese civilization posed by a handful of novelists and screenplay writers.

This style of rhetorical warfare was born of militant socialism and ideological sectarianism, a war that enlisted cultural surrogates. Of course, there was a notional opposition in the temper, if not the views, of novelists like Zhang Chengzhi and Wang Shuo, writers with markedly different personal and generational experiences. Both of them were used in the friction between Wang Meng and his supporters and Xiao Xialin. And the clash was about not only vague literary and cultural values but also cultural hegemony in the sphere of nonofficial letters. The contest was over popular culture, but the spoils of war would be in the realm of the elite. During the debates of the mid-1990s, it was more than evident that the protagonists did not welcome a pluralistic critical environment that would allow room for their opponents.

What was the culture that writers like Xiao Xialin, Zhang Chengzhi, and Liang Xiaosheng expected to create? Did the realities of an aging, money-oriented People's Republic that had fallen from the heights of revolutionary zeal in the 1960s to the grubby depths of materialistic atavism in the 1990s disgust them so much that they preferred a return to the cultural restrictions—not to mention the erratic politics—of the past? Did they honestly think that an imaginary coalition of writers and critics consisting of people like Wang Shuo and Wang Meng were dragging the once spiritually pure Chinese down the road of cultural degradation and ruination? Were they alarmists who were giving in to a political paranoia nurtured by decades of party-inspired conspiracy theories about plots against the state that were engineered by enemies of the people and international capital?

Those who declared themselves unwilling to "kowtow to the vulgar" were attempting to exploit the particular political economy of socialism. Whereas money was the general equivalent of goods in reformist China, they traded on language, particularly their own party-generated rhetoric, as the equivalent of ideas. "With the aid of language, people have the opportunity to enrich themselves and impoverish their enemies—ideologically." Of course, the value of words was, like that of money, in a constant state of flux. The highest exchange value in the mid-1990s debate described in this chapter belonged to terms like "war of civilizations" and "Great Wall of the Spirit." They were a nonfiscal currency used to buy power, influence, work, and opportunity.[95]

The cultural marketplace was perhaps a more honest master than the fickle fiats of the party, but when the two combined during the 1990s, the socially engaged independent artist had perhaps less rather than more room in which to maneuver. This was a situation by no means unique to mainland China. As the Polish writer Ewa Kuryluk commented in an essay entitled "A Plea for Irresponsibility":

> The avant-gardists, blue birds, and lonely riders who refuse to subscribe to some goodness or truth, seem to be an endangered species, and the number of single-minded dealers, critics, and beholders who share their dreams and are able to defend them from the claws of the political cats and the appetites of the commercial sharks keeps shrinking as well. The sharks, on the other hand, grow into killer whales, and, consumed by their greed for global profits, develop ever more perverse skills in producing and promoting best-sellers only. Squeezed in between the pursuers of politics and the pressure of the market, the artist is about to break down and succumb to propaganda or soap opera. . . .
>
> Let's start whispering into the ear of the public: The art that's best for you—now and in the future—is not a commodity but an inspiration. A cu-

rious communication between me, the creator, and you, the recreator of hidden patterns and secret suggestions, art is a coded love letter and a private plea: to retrieve from the river of blood and time what's irresponsible and mutual.[96]

This observation also applies to the dilemmas of the cultural politics (not to say policies) of a fragmented totalitarian environment like that of China. The well-meaning but wishy-washy whateverism of Wang Meng's liberalism undermined anything with a political and ideological edge. This served the status quo which, it should not be forgotten, was one in which Wang Meng and many of his allies, both past and present,[97] were deeply mired. Wang Meng himself was also, after all, the minister of culture for a time. Wang Binbin and Xiao Xialin may just have been popinjays out to make a quick name for themselves and cash in on the flaccid ideology of established writers (the two Wangs and others), yet no matter how questionable their motives and tactics, there is no denying the fact that they had a point. Outspoken dissent had been quelled in the late 1980s, and during the early 1990s the cultural opponents of authoritarianism generally cast themselves as ironists who cordoned off their sentiments in quotation marks. There was little room left for a concerted opposition articulated by individuals of conscience who tried to find a way between the reasoned sophistry of Wang Meng and the faux idealism of Zhang Chengzhi. As the Romanian writer Norman Manea has observed,

> Caution toward ideologies and suspicion toward politics do not, however, necessarily lead to moral stability. The noncommittal stance doesn't only have positive effects. Among its frequent consequences are, unfortunately, compromise and complicity. The deformation of high principle to the point of caricature can discredit faith in principles as such. The social mechanism imperceptibly begins to function in the good old "natural" ways, by mutual favors and force of circumstance, proliferating corruption, Byzantinism, demagogy, abuse of power, and nepotism on a truly fantastic scale.[98]

Old-style ideological conservatives like Zheng Bonong, the former editor of the *Literary Gazette* and an ideological enemy of Wang Meng (discussed in the section "A Storm in a Rice Bowl" in this chapter), were sympathetic to the moralizing of the writers who "refused to capitulate." In late 1995, when Party General Secretary Jiang Zemin issued a call for party members to "talk up politics," *jiang zhengzhi*, Zheng took it to be a timely plea to stave off the corrupting influences of the West and to attack cultural pluralism once more. Jiang's policy was part of a revival of cultural rectitude or, in party code, "the construction of spiritual civilization"[99] that was pursued with increased vigor in 1996–1997 and saw the temporary purge of a number of writers (including Wang Shuo) and the banning of important elite cultural forums, like the journal *Orient*.

Writing for *Mainstay* in early 1996, Zheng said that apart from healthy competition in the arts world, there also was intense struggle. It was an ongoing conflict between correct and erroneous thinking, a war between proletarian and bourgeois ideology. "The inimical forces of the West want to force us to 'Westernize'," Zheng wrote. "They plot to divide us and engage in ideological subversion." He appealed to his readers to be wary of Western attempts to undermine China's worldview, historical perspective, and value system. Quoting Jiang Zemin he said, "It is essential that we remain alert and continue the fight."[100] Here, too, was a warning against capitulationism. "There are comrades who avoid and cover up ideological contradictions. They take a lackadaisical and laissez-faire stance toward the corrosive ideology of the exploitative classes." Chairman Mao's philosophical guide to class struggle, "On Contradiction," Zheng opined, was still the beacon for those who supported the dangerous capitulationism of eclecticism. Such people, Zheng cautioned, may believe they were upholding "stability and unity," yet in reality their actions threatened the nation with long-term destabilization. With Wang Shuo eclipsed during the purge of 1996, once again the conservatives turned their attentions to Wang Meng, and in early 1997 *Mainstay* published the most vicious (and clearly argued) attack on the novelist to date.[101]

It was in the trenches of ideological warfare where the harangues of party hacks like Zheng found fellowship with the odious philippics of Xiao Xialin and Zhang Chengzhi. They may well have been unhappy in each other's company, but in the tone and style of their pedagogical warnings they were united in a reverie for the high age of idealism and the "totalitarian nostalgia" that is the subject of the concluding chapter.

In 1989, writing for the *Literary Gazette* on the eve of the Beijing massacre, Qian Liqun, a leading literary historian at Peking University, observed with trepidation the growth of new ideological camps among intellectuals and writers:

> On one level China's modern history is a record of intellectuals caught up in the process of mutual destruction. I had a "dream" that in the not too distant future famous intellectuals who are presently most active in the intellectual and cultural spheres, people who have different "strategies for national salvation," will finally draw up battle lines and fight to the death. . . .
>
> In their investigations of the history and condition of Chinese intellectuals and writers [in the 1930s] the brothers Zhou Zuoren and Lu Xun came to a similar conclusion: Zhou Zuoren lumped "intellectuals," "the emperor" and *liumang* together; Lu Xun said that in the Chinese intellectual world there were only "official souls" and "bandit souls."

While contemplating today's famous intellectuals—regardless of whether they are my seniors, peers, or juniors—I always find in them something of the "imperial air" (hegemon) or a "touch of the *liumang*" (a breath of the bandit). It is there in all of them, be it to a greater or lesser extent, obvious or disguised, consciously recognized or unconscious.

Furthermore, I find the very same thing in myself.

There have always been intellectuals who have been the accomplices or handmaidens of the rulers. When feudal authoritarianism saturated the national spirit as a whole, intellectuals got a big dose of it. Thus, in China we not only have autocracy and the autocracy of the ignorant, we even have the autocracy of the intellectuals. People say the rule of the ignorant is fearful because it means that the "unbridled masses" go wild; but the terrifying thing about the dictatorship of intellectuals is that it poses as being "scientific" and "legitimate," precise and exacting. In its respect for power and unity of thought, its opposition to individualism, freedom, the minority, heretics, dissonance and pluralism . . . its purpose is at one with the rule of the kings or dictatorship of the ignorant.[102]

CHAPTER TWELVE

Totalitarian Nostalgia

A NOSTALGIC MOOD

"Totalitarian nostalgia," as Svetlana Boym writes, is "primarily an aesthetic nostalgia for the last grand style in the twentieth century—the Stalinist Empire Style—and even more, a 'nostalgia for world culture'."[1] Boym also points out that in 1990s Russia, totalitarian nostalgia was the product of an environment in which culture had "to survive a balancing act between the old . . . ideology and mentality, the demands of art, and new commercial imperatives."

This concluding chapter discusses aspects of totalitarian nostalgia in contemporary mainland China. It argues that the totalitarian temper in 1990s China constantly harks back to and feeds off lingering totalistic and totalizing temptations. These are temptations that have been evident in Chinese political and cultural debates since the end of the nineteenth century; they are present in the intellectual and political projects that seek to formulate holistic systems, paradigms, and arguments for the salvation of China; they persist despite the relative decline of the official ideocracy since the 1970s.

As we saw in the preceding chapter, when faced with the decay of sociopolitical coherence, even if the coherence that had once existed was premised on an unjust and inhumane system, some writers in the 1990s called for a moral revival, identifying various devalued ideals of the past as a touchstone for the present. They chided artists who would seek answers in the cultural marketplace; they lambasted those who rejected the notion that literature must serve the higher cause of politics and Kultur. They despised the writers and intellectuals who took heart in the growth of a pluralistic culture that could respond not only to the impulses of the individual artist but also to the needs of a varied public. They mourned the loss of their presumed position as the cultural arbiters of the nation, their role as the conscience of society. They resiled from the complex reality in which their obnoxious rhetoric and overblown bombast occupied nothing more than a quaint market niche. They were nostalgic for the grand purpose of history, their avowed role (as actor and/or victim) in it and longed for its return.

Totalitarian nostalgia was not the sole province of a knot of displaced literati, nor was it merely a commodified social mood sated simply by the revenant Mao cult of the early 1990s or a crude retro Cultural Revolution longing that fed the success of works like Jiang Wen's 1995 film *Under the Radiant Sun*.[2] Rather, it was a nostalgia for a style of thought and public discourse; it was a nostalgia for a language of denunciation that offered simple solutions to complex problems. It was a style in which China's dissidents and democratic oppositionists all too often chose to express themselves. It is a style that reinforces itself by its appeal to well-worn paths that lead to the past.

The word *nostalgia* originally connoted a longing for or painful yearning to return home. It was coined by the Swiss physician Johannes Hofer to describe a malady, an "extreme homesickness among Swiss mercenaries fighting far from their native land in the legions of one or another European despot." He identified the symptoms of the illness of nostalgia as leading to despondency, melancholia, lability of emotion, anorexia, and, in some cases, suicide.[3] The condition was variously treated with leeches, opium, a range of emulsions, and exposure to curative alpine air.

Nostalgia is a condition of being lost to a familiar abode, an exile from home and, as such, is said to be closely related to the homing instinct. What was in the nineteenth century viewed as a physical condition, nostalgia has today become a general state of mind. Indeed, how many of us are nostalgic for a time when people were not nostalgic? The widespread condition of nostalgia can be symptomatic of a social interior dialogue regarding the irrevocable past, an identification with what is perceived as having been lost. The dynamics of the dialogue between past and present that finds expression in various forms of public nostalgia are complex. In the case of mainland China, that dialogue has generally been muted and more often than not forestalled by government fiat. There is much that has been left unsaid about the recent past in mainland China, and much of what has been concealed excites new waves of nostalgia and longing. This disjointed dialogue with the past thus, by necessity, continues in fits and starts, and not just among the elderly or ex–Red Guards. In the ranks of the young, the past can also be a resource on which they rely and prey, and can exploit for their own uses.

Nostalgia does not necessarily mean that a longing for the past and hand-wringing over the present will be a negative or noncreative venture. The mechanism of public nostalgia, especially when it is manipulated by the media, often makes the past more palatable and handy for shoring up present exigencies. Given the perceived burdens of the Chinese past and its complex mesh of historical precedents, the various lapses in collective memory that have occurred over the past two decades may not, however, have been such a bad thing. They may well have allowed people a chance to clear the way to the future without the pressures of earlier horrors constantly invading and overwhelming the present.

From the official end of the Cultural Revolution in 1976, the leadership of the Communist Party rose in public esteem on a wave of nostalgia for the past. The authorities instituted a program of "bringing order out of chaos and returning to the rectitude [of the past]"; they spoke of "giving things back their original appearance" and "turning an inverted history on its head."[4] As the government undertook the nationwide process of rehabilitating cadres and individuals purged during the Cultural Revolution and before, old films, songs, and books were re-released during the late 1970s, and they fed the frenzy to recover the past. The media also began depicting the first years of Communist Party rule in the early 1950s, before radical socialization and the aberrant economic policies of Mao Zedong took hold, as having been a halcyon age of simplicity and purity in which a nation newly born from the terrors of civil war was united by a common goal and inspired by an idealistic purpose.

As Dai Qing, a journalist turned historiographer-*cum*-dissident, wrote in 1988:

> Since 1978, the intellectuals and pseudo-intellectuals of China, regardless of their age (from twenty to ninety), no matter whether they have been attacked by others or have attacked others, have all witnessed with a mixture of pain, delight, bitterness and relief the yellowing pages extracted, one by one, from old files. This has been translated into tearful family reunions and sighs for the months and years that have irrevocably passed . . . [B]y now the Chinese all know that a prosperous and strong China depends on its people being intelligent and enthusiastic, and for them to be both of these things they must be able to understand historical truth, for indeed it entwines them at every turn.[5]

Of course, the past was also used to sanction the policies and actions of the present. Independent political and cultural trends were attacked for being part of a concerted effort by maladjusted individuals or groups to negate the heritage of the revolution and betray the sacrifices made by the party's martyrs.[6] Writers and historians who attempted to formulate their own version of the past were often banned or criticized, and broadly speaking, the official party line on the past continued to dominate the mass media view of history.

In his sociology of nostalgia, *Yearning for Yesterday*, Fred Davis outlines an "ascending order of nostalgia." He speaks of simple nostalgia, "a positively toned evocation of a lived past in the context of some negative feeling toward the present or impeding circumstance"; reflexive nostalgia, in which the individual "in perhaps an inchoate though nevertheless psychologically active fashion . . . summons to feeling and thought certain empirically oriented questions concerning the truth, accuracy, completeness, or representativeness of the nostalgic claim"; and interpreted nostalgia, an attempt to objectify the sense of nostalgia and question the reasons behind the nostalgic mood and its significance for the present.[7]

Nostalgia is a central feature in how people form, maintain, and reconstruct a sense of self and the place of the individual in the world. Nostalgia develops usually in the face of present fears, disquiet about the state of affairs, and uncertainty about the future. Confronted with social anomie and disjuncture, nostalgia provides a sense of continuity. Nostalgia has politically often been used for extremist, particularly totalitarian and nationalist, ends.[8] In mainland China, nostalgia was institutionalized by the Communist Party and its claims to legitimacy that emphasized its role as the inheritor and protector of a codified body of national traditions and that were summed up in terms of China's unique "spiritual civilization."[9]

In the mid-1980s, as the publishing and media industries became economically more independent, reprises of the past accrued a market value. Mainland China entered the age of spontaneous (or commercially enhanced and manufactured), and not merely state-directed, revivals. Again, Hong Kong and Taiwan played a crucial role in this by providing a ready audience for films and books that dwelled on the imperial past, the decadent late-Qing period, the republican era, and even socialism. On the mainland, a commercial nostalgic revival of the Cultural Revolution, for example, can be dated from the mid-1980s with the release of the first disco versions of revolutionary Model Beijing Operas, *geming yangbanxi*, and the publication of sensational accounts of the period.[10]

The Communist Party's post–4 June "state-of-the-nation education" campaign (see chapter 10, "To Screw Foreigners Is Patriotic") included the rerelease of old revolutionary films and the distribution of karaoke tapes of "classic" revolutionary songs. It was hoped that such material would inculcate a sense of positive nostalgia among the young. Thus, old war films dating from the early 1950s were screened on prime-time television, and heavily publicized contemporary historical films, including the story of Deng Xiaoping's youthful military career (*The Bose Uprising*, Bose qiyi) and the epic-length extravaganza on the founding of the People's Republic (*The Birth of a Nation*, Kaiguo dadian) also were produced. Furthermore, in 1990, the 150th anniversary of the first Opium War was commemorated amid considerable talk of the blood shed by patriotic martyrs and revolutionaries for the cause of national independence. The message was simple: the blood debt of the past was so great that no citizen today had the right to renege on the final choice of history for China: Marxism-Leninism and the leadership of the Communist Party.

DREAMING OF CHAIRMAN MAO

Commenting[11] on the 1990s reinvention of Stalin in Russia, Svetlana Boym wrote that the Soviet leader had been transformed into "a truly postmodern hero, subject to demystification and remythologization, to documentary exposure and fictional recreation, moving back and forth between irony and nostalgia."[12] In mainland China, the new Mao cult of the late 1980s and early 1990s also was caught in a dialectic of irony and nostalgia.

For many people, the late 1980s was a time when the reforms had reached an impasse; corruption, nepotism, and economic ineptitude had led to widespread disgruntlement; and the party leadership, its attempts at substantial political reform thwarted by infighting, appeared to be increasingly out of touch with everyday realities. Mao, a strong leader who in the popular imagination was above corruption and a romantic unfettered by pettifogging bureaucratic constraints, was for many the symbol of an age of economic stability, egalitarianism, and national pride. Gradually, the image of Mao, long since freed from his stifling holy aura and the odium of his destructive policies, became a "floating sign," a vehicle for nostalgic reinterpretation, unstated opposition to the status quo, and even satire.

For the young, the general mood of helplessness only added to the nostalgia for the past. Victor Zaslavsky's comments on attitudes of Soviet youth in the 1960s adumbrate some of the attitudes that appeared among various strata of China's urban youth in the early 1990s: "The young neither fight against communism, argue against it, nor curse it; something much worse has happened to communism: they laugh at it." In the Soviet Union, the young—workers, students, and others—were witnessing their society turning into a realm of consumers and found their own lives increasingly meaningless and without goals. Their creativity frustrated and deprived of a positive direction, they "look[ed] back nostalgically to the period of social revolution inseparably linked with Stalin's name."[13]

There was, however, another level of the abiding reputation of Stalin in the Soviet Union. As the dissident Soviet philosopher Alexander Zinoviev observed, Stalin's rule was the ultimate expression of popular will and the mass personality.[14] He was the embodiment of both history and the national spirit, so to deny him would be to negate not merely one's own history but also vital facets of the national character. Large numbers of people had participated in the terror that marked Stalin's rule, just as in China the nation had enthusiastically responded to the Great Leap Forward, the Cultural Revolution, and the ceaseless political purges that Mao had directed, starting in the early 1950s. To "rediscover" Mao in a period of rapid change and social dislocation was for many also a grounding act of self-affirmation.

In China, the events of 1988 and 1989—natural disasters and economic uncertainty followed by a fear of national collapse and mass protests against corruption, and the lack of freedoms followed by the ill-managed government suppression of the 1989 protests, the equivocal response of the Western democracies, and the fall of Communism in Eastern Europe—all served to encourage the nascent Mao cult. As is so often the case when people face economic uncertainty and social anomie, old cultural symbols, cults, practices, and beliefs are spontaneously revived to provide a framework of cohesion and meaning for a threatening world. To many, Mao was representative of an age of certainty and confidence, of cultural and political unity, and, above all, of economic equality and incorruptibility.

The Maoist past reflected badly on Deng's present. Yet perhaps it was only with the relative economic freedoms allowed by the reforms that people could afford to indulge in an anodyne wave of pro-Mao nostalgia. Certainly, the new cult suggested alternatives to the reformist economic and social order, but it did not offer new or viable political solutions to China's problems. If anything, the Mao cult looked fondly on strong government, coherent national goals, authority, and power. Mao was, first and foremost, an unwavering patriot who led the nation against imperialism and expelled foreign capital. The formulas of the Mao era also offered simple answers to complex questions: direct collective action over painful individual decisions, reliance on the state rather than a grinding struggle for the self, national pride as opposed to self-doubt. Many could indulge in Mao nostalgia because due to bans on remembering the past, they had forgotten its horrors. Unlike Europeans, for example, who still are exposed to a continuous media barrage related to World War II, the Chinese government's censorship of most information on the Great Leap Forward and Cultural Revolution meant that the populace did not have to confront the unadulterated memory and horror of those periods in film, television, newspaper articles, memoirs, and so on. Emotionally, therefore, many people, and especially the young, could partake in the luxury of a nostalgia for the past.

The most daring public criticism of the residual longing for Mao among mainland Chinese was published by the Shanghai critic Li Jie in early 1989. In "The Mao Zedong Phenomenon: A Survivor's Critique," Li reflected on the reasons for the widespread nostalgia for Maoist totalism and traced the growth of both *liumang* culture and the moral revivalism of contemporary China back to the demise of the chairman:

> The secret of Mao's success lies in the fact that he created a belief system for the masses and launched a grand enterprise. The victorious Mao combined the elements of sage-ruler (based on a belief system) with that of the political hero (realized through his autocracy). He reached a pinnacle of success unprecedented in the thousands of years of Chinese history. The

power of belief cannot be underestimated. The emperors Qin Shihuang, Han Wudi, Tang Taizu, and Song Gaozu all enjoyed periods of ultimate power, but which of them became a popular god? Mao's success was, primarily, the success of popular faith in him. . . .

The greatest secret of Mao Zedong's achievement lies in the understanding of the Chinese that he shared with Lu Xun. Whereas Lu Xun used his insight to criticize the Chinese, Mao utilized the weaknesses of the Chinese to further his own Mao-style revolution. . . .

During those years [of the Cultural Revolution,] anyone who had a modicum of power as a rebel leader would turn into a mini-Mao. The way they talked, their enunciation, speech patterns and even grammar were all à la Mao. The most convincing evidence of this was the use of Mao quotes by both sides as a weapon during every debate and bloody skirmish. They all cried "We swear to protect Chairman Mao with our lives." The Chinese weren't fighting with each other; two Mao Zedongs were locked in mortal combat. . . .

The cultural ramifications of the personality split Mao suffered in his last years have only been fully realized in the 1980s. Mao came to embody the moral and political icons (sage-emperor) so dear to the hearts of the Chinese. The moment that the living icon Mao and the worship of him came to an end, the Chinese lost all cultural coherence. The Chinese of the 1980s are a discombobulated people. Their icon has crumbled and, with it, their psychological linchpin has disappeared. Extreme mental imbalance has either turned them into unprincipled louts or forced them to search for a new spiritual goal. . . .

. . . Mao's shadow can be seen everywhere. Whenever you see a shop assistant rudely ask a customer what they want; whenever a concierge shouts at a visitor; whenever a policeman lectures someone who has violated traffic regulations in an imperious manner; whenever an official makes a report in front of a microphone in a droning monotone . . . you can always make out the shadow of Mao in the background.[15]

A strikingly different view came from the novelist Zhang Chengzhi, one of the leading combatants in the mid-1990s war of resistance discussed in the previous chapter. Like many members of his generation, Zhang was a fervent disciple of Mao and Mao Thought. As a prominent activist in the Red Guard movement, he also achieved a certain media recognition in the 1960s, and pictures of him studying Mao's works can be found in the pages of official propaganda publications of the time. Like Li Jie, Zhang Chengzhi was fascinated with the legacy of Chairman Mao. In contrast, however, Zhang found the spirit of Mao sadly lacking in contemporary China. On the anniversary of the centenary of Mao's birth in 1993, he wrote an essay entitled "Chairman Mao Graffiti" for the Japanese journal *Sekai*:

> No matter how you look at it, Chairman Mao remains an outstanding individual, a man with great charisma, as everyone says. . . .
>
> Following the collapse of the Socialist Bloc and during the Gulf War, the international powers led by America and England set out to destroy the Islamic world which they perceived as being a potential enemy. The infamous Monroe Doctrine formulated to deal with the forces of self-determination in Latin America is an old weapon in the U.S. arsenal. The most recent example of its application was the Panama invasion. Next time it will be China's turn. China, not Communist China, but China a massive cultural entity, is next on the hit list of the New World Order. Although we are confronted by this international situation, Chinese intellectuals (and here I include the majority of Chinese studying overseas) are still unashamedly pro-American. . . .
>
> With Mao's death, China's age of great men came to an end. The masses feel a sense of loss. They have not yet found an alternative. That is to say that despite the passage of time, when the masses feel themselves discriminated against and oppressed, they can think of no other leader than Mao Zedong.
>
> Regardless of the talk of international peace for our ancient motherland of China, the New World Order is a pitiless killer and every Chinese will have to face its onslaught one day. In the future, world justice will continue to be frustrated, and there will be no such thing as compassion, nor will anyone stand up for the dispossessed.
>
> The name Mao Zedong will remain eternally a symbol of rebellion against this new order. His prestige may well gradually rise among the masses once more. Of course, Mao Zedong must be criticized in human terms, but ironically, for Chinese like me who continue to oppose neo-colonialism, the international balance of power makes it necessary for us to look to him as a bastion of human dignity.
>
> Seen in this light, for the people of China and of the poor nations throughout the world who are confronted with the new international scene, it is possible that Mao Zedong will gain a new lease on life.[16]

There was more to the Chairman Mao revival, however, than just concerns about the new world order. Despite all its horrors, for many people, the Mao era was a time of deeply stirred passions and beliefs firmly held. In the glow of nostalgic reverie and from the comfortable perspective provided by the passing of two decades, the Cultural Revolution appeared to many—on certain levels of consciousness at least—to have been a period of simple emotions and plain living. Soap operas like *Aspirations* (see chapter 5, "The Graying of Chinese Culture") and films like *Under the Radiant Sun* (1995), a coming-of-age story of a group of childhood friends set in the 1960s, affirmed this sense of lost innocence. Furthermore, as the early years of the reform era passed into history, material prosperity altered forever the pace of Chinese urban life. Even the 1980s, an age when party cells, personnel dossiers, and street committees still held sway over every aspect of life, shone with an increasingly nostalgic glow, perceived as a period of possibilities and simple choices. As for the earlier era of political maelstrom, the mood of totalitarian nostalgia lent these a near-romantic aura, especially for the young, that was in stark contrast to the mundane realities of the 1990s economic boom.

As J. M. Coetzee commented on the abiding power of Stalin:

> Stalin and his apparatus castrated a generation of writers, robbing it not only of it generative power but of its power of historical witness and therefore its political power. By the wounds he inflicted, Stalin in effect ensured that he could not be repudiated even after his death; by this means he intended to guarantee himself a backhand immortality.[17]

REINVERTING THE PARTY

In their comments on the Khrushchev thaw of the 1960s, the Russian dissident artists Komar and Melamid, masters of a painterly school of nostalgic socialist realism, what they called *sots art*, gave voice (although in a more sardonic and unaffected tone) to sentiments that became familiar to Chinese artists from the 1980s:

> We understand now that the culture of the thaw was so light, so incredibly bad—Yevtushenko and so on. We thought they were good because, after Stalin's dark time—a terrible time, of course, a bloody time—there came new times. But these new times were so easy, so light. The real Stalin time was about life, death. Blood. It was a terrible time but a deep one, the real time. The cultural life of Russia under Stalin. The radio played Brahms, Beethoven. The time of the thaw was about nothing. What was Yevtushenko? It's like the beatnik generation in the United States. What was it about? What was this bullshit? Committed art. Committed to what? What's the problem? What are you solving with this idiotic poetry?[18]

Komar and Melamid's *sots art* mocked the Soviet Union's official culture, but it was a mockery based on imitation, that most sincere form of flattery. Komar and

Melamid did not simply dismiss out of hand official propaganda and its style, for they recognized how it had shaped their own perceptions, just as advertising culture shaped the artistic vision of pop artists in the West.

Chinese ironists and writers in the 1980s and 1990s also attempted to divert some of the power of state culture to their own enterprise. In the process, they produced a body of intriguing and, at times, heartfelt work. Unlike the late Soviet Union, however, the Chinese state was far from being a stagnant and ossified command economy with a rigid cultural structure on which the parasitical artist could simply feed in an ironic frenzy. As we have seen repeatedly in the preceding pages, the state's vitality and complicity in encouraging economic and cultural changes that both threatened and enlivened its autocracy frustrated many artists.

As we observed in chapter 9, "ccp™ & Adcult PRC," the existence of the great divide between high and low art remains, literally, academic. For decades, elements of high art have been feeding the wellsprings of advertising culture, as James Twitchell eloquently demonstrated in his study of the subject.[19] Meanwhile, lowbrow or vernacular culture has often taken gimmicks, techniques, motifs, subject matter, and styles from high modernism. That avant-garde Chinese culture has similarly fed the party's advertising culture comes, therefore, as no great surprise. We are reminded of an observation made by Arthur C. Danto, a philosopher of art, in "Bad Aesthetic Times":

> An awful lot of what was introduced in a kind of anti-establishment spirit has — such is the irony of things — found its way into the highest precincts of contemporary high art, as if cooperation were irresistible, and the art world, like the commercial world, feeds and flourishes on what was intended to call it in question and overthrow it.[20]

"Disturbatory art," to use Danto's expression, the various efforts of the mainland Chinese avant-garde of the 1970s and 1980s, appeared initially aesthetically unsettling and "bad" to those nurtured in the tradition of the party's artistic canon. During the 1990s, however, the techniques and poses of the avant-garde were well on the way to becoming part of accepted standards, and they were increasingly employed as the means for teaching and communicating what are good aesthetics in educational institutions and the media, thereby aiding in the creation of an alternative or, at least dilated, canon of taste.

One is inevitably tempted to ponder future possibilities. When, for example, revivals of mainland Chinese 1970s and 1980s modernism and post-1976 culture are spawned in the future, will the canonized avant-garde appear as dreary and pedagogical compared with the revitalized and commodified mainstream (official and commercial) culture, as modernism so often does today in Euro-America when it is juxtaposed with the more vital vernacular arts like graffiti, caricature, comics, and advertising? Similarly, following the first wave of avant-gardist inversions of communist symbolism since 1976 and the subsequent retakes of these inversions by commerce and party cult since the late 1980s, can we not also expect to see nonofficial artists and writers further plunder the new advertising culture for their work, to indulge themselves in CCP-based bricolage? Then, party artists may well respond with counterbricolage.

To keep abreast of the demands of the market—the international arts and film circuit, advertisers' needs, party initiatives—the avant-garde must, perforce, attempt ever new innovations of the stock of Chinese-based sign systems and values. They are sign systems that have been formulated and articulated predominantly by the authorities for nearly half a century, and the further appropriation of them by the avant-gardists may give birth to the type of "second-degree kitsch" that is so common in postindustrial societies.[21] Presumably, the avant-garde will also compose anthologies of previous avant-garde strategies, enabling them to be recirculated into mainstream political and commodity culture, thereby creating a nostalgic revival of posttotalitarian tropes that have been colonized by the totalitarian state.

THE RHETORIC OF DENUNCIATION

The language of totalitarianism itself operates according to rules and an internal logic that aid and abet a thought process conducive to its continued purchase on power and authority. In the decades of its ascendance, as well as in the long years of tenacious reform, the totalitarian in China has exhibited an intriguing versatility, "commodifying" culture, ideas, and even opposition in the general cause of its redefinition and self-affirmation.

It is the concern of many students of things Chinese that the yawning gap between reality and rhetoric must surely, in the long run, make things untenable or lead to some dramatic collapse of the vestigial ideological power of the party-state. I would argue, rather—again taking a sideward glance at the parallels between Soviet and Chinese socialism—that communist rule in China has created a range of ideological simulacra that have, to date, incorporated cultural alternatives and opponents in a postmodern pastiche of the kind described in the Russian philosopher Mikhail Epstein's work on the Soviet ideological landscape.[22]

In his work on relativistic patterns in totalitarian thinking, Epstein analyzes totalitarianism as "a specific postmodern model that came to replace the modernist ideological stance elaborated in earlier Marxism."[23] He argues that the use of "descriptive-evaluative" words, that is, terms that combine both descriptive and evaluative meanings—what Epstein calls "ideologemes"—deployed universally in Soviet speech communicated not only information but also a particular ideological message, or concealed judgments that take the form of words. Although his arguments are too elaborate to reproduce here in full, Epstein's analysis of how ideologemes functioned in Soviet public discourse has striking parallels in contemporary China. In short, he notes that a key to the function of ideologemes is that they can embrace both leftist and rightist concepts, encompassing the spectrum of utilitarian shifts made in a totalitarian or totalizing system. A simple example of this can be found in the Chinese usage of the expression "socialist market economy." It is a term created to convey the extreme contradictions of contemporary economic realities and to allow for an ideological underpinning to what, superficially at least, appears to have been an example of the party's retreat from its avowed Marxist-Leninist-Maoist ideals. According to Epstein, this kind of linguistic formulation is not the result of clumsy pragmatism but, rather, is the reflection of the core philosophy of totalitarian politics which "uses leftist slogans to defeat the right, rightist slogans to defeat the left" while maintaining its own primacy.[24]

Totalitarian speech is marked by its ability to employ ideologically laden words to weaken opposing sides while taking advantage of the resulting confusion. The Chinese language has a rich and venerable lexicon of words that have been converted under communist rule to act as "ideologemes." It is a lexicon that was, according to tradition, first formulated by Confucius when he edited the history of the state of Lu, the *Spring and Autumn Annals*, judiciously choosing expressions to describe political actions in moral terms. Classical scholars claimed that the Sage thereby created a "Spring and Autumn writing style," *chunqiu bifa*, which relied on a vocabulary of *baobianci*, or judgmental words, to praise, *bao*, or to censure, *bian*, every political act and event contained in the annals of Lu. In modern usage, all activities beneficial to the party-state are represented by words with positive connotations, *baoyici*, whereas those that are deleterious in nature are condemned with negative verbs, nouns, and adjectives, *bianyici*. The growth or maturation of socialist society has led to linguistic accretion, incorporating Maoist doublethink with the left-right parole of reform. The general party line exists in a state of constant tension with both right and left deviations, maintaining a rhetorical and practical balance between the two and thus betraying and being betrayed as it maintains its grip on society. One could postulate, as Epstein does for Soviet Marxism, that "socialism with Chinese characteristics" is an enigmatic and hybrid phenomenon that "like postmodern pastiche . . . combines within itself very different ideological doctrines."[25]

There is reason to believe that Soviet Marxism, which survived for seventy years as the dominant ideology of the Soviet Union, accommodating itself to enormous historical change in the process, has become de-ideologized in direct proportion to its expansion. This ideology exceeded and absorbed all other systems until it approached the limits of ideological imagination. Over the course of seven decades, Soviet Marxism lost its specificity as a particular ideology and became instead an all-encompassing system of ideological signs that could acquire any significance desired.[26]

In China, too, the ruling ideology has gone through a transmogrification rather than a collapse, absorbing both communist and capitalist ideas. And as Epstein observes, "ideology becomes simply a habit of thinking, a manner of expression, the prism through which all views and expressions are refracted without depending on particular views and ideas—a sort of universal network that may be compared to the advertising networks of Western nations."[27] As goods are exchanged for money in a capitalist environment, so facts can be exchanged for ideas in the totalitarian realm. As a form of currency, ideas accrue their own "ideological capital." Their value lies in their ability to shore up the "correctness" of the ideology of their proponents, and it is this correctness that compensates people for their sacrifices to the cause and recoups the cost of policy errors. Such ideological capital has outgrown the limitations of particular personalities and systems of ideas to "become an omnipresent mentality, appropriating any fact to serve any idea."[28]

The style of denunciation born of this "universalist ideology" is by no means limited to Maoist revanchists or writers like Zhang Chengzhi and Xiao Xialin. As we have seen throughout this book, modes of criticism in mainland culture readily fall back on the habits of mind and language inculcated by decades of party rule. Even in an environment of increased free speech and media openness, the rhetorical style of totalitarianism—and its refusal to allow for critical self-reflection—maintains its appeal for writers and thinkers of all persuasions.

In April 1995, a heated controversy erupted in the dissident Chinese community overseas. It centered on the role of radical student activists during the 1989 protest movement as depicted in the documentary film *The Gate of Heavenly Peace* (hereafter referred to as *Gate*). The debate surrounding issues raised by the film quickly revealed the style of political rhetoric typical of extreme Chinese radicals. Whereas the nature of the debate was not surprising—the film *Gate* touched on some of the most contentious areas of contemporary political life—what was interesting was that some of the internationally feted members of the exiled dissident community articulated their views in a language reminiscent of the ideological newspeak of mainland Chinese politics. It was the language of totalitarianism, and its deployment—for readers versed in Cultural Revolution venom—held a certain nostalgic charm. It also revealed much about Chinese "democratic dissidents" that is rarely discussed in non-Chinese-language works.

Before continuing, I should point out my own interest in *Gate*.[29] I was involved with the project from an early stage and acted as both a scriptwriter and an associate director for the final three-hour film.

On 22 April 1995, Hsüeh Hsiao-kuang, a prominent Hong Kong–based reporter for the Taiwan newspaper *United News Daily*,[30] published a story about the as-yet-incomplete film. Hsüeh's article focused on an interview featured in the film with the student leader Chai Ling, the commander of the Defend Tiananmen Square headquarters in the last days of the protest movement. Chai had chosen to speak to the American journalist Philip Cunningham on 28 May 1989, a crucial moment on the eve of the 4 June Beijing massacre. In the interview, Chai articulated her views on the student movement and her role in it. Hsüeh Hsiao-kuang's article, which was based principally on materials provided by Carma Hinton, one of the film's directors, who gave her a rough cut of the film, discussed the issues raised by that interview and questioned the responsibility that Chai Ling shared for the final bloody outcome of the student movement. The piece was published on the Mainland News page of Hsüeh's paper in Taipei and reprinted on 26 April 1995 in the New York edition of *World Journal*, the leading North-American Chinese daily.[31]

In that article Hsüeh quoted from the Chai interview as follows:

CHAI LING: My fellow students keep asking me, "What should we do next? What can we accomplish?" I feel so sad, because how can I tell them that what we actually are hoping for is bloodshed, the moment when the government is ready to butcher the people brazenly? Only when the square is awash with blood will the people of China open their eyes. Only then will they really be united. But how can I explain any of this to my fellow students?

And what is truly sad is that some students, and famous, well-connected people, are working hard to help the government, to prevent it from taking such measures. For the sake of their selfish interests and their private dealings, they are trying to cause our movement to disintegrate and get us out of the square before the government becomes so desperate that it takes action. . . .

That's why I feel so sad, because I can't say all this to my fellow students. I can't tell them straight out that we must use our blood and our lives to wake up the people. Of course, they will be willing. But they are still so young (*cries*) . . .

INTERVIEWER: Are you going to stay in the square yourself?

CHAI LING: No.

INTERVIEWER: Why?

CHAI LING: Because my situation is different. My name is on the government's blacklist. I'm not going to be destroyed by this government. I
want to live. Anyway, that's how I feel about it. I don't know whether
people will say I'm selfish. I believe that people have to continue the
work I have started. A democracy movement can't succeed with only
one person. I hope you don't report what I've just said for the time
being, OK?[32]

Hsüeh acknowledged that when Chai spoke of Tiananmen Square's being
"awash with blood," she could not have known about the violence that awaited
the protesters on 3–4 June; she may have thought that the government would use
only rubber bullets and batons to quell the demonstrations. Nonetheless, Hsüeh
asks, as one reads Chai's chilling comments one cannot help but wonder "what
type of environment could have produced a value system that has resulted in the
attitudes of this post–Cultural Revolution generation of Chinese youth?" Although emphasizing that the Chinese government was responsible for the bloodshed of 4 June, Hsüeh observed that surely student leaders like Chai Ling and Li
Lu (Chai's erstwhile cohort who also went on to become something of a U.S.
media star), through their constant refusal to leave the square even as disaster
loomed ever closer, also were responsible in part for the continued escalation of
the conflict and its tragic denouement.

Hsüeh Hsiao-kuang's article also quoted Ding Xueliang, then a lecturer at the
Hong Kong Polytechnic University and a prominent analyst of mainland Chinese
affairs, on the reasons that extremism had won out among the students toward the
end of the protest movement. Ding responded that those who had felt that remaining on in the square was pointless gradually left, and those who thought that
they had no alternative but to struggle on stayed behind. In turn, these extremists
supported and elected even more extreme people to lead them. He further commented that all this had to be understood in the context of the collapse of moral
values and self-restraint in post-Mao China, as well as in light of the communist-
style rhetoric of the students during the movement itself.

On 27 April 1995, Chai Ling published a rebuttal of Hsüeh's article in the Features page of World Journal. It was a heavily edited-down version of a much longer
piece that appeared in full in Beijing Spring, the leading Chinese dissident publication based in New York, and again in Tiananmen, a radical dissident journal
that was first published in June 1995.[33] In her response, Chai described the reasons for Hsüeh Hsiao-kuang's critique:

Certain individuals have, for the sake of gaining the approval of the authorities, racked their brains for ways and means to come up with policies

for them. And there is another person with a pro-Communist history [Carma Hinton] who has been hawking [her] documentary film for crude commercial gain by taking things out of context and trying to reveal something new, unreasonably turning history on its head and calling black white. First, last year, there was Dai Qing who clamored for Chai Ling to be "given a stiff sentence," for being "guilty of interfering with traffic"; now today Chai Ling has become a person with extremely selfish motives who "will let others shed blood while she saves her own skin."[34]

個別的人為了利欲討好當政者，挖空心思地為當政者出謀劃策；另一個有親共歷史的人為了牟取商業暴利推銷自己的紀錄片，斷章取義企圖要標新立異，硬要把歷史的黑白顛倒過來，先是去年戴晴叫嚷的"柴玲"要判重罪，"擾亂交通治安罪"；今天柴玲又成了個讓"別人流血，而自己求生"的極端自私自利的人。…

Chai's defense of herself—one that was given considerable coverage in both the U.S. and Kong-Tai media—is not our particular concern here. Rather, we are attracted to the revealing use of rhetoric as we contemplate the question of totalitarian nostalgia. Chai's language is so colorful and ideologically laden that it is useful to list in Chinese (plus their translations) some of the ideologemes she uses:

weile liyu taohao dangzhengzhe: to engage in an act beneficial to ingratiating [oneself] with the government for the sake of personal gain.

wakong xinsi wei dangzhengzhe chumou huace: to rack one's brains to mastermind a scheme on behalf of the government.

mouqu shangye baoli: to reap staggering [and immoral] profits.

tuixiao yingpian: to hawk a film.

duanzhang quyi qitu yao biaoxin liyi: to quote out of context in an attempt [negative connotation] to do something new, just to appear different.

ying yao ba lishide heibai diandao guolai: obstinately wanting to turn the black and white of history on its head.

Dai Qing jiaorang: Dai Qing clamored/shouted/howled . . .

Chai's is a parole replete with the connotative-evaluative messages that Epstein dissects in his work on relativistic patterns in totalitarian thinking. It is a language that is steeped in the discursive style of the official Chinese media and one that is also highly reminiscent of the emotive mode of denunciation commonly employed in the Cultural Revolution. Furthermore, it is a fulsome expression of the megalomaniac rivalry that built up between trenchant members of the Chinese government and their opponents. Chai Ling's language was not the only element of the article that bespoke a totalitarian inertia in her mental habits. In defense of her comments to Cunningham, she ignored the verbatim quotation given by Hsüeh: "I feel so sad, because how can I tell them that what we actually are hoping for [*qidai*] is bloodshed, the moment when the government is ready to butcher the people brazenly?" Instead she uses what is for her, and her defenders like Ruan Ming (a former party curmudgeon who became a democrat in the late 1980s and a dissident in the '90s), a sanitized English word, "expect," to occlude the idea and connotation of desirability that is inherent in the Chinese term *qidai*.[35]

Chai also claimed that during the movement, "our demands never exceeded the freedoms and rights granted to citizens by the constitution."[36] Here again, she ignores what she said to Cunningham, to wit: "Unless we overthrow this inhuman government, our country will have no hope! Our people will have no hope!"[37] During the 1990s, faced with the implacable rule of the Communist Party and the erratic policies of the Clinton administration in regard to China, it became politic for the extremist dissidents of 1989 to become supporters of "constitutional change" and "gradual reform" in China. As the mainland economy boomed, they tactically repositioned themselves. Whereas they once had vociferously opposed the U.S. government's granting most-favored-nation status only a few years earlier, they now lobbied for constructive engagement with China. It was perhaps no coincidence that a number of them now spoke on behalf of the American business interests that now employed them. The truth remains, however, that in the days leading up to 4 June 1989, many of this group had indeed agitated for the overthrow of the Communist Party and hoped to carry out a totalistic, avowedly "democratic," revolution.

The conflation of time and space into a realm of the permanent ideologically correct present is also central to the totalitarian habit. In responding to Hsüeh's article and in many of the vociferous attacks on *Gate*, critics readily passed over the actual circumstances of the interview that Chai Ling had given on that day in May. It came about shortly after the Joint Liaison Committee of groups concerned with the movement voted on 27 May in favor of leaving the square. The committee was an ad hoc body of people set up in an attempt to coordinate the protests. It consisted of leading figures among the student protesters, the intellectuals of Beijing, and the workers. On that day, the committee was told that the situation in the square was chaotic and unhygienic. It was argued that it was better to declare the movement victorious, end the occupation of the square on 30 May, and encourage the students to return to their schools to continue agitating for change there. The Liaison Committee included the student representatives Chai Ling, Wang Dan, and Wuer Kaixi. Chai voted in favor of the motion along with everyone else (there was reportedly only one abstention).

The decision of the Liaison Committee was subsequently announced at Tiananmen by Wang Dan. It was only then that Chai Ling, having been advised by her lieutenant Li Lu (who was not at the meeting that voted to persuade the students to leave) and others, unilaterally overturned the decision and called on the students to remain in the square indefinitely. She was considering leaving Beijing herself. Then, on May 28, Chai Ling approached Philip Cunningham and offered him an interview that was nothing less than a political testament. That she later changed her mind regarding her tactics may have been for the most laudable reasons, but her support for the decision to leave the square, her sudden about-face, and then her comments on the need for bloodshed, talk of conspirators and capitulationists, and the other revelations about her view of her sacrifice for "the Chinese people" that she made to Cunningham are part of the historical, and now public, record.

If one reads all of Chai's article and the numerous other attacks on *Gate* by the extremist Chinese dissident exiles (they constitute, it should be noted, only one faction in a large and complex community) published in the Chinese media in April–July 1995—a veritable mini-mountain of material that comprises many dozens of pages—one will discover many curious things. Some of the articles darkly hint at "international plots" to discredit the Chinese dissidents—one author claims that Patrick Tyler (the *New York Times* Beijing correspondent) and the *New York Times*, which also ran a controversial story on *Gate* in late April 1995, were part of a conspiracy to discredit the dissident exiles and help China's communist reformers.[38]

THE UNITY OF OPPOSITES

Over the years, the factional opponents of ideological extremism in China have been all too ready to use the language of their enemies when writing their denunciations and attacking their foes at various forums.[39] On one hand, they have done so as an ironic inversion of party language, but on the other, such writing also betrays the fact that even many of China's self-styled free thinkers were infected by the same type of sectarian narrowness and virulence that they so abhorred in their adversaries.[40]

It is not surprising, therefore, that a writer for *Mainstay*, the mainland "retro-Maoist" journal founded after 4 June to propagate the cultural line of right-thinking ideologues, published a critique of Cultural Revolution–style diction as used by supposedly liberal journalists. In what is a classic example of the pot calling the kettle black, the writer of the piece noted that the rabid, *yaoya qiechi* (literally "teeth gnashing" or vituperative), style of language reflected an abiding Cult-Rev psychology. The writer also noted that the so-called enemies of such linguistic reaction—in particular, liberals who took advantage of Deng Xiaoping's tour of the south to denounce extreme "leftists"—readily indulged themselves in such histrionics.[41] An example of this "liberal" demagoguery, the article said, was to be found in Zhao Shilin's preamble to *Aide-Mémoire on Preventing "Leftism,"* a popular collection of essays produced in 1992 in response to Deng's critique of post-1989 ideological extremism. The best-selling volume featured work by Wang Meng, Liu Xinwu, Li Zehou, and Yuan Hongbing, among others. As Zhao, the anti-leftist liberal editor, noted:

> At the crucial moment when the powers of extreme "leftism" and their in-house theoreticians, swollen with arrogance, had set their sights on striking out wantonly against reform, Comrade Deng Xiaoping resolutely toured the south. He issued speeches in which he stated categorically: "We must guard against rightism, but more important, we must prevent 'leftism'!" One simple sentence, but each word bears the weight of greatness, an uncompromising statement, one that resounds with authority. Finally, Comrade Deng Xiaoping has turned around the ship of state, guiding us with his eye of wisdom, his genius and daring. Although an octogenarian, he has thought nothing of thus exerting himself, and at this key moment he has repulsed the evil current of leftism. Oh, how fortunate the reforms! How blessed are our people![42]

Turning once more to the debate over *Gate* in 1995, we find in the overblown language of Chai Ling's supporters the habits of mind bred from the relativistic logic of communist ideology. Bai Meng, the student in charge of the public address system at the Monument to the People's Heroes when Chai Ling was commander in chief of the Defend Tiananmen Square headquarters, and a coauthor of the Student Hunger Strike Declaration, wrote a long critique, entitled "Tiananmen Trials," of Carma Hinton and *Gate* in the inaugural issue of the journal *Tiananmen*. It is so characteristic of the style of democratic denunciation used by extremist dissidents to attack their enemies—to both the left and the right—that it deserves to be quoted here at length:

> I feel compelled to point out that I have lost faith in the fairness of the media in the "Free World." Ever since Dai Qing, a woman who poses as a "political dissident," first clamored about wanting to "put Chai Ling on trial" two years ago, this tune has been echoed a number of times both in- and outside China. Now we are finally hearing a chorus of support. It comes with the emergence of the film *The Gate of Heavenly Peace*. It is produced by Carma Hinton, an American who grew up in China like a privileged aristocrat, a person who maintains deep ties with the highest levels of the Chinese Communist Party. She has gathered around herself a group of

people with dubious political pedigrees and selectively used materials taken out of context to scrape this film together.

Carma Hinton is the daughter of William Hinton, the author of *Fanshen*, a renowned account of the communist land reforms of the late 1940s and a man known for his long-term support of the Chinese revolution. On the strength of these blood ties, Chai, Bai and their coevals labeled Carma a pro-Communist (although as a youth in China she never joined any Communist Party youth organization or the Chinese Communist Party itself). It was an intriguing accusation, since virtually all the famous exiled dissidents shared a far more venerable "pro-Communist" history than did Hinton, who moved to the United States in 1970. Indeed, most of these dissidents grew up as members of the Communist Party's Young Pioneers or the Youth League or even joined the Communist Party itself. In 1982, at the age of sixteen, Chai herself was named one of the Communist Youth League's top one hundred students.[43]

Bai Meng continued in this vein of genealogical investigation and examined the personal histories of each of the dubious characters involved in *Gate* and the resultant controversy: Dai Qing, Hsüeh Hsiao-kuang, Liu Xiaobo, Zhou Duo, and Gong Xiaoxia. The upshot of his inquisition was that all were found to be tainted by serious political problems; indeed all, except for Hsüeh, had been jailed by the Communists. Bai then declared that through their words and deeds, these heinous individuals had "aimed weapons that are even more lethal than those used by the Chinese government at us, the children of Tiananmen." He went on to say:

> Although they are opportunists, the filmmakers have shown considerable foresight. The ideas they've come up with to aid and abet those in power are even more crafty than those the authorities could concoct for themselves. That's because they [the filmmakers] know that by posing as "intellectuals" and "dissidents," they can deceive more people. . . .
>
> As long as they call themselves intellectuals, their flagrant distortion of history is nothing less than criminal. Although the actual trials of Tiananmen are yet to take place, the trial of souls is already under way. The verdict is that they [the filmmakers] are not independent intellectuals exercising independent value judgments. They are nothing more than a bunch of flies. They are the scourge of our age.[44]

Ye Ren, a mainland resident in the United States familiar with the ins and outs of this acrimonious debate, observed in a more phlegmatic mood:

> Chai Ling, who is at the center of the controversy, displayed an even more acute insight than her former deputies. In an interview published in the

World Journal just before the sixth anniversary of 4 June [in 1995], she pointed out, "Recently, a small number of people in the Western media have
tried to divide the students from Tiananmen into radicals and moderates.
By using the tactic of currying favor with some and attacking others, they
intend to transfer the blame for the bloodshed onto the so-called hard-line
students. Following this attempt, the Chinese Communist news agency
Xinhua clamored about opposing radicalism. We must be vigilant and pay
close attention to this well-planned and well-organized attempt to divide
the forces for democracy." Is Chai Ling suggesting that through their plotting the Chinese Communists have joined up with Chinese-language
newspapers abroad, *The New York Times*, and American filmmakers in a co-
ordinated effort with its own official media to transfer the blame for the
Massacre onto people like herself? I find it hard to believe that even in its
wildest dreams the Communist Party could ever create such a united front.

What we see here is a very peculiar phenomenon. Those who promote
themselves as having devoted their lives to the cause of democracy are unwilling even to use democratic methods to discuss an issue. Their treatment
of people who hold different opinions is to immediately check their family
background, investigate the history of their political attitudes, and try to un-
cover an "evil master-mind" behind them. The language they use, such as
"characters with dubious political background," "a small number of people
in the media," and "curry favor with some and attack others," reminds one
of the terms used in the days of political persecution in China. Their behavior resembles that of the Communist Party, and the way they go about
advocating democracy resembles nothing so much as McCarthyism.[45]

Zheng Yi, a prominent exiled writer, also went on the defensive on Chai Ling's
behalf. Quoted by the *World Journal*, he stated that Carma Hinton was a person
with well-known communist sympathies. Zheng—who knew of Hinton from
their school days—an ex–Red Guard, a mainland novelist, and a 1989 dissident
who achieved a measure of media prominence for his book on cannibalism during the Cultural Revolution, published another article on the subject in *Tiananmen* entitled "In Defense of Chai Ling":

Journalist Patrick Tyler and filmmaker Carma Hinton: both of you have
wantonly manipulated history and fabricated crimes that you interpolate
onto the democracy movement, concocting in the process a story about
there being some sort of "hidden strategy" [among student leaders]. Don't
you think you have violated professional ethics and acted unconscionably?
The United States is a Christian country that regards lying as a sin. I do not
know whether you are Christians. But would you honestly be able to put

your hand on the Bible and swear that you are not telling lies for some unspeakable motive?[46]

Zheng went on to claim that *Gate* would have the most deleterious effect on China:

Whether or not you [Hinton and Tyler] were involved with a premeditated political plot, you have already created a massive obstacle to the overturning of the official verdict on 4 June. This is an important issue that affects the fate of 1.2 billion people. But you have acted as though this is but a ploy in your pursuit of personal fame and financial gain![47]

Speaking on behalf of the "1.2 billion people" of China is a favorite pastime of propagandists from both ends of the political spectrum. Although the official mainland response to the film was slow, when it came, it proved to be as equally unimaginative and cliché prone as that of the extremist exiles. After the New York Film Festival announced that *Gate* was to premiere at the festival in October 1995, the Chinese authorities demanded that it be withdrawn. When the organizers failed to comply, the Chinese attempted to ban Zhang Yimou's new film, *Shanghai Triad*, from opening the festival. After this, too, was frustrated, Zhang himself was forbidden to go near New York. In their subsequent efforts, the Chinese authorities were sometimes more successful in their intimidation, and a number of high-profile festivals either dropped plans to screen *Gate* or sidelined the film.

Approximately one year after the original debate about *Gate* appeared in the U.S. press, the Chinese finally felt compelled to put their protest in writing. In a letter dated 19 April 1996, to the director of Filmfest DC, who was preparing to screen *Gate*, the press consul of the embassy of the People's Republic of China in Washington, wrote:

As is well known, a very small number of people engaged themselves in anti-government violence in Beijing in June 1989 but failed. The film *The Gate of Heavenly Peace* sings praise of these people in total disregard of the facts. If this film is shown . . . it will mislead the audience and hurt the feelings of 1.2 billion Chinese people. Therefore, it is necessary and appropriate to withdraw this film from the festival.

The director of Filmfest DC found it both unnecessary and inappropriate to satisfy this request.

In reviewing this contretemps, one is reminded of a controversy over an earlier documentary on China: the Italian director Michelangelo Antonioni's 1973 film *Zhongguo*. The *People's Daily* and *Red Flag*, the official communist propaganda organs of the time, published lengthy denunciations of Antonioni, and the party called on the nation to engage in a frenzied vilification of his film, one that tried to depict, with a goodly dose of irony, some of the sodden realities of revolutionary New China. Antonioni was pilloried for "being possessed of an inimical attitude toward the Chinese people." He "had ulterior motives and employed extremely despicable methods, taking unfair advantage of an opportunity to visit China with the sole aim of raking up material so as to vilify China in order to achieve his unspeakable political ends."[48] Numerous articles and speeches attacking the film in this vein were published. Needless to say, to ensure the ideological health and protect the "feelings of the Chinese people," the authorities never let China's outraged critics or masses actually see the object of their outrage.

BEGINNING AT THE END

The Gate of Heavenly Peace follows the history of the 1989 protest movement while weaving into its structure the prehistory of those events and commenting on the political habits and attitudes that have come to inform public life in China over the past century. It documents the development of the movement and, in so doing, reflects the drama, tension, humor, absurdity, heroics, and many tragedies of those six weeks from April to June in 1989. Through this process, the film attempts to reveal how moderate voices in both the government and among the protesters (including students, workers, and intellectuals) were gradually cowed and then silenced by extremism and emotionalism on both sides. This extremism was couched in terms of "plots" and "conspiracies," reflecting the kind of political scare tactics and totalitarian rhetoric that had developed, especially under Maoism.

In 1989, the end result of the protests was the erasure of the middle ground: Liberal and moderate figures in the government were ousted; leading forums for public debate were closed down; and independent activity in the society was crushed for some years.

The style of demotic denunciation, the pattern of crudely confrontational argumentation that has generally held sway on mainland China since then, benefits ideological opponents. It stifles reasoned opinion, abolishes intermediate and self-reflective analyses, and appeals to emotional and linguistic extremism while claiming for itself the language of both revolution and reform. At one moment, it can veer to the left; at another, to the right. As we have pointed out, this mind-set, be it expressed by conservative auto-orientalists or democratic firebrands (or, for that matter, "globalized" po-mo elites) thus shares a bond with the habits and linguistic style of totalitarianism.

As J. M. Coetzee remarked regarding the nature of politics as a "totalizing category,"[49] it lends itself to "a certain idiom of outrage and vituperation that belongs to the levels of escalation at which debate is no longer possible."[50] "Through the means of provocative insult, the monologic ground of official denunciation is redefined . . . as the dialogic ground of polemical strife, that is to say, redefined as a ground on which it is possible for the opposing voice to *win*."[51]

In this and the previous chapter we have considered a number of debates in the realm of ideas and culture on the mainland and have observed, again to quote Coetzee, what could be construed as "the dynamic of spiraling mimetic violence precipitated by the collapsing of distinctions."[52] Despite the vast transformations since the advent of the reform era that mainland Chinese society has witnessed in the realm of ideology—and here culture and politics are included in our definition—self-identification in relation to polemic enemies has remained a central feature of the mindscape. Although the shifting sands of debate have meant that the identity of "enemies" has seemingly changed over the years, in terms of rhetorical strategies and intellectual paradigms, we have seen that in the realm of contending power hierarchies, both tyrant and revolutionary, establishment and opposition, are often more alike than different. The imitative violence of these polemics repeatedly defines the contours of debate and leads into the thrall of what we have called totalitarian nostalgia.

The former Soviet artists Komar and Melamid speak of "the aesthetics of ideological advertisement"[53] when discussing their own nostalgic bent, but they also use the word *necrology*, an examination of the dead past, as a sardonic description of their practice of repeatedly returning to the past for the inspiration of their work. "Their nostalgia helps them persevere into the future, for every step backward directs them forward, toward some fresh nuance of meaning."[54] Such a necrology, even a necrophilia, has certainly been evident in China in the 1990s, although as I have attempted to demonstrate in this book, the double bind of the party-state and the marketplace (both socialist and offshore) has had a profound influence on the way artists have evoked the spirit of the past.

Up to the mid-1990s, with a few notable exceptions, there was little attempt by resident mainland intellectuals who were involved in the major public cultural debates of the day to employ self-reflective critical and theoretical tools to analyze China's long-term historical predicament per se (although mainland-born scholars working overseas were energetic in doing so, often to the chagrin of their homebound fellows). Since the 1980s, there has been a strong undercurrent of discussion in China concerning the development of the "modern" (that is, post-Ming) state, the manipulation of symbols to maintain social and cultural cohesion, the rearticulation of national-racial icons like the Yellow Emperor and the

"Chinese race," *Zhonghua minzu*, to define ultra-Chinese sensibilities, as well as debates about the shape of a future Chinese commonwealth in terms of federalism, regionalism, and so on. One could have presumed that the resultant cultural and historical melee would have led to a concomitant interest in dissecting the Manchu-Han creation of "China" dating from the expansionist phase of the Qing dynasty in the eighteenth century. Similarly, the discussion of issues related to the confabulation of a dominant Han (Yellow River) culture and its "othering" effects on regional Han and non-Han cultures could benefit greatly from theoretical perspectives that have been introduced from "the West."[55] Nonetheless, in the mid-1990s atmosphere of Sino-Western *Kulturkampf*, conservative writers have been at pains to deny the universalist presumptions of Western academic approaches and call for scholarship with "Chinese characteristics."[56]

Indeed, "Chinese characteristics" became an adjectival intellectual catchall used by canny writers to reject Chinese (and, by association, Western) Enlightenment narratives while accommodating ideological positions of the most conservative bent, or at least laying the foundations for a reaffirmation of the history of Maoist "modernity."[57] Among the disarmed liberal intelligentsia, there was a widespread belief that the rejection of authoritarian habits of thinking also required the abandonment of ideological commitment. This "deconstructive imperative" in turn fed all too readily into a parlous situation in which liberal intellectuals and nonpartisan thinkers shied away from anything more than a reactive approach to the cultural issues of the day. Although a justifiable and, one could argue, sincere stance for the individual, in practice—given the continued and manipulative hegemony of the Communist Party and the acuity of its sentimental hangers-on—the marginalization of independent thought seemed to be leading to the kind of cultural bifurcation of earlier eras.

As I have attempted to demonstrate, this culture is a complex and contradictory miscegenation. Cultural intermediaries—among them educators, journalists, academics, and writers—have also used the language of political, social, and literary theory to reformulate and articulate anew their own definitions of identity. Much of what these figures have been engaged in in recent years has been grounded in nativist cultural assumptions which, through the appropriation of the most modern, international, and Western elements of discourse, have gained a new validity and cultural cachet. It may be theoretically valid to talk of the postmodern global capitalist decay of the intellectual as a vital force in society and claim that many of the issues discussed here are the bleatings of a dying caste. However, I hesitate to join in the po-mo frisson of self-abnegation that such a hasty conclusion may produce. It is, I would argue, somewhat premature to declare the demise of the Chinese intellectual elite. Rather, this book has found that the Chinese intelligentsia has, again to take a line from Svetlana Boym with whom we began this chapter, "been playing hide-and-seek with its cultural mission; at times it has been ostracized, but only to be redeemed later, in the unofficial or dissident culture."[58]

In early 1996, the Shanghai-based cultural historian Xu Jilin observed that "the past has shown us that truly independent thinkers who maintain an individualistic stance are doomed to be ignored by the broader public and fated to be misinterpreted by both sides [of the political/ideological divide]. Invariably they live a solitary and isolated existence on the sidelines."

In the highly politicized atmosphere of China, extremists have consistently avoided the fate of such marginalization, either politically or culturally. As Xu says, "They play the central roles everyone takes notice of, be they tragic or comic."[59]

For editors like Liang Xiaoyan, one of the guiding forces behind the journal *Orient* and a commentator who was featured prominently in the film *Gate*, the relationship between extreme political and cultural opinions could be negotiated only with increasing difficulty. At pains to turn *Orient* into an open forum for a range of opinion in what was far from being an environment free of censorship and control, she risked supporting indirectly those who would use ideas and political posturing to stake a claim on further cultural oppression. To make *Orient* into a kamikaze vehicle for openly dissident views, on the other hand, would have resulted in its immediate closure. The spirit of skeptical rationalism, rejected through the mid-1990s by Chinese po-moists and nativists (or conservatives) alike, all too readily sowed the seeds of its own destruction.[60] As Lu Xun had realized in the heavily policed literary environment of 1930s Shanghai, fair play works only when everyone plays by the same rules. In mid-1996, Liang Xiaoyan was forbidden to edit *Orient*, and at the end of the year, the authorities closed down the journal.[61] In 1997, Liang became a freelance editor and, along with similarly minded writers and editors, was involved once more in efforts to establish and maintain a few publishing outlets for independent opinions.

Xu Jilin's concerns about the fate of independent intellectuals are deeply felt. He was but one of a number of younger scholars whose studies of the melancholic history of the would-be independent Chinese intelligentsia in the twentieth century directly inspired their engagement in cultural debate in the 1980s.[62] In reviewing the progress of the May Fourth movement in 1989 (referred to in chapter 3, "Traveling Heavy"), Xu wrote, for example, that the general trend in favor of cultural reassessment that developed in China at either end of the century "was in itself inspired by a mood of political utilitarianism rather than being part of a quest for knowledge. All the cultural debates that resulted from it have invariably been tinged with an ideological hue and marked by a desire for immediate results."

The quick fixes of the Deng Xiaoping era, so eloquently, even if inelegantly, summed up by the late grand architect of reform as "crossing the river by feeling for the stones," *mozhe shitou guo he*, conceal habits of mind that we have chosen to characterize under the rubric of totalitarian nostalgia. The true attraction of the totalitarian, however, is not merely intellectual, for it contains an awe-inspiring mixture of the divine and the demotic, a beguiling union that characterizes the totalitarian project to transform the world and reorder history. When such a mission is combined with a sense of national purpose and global capitalism, it can produce a heady mix indeed.

We have also argued that outside the relationship of those in power and the individuals and groups sequestered politically and economically, the alternative cultural figures of the past decade or so have in their own right appropriated the lives, style, language, and culture of other subordinated groups, and through those acts of usurpation, they have effectively established their own authorizing voice. And so it is that they have negotiated a position of cultural prominence for themselves that trades on their international or local reputation, contributing thereby to the establishment of new cultural hierarchies.

The trickster, characterized in this book by Wang Shuo (and, to a lesser extent, Kong Yongqian and various pop artists), developed a cultural balancing act that delighted and thrilled spectators in the early 1990s. This conspiratorial charm gradually waned, devolving not so much into a new strategy for subversion or independence as the means for occupying a certain market niche. It has often been argued in regard to post-1976 Chinese art that in the long run, mainland cultural entrepreneurs, be they investors or producers, have helped stake out the perimeters for greater movement in the society. Even though such a progressivist view might be highly laudable and might be a reflection of one perception of reality, it has not been our aim here to validate further such claims but, instead, to analyze the cultural contexts of avowedly new and significant phenomena. By questioning common narrative interpretations of contemporary Chinese culture in this way, this book has proposed a slightly more nuanced appreciation of the mainland environment.

Similarly, to explain official ideology in terms of its utilitarian pragmatism may be of some help in describing its recent history but fails to account for its vitality outside the boundaries of party pronouncements and mainstream discourse. Beyond economic pragmatism lies a realm of ideas. Time and space have been reduced through the official media to construct a historical narrative only cursorily related to historical events and detail. Again, Mikhail Epstein argues that a similar process of de-ideologization in the Soviet Union was marked by the end of any " 'particular' ideology that originally had a definite class character, social ideals, and aimed to inspire the proletariat to launch a socialist revolution and construct communism."[63]

In China, de-ideologization led to a proliferation and not an end of ideologies. Just as people were finding and creating spaces during the reform era in which alternative identities could be developed and expressed, these spaces were also occupied, co-opted, diverted, or claimed by a concatenation of cultural forces. Those who led the push to give voice to these alternatives themselves, though not simply subsumed by commercial socialism, were transformed by it.

In addition, the role of the cultural purge or minicampaign has changed since the mass movements of the Maoist years. As we have observed, since 1976 there has been some form of cultural putsch—or, concomitantly, a period of relaxation—on an average of every two years. The cumulative effect of these repeated and erratic cultural contractions has not been to eliminate independent artistic activity but, rather, to engender an environment in which creative individuals and groups have been able to negotiate a space for themselves within the ambit of reformist culture. Regular policing and bans have helped socialize (in both senses) the aberrant artist and thinker.

The merchant class, excoriated throughout the history of mainland Communism, has risen in a fanfare of get-rich-quick stories. Gradually, it is making its impact felt not only on the society as a whole but within the realm of culture as well. They, too, are new compradors of influence and taste. Many of the cultural enterprises discussed in this book—art, film, TV series, literature, and even intellectual journals and, by association, the cultural debates they promoted—have in part been funded by the entrepreneurial class. But our interest has been to study certain aspects of cultural entrepreneurs and their devil's dance with both official and nonofficial cultural forms.

During the 1990s, the mainland experienced many facets of totalitarian nostalgia. The childhood and adolescence of socialist China, the 1950s and 1960s, was imbued with a romantic incandescence; it became a hazy past that was reflected in revived heroic films and mass culture that depicted a national youthfulness and vitality. Then there was the complex fad for Chairman Mao that saw him finally enter the popular pantheon of Chinese Worthies; the works of younger film directors recalling the Cultural Revolution in cinematic reverie, the general longing for a mythic past of egalitarianism and shared suffering, an attachment among ideologues to a party culture that molded rather than reacted to popular culture, a cleaving of both the entrenched power holders and their opponents to simplistic styles of political confrontation, and the growth of a populist, commercial nationalism fed by party propaganda that divided the world into "China" and its enemies. In an era in which the individual as producer and consumer had more and more choices to make, the obliteration of personal responsibility in regard to the past provided a welcome diversion from the present and created the mental wallpaper of a revenant China.

Svetlana Boym distinguishes two types of nostalgia in her study of Russia after the dissolution of the Soviet Union: utopian nostalgia, which was reconstructive and totalizing, and ironic nostalgia, which was inconclusive and fragmentary.

The former stresses the first root of the word, *nostos* (home), and puts the emphasis on the return to that mythical place on the island of Utopia where the "greater patria" has to be rebuilt, according to "its original authentic design." Ironic nostalgia puts the emphasis on *algia*, longing, and acknowledges the displacement of the mythical without trying to rebuild it.[64]

In this book, I have tried to demonstrate that in the Chinese party-state of the 1990s, these two kinds of nostalgia (not to mention the innumerable intermediate and contradictory positions between these presumed poles of difference) were increasingly complementary. The relationship may have been fraught with tension and antagonism. But the two were united more than divided in the realm of totalitarian nostalgia, a realm where there is both a "longing for a total reconstruction of a past that is gone"[65] and the employment of a refurbished past in beginning a new history, one that begins at the end.

Springtime in Beijing

The eight-part China Central TV documentary *Tiananmen* was completed in 1991. The work of two young Beijing directors, Chen Jue and Shi Jian, the eight-hour series was begun at the height of cultural liberalism in the late 1980s and edited during the political purge that followed the 4 June Beijing massacre. Each episode contained elements—in both the montage of images and the narration—that reflected this momentous shift in public life. The narration, cowritten with Guang Yi, was couched in highly symbolic language and expressed eloquently what Miklós Haraszti would have recognized as "civilization between the lines."

In "Going Places," episode 5 of *Tiananmen*, as images of adults and children skating on the frozen waters of the river-moat encircling the imperial palace at the heart of Beijing appear on screen, the narrator tells the audience:

> In this ancient city, as soon as the ice is thick enough, people come here to skate. Such freedom is a thrill, as is the ease with which you can constantly change speed and posture.
>
> The moment you put a foot on the ice, you realize you have to change the way you walk. You also know that if you stop now, you'll have no other choice but to leave quietly or stand aside and watch the others.
>
> Observing them, you may eventually be emboldened to start again. Your first fall will leave you dejected. People speed on past, but you'll see that you're not the only one who has faltered. This will give you the courage to stand up. You may fall again, but you'll keep trying. This is the beginning of understanding.
>
> You learn how to modulate your pace and movements. You decide what path you'll take and learn to keep your emotions in check. Initially everything seems unfamiliar, but gradually you get the hang of it.
>
> The ice begins to melt. The season is nearly over. Much has been learned, some things better than others. You treasure the carefree sensation of gliding over the ice and you wait, wait for the next season.[1]

CAN THE SPRING BE FAR AWAY?

In traditional China, autumn was a season of great moment. At the Autumn Assizes, for instance, condemned prisoners would have their death sentences confirmed or reduced. It was also in the autumn and winter months, the seasons of decay and death, that major legal proceedings were undertaken and executions carried out. For farmers, the autumn was harvest time, after which came the annual reckoning when outstanding accounts were settled. Throughout the history of the People's Republic, hopes and trepidations for the spring in Beijing always built up in the preceding autumn and winter.

In September 1997 another congress of the Communist Party of China (this time the fifteenth) introduced national policy directions that would guide the country into the twenty-first century. It signaled, above all, a new move toward the market. The congress was lauded as signaling a "thought liberation movement," *sixiang jiefang yundong*. The liberation was simple: it was necessary to admit that China's unprofitable public sector—in particular, the massive, inefficient state enterprises—required downsizing and basic structural renovation if the economy was to continue to grow. The bureaucracy itself, bloated and corrupt beyond control despite numerous attempts to rein it in, was to be radically reshaped, and a series of reforms under a new premier (Zhu Rongji, appointed in the spring of 1998) were to be launched. The face of Chinese socialism, which had already undergone a radical makeover since the late 1970s, was to be further altered.

It was also in the autumn of 1997 that the cultural world experienced the first hint of what in 1998 would be dubbed internationally as yet another "Beijing Spring."

There have been any number of political and cultural thaws on mainland China since 1978. Presaged by some shift in central government policy or factional realignment, and burgeoning amid an outpouring of controversial cultural activity, ideological lobbying, and sometimes even public protest, each "spring" in the past waxed in tandem with political need or economic bullishness and waned as the situation deteriorated. Every spring blossoming had invariably been followed by a harsh winter of Central Committee discontent. Sensitive to the seasonal mood of the policymakers and long before the actual spring of 1998, astute political writers and cultural commentators took advantage of the relaxation augured by the party congress to "settle scores after the autumn harvest," *qiuhou suanzhang*. The main object of their scorn were the fall guys of the reform age, the political stalwarts of the Maoist past: China's lunar left.

In the late 1970s, Deng Xiaoping helped lead the party and nation away from Maoism by supporting a theoretical debate about "practice being the sole criterion of truth."[2] It was a discussion that enabled party thinkers to formulate a rationale for economic reform that would maintain the facade of Mao Thought while emptying it of all content. These ideological acrobatics were hailed as constituting a "second liberation" for the Chinese nation, a liberation of thought that was virtually on a par with the liberation of mainland China in 1949 when the Communist Party came to power. It allowed the party to liberate itself from the personality cult of Mao Zedong and the Marxist-Leninist fundamentalism that went with it.

Then in early 1992, with the economic reforms in the doldrums and political life cauterized by the 1989 purge, Deng Xiaoping traveled to the south of China and issued a call for yet another wave of sweeping market-oriented change. He warned the party and the nation that they could no longer afford to neglect much-needed restructuring or continue to dissipate time and energy on niggardly debates about whether China was socialist or capitalist, *xing "zi" haishi xing "she."* He admonished the cadre of communists to forge ahead with bold economic reforms, regardless of their ideological doubts or, if not, suffer the fate of the Soviet Union. Deng's tour of the south and the ideas he propounded were eulogized as a "second liberation of thought" that freed people from reliance on the planned economy of socialism.

Shortly after the grand architect's demise in February 1997, Jiang Zemin authored his own "liberation of thought" campaign; it was the third in twenty years. Deng Xiaoping Theory was enshrined in the party catechism; socialism with Chinese characteristics was the latest milestone in the development of Marxism-Leninism. The new stage of national development was to be a radical transformation of state ownership (particularly of state enterprises, the core of the old command economy) and further wide-ranging privatization.

These policies rejected "leftist" objections that had been leveled at party programs since 1992. In a series of lengthy petitions to the Central Committee, the proto-Maoists, often dubbed "red fundamentalists" by their critics, warned that party rule in 1990s China faced a crisis like that experienced in the twilight years of the Soviet Union; that economic inequities were generating serious social conflicts and even new class warfare; that ideological decay was corrupting the heart and mind of the party, as well as causing mass disaffection within China; and that bourgeois liberalism and cultural decay now threatened to undermine what remained of socialist thought. Given the hegemonic position of the United States, they cautioned, the nation must be on constant guard against the enemy within, one that was in league with global capital to achieve the "peaceful evolution" of China into a bourgeois country. Unless resolute action was taken, they declared, counterrevolution and widespread civil strife would be inevitable.

Since the early 1990s, the voices of these advocates of state socialism, central planning, and communism had been all but silenced in the mainstream media.

Although hardly subject to the rigorous bans that were applied to proponents of liberal democracy, by 1998 despite their continued ascendancy in key areas of the bureaucracy, official Maoists held sway over only a few lackluster publications in the Chinese capital and the provinces that catered to a feeble audience. In terms of both its size and its age, their constituency was not that dissimilar to the corps of faithful but elderly patrons of traditional Beijing opera. Just as they had once repressed alternative visions to their agenda (and paradoxically inculcated the very political culture that led to their dwindling influence), the "leftists" were now out of step with the prevailing party line and were publicly excoriated for their recidivism.

As in traditional times, so too in reformist China, seasonal change was a time for the settling of old scores. From late 1997 through to the spring and summer of 1998, the new phase in the capitalization of China engendered another round of relative freedom in the media and the cultural sphere. The opponents to further radical economic restructuring had secretly circulated within the party their dire predictions about the future. During the spring of 1998, however, these warnings were reproduced—and denounced—in a pro–Jiang Zemin book that gave a history of the internal ideological strife of the previous years. Entitled *Crossed Swords—A Veritable Record of Three Movements to Liberate Thought in Contemporary China*, the volume was part of a series released under the auspices of Liu Ji, vice president of the Chinese Academy of Social Sciences (CASS) and a man rumored to be a think-tank adviser to Jiang.[3] Other volumes in the series Reports on China's Problems[4] were *The Pitfalls of Modernization* and *China Will Never Be a "Mr. No"* (a title that played on the name of the xenophobic best-seller of 1996, *China, Just Say No!*),[5] and they depicted the overall economic and social condition of the country with a measure of frankness rare in recent years. Once more, it seemed, a crisis literature of the kind that had appeared in the late 1980s and again in the early 1990s was being produced that reflected the seemingly overwhelming problems that confronted China.

Jiang Zemin followed the September 1997 party congress with a state visit to the United States which, in its own way, contributed directly to the cultural license of 1998. Before the Chinese president's visit, Liu Ji of CASS was invited to speak at the Fairbank Center for East Asian Research at Harvard University. Liu's remarks on the history and future of the Sino-American relationship were taken to be something of a weathervane for the bilateral relationship, and the full text of Liu's speech was eventually published in China on the eve of President Bill Clinton's June 1998 trip to Beijing.

In his speech Liu made a critical assessment of *The Coming Conflict with China*, a 1997 best-seller by Richard Bernstein and Ross Munro (see the appendix, "Screw You, Too"). He also cautioned his audience that, like America, China was prone to waves of antiforeign sentiment and irrational nationalism. To keep these forces at bay, he announced, "The Chinese government has formulated a policy of 'non confrontation, reducing conflicts, increasing mutual understanding and enhancing cooperation'."[6]

The foreign affairs offensive launched by China in response to American attempts to engage that country in a constructive relationship had immense regional, political, and economic significance. It also had an immediate impact on the intellectual and cultural life of the mainland, areas that were particularly sensitive to every nuance of the turbulent relationship between China and America.

Speculation about the underlying reasons—both pragmatic and long term—for the Jiang Zemin–led thaw with the United States was rife beginning in 1997. Meanwhile, a raft of policy shifts in the arts had a delightfully bizarre effect in China. Among other things, for example, Party General Secretary Jiang exhorted his Politburo colleagues to study James Cameron's Hollywood blockbuster movie *Titanic*. He interpreted it to be a moving depiction of class tensions and love. One of the most visible by-products of the party leader's enthusiasm was the high profile of the film's actors, and during the first half of 1998, the adolescent mien of Leonardo DiCaprio graced the covers of numerous mainland glossy publications.

If only the Communist Party could deliver its wholesome political message with the sleek style of Hollywood, the apparatchiki reasoned, propaganda would have a glorious future. Dexterous semi-independent filmmakers immediately took up the challenge and, in one instance, produced a sycophantic documentary about Jiang's U.S. trip that was released on the eve of Bill Clinton's arrival in China. Bearing the chinoiserie title "As the Sun Rises, the Waves on the River Glisten Brighter Than Fire," the film was a collation of sound bites from a range of Americans about the statesmanlike Jiang Zemin. All those interviewed—from ponderously self-important public figures and obsequious overseas Chinese to civilians in the street—expressed the view that the Chinese leader's visit marked a historical turning point. In the interstices, the off-screen narrator gushed about Jiang's masterful glad-handling of his American hosts and spoke glowingly of how he impressed everyone with his warmth, humor, social graces, and presidential musical talents. The advertising hype on the cover of the video version of the film that was released in mid-1998 summed it up with a dose of Sino-spin (*mais sans ironie*): "What do Americans say about Jiang Zemin? 'He is very cool!' "[7]

In keeping with this gleeful Americophilia, Ding Guangen, the glum Politburo stalwart whose policies had cast a pall over the arts for years, now gave voice to the shift in government thinking. He encouraged film and TV makers to be more daring in their work. With the fiftieth anniversary of the People's Republic, the eightieth anniversary of the May Fourth movement, the return of Macao to the motherland, and the cusp of the millennium all coming up in 1999, large state budgets were allocated to stage, screen, and publishing ventures. It was hoped that the nation's culture workers could successfully marry official homilies to commercial entertainment, and many edgy arts figures willingly responded to the state's advances. Since 1999 would also mark the tenth anniversary of the 1989 protests and 4 June, overseas activists also prepared for their own media offensive.[8]

WHOSE PEKING UNIVERSITY?

Not all anniversaries were that far off, however, and Peking University celebrated its centenary in mid-1998. It was perhaps an unhappy coincidence that one of the internationally most famous students from the university, Wang Dan, a leader during the 1989 protests, was expelled from China just as his alma mater was preparing for its birthday.

Wang's involvement in a democracy salon at the university had led to his active participation in the mass protests that brought the capital to a standstill for nearly two months in 1989. A moderate voice amid shrill calls for radical if not revolutionary change, Wang was eventually purged by his fellow activists before 4 June. As a ringleader named by the government for instigating the disturbances, however, he was jailed following the Beijing massacre. His eventual release and expulsion to the United States in 1998 came at time when many scholars and writers were recalling the original spirit of Peking University and the tradition of free speech and intellectual commitment that had been nurtured there in the 1910s and 1920s and that had inspired Wang Dan and many of his classmates in 1989.

The authorities held a lugubrious ceremony for the school in the Great Hall of the People on the west flank of Tiananmen Square on 4 May, the symbolic Youth Festival of China that itself commemorated the antigovernment patriotic student demonstrations of 1919. In his congratulatory message to the meeting, Jiang Zemin lauded the university's "glorious tradition of patriotism, progress, democracy, and science" and enjoined students throughout the country to "revive the nation with science and learning," *kejiao xing guo*, while inculcating in themselves a correct communist worldview inspired by "the older revolutionaries and the people."[9] The occasion was variously marked by cultural performances, seminars, and lavish building projects. Far from the pomp and ceremony of the Great Hall, others took the opportunity to reconfirm what they saw as the true heritage of the university.

Qian Liqun, the Peking University professor of twentieth-century literary history whose comments conclude chapter 11, "Kowtowing to the Vulgar," wrote about the spirit of the university in the lead story of the May 1998 issue of *Reading*. In it he spoke in particular of Cai Yuanpei (1868–1940), the chancellor of the university during its heyday as the focus of China's New Culture Movement from 1916. Cai had defined the university as the home for "absolute academic freedom and the unhindered expression of divergent theories," *sixiang ziyou, jianrong bingbao*. As Qian commented, "Cai attempted to transform Peking University into a haven for intellectual freedom. He wanted to create a space in which the intelligentsia could cast aside the shackles of the past and be liberated from the spiritual frustrations under which they labored."[10]

Those halcyon days were short lived, although it was not until the 1950s that the university was purged in order to conform to the needs of socialist construction. Over the past two decades since the inception of economic reform, Qian Liqun observed, a mood of independence had once more flourished on the campus. Nonetheless, pressures on the university to "constantly provide the machinery of state with 'exploitable' talents" were enormous, and this utilitarian approach to education was at loggerheads with the ideals propounded by Cai Yuanpei. He had made Peking University a training ground for independent intellectuals who were "outside the state establishment; people endowed with an eternally critical spirit who would not be obsessed with constantly weighing up the cost of their independence and its consequences." At the dawn of the new millennium, Qian wrote, the university was confronted by the same question that it had faced in Cai Yuanpei's day; that is, what type of university should it be?

> In my view, its central task should be to encourage people with independent critical faculties. It should concern itself with how it can contribute to the long-term benefit and fate of this nation in particular and humanity in general. It should provide an environment for thinkers and writers to formulate new ideals and approaches not only for China but for humankind.[11]

Qian Liqun was concerned not only with commemorating the past, short-lived glories of his university. He also wrote a powerful preface to a volume of essays entitled *Fire and Ice* by a student at the university who was immediately lauded as one of China's most outspoken new writers.

Yu Jie was a twenty-five-year-old student of Chinese literature. His writings, which ranged from somewhat juvenile meditations on youth, integrity, and life to book reviews and critical essays, *zawen*, in the acerbic style of literary feuilletons, had previously enjoyed considerable currency as "literature hidden in the drawer," *chouti wenxue*. His work had reportedly circulated for some time among students at the universities in the Chinese capital; a number of the essays had even appeared in provincial literary journals, to considerable praise.

Yu was conscious of both the controversial traditions of Peking University and the atmosphere of liberalization that now made it safe for circumspect writers to speak out. In "The Lost May Fourth," an essay in *Fire and Ice*, he observed that the slogans formulated during the 1919 student-led May Fourth movement advocating "freedom, democracy, science and human rights" had a particular resonance for Peking University. That early spirit of protest, however, had been diminished, so much so that "now the May Fourth is nothing more than a distant backdrop . . . we don't really know what it means at all." Certainly, he said, today the authorities were right to claim that the May Fourth period had generated a modern strain of patriotism, but it had also given birth to the twentieth-century Chinese tradition of intellectual independence, freedom, and democracy. "What was really unique to the May Fourth period were these latter values; they are what the powerholders fear. That is why the May Fourth has been subverted, dressed up in a garish costume to perform in public. Now it is little more than a draw card for curious onlookers." In 1998, Yu Jie wrote, it was far too early to heed the propaganda line about "moving on from" or "surpassing" the May Fourth tradition. "What we need to do is to make a concerted effort to appreciate what it was really all about."[12]

Fire and Ice appeared in April 1998, promoted by the publishers, the *Economic Daily*, an entrepreneurial official organization in Beijing, as the work of another "dark horse." As we noted earlier, in 1986 the critic Liu Xiaobo had been branded—and depicted in the relatively primitive media market of the time—a dark horse when he derided the self-congratulatory writers and artists of that period, rocking the literary establishment and its leaders (in particular Wang Meng, Liu Zaifu, and Li Zehou) in the process. In the mid-1990s, Wang Meng himself had used the diminutive expression "black colt" to condemn the PLA critic Wang Binbin for having the gall to chide the former minister of culture for "shunning the sublime" and selling out to the market. Now, in 1998, a mainstream publisher packaged a "Dark Horse Collection," *Heima congshu*, of books to promote controversial works by its stable of authors, the leader of the herd being the latest literary firebrand, Yu Jie.

The new dark horse had far more in common with the Liu Xiaobo of the 1980s than the Wang Binbin of the 1990s. Yu Jie's caustic style and literary persona partook of a grand twentieth-century lineage of Chinese essayists and writers who were committed to being different, even superciliously superior. Advertised as "the first Li Ao on the Chinese mainland" and Peking University's "second Wang Xiaobo,"[13] Yu chose as his targets the autocratic habits of traditional Chinese culture and politics, fascism in twentieth-century Europe, and the suppression of free thought. In the war of the two Wangs and the debate over "kowtowing to the vulgar," he was a partisan of Wang Meng. In particular, he was an unabashed critic of Zhang Chengzhi, the man who "refused to capitulate."

Zhang Chengzhi is unequivocal when he proclaims: "Despite everything I still champion the great age of the 1960s. I call on people to take the full measure of Mao Zedong, perhaps the last great man of Chinese history, and a solitary figure."

Statements like this absolutely horrify me. In his inaugural address as rector of Freiberg University on 27 May 1943, Martin Heidegger extolled the Führer principle and the concept of the Führer being the natural leader of Germany, the embodiment of the nation's reality and law. The Nazi sword of Damocles was hanging over his head as he spoke. It is quite a different matter for Zhang Chengzhi to talk as he does in 1990s China.

His statements beg the questions: as spokesman for the masses, what has Zhang got to say about the 30 million people who starved to death during the so-called three years of natural disasters?[14] How does he react when contemplating the countless tormented souls of those who hanged or drowned themselves or were beaten to death [in the Cultural Revolution]?

Of course, the utopian vision of some proffered Great Harmony is a tantalizing one, but it is nothing more than a desert mirage. We must ask ourselves: how many silent corpses are buried in those pitiless sands?

I was born in 1973, so I never had the chance to experience the "great age" of which Zhang Chengzhi speaks. But I do know one thing: poverty and ignorance, cruelty and violence, dictatorship and autocracy can never give birth to "purity."[15]

Yu Jie aligned himself with Wang Meng's characterization of Zhang's "red fundamentalism," *yuan hongzhizhuyi*, and deplored his phony "antiestablishment stance." He even quoted Liu Xiaobo—presumably the first time in years the dissident who had been sentenced to three years' labor reform in 1996 had been referred to in the mainland media in a positive context—to the effect that "when people are deprived of the freedom of choice, when they have no alternative between despotism and deceit, they are also stripped of their individuality; they are nothing more than the tool and plaything of the rulers."[16]

In his reviews of the writings of Osip Mandelstam, Stefan Zweig, Joseph Brodsky, George Orwell, Alexis de Tocqueville, and Milan Kundera, Yu Jie meditates on the state of literature, culture, and politics in late 1990s mainland China. Although *Fire and Ice* was undoubtedly the most provocative book of its kind to have appeared for years, its reception even among unaligned intellectuals and readers was not one of unalloyed delight. Even though many would have agreed with Yu's sentiments—if not always appreciating his precocious and barbed style—the packaging and marketing of the book caused some critics to reflect on the fate of controversial opinion in China's modern market socialism. Advertised by the publisher *Economic Daily* as underground literature, people were skeptical of the new star's work. The critics that I spoke to about the book in May 1998, though deploring the political censorship that kept such work from appearing in the past (and would most probably stymie similar books at some future date), were also repulsed by the hype surrounding this young writer of middling talent, and wondered whether he would turn out to be a pliant media maverick. They protested that the right stuff was being published and hawked for the wrong reason. It was no small irony that whereas socialism had made people cynical about official politics, the market had engendered a wariness of dissident writing and committed literature even among some of its avowed supporters.

Writers like Yu could, for a time, utilize a freedom from innuendo to express controversial ideas directly to the reading public. As has been usual during periods of liberalization over the past twenty years, few people were willing to let such an opportunity for graphomania pass them by. Even petitions to the government regarding 4 June and the 1989 student movement proliferated.[17] But as had been the case many times before, the cultural relaxation was the result of political largesse and a period of officially ordained "liberated thought." The publishing surge was not a victory for cultural diversity as such; it was more a by-product of the state's constant incursions into and manipulation of the marketplace of ideas.

One of those who articulated these concerns was Liu Junning, the editor of the main forum for liberalist thought on the mainland, Res Publica.[18] Like Qian Liqun, Liu availed himself of the centenary celebrations for Peking University to declare that "not only has the spirit of the university not died, it is on the road to a rebirth." In his preface to a collection of essays about the university entitled Heralds of Liberalism, Liu wrote:

> As early as the 1930s, Yang Xingfo [1883–1933], the noted human rights activist who sacrificed his life in the defense of liberty, declared with a heavy heart that "[in Europe and America] the struggle for the protection of individual rights was a battle that belonged to the eighteenth century. Tragically, we in twentieth-century China are still fighting that old campaign."[19] In global terms, human rights was but one of the important fruits of liberalism. In the West, in particular in England and the United States, human rights have been an issue for more than two centuries. In China it has been on the agenda for only the past one hundred years. The way things look at the moment, however, I fear the Chinese will still be striving to achieve human rights well into the twenty-first century.[20]

Regardless of the relative freedom to debate issues related to the state of the nation and its future, Liu Junning was dubious about the latitude that committed intellectuals and citizens throughout the society really enjoyed. For whatever greater public scope for expression and circumscribed political debate existed, it remained the prerogative of particular leaders, indulgences accorded by policy shifts, rather than the outcome of a fundamental or systemic change. "For

China's liberals, the question is how we can transform a tolerance for divergent views into a mechanism for the protection of liberalism so that we will not constantly be at the mercy of individual personalities. . . . If the situation does not change, any improvements will prove to be transitory."[21]

By the time Bill Clinton went to Peking University on 29 June 1998 to lecture the student body on the need to protect individual rights, media freedom, and democracy, there was nothing much he could say that had not been prefigured in books and magazines freely available in the city in the months prior to his visit.

CONSTRICTIVE PARTNERSHIPS

In 1989, Qian Liqun had expressed fears that China's intellectuals would, sooner or later, draw up battle lines and engage in a process of mutual destruction. Deprived of channels for direct political participation or a means with which to test their ideas in opposition to the party status quo—although freer in the late 1990s to debate issues in public forums than at any time in recent history—the intelligentsia was increasingly riven by its own ideological differences.

Some of the fundamental fissures in intellectual life were articulated during the last months of 1997 in a lengthy analysis by Wang Hui published in *Frontiers* and another by Li Tuo in *Reading*. The provenance of the two authors and their choice of publication venues were themselves suggestive: Wang Hui was the editor of *Reading* in Beijing, and Li Tuo was an acquiring editor for *Frontiers*, which was produced in Hainan Province, an island in the South China Sea. Few readers who were *au fait* with the positioning of elite public opinion failed to notice this fortuitous juxtaposition.

After presenting in his essay a personal overview of intellectual developments in China from the late 1970s, Wang Hui went on to question the evolution of a state-directed, market-oriented society and its impact on issues like democratization and civil society. He was profoundly equivocal about people who claimed that there was a clear delineation between the state and the civil, cultural entanglement and intellectual independence.[22] In what was regarded from the time of its publication as a key review of the failures of independent thinkers to analyze and adequately address the issues engendered by China's recent history of modernization, Wang also rearticulated concerns about the nation's increased involvement in the process of globalization and the political, social, economic, and cultural consequences of the growth of a runaway capital-fixated consumer society. To break free of the stultifying rule of state socialism only to fall prey to the machinations of the international market and state capitalism was the specter that thinking individuals now contemplated with growing disquiet.

Li Tuo, or "Master Tuo" as he was often called by friends and foes alike, had the reputation of being someone who always wanted to have the last word first.[23] A thoughtful and often insightful critic of popular cultural phenomena, in 1998 Li called on the intelligentsia to reassess the import of the Frankfurt school and the relevance of its critique of modernity to China.[24] "New issues are confronting the Chinese with added urgency," he wrote in the high-brow declamatory style of prose replete with the kind of interrogative "ideologemes" discussed in chapter 12, "Totalitarian Nostalgia."

> As a leading Third World country, China must, of course, develop. But in the face of the tide of "globalization," in what kind of context should that development be placed? How should China deal with "globalization"? How should China respond to the issues presented by the process of modernization? How should the various theories regarding modernization and development be treated? Should a self-conscious stance be articulated after a critical assessment of these theories so that we can decide which of them conform with our needs? Should we not gradually formulate our own developmental theory?[25]

They were questions for which a swath of Chinese thinkers and writers sought answers. That this series of interrogations came from one of the most voluble elitist critics in the country, however, confirmed many in the belief that there was a trend among mostly Beijing-based writers and thinkers to reformulate ideas about Chinese exclusivity, but this time with a new twist. These thinkers argued that China was somehow different, its search for a path to modernity unique to itself. They posited a view that Western post-Enlightenment values were not necessarily universal, and this included ideas about humanism, democracy, economic liberalism, and so on. Furthermore, China's history under the Communist Party had indicated that surely there was another route that developmental modernity could take. Even the Great Leap Forward and Cultural Revolution, disastrous though they had been in many ways, could and should be appreciated as part of a bona fide attempt to forge a path that differed from that of other nations.

For readers outside the charmed circle of Beijing-Shanghai salon debate, however, both this train of thought and its proponents were distasteful. Chagrin and resentment mixed with a sense of being out of the loop. One group of readers in Nanjing, the provincial capital of Jiangsu, disaffected by the increasingly haughty and pedagogical tone of elite journals like *Reading*, gave vent to their frustrations by lambasting what they called "Green Card" writers, that is authors with foreign (or, rather, U.S.) residency status.

> Articles in *Reading* reek of Green Card confidence, and it is intolerable. . . .
> In particular [the attitude of Li Tuo] is typical of the "cool" [*ku*] style promi-

nent today, suffused as it is with a sense that he's a Great Leader calling on the masses to support him. . . . [The author quotes the preceding passage and goes on to say:] Maybe because he has spent so much time overseas, he does not realize that he is out of touch. But that's not the real problem. What rankles is his hegemonic style of discourse.[26]

These criticisms—and there were many such gibes aimed at *Reading*, not only in newspapers but also in the jottings of people like Yu Jie[27]—were in part a result of the disgruntlement people felt with a style of intellectual debate that had disenfranchised the broader readership. Deprived of political democracy, there was a sense that what little intellectual democracy existed was being frustrated by self-serving elitist factions that were imbricated in their own agendas. The frequent use of Western theory, Anglo-French terminology, and the tendency to dismiss basic social and political concerns in the name of debunking Enlightenment values and the affirmation of antielitist discourse disaffected the reading public. Once more, a caste of superior intellectuals seemed to be assuming the right to raise the consciousness of the unthinking masses (including their misguided fellow intellectuals), as though they had some unique purchase on a privileged, ideal cultural and intellectual program that was simply beyond the ken of more pedestrian minds. In claiming to debunk Enlightenment values, it appeared to their critics that the self-appointed elite was engaged in its own project of self-righteous enlightenment. Was this, like that earlier revolution, also to be carried out in the name of the people? And did these new textual strategies not amount to an elaborate set of evasions of the unpleasant realities of contemporary politics that also nullified the 1950s and 1960s holocaust?

Particularly galling was the fact that some of the most vocal critics of America and globalization themselves made an annual pilgrimage to the enemy camp to "nurture their Green Card," *yang lüka*. By so doing, they maintained their privileged position in the coterie of the migratory intelligentsia. They had joined the ranks of the postmodern tourist,[28] the globally mobile who shuttle between their authenticating home territory (where the mission of postmodern enlightenment engages their attention) and the Euro-American metropoles. It was a migration that reinforced their heartfelt need to reject the West while at the same time giving them access to the latest intellectual high firepower with which to join the next skirmish in an avowed war of independence.

Thus, leading intellectual critics of the status quo in late-1990s China were tending to fall (although not exclusively) into opposing camps. It was a tendency that was, as we have seen, reinforced by rhetorical habit and a certain ideological mind-set, not to mention cultural expediency. One grouping engaged in a critique of globalization and shared much with internationalized left-leaning academia, as well as finding favor with its institutions and publications. The other, proliberal, pro–Western center-left thinkers, shared a fellowship with the global and the market, possibly to the detriment of the very cause of local democratization that they ostensibly espoused.

The novelist and TV writer Wang Shuo was a pop cultural figure who had profitably mocked the bombast of the intelligentsia as well as official ideology. Under a ban imposed in mid-1996, he traveled to the United States, partly as a self-sentenced exile but also to capitalize on the appearance of his first novel in English translation. In early 1998 after returning to China, he published a literary swan song in the form of a selection of his fiction. The preface to the collection was in his signature style of tongue-in-cheek self-deprecation. He declared: "I have destroyed myself; my language is dead."[29] He then proceeded to bewail the fact that his years as a professional writer had turned him into the very thing that he most detested: an intellectual.

Critics had often averred that Wang's lack of a college education had left him with an inferiority complex, a resentment about his own inadequacies expressed itself as a literature of revenge on the Chinese intelligentsia.

> I admit that I promised myself that I'd never become a so-called intellectual. I suppose my prejudices were nurtured by my high school teachers. Since they thought they had knowledge on their side, they felt justified in being insensitive, self-important, and overbearing. For them, learning was an excuse to bully people.
>
> Too often did I see knowledge abused, blindly worshiped, and manipulated to pervert human nature. My trust in the guardians of knowledge was undermined. At first I merely rejected them; only later did I learn to despise them.
>
> Yet I must admit I have also met people who deserve respect. They have made me aware of my own narrow-mindedness. But just as I was about to reconsider my views, I would encounter another intellectual who would only confirm my original bias.
>
> This too, then, is human nature. Just as having a little money corrupts people, so acquiring a bit of knowledge makes people think they can deceive the public. Once I thought one could distinguish between knowledge [zhishi] and intellectuals [zhishifenzi]. In particular, I thought I could escape the vulgar fate [miansu] of being like others and maintain my natural state. I was wrong. How could I be unaffected? Years of writing have turned me, also, into one of them, an intellectual. It makes me extremely uncomfortable, but I am powerless.[30]

Being a reluctant self-proclaimed intellectual, zhishifenzi, was one thing. Having exhausted the possibilities of his style of fiction, both commercially and politically, Wang Shuo used his departure from the literary scene to launch this final salvo. It was an act that said as much about his own benighted state as it did about the chattering classes he so abhorred. Wang's parting shot brings to mind a slang expression that describes neatly the haughty members of the educated classes, the intelligentsia of which Wang Shuo now claimed membership, who presume to speak on behalf of all Chinese. A near homophone of the word *zhishifenzi*, it was as crude as it was eloquent; the expression was *chishifenzi*, "shit eater."

THE PROMOTION OF THE POWERLESS

Censorship and its polar opposite, self-expression or resistance, are at their most comforting when egregious and uncompromising. The black and white of lies and truth can be circumscribed neatly and remorselessly by the red, surgical incisions of the censor's pen. But when the red is used to highlight and overstate, self-promotion often fixates the expressive, and the desire to be heard regardless of what the clamor may mean often comes to rule the day. When censorship is more a matter of negotiation than negation, when compromise replaces the cudgel and opportunism is married to opposition, the rules of censorship are finessed and categories blurred. If the openness of 1997–1998 was built on the "positive censorship" of unpopular opinion within the party then, it did not evince a change in political culture so much as a shift in priorities.

In 1978 the Czech playwright Václav Havel wrote one of his most famous essays, "The Power of the Powerless." Translations of this and many of Havel's other writings had circulated in mainland China during the 1990s. In that essay Havel declared that those deprived of political rights and freedoms in a totalitarian environment had a particular kind of power. For it was in such a society in which "'living within a lie' confronts 'living within the truth,' that is, where the demands of the post-totalitarian system conflict with the real aims of life . . . [that] every free human act or expression, every attempt to live within the truth, must necessarily appear as a threat to the system and, thus, as something which is political *par excellence*."[31]

Havel argued that "modest expressions of human volition" would work to undermine the primacy of the state and militate against the regime of lies that distorted the lives of all who lived under it. The "parallel structures" that developed around individual initiatives were, he believed, most highly developed in the cultural sphere. Havel was responding to conditions in Eastern Europe in the 1970s, a time and place at a considerable remove from 1990s Chinese market socialism. The parallel *polis* that developed in China, however, was not necessarily a liberated zone, for it bordered on both the state system and the hungry world of commerce. In an observation about a very different nation, but a not dissimilar state of affairs, Thomas Frank remarked: "As business replaces civil society, advertising is taking over the cultural functions that used to be filled by the left."[32]

In May 1998, Cui Jian, the leading dissident rock 'n' roll star of Beijing, released his latest album. The Chinese title "Wunengde liliang" seemed innocuous enough; the English name that Cui chose for this long-awaited work was far more media savvy: *The Power of the Powerless.* The cover of the cassette featured a blob-like infant nursing a baby bottle as if it were a rifle.

Cui Jian had often been hailed as "China's Bob Dylan," but he was not working in some Far Eastern "invisible republic." The new album was released by the state-run China Music Company and marketed by the singer-songwriter's own Beijing East-West Music Manufacturing Corporation. From midyear, it was on sale at music stores throughout the country. Widely promoted in the media, its appearance was accompanied by a blitz of music store posters featuring the some-times-banned star. In mid-June, *Mandopop!*, the Internet Chinese entertainment news sheet, reported that the collection had fueled a Beijing-wide increase in record sales, with 200,000 units being moved in the first few days of its debut, "earning him [Cui] rare praise from music industry suits."

Quoting diehard fans, *Mandopop!* described the release as "a modern classic, combining Cui's trademark buzz-saw guitars and intense lyrics with leading-edge jungle loops."[33] For this jaded listener, it was the lyrics of Cui's "Fresh New Rock 'n' Roll," however, that struck a familiar chord:

Your style's the same as decrepitude
You both use lies to maintain pedestrian joys.
You embrace a guitar, eyes wide open
Lookin' for new lovers of rock 'n' roll.[34]

Don't fixate on the lyrics, people argued, northern rock was still better than southern bubble gum pop, somehow more authentic and pure. And as Cui himself said in defense of his songs: "People try to read so much meaning into every contemporary Chinese cultural work. Hey, it's really not so serious. It's only rock and roll."[35]

The new album also enjoyed an immediate laying on of hands from the cool capital media, including a cover story in the expat English weekly, *Beijing Scene.* The paper was known for its enthusiastic reporting on capital youth culture and faux chinoiserie, which the editors couch in a wonderfully brassy West Coast American-colonial style. *Beijing Scene* was itself a benefactor of the 1998 spring fever, and its founding editor, Scott Savitt, returned from a period of "self-imposed exile" in New York to revive it after an enforced hiatus in 1997.

In an interview with a correspondent from that paper, the no-longer young rock star Cui opined: "Pop music as a strictly commercial product, that is for money only, I am not interested in and am indeed opposed to."[36] Deprived of opportunities to perform regularly in Beijing and Shanghai, Cui surprisingly still managed to irritate some of those in authority while being typecast internationally as a "rebel rocker." As both he and his music mellowed, though, like aging pop icons elsewhere, Cui Jian found the market, whether in political or commercial guise, to be an indulgent if fickle master. During the 1990s he had repeatedly proved himself capable of playing both and prospering. And as for that teflon rebel-without-a-cause pose he continued to strike as he was enjoying another commercially successful comeback, one could only muse that—as is so often the case—"It's the difference between personality and a persona: one's something you live, the other's just one more thing to sell."[37]

CULTURAL DEFICITS

Even though books like Ma Licheng and Liang Zhijun's *Crossed Swords*, Yu Jie's *Fire and Ice*, and Wang Shuo's *Selected Fiction*, and Cui Jian's new album were among the success stories of the cultural market in 1998, the long-term effects of political manipulation and censorship were increasingly evident in the realm of serious debate and social agitation.

In 1996 as part of a renewed party campaign for the "construction of spiritual civilization," a number of important cultural and intellectual journals had been banned. Although other forums for concerned writers and thinkers continued to flourish and many important books were published, their audience was generally limited to the urban cognoscenti who, through their access to bookstores and insider gossip, enjoyed a privileged knowledge of such work while the society at large remained generally unaware of its existence. The authorities, in their wisdom—and as a result of the decades during which controversial works (books, essays, films, theater productions, and poetry) had enjoyed a wide cachet because they had been criticized (*bei pichu ming lai*, as the expression goes)—adopted a laissez-faire attitude. This control through neglect, or passive censorship, though certainly an improvement on the past, raised complex issues that belie simplistic observations that free-market principles evolving in the publishing sphere functioned outside China's particular political culture, or without constant reference to it.

The combination of party censorship (even in its more benign late 1990s guise) and market forces (which are neither as invisible nor as free as is generally imagined) continued to stifle the growth of the public realm and awareness of issues of social and political import. As Liu Junning said when commenting on the tradition of liberal thought at Peking University: Without systemic change, any toleration of divergent views in China would be chimerical.

Mao Zedong once predicted that eventually intellectuals, workers, and peasants would speak "the same language, not only the common language of patriotism and of the socialist system, but probably even that of the Communist world outlook." In the new China at the end of the twentieth century, however, there was more than ample evidence to suggest that fewer people in any group spoke the same language at all, and despite greater latitude, many were increasingly speaking at cross-purposes.

Yet what was happening was—to use another expression from Václav Havel— an "existential revolution." Perhaps it was not the untroubled development of civil society about which so many had speculated, nor did it necessarily mean that the realization of radical political agendas would make much difference. Nonetheless, the proliferation of ideological stances and cultural possibilities— albeit hamstrung and distorted, as we have seen in the preceding pages—allowed for an unprecedented opportunity for debate and dissension in the history of the People's Republic.[38] The lack of adequate public institutions that could provide avenues for constructive change and wide-ranging practical reform meant that the transformation was not neatly discernible or particularly dramatic, but it was continuing apace nonetheless.

In 1991, writers for *Beijing Youth News* had noted with disquiet that during the Jiao Yulu and San Mao debate, discussed in chapter 5, "The Graying of Chinese Culture," many young people had affirmed the value of the self-sacrificing communist cadre Jiao in terms of humanistic value: he was a good man who acted with compassion and decency. Despite the dire warnings of theoretically superior individuals and the hand-wringing of party hacks, the change in public normative values that resulted from the economic and cultural growth of the country fostered many positive changes in the society as a whole. The affirmation of a common humanity and social conscience was not only underpinned by party concerns or commercial interest. This was something that found public expression, for example, every time students and citizens voluntarily contributed to flood relief appeals or charitable causes and in the efforts made by individuals and groups to ameliorate the plethora of social ills. Similarly, it was evident in the countless private moments of decency that marked a society freed from the harsh political dictates and utilitarianism of the past. Nugatory moments for the thinkers and social engineers, perhaps, but "humanly meaningful" all the same. It was just these moments, as well as through the quiet work of social activists within the state apparat as well as the private sphere and in elite cultural circles, that what Václav Havel called "the art of the impossible," that is, "the art of improving ourselves and the world," was finding expression in China as it entered the twenty-first century.[39]

The Beijing artist Ai Weiwei had been a member of the 1970s artists' collective the "Stars." He moved to the United States in the early 1980s, returning to work in China a decade later. Back in Beijing he pursued his art while editing an annual nonofficial arts journal with Zeng Xiaojun. In the late 1997 edition of the journal *The Gray Book*, he published a photographic triptych, "A Study in Perspective: 1995, 1996, 1997." It consisted of three photographs: one of the White House in Washington (1995), the second of Hong Kong Harbor (1996), and the third of Tiananmen Square in Beijing (1997). In the foreground of each image the artist's hand is seen giving the finger to each of the iconic scenes.[40]

In an essay that accompanies this image, entitled "Making Choices," Ai gives voice to the concerns that a committed artist felt as he faced the dilemmas of working in an environment with a cultural deficit, one that we have discussed throughout this book as being "in the red":

> The unpleasant truth of the matter is that although you can import modern technology and lifestyles, you cannot introduce spiritual awareness or a sense of justice and moral strength in the same way; nor can you import soul.
>
> The history of modern China is a history of negation, a denial of the value of humanity, a murder of individuality. It is a history without a soul. . . .
>
> The investigation of all kinds of language, the deployment of a sparkling array of methodologies and media, the plagiarism of styles and content— none of these things can disguise the cultural deficit, a lack of self-awareness, social critique, and creative independence. Instead, artists celebrate their craven pragmatism and opportunism. They reflect degraded standards and a lack of heartfelt values.
>
> Only when the obsession with fleeting fashions is replaced by a fascination with the individual, only when stylistic faddism gives way to an investigation of the human condition and the values of the spirit will art come to life.
>
> This will necessarily be a slow and tortuous journey.[41]

Screw You, Too

The Communist Party leadership has, throughout its history, relied on intellectuals and ideologues to rationalize the quirks and shifts of its decision making. The more talented and astute of this caste serve a function not entirely dissimilar to that of advisers or censors at the imperial court, or perhaps their role can be likened to the itinerant "lobbyists," *youshui zhi shi*, or the "strategists," *zonghengjia*, literally "those who suggest lateral and horizontal alliances," of the Warring States period. In the "Five Pests" chapter of the classical philosophical text *Hanfeizi*, strategists are singled out along with scholars, knights-errant, fawners, merchants, and artisans as being the true enemies of the state.

Sometimes these hired hands—although voluntary careerists also feature prominently—have proved to be highly capable. This was true in the case of crafty party apparatchiki like Chen Boda, Zhou Yang, and Hu Qiaomu in the 1940s and 1950s or others like Yao Wenyuan in the 1960s. In the 1980s and 1990s, there has been no dearth of men and women ready to offer policy advice to the power holders. Similarly, in the commercial environment, ideas too have become a commodity, and a futures market in ideology has seen a steady growth. Think tanks and newly founded journals vie for the attention of both a public readership and the elitist cognoscenti. It is invariably the fate of the passive-aggressive intellectuals that their ideas are used by the victors in a given political struggle to justify their actions, and for the modern *zonghengjia*, this is one of the chief aims of their intellectual activity. But there can be hidden dangers also for the volunteer strategist, for in periods of political crisis, their carefully balanced advice can also be used to support irrational policy decisions and to damn the author who has so eagerly sought the attention of his leaders.

Over the years, many talented intellectuals have written for the party leadership, and although they have generally remained hidden from view in their preferred role as authors of internal reports, they have often enjoyed considerable influence. Their true importance is sometimes revealed only after the passage of time or, suddenly, by purges of the party's ranks. In the past, many memorialists were satisfied with positions as crucial members of some high-level writing group or as *rōnin* intellectuals in search of patronage from the powerful. But in the China of the 1980s and 1990s, the market of ideas has been bullish and the competition fierce. Political patronage has not been enough, especially in the case of the politically or economically ambitious critic.

The commercial publishing industry provides assiduous thinkers with many public forums to present their ideas, and seminars and symposia offer a stage for them to hone their presentation skills and build alliances. Political factions and the complexity of socioeconomic issues throughout China have given many people an opportunity to tender advice and build careers as latter-day strategists. While the Communist Party flourishes, they add their support to rationalizing and legitimizing its rule, donning all the while the guise of the critical patriot. If it should falter or a new crisis lead to a political upheaval, they will be ready to parade their talents for the newcomers.

The postures of those who chose to service the needs of the status quo at times seem strikingly similar—and often the strategy is essentially the same—to those of commercial hacks who churn out think pieces and editorial comment for the hungry maw of the popular media. The rash of loony-nationalist screeds produced in China in 1996–1997 was ample proof of this. On the other side of the Pacific Ocean, similarly alarmist work was appearing in fiction, film, and journalism. Some of it, however, though no less alarmist, was far more polished. For example, there was one thing certain about Richard Bernstein and Ross H. Munro's *The Coming Conflict with China*,[1] which appeared amid considerable fanfare in the United States in early 1997: it could have been a runaway best-seller in China itself.

There were a number of reasons for this: It created a mini-sensation in the international press; it was written by two former Beijing-based foreign correspondents from major North American newspapers; and it was a work about a subject that holds an abiding fascination for many readers—the Sino-American relationship. But there was another reason that *The Coming Conflict* was set to make such a splash. For all the surface objectivity and polish, it was essentially a polemic limned in the "primary colors" of political rhetoric: black and white. These are colors that suffuse public discourse in China, and they provide a reassuring simplicity of vision.

In recent years, Chinese readers and leaders have been fed a constant diet of what is known as *zouzhe wenxue*, "memorial literature." It is a genre that refuses to get bogged down in the messy gray zones of complex realities and nuanced scenarios. It delights in broad brush strokes and knowing, expert prognostications. It is the apocalypse-now version of realpolitik thinking. In China today, memorial literature is produced by state intellectuals, ambitious journalists, literary critics, and just about every political wannabe in the country. Local hacks constantly formulate advice papers for regional government agencies and bureaus; Shanghai and Beijing thinkers (even some regarded by the West as "liberals") concoct with a furious energy strategy memorials for the leaders in China's two major cities.

It is a type of literature that would be familiar to U.S. readers of *The Coming Conflict*. All such writing advertises itself under the name of national interest, and it is the avowed "national interest" that is used to rationalize the contentions made by the authors of memorial literature. Moreover, historical mission is wedded to national interest by writers who argue that what is good for us is good for everyone else. In such writing, the Other (China or the United States, depending on what postmodern critics call your positionality) is demonized and, above all, depicted as a monolithic, malevolent, and purposeful polity set on a course of economic expansion and regional domination.

Authors of memorial literature serve up large doses of up-to-the-minute data, state-of-the-art statistics, and revelations from confidential government think-tank reports. So as not to lay themselves open to accusations of blatant bias, they are always careful to make passing reference to evidence and factors that may contradict the main thrust of their argument, quoting learned opinion and moderate comments to leaven their lead-weighted fare. But make no mistake, the aim of the memorialist is always the same: to promote specific scenarios, provide enough alarmist evidence to focus the reader's mind on the looming horrors, and suggest policy options for the future with an eye to influencing both public opinion and patrician decisions.

Previously in China, writing successful "memorial literature" was a shortcut to promotion within the ranks of officialdom. Today, in keeping with the commercialization of the publishing industry, it has also become a way to package a bestseller. In the mid-1990s, as anti-American sentiment blossomed on the mainland, there was a deluge on the market of books similar to *The Coming Conflict*, albeit ones that presented the other side of the debate. The formidable polemicist He Xin, formerly of the Academy of Social Sciences in Beijing whose post–4 June role was mentioned in chapter 3, "Traveling Heavy," edited his anti-U.S. advice papers written for the Politburo as glitzy popular tomes with titles like *The Revival of China and the Future of the World*.[2] Other frustrated dissidents and ne'er-do-wells produced highly emotive attacks on the United States and their fellow Chinese, whom they denounce for pro-foreign attitudes like *China, Just Say No!*, a national best-seller in the summer of 1996. Still others championed the cause of "Asian values" as the dominant conservative ideology behind the pre-1998 Asian "economic miracle."[3]

"Memorial literature" might never be in the running for the Nobel Prize, but some of its more persuasive products may have an international influence the like of which Nobel laureates could only dream. Bernstein and Munro's speculative jeremiad is a successful and sobering example of U.S. "memorial literature." The authors skillfully contend that China is rapidly becoming a major destabilizing influence in Asia. They are correct in pointing out that state-manipulated media of that country have successfully demonized America in Chinese eyes (though it is not particularly in their interest to point out that the same is also generally true of the U.S. media vis-à-vis China), and they accurately assess the long-term cultural and ideological impact of the 1989 student protests in Beijing and the bloody massacre and purge that followed in its wake. The authors are also masterful at depicting the confused and contradictory policies of the Chinese Communist Party and government as reflecting greater purposefulness and coherence than is probably the case. But then again, the Chinese strategy and foreign affairs advisers with whom I have spoken in Beijing and Shanghai over the years often assume a guiding wisdom behind American machinations that verges on the absurd.

Certainly, *The Coming Conflict with China* is a spellbinding read and far more polished in terms of style and presentation than its Chinese siblings. It gets especially exciting when the authors indulge in a little futurology in the "War Game" chapter at the end of the book. That is where they speculate on the blow-by-blow details of a military standoff between China and the United States over Taiwan in 2004.

Without doubt, for the foreseeable future, China is going to be a complex and difficult power in both the Pacific Rim and elsewhere. But developing a complex and layered appreciation of both Chinese and regional realities—not to mention overweening U.S. expectations—is a burdensome task for the mass media and specialists alike. Sadly, given the market forces and ideological imperatives that rule the day on all sides, it is more likely that the purveyors of memorial literature will do their best to make sure the future is on their side.

On 17 and 18 November 1995, the editors of the conservative, PLA-backed and Beijing-based journal *Strategy and Management* organized a gathering in Shenzhen, the southern Special Economic Zone bordering on Hong Kong. Held at the local Intercontinental Hotel, this "Academic Symposium on 'Nationalism at the Turn of the Century' and the 1995 Colloquium of North-South [Chinese] Academics" (Shiji zhi jiaode minzuzhuyi xueshu taolunhui ji '95 Nan-Bei xuezhe duihuahui) provided a forum for writers, commentators, editors, and scholars from a range of backgrounds to discuss the issue of nationalism/patriotism. According to the participants, one of the topics covered was my essay "To Screw Foreigners Is Patriotic," which appears as chapter 10 in this book.

Indeed, not only was it discussed, but the organizers of the conference translated material from it for a criticism *in absentia*. This is not surprising, considering the content of the article and the ideological bent of the editors of *Strategy and Management*, two of whom, Wang Xiaodong and Yang Ping, are mentioned in the essay. The January 1996 issue of *Strategy and Management* carried a riposte by way of reviewing the piece. As Wang, writing again under his polemic pen name Shi Zhong, stated:

> The reason we are introducing Barmé's views is that we believe it is important for the Chinese academic world to understand what extremist, albeit seductive, ideas are current in the West. It is just such views that are fashionable in the Western media, which are themselves much given to sensationalism.[4]

Shi Zhong continues in this magisterial vein to comment that although "Screw" contains some accurate data on the mainland intellectual world, "that does not mean that [Barmé] has thereby been able to depict a vision of China that is in any way more pertinent than that presented by other Western academics." In a lengthy disquisition, however, Shi Zhong gives a potted summary of "Screw" and quotes from it liberally, picking and choosing things from the original skein of argument that suit his own purposes while doing it less than complete justice. It is an effective polemical strategy nurtured over the past half century by a regime of media and intellectual censorship that, far from allowing an atmosphere of free debate, has drawn its strength from selectively quoting from the authors and works being critiqued.

Although the rebuttal of "Screw" was hardly simplistic and dismissive, the author repeatedly glides over material that does not suit his own purposes, something he claims as being representative of the consensus of thoughtful mass opinion in China. He avers that essays like "Screw" are the product of an extremist stance of highly questionable validity and one that in the final analysis is academically unworthy, for it primarily benefits the Western media and serves Western national strategies in dealing with China. Shi Zhong concludes, naturally enough, that Westerners of this ilk cannot fully "understand China," something of which he is even more convinced "after reading the work of Barmé and other Western academics."[5] Such obloquy is universally applied to unpopular or aberrant offshore views by those who lay exclusive proprietorial claim to the nation-state, as well as all that is beholden to it. In December 1996, Wang Xiaodong remarked to me that he had originally hoped some other writer would have rushed into the breach opened by my essay and produced a rebuttal. In the absence of any suitable material, however, he was left to write his own mild and overly circumspect response. After Sino-American relations entered an uneasy period of reconciliation in mid-1997, Shi Zhong (Wang Xiaodong) and his colleague Yang

Ping, the hands-on editor of *Strategy and Management*, were relieved of their positions, and the editorial tone of the journal mellowed somewhat in 1998. Yet again, energetic strategists were shunted aside by the very leaders for whom they had assiduously provided macrotheoretical policy advice.

Without public intellectuals, a free press, or open debate, few of the more extreme, often party-sanctioned, opinions that do appear, and reach mass audiences, are ever seriously challenged. Thus, best-selling books like Wang Shan's 1994 *China Through the Third Eye* or the 1996 *China, Just Say No!* as well as the 1997 anti-U.S. media screed *Behind the Demonization of China*[6]—one of the most tasteless examples of this genre of writing, replete as it is with racist and sexist vitriol—have earned sizable amounts of both cash and celebrity for authors and publishers. Since they were not produced by old-fashioned party hacks but by younger writers fluent in the style of populist prose, these works have also had an incalculable effect on shaping public opinion in urban centers, where they were eagerly greeted by their readers. This situation, though dolorous for thinking readers in China, has been, however, a godsend for the overseas (including Taiwanese and Japanese) media, for whom the high dudgeon and venomous anti-Western sentiment that suffused these tomes have provided good copy.

Concerted attempts were made to respond to the wave of publishing extremism and the commercial exploitation of nationalist sentiment in the semi-independent journals produced in Beijing, but the publishing purge initiated in early 1996 as part of a new "spiritual civilization" campaign (for which one should read "promotion of trite party values and vacuous cultural nostrums") carried off the best forum for debate, *Orient*, and for a time saw the retreat of many writers from their former outspokenness. Not daunted by the plangent fate of publishing on the mainland, however, a group of "independent intellectual" essayists banded together and in early 1997 produced *How China Faces the West*, a collection of articles that debates the East-West divide and attempts to respond thoughtfully to issues highlighted by populist nationalism.[7]

The introductory chapter of *How China Faces the West* identifies, succinctly and precisely, the significance of the fashion for xenophobic screeds in recent years: "Propagating nationalism is the safest form of political opportunism there is [in China today]. It is also a way of achieving the greatest economic return." Who in China today, the writer continues, doesn't have at hand a few examples of how foreigners, particularly Americans, have lorded it over them or at least can report a few rumors that they've heard to this effect? How much more common are examples of shameless pandering to foreign interests?

As the writers generally point out, officially tolerated and manipulated nationalism had, to date, evinced no signs of becoming an ideology for Chinese expansion and aggression. Rather, it had been reified in an environment in which a new sense of aggrieved national sentiment played a pivotal role in providing political coherence and creating a framework of consensus in dealing with pressing international issues, like Hong Kong, Sino-U.S. relations, Taiwan, and Japan. A number of contributors to this volume also pointed out that the rise of rhetorical nationalism in the public media has been greatly enhanced by the writings of people like Samuel P. Huntington, the Harvard professor whose *The Clash of Civilizations*, an essay later expanded into a book, had been a gift to the neonationalists in China.

One of the authors of *How China Faces the West* was Xu Jilin, the prominent Shanghai intellectual historian and cultural commentator who has appeared many times in this book. He said that what China needed in response to such fanciful prognostications was not a narrow, xenophobic nationalism, condemning it to remain a self-important pariah—something that would only exacerbate that country's efforts to deal with its burdensome traditions and modern dilemmas—but an open-minded and outward-looking patriotism that would permit China to enter the family of nations with confidence.

The problem for thoughtful readers and observers is that in the face of the rhetorical extremism of both China and the West, and given the ideological controls on China, especially after the mid-1990s, rebuttal—whether impassioned or coolheaded—has been all but impossible. Reasoned and measured reactions are, during times of cultural containment, quite literally unpublishable. *How China Faces the West* was edited surreptitiously on the mainland and published in Hong Kong.

China watching, like Kremlinology among former Soviet analysts, has accrued a certain odium in recent decades. The track record of specialists in Chinese current affairs, like that of many Sovietologists, has been fairly abysmal. Few managed—either in China or overseas—to get it right: the antirightist purge of the 1950s, the murderous famines of the 1960s, the meaning of Mao Zedong's apotheosis, the Cultural Revolution, the fall of Marshal Lin Biao, the ineluctable rise of Deng Xiaoping, the fall from grace of Hu Yaobang in 1986 and Zhao Ziyang in 1989, and even the waning of Qiao Shi's star in 1997.

Sinologists themselves recognize that China watching is an arcane pursuit, its object more elusive by far than the study of oracle bones or Shang dynasty bronzes. For it demands of its practitioners accurate predictions about the political future of a restive nation whose rulers have all too often found themselves to be out of step with the times or simply ill informed.

Thus it was with good reason—and no little venom—that Simon Leys (nom de plume of the Canberra-based Sinologist Pierre Ryckmans) wrote some years ago: "Paris taxi drivers are notoriously sophisticated in their use of invective. 'Hé, *va donc, structuraliste!'* is one of their recent apostrophes—which makes one wonder when they will start calling their victims 'China Experts!' "[8]

While expletives like *"Hé, va donc, post-moderniste!"* may be passé in today's Paris, in light of the 1997–1998 Asian economic crisis, you can't help wondering how long it will be before Sydney or Melbourne taxi drivers add a new line of spleen to their deprecations: "Watch where you're goin' you fuckin' economist!"

How tiresome indeed it has been over the past decade to hear the *nouveau* converts to Asia literacy lecture all and sundry on the virtues of the Asian world. "Asian values" have been touted as some unique concatenation of spiritual and cultural factors that since the 1970s have been at the core of the extraordinary economic developments from Japan through to India, China down to Indonesia.

There have been clamorous proponents of Asian uniqueness throughout the region and calls in my own country of Australia for us to understand and enmesh the nation with the values of this mysterious region in some meaningful and constructive way. It is an approach that has also served well the political and cultural pragmatists of countries like China. In particular, since the 1996 campaign launched in Beijing to promote "spiritual civilization," these values have been reiterated as fundamental to China's "culture of consensus," *hehe wenhua*.

Since the harsh reality and deeper significance of the economic and political events in Asia during 1997–1998 will probably do little to undermine the mythologizers' confidence in their thesis, it is instructive here as we conclude our discussion of Chinese nationalist rhetoric and its proponents from He Xin to Wang Xiaodong to put on record the ten most popular "Asian values" familiar to anyone who has dealt with apologists for the status quo, whether they be in China or elsewhere in the region. While the list of positive values is taken from a 1997 work entitled *The Tyranny of Fortune: Australia's Asian Destiny*,[9] these "values" will be familiar to anyone who has sat through briefings on doing business in Asia and had to hear learned cultural experts, economic toffs, self-important media converts to Asia, and know-it-all bureaucrats prattle on about the special cultural dimensions of the economic transformation of the region.

Asian values have given a raft of authoritarian rulers, their propagandists, bureaucrats, and business people (not to mention those from liberal democracies who are ready to read cultural difference as something bordering on the racial) a legitimizing veneer of "the thick and black," *houhei* (see chapter 4, "The Graying of Chinese Culture"), as they pursue their own agendas. They have also acted as a cultural caveat used to dismiss independent comment and analysis as liberal wrongheadedness, cultural imperialism, and orientalist revanchism.

In listing these values, I will use a metaphor taken from a hoary Australian cultural convention, the game of two-up in which gamblers use a pair of coins to determine who wins and who loses, to contrast the idyllic "Asian values" foisted on the gullible with those that people with a more somber and realistic appraisal of the situation in many Asian nations would feel somewhat closer to the mark.

When things go wrong, values go south. The list of negative values that I offer here is compiled from a range of works both classical and contemporary published in China. It is not a list of absolutes, or of unique values, but a catalog of what comes into view when we choose to see through the Asian leaders' new clothes.

Obligation

Heads: An emphasis in society on obligation rather than rights, and a complex tradition of mutually interacting pressures to ensure that all members are caught in the network of obligation and share both responsibilities and rewards.

Tails: Obligations forged on the basis of hierarchical pressure and unspoken principles of deference entrap individuals in a strangling network of "sentiment deficits" that lead to stagnation or, under the pressure of rapid change and the collapse of interpersonal relations, to unbridled avarice and systemic indecision or miscalculation.

Rule of Virtue

Heads: An emphasis on rule by people or virtue rather than the law, which maximizes the harmony and cohesion possible in society, stresses ritual or rites, and tends to ensure that competition is pursued within a framework of established ceremony and courtesy that preserves social consensus.

Tails: Leaders grow old, ineffectual, or senile. Their rule by virtue is often the result of ossified political habits that do not admit change or social maturation. When economic performance slows or social friction comes to the fore, people soon discover that behind every virtuous leader is a strong military, well-equipped police force, and courts that will do the bidding of entrenched interests, local or global.

Education

Heads: A high emphasis on rigorous, even ruthless, competitive education, which instills lifetime standards of excellence in all and allocates lifetime positions of national bureaucratic and other authority to the victors of that educational competition.

Tails: Elite education is available to those with the sociopolitical connections and money to afford it. The binding ties between the progeny of hereditary power holders and the newly rich limit the impact of entrepreneurial talent on the system as a whole. Meanwhile, the majority who are lower down on the food chain are taught to be satisfied with their lot. Disenfranchised on all levels, they become restive and resentful when the sacrifices they make for the nation-state do not pay off or when the improvement of their lot is eroded by political and economic decisions made by ensconced jet-setting elites.

History

Heads: An acute sense of linkages between past and present that promotes a keen awareness of historical time and the long-term commitment necessary for major institutional and related achievements, contrasting rather strongly with the Western short-term emphasis on the bottom line and cost effectiveness.

Tails: In an environment where free and informed media and academic debate are hamstrung by rules of censorship and self-censorship, historical fallacy or egregious historical rationalizations are used by the power holders to promote their own policies and narrate a history that depicts them as being the pinnacle of national development. These distortions are useful as social levers to induce people to make sacrifices for the nation, to bring about a renaissance or return to former glory, but when things go wrong, it is these unchallenged myths that feed a sense of aggrieved nationalism and shepherd a tendency for the politics of revenge.

Community

Heads: A high sense of the value of human community and order, rather than material possessions and accumulation, with the ultimate economic authority being placed in the hands of those with noncommercial motivations of a high order but a shrewd and hardheaded understanding of commercial reality.

Tails: Mao Zedong is still spoken of as the most selfless leader China has produced for centuries. He even gave up eating meat for a time when his lunatic economic policies (the "Great Leap Forward") led to one of the most harrowing man-made famines of all time. In the more export-oriented regimes of Asia, local consumption has been reined in to encourage rapid growth. People are now scrambling to find a few high-minded and sagelike leaders or their cronies who have not soiled their hands with cash, kickbacks, or other corrupt practices.

Intuition and Intellect

Heads: A high regard for logic and rationality, balanced by a strong sense of the need for intuitive and emotional checks, reflected in some ways by the complementary spiritual traditions of Confucianism and Taoism.

Tails: The retro New Age philosophy of rationality embedded in emotionalism is used to legitimate the rule of authoritarianism. When the acquiescence imposed on the public becomes too great a burden, emotional repression can easily fuel indignation and moral outrage against the power holders and their cronies.

Yin and Yang

Heads: An acute awareness of the changing nature of reality and the need for polar opposites to complement rather than conflict with each other, reflected respectively in the *Book of Changes* and *yin-yang* teachings.

Tails: Chairman Mao, that East Asian dialectical materialist, drew on a line of argument inspired by Hegel and Marx to declare that "in a suitable temperature an egg changes into a chicken, but no temperature can change a stone into a chicken" (from "On Contradiction," 1937).

Fusion

Heads: A unique perception of commerce, technology, and science, with a healthy tension between market-driven innovation and environmental caution, producing less interest in scientific breakthroughs but a keen attention to the possibility of fusion of diverse technologies, as in robotics, to better serve community interests.

Tails: Once the age of technology transfer and catch-up economics passes, it is exactly the need for innovation in every field that helps feed the growth of a society. The plundering of the environment and squandering of limited national resources are finally being realized in many "tiger economies" (as well as others) to be a short-term strategy that will condemn future generations to a degraded world.

Officialdom

Heads: A strong instinct for institutional pragmatism and innovation in response to problems, reflecting the authority and responsibility carried by the officials who regulate society in a manner unthinkable in non-Confucian communities.

Tails: Bureaucracies are so byzantine and enmeshed with cushy deal making that infighting is endemic and threatens long-term planning at every turn. What appears to be stability becomes, in times of dysfunction or uncertainty, a mechanism for shedding responsibility and avoiding hard decisions. By stifling civil society and preventing citizens from a mature involvement in the political process, the ruling class and business elites cut themselves off from public support.

Cultural Pollution

Heads: A profound concern to avoid the evils of spiritual pollution associated with Westernization and individualism, such pollution being identified almost as a crime because of its capacity to weaken and leave vulnerable the larger community and state.

Tails: Even the term *spiritual pollution* is transposed from European discourse. Societies hell-bent on growth and positive economic indicators at the price of all else have, over recent decades, publicly refused to admit that the economic forces they have unleashed are themselves often the greatest source of socially destabilizing "pollution." The canker includes widespread corruption and graft, bureaucratic inefficiencies on a monumental scale, crime, and social dislocation caused by increasing disparities in incomes. With few concomitant "modernized" social values to ameliorate these extreme and abrupt changes, an increasing sense of popular disenfranchisement, consumerism, info-tainment, and reckless hedonism become the international staple.

We should not overlook the fact that both business and governments have been active in promoting the myth of Asian values and the Asia-Pacific century to further their own interests and the direction of public policy. This simplified list of values—and the parody of opposites that I have composed—should not be taken, however, as an argument to ignore the sociocultural dimensions of the changes taking place throughout Asia. Rather, we should be careful not to mystify or segregate the experience of those in the Asia-Pacific region from the realities of social, political, and economic change and tumult that most countries are experiencing and will continue to experience. One thing the Asian economic crisis seems to indicate is that capitalism freed of the bonds of social responsibility can easily lead to a politics of plunder, markets without a concomitant leavening of democracy, and growth without equity. It is a politics that presumably works in favor of IMF intervention and multinational imperialism in some cases or just good old homegrown authoritarianism in others.[10]

Over the past few years, I have often wondered how the Great Asian Values debate of recent memory will be seen in a few decades. Also, as South Asia, that is, the Indian subcontinent, experiences its own economic boom, one wonders whether the cultural and economic rationalists will now lecture us about ancient Vedantic lore and kundalini yoga, the practice of nurturing and releasing the productive energies to achieve the sublime state of . . . what, global consumerism? After all, it is worth remembering that it was Indian fakirs like Swami Vivikenanda who, at the turn of the last century, first promoted the concept of unique Asian spiritual values among the Theosophists, and cultural gurus like the Bengali poet Rabindranath Tagore who championed Eastern thought over that of the mercantile West both in India and on a lecture tour to China in the 1920s.

NOTES

INTRODUCTION

1. Those present included, of course, Wang Meng, as well as Liu Binyan, Bai Hua, Wang Zengqi, Lu Wenfu, Zhang Xinxin, Wang Anyi, Shu Ting, and many others. The controversial Shanghai writers Wang Ruowang and Dai Houying were present only for the official receptions. For a report on the proceedings, see Bai Jieming (Barmé), "Mianxiang shijiede dangdai dalu wenxue—Zhongguo zuoxiede Shanghai guoji taolunhui," *Jiushi niandai yuekan*, 1986:12, pp. 82–85.

2. Geremie Barmé and John Minford, eds., *Seeds of Fire: Chinese Voices of Conscience* (Hong Kong: Far Eastern Economic Review, 1986), 2nd ed. (New York: Hill & Wang, 1988).

3. Milan Kundera, *The Book of Laughter and Forgetting*, trans. Aaron Asher (London: Faber & Faber, 1996), p. 147; and for my remarks, see Bai Jieming (Barmé), "Zhongguo dalu 'xin shiqi' de gexing sanwen," *Jiushi niandai yuekan*, 1986:11, pp. 96–99, esp. p. 99.

4. See my contributions to John Minford and Stephen C. Soong, eds., *Trees on the Mountain, Renditions* nos. 19 and 20 (Hong Kong: Chinese University of Hong Kong, 1983); Barmé and Minford, *Seeds of Fire*; Geremie R. Barmé and Linda Jaivin, eds., *New Ghosts, Old Dreams: Chinese Rebel Voices* (New York: Times Books, 1992); and Geremie Barmé, *Shades of Mao: The Posthumous Cult of the Great Leader* (Armonk, N.Y.: Sharpe, 1996).

5. See my two volumes of Chinese essays published under the name Bai Jieming, *Xiyangjing xia* (Xianggang: Bowen shuju, 1981), and *Zixingche wenji* (Xianggang: Tiandi tushu youxian gongsi, 1984), as well as my columns in the *Nineties Monthly* (Jiushi niandai yuekan), 1985–1991.

6. See Thomas Frank, "The New Gilded Age," in *Commodify Your Dissent, Salvos from the Baffler*, ed. Thomas Frank and Matt Weiland (New York: Norton, 1997), pp. 24, 26.

7. Quoted in Matt ffytche, "Virtual banality," *Modern Review* (London) 1, no. 16 (August/September 1994), p. 27.

8. Thomas Frank, *The Conquest of Cool: Business Culture, Counterculture, and the Rise of Hip Consumerism* (Chicago: University of Chicago Press, 1997), p. 8.

9. Tom Wolfe, "The Apache Dance," in his *The Purple Decades* (Harmondsworth, Middlesex: Penguin Books, 1984), p. 345.

10. George Orwell, "The Art of Donald McGill," in *The Collected Essays, Journalism and Letters of George Orwell*, ed. Sonia Orwell and Ian Angus, vol. 2: *My Country Right or Left 1940–1943* (Harmondsworth, Middlesex: Penguin Books, 1968), p. 192.

11. Cosmo Landesman, "American Myths: 1. Americans Have No Irony," *Modern Review* 1, no. 8 (April/May 1993), p. 9.

12. Norman Manea, *On Clowns: The Dictator and the Artist* (New York: Grove Press, 1992), p. 147.

13. Ibid., p. 173.

14. Chen Maiping, "What Has Replaced 'Socialism' or 'Communism'? — The Grotesque Cultural Landscape of Fin-de-Siècle China," Institute of Oriental Languages, Stockholm University, paper presented at the Nordic Symposium on Nation, Culture, and Character in China, Oslo, 1–4 June 1996.

15. Naomi Miller, *Heavenly Caves, Reflections on the Garden Grotto* (New York: Braziller, 1982), p. 10.

CHAPTER I

1. The writer Ba Jin, a veteran leftist writer from the 1920s and former enthusiastic people's artist, provided a fascinating, if not explicit, comment on his own "rites of passage" in his five volumes of memoirs, *Random Thoughts*. See Ba Jin, *Suixiang lu* (Xianggang: Sanlian shudian, 1988); and Ba Jin, *Random Thoughts*, trans. Geremie Barmé (Hong Kong: Joint Publications, 1984). In 1996, Ba Jin published another volume of essays related to these issues. See Ba Jin, *Zaisi lu* (Xianggang: Sanlian shudian, 1996).

2. This is a reference to Lung-kee Sun's (Sun Longji) influential study of what he called the "deep structure" of Chinese culture. See Sun, *Zhongguo wenhuade "shenceng jiegou"* (Xianggang: Jixianshe, 1982).

3. Geremie Barmé and John Minford, eds., *Seeds of Fire: Chinese Voices of Conscience*, 2nd ed. (New York: Hill & Wang, 1988), p. 386.

4. Yang Jiang, *Xizao* (Xianggang: Sanlian shudian, 1988), also published in Beijing and Taipei in early 1989 and advertised as the first work by a mainland writer to appear in all three cities "simultaneously." See *Wenyi bao*, 17 December 1988. I translate the title of the work as *Washing in Public* in the hope of conveying some of the connotations discussed by Yang in the preface to the book.

5. Yang Jiang, *Xizao*, p. 1.

6. See *Ganxiao liuji* (Beijing: Sanlian shudian, 1981), and "Bingwu dingwei nian jishi," in *Jiang yincha* (Beijing: Sanlian shudian, 1986), reprinted in Yang Jiang, *Yang Jiang zuopin ji* (Beijing: Zhongguo shehui kexue chubanshe, 1993), vol. 2, pp. 3–52, 154–183, and translated by Barmé, *Lost in the Crowd: A Cultural Revolution Memoir* (Melbourne: McPhee Gribble, 1989). Yang also wrote about the history of her own sister's "remolding" in the 1950s and 1960s. See Yang Jiang, "Ji Yang Bi," reprinted in

Lin Daoqun and Wu Zanmei, eds., *Zhe ye shi lishi—cong sixiang gaizao dao wenhua geming 1949–1979* (Xianggang: Niujin daxue chubanshe, 1993), pp. 223–235.

7. Literally "washing the heart and changing the skin on one's face," that is, to repent and change one's ways. This compound expression originates in *The Book of Changes* (Zhou Yi). Chapter 10 of the Xici reads, "In this way the holy sages purified their hearts," *shengren yi ci xi xin*. The explanation of the sixth line of the hexagram "Revolution," *ge*, reads: "The superior man changes like a panther. The inferior man molts in the face," *junzi bao bian, xiaoren ge mian*. See Richard Wilhelm, *The I Ching or Book of Changes*, trans. Cary F. Baynes (London: Routledge & Kegan Paul, 1970), p. 192.

8. See Yang, *Xizao*, pp. 215–218, 230–237, 238, 255–256.

9. Ibid., pp. 238–342.

10. "Snakes and Ladders: Or Three Days in the Life of a Chinese Intellectual," trans. Geremie Barmé and Linda Jaivin, in Shen Rong, *At Middle Age* (Beijing: Foreign Languages Press, 1987), pp. 119–236.

11. In broader terms, both works belong to what could be called "meeting art," *huiyi wenyi*. The narration revolves around political meetings, as did the lives of mainland citizens for more than forty years. In the 1980s, the old satirical saying that "the KMT taxes you to death, the CCP does it with meetings" (*Guomindang shui duo; Gongchandang hui duo*) finally found a reflection in art.

12. Miklós Haraszti, *The Velvet Prison: Artists Under State Socialism*, trans. Katalin and Stephen Landesmann (New York: Basic Books, 1987).

13. Whereas in this chapter I quote exclusively from Miklós Haraszti, many other socialist-bred writers have commented perceptively on this subject. The work of the eccentric Soviet philosopher-novelist Alexander Zinoviev is a case in point. See, for example, his collection of essays *Nous et l'occident*, trans. Wladimir Berelowitch (Lausanne: Editions L'Age d'Homme, 1981), and *Homo Sovieticus*, trans. Charles Janson (London: Paladin, 1986).

14. In the late 1980s, two prominent mainland critics were particularly outspoken in declaiming the disastrous ecological impact of tradition on the Chinese cultural landscape. Liu Xiaobo was well known for his iconoclasm, for some choice examples of which see Barmé and Minford, *Seeds of Fire*, pp. 395–397; and Geremie Barmé and Linda Jaivin, eds., *New Ghosts, Old Dreams: Chinese Rebel Voices* (New York: Times Books, 1992), pp. 33–48. The Shanghai critic Zhu Dake, active since 1986, was less of a media personality in China and little known overseas. He came to prominence in Shanghai when he attacked Xie Jin, mainland China's leading film apparatchik. See Zhu's "Xie Jin dianying moshide quexian," *Wenhui bao*, 18 July 1986, in which he derided Xie for making "Confucian films," *ruxue dianying*, that served party prerogatives.

15. This school of thought should not be confused with neo-Confucianism, *lixue*. I think of the term post–neo-Confucianism or capitalist-Confucianism as being somewhat akin to the uses of "postmodernism," which has become in effect a grab bag for late-twentieth-century intellectual fashions. While championed for many years by a group

of overseas-based Chinese intellectual activists, the discovery of this school's utilitarian aspect was realized on mainland China only in the 1980s. The fact that the *People's Daily* published a long article introducing post–neo-Confucianism was something of an indication of the increasing popular awareness of this school of thought. See Li Zonggui, "Xiandai xin ruxue sichao—youlai, fazhan ji sixiang tezheng," *Renmin ribao*, 6 March 1989. For a valuable source of discussions of Confucianism and reform in China, see Silke Krieger and Rolf Trauzettel, eds., *Confucianism and the Modernization of China* (Mainz: v. Hase & Koehler Verlag, 1991).

16. Up to 1990, one important exception was Lu Feng of the Academy of Social Science in Beijing who studied the origins, history, and influence of the work unit, *danwei*, the basic building block of party control in China. See Lu Feng, "Danwei: yizhong teshude shehui zuzhi xingshi," *Zhongguo shehui kexue*, 1989:1, pp. 71, 88. Since Lu's work first appeared, a number of incisive studies have been produced on the work unit.

17. Wang Xiaodong and Qiu Tiancao, "Jiqingde yinying—ping dianshi xiliepian 'Heshang'," *Zhongguo qingnian bao*, 10 July 1988. See also Geremie Barmé, "TV Requiem for the Myths of the Middle Kingdom," *Far Eastern Economic Review*, 1 September 1988, p. 43. In 1993, Wang Xiaodong became one of the founding editors of the conservative monthly *Strategy and Management* (Zhanlüe yu guanli). The role of this magazine and Wang's own work are discussed in chapter 10, "To Screw Foreigners Is Patriotic," and again in the appendix, "Screw You, Too."

18. In a directive written in February 1962 on a letter from the Central Conservatorium, Mao Zedong declared that in the realm of culture, China had to "make the past serve the present and foreign things serve China," *gu wei jin yong, yang wei Zhong yong*. The more traditional expression for "manipulating the past to attack the present" is *jie gu feng jin*.

19. Haraszti, *The Velvet Prison*, p. 44. See also Zinoviev, *Homo Sovieticus*, pp. 17–18, for some comments on this subject by a man who declined to live between the lines.

20. Haraszti, *The Velvet Prison*, pp. 144–145, my italics.

21. See, for example, Bo Yang, *The Ugly Chinaman and the Crisis of Chinese Culture*, trans. and ed. Don J. Cohn and Jing Qing (Sydney: Allen & Unwin, 1992); and Lung-kee Sun, in Barmé and Minford, *Seeds of Fire*, pp. 30–32, 163–165.

22. Benjamin Schwartz, "The Intelligentsia in Communist China: A Tentative Comparison," in *The Russian Intelligentsia*, ed. Richard Pipes (New York: Columbia University Press, 1961), p. 178. Schwartz based his observations on the events of the Hundred Flowers period of 1956–1957. He stated that during this episode, "not only were the literary and cultural policies of the regime attacked; not only did professionals challenge the authority of the party within their areas of competence; but there were even those who raised the dread questions of power itself. The very grounds on which the Communist Party claimed political infallibility were challenged. . . . Any notion of a natural proclivity on their part for limitless dosages of totalitarianism must certainly be rejected after this episode" (p. 180). Interestingly, the debates and even the personalities of those years were still at the center of political discussions in late-1980s China. This was particularly in evidence in 1987 when the journalist Liu Binyan, pre-

viously denounced in the late 1950s, claimed that he was purged from the party a second time for, among other things, his part in planning a commemorative symposium on the thirtieth anniversary of the 1956 Hundred Flowers campaign.

23. I have commented elsewhere on the reasons why both Chinese commentators and some China scholars have been inclined to maintain that the Chinese intelligentsia is "simply a temporarily displaced bureaucratic class," to quote Schwartz once more. See my "Letter of Protest Opens Chinese Eyes," *Far Eastern Economic Review*, 2 April 1987, and "The Man Who Speaks Too Much, Too Often," *Far Eastern Economic Review*, 22 October 1987.

24. Li Xianting was an editor of and writer for *China Fine Arts Press* (Zhongguo meishu bao), a Beijing weekly that published from 1985 until being banned after 4 June 1989.

25. I say more about Zhu Dake later. Liu Xiaobo has been widely written about and published outside the mainland. For more on Li Jie, see chapter 12, "Totalitarian Nostalgia." Dai Qing's studies of Wang Shiwei (a party cultural dissident executed in the late 1940s) and Chu Anping (an independent journalist silenced during the antirightist movement of 1957) had a considerable popular impact in the late 1980s. For more details of the significance of Dai's work, see Geremie Barmé, "Using the Past to Save the Present: Dai Qing's Historiographical Dissent," *East Asian History*, no. 1, June 1991, pp. 141–181; and Barmé and Jaivin, *New Ghosts, Old Dreams*, pp. 358–362.

26. Interestingly, Wang Yihua, writing in Hong Kong, was one of the few commentators who made explicit comments about the culture of "military communism," *zhanshi gongchanzhuyi*, and its aftereffects in 1980s China, much of which parallels Haraszti's analysis. See Wang Yihua, "Dui dangjin Zhongguo 'wenhua re' de sikao," *Mingbao yuekan*, 1989:4, p. 36.

27. See the dust jacket of *The Velvet Prison* for this quotation from Leys. I am grateful to Simon Leys for bringing my attention to Haraszti's work in 1987. Josef Skvorecky, the Czech writer whose works include *The Engineer of Human Souls*, wrote that "not since Koestler's *Darkness at Noon* has there been a book on communism as frightening as Haraszti's *The Velvet Prison*."

28. See "Doing Without Utopias: An Interview with Václav Havel," *Times Literary Supplement*, 23 January 1987, an interview conducted by Erica Blair and translated by A. G. Brain.

29. See Liu Zaifu, "Xin shiqi wenxuede zhuchao," *Wenhui bao*, 8 September 1986; and Geremie Barmé, "Confession, Redemption, and Death: Liu Xiaobo and the Protest Movement of 1989," in *The Broken Mirror: China After Tiananmen*, ed. George Hicks (Essex: Longman, 1990), pp. 72–73.

30. In 1986, Deng Xiaoping said that "bourgeois liberalization means rejection of the party's leadership."

31. The open door and reform policies, *gaige kaifang*, were initiated by the Communist Party of China in late 1978 as part of a strategic policy shift to economic work.

32. Haraszti, *The Velvet Prison*, p. 113.

33. Ibid., p. 114.

34. Ibid.

35. See chapter 8 and Geremie R. Barmé, *Shades of Mao: The Posthumous Cult of the Great Leader* (Armonk, N.Y.: Sharpe, 1996), pp. 45–46, 100, 215–220.

36. See "Wang Meng xiang Luomaniya pengyou jieshao gaige shinian wentan xinmao," *Wenyi bao*, 7 January 1989.

37 Haraszti, *The Velvet Prison*, pp. 113–114.

38. Ibid., p. 95.

39. Ibid., p. 75.

40. Ibid., p. 98.

41. The Four Basic Principles, *sixiang jiben yuanze*, are (1) adherence to the socialist road; (2) adherence to the democratic dictatorship of the people; (3) adherence to the leadership of the Communist Party; and (4) adherence to Marxism-Leninism and Mao Zedong Thought .

42. For a more complete list, see Barmé and Minford, *Seeds of Fire*, pp. 343–353.

43. A basic thesis of *Seeds of Fire* was that "the energies and enthusiasms [the democracy movement of 1979] released are still active and in a sense more potent than ever. They have simply been pushed underground. or channelled into less obviously political areas." As we noted in that book, "The main activists have been jailed, but their writer and artist contemporaries (with whom they were always closely associated) continue to experiment and search for new modes of self-expression, in many cases abandoning their demands for political reform in favor of a more individual quest." See the introduction to the 1986 edition of *Seeds of Fire*, p. xiii. In early 1989, events forced Bei Dao (and other poets of the *Today* group like Mang Ke, Yang Lian, and Gu Cheng) to take a public political stance once more.

44. See Ouyang Bin, "Qiqu minzhu lu," a chronicle of the events following Fang's January letter in *Mingbao yuekan*, 1989:4, pp. 3–6; also *Jiushi niandai yuekan*, 1989:4, pp. 16–28.

45. See Barmé and Minford, *Seeds of Fire*, pp. 368–372.

46. Haraszti, *The Velvet Prison*, pp. 150–153.

47. In early 1986, Hu Yaobang outlined methods by which the state could encourage disaffected and unemployed samizdat writers to join in the fold. The activities of Hu Yaobang, Hu Qili, and Wang Meng in 1986 may be taken as signifying the formal initiation of China's velvet prison culture, although writers like Sha Yexin (author of "The Imposter"), Bai Hua (who wrote *Unrequited Love*) and Ye Wenfu (the army poet who composed "General, You Can't Do That!"), who all had been attacked in 1980–1982, had been seduced some years earlier. As a result of Hu Yaobang's comments on nonofficial culture, both Bei Dao and Gu Cheng were sought out by functionaries of the party's Propaganda Department regarding prospective employment. They declined.

48. After becoming the minister of culture in 1986, Wang Meng treated Bei Dao (as opposed to other ex-*Today* writers) with particular favor. For example, Wang attended the opening of an exhibition of paintings by the former "Stars," Xingxing, artist Shao Fei, Bei Dao's wife, the same day he announced that he had become minister in 1986, and on another occasion, he expressed his wish to Bei Dao that he travel to France to take part in a writers' conference with him in 1988, and so on.

49. *Xiandai hanshi*, edited variously in the early 1990s by Tang Xiaodu, Mang Ke, and others.

50. Haraszti, *The Velvet Prison*, p. 153.

51. Ibid., pp. 155–159.

52. Ibid., pp. 158–159. See also chapter 5, "The Graying of Chinese Culture," and chapter 9, "CCP™ & Adcult PRC."

53. Haraszti, *The Velvet Prison*, p. 79.

54. See "Zhonggong zhongyang guanyu jin yibu fanrong wenyide ruogan yijian," passed by the party's Central Committee on 17 February 1989. This document was, to an extent, a response to criticisms of the party and government by National People's Political Consultative Congress members in 1988. See "Gaige, she ci bie wu xuanze," *Wenyi bao*, 9 April 1988, and "Zuojia zuiguangdade chuangzuo ziyou shi mianxiang gaige," *Wenyi bao*, 3 December 1988.

55. Naturally, this was only one of a series of policy statements, speeches, and directives made since the late 1970s by party leaders on the subject of culture. It was important, however, in that it was attributable to the collective party will rather than being the fiat of any single, transient leader. The introductory paragraph of this lengthy policy statement provides the center's view of the role of culture: "To implement the party's basic line during the initial phase of socialism, to draw lessons from the historical experience of the last forty and, in particular, the last ten years, to enhance and strengthen the party's leading role over the cultural industry, and to persevere with the general and specific cultural policies aimed at developing culture *are of considerable importance in consolidating and furthering stability and unity, to the democratic and harmonious political situation, and to advancing the construction of socialist material and spiritual culture* at the same time as further enhancing our socialist art and literature." (my italics)

    Using similar although less turgid phraseology, Deng Xiaoping said as much in his famous speech of 30 December 1986: "Our socialist construction can be carried out only under leadership, in an orderly way and in an environment of stability and unity."

56. See "Cujin wenyi shiye changqi wending fazhan," *Renmin ribao*, 14 March 1989. Clearly, "Opinions" did not go far enough in satisfying the hopes of some state artists, and during the March 1989 session of the Chinese People's Political Consultative Congress, five delegates (Wu Zuqiang, Cao Yu, Zhang Junqiu, Xie Jin, and Feng Jicai) called for an "art and literature law" to protect "artists' lawful rights and interests, especially their economic rights and interests in this period of economic retrenchment." See "Law Urged to Protect Writers and Artists," *China Daily*, 27 March 1989.

57. *Renmin ribao*, 14 March 1989; my italics.

58. "Opinions," 2:1 and 5:2, respectively.

59. *hongguan tiaojie he yindao zuoyong*. See "Opinions," 3:1.

60. A useful point-by-point comparison could be made of the two documents.

61. See Mao Zedong, *Mao Zedong xuanji* (Beijing: Renmin chubanshe, 1969), vol. 3, pp. 806–808, 811–815; "Opinions," 2:1.

62. See *Mao Zedong xuanji*, vol. 3, p. 805.

63. Haraszti, *The Velvet Prison*, pp. 78–79.

64. *Renmin ribao*, 14 March 1989.

65. Haraszti, *The Velvet Prison*, pp. 99–100, 104.

66. Ibid., pp. 86, 88.

67. See, for example, Fan Xiaoda, "Devalued Education Foils Book Publishing," *China Daily*, 27 March 1989.

68. In this context, see the discussion of Jia Pingwa's *The Abandoned Capital* in chapter 7, "Packaged Dissent."

69. A number of publications were banned or exposed to heavy official pressure even before 4 June. See *South China Morning Post*, 23 March 1989; Xu Xing, "Poxiao shifende Xin qimeng," *Jiefang yuekan*, 1989:3, pp. 34–35, 42; Yang Manke, "Cong Xin qimeng kan Zhongguo minkan," *Jiushi niandai yuekan*, 1989:4, pp. 62–63; and Xiao Chong, "Dule shuwu liangci guanbi fengbo," *Zhengming*, 1989:4, pp. 14–15.

70. See, for example, Lucian Pye's *The Mandarin and the Cadre: China's Political Cultures* (Ann Arbor: University of Michigan Press, 1988). Pye also comments on the relevance of Haraszti's work; see pp. 169, 196–197, n. 15.

71. In an essay written in early 1988, the novelist Liu Xinwu suggested that if only writers and readers were allowed greater scope for "self-regulation," *ziwo zhiyue*, bans would not be needed to outlaw controversial works. See Liu Xinwu, "Jinguo xiaoying," *Wenyi bao*, 9 April 1988. See also the incisive comments on this subject by the Yugoslav writer Danilo Kiš, "Censorship/Self-Censorship," in his *Homo Poeticus: Essays and Interviews*, ed. and introduced by Susan Sontag (New York: Farrar, Straus & Giroux, 1995), pp. 89–94.

CHAPTER 2

1. Deng Xiaoping, "Zai Zhongguo wenxue yishu gongzuozhe di sici daibiao dahui-shangde zhuci (1979 nian 10 yue 30 ri)," in *Deng Xiaoping wenxuan (1975–1982 nian)* (Beijing: Renmin chubanshe, 1983), p. 182.

2. Deng's statement on culture quoted earlier was included in a *People's Daily* editorial in October 1989. See "Cujin shehuizhuyi wenyi shiyede jin yibu fanrong," *Renmin ribao*, 5 October 1989.

3. Similar circulars were regularly issued during political campaigns. A thorough purge of publishing had been carried out at the end of the Cultural Revolution when works described as "peddling the black wares" of the ousted Gang of Four were banned. See Michael Schoenhals, "Weeding out the 'Gang of Four'," *Index on Censorship*, 1988:6, pp. 12–14, 26.

4. *Jinzhi xiaoshoude shukan mulu*. The copies of the 1989–90 booklets I have acquired were edited and printed by the Beijing Municipal News and Publishing Bureau. Similar booklets were produced by province-level publishing administrators throughout China.

5. The works of prominent intellectuals and writers who had appeared in Tiananmen

Square during the 1989 demonstrations and who were subsequently named in the official government report on the student-led insurrection, along with those involved in producing the television series *River Elegy*, were included in this ban. The philosopher Li Zehou's work was eventually rehabilitated, and his collected writings were published amid considerable fanfare in 1995. For a critique of Li's "spiritual collaboration" with Marxist orthodoxy in China, see Gu Xin, "Hegelianism and Chinese Intellectual Discourse: A Study of Li Zehou," *Journal of Contemporary China*, no. 8 (Winter/Spring 1995), pp. 1–27. Meanwhile, He Xin, the intellectual political careerist discussed in the following chapter, praised Li Zehou's ideological stance and the value of his academic work. See He Xin, "Shehui anding yu wenyi zhengce," in *He Xin zhengzhi jingji lunwen ji (neibu yanjiu baogao)*, 1993 (no publisher), pp. 269–270. Other figures, like Yu Haocheng, Li Honglin, Jin Guantao, Liu Qingfeng, and Dai Qing, were not as favored as Li, and their writings remained banned.

6. A fourth volume in this series of indexes appeared in August 1990. Along with the titles and publishers of the offending materials, a column listing the "nature," *xingzhi*, of the works' ideological offense was also included. Short, titillating descriptions are given for each item, like "promotes idealism," "illicit," "contains sexually explicit material," "obscene," "promotes superstition," "promotes sexual license," "violent content," "vulgar," "contains political errors," "pirated," and "promotes terror," as well as the catchall expression "[published] in contravention of the relevant regulations." This is followed by a "decision on the method of disposal," the most common being "confiscate and incinerate," *shoujiao, xiaohui*.

7. These included the reportage writers Zhao Yu, Wang Luxiang (one of the authors of *River Elegy*), Dai Qing, and the critic Liu Xiaobo. In the provinces, numerous poets, essayists, and others also were incarcerated for varying periods of time. For details, see Asia Watch, *Detained in China and Tibet: A Directory of Political and Religious Prisoners* (New York: Human Rights Watch, 1994).

8. See Wang Shuo, *Qianwan bie ba wo dangren, Zhongshan*, 1989, nos. 4, 5, 6.

9. See "Wenyijie haozhao jianchi sixiang jiben yuanze qieshide fandui zichanjieji ziyouhua," *Renmin ribao*, 8 July 1989.

10. Yu Xiaoxing, "Haiwai Zhongguo zuojia taolunhui jiyao," *Jintian*, no. 2 (1990), pp. 94–103.

11. Kong Jiesheng, "Wentan jinkuang," *Xinwen ziyou daobao*, 21 December 1990. This view was being reinforced in otherwise well-informed works like Xiaomei Chen's *Occidentalism* (Oxford: Oxford University Press, 1995), as late as 1995 (Chen, p. 157 inter alia).

12. Zang Kejia, " Quanguo Zhengxie liujie wuci huiyi bufen weiyuan fayan zhaiyao (5)," *Renmin ribao*, 7 April 1987; and Geremie Barmé and John Minford, eds., *Seeds of Fire: Chinese Voices of Conscience*, 2nd ed. (New York: Hill & Wang, 1988), p. 391.

13. "Bufen wenyijia zai Jing zuotan pipan zichanjieji ziyouhua: jianyi jinxing yici xinde wenyi zhengfeng," *Renmin ribao*, 13 July 1989.

14. This group included figures like the "poet" He Jingzhi, who became the acting min-

ister of culture, and others like Lin Mohan, Wei Wei, Yao Xueyin, Liu Baiyu, and Ouyang Shan.

15. For more details on the series, see Su Xiaokang and Wang Luxiang, *Deathsong of the River: A Reader's Guide to the Chinese TV Series Heshang*, introduced, translated, and annotated by Richard W. Bodman and Pin P. Wang (Ithaca, N.Y.: Cornell University Press, 1991); Chen Fong-ching and Jin Guantao, *From Youthful Manuscripts to River Elegy: The Chinese Popular Cultural Movement and Political Transformation 1979–1989* (Hong Kong: Chinese University Press, 1997); and Christina Neder, *Flusselegie Chinas Identitätskrise: Die Debatte um die chinesische Fernsehserie Heshang 1988–1994* (Dortmund: Projekt Verlag, 1996); and Geremie Barmé and Linda Jaivin, eds., *New Ghosts, Old Dreams: Chinese Rebel Voices* (New York: Times Books, 1992), pp. 138–164.

16. See, for example, Cui Wenhua, ed., *"Heshang" lun* (Beijing: Wenhua yishu chubanshe, 1989); and Cui Wenhua, ed., *Haiwai "Heshang" da taolun* (Haerbin: Heilongjiang jiaoyu chubanshe, 1988). The latter volume includes critiques by well-known cultural figures in Taiwan and Hong Kong like Bo Yang, Jiang Xun, Xi Murong, and Hu Juren.

17. Su Xiaokang and Wang Luxiang, *Heshang* (Beijing: Xiandai chubanshe, 1988).

18. Such views were expressed in letters to the directors collected in an internal reference booklet compiled by China Central TV in mid-1988.

19. See the editorial note at the beginning of Hua Yan, ed., *"Heshang" pipan* (Beijing: Wenhua yishu chubanshe, 1989). The expression *microclimate* comes from Deng Xiaoping's remarks on the causes of the 1989 demonstrations. See Deng Xiaoping, "Zai jiejian shoudu jieyan budui jun yishang ganbu shide jianghua" (9 June 1989), reprinted in Zhonggong zhongyang wenxian yanjiushi, ed., *Deng Xiaoping tongzhi lun gaige kaifang* (Beijing: Renmin chubanshe, 1989), p. 119. The "international climate," *guojide daqihou*, refers to the supposed plot of the Western powers led by the United States to overthrow the Chinese Communist Party and turn China into a bourgeois vassaldom.

20. See the *People's Daily* editorial note to Yi Jiayan, " 'Heshang' xuanyangle shenme?" *Renmin ribao*, 17 July 1989.

21. Yi Jiayan, " 'Heshang' xuanyangle shenme?"

22. Collected in Li Fengxiang, ed., *"Heshang" baimiu* (Beijing: Zhongguo wenlian chuban gongsi, 1990). Although published as part of a political vendetta against liberal writers and thinkers in China, many of these critiques did point out factual errors in the series.

23. "Bufen wenyijia zai Jing zuotan pipan zichanjieji ziyouhua: jianyi jinxing yici xinde wenyi zhengfeng."

24 See Dai Qing, *Wang Shiwei and "Wild Lilies": Rectification and Purges in the Chinese Communist Party 1942–1944* (Armonk, N.Y.: Sharpe, 1994); and Gregor Benton and Alan Hunter, eds., *Wild Lily, Prairie Fire: China's Road to Democracy, Yan'an to Tianan'men 1942–1989* (Princeton, N.J.: Princeton University Press, 1995), pp. 69–84.

25. See the editorial note to Yi Jiayan, " 'Heshang' xuanyangle shenme?"

26. "Quanguo xuanchuanbuzhang huiyi zai Jing bimu qiangdiao renqing xingshi zhenfen jingshen dali jiaqiang xuanchuan sixiang gongzuo," *Renmin ribao*, 22 July 1989.

27. He's appointment was announced in *Renmin ribao*, 5 September 1989; and see David E. Sanger, "China Dismisses Culture Minister," *International Herald Tribune*, 5 September 1989.

28. The *sankuan*, or "three *kuan*," were *kuanrong*, *kuanhou*, and *kuansong*. See, for example, Xiao Hong, "Nilin tan 'sankuan'," *Renmin ribao*, 27 April 1990.

29. See Hu Qili, "Zai Zhongguo wenxue yishujie lianhehui di wuci daibiao dahui-shangde zhuci (1988 nian 11 yue 8 ri)," *Renmin ribao*, 10 November 1988.

30. Xiao Hong, "Nilin tan 'sankuan' "; also Yi Ren, "Zhuozhou huiyide qianqian houhou," *Renmin ribao*, 14 February 1990.

31. The name of the journal, *Zhongliu*, comes from the expression *zhongliu dizhu*, "a pillar [or firm] rock in midstream," that is, a tower of strength or cornerstone. This saying dates from the early classical text *Spring and Autumn Annals of Master Yan* (Yanzi chunqiu). A "theoretical" sister publication of *Mainstay* was also established around this time. This was *Front* (Zhendi), "ideological front." See "*Zhendi* fakanci," *Wenhui bao*, 20 January 1990.

32. "Relie huijian qinqie jiaotan—*Zhongliu* chuangkan zuotanhui fayan zhaideng," *Zhongliu*, 1990:4, pp. 18–26. See also the inside of the cover of this issue for photographs of this occasion.

33. The autocratic pre–Cultural Revolution minister of culture, Zhou Yang, was derisively spoken of as a "cultural czar," *wenhua shahuang*. It seems appropriate to dub the feeble conservatives who regained power in 1989 as "cultural mini-czars." In his post–Cultural Revolution career, Zhou Yang, a man with much blood on his hands, was contrite. See, for example, Wei Junyi, "Zhou Yangde chanhui," *Wenhui dushu zhoubao*, 6 March 1993.

34. *Wenyi bao*, 21 April 1990.

35. The conveners of the Zhuozhou Conference were the literary departments of *Red Flag* (Hongqi), the party's official theoretical propaganda organ; *Guangming Daily*; and *Literary Theory and Criticism* (Wenyi lilun yu piping), acting under the aegis of the Department of Propaganda. For a translation of one of the speeches at that meeting, see "These Are a Few of My Least Favorite Things: Comrade Xiong Fu Speaks," in Barmé and Minford, *Seeds of Fire*, pp. 403–406.

36. Yi Ren, "Zhuozhou huiyide qianqian houhou," *Wenyi lilun yu piping*, 1990:1, reprinted in *Renmin ribao*, 14 February 1990. Yi Ren was the pen name of the literary critic Cheng Daixi.

37. See Bai Jieming (Barmé), "Dalu wentan laozuode Baoding huiyi," *Jiushi niandai yuekan*, 1990:8, pp. 68–69; and Teng Jinxian, "Guanyu Zhongguo dianyingde zhu xuanlü," *Renmin ribao*, 7 February 1991. The concept of a "keynote" culture was first formulated by the Film Bureau and presented at a national conference on feature films held in March 1987, at the height of the anti–bourgeois liberalization campaign begun after the fall of Party General Secretary Hu Yaobang. The slogan the Film Bu-

reau suggested was "Emphasize the keynote, persist with cultural diversity," *tuchu zhu xuanlü, jianchi duoyanghua.*

38. He Jingzhi, "Zhengqu minzude shehuizhuyide geju yishude xin fanrong," *Renmin ribao,* 6 December 1990.

39. *Wenyi bao,* 28 April 1990.

40. *Wenyi bao, Zhongguo wenhua bao, Zuopin yu zhengming, Wenyi lilun yu piping,* and *Zhongliu,* respectively.

41. "Jiushi niandaide zhaohuan," *Renmin wenxue,* 1990:7–8, p. 4.

42. "Jiushi niandaide zhaohuan," p. 5. Liu Xinwu's editorial impact on *People's Literature* was thoroughly rejected by Cao Mu. See "Shandongde shenme chibang?—chongdu *Renmin wenxue* 1987 nian 1–2 hekan," *Zhongliu,* 1990:4, pp. 38–41.

43. In Chinese, these titles are *Zhongshan, Shouhuo, Huacheng,* and *Wenxue ziyou tan.*

44. *Wenhui kuoda ban,* subsequently renamed *Wenhui dushu zhoubao.*

45. J. M. Coetzee, *Giving Offense: Essays on Censorship* (Chicago: University of Chicago Press, 1996), p. 35.

46. *Wenyi bao,* 28 October 1990.

47. Xia Zhongyi, "Lishi wuke bihui," *Wenxue pinglun,* 1989:4, pp. 5–20.

48. Zhang Jiong, "Mao Zedong yu xin Zhongguo wenxue," *Wenxue pinglun,* 1989:5, pp. 5–18, 159; Yang Zhenduo, "Wufa huibide bianlun—guanyu yishu benzhi ji qita wenti yu Xia Zhongyi tongzhi zai shangque," *Wenxue pinglun,* 1989:6, pp. 33–39.

49. Zhang Jiong, "Mao Zedong yu xin Zhongguo wenxue," p. 5.

50. Li Jie, "Lun Mao Zedong xianxiang," translated in Geremie R. Barmé, *Shades of Mao: The Posthumous Cult of the Great Leader* (Armonk, N.Y.: Sharpe, 1996), pp. 144–145.

51. See Yu Piao, "Guanyu Mao Zedong wenyi sixiang wentide lunzheng," *Wenyi bao,* 19 May 1990, p. 3; and "Jianchi Mao Zedong wenyi sixiangde zhidao diwei—zuotanhui fayan," *Wenyi lilun yu piping,* 1991:1, pp. 51–58. For a detailed "history" of the attacks on Mao's cultural thought in the 1980s, see Jin Sheng, "Huigu dui Mao Zedong wenyi sixiangde yichang 'weijiao'," *Zhongliu,* 1991:5, pp. 36–45; and Geremie Barmé, "History for the Masses," in *Using the Past to Serve the Present: Historiography and Politics in Contemporary China,* ed. Jonathan Unger (Armonk, N.Y.: Sharpe, 1993), pp. 268–269.

52. Jin Sheng, "Huigu dui Mao Zedong wenyi sixiangde yichang 'weijiao'," p. 45.

53. *Renmin ribao,* 20 September 1989.

54. See *Renmin ribao,* 14 September 1989.

55. See Li Ruihuan, "Fanrong wenyi bixu dali hongyang minzu youxiu wenhua," *Renmin ribao,* 12 January 1990; and "Guanyu hongyang minzu youxiu wenhuade ruogan wenti—zai quanguo wenhua yishu gongzuo qingkuang jiaoliu zuotanhuishangde jianghua (1990 nian 1 yue 10 ri)," *Renmin ribao,* 15 May 1990.

56. For an example of Li's line, see "Li Ruihuan tan wending dangqian daju," *Yangcheng wanbao,* 30 April 1990.

57. *Yangcheng wanbao,* 23 February 1990.

58. "Zhongyang guanyu yishi xingtai wentide zhishi (1989 nian 6 yue—1990 nian 6 yue)," *Zhongguo wenhuabao,* 24 June 1990.

59. "Quan dang fucong Zhongyang," *Zhongguo wenhuabao*, 24 June 1990.

60. Alexander Zinoviev, *Homo Sovieticus*, trans. Charles Janson (London: Paladin, 1986), p. 73.

61. Ibid., p. 12.

62. Zheng Wang and Ji Kuai, eds., *Liu Xiaobo qiren qishi* (Beijing: Zhongguo qingnian chubanshe, 1989). Liu commented to friends that he was delighted that the book reproduced some of his most provocative articles. The forty pages of Liu's own works contained in the book—which took up approximately a third of the whole volume—also included some of his best speeches and articles from 1989. See *Liu Xiaobo qiren qishi*, pp. 82–139. See also Shi You, ed., *Zhongguo dangdai "jingying" de zhenmianmu* (Beijing: Guangming chubanshe, 1990); and Zhao Wang et al., eds., *Wangming "jingying" qiren qishi* (Beijing: Zhongguo qingnian chubanshe, 1991).

63. Xu Weicheng worked in the Beijing Municipal Committee until the Cultural Revolution, after which he became a leading editor at the *Beijing Daily* (Beijing ribao). After a period in disgrace, he became an active propagandist in the last years of the Cultural Revolution and staged a skillful comeback in the 1980s. For some details of Xu's irrepressible rise, see Hu Nan, "Fengpai renwu Xu Weicheng xiang dang Zhonggong xuanchuan buzhang," *Zhongguo dalu*, 1992:5, pp. 17–20.

64. See Yu Xinyan, *Shengsi cunwang* (Chengdu: Sichuan renmin chubanshe, 1990); and Ouyang Shan, *Guang yusi* (Beijing: Guangming chubanshe, 1991). Xu was based in Beijing, and Ouyang lived in Guangzhou, in the south. Shanghai produced its own literary assassin in the person of Yi Mu (Luan Baojun), who concentrated his invective on denouncing Wang Ruowang, the Shanghai dissident writer, and praising the efforts of the workers' militia in quelling the student protests in the city in June 1989. See Luan Baojun, *Zhiyan lu—Luan Baojun (Yi Mu) zhenglun zawen xuan* (Shanghai: Shanghai renmin chubanshe, 1991), esp. pp. 218–269.

65. See Yu Xinyan, *Shengsi cunwang*, pp. 1–2, 19–20, 68–69. The term for AIDS in Chinese—*aizi bing*—is a homonym for "afflicted with a love of capital."

66. See Zheng Wang and Ji Kuai, *Liu Xiaobo qiren qishi*, p. 154.

67. See, for example, Dong Xuewen, "Lun Liu Zaifu 'wenxue zhutixing' lilunde shizhi," *Qiushi*, 1991:1, pp. 25–31; and Lan Yan, "Lun 'Liu Zaifu xianxiang'," *Qiushi*, 1991:4, pp. 22–31.

68. See, for example, *Renmin ribao*, 29 August 1989, p. 6.

69. *Qiushi*, 1991:1, pp. 25–31; and *Zuopin yu zhengming*, 1991:5.

70. For examples, see *Suibi*, 1990:2, 3, 4; 1991:1, 2.

71. See Barmé and Minford, *Seeds of Fire*, pp. 153–160, 361–367; and Barmé and Jaivin, *New Ghosts, Old Dreams*, pp. 50–53.

72. *Suibi*, 1991:1, 2.

73. These anecdotes and illustrations were taken from Huang Yongyu, *Yongyu sanji*, 3 vols. (Xianggang: Sanlian shudian, 1983). Huang's name also appeared in the pages of the Shanghai *Wenhui Book Review*. See Huang Yongyu, "Wo yao yin baben shu," *Wenhui dushu zhoubao*, 7 November 1992. Huang had frequently contributed satiri-

cal essays to the liberal Beijing journal *New Observer* (Xin guancha), edited by Ge Yang, before its closure in 1989. For a collection of these, see *Wu Shimang luntan* (Xianggang: *Ming bao* chubanshe, 1989). After an absence of some years, Huang made a private visit to the mainland in late 1995, and settled in Beijing in 1998.

74. Dai Qing, *Wode ruyu*, serialized in *Ming Pao Daily* (Ming bao) in May 1990 and published in book form shortly thereafter. For a partial translation of "My Imprisonment," see Geremie Barmé, "The Trouble with Dai Qing" and "My Imprisonment," in *Index on Censorship*, 1992:8, pp. 15–27.

75. See, for example, Dai Qing, *Wode sige fuqin* (Xianggang: *Ming bao* chubanshe, 1995); and *Zai Qincheng zuolao* (Xianggang: *Ming bao* chubanshe, 1995).

76. For the details of this incident, see Barmé and Minford, *Seeds of Fire*, pp. 368–372; and Wu Zuguang, *Wu Zuguang xianwen xuan* (Xianggang: *Ming bao* chubanshe, 1989).

77. See, for example, Wu Zuguang, "Feiqin zoushou, nimen yuanwang," *Ming bao*, 25 February 1991. The Shanghai dissident Wang Ruowang (and also Bai Hua) had his memoirs published in Hong Kong following his release from detention. See Wang Ruowang, *Wang Ruowang zizhuan* (Xianggang: *Ming bao* chubanshe, 1991).

78. Yang Xianyi, *Yinqiao ji* (Xianggang: Tiandi tushu youxian gongsi, 1995).

79. Joseph M. Lau, "Text and Context: Toward a Commonwealth of Modern Chinese Literature," in *Worlds Apart: Recent Chinese Writing and Its Audience*, ed. Howard Goldblatt (Armonk, N.Y.: Sharpe, 1990), pp. 11–28.

80. See He Jingzhi, "Guanyu jianshe you Zhongguo tesede shehuizhuyi wenhuade jidian kanfa," *Zhongguo wenhuabao*, 20 March 1991.

81. Chen Yong, "Guanyu shehuizhuyi wenyi," *Renmin ribao*, 10 January 1991; and Li Zhun, "Shehuizhuyi wenyi he lixiangde zhuiqiu," *Renmin ribao*, 24 January 1991.

82. *Renmin ribao*, 10 February 1991.

83. Yan Zhaozhu, "Lun wenxue benzhi duoyuanhualunde shizhi," *Wenyi lilun yu piping*, 1991:1, reprinted in *Zhongguo wenhua bao*, 3 February 1991.

84. "Dang zhongyang yaoqing wenyijie zhiming renshi zuotan," *Renmin ribao*, 2 March 1991; and *Wenyi bao*, 9 March 1991.

85. They included Liu Baiyu, Yao Xueyin, Guan Hua, Wei Wei, Liu Changyu, and Dong Xuewen.

86. "Dang zhongyang yaoqing wenyijie zhiming renshi zuotan."

87. These quotations are from Shen Rong's unpublished speech "Small Hope" (Yidian xiwang), 1 March 1991. The full text of Shen's speech is as follows:

SMALL HOPE (BY SHEN RONG)

As a newcomer to the field of fiction writing, I know that what my readers hope of me is that I produce more novels. Ba Jin has remarked: "An author's name should appear on their works [and nowhere else]." I couldn't agree more. If a writer's name is secondary to their official title or appears primarily in a list of people who have participated in some meeting or other, how can they really be called a writer?

Today, all I'd like to do is express a few hopes.

I hope there'll be a little less noise pollution, less interference, so that we can get on with our writing in peace. For example, the moment Party Central called for the "sweeping away of pornography," we heard complaints from some quarters that "the purge of pornography cannot replace the movement to oppose bourgeois liberalism." When the center said: "On the one hand, we must carry out a cultural shake-up, but on the other, we must ensure the arts continue to flourish," immediately someone else piped up: "We can achieve cultural health only if there is a rectification." The center may appeal for "developing the arts," but someone immediately jumps out and cries: "What do you mean by the arts? We must develop the culture of socialism, not the culture of capitalism."

Now, I don't have any idea where all this acrimony and bickering over terminology come from, or what kind of authoritative backing it might have, but I do know that it's all pretty scary.

For a writer like me, you feel like you're walking into a minefield. You never know when you're going to write something that'll set off an explosion, making you dive for the ground in terror.

Let me ask you: how can a writer produce anything of value if they're always scared? In my opinion, if there really is a debate about all the issues I've just mentioned, I would hope that the leadership first fights it out among yourselves. When you're through, write up your decisions in a Party Central document, and just let us know.

Since the leaders of the party Department of Propaganda are present today, I would like to express a wish to them as well: don't just act as cultural watchdogs, constantly on the lookout for suspicious activity among the enemy. You should be like sappers who go in to clear out the minefields and open up a way for the prospering of the arts. Of course, I should hasten to add that when I talk about art and culture, I'm talking about socialist culture, not capitalist culture.

Thank you for your attention.

88. Wei Wei, "Yuanxiao," *Zhenlide zhuiqiu*, 1991:5, reprinted in *Zhongguo wenhua bao*, 2 June 1991.

89. Mao Zedong, "Ode to the Plum Blossom — To the Tune of *Pu suan tzu* (Yung mei)", December 1961, in Mao Tsetung, *Poems* (Peking: Foreign Languages Press, 1976), p. 43.

90. Zhonggong zhongyang Xuanchuan bu, Wenhua bu, Guangbo dianying dianshi bu, "Guanyu dangqian fanrong wenyi chuangzuode yijian (1991 nian 3 yue 1 ri)," published in *Zhongguo wenhua bao*, 15 May 1991.

91. Bi Hua, " 'Shao ganyu, shao jieru'? Jiangui qu ba!" *Jiushi niandai yuekan*, 1991:8, pp. 38–39.

92. For details of the wealth of literature that appeared between 1989 and 1991, see Geremie Barmé, "An Iron Fist in a Velvet Prison: Literature in Post–June 1989 China," *China News Analysis* 1443, 15 September 1991, pp. 4–7.

93. Zhou Lunyou, "Jujuede zitai," *Xiandai hanshi (wenxue jiaoliu ziliao)*, Spring/Summer 1992, p. 116.

CHAPTER 3

1. From a letter to me dated 2 October 1989, quoted with permission. See He Xin, "Letter from Beijing," translated and annotated by Geremie Barmé, *Australian Journal of Chinese Affairs*, no. 24, July 1990, p. 343.

2. Ibid., pp. 343–344.

3. Never slow at self-promotion, in the early 1990s He Xin used vanity publications to share his sage views with a select audience. One of these volumes was his *He Xin zhengzhi jingji lunwen ji (neibu yanjiu baogao)*, 1993 (no publisher). Other published works that reflect his political views include He Xin, *Dongfangde fuxing—Zhongguo xiandaihuade mingti yu qiantu* (Haerbin: Heilongjiang jiaoyu chubanshe / Heilongjiang renmin chubanshe, 1991), and *He Xin zhengzhi jingji lunji* (Haerbin: Heilongjiang jiaoyu chubanshe, 1995). An acquaintance passed on a copy of the latter to me in 1996 with an inscription from He Xin that simply read: "A book that influenced history."

4. See Jirina Siklov, "The 'Gray Zone' and the Future of Dissent in Czechoslovakia," *Social Research* 57 (2), Summer 1990, pp. 347–363.

5. *Zhongguo minzhu zhenxian*, or *Minzhen* for short.

6. *Jintian* and *Wenhua guangchang*, respectively.

7. *Zhongguo minzhu tuanjie lianmeng*, or *Minlian*.

8. Details of Wuer Kaixi's views and antics following June 1989 can be found in Joseph F. Kahn's "Better Fed Than Red," *Esquire*, September 1990, pp. 186–197. See also Orville Schell, "Children of Tiananmen," *Rolling Stone*, December 1989, pp. 185–195, 247, 249.

9. Alexander Zinoviev, *Homo Sovieticus*, trans. Charles Janson (London: Paladin, 1986), p. 116.

10. Lu Keng, "Minyunde jiazhi hezai?" *Xinwen ziyou daobao*, 12 October 1990.

11. The text of Hu's "Lun yanlun ziyou" can be found in Hu Ping et al., *Kaituo—Beida xueyun wenxian* (Xianggang: Tianyuan shuwu, 1990), pp. 31–77. Wang Dan's "Lun fanduipaide yanlun ziyou" was published in *Jiushi niandai yuekan*, 1989:9, pp. 72–73.

12. Hu Ping, "Haiwai minyun xiayibu," *Xinwen ziyou daobao*, 12 October 1990.

13. Ibid.

14. See Ou Lu, "Cong Bali zhuanxiang Beimei," *Kaifang zazhi*, 1990:8, pp. 75–77; and Tan Liyan, "Pulinsidun xuepai yu Zhijiage xuepai," *Kaifang zazhi*, 1990:10, pp. 50–51.

15. *Dangdai Zhongguo yanjiu zhongxin*. Exile gave Chen an opportunity to record his version of the history of China's reforms in the 1980s. See Chen Yizi, *Zhongguo: shinian gaige yu bajiu minyun—Beijing liusi tushade beihou* (Taibei: Lianjing chuban shiye gongsi, 1990).

16. Chinese folklore held that eating a steamed bread *mantou* dipped in the blood of a recently executed person could prolong life or cure disease.

17. Zhao Chu, "Guoge rengede lianjia da paimai," *Renmin ribao*, 23 October 1990.

18. This has been noted by Lee Yee (Li Yi) in " 'Liusi' wailiu renshide kun'ao," *Jiushi niandai yuekan*, 1990:10, p. 33.

19. This is the way Li Lu was written up in a flyer issued by St John the Divine in New York, where he addressed a gathering on 4 June 1995. Li Lu's autobiography, *Moving the Mountain*, became the basis for David Apted's 1994 documentary of the same name. For details of the hedge fund (Himalaya Capital Partners L.P.), see Carrie Cunningham, "Tiananmen Square to Wall Street: Li Lu Hits the New York Jackpot," *New York Observer*, 18 May 1998.

20. See Gao Luji, "Congshan ruliude gaiguo," *Jiushi niandai yuekan*, 1990:10, p. 36.

21. *Ershiyi shiji.*

22. From an editorial note in the magazine's promotional pamphlet.

23. Liang Heng was known to English readers for *Son of the Revolution*, coauthored with Judith Shapiro.

24. *The Nineties Monthly* tended to favor the post–4 June intellectual exiles like Su Xiao-kang, Yan Jiaqi, and Liu Binyan, whereas *Open Magazine* gave greater prominence to people associated with the older and consistently rebellious members of Hu Ping's alliance. One of the most indicative examples of this type of favoritism can be seen in the support that *The Nineties Monthly* gave to the artist Huang Yongyu after 1989, whereas *Open Magazine* championed Huang's nemesis, the painter Fan Zeng. Both Huang and Fan were former darlings of Communist Party gerontocrats.

25. Zhu Dake, "Kongxinde wenxue," in his *Ranshaode mijin* (Shanghai: Xuelin chuban-she, 1991), pp. 109–111. Zhu himself was investigated after 4 June for his role in writing a petition calling for creative freedom. In the early 1990s, he was able to travel overseas; thereafter he shuttled between Shanghai and Sydney.

26. See Lin Ching-wen and Lina Hsu, "Marx, Not Confucius, Blamed," *Free China Journal*, 11 January 1990.

27. See Werner Meissner, *Philosophy and Politics in China: The Controversy over Dialectical Materialism in the 1930s*, trans. Richard Mann (London: Hurst , 1990), pp. 1–15, 174–192. My thanks to W. J. F. Jenner for directing my attention to this fascinating study.

28. Quoted in Tan Xia, "Qishiyi nian lishi, sidairende huigu — cong Wusi dao Liusi," *Zhongguo zhi chun*, 1990:7, pp. 19–20. Similar sentiments were often expressed in the émigré press. See, for example, Wang Huiyun, "Minzhu shi yizhong shenghuo fang-shi," *Xinwen ziyou daobao*, 16 November 1990.

29. Hai Feng, "Tashuo: ta jiang yi wu fan gu — benbao jizhe zhuanfang Hou Dejian," *Xinwen ziyou daobao*, 30 July 1990.

30. Yuan Zhiming, "Heishou haishi qishou?" *Xinwen ziyou daobao*, 20 January 1990.

31. See, for example, Liu Xiaobo's criticism of Liu Binyan and his fellow "closet dissidents" in Geremie Barmé and Linda Jaivin, eds., *New Ghosts, Old Dreams: Chinese Rebel Voices* (New York: Times Books, 1992), pp. 33–48.

32. Danilo Kiš, "Censorship/Self-Censorship," in his *Homo Poeticus: Essays and Interviews*, edited and introduced by Susan Sontag (New York: Farrar, Straus & Giroux, 1995), p. 93.

33. See, for example, Liu Binyan, "Daobian yu tianbian—lianzhide duanlie ji fanxing," *Guangchang zazhi*, 1990:6, pp. 6–11; and "Women hulüele xinling zhi ai—Haweier-de qishi," *Minzhu Zhongguo*, 1990:8, pp. 7–11. Also see Xu Xing, "Diceng liliang yu zhishifenzi," *Kaifang zazhi*, 1990:11, pp. 30–33.

34. See Merle Goldman's foreword to Liu Binyan, *China's Crisis, China's Hope: Essays from an Intellectual in Exile*, trans. Howard Goldblatt (Cambridge, Mass.: Harvard University Press, 1990), p. x.

35. Bei Ling, "Zhongguo zuojiade zhengzhi sucai," *Kaifang zazhi*, 1990:10, p. 92.

36. Bei Ling, "Xinwende zhenshi yu xianjing," *Zhongguo shibao zhoukan*, 1990:5, pp. 12–18.

37. See Tao Gang, "Lun quxian jiuguo," *Kaifang zazhi*, 1990:11, p. 80. Tao refers to certain exile groups that warn of "democracy harming the nation" and oppose the mindless and emotional prodemocracy faddism of many dissident discussions. See also Zhang Hao, "Pan Zhongguo minzhu shenggen, zouchu lishi xunhuan," *Ershiyi shiji*, 27 October 1990 (inaugural issue), pp. 9–10.

38. See, for example, Lin Yü-sheng's *The Crisis of Chinese Consciousness: Radical Anti-traditionalism in the May Fourth Era* (Madison: University of Wisconsin Press, 1979).

39. For some relevant comments by Lin, see his conversation with Benjamin I. Schwarz in Lin Yusheng, *Sixiang yu renwu* (Taibei: Lianjing chuban shiye gongsi, 1983), pp. 464–465.

40. Lin Yusheng et al., *Wusi: duoyuande fansi* (Xianggang: Sanlian chubanshe, 1989), p. 242.

41. Xu Jilin, "Xiandai wenhuashishangde 'wusi guaiquan'," *Wenhui bao* (Shanghai), 21 March 1989.

42. Hua Sheng in "Tantao weilaide daolu," *Minzhu Zhongguo*, 1990:6, p. 40.

43. Xu Xing, "Diceng liliang yu zhishifenzi," p. 33.

44. See Hu's report to the Twelfth Congress of the Central Committee of the Chinese Communist Party made on 8 September 1982, published as a booklet entitled *Quanmian kaichuang shehuizhuyi xiandaihua jianshede xinjumian* (Beijing: Renmin chubanshe, 1982), p. 24.

45. See Lucien W. Pye, *The Spirit of Chinese Politics, A Psychocultural Study of the Authority Crisis in Political Development* (Cambridge, Mass.: M.I.T. Press, 1968), pp. 135–137, and the chapter "Organizational Behavior and the Martial Spirit." Also see Pye's "Tiananmen and Chinese Political Culture: The Escalation of Confrontation," in *The Broken Mirror: China After Tiananmen*, ed. George Hicks (Essex: Longman, 1990), pp. 162–179.

46. He Xin, "Zhongguo dangdai wenhua beiwanglu—wode kunhuo yu youlü," *Jingjixue zhoubao*, 8 January 1989.

47. Formerly a party propagandist and historian who, following the Cultural Revolution, became a leading figure in the liberalization of historical studies. He died in December 1988.

48. Dai Qing, *Wode ruyu* (Xianggang: *Ming bao* chubanshe, 1990), p. 42. For a translation of this work, see Dai Qing, "My Imprisonment, an Excerpt," trans. Geremie

Barmé, *Index on Censorship*, 1992:8, pp. 20–27. The debate on the gradual transformation of the polity, as opposed to revolutionary change, began in the late Qing dynasty. See Andrew J. Nathan, *Chinese Democracy: The Individual and the State in Twentieth Century China* (London: I. B. Tauris, 1986), pp. 130–131.

49. Li Yi, " 'Liusi' wailiu renshide kun'ao."

50. See Robert Delfs, "Thought Control," *Far Eastern Economic Review*, 8 November 1990, p. 19, for a comment on the heated debate in the Chinese leadership concerning rehabilitation at that time.

51. For an elucidating study of the nature of the shifting sands of Chinese political alliances, see Andrew J. Nathan, "A Factionalism Model for CCP Politics," in his *China's Crisis: Dilemmas for Reform and Prospects for Democracy* (New York: Columbia University Press, 1990), pp. 23–37.

52. For these quotations, see Liu Xiaobo, "Pingfan! Zhongguo zuidade beiju," *Tiananmen 1989*, ed. *Lianhebao* (Taibei: Lianjing chuban shiye gongsi, 1989), p. 277.

53. Ou Lu, "Cong Bali zhuanxiang Beimei," p. 77.

CHAPTER 4

1. See "Bixu qizhi xianmingde fandui dongluan," *Renmin ribao*, 26 April 1989. Throughout the 1980s, the party described the Cultural Revolution as "ten years of turmoil," *shinian dongluan*, and books about that period often used the word "turmoil," *dongluan*, in their titles. See, for example, Hei Yannan, *Shinian dongluan* (Xi'an: Guoji wenhua chuban gongsi, 1988); and Wang Nianyi, *1949–1989 niande Zhongguo: Da dongluande niandai* (Kaifeng: Henan renmin chubanshe, 1988). In representing the 1989 protests as "turmoil," the authorities were claiming they were but a replay of that earlier period of chaos.

2. These three were first lumped together by He Xin in "A Word of Advice to the Politburo," *Australian Journal of Chinese Affairs*, no. 23, January 1990, p. 67. Li Ruihuan, the Politburo propaganda chief, also attacked this trinity of bourgeois liberalization-mongers in his 1989–1990 speeches.

3. *wending yadao yiqie*.

4. Although the word Shuo, "New Month," or "Northern," is romanized with an "h," it is generally pronounced as "Suo" in Beijing. Wang Shuo himself pronounces his name as Wang Suo.

5. Of course, this is not unique to the terminal phase of communist culture in China. The same was true of many Eastern European countries and the Soviet Union in the 1970s and 1980s. For some observations on the latter, see, for example, Martin Walker, *The Waking Giant, the Soviet Union Under Gorbachev* (London: Abacus, 1986), pp. 171–175; Andrew Wilson and Nina Bachkatov, *Living with Glasnost, Youth and Society in a Changing Russia* (London: Penguin, 1988), pp. 141–147; and Anthony Barnett, *Soviet Freedom* (London: Picador, 1988), pp. 245–252 ("The Role of Rock") and 253–270 ("The Sixties Come to the Soviet Union"). Interesting parallels can be drawn between Wang Shuo's fiction and works from the Soviet Union and Eastern Europe.

There seem to be, for example, elements of similarity in the Soviet writer Venedikt Yerofeyev's samizdat novel *Moskva-Petushki*. See Zinovy Zinik, "Silence, Exile & Glasnost: A Bilingual Minority," *Encounter*, June 1990, p. 67. My thanks to Brian Martin for bringing this article to my attention. See also Jan Pelc, "It's Gonna Get Worse," *Index on Censorship*, 1986:6, pp. 27–30.

6. The writer Zhou Zuoren preferred the translation "picaroon," from the Spanish *pícaro*, or "rogue." See his 1924 essay "Pojiaogu," in *Zhou Zuoren zaoqi sanwen xuan* (Shanghai: Shanghai wenyi chubanshe, 1984), p. 23.

7. From John Minford, "Picking up the Pieces," *Far Eastern Economic Review*, 8 August 1985, p. 30. I have benefited greatly from discussions in 1985–1986 and 1989 with Minford on the question of the *liumang*.

8. See Ge Zhixu, *Huyou zaji*, first published in 1876 and reprinted in the *Shanghaitan yu Shanghairen congshu*. Ge Zhixu et al., *Huyou zaji, Songnan mengying lu, Huyou mengying* (Shanghai: Shanghai guji chubanshe, 1989), p. 22. Also in the same book, see Huang Shiquan's 1883 *Songnan mengying lu* for a further comment on the term (p. 101). My thanks to Ye Xiaoqing for pointing out these references.

9. See Wu Yu, Liang Licheng, and Wang Daozhi, *Minguo heishehui* (Nanjing: Jiangsu guji chubanshe, 1988). This book has a section on the *liumang*'s tricks of the trade on pp. 113–136.

10. In the past, the two expressions *dipi liumang* were often used in combination. In recent years *dipi* appears to have fallen out of favor. Another word close in meaning to *liumang* and *dipi* is *wulai*, which Lin Yutang translated in the 1930s as "ne'er-do-well." The northern Shaanxi dialect expression *erliuzi*, "idler" or "bum," is another term often used in this context; as is *afei* in Shanghai.

11. In 1988, one judge described the ten signs of aberrant adolescent behavior that presaged a criminal future. These included such traits as a generally negative attitude toward authority figures, a penchant for fighting, sexual dalliances, irregular habits, interest in clannish gangland activities, gambling, and harassing the opposite sex. It was nothing less than a pen portrait of the *liumang* as depicted in Wang Shuo's fiction. See "Qingshaonian fanzui shizhong xianzhao," *Renmin ribao*, 6 November 1988.

12. Zhou Zuoren, "Liangge gui," in *Zhou Zuoren zaoqi sanwen xuan*, p. 98. For an episode early on in Zhou's career when he was friendly with a gang of Shaoxing *liumang*, see his essay "Pojiaogu," in the same volume, pp. 21–23; and "Jihu chengle xiao liumang," in Zhou Zuoren, *Zhitang huixiang lu* (Xianggang: Sanyu tushu youxian gongsi, 1980), pp. 61–64.

13. Zhou, "Liangge gui," p. 99.

14. Ibid.

15. Chen Ziming, "Shei shi lishide zuiren—wode bianhushu zhaiyao (er)," *Xinwen ziyou daobao*, 12 July 1991.

16. Yi Shuihan, "Wuchanjiejide liumang yishi weihai shehui," *Jingjixue zhoubao*, 27 November 1988, excerpted in *Chaoliu yuekan* (Hong Kong), no. 25, 15 March 1989, p. 22. A lively portrait of an entrepreneur/reformist in Wuhu, Anhui, can be found in Lu Yuegang's reportage "Chuangshiji huangdan," in Shan Li, ed., *Zhongguode xin da-*

heng (Beijing: Beijing shiyue wenyi chubanshe, 1989), pp. 205–256. For a comment on a similar phenomenon in East Europe, see George Konrád, "Letter from Budapest," reprinted in *Cross Currents*, 1982, pp. 12–13.

17. Yü's list is *dipi, liumang, guanggun, wulai, budi xiucai.*

18. The term *liumang* politician, *liumang zhengzhijia,* has been used at various times as an epithet to describe such disparate figures as Chiang Kai-shek and Jiang Qing.

19. Yu Yingshi, "Dai congtou, shoushi jiu shanhe," *Ershiyi shiji,* no. 2, December 1990, p. 6.

20. It is interesting to note that during the 1989 protest movement, the epithet *liumang* was applied freely by both the authorities, who derided those who took part in protests in late May as *liumang,* and by the demonstrators, who denounced the leaders who imposed martial law on Beijing, pitting the army against the people, as the ultimate *liumang.*

21. During the Bolinas China '89 Symposium held in April 1989, Wu Guoguang, a former *People's Daily* writer, spoke at considerable length about the *"liumang* air," *liumangqi,* or "monkey spirit," *houqi,* of Mao Zedong and his fascination with Monkey (Sun Wukong), the hero of *Journey to the West.* At the same symposium, the playwright Wu Zuguang remarked that Deng Xiaoping's response to the April student demonstrations was that of a *liumang.* See Wu's comments in Geremie Barmé, ed., "On the Eve," on the web site for the documentary film *The Gate of Heavenly Peace,* <www.nmis.org/gate>.

22. See Wang Yi, "Liumang zhengzhi ji Zhang Tiesheng xianxiang," *Ershiyi shiji,* no. 8, August 1991, pp. 132–137. Wang's observations on *liumang* politics were hardly original. Sa Mengwu expressed a similar view in his 1930s *Shuihu zhuan yu Zhongguo shehui,* repr. (Changsha: Yuelu shushe, 1987), pp. 3–12.

23. See Qu Yanbin, *Zhongguo qigai shi* (Shanghai: Shanghai wenyi chubanshe, 1990), pp. 228–235. Qu also referred to the *Jingjixue zhoubao* article mentioned earlier; see p. 232.

24. See, for example, Chen Baoliang, *Zhongguo liumang shi* (Beijing: Zhongguo shehui kexue chubanshe, 1993); and Wanyan Shaoyuan, *Liumangde bianqian: Zhongguo gudai liumang shihua* (Shanghai: Shanghai guji chubanshe, 1993).

25. Wang, "Yidian zhengjing meiyou," *Zhongguo zuojia,* 1989:6, p. 138.

26. Zhang Zheng, " 'Wanzhu' Wang Shuo," *Zhongguo dianyingbao,* 5 November 1988. Synopses of all four films were included with Zhang's article. For an early critical response to the "Wang Shuo fad," see Ming Qi, "Zhongshuo fenyun 'Wang Shuo re'," *Zuoping yu zhengming,* 1989:9, pp. 79–80.

27. Huang Shixian, "E zhi hua: zuo'e yu congshande mofang," *Zhongguo dianyingbao,* 15 July 1989.

28. *The Operators,* from the story of the same name, will be discussed later. *Samsara* was based on Wang's story "Flotsam" (Fuchu haimian), although the director also "sampled" scenes and characters from two other stories by Wang Shuo, namely, "Hot and Cold, Measure for Measure" (Yiban shi haishui, yiban shi huoyan) and "Rubber Man" (Xiangpi ren). For the significance of this film in the context of urban *liumang* in the age of economic reform, see the director Xie Fei's comments in *Dianying yishu*

cankao ziliao, 1989:1 (issue 197), restricted circulation, pp. 2–5; and Paul G. Pickow-icz, "Huang Jianxin and the Notion of Postsocialism," in *New Chinese Cinemas: Forms, Identities, Politics*, ed. Nick Browne et al. (Cambridge: Cambridge University Press, 1994), pp. 73–78.

29. Xie Fei's 1989 film *Birth Year* (Benming nian) was another important tale of entre-preneur tragedy. It was based on *Black Snow* (Heide xue), a novel by Liu Heng, one of Wang Shuo's close associates. Praise for Xie's film, which was released after June 1989, was often premised on negative reviews of the Wang Shuo films. See *Dianying yishu cankao ziliao*, 1990:9 (issue 217), pp. 2, 3, 7.

30. Zuo Shula, "Buru 'liu' zide qile, xiexie Wang Shuo," *Dangdai* (Taibei), 1989:4, p. 129. For more from Zuo's article in translation, see Geremie Barmé and Linda Jaivin, eds., *New Ghosts, Old Dreams: Chinese Rebel Voices* (New York: Times Books, 1992), pp. 218–226. A shorter version of Zuo's article appeared on the mainland under the title "Wang Shuo—yige ganyu miaoshi changguide 'suren'," in *Dazhong dianying*, 1989:5, pp. 14–15, and 1989:7, pp. 10–12.

31. Zuo, "Buru 'liu' zide qile," p. 130.

32. Wang Shuo, "Dengdai," *Jiefangjun wenyi*, 1978:11, pp. 25–29. Set in the late Cultural Revolution, the story is narrated by a frustrated and rebellious young girl. Her mother keeps a tight rein on her, fearful that she will fall prey to the *liumang* who are suppos-edly running riot in the city (pp. 26, 27, 29). It is a relatively inoffensive example of the formulaic "literature of the wounded," *shanghen wenxue*, that flourished in 1978–1979.

33. Yao was a veteran writer known for his epic novel on the late Ming rebel Li Zicheng. Wang came to prominence in the late 1970s by writing about the police.

34. He became a blackmarketeer, *daoye*. Some of Wang's experiences in the south found their way into the novella "Rubber Man." See Wang, "Xiangpi ren," *Xiaoshuo xuan-kan*, 1987:1, pp. 5–49.

35. Wang Shuo, "Kongzhong xiaojie," *Dangdai* (Beijing), 1984:2, pp. 162–184. One of the points of interest in the story is that it describes a man who, after leaving the navy, be-comes a *wulai*, a "no-hoper," who lives off his flight attendant girlfriend until she breaks up with him. There are elements of the idealistic romanticism in the story that appear in a number of Wang's later works, in particular his late-1989 story "Love Lost" (Yong shi wo ai).

36. Zuo, "Buru 'liu' zide qile," pp. 131–133.

37. Ibid., p. 133.

38. *shehui xiansan renyuan*. See Thomas B. Gold, "Guerrilla Interviewing Among the Getihu," in *Unofficial China: Popular Culture and Thought in the People's Republic*, ed. Perry Link, Richard Madsen, and Paul G. Pickowicz (Boulder, Colo.: Westview Press, 1989), p. 185. "Idle person," *xiansan renyuan*, is also the term the protagonist of "Rub-ber Man" uses to describe himself and his fellows. See Wang Shuo, "Xiangpi ren," p. 6.

39. Quoted in Zhang Zheng, " 'Wanzhu' Wang Shuo." In this context, see also Zuo Shula, "Buru 'liu' zide qile," p. 136.

40. *houbu zuifan*. See Wang Ping, "Wang Shuode ezuoju," *Wenxue ziyoutan*, 1989:4, p. 100.

41. Zuo, "Buru 'liu' zide qile," p. 134.

42. Ibid., p. 130.

43. Wang Shuo, "Wanzhu"; see *Wang Shuo xiequ xiaoshuo xuan* (Beijing: Zuojia chubanshe, 1990), pp. 63–66. It is the same style of dialogue and, to a certain extent, a similar relationship that were central features of Wang's 1991 novel *I'm Your Dad* discussed later.

44. Obvious early examples are to be found in the 1979 play *The Imposter* (Jiaru wo shi zhende) by Sha Yexin, Li Shoucheng, and Yao Mingde; Wang Jing's scenario "In the Archives of Society" (Zai shehuide dang'anli); and Li Kewei's "The Woman Thief" (Nüzei).

45. Wang Ping, "Wang Shuode ezuoju," p. 100.

46. Yan Jingming, "Wanzhu yu dushide chongtu—lun Wang Shuo xiaoshuode jiazhi xuanze," *Wenxue pinglun*, 1989:6, p. 87.

47. As one outraged reader remarked: "There's a similar tenor here to the 'three emphases' [*san tuchu*] of the 'Gang of Four.' . . . [Wang] flaunts and exaggerates the penises of sexual fiends, the thighs of sluts, the hands of gamblers, and the bellies of gourmets." See Zhang Xiaoping, "Zatan Wang Shuo, Fang Fang deng rende xiaoshuo," *Wenxue ziyoutan*, 1990:2, pp. 38–39.

48. *Xin jingwei xiaoshuo.* See the blurb on the back cover of *Wang Shuo xiequ xiaoshuo xuan.*

49. Li Ke, " 'Liumang wenxue,' xiaoshuo yu ni," *Wenyi pinglun*, 1989:4, pp. 88–89.

50. These novelists included Liu Shaotang, Wang Zengqi, Deng Youmei, Han Shaohua, Chen Jiangong, Hao Ran, and Su Shuyang. For a selection of their works, see Liu Yingnan and Xu Ziqian, eds., *Jingwei xiaoshuo bajia* (Beijing: Wenhua yishu chubanshe, 1989). Liu Xinwu, the author of such works as "The Talisman" (Ruyi) and *The Clock and Drum Towers* (Zhonggulou), was also considered a major author of this "school." In this context, see also Song Yongyi, *Lao She yu Zhongguo wenhua guannian* (Shanghai: Xuelin chubanshe, 1988), p. 111; and the academic studies of Beijing literature by Xu Daoming, *Jingpai wenxuede shijie* (Shanghai: Fudan daxue chubanshe, 1994); and Lü Zhimin, *Hua su wei ya de shijie—jingwei xiaoshuo tezheng lun* (Beijing: Zhongguo heping chubanshe, 1994).

51. Yan Jingming, "Wanzhu yu dushide chongtu," p. 87.

52. Wang Shuo, "Yiban shi huoyan, yiban shi haishui," first published in *Zhuomu niao*, 1986:2, and reprinted in *Xin shiqi zhengming zuopin xuan* (Xi'an: Xibeidaxue chubanshe, 1988), pp. 198 ff. An excerpt from the first half of this story is translated in Barmé and Jaivin, *New Ghosts, Old Dreams*, pp. 227–244.

53. Chen Yishui, "Xing fanzuide jiaokeshu: ping 'Yiban shi huoyan, yiban shi haishui'," in *Xin shiqi zhengming zuopin xuan*, pp. 299, 300, 307.

54. Quoted by the film critic Zhong Chengxiang in an official seminar on *Samsara*. See *Dianying yishu cankao ziliao*, 1989:1 (issue 197), p. 13. At the April 1990 Baoding Conference (see chapter 2, "An Iron Fist in a Velvet Glove"), Zhong reserved particular venom for his attacks on the Wang Shuo films. In early 1927, Mao Zedong rejected claims that the Hunan peasant movement was a *"pizi* movement." See his "Report on

the Hunan Peasant Movement" (Hunan nongmin yundong kaocha baogao), *Mao Zedong xuanji* (Beijing: Renmin chubanshe, 1969), vol. 1, pp. 18, 19, 21.

55. *"xipishi" de "youxi rensheng."*

56. See Zhong in *Dianying yishu cankao ziliao*, p. 13.

57. A good example of this usage can be found in "The Young Worker" (Qinggong) in Zhang Xinxin and Sang Ye's *Beijingren: 100 ge putongrende zishu* (Shanghai: Shanghai wenyi chubanshe, 1986), p. 211.

58. See Fu Min and Gao Aijun, eds., *Beijinghua cihua* (Beijing: Beijing daxue chuaban she, 1986), pp. 234–235; and Xu Shirong, *Beijing tuyu cidian* (Beijing: Beijing chubanshe, 1990), pp. 406–407.

59. See "Lü ao," in *Shujing* (Shanghai: Shanghai guji chuban she, 1987), p. 79.

60. The China of the 1980s and 1990s was not only a paradise for Chinese adventurers. Wu Mingli records the history of a foreign *liumang* in "Yang hunzi," *Zhongguo zhi chun*, 1991:6, pp. 87–90.

61. *ti ren jie nan, ti ren jie men, ti ren shou guo.* See Wang Shuo, "Wanzhu," p. 4.

62. Wang Shuo, "Wanzhu," p. 13.

63. Zhao's personal name, Yaoshun, is made up of the two words for the mythical sage-emperors Yao and Shun. It may also be a reference to Mao's 1958 poem "Sending off the God of Disease" (Song wenshen), in which the chairman spoke of the Chinese people as being "six hundred million Yaos and Shuns."

64. This line is taken from the Confucian philosopher Mencius, see "Jinxin shang" in *Mengzi*, 13A: 9. See *Mengzi*, ed. and trans. Yang Bojun (Beijing: Zhonghua shuju, 1984), p. 304.

65. Wang Shuo, "Wanzhu," p. 69.

66. Ibid., p. 59.

67. Yan Jingming, "Wanzhu yu dushide chongtu," p. 90. A similar but even more virulent attack on "The Operators" was published in *Zhongliu*, the post–June 1989 conservative literary journal mentioned in chapter 2, "An Iron Fist in a Velvet Glove." See Yu Li, " 'Pizi wenyi' yu 'zilianzhuyi'," *Zhongliu*, 1990:5, pp. 44–45.

68. Dai Jinhua, "Yishixingtai, Wang Shuo, 1988," *Zhongguo dianying zhoubao*, 2 March 1989.

69. See Liu Qing, "Wang Shuode 'guiji'," *Wenhui dushu zhoubao*, 29 June 1991.

70. Mi Jiashan's film version of "The Operators" was released in 1989 by the Chinese Film Corporation under the English title *Three T Company*. It became one of the most popular films of the year. See reviews of the film in the Filmmakers' Association restricted-circulation reference booklet, *Dianying yishu cankao ziliao*, 1989:6 (issue 202). After 4 June, *Three T Company* was repeatedly criticized. See, for example, "Quanweide fayan—yifen laizi jiceng dianying guanzhongde diaocha baogao," *Dazhong dianying*, 1990:11, pp. 4–5.

71. Zhang Wei, "Zhengfu liangji xianxiang," *Zhongguo dianying zhoubao*, 2 March 1989. The disco scene does not occur in the original story "The Operators." After the award giving, there is a frantic rush for free beer.

72. See Benjamin L. Liebman, "Reluctant Ruffians: Language, Authority, and Alienation in Wang Shuo's Fiction," senior essay, Yale University, April 1991, p. 7, n. 10.

73. Zhu Dake, "Kongxinde wenxue," *Ranshaode mijin* (Shanghai: Xuelin chubanshe, 1991), p. 98.

74. Wang Shuo, "Yidian zhengjing meiyou," pp. 110–140.

75. Ibid., p. 126. Fang Yan, incidentally, is not in his eighties but is a young man.

76. Another memorable episode in Wang's fiction dealing with self-important university students can be found in "Hot and Cold, Measure for Measure," pp. 206–208. When one of the *liumang* protagonists is told by a woman university student to listen quietly to a lecture on morality and patriotism, he turns on her and says: "Just look at you! . . . All this fuckin' education and you've still got shit for brains. What a joke" (p. 207).

77. The term used in Chinese is *jingying*, the select group of intellectual opinion makers who were supposedly the leading cultural force in late 1980s' China. After 4 June 1989, they were accused en masse of collusion with foreign powers plotting to overthrow Communist Party rule.

78. Wang Shuo, "Yidian zhengjing meiyou," p. 126.

79. For a comment on this, see Mu Gong, "Wang Shuo—zhishifenzi wenhuade bishizhe," *Zhongshan*, 1991:1, p. 152.

80. Wang Shuo, "Yidian zhengjing meiyou," p. 127.

81. Ibid., p. 127.

82. Jin Sheng, " 'Wan wenxue' de shizhi jiqi weihai," *Guangming ribao*, 5 August 1990.

83. Liu Runwei, "Wenyijiade shehui zerengan," *Renmin ribao*, 29 May 1990. A similar line of thinking informed Kui Zeng's " 'Wan wenxue': meiyou chuxide ezuoju," *Zhongliu*, 1990:5, pp. 41–43.

84. Yang Shu, "Wang Shuo: zai 'zhenren' yu xieduzhe zhi jian," *Wenxue bao*, 8 February 1990.

85. Zuo Shula, "Buru 'liu' zide qile," p. 135.

86. He Xin, "Dui Zhao wende jidian dafu," in his *Yishu xianxiangde fuhao—wenhuaxue chanshi* (Beijing: Renmin wenxue chubanshe, 1987), pp. 162–163.

87. Xu Xing, "Wuzhuti bianzou," *Renmin wenxue*, 1985:7, pp. 29–37. Excerpts from Xu's story are translated in Barmé and Jaivin, *New Ghosts, Old Dreams*, pp. 256–259.

88. For this episode in the career of Liu Ling, see the "Rongzhi" chapter in Liu Yiqing's fifth-century anthology of anecdotes, *Shishuo xinyu* (Shanghai: Shanghai guji chubanshe, 1982), vol. 1, p. 29.

89. Ji Gong, or Ji Dian, is the Southern Song dynasty hero of a popular romance, the *Life of Master Ji* (Ji Gong zhuan), written by Guo Xiaoting of the Qing dynasty. The carousing monk was famous for helping the poor and deriding officialdom. The Master Ji cult saw a mass popular revival in the 1980s with new publications and a major television series devoted to his adventures. He is honored at the Hupao Temple in Hangzhou.

90. He Xin, "Dangdai wenxuezhongde huangmiugan yu duoyuzhe," *Dushu*, 1985:11, p. 11. See also He Xin, "A Word of Advice to the Politburo," trans. Geremie Barmé, pp. 51–52 and n. 9.

91. He Xin, "Gudu yu tiaozhan, 3: zai heishehuide bianyuanqu," *Zixue zazhi*, 1989:3, pp. 15–22.

92. The term "hippy," *xipishi*, is applied with considerable abandon by Chinese writers when referring to the range of personality traits associated with either the bourgeois West or the quirky individualism of traditional China. More will be said about this later. Another popular term used by mainland critics when discussing Wang's works is "the beat generation," *kuadiaode yidai*.

93. Liu Xiaobo, "Yizhong xinde shenmei sichao—cong Xu Xing, Chen Cun, Liu Suo-lade sanbu zuopin tanqi," *Wenxue pinglun*, 1986:3, p. 36. After 1985, Xu Xing contin-ued to write but to little critical acclaim. He went into voluntary exile after 4 June 1989 and returned to China from Germany in 1993 to dabble in various media ven-tures. Chen Cun became a mainstream official novelist, and in the late 1980s, Liu Suola went to live in London, where she enjoyed a career as a singer and performer. In the mid-1990s, she devoted her energy to developing a strain of hybrid music she called "Chinese blues," *landiao*, which she promoted in the mainland in 1996. Both Xu and Liu became editorial committee members of the revived *Today* literary jour-nal in 1990.

94. See Barmé and Jaivin, "Portraits of Individualists," in *New Ghosts, Old Dreams*, pp. 191–206.

95. Ma Jian achieved considerable notoriety in 1987 with the publication of his voyeuris-tic story "Liangchu nide shetai huo kongkong dangdang," *Renmin wenxue*, 1987:1–2, translated as "Stick out Your Furry Tongue, or Fuck All," in Geremie Barmé and John Minford, eds., *Seeds of Fire: Chinese Voices of Conscience* (Hong Kong: Far Eastern Economic Review, 1986), 2nd ed. (New York: Hill & Wang, 1988), pp. 438–447. Liu Yiran, a PLA novelist, created a furor with his 1988 story "Rock 'n' roll Youth" (Yaogun qingnian), which was attacked by one incensed critic for its use of excessively foul lan-guage. See Han Wuxi, "Guoma jihui," *Wenxue ziyoutan*, 1989:4, p. 89. For a partial translation of Liu's story, see "Rocking Tiananmen" in Barmé and Jaivin, *New Ghosts, Old Dreams*, pp. 5–22.

96. See Sha Tan, "Pizi yishi yu guizu yishi," *Wenxue ziyoutan*, 1990:2, pp. 50–53.

97. Zuo Shula, "Buru 'liu' zide qile," p. 136.

98. Kai Fangyi, "Ge zhu yinyang," *Qingchun*, 1987:2, pp. 29–38.

99. Qu Yanbin comments on the connection in his *A History of Chinese Beggars* (Zhong-guo qigai shi), p. 235, where he says that from the first chronicles of knights-errant, "Biographies of Knights-errant" (Youxia liezhuan), ch. 124 of Sima Qian's *Historical Records* (Shiji), through descriptions of the adventures of *wuxia, youxia*, and *jianghu xiake*, there is no lack of evidence that they often displayed what he calls "the tricks of wandering beggars," *liugai jiliang*. He also equates this to the *liumang* mentality.

100. See James J. Y. Liu, *The Chinese Knight-Errant* (London: Routledge & Kegan Paul, 1967), pp. 86–99.

101. Ibid., pp. 4–7. Also see Yang Xing'an, "Woguo haoxia jingshende tese," *Mingbao yuekan*, 1991:1, pp. 113–117. Lin Yutang was a great admirer of what he called the spi-rit of the "vagabond," the free individual. The vagabonds he praised were at the cul-

tivated, literati end of the spectrum of *liumang*. In this context, see Lin's comments on the Ming writer Tu Long's *Travels of Mingliaozi*, in Lin Yutang's *The Importance of Living* (London: Heinemann, 1962), pp. 320–321.

102. *Wuhu jiang*, directed by Zheng Xinyan and Fu Qi.

103. Zhang Huaxun's debut kungfu film exploited both the massive carved Buddha at Le-shan in Sichuan and the box-office popularity of the actress Liu Xiaoqing, who plays a female warrior (*nüxia*) pitted against an unintentionally comic masked foe. In the following decade, more than one hundred martial arts films were made on the main-land (including coproductions with Hong Kong). See Yang Zhiyong, "Xinshiqi shi-nian wuxiapiande liubian," *Yishu guangjing*, 1991:3, p. 34.

104. *Shaolin Temple* (Shaolin si) was coproduced with a mainland-controlled film stu-dio in Hong Kong and made by Zhang Xinyan, the codirector of *Treasure Island*. There was a spate of Shaolin films in Hong Kong during the mid-1970s, and it was these that now inspired mainland directors. See Sek Kei, "The Development of 'Martial Arts' in Hong Kong Cinema," in *A Study of the Hong Kong Martial Arts Film, the 4th Hong Kong International Film Festival* (Hong Kong: Urban Council, 1980), p. 19. Similarly, access to the real Shaolin Temple in Henan, or, rather, what remained of it, was also a lure to Hong Kong filmmakers. The attraction of the made-to-order mainland actor Jet Lee was that he was a professional martial arts athlete and handsome to boot. He was promoted in the hope that he would eclipse local Hong Kong kungfu stars. The film *Shaolin Temple* inspired numerous film and literary imitations.

105. Jin Yong was the pen name of Louis Cha, or Zha Liangyong, former editor of *Ming Pao*.

106. Other popular modern martial arts novelists are Gu Long, Liang Yusheng, Wen Ruian, and Ni Kuang. In the late 1970s, Shaw Brothers made screen versions of a number of Jin Yong's most famous novels, and the Hong Kong woman director Ann Hui (Xu Anhua) made a two-part film of Jin's *Revenge of the Book and the Sword* (Shu jian enchou lu) in the mainland, using the scenery of Hangzhou and Xinjiang. The genre has been more readily adapted to lengthy television serials. For details of Jin Yong's career, see John Minford, translator's introduction to "The Deer and the Caul-dron—The Adventures of a Chinese Trickster," *East Asian History*, no. 5, June 1993, pp. 1–14.

107. Yang Zhiyong, "Xinshiqi shinian wuxiapiande liubian," p. 34.

108. Wang Zheng, "Shusheng zhi qing jiyu shu—zhishijie wuxia xiaoshuomi xintai chutan," *Renmin ribao*, 3 March 1989.

109. Ibid.

110. Ibid.

111. Ibid.

112. Chen Pingyuan, a literary historian who studied kungfu literature, hinted that the post–4 June situation in China was even more conducive to the appeal of escapist martial arts fiction among students and intellectuals. See Chen Pingyuan, "Ye yu wuxia xiaoshuo jieyuan," *Dushu*, 1991:4, pp. 58–61.

113. Ibid., p. 58.

114. Chen Pingyuan, "Wuxia xiaoshuo, dazhong qianyishi ji qita: huiying Zheng Shusen xiansheng," *Ershiyi shiji*, no. 5, June 1991, pp. 157–158.

115. Zhou Zuoren, "Pojiaogu," p. 23.

116. For a translation of this novel, see Louis Cha, *The Deer & the Cauldron*, ed. and trans. John Minford, 3 vols. (Hong Kong: Oxford University Press, 1997–1998). That is not to say that some of Jin's more traditional heroes never engage in *liumang* antics. See, for example, the *liumang* verbal encounter between Linghu Chong and the loutish Tian Boguang in the "Huiyan Pavilion" episode of *The Smiling, Proud Wanderer*. Jin Yong, *Xiaoao jianghu*, rev. ed. (Xianggang: Minghe she, 1984), pp. 130–151.

117. In "The Operators" (pp. 66–67), Yu Guan berates Ma Qing for having taught a young woman camp follower all the dirty slang he knows, or what he calls all his "martial arts," *wuyi*.

118. They are the protagonists of "The Operators," *Living Dangerously*, "An Attitude," and, to a certain extent, *No Man's Land*.

119. The pre-Qin philosopher Han Feizi includes "those who carry swords," *daijianzhe*, in his list of the "five poisons," *wudu*, that inculcate disorder. His most often quoted comment on the knight-errant is "The *xia* breaks taboos by fighting" (*xia yi wu fan jin*). See "Wudu" in *Han Feizi* (Shanghai: Shanghai guji chubanshe, 1989), p. 155.

120. *kan* is a popular word in Beijing slang, meaning "to speak without reservation," "to exaggerate," "to tell tales," "to talk on at great length," or "to enjoy hearing the sound of your own voice," or simply "to bullshit." It is used in expressions like *kan dashan*, literally "to talk a great mountain," and *kan gushi*, "to come out with a tall tale." Big talkers, or bullshit artists, are called *kanye*, which is also a popular term for cultural critics. There is some dispute as to the origin of the term. One interpretation is that it comes from *kan*, "to cut," and another holds that it is from the classical expression *kankan er tan*, "to speak with fervor and assurance." Regarding this disputation, see Sang Ye, "Guanyu 'Zai hua yuci'—he Wang Meng xiansheng taigang," *Dushu*, 1991:2, p. 72. In the late 1980s, a popular rhyming saying summed up the universality of *kan* in the mainland: "[In China there are] ten hundred million people, nine hundred million [spend their time] *kan*, leaving one hundred million to do the real work," *shiyi renmin jiuyi kan, haiyou yiyi zai fazhan*.

121. Wang Shuo, "Fuchu haimian," p. 283. Earlier in the story, Shi Ba remarks that as a youth, he wanted to be a dancer like his prospective girlfriend Yu Jing, but the only kungfu or skill he really ever practiced was *zuipizi gongfu*, that of a quick tongue (p. 258). The word *kan*, "to talk," is often written with a character meaning "to chop" or "cut with a sharp instrument." Shi Ba uses the expression "dig away at a big mountain," or *kan dashan*. This is a play on both the classical story of the Foolish Old Man who moved the mountains through his unstinting daily labors and that of his descendants (see the "Tang wen" chapter in the pre-Qin philosophical text *Liezi*) and Mao Zedong's speech "The Foolish Old Man Who Removed the Mountains," in which Mao compared the Communist spirit with that of the indomitable old man of legend.

122. When reading the exchanges between some of Wang's heroes and intellectuals (like Zhao Yaoshun in "The Operators"), the classical expression *she zhan qun ru*, literal-

ly "defeating the amassed scholars with one's tongue," comes to mind. This saying was originally used to describe Zhuge Liang, the wily talker and strategist of the Three Kingdoms period, *Zhuge Liang she zhan qun ru.*

123. Wang's *Living Dangerously,* in which the game is murder, is an ideal example of tricksters at work.

124. This is obvious in the case of Yu Guan in "The Operators." His father is described as being surrounded by all the paraphernalia of a retired "revolutionary cadre." See Wang Shuo, "Wanzhu," pp. 63 ff. Wang is the descendant of Manchu bannermen, *qiren,* whose decadent lifestyle and unique literature were a feature of late-Qing China. See Teng Shaozhen, *Qingdai baqi zidi* (Beijing: Zhongguo huaqiao chuban gongsi, 1989), pp. 251–286. Although somewhat anachronistic, the term *gongzige'r,* "playboy," could be applied to some of Wang's *liumang* heroes.

125. For some examples from 1988–1989, see Yu Jiwen, "Beijing xin yaogun," *Jiushi niandai yuekan,* 1989:6, p. 104. These were shoddy recordings of often scurrilous songs by *pengchong* (literally "studio insects") produced for a fast buck. Some musicians disassociated themselves from this "lowbrow" material, as they aspired to the more formal, mainstream style of Cui Jian.

126. See Wang Shuo, *Wande jiu shi xin tiao,* originally published in *Wenxue siji (qiu zhi juan),* 1988:1, pp. 174–255, and later produced as a book (Beijing: Zuojia chubanshe, 1989). For this episode, which revolves around a few lines of Cui Jian's song "Nothing to My Name," see p. 141. For an English version of this book, see Wang Shuo, *Playing for Thrills,* trans. Howard Goldblatt (New York: Morrow, 1997).

127. Between 1991 and 1993, Li Xianting (Hu Cun) wrote about a number of younger artists throughout China whose works revealed what he called a *"popi* style humor." See the section "Export, Exploit, Expropriate" in chapter 8, "Artful Marketing." *Bopi* is a classical equivalent of *liumang* used in late-imperial vernacular novels like *The Water Margin* (see, for example chapter 12 of this book regarding the fate of the blustering *popi* Niu Er), *The Scholars,* and *The Story of the Stone.*

128. See Wei He, "Beijing 'mangliu' yishujia yinxiang," *Zhongguo meishubao,* 31 October 1988. The "floating artists" were part of the *liumang* cultural scene of the capital who, with the help of diplomats, journalists, overseas Chinese, and "foreign experts," have brought segments of the *liumang* subculture into direct contact with the outside world. See also Sang Ye, "Fringe-Dwellers: Down and out in the Yuan Ming Yuan Artists' Village," trans. Geremie R. Barmé, *Art AsiaPacfic,* no. 15, June 1997, pp. 74–77.

129. Bai Hua, one of the protagonists in the poet Bei Dao's early novel *Waves* is a typical, modern *liumang* figure, a heroic hobo with a touch of the knight-errant. See excerpts from the novel translated by Susette Cooke in *Trees on the Mountain: An Anthology of New Chinese Writing,* ed. John Minford and Stephen C. Soong (Hong Kong: Chinese University Press, 1984), pp. 134–135, 139–142 ff.

130. Xu Shirong, *Beijing tuyu cidian,* p. 145.

131. Fu Min and Gao Aijun, *Beijinghua cidian,* p. 90.

132. Feng Lianhui et al., eds., *Jingshen wenming cishu* (Beijing: Zhongguo zhanwang chubanshe, 1986), p. 735.

133. Ibid.

134. Wu Huan was a novelist turned screenwriter. For an example of his early satirical writing, see his "An Urbling Spot" in Barmé and Minford, *Seeds of Fire*, pp. 103–104.

135. Another writer who employed this language was Zhong Jieying, a stodgy middle-aged novelist who was the first to use the term *gemen'r* in 1987 in a hit mainstream play, Gemen'r *on the Make* (Gemen'r zheteng ji).

136. For an example of a similar phenomenon in the Soviet Union, see Brian Cooper, "Russian Underworld Slang and Its Diffusion into the Standard Language," *Australian Slavonic and East European Studies* 3 (2) (1989), pp. 61–89.

137. Li You, "Lun 'gemen'r'," *Beijing wenxue*, 1987:11, pp. 69–70.

138. C. T. Hsia, "Comparative Approaches to *Water Margin*," in *Yearbook of Comparative and General Literature*, no. 11 (Bloomington: Indiana University Press, 1962), pp. 121–128; W. J. F. Jenner, *The Tyranny of History: The Roots of China's Crisis* (Harmondsworth, Middlesex: Penguin Books, 1994), pp. 205–208; and W. J. F. Jenner, "A Knife in My Ribs for a Mate: Reflections on Another Chinese Tradition," paper delivered at the Fifty-Fourth George Ernest Morrison Lecture in Ethnology, 1993, Canberra, Australian National University, 1995, published as "Tough Guys, Mateship and Honour: Another Chinese Tradition," *East Asian History*, no. 12, December 1996, pp. 1–34. See also Sa Mengwu, *Shuihuzhuan yu Zhongguo shehui*, pp. 3–12; and Yang Xing'an, "Woguo haoxia jingshende tese," pp. 113–117, where he quotes Sa.

139. Lao Gui, *Xuese huanghun* (Beijing: Gongren chubanshe, 1987), or for the English version, see Ma Bo, *Blood Red Sunset: A Memoir of the Chinese Cultural Revolution*, trans. Howard Goldblatt (New York: Viking Press, 1995); and Chen Pingyuan, "Wuxia xiaoshuo, dazhong qianyishi ji qita," pp. 155–157.

140. From the editorial note above the table of contents in *Wenxue siji*.

141. Benjamin L. Liebman discusses this complex novel in "Reluctant Ruffians," pp. 30–60. The last section of *Living Dangerously* follows the *liumang* degradation of a group of *gemen'r* fresh out of the army (pp. 184–242).

142. Wang Shuo, *Wan'rde jiushi xintiao*, p. 218.

143. Wang Shuo, "Yidian zhengjing meiyou," p. 133.

144. Ibid., p. 134.

145. Ibid.

146. Zhou Zuoren, "Pojiaogu," p. 23.

147. Yang Jiang, the Chinese translator of *La Vide de Lazarillo de Tormes*, the first picaresque novel, entitled her translation simply *xiao laizi*, "little scabby one." She was making a reference to the scabious Lazarus of The Gospel According to St. Luke in the New Testament, from whom the hero of the Spanish novel got his name. In discussing her translation, Yang said that "by using the name *xiao laizi*, I did not mean to say he was scabby. The term simply refers to any *liumang* or ruffian." See Yang Jiang, "Jieshao *Xiao laizi*," in her *Guanyu xiaoshuo* (Beijing: Sanlian shudian, 1986), p. 103.

148. Wang Shuo, *Qianwan bie ba wo dang ren*, serialized in the Nanjing literary bimonthly *Zhongshan*, 1989, issues 4–6 (September–December), pp. 4–37, 125–148, and 4–46, respectively.

149. Stuart Miller, *The Picaresque Novel* (Cleveland: Case Western Reserve University Press, 1967), p. 10.

150. Ibid., p. 56.

151. Ibid., pp. 133–134.

152. See the editorial page of *Zhongshan*, 1989:4.

153. Wang Shuo, "Yidian zhengjing meiyou," p. 133. This exchange with foreign "China experts" led to Fang Yan's calling them *shabi* (stupid cunts) to their faces.

154. Ibid.

155. For example, Wang Shuo, "Xiangpi ren," p. 42.

156. For example, Situ Qiao and Ruan Lin's grotesque attempts at *qigong* sublimation in Wang Shuo's story "The Idiots" (Chiren). See *Wang Shuo xiequ xiaoshuo xuan*, pp. 201–203.

157. Wang Shuo, *Qianwan bie ba wo dang ren*, in *Zhongshan*, 1989:4, p. 6.

158. Ibid., p. 7.

159. Bruce Lee's films, for example, feature the kungfu master pummeling sly foreigners. A number of the Tianjin writer Feng Jicai's novellas, like *Magic Fists* (Shenquan) and *Magic Queue* (Shenbian), deal with similar subjects. The film version of *Magic Queue*, for instance, ends with the kungfu master turned Boxer rebel using his whip-like pigtail to flagellate the foreign invaders. Similarly, Feng's "Tianjin Anecdotes" (Tianjin yishi) tell of a Chinese soccer team that succeeds in beating its foreign opponents only when it resorts to the martial arts.

160. Wang Shuo, *Qianwan bie ba wo dang ren*, *Zhongshan*, 1989:4, p. 27.

161. Ibid., pp. 30–33.

162. Ibid., pp. 8, 22.

163. See Wang, *Qianwan bie ba wo dang ren*, *Zhongshan*, 1989:6, pp. 12–13. From the mid-1980s, critics like Liu Xiaobo repeatedly railed against the "collective impotence," *jiti yangwei*, of the Han Chinese. Despite—or, rather, because of— this anxiety, there was a common emphasis on the "tough guy," *ying hanzi* or *nanzihan*, hero in 1980s Chinese fiction and increasingly in film (for example, Jiang Wen's character in Zhang Yimou's *Red Sorghum*). See Cui Wenxuan, *Zhongguo bashi niandai wenxue xianxiang yanjiu* (Beijing: Beijing daxue chubanshe, 1988), pp. 251–267; and Kam Louie, "The Macho Eunuch: The Politics of Masculinity in Jia Pingwa's 'Human Extremities'," *Modern China* 17 (2), April 1991, pp. 163–187.

164. Tang Guotao is a name that brings to mind the early Communist Zhang Guotao, a "splittist" party leader of the 1930s excoriated by Mao Zedong for undermining the revolution.

165. See, for example, Wang Shuo's short story "Damned If You Don't" (Wangran bu gong), *Zhuomu niao*, 1987:1, pp. 4–28, one of a series of "detective Shan Liren" stories. The interrogation of the murder suspect in this story, his written account of his actions on the night of the murder and the evidence of four of his former lovers, is a keenly observed study of the *liumang* under pressure.

166. For these episodes, see Wang Shuo, *Qianwan bie ba wo dang ren*, in *Zhongshan*, 1989:4, pp. 22–23, 23–24, 26–27; 1989:5, pp. 127–128, 133–134, 145–146; 1989:6, pp. 35, 43.

In a review of Alexander Zinoviev's *The Radiant Future*, Clive James makes a number of interesting remarks about the nature of Zinoviev's use of satire in both this novel and *The Yawning Heights*, which he identifies with the postrevolutionary humorous tradition of Soviet satire as found in Zamyatin's *We*. "In this satirical tradition," James says, "the true state of affairs is found to be already so exaggerated that its enormity can be conveyed only by analysis. Rather than to create a fantasy, the main effort is to understand a fantasy that is already there." Clive James, *From the Land of Shadows* (London: Picador, 1982), p. 271. In 1983, the Chinese playwright Gao Xingjian commented that one of the reasons the theater of the absurd attracted so little attention in China at that time was that real life was far more bizarre than anything that could be put on the stage.

167. Wang Shuo, *Qianwan bie ba wo dang ren*, in *Zhongshan*, 1989:6, p. 43.

168. Ibid., pp. 43–46.

169. An obvious example is the work of the Shanghai writer Chen Cun. See the quotation from Chen given by Liu Xiaobo in "Yizhong xinde shenmei sichao," p. 35.

170. Wang Shuo, *Qianwan bie ba wo dang ren*, in *Zhongshan*, 1989:6, p. 41. A full translation of the letter can be found in Geremie R. Barmé, *Shades of Mao: The Posthumous Cult of the Great Leader* (Armonk, N.Y.: Sharpe, 1996), pp. 224–227.

171. See, for example, "Guanyu 'Wang Shuo dianying' de taolun," *Wenhui bao* (Shanghai), 3 April 1990. This article contains excerpts from a discussion attended by an assortment of party members and workers. Only three of the eleven speakers make positive comments on the films.

172. See Wang Shuo, *Wo shi ni baba*, in *Shouhuo*, 1991:3, pp. 116–208.

173. This is illustrated by an incident in which Ma Rui corrects the pronunciation of his politics teacher at school. The teacher is outraged at his insolence, and although his father is secretly sympathetic, Ma Linsheng beats the boy and forces him to hand in a fawning self-criticism that he writes for him. See Wang Shuo, *Wo shi ni baba*, pp. 127–136.

174. Ibid., pp. 142 ff. The psychological complexities and fluid nature of the relationship are "flagged" by Wang's dexterous use of the second-person pronoun *you* in its plain and respectful forms (*ni* and *nin*).

175. Ibid., pp. 174 ff. Ma Lingsheng finally decides to give his son a lecture on the art of survival and criticizes him for all the martial arts novels and love stories he reads. The individual code of honor of the kungfu novel is particularly dangerous, the father says, "If you're in trouble, you should rely on the [party] organization. After all, what are the police there for? You might train yourself so you'll be able to solve all your own problems, but then what's going to happen to all the fathers, mothers, and teachers? If you read too much of this stuff, you'll end up with no respect for anyone." The speech is typical of Wang's parody of traditional Chinese moral preaching and party jargon. Ma Linsheng concludes with a reworked quotation from Chairman Mao: "It is not hard for a person to do a little good; the real difficulty is being good for your whole life—the key is always to keep your tail between your legs and act properly [*zuoren*]." See Wang Shuo, *Wo shi ni babao*, p. 180.

176. Part of the story takes place around the time of the September 1990 Asian Games held

in Beijing. Since the authorities feared there would be popular unrest during this important post–Beijing massacre public relations exercise, it was a period of considerable political tension. Wang hints at the state of near martial law by depicting the city as being in a state of unbridled mass delirium (pp. 147–148, 150, 187). He has Ma Linsheng get drunk and throw up at the base of a mechanical Panda Panpan, the symbol of the games (p. 155) and gives chilling details of the excessive police presence throughout Beijing both before and during the games (pp. 150–153, 196).

177. See the editorial note on the front page of *Wenhui dushu zhoubao*, 22 June 1991.

178. Wang Shuo, *Wo shi ni baba*, p. 208. See also the discussion on the novel in Su Mang, "Cong 'fuqin' dao 'baba'—du Wang Shuo xinzuo *Wo shi ni baba*," *Wenhui dushu zhoubao*, 29 June 1991; and Zheng Yiwen, "Yizhong mishi—ye du Wang Shuo xiaoshuo *Wo shi ni baba*," *Wenhui dushu zhoubao*, 13 July 1991.

179. Wang Shuo, "Wode xiaoshuo," *Renmin wenxue*, 1989:3, p. 108.

180. Wang Shuo, *Wang Shuo wenji*, 4 vols., ed. Sun Bo and Du Jianye (Beijing: Huayi chubanshe, 1992).

181. Zhu Dake, "Kongxinde wenxue," p. 97.

182. For a description of this group, see Ma Weidu, Liu Yiran, Zhu Xiaoping, and Wu Bin, "'Haima' renwu sumiao," *Zhongguo dianying zhoubao*, 30 March 1989; and Ge Xiaogang, "Wei Dongsheng jianying," *Zhongguo dianying zhoubao*, 20 April 1989. In 1991, some members of the group invested in the Seahorse Club, Haima julebu, a karaoke restaurant in Dongsi shitiao in central Beijing.

CHAPTER 5

1. See "Dierdai ren ru shi shuo: 'Women bing bushi huisede'," *Beijing qingnian bao*, 1 January 1991. This "second generation" was spoken of by one author as the "third generation" (those ranging in age from thirty-two to forty-seven). See Yang Fan, *Gongheguode disandai* (Chengdu: Sichuan renmin chubanshe, 1991).

2. This is not to overlook the significance of repeated efforts to do away with the tide of pornography during the 1990s. According to official Ministry of Culture statistics (an unreliable source of hard facts at the best of times), the 1991 winter-to-spring purge of pornography led to the banning of nearly 7 million illegal publications, 3,000 pornographic works, 1,300 "reactionary books" and periodicals, and more than 1 million illicit calendars. See the report "'Saohuang' chengguo leilei," *Wenhui dushu zhoubao*, 28 December 1991. "Pornographic culture," *huangse wenhua*, was regarded as resulting from the ideological laxity of the 1980s. Due to bourgeois liberalization, the "mosquitoes and flies" of foreign corrupting ideas and lifestyles had been able to penetrate China through the "open door" that was part of the economic reform process. In 1989, Party Central called for the elimination of "yellow culture" and the "six pestilences." For details of the 1990s' purges, see Tao Qingliang, *Saohuang—shenshengde shiming* (Beijing: Zhonggong zhongyang dangxiao chubanshe, 1992), pp. 1–2. The six pestilences were (1) prostitution; (2) the production, sale, and distribution of pornography; (3) trade in women and children; (4) the production, consumption, and sale

of drugs; (5) gambling; and (6) the exploitation of feudal superstition with the aim of extortion. See "Gonganbu yinfa 'Guanyu zai quanguo kaizhan saochu maiyin piaochang deng "liuhai" tongyi xingdongde fang'an' de tongzhi," 21 November 1989, reprinted in Zhonggong Fujian shengwei zhengfa weiyuanhui and Zhonggong Fujian shengwei zhengce yanjiushi, eds., *Shehui zhi'an zonghe zhili zhengce fagui huibian*, restricted circulation (Beijing: Qunzhong chubanshe, 1992), pp. 145–149.

3.   There was talk of *saohui*—literally "eliminating gray," as in "gray culture," *huise wenhua*, and "gray attitudes," *huise qingxu*. See, for example, Zheng Tong, " 'Huang' ji 'hei,' 'bai,' 'hui'," in *Fang "zuo" beiwanglu*, Zhao Shilin, ed. (Taiyuan: Shuhai chubanshe, 1992), p. 336.

4.   Gayle Durham, "Political Communication and Dissent in the Soviet Union," in *Dissent in the U.S.S.R.*, Rudolf L. Tükés (Baltimore: Johns Hopkins University Press, 1975), p. 257.

5.   Officially called *Huiban jin Jing*. See Xu Chengbei, " 'Hongdeng ji' xiemu suixiang," *Wenyi bao*, 9 March 1991.

6.   See Jianying Zha, *China Pop: How Soap Operas, Tabloids, and Bestsellers Are Transforming a Culture* (New York: New Press, 1995), pp. 25 ff. The term *feizaoju* or *zaoju* is the preferred translation of the English "soap opera" used in Hong Kong and Taiwan. On the mainland, however, common terms are *dianshiju, lianxuju, xilieju, shineiju, qingjieju*, and even *qingjing xiju*. Numerous television series have been produced in China since the early 1980s. For some details of these earlier series, see Nie Dajiang's speech, " 'Kewang' de jiji yiyi," *Wenyi bao*, 5 January 1991; and Zhong Yibing et al., eds., *Zhongguo dianshi yishu fazhan shi* (Hangzhou: Zhejiang renmin chubanshe, 1994), pp. 46–146. American (including Latin American), Hong Kong, and Taiwan soaps had been screened in China for some years and directly influenced the style of mainland soap operas and informed popular taste.

7.   For some details of the *Aspirations* craze, see Zhang Weiguo, " 'Kewang' chongjibo," *Beijing qingnian bao*, 8 January 1991; Zhang Weiguo, *"Kewang" qiandong yiwan renxin* (Beijing: Renmin ribao chubanshe, 1991); and " 'Kewang' guanzhongde zhongzhong xintai," *Beijing qingnian bao*, 11 January 1991; and Diandian, "Jingzheng yu youhuan," *Beijing qingnian bao*, 22 February 1991. Publishers and editors were quick to exploit the popularity of the series, leading to a flurry of instant books. Magazine and newspaper editors hastily organized special forums and readers' discussions of the series. Two of the scriptwriters of *Aspirations* even produced a "quickie" novelized version; see Zheng Wanlong and Li Xiaoming, *Kewang* (Beijing: Shiyue chubanshe, 1991).

8.   In a rare moment of candor, the saintly Liu Huifang (constantly described in traditional terms as a "virtuous wife and good mother," *xianqi liangmu*) reveals to Song Dacheng that the reason she is obsessed with Xiaofang is that as a failure in her own life (she never went to university, etc.), she wants to make the child a success and through her realize her own frustrated ambitions (see *Aspirations*, episode 16). Her sacrifice is at heart selfish and destructive. This is a point made by one reader in response to the *Chinese Women's News* (Zhongguo funü bao) debate on the series. See

Ni Yongsheng's comments "Zongqing ru zonghuo," in "Tade hunyin weishenme hui shibai?" *Zhongguo funü bao*, 8 February 1991. See also Yang Ping, "Liu Huifang— dang buzhude ganjue: tantan you xie ren ganma gen Huifang guo buqu," *Zhongguo funü bao*, 4 January 1991.

9. Wang Yaru wields authority in her father's absence in the first twenty episodes; when he returns, she becomes impuissant. Mother Liu is the matriarch who can rule because of the death of her husband. The weak and indecisive Song Dacheng is married to the feisty Xu Yuejuan, who is effectively "castrated" because she is unable to have children; her success as an entrepreneur is thus belittled.

10. Zheng Wanlong's comment in " 'Kewang' cehuaren tan 'Kewang'," in *"Kewang" zhi mi*, ed. Xing Hua (Beijing: Xinhua chubanshe, 1991), p. 20.

11. Sandra Tsing Loh, *Depth Takes a Holiday: Essays from Lesser Los Angeles* (New York: Riverhead Books, 1996), pp. 211–212.

12. In April 1990, Li lectured the paper's editors on the need for mild propaganda that would "mollify popular sentiment"—*lishun rende qingxu*—rather than making people flee in disgust. See "Li Ruihuan tan wending dangqian daju," *Yangcheng wanbao*, 30 April 1990.

13. *Guangming ribao*, 9 January 1991.

14. National nihilism, *minzu xuwuzhuyi*, had become one of China's great cultural bugbears. Anything that attempted a critical reappraisal of traditional culture, its values, or the national character of the Chinese could, if it failed to conform with the prevalent party orthodoxy, be labeled as "national nihilism," a form of cultural treason. For a detailed exposition in favor of this approach, see Gong Shuduo, Liu Guisheng, and Wang Junyi, eds., *Minzu wenhua xuwuzhuyi pingxi* (Beijing: Zhongguo renmin daxue chubanshe, 1990).

15. " 'Kewang' cehuaren tan 'Kewang'," in *"Kewang" zhi mi*, p. 24. In late 1990, Wang was hopeful of writing the script for a film sequel to *Aspirations*. He envisaged Liu Huifang's becoming entangled with an intellectual/*liumang* character who would inspire love and disgust in equal parts. But the director of the proposed film abandoned the project, fearful that neither the authorities nor the "grannies of Beijing" would tolerate the story.

16. *huise wangguo*. See Huang Shixian, "Huise youhuo: meisu, fuzaode wenhua xintai— Wang Shuo dianying sanlun zhi si," *Zhongguo dianying bao*, 25 July 1989, reprinted in Wang Shuo, *Qingchun wuhui—Wang Shuo yingshi zuopin ji*, pp. 369–373.

17. The others were Zheng Xiaolong, assistant chief of the Beijing Television Art Center, and Li Xiaoming, editorial chief of the same organization. Zheng Wanlong, known for his works of "roots fiction," *xungen wenxue*, was an editor of the *October* (Shiyue) literary bimonthly. After the success of the series, some of the writers fell out over the question of the novelization of the story and its royalties. See Xia He, "Li Xiaoming shi 'Kewang' weiyide bianju ma? Wang Shi, Zheng Xiaonong shuo: bu!"; and Xi Ling, "Wang Shi, Zheng Xiaonong shifou yinggai shu bianju? Li Xiaoming shuo: bu!" *Zhonghua gongshang shibao*, 27 February 1991.

18 " 'Kewang' cehuaren tan 'Kewang'," in *"Kewang" zhi mi*, p. 19.

19. See, for example, Wang Wenying, " 'Kewang' wenhua yiyunde liangmian guan," and Ming Ya, "Huayu yu yinyu" in "Hua shuo 'Kewang'," *Shanghai wenlun*, 1991:2, pp. 10–11 and 13, respectively.

20. Wang Wenying, " 'Kewang' wenhua yiyunde liangmian guan," p. 10.

21. Jin Zhaojun, "Hao ren yi sheng ping'an — 'Kewang' suixiang," *Dangdai wentan bao*, 1991:2, pp. 4–7.

22. Chen Sihe, "Tan 'Kewang' de wenhua yuanxing," in the published accounts of the SASS forum, "Hua shuo 'Kewang'," *Shanghai wenlun*, 1991:2, p. 5.

23. Zhu's comments can be found in " 'Kewang' qishilu," *Wenhui bao*, 17 January 1991. Over the next few years, Zhu became increasingly critical of elite culture and what he perceived as being the failure of intellectuals to oppose the rising tide of commercialization.

24. Wen Yan, " 'Kewang' rede beijing xiaoying," *Beijing qingnian bao*, 11 January 1991.

25. See " 'Kewang' qishilu," *Wenhui bao*, 17 January 1991.

26. Malaqinfu, " 'Kewang' gei rende qishi," *Wenyi bao*, 5 January 1991.

27. Li Shaohong, *Xuese qingchen* (Beijing: Beijing dianying zhipian chang, 1990).

28. See Mu Zi, "Haishi dao shenghuozhong zou yi zou," *Dazhong dianying*, 1991:5, pp. 4–5.

29. Lu Xun made a similar point about the import of the highly popular 1933 film *Flower Sisters* (Zimeihua). See his essay "Fate" (Yunming) in *Lu Xun quanji* (Beijing: Renmin wenxue chubanshe, 1981), vol. 5, pp. 442–443.

30. "Renqing, Zhongguo jingjide yida zainan," *Wenhui dushu zhoubao*, 27 March 1993.

31. Soap operas and period dramas developed apace, with a number of big-budget traditional costume series like *Wu Zetian* and *The Romance of the Three Kingdoms* being added to the earlier modern dramas. See Hao Jian, "Dianshi feizaoju: chuangkou haishi heidong," *Sanlian Shenghuo zhoukan*, 1996:3, pp. 50–51.

32. Nationwide Lei Feng campaigns were launched in 1963, 1977, 1983, and again in 1990. See Beate Geist, "Lei Feng and the 'Lei Fengs of the Eighties' — Models and Modelling in China," *Papers on Far Eastern History*, no. 42, September 1990, pp. 96, 107–108.

33. *Lei Feng jingshen sanyue laile siyue zou.*

34. "Li Ruihuan tan wending dangqian daju." Jiao Yulu was the model for the middle aged. Lai Ning, an adolescent who was incinerated while fighting a forest fire, was an idol held up to teenagers as a paragon. In 1995–1996, the new model cadre who had a special television series devoted to his life was Kong Fansen, a man who had sacrificed his life in service to the Tibetan Autonomous Region.

35. "Shoudu juxing *Jiao Yulu* shouyingshi," Xinhua she, 26 February 1991.

36 See the news item in the Shanghai *Wenhui bao*, 10 February 1991. For official praise of the film, see "Renmin xinzhongde yizuo fengbei — dianying 'Jiao Yulu' zuotanhui jiyao," *Dazhong dianying*, 1991:3, pp. 2–4.

37. This was particularly true in the case of student leaders like Wuer Kaixi, Chai Ling, and Li Lu.

38. Yang Ping was an example of one of these editors who often organized forums in the newspaper that were chauvinistic and highly patriotic but couched in an appealing

reformist-style rhetoric. For some examples of Yang Ping's work, see chapter 10, "To Screw Foreigners Is Patriotic."

39. A five-volume collection of articles from the paper was published in celebration of ten years of the paper's post–Cultural Revolution publication. See *Beijing qingnian bao congshu* (Beijing: Zhongguo chengshi wenhua chubanshe, 1991).

40. See, for example, Li Ren, *Yisi jing tianxia—San Mao zishade qianqian houhou* (Beijing: Zhongguo jiaoyu guangbo chubanshe, 1991), a best-selling instant book available on Chinese bookstalls in January 1991. Also see Gu Jitang, *Pingshuo San Mao* (Beijing: Zhishi chubanshe, 1991). San Mao's popularity among young (generally middle-school age) readers, along with that of the poet Xi Murong, followed earlier crazes for the Taiwan novelist Qiong Yao and the Hong Kong writer Yi Shu. For some details of the San Mao craze up to her death, see Niu Ming, "San Mao sui feng qu," *Beijing qingnian bao*, 18 January 1991. For more on the appeal of the San Mao persona, see Miriam Lang, "San Mao Goes Shopping: Travel and Consumption in a Post-Colonial World," *East Asian History*, no. 10, December 1995, pp. 127–164.

41. Xia Hong, "Jiao Yulu yu San Mao liangju mingyan, ni zuo he xuanze?" *Beijing qingnian bao*, 2 April 1991.

42. San Mao was the name of a raffish homeless boy depicted in the Shanghai artist Zhang Leping's late-1940s cartoons. Chen Ping, a fan of San Mao comics as a child, took her pen name from this character and called Zhang Leping "Daddy" when she met him in 1989.

43. The contrast between revolutionary and reactionary death was made even more explicit in an article published by the magazine *Comedy World* (Xiju shijie) in February 1991, entitled simply "Applause for San Mao's Suicide." See Zhu Jianguo, "Wei San Mao zisha guzhang," *Xiju shijie*, 1991:2, p. 35; and a reader's response in the March issue of the same magazine (p. 64).

44. Xia Hong, "Jiao Yulu yu San Mao liangju mingyan, ni zuo he xuanze?" In Chinese, the word *chore* is *lei*, literally "tired or exhausted."

45. *Beijing qingnian bao*, 2 April 1991.

46. The cartoon series was screened on Chinese television through the early 1990s. In Chinese it is called *Renzhe shengui*.

47. *Beijing qingnian bao*, 2 April 1991.

48. Wang Ronghui, "Bing fei eryuande xuanze," *Beijing qingnian bao*, 23 April 1991.

49. According to the final evaluation of the discussion, more than eight hundred letters were received from readers in eighteen provinces, cities, and autonomous regions throughout China. See Xia Hong, "Muguang yueguo xuanze," *Beijing qingnian bao*, 4 June 1991.

50. The concept of "abstract human value" had been rebuked time and again during the 1980s as a dangerous, bourgeois concept. It was held that there was no such thing as a human value that was not entirely conditioned by class relationships. See Geremie Barmé, "China Blames the West for 'Cultural Pollution'," *National Times* (Sydney), 12–19 January 1984; and Wang Ruoshui, "Writings on Humanism, Alienation and Philosophy," ed. and trans. David Kelly, *Chinese Studies in Philosophy*, Spring 1985.

51. Xia Hong, "Muguang yueguo xuanze."

52. Zhang Qian, "Jiao Yulu yu disidai rende jiazhi xuanze," *Beijing qingnian bao*, 23 April 1991.

53. Xia Hong, "Muguang yueguo xuanze."

54. Ibid.

55. Ibid. See also the final exchange between an editor and an unnamed "scholar" on the subject: Xue Xiao, "Geren yu shehui—ni shike dou zai xuanze liangzhong liyi," *Beijing qingnian bao*, 28 June 1991.

56. Stall owners who sold the shirts, as well as their customers, usually referred to them more colloquially as "[T-shirts] with writing on them," *dai zi'rde [beixin]*.

57. Xian Yi, " 'Wenhuashan' zhi you," *Zhongguo qingnian bao*, 17 July 1991.

58. Rong Ya, "Ruci 'wenhuashan' xianxiang," *Jingji ribao*, 11 July 1991, italics in the original.

59. Xia Hong, " 'Lei' yu 'fan' yinchude sikao—qingchun shi yi ben shenme yangde shu?" *Beijing qingnian bao*, 29 October 1991.

60. See the editorial note to "Jie ling hai xu xi ling ren—'Lei yu fan yinchude sikao' shi ren tan," *Beijing qingnian bao*, 27 December 1991.

61. For examples, see *Beijing qingnian bao*, 1, 15, 22, and 29 November and 10, 13, and 20 December 1991.

62. Zhang Hongmei, "Liu Hulan hui shuo 'lei' he 'fan' ma?" *Beijing qingnian bao*, 29 November 1991.

63. See Beverley Hooper, *Youth in China* (Harmondsworth, Middlesex: Penguin Books, 1985), pp. 161–162.

64. Zhao Tianzhu, "Qing wei 'lei' he 'fan' guzhang," *Beijing qingnian bao*, 29 November 1991.

65. "Jie ling hai xu xi ling ren—'Lei yu fan yinchude sikao' shi ren tan."

66. This observation is based on my discussions with people in their teens and twenties in Beijing and Shanghai during 1991.

67. One of the most painful moments of "Youth Knows No Regrets" (Qingchun wu hui), scripted by Wang Shuo and Wei Ren and directed by Zhou Xiaowen (Xi'an Film Studio, 1991), was a scene during which a family gathers to sing with a karaoke machine at home and attempts to force the son's fiancée to join in. Little wonder that this was the last straw in an already strained relationship.

68. See Dong Qing, "Niannei tuichu 1000 shou dalu kala OK xinzuo," *Beijing qingnian bao*, 26 March 1991.

69. Wang Dongyuan, "Kala OK re Jingcheng," *Beijing qingnian bao*, 11 June 1991.

70. As karaoke machines insinuated their way into the lives of Sydney-siders in Australia, one writer listed possible reasons for their popularity. Karaoke makes you famous (for about three-and-a-half minutes) and gives you the opportunity to perform your favorite music (mushy kitsch); karaoke Heads are defiant Hits and Memories groupies; it makes you sound even better than you do singing in the shower; it is best when drunk; it lets you impersonate pop stars with impunity; it offers an alternative to group therapy and/or head shrinkery; it brings people together; and, it can

initiate liaisons that might never otherwise have occurred. See Jean Norman, "Singing for Your Sushi," Metro supplement of *Sydney Morning Herald*, 14 February 1992.

71. "Zhonghua dajia chang (kala OK) quku zai Jing shoufa," *Zhongguo wenhua bao*, 5 June 1991.

72. See Gu Xiaoming, "Mianxiang renmin dazhong yanjiu zishen guilü," *Wenhui dushu zhoubao*, 9 June 1990.

73. I noted this on Beijing television in October 1991.

74. Sang Ye came to fame with Zhang Xinxin in the 1980s with the publication of a series of Studs Terkel–style interviews. See Zhang Xinxin and Sang Ye, *Chinese Lives: An Oral History of Contemporary China*, ed. W. J. F. Jenner and Delia Davin (New York: Pantheon Books, 1987).

75. Sang Ye, "Mudu Beijing ciwenhua," *Kaifang zazhi*, 1991:8, p. 19.

76. Sang Ye, "Zai Beijingde yitian," *Zhongshi wanbao*, 3 August 1991.

77. *yi bupa ku, er bupa si, ye bupa ni.* The first two clauses were printed in red, the last in black ink. The original quotation was popularized in the 1965 army campaign to learn from Wang Jie, the PLA soldier dismembered when he leaped onto a live hand grenade during a militia exercise, thereby saving his comrades. At the Ninth Party Congress in April 1969, Mao Zedong said, "I approve of the slogan: I'm not scared of hardship, I'm not scared of dying."

78. The large budgets provided by the state for these "leader epics," *lingxiu pian*, and "gift presentation films," *xianli pian*—that is, propaganda epics made for such official occasions as National Day and the party's birthday (1 July)—were said to have saved many studios from economic disaster.

79. See Geremie R. Barmé, *Shades of Mao: The Posthumous Cult of the Great Leader* (Armonk, N.Y.: Sharpe, 1996).

80. Comic skits, *xiaopin*, became increasingly popular after 1990, turning into a craze during 1991. What I would call the "revolutionary skit" featuring the leaders is not entirely unlike the appearance of martial figures in traditional operas or in *zhezi xi*, highlights from well-known operas.

81. See Andrew Ross, "Uses of Camp," in his *No Respect: Intellectuals & Popular Culture* (New York: Routledge, Chapman and Hall, 1989), p. 139.

82. Ibid., p. 140.

83. Susan Sontag, "Notes on Camp," in her *A Susan Sontag Reader* (Harmondsworth, Middlesex: Penguin Books, 1983), p. 114.

84. An important example of just such a series was the *Across the Century Series* (Kua shiji congshu) published in Sichuan in mid-1991. With a general introduction by Yuan Mu, the most odious of China's official propagandists and State Council spokesman during the 1989 demonstrations, the five-volume series was obviously aimed at readers familiar with the *Toward the Future Series* (Zou xiang weilai congshu) edited for the same publisher by Jin Guantao and Bao Zunxin, both of whom were purged after 4 June. The books include volumes on student protests (*Xuechao xianxiang*), the rise

of conservative princelings (*Gongheguode disandai*), and one on the value of traditional culture (*Huahun gaoyang*), which was coauthored by Liu Dong, the philosopher Li Zehou's prize student.

85. Despite earlier leanings toward a more liberal ideological approach, Qin had been involved in a 1989 production written both as a reply to *River Elegy* and as part of the propaganda merriment of the fortieth anniversary of the People's Republic. See Qin Xiaoying et al., *Zhongguo hun* (Beijing: Zhonggong zhongyang dangxiao chubanshe, 1989). Qin also was active in the mid-1990s as a propagandist working for younger nationalist politicians like Pan Yue, a leader in the National Administrative Bureau of State-Owned Property.

86. See Geremie Barmé, " 'Road' Versus 'River'," *Far Eastern Economic Review*, 25 October 1990, p. 32.

87. *Shenzhou yin.*

88. For the narration to this series, see Tao Taizhong et al., *Wang Changcheng* (Xianggang: Tiandi tushu youxian gongsi, 1992). Also see Xiao Rong, "Changcheng—yibu du bu wan, kan bu toude dashu," *Wenxue bao*, 30 January 1992.

89. Zhou Zhentian et al., *Guohun* (Shenyang: Liaoning renmin chubanshe, 1991).

90. Tian Bingxin and Wang Zhigang, "Guangzhou: yizuo bu shefangde chengshi," *Yue-Gang xinxi bao*, 5 October 1991. It is surprising that political television specials like the late-1991 recitation of the Chinese government's white paper *Human Rights in China* were not sponsored by local enterprises, or, better still, reform-through-labor factories and farms.

91. The *Guanggao jiemu*, as it was called, later ran to 160 minutes.

92. In the late 1980s, there was one independent TV advertisement production company in Beijing, run by Zhong Xingzuo, the younger brother of the writer Ah Cheng. Zhong's film unit—Xingzuo's Ad Workshop (Xingzuo guanggao zhizuo suo)—was featured in "On the Way" (Zoutai), the seventh part of the eight-part documentary *Tiananmen*, produced by Shi Jian and Chen Jue in May 1991.

93. The editors of *Shanghai wenlun*, the humanities journal of the Shanghai Academy of Social Sciences, did, however, indicate an interest in the relationship between popular culture and commercialism, in a new column started by the journal in early 1991. See "Guanyu dazhong wenyide bitan," *Shanghai wenlun*, 1991:1, pp. 15–25. Bao Yaming, a young critic and editor with this journal, applied some relatively modern Western theory—Adorno, Jameson, Sartre—à la the Frankfurt school to the questions of popular culture in his "Xiaofeizhongde chenlun yu jiushu," *Shanghai wenlun*, 1991:2, pp. 16–23.

94. Zhongyang was originally a short form of the "Central Committee of the Chinese Communist Party," also called Dang zhongyang, or "Party Central." There was also the "Central People's Government," Zhongyang renmin zhengfu. The expression Zhongyang became a synecdoche covering the center of power and, through association, Beijing as a whole.

95. The love song "Heri jun zai lai" featured in the 1937 film *Three Stars Accompany the Moon* (Sanxin ban yue). The song's popularity in 1980 on the mainland led to a pro-

tracted debate in the press, and it was repeatedly criticized as a "pornographic song." See, for example, Nan Yong, "Huan lishi benlai mianmu—guanyu 'Heri jun zai lai' wenda," *Renmin yinyue*, 1980:9, reprinted in *Renmin yinyue* bianjibu, ed., *Zenyang jianbie huangse gequ* (Beijing: Renmin yinyue chubanshe, 1983), pp. 44–45. On the origins of the song, see Ying Guojing, "Ye tan 'Heri jun zai lai'," *Wenhui bao*, 17 August 1980.

96. See "Deng Lijun xianxiangde zhengzhi, wenhua he meiti fansi," *Mingbao yuekan*, 1995:6, pp. 46–63. W. J. F. Jenner has called Teresa "the Vera Lynn of the KMT."

97. See *Gaobiede yaogun* (Hubei/Xianggang/Beijing: Hubei yinxiang yishu chubanshe, Xianggang Jinlin yule zhizuo youxian gongsi, and Beijing Jin xuanlü yinxiang zhongxin, 1995).

98. Ranging from the essays and romances of writers like Qiong Yao, Yi Shu, and San Mao to the martial arts novels of Jin Yong, Gu Long, Liang Yusheng, and Wen Ruian.

99. Published by the formerly staid and later economically strained Joint Publishers (Sanlian shudian) in Beijing, the Taiwan artist Cai Zhizhong's cartoon-illustrated rewrites of everything from the Confucian *Four Books* (*The Analects, Mencius, The Great Learning,* and *The Way of the Mean*) to Taoist philosophy and ghost stories became best-sellers on the mainland in the early 1990s. Just as children's and adults' comic books, *lianhuan hua* or *xiaoren shu,* had propagated party heroes for decades, in the 1980s comics from Hong Kong and Taiwan facilitated the revival of traditional Chinese classics using this accessible and vernacular format.

100. Although in conversational Chinese, Hong Kong and Taiwan are referred to in that order (Gang-Tai, a short form of Xiang*gang* and *Tai*wan), for political and cultural reasons, the official formulation is Tai-Kong (Tai-Gang).

101. Many Hong Kong and Taiwan expressions percolated north from the mid-1980s, and in 1990, an Anhui publisher produced what was perhaps the first dictionary of the faddish new terms. See Huang Lili, Zhou Shumin, and Qian Lianqin, eds., *Gang-Tai yuci cidian* (Hefei: Huangshan shushe, 1990). See also Zhu Guangqi, ed., *Dangdai Gang-Tai yongyu cidian* (Shanghai: Shanghai cishu chubanshe, 1994). In early 1991, a Hong Kong report even noted a "Cantonese craze" in the clubs of Shanghai. See Zhou Wei, "Shanghai wuting xianqile yueyure," *Ming bao,* 9 March 1991. Although Cantonese-accented Mandarin remained the object of derision in film and television, fashionable northerners and businesspeople readily displayed Cantonese expressions and Taiwanese turns of phrase in their everyday speech.

102. What was originally termed *tongsu* or *dazhong wenhua* by traditional engineers of human souls was eventually supplanted by the Kong-Tai expression *liuxing wenhua* and the older term *su wenhua.* See Thomas B. Gold, "Go with Your Feelings: Hong Kong and Taiwan Culture in Greater China," *China Quarterly,* no. 136, December 1993, pp. 909–13.

103. See Tian Bingxin and Wang Zhigang, "Guangzhou: yizuo bu shefangde chengshi." This extraordinary conversation between two New China Newsagency correspondents was pointedly in favor of Guangzhou's "democratizing" commercial culture, as opposed to what was described as Beijing's backward political ethos.

104. See Tu Wei-ming, "Cultural China: The Periphery as the Center," *Daedalus*, Spring 1991, pp. 1–32.

105. Perhaps the most notorious example in 1991 was the Hong Kong and Taiwan publication of the novel *Yellow Peril* (Huanghuo) by "Bao Mi" (Secret), 3 vols. (Taibei: Fengyun shidai chuban youxian gongsi, 1991). This futuristic novel about the collapse of Communism in China and the outbreak of a civil war that leads to a global conflagration was written by the Beijing writer Wang Lixiong. The book circulated on the mainland in manuscript, computer printouts, and even on computer disks. It seemed to be far more popular with readers who had access to it there than in either Hong Kong or Taiwan.

106. See in particular the comments by Wu Zuguang, Liu Xinwu, Shu Ting, and Bai Hua in "Xiangfeng zai Guangzhou," *Lianhe bao*, 14–15 May 1991.

107. *Sanlian Shenghuo zhoukan*, edited after 1995 by Zhu Wei, formerly a fiction editor under Liu Xinwu at *People's Literature*. Previous editors of *Life* were the PLA reportage writer Qian Gang, the Shanghai Rousseau expert Zhu Xueqin, and Yang Lang.

108. See the photo report in *Beijing wanbao*, 20 June 1991; and Zhangwu, "Zhao Chuan: 'fengkuang' Beijing qingnian," *Beijing qingnian bao*, 21 June 1991.

109. *Wo hen chou, keshi wo hen wenrou*. For a time, this song title was also associated by Beijing cultural figures with the mild if unprepossessing person of Li Ruihuan.

110. From Lo Tayu's "The Maxim of Love" (Aide zhenyan) in his 1983 album *Weilaide zhurenweng* (Taibei: Gunshi gongsi, 1983).

111. Lo's "Love Song 1990" (Lianqu 1990) was named the most popular pop song on the mainland in 1990. See Li Jun, ed., *90 zai huishuo* (Beijing: Zhongguo guoji chubanshe, 1991), pp. 1–3. The song was from Lo's earlier album *Comrade Lover* (Airen tongzhi).

112. "Huanghou dadao dong," lyrics by Lin Hsi, music by Lo Tayu, and produced by Lo's Music Factory, Yinyue gongchang. For an interview with Lo and general remarks on political music in Hong Kong, see Fang Su, "Zhengzhi liuxingqu: cong Taiwan changdao Xianggang," *Jiushi niandai yuekan*, 1991:9, pp. 66–68.

113. This song does in music what the Hong Kong–based satirist Yau Mai Tei, the pen name of the Beijing exile Xiao Tong, achieved in his 1997 *Rhapsody—A Prophetic Film Documentary* written in 1982. See *Renditions, Special Issue: Hong Kong*, nos. 29 and 30 (1988), pp. 346–353.

114. The term *new ideas* was a play on former Soviet leader Mikhail Gorbachev's "new thinking" and China's Deng thought. For some interesting reflections on both Lo Tayu and Cui Jian's songs, see Rey Chow, *Writing Diaspora: Tactics of Intervention in Contemporary Cultural Studies* (Bloomington: Indiana University Press, 1993), pp. 144–161.

115 See, for example, Andrew F. Jones, *Like a Knife: Ideology and Genre in Contemporary Chinese Popular Music* (Ithaca, N.Y.: Cornell University Press, 1992). Jones's book itself is a significant pop culture artifact, researched and produced at a time when many of the phenomena he was investigating had gone a long way toward being tamed. See also Peter Micic, " 'A Bit of This a Bit of That': Notes on Pop/Rock Genres in the Eighties in China," *Chime Journal*, no. 8, Spring 1995, p. 78.

116. See Gu Tu, "Cong 'Yi wu suo you' shuodao yaogunyue—Cui Jiande zuopin wei shenme shou huanying?" *Renmin ribao*, 16 July 1988; and Bai Jieming (Barmé), "Yaogun fanshenle?" *Jiushi niandai yuekan*, 1988:11, pp. 94–95.

117. See Zeng Yi, " 'Qiuge' de fengxing shuomingle shenme?" *Guangming ribao*, 19 October 1988.

118. See Yu Jiwen, "Beijingde xin yaogun," *Jiushi niandai yuekan*, 1989:6, pp. 104–105; and Geremie Barmé and Linda Jaivin, eds., *New Ghosts, Old Dreams: Chinese Rebel Voices* (New York: Times Books, 1992), p. 252.

119. Reported in *Beijing wanbao*, 26 November 1989, and quoted in the explanation of the term "rock 'n' roll band," *yaogun yuedui*, in Yu Genyuan et al., eds., *Xiandai Hanyu xin ciyu cidian* (Beijing: Zhongguo qingnian chubanshe, 1994), p. 1053.

120. Miklós Haraszti, *The Velvet Prison: Artists Under State Socialism*, trans. Katalin and Stephen Landesmann (New York: Basic Books, 1987), p. 159.

121. See Geremie Barmé, "Official Bad Boys or True Rebels?" *Human Rights Tribune* 3 (4) Winter 1992, p. 17.

122. Ping Fang and Ma Mu, "Yi wu suo you, yaogun yu touji: wei Yayunhui juankuan yibaiwan yuan yiyan jishi," *Xiju shijie*, 1990:3–4, pp. 2–11.

123. The earlier 1989 work was *Xin changzheng lushangde yaogun: Cui Jian zhuanji* (Beijing: Zhongguo difang lüyou chubanshe, 1989).

124. Cui Jian, *Jiejue* (Beijing: Beiji gongsi, 1991).

125. "Red Cloth" (Yikuai hongbu), "Come on, Let Me Go Wild in the Snow" (Kuai rang wo zai zhe xuedishang sa dian'r ye), and "Parting Shot" (Zuihou yiqiang). It is noteworthy that in the printed sheet of lyrics that were sold with the tape, the producers broke one of the greatest of the party's cultural taboos by "opening a skylight," *kai tianchuang*, that is, leaving a space where (self-)censored material had been deleted. The lyrics of two songs, "Like a Knife" (Xiang yiba daozi) and "Parting Shot," were missing, presumably because of their controversial nature. Cui so often sings in a fashion bordering on the incoherent that it would be very difficult for the politically correct—many of whom were aged and hard of hearing, in any case—to make out the words. Opening skylights was common under the KMT government before 1949 when many leftist and other publications were censored. Under the Communists, however, the first widely recognized "skylight" was opened in early 1987 when an article by the recently purged Liu Binyan was deleted from Liu Zaifu's journal *Literary Criticism*. Because of the odious associations of such an act, the incident led to an uproar in the party.

126. These were the works of the Guangzhou-based director Sun Zhou. Sun did a series of music television videos for the songwriter/singer Hou Te-chien and his de facto wife Cheng Lin, which borrowed heavily from the animated version of Pink Floyd's "The Wall," dubbed Hong Kong television video copies of which had been circulating on the mainland since 1986. One of the most interesting and earliest videos of mainland commercial rock was "Red Socks," made by the Hong Kong experimental film director Jim Shum (Shen Desheng) in 1988, which featured Cui Jian intercut with PLA propaganda and TV commercials.

127. See Shen Yanping, "It's Only Rock 'n' Roll," *Beijing Weekend (China Daily)*, 25–27 October 1991, pp. 1, 8–9. Favorite rock performance venues included Maxims, the Restaurant for Diplomatic Missions, Poacher's Inn, and the Friendship Hotel.

128. From Grzegorz Ociepa, "Rock 'n' roll the Polish Way," *The Insider*, 5 September 1991. I am grateful to Linda Jaivin for bringing this delightful morsel to my attention.

129. In the middle of the year, a widely popular book devoted to Cui Jian was banned by the authorities. See Hong Bo, Ye Guigang, and Cai Yuanjiang, *Cui Jian xianxiang: yaogunyue youhuo zhi mi* (Beijing: Xueyuan chubanshe, 1990). For a critique of the book, see Jiang Yonglin, "Ping *Cui Jian xianxiang*," *Zhongguo tushu pinglun*, 1991:4, pp. 15–16. Shanghai scholar Xu Jilin reviewed the book favorably but was castigated for his efforts. See Xu Jilin, "Wo suo lijiede Cui Jian," *Wenhui dushu zhoubao*, 8 June 1991; and Zhang Shiping's letter to the editor, "Yipian bugai fabiaode cuowu wenzhang," *Wenhui dushu zhoubao*, 24 August 1991, which refers to the ban on the book.

130. See Zhu Yu, "Mengzhong: wan yaogunde zhongxuesheng," *Beijing qingnian bao*, 5 April 1991.

131. *Haixia liang'an yaogun yinyue zhi weilai.*

132. See, for example, Guo Heng, "Shenghuo huanjing you bie ganshou bu tong, Cui Jian chuyan bu xun rexia weiyan," *Ming bao*, 4 April 1991.

133. Xia Miaoran, "Hou Dejian, Cui Jian: Haixia liang'an yaogunyude zhengzhixing," *Ming bao*, 3 April 1991.

134. Cui made this comment to Linda Jaivin in Beijing in November 1991.

135. See *Heibao*, produced by Kinn's Management Ltd., Hong Kong, 1991; Chang Kuan, *Chongxin jihua xianzai* (Hong Kong: Dadi Production Ltd., 1991); and *Ling yizhi yan kan Zhongguo—Hei yueliang* (Hong Kong: CZ Music Production Co., 1991). See also Chen Zhe, "Guanyu 'Ling yizhi yan kan Zhongguo—Hei yueliang' changpiande zhizuo ji qita," *Top Music Magazine*, July 1991, pp. 92–95.

136. John Heileman, "Rouble Without a Cause," *Modern Review* 1, no. 1 (Autumn 1991), p. 6.

137. Ibid.

138. Shuang Qing, "Gei Zhongguo yaogun yi jihui," *Beijing qingnian bao*, 19 April 1991.

139. See Zhou You, ed., *Beijing yaogun buluo* (Tianjin: Tianjin shehui kexue chubanshe, 1994). Zhou's book contains a chronology of Beijing rock, as well as a fairly comprehensive list of local rock stars and their work.

140. Heavy Metal Heaven was on the southwest corner of Xidan at Chang'an Boulevard. For a list of the hot discos in mid-1996, see Charlotte Kilroy, "Beijing Boogie," *Beijing Scene* 2, no. 19, 2–15 August 1996, pp. 4–6.

141. *Shen wa dong, guang ji liang, bu cheng ba; Beizhan, beihuang, wei renmin;* and *Shijie shi nimende, ye shi womende, dan guigen jiedi shi nimende. Nimen qingnianren zhaoqi pengbo, haoxiang zaochen ba, jiu dianzhongde taiyang, xiwang jituo zai nimen shenshang.* The shopping bag was designed by the Sunflower Design Company (Xiangrikui sheji zhizuo gongsi).

142. This was previously more obvious in the literary field, with Taiwan publications of

mainland works between 1987 and 1990 helping keep a number of prominent writers out of the red. See chapter 1, "The Chinese Velvet Prison."

143. It was reported that in late 1991, film bureaucrats alarmed by this tendency attempted to interfere and even stop certain Taiwan-financed productions. Initially, their efforts were unsuccessful, although new regulations in 1996 made the situation far more difficult for a time.

144. Sang Ye, "Mudu Beijing ciwenhua." For an interview with Ai Jing, see Zi Ye, "Liulangde yanzi ma?" *Zhongguo daobao*, 1993:2, pp. 18–20.

145. Some of the most important examples of this genre were the following books: Lu Yi, ed., *Qiuji: yige shijixingde xuanze* (Shanghai: Baijia chubanshe, 1989); Li Ming, ed., *Zhongguode weiji yu sikao* (Tianjin: Tianjin renmin chubanshe, 1989); and He Bochuan, *Shan'aoshangde Zhongguo*, rev. ed. (Xianggang: Sanlian chubanshe, 1990). See also Barmé and Jaivin, *New Ghosts, Old Dreams*, pp. 165–170.

146. Su Ya and Jia Lusheng, *Shei lai chengbao?—Zhonguo jingji xianzhuang toushi* (Guangzhou: Huacheng chubanshe, 1990). The cover has a large question mark over a map of China, thus the title is often given as *Shei lai chengbao Zhongguo?*

147. Ōjima Tsutomu's (Wangdao Mian), *1999 nian renlei da jienan* (Beijing: Xueyuan chubanshe, 1990), criticized for encouraging popular hysteria by Li Ming, "Xuwang yuyan *1999 nian renlei da jienan*," *Zhongguo tushu pinglun*, 1990:2, pp. 77–79.

148. Sheng Bin and Feng Lun, eds., *Zhongguo guoqing baogao* (Shenyang: Liaoning renmin chubanshe, 1990); and Hu Angang, *Zhongguo: zouxiang 21 shiji* (Beijing: Huanjing kexue chubanshe, 1991). Hu was a member of the Research Group on the State of the Nation, Guoqing fenxi yanjiu xiaozu, attached to the Academia Sinica. An earlier example of his work in this area is the book he coauthored with Wang Yi, *Shengcun yu fazhan* (Beijing: Kexue chubanshe, 1989).

149. See Shi Zhongwen, *Zhongguoren: zouchu si hutong* (Beijing: Zhongguo fazhan chubanshe, 1991); and Wang Zhigang, *Zhongguo zoushi caifanglu* (Guangzhou: Guangdong gaodeng chubanshe, 1990).

150. For a discussion of the "*Book of Changes* fever" that swept the mainland after 1989, see the series of articles in *Zhongguo tushu pinglun*, 1990:2, pp. 26–37. See also "The Cultural Kaleidoscope," *China News Analysis* 1522, 15 November 1994, pp. 6–7; and, Cheng Ying, "Qiren, qishi, qishu—dadu yizhan xinxing Zou Weihua," *Jiushi niandai yuekan*, 1991:8, pp. 66–67.

151. On the Zen fad, see, for example, Ke Shiyu, "Chanzong re yu Zhongguo zhishifenzi xintai," *Zhongguo tushu pinglun*, 1990:1, pp. 37–40; Huang Jiazhang, "Ye tan chan wenhuare yu Zhongguo zhishifenzi xintai," *Zhongguo tushu pinglun*, 1990:4, pp. 27–29; and He Zhiyun, "*Chande gushi* guaqi yizhen chanfeng," *Zhongguo shibao zhoukan*, 26 January–1 February 1992, p. 65.

152. A hotly discussed and eagerly sought-after work among Beijing readers in 1991 was Chen Kaiguo and Zheng Shunchao's *Dadao xing—fang fudu jushi Wang Liping xiansheng* (Beijing: Huaxia chubanshe, 1991).

153. See Zhuge Xihan, *Chaoren Zhang Baosheng* (Guangzhou: Guangdong renmin chubanshe, 1991). Among other miracles, Zhang is credited with having used his *qi*

to keep a number of China's political elders alive long beyond their allotted time. Both Zhang and Ke Yunlu (as well as others of their ilk) were pursued tirelessly by media skeptics like Sima Nan from 1990. See Zhao Bin, "Sima Nan tanxun Ke Yunlu jingying zhi dao," *Zhongguo jingyingbao*, 26 May 1998.

154. For this translation and more from Li's work, see Barmé and Jaivin, *New Ghosts, Old Dreams*, pp. 448–449.

155. Li Zongwu, *Houheixue xubian* (Beijing: Tuanjie chubanshe, 1990); and Zhang Mosheng, *Houheixue jiaozhu zhuan* (Shijiazhuang: Huashan wenyi chubanshe, 1991).

156. See, for example, Wei Guan, " 'Houhei' chubanshede mishi," *Zhongguo tushu pinglun*, 1990:1, pp. 71–73; and Yang Xianyi's comments on the phenomenon in "Renda daibiao, zhengxie weiyuan fayan zhaideng," *Zhongguo wenhua bao*, 10 April 1991.

157. Shi Tao, "Shushi chuiqi 'hei xuanfeng'," *Wenhui dushu zhoubao*, 30 January 1993.

158. See the series edited by Yan Feng and others, *Aiqing houheixue, Facai houheixue, Tuixiao houheixue, Qiuren houheixue,* and *Koucai houheixue* (Xi'an: Shaanxi lüyou chubanshe, 1992–1993).

159. See Wu Mengqian, *Fan houheixue—renjian zhinan* (Beijing: Minzu chubanshe, 1993).

160. Chiu-ning Chu, *Thick Face Black Heart: Thriving and Succeeding in Everyday Life and Work Using the Ancient Wisdom of the East* (London: Allen & Unwin, 1992).

161. See Wang Dayou, *Houheixue manhua ben* (Beijing: Huaxia chubanshe, 1993).

162. Published by the Xuelin chubanshe in Shanghai, the two books were translated as *Shi, Dachen* and *Shi, Shouxiang*, respectively. For details, see "Shi, Shouxiang," *Wenhui dushu zhoubao*, 4 September 1993.

163. General editions of the book were reprinted a number of times, including *Caigen tan*, compiled by Hong Yingming (Hong Zicheng) and reedited by Zhang Xijiang (Shanghai: Shanghai renmin chubanshe, 1989); and *"Caigen tan" zhushi*, by Hong Yingming, annotated by Wang Tongce (Hangzhou: Zhejiang guji chubanshe, 1989). See also Hung Ying-ming, *The Roots of Wisdom: Saikontan*, trans. William Scott Wilson (Tokyo: Kodansha International, 1985). My thanks to Benjamin Penny and James A. Benn for this last reference.

164. In the popular imagination, the Wanli Reign period (1571–1619) was a time of political corruption, social decadence, and economic uncertainty. During the unsettling years of 1985 to 1989, a Chinese version of Ray Huang's (Huang Renyu) study of the Wanli period, *1587, a Year of No Significance* (Wanli shiwu nian), was taken by many people to parallel China's contemporary economic and political fate. This was also the case in 1991–1992 with the publication of Yu Xingming's *Shanghai, 1862 nian* (Shanghai: Shanghai renmin chubanshe, 1991), a book about the colonization of Shanghai in the last century.

165. "Yaosui *Caigen tan*: yanmai yijiude *Caigen tan* weishenme fengxing yishi," *Beijing qingnian bao*, 29 October 1991.

166. Ibid.

167. Han Xu in "Yaosui *Caigen tan*: yanmai yijiude *Caigen tan* weishenme fengxing yishi."

168. Gu Yueren in "Yaosui *Caigen tan*: yanmai yijiude *Caigen tan* weishenme fengxing yishi."

169. See Yang Jianmin, "Ling ren shengyande *Caigen tan*," *Zhongguo tushu pinglun*, 1991:1, pp. 62–64.

170. Ke Yunlu, *Da qigongshi* (Beijing: Renmin chubanshe, 1989).

171. See "*Qigong*: The Ultimate Revolution," in Barmé and Jaivin, *New Ghosts, Old Dreams*, pp. 374–385.

172. See "Xinshu yugao," back cover of *Shiyue*, 1991:1.

173. Ke Yunlu, *Xin shiji*, 2 vols. (Huhehaote: Neimenggu daxue chubanshe, 1992).

174. "Haoren huo qiangzhe, jiu ti xin yi: Song Dacheng yu Bulaike, ni xuanze shei?" *Beijing qingnian bao*, 29 November 1991.

175. Lin Sheng, " 'Huise wenhuashan' xianxiang," *Neibu xiaoxi*, a restricted-circulation monthly published by *Beijing Youth News*, 1991:9, p. 46.

176. The series was conceived in late 1989 and completed in November 1991. It featured some of China's most popular comic performers, including Ge You, Hou Yaohua, and Lü Liping.

177. See Wang Shuo et al., "*Bianjibude gushi*" — *jingcai duibai xinshang* (Beijing: Zhongguo guangbo dianshi chubanshe, 1992); and Wang Shuo et al., *Bianjibude gushi* — *youmo dianshi gushi*, 2 vols. (Shenyang: Shenyang chubanshe, 1992).

178. Yang Ping, "Zhongguode xipi yu yapi," *Beijing qingnian bao*, 5 August 1993.

CHAPTER 6

1. "Attitude T-shirts" have been common since the 1960s, and they became a highly marketable item starting in the 1980s. See the entries "Coed Naked" and "No Fear" in Steven Daly and Nathaniel Wice, *alt.culture an a-z guide to 90s america* (London: Fourth Estate, 1995), pp. 49 and 163. See also Rosalie Grattatori, ed., *Great T-shirt Graphics* (Rockport, Mass.: Rockport Publishers, 1993). Japanese weird-slogan T-shirts have also been current for decades. See, for example, Sally Larsen, *Japlish — Photographs by Sally Larsen* (San Francisco: Pomegranate Artbooks, 1993).

2. *T xu*, pronounced *T xuet* in Cantonese, is the Hong Kong sinification of the English expression T-shirt. *T xu shan*, or simply *T xu*, has been current on the mainland since the early 1980s. Another, lexically more rigorous, term, is *T xing chenshan*.

3. ACT UP (AIDS Coalition To Unleash Power) was a direct-action group started in America that used graphics and bitingly humorous slogans to remind and confront the government and public about the many issues surrounding the AIDS crisis in the late 1980s.

4. Kong Yongqian belongs to the seventy-fifth generation of the Confucius clan. Yongqian's father, Kong Fanli, was named in accordance with clan tradition, the word *li* or "propriety" appearing in his name. He refused, however, to give his son the appropriate generational name, which would have required that he be called Kong Xiang xxx. Fanli, branded a rightist in the late 1950s, chose instead to name his son

Yongqian, literally "eternally humble." Kong Fanli was of the same generation as Kong Fansen, the early 1990s' model party martyr who had worked in Tibet.

5. These were with the Beijing Youth Film Studio, the Science Publishing House, Shenzhen University, and 1 August Film Studio.

6. This biographical information is based on interviews with Kong Yongqian at Liubukang in Beijing, 11 November 1991, and his own unpublished notes on the T-shirts.

7. See, for example, Cheng Shi et al., eds., *Wenge xiaoliao ji* (Chengdu: Xinan caijing daxue chubanshe, 1988); and the more recent material on Cultural Revolution–period jokes in Yang Jian, *Wenhua dagemingzhongde dixia wenxue* (Beijing: Zhaohua chubanshe, 1993), pp. 339–341; as well as the major collection of *geyao* in Duan Baolin, editor and annotator, *Dangdai fengci geyao* (Shenyang: Liaoning renmin chubanshe, 1993). Duan's collection has an introduction written by Wang Meng.

8. See Wu Jincai, "Minyao: dongnan xibei feng," *Guoqing yanjiu*, 1989:2, pp. 65–67. The journal in which this essay was published, *Studies on the State of the Nation*, was a restricted-circulation magazine that was banned after only a few issues.

9. The rhyming Chinese original reads *da "Benchi" di, lou waiguo mi, chou guizi yan, he Weishiji, chuan xinchao yi, zheng huohong T, de Aizibing, xi sangna yu, wan'r baoling, zuo dianzi, zande mubiao shi geti, kaichu gongzhi he suo ju?*

10. See He Xin, "Tongzhang ehua ji jinggai shibaide yuanyin," in two parts, in *Mingbao yuekan*, 1988: 2, p. 17, and 1989:2, pp. 59, 60.

11. *shiyi renmin jiuyi shang, tuanjie yizhi pian zhongyang. Dang zhongyang ye bu pa, laile ge quanmian da zhangjia.*

12. See Pu Su, "Yaoyan he minyi," *Wenyi bao*, 7 March 1992.

13. *fule haibiande, fale baitande, kule shangbande, qiongle jiaoshude, zuile dangguande.* See Duan Baolin, *Dangdai fengci geyao*, p. 117.

14. *Zhou sile esi zhu/zhu sile meiyou mao/mei mao hua yige/hua bu hao hu yige/hu bu xiang zhao yige/zhao bu cheng jiangjiuzhe.* See Geremie R. Barmé, *Shades of Mao: The Posthumous Cult of the Great Leader* (Armonk, N.Y.: Sharpe, 1996), p. 282.

15. Gregor Benton, "The Origins of the Political Joke," in *Humor in Society: Resistance and Control*, ed. Chris Powell and George E. C. Paton (London: Macmillan, 1988), p. 41. For examples of what Benton is talking about, see Greg Benton and Graham Loomes, *Big Red Joke Book* (London: Pluto Press, 1976).

16. Such slogans included, for example, "The water can either carry or sink a boat" (*shui ke zai zhou yi ke fu zhou*, originally *shui ze zai zhou, shui ze fu zhou*, from the "System of the Ruler" chapter of the pre-Qin philosophical work *Xunzi*), an expression traditionally used to urge officials and rulers to be upright. Kong recalled seeing a group of middle-school teachers carrying a placard with this written on it.

17. Unbeknownst to most mainland people, many pro-student T-shirts were also produced in Hong Kong. These included pictures of the student "stars" Chai Ling, Wuer Kaixi, and Wang Dan and other shirts carrying slogans. A personal favorite of mine was a Giordano shirt with a big exclamation mark on it and the line "How are you?" followed in small print by: "Please get out [of politics]," *qing nin xialai.* T-shirts have been and are an instrument of politics and social debate in many countries. For ex-

ample, a T-shirt related to the Rodney King incident in Los Angeles in 1992 read "L.A.P.D. We Treat You Like A King."

18. Designed and printed by students at the Central Art Academy, most of these shirts were confiscated and destroyed by the police.

19. Throughout the movement, signatures on T-shirts were an important element of self-validation. See Geremie Barmé, "Beijing Days, Beijing Nights," in *The Pro-Democracy Protests in China*, ed. Jonathan Unger (Armonk, N.Y.: Sharpe, 1991), pp. 44–45.

20. Kong Yongqian, "Geren jianli," 24 October 1991, unpublished manuscript, p. 2.

21. Tang Chenglin, " 'Bukan ladao'—xinchao wenhua shan xunji," *Zhongguo jingying bao*, 2 July, 1991; and Mu Yelin, "Wenhua shande beihou," *Ming bao*, 24 July 1991.

22. See Xian Yi, " 'Wenhuashan' zhi you," *Zhongguo qingnian bao*, 17 July 1991.

23. See Wang Lin, "1991 nian Jing cheng 'wenhuashan' xianxiang," *Qingnian yanjiu*, 1992:4, p. 1.

24. In June 1992 a stall near Beijing University was also selling Cui products: a T-shirt with the image of a shot-up bull's-eye and the title of Cui's song "Parting Shot" (Zuihou yiqiang) on it.

25. This line of shirt continued to be sold in China. Boddhisattvas and a range of traditional Chinese Buddhist images also became common during the 1990s.

26. Todo Akiyasu et al., eds., *Saishin Chūgoku jōhō jiten* (Tokyo: Shōgakukan, 1985).

27. Restricted-circulation dictionaries of new political expressions were, however, compiled during the Cultural Revolution.

28. *Saishin Chūgoku jōhō jiten*, p. 683. The Four Bigs were big opinions, big discussions, big-character posters, and big arguments. The Four Great Freedoms were the freedom to rent, buy, and sell farmland; the freedom to lend and borrow money; the freedom to hire wage workers; and the freedom to trade. The Four Pests were flies, mosquitoes, rats, and sparrows (or bedbugs); or, alternatively, the Gang of Four consisting of Wang Hongwen, Zhang Chunqiao, Jiang Qing, and Yao Wenyuan.

29. See *"ping piaozheng gongying"* and the illustration *haikyū kippu* in *Saishin Chūgoku jōhō jiten*, p. 552.

30. Sun Longji, *Zhongguo wenhuade "shenceng jiegou,"* rev. ed. (Taibei: Tangshan shudian, 1990); hereafter simply referred to as *Shenceng jiegou*. Kong would have read one of the edited versions that appeared clandestinely on the mainland in 1986.

31. *te laoshi, te pushi, te tashi, te benfen, te tinghua, tebie guai.*

32. See Sun Longji, *Shenceng jiegou*, pp. 182–185.

33. Ibid., pp. 182–185, 239–241.

34. Ibid., pp. 62–142. The shirt was to read *"xinleng, xinre, xin lianzhe xin, guanxin, aixin, shangxin, tiexin, shangxin, pingxin er lun, yixin yiyi, yixin buke er yong, jiang xin bi xin, xinxin xiang yin, jiaoxin . . . ai mo da yu xin si."* From remarks made by Kong Yongqian, April 1993.

35. Wang Shuo, *Wang Shuo xiequ xiaoshuo xuan* (Beijing: Zuojia chubanshe, 1990).

36. Wang Meng, "Duobi chonggao," *Dushu*, 1993:1, p. 15.

37. See Wang Shuo, *Wang Shuo xiequ xiaoshuo xuan*, pp. 8, 82, and esp. pp. 92 and 122.

38. *you xiege shi ni yue na ta dang shi ta jiu yue shi ge shi.*

39. *te*, so overused by the mid-1990s as to be hackneyed was, after 1992, marginally overshadowed by the cloying Taiwanese adjective/adverb *haohao*. Local dialect variations
of the T-shirt language appeared in Shanghai, and some shirts in Beijing used the
northeast dialect word *zei* (very) instead of *hen* or *te*. See Lin Sheng, " 'Huise wenhuashan' xianxiang," *Neibu xiaoxi*, a restricted-circulation monthly published by the
Beijing Municipal Committee of the Chinese Youth League, 1991:9, pp. 44–45. For
an array of this kind of language and its English equivalents, see James J. Wang, *Outrageous Chinese: A Guide to Chinese Street Language* (San Francisco: China Books
& Periodicals, 1994); and Zhou Yimin and James J. Wang, *Mutant Mandarin: A
Guide to New Chinese Slang* (San Francisco: China Books & Periodicals, 1995).

40. These details on the origins of the shirts are taken from Kong Yongqian, "Wen-
huashande zhege nage," an account written in longhand in August and September
1992, and from comments made to me in April 1993.

41. One features a *neizhao tu*, a side view of a dissected human being with all the organs
named; the other, *Xixin tuizang tu*, is taken from a meditational text, it bears an English legend on the bottom right-hand corner that reads: "He acts so weird that I just
can't stand it," signed Kong Long, May 1991. My thanks to Benjamin Penny for "sharing" these shirts with me.

42. Kong Yongqian, "Jushen jingguo," an unpublished handwritten account, p. 16. Many
points in this account parallel Wang Lin's article "1991 nian Jing cheng 'wenhuashan'
xianxiang'," which would appear to have been based on police reports of Kong's 1991
interrogation.

43. *Shijingshanqu jundui lixiu tuixiu disan ganbu xiuyangsuo.*

44. These details come from Kong's copy of the Letter of Agreement with the Facility.

45. *Zhenxing gongyipin chang.*

46. These details come from Lin Sheng, " 'Huise wenhuashan' xianxiang," p. 45. This
article is said to be based on official police sources. On p. 44 there is a photograph
of Kong Yongqian taken from the police video made during his detention in early
July 1991.

47. Kong Yongqian, "Geren jianli," p. 3. A clothing factory in Changping County was
contracted to this end, but Kong's detention in early July signaled the bankruptcy of
the project. At the height of the T-shirt fad, Kong was approached by representatives
of factories and companies in Tianjin, Guangdong, Fujian, Nanjing, Shanghai,
Xi'an, Chengdu, Shijiazhuang, and Kunming that hoped to set up production facili-
ties outside Beijing.

48. Lin Sheng, " 'Huise wenhuashan' xianxiang," p. 43.

49. Sun Jie, "Beijing liuxing 'wenhuashan'," in *Jinri redian jishi*, written and edited by
Sun Jie (Changchun: Shidai wenyi chubanshe, 1992), p. 94.

50. See Barmé, *Shades of Mao*, p. 96, figs. 28, 29.

51. *Beijing tuhua* reads in full: *zhentie zhentu zhenhei zhenniu gaile gailemao tulaomao
zhenshuai zhenfen'r bafen'r jiaofen'r zhenle fule juele shenle meilezhile meizhe meixi
meimen'r youmen'r pingle tefan tetie teci temu teshui zhenfan zhenlei zhencan zhende.*

52. Wang Lin, "1991 nian Jing cheng 'wenhuashan' xianxiang," p. 3.

53. *shangdiao mei dan, poufu mei dao, fudu mei yao, tiaolou mei men. hai huozhe.* See Wang Lin, "1991 nian Jing cheng 'wenhuashan' xianxiang," p. 3. Dorothy Parker's poem "Résumé" reads: "Razors pain you; / Rivers are damp; / Acids stain you; / And drugs cause cramp. / Guns aren't lawful; / Nooses give; / Gas smells awful; / You might as well live."

54. Another shirt that Kong was interrogated about bore the legend "Can't blame the government if I got a bum hand [a reference to mahjong]," *dian'rbei buyuan zhengfu*, an alternative line was *dian'rbei buyuan shehui.*

55. From a recorded interview with Kong Yongqian, 10 November 1991, Liubukang, Beijing.

56. See Barmé, "Beijing Days, Beijing Nights," p. 37.

57. "Beijing slang" also inspired a T-shirt that read "Real Buddies," *teci.*

58. Lin Sheng, " 'Huise wenhuashan' xianxiang," p. 44. The wholesale price of Kong's shirts was 5 *yuan*, and they sold for 7 to 10 *yuan.*

59. Tang Chenglin, " 'Bukan ladao'—xinchao wenhua shan xunji."

60. Kong Yongqian, "Geren jianli," p. 4.

61. See Tang Chenglin, " 'Bukan ladao'—xinchao wenhua shan xunji." Kong did the handwritten title of the piece.

62. Ibid.

63. For a full translation of the song, see Geremie Barmé and John Minford, eds., *Seeds of Fire: Chinese Voices of Conscience* (Hong Kong: Far Eastern Economic Review, 1986), 2nd ed. (New York: Hill & Wang, 1988), pp. 400–401.

64. Tang Chenglin, " 'Bukan Ladao' "

65. Sang Ye, "Mudu Beijing ciwenhua," *Kaifang zazhi*, 1991:8, p. 19.

66. *xiongpushangde minzhuqiang.* See Gao Xiong, "Yaofeng cong nali lai?" *Kaifang zazhi*, 1991:7, pp. 7–8.

67. *nongsuolede biaoyu kouhao.* Kong Yongqian, "Geren jianli," p. 5.

68. From Sang Ye's notes on the T-shirts written in mid-1991.

69. *xingxing zhi huo, keyi liao yuan.* See Mao Zedong, *Mao Zedong xuanji* (Beijing: Renmin chubanshe, 1969), vol. 1, pp. 94–104.

70. *buxu fangpi, shikan tiandi fanfu.* From Mu Yelin, "Wenhua shande beihou." The antiseptic official translation of this line is "Stop your windy nonsense! Look, the world is being turned upside down." See Mao Tsetung, "Two Birds: A Dialogue—To the Tune of *Nien Nu Chiao*, Autumn 1965," in Mao, *Poems* (Peking: Foreign Languages Press, 1976), p. 52.

71. Sang Ye, "Zai Beijingde yitian," *Zhongguo shibao*, 3 August 1991. A variation on this T-shirt was "I'm not afraid of hardship, nor am I afraid of being poor," *yi bupa ku, er bupa qiong.*

72. *geming zhanshi shi kuai zhuan / nali xuyao nali ban.*

73. From an interview conducted by Carma Hinton with Kong Yongqian in Boston on 16 June 1994.

74. Lin Sheng, " 'Huise wenhuashan' xianxiang," p. 45. Lin's report was based on inter-

views with the Marketplace Office of the Beijing Municipal Industry and Commerce Supervisory Bureau.

75. From "Guanyu yanjin zhi shou dai you bujiankang tu'an wenzi shangpinde tong-gao," 29 June 1991. See Lin Sheng, " 'Huise wenhuashan' xianxiang," p. 46.

76. "Guanyu dui weifa zhi shou 'wenhua shan' anjian dingxing chuli wentide tongzhi," Jing gongshang jianzi (1991) 25 hao. This document is quoted in the notification Kong received concerning the official decision on the shirts in January 1992.

77. These details come from Lin Sheng, " 'Huise wenhuashan' xianxiang."

78. Interview with Kong Yongqian and from his "Jushen jingguo," pp. 9 ff. The Special Trades Section was the Tezhong hangyeke.

79. Kong Yongqian, "Jushen jingguo," pp. 1 ff.

80. Ibid., p. 9.

81. From a comment made by a worker in a clothing store in Di'anmen, reported to me by friends.

82. This was also the name of a popular TV dating program.

83. *zuohuai buluan* is a saying that refers to a tale from the Spring and Autumn Period (eighth to fifth centuries B.C.) and is used to describe platonic relations between the sexes.

84. *lajia daikou: yuepiao, liangpiao, bupiao, youpiao, fancaipiao, gongzuozheng, xue-shengzheng, jiehunzheng, jumin shenfenzheng, hukouben, jumin gouhuo ben, zi-xingche zhizhao, xiao jinku, chumenzheng, jieshaoxin, mingpian.*

85. Sang Ye, "Mudu Beijing ciwenhua," p. 19.

86. Kong Yongqian, "Jushen jingguo," pp. 6–7, 9, 12.

87. Ibid., p. 12.

88. Ibid., p. 13.

89. In the seventeenth episode of the series *Never Try to Help Anyone* (Bang ren leisi ren), there is a direct use of the expression "making ends meet," *lajia daikou,* meaning "I have a family (and am weighed down by all that entails)." See Wang Shuo, Su Lei, and Wei Ren, *Guanggaoren* (Beijing: *Renmin Zhongguo* chubanshe, 1993), vol. 2, p. 369.

90. *yishi wu cheng: yao zousi mei dan'r / xiang dangguan'r shao xinyan'r / hun rizi za fan-wan'r / qu liantan'r mei ben'r.* The word *guan'r,* "bureaucrat or official," was blanked out in versions of the shirt produced after Kong's first interrogation on 18 June. A somewhat similar message was contained in a T-shirt that featured a man holding his head in his hands with a pained expression on his face, under which is written: "What should I do: stick with my office job or start up a street stall?" *daodi shi shangban'r haishi liantan'r.*

91. Kong Yongqian, "Jushen jingguo," pp. 15–16.

92. Ibid., pp. 10–11.

93. Ibid., p. 13.

94. Ibid., p. 17.

95. Ibid., p. 18.

96. Ibid., p. 19.

97. "Wo shi youguan bumen lianhe xingdong: qingli 'wenhua shan' shichang jinghua shehui fengqi," *Xi'an ribao,* 8 August 1991.

98. "Beijingshi Shijingshanqu gongshang xingzheng guanliju: Anjian chufa jueding-shu," Shigongshang (91) jingjian zi di 11 hao.

99. Kong Yongqian, "Geren jianli," p. 5. Kong suggested that it was more than possible that some of the shirts reportedly confiscated and destroyed were hidden away by stall owners during the purge and subsequently sold at inflated prices on the black market.

100. Ibid., p. 4.

101. See Sang Ye, "Zai Beijingde yitian." T-shirts with the images of stars on them were popular starting in the early 1990s. The expression "star T-shirt," *mingxing shan*, was current from 1992. Used in the *Wenhui bao* on 17 May 1992, it is recorded in Yu Genyuan et al., eds., *Xiandai Hanyu xin ciyu cidian* (Beijing: Zhongguo qingnian chubanshe, 1994), p. 631.

102. Wang Lin, "1991 nian Jing cheng 'wenhuashan' xianxiang," p. 6.

103. Rong Ya, "Ruci 'wenhuashan' xianxiang," *Jingji ribao*, 11 July 1991. This article was reprinted the following day in the *People's Daily*; italics as in the original.

104. From a conversation with Kong Yongqian. See also his "Jushen jingguo," p. 17.

105. Kong Yongqian, "Jushen jingguo," p. 16.

106. From the Carma Hinton interview, Boston, 16 June 1994.

107. See Mu Yushi, " 'Wenhuashan' yu 'fan wenhua'," *Beijing qingnian bao*, 19 July 1991.

108. Xian Yi, " 'Wenhuashan' zhi you."

109. See "Beijing qingnian aichuan 'wenhua shan'," *Zhongyang ribao*, 12 July 1991.

110. " 'Wenhua shan' hongtou Jing cheng," *Xinmin wanbao*. I have been unable to locate the original of this article.

111. This was the *Shenghuo bao*. For a report on this, see " 'Buliang' T-xu shi yishupin," *Ming bao*, 22 July 1991.

112. See Wang Lin, "1991 nian Jing cheng 'wenhuashan' xianxiang," pp. 1–3. The journal in which Wang's article appeared, *Youth Research*, was a restricted-circulation publication produced by the Chinese Academy of Social Sciences.

113. See also Bai Jieming (Barmé), "Didangbuzhude ganjue—dalude huise langchao," *Zhongguo shibao zhoukan*, 8–14 March 1992.

114. See "The Youth," in *China News Analysis* 289, 21 August 1959, p. 6. My thanks to Nicholas Standaert for bringing this item to my attention.

115. See Li Yaoming, "Dalu huangchao gungun lai," *Jiushi niandai yuekan*, 1993:6, p. 49.

116. Kong Yongqian, "Jushen jingguo," p. 5.

117. Lin Sheng, " 'Huise wenhuashan' xianxiang," p. 46.

118. Cao Zhiqian, " 'Wenhua shan' de leng sikao," *Nanfang ribao*, 13 September 1991.

119. Wang Weixiang, "Guanyu 'wenhua shan' de sikao," *Gongren ribao*, 12 October 1991.

120. This was the "Shoudu yanyijie renshi zhenzai mujuan yiyan" held in August 1991. Another one of the shirts had the words "It's everybody's home," *gongyoude jiayuan*, printed on the front and a page from the *Beijing Youth News* on the back.

121. The "New Generation Art Exhibition," Xinshengdai yishuzhan, was sponsored by the *Beijing Youth News* and held in the Museum of Chinese History on Tiananmen Square, 9–14 July 1992.

122. See "*Beijing qingnian bao* CI xin xingxiang sheji," *Beijing qingnian bao*, 29 April 1994. Corporate identity design became a focus for many organizations in 1993–1994.

123. See *Fengci yu youmo* (*Renmin ribao fukan*), 20 October 1991, no. 296.

124. For an illustration of this shirt, see Barmé, *Shades of Mao*, p. 96, fig. 28.

125. *Xiaoping tongzhi renmin zhichi ni*! and *Xiaoping tongzhi dailing women zouxiang shehuizhuyi qiangguo zhi lu*, respectively. See the photograph issued by the China News Agency in *Dagong bao*, 12 July 1992.

126. *Wenhua shan yanjiuhui.*

127. Liu Shaojun, " '92 Beijing wenhua shishang," *Zhuiqiu*, 1993:2, p. 9. See also Li Tiezheng, "Da beixinde qifa," *Jingji ribao*, 19 July 1992.

128. See the Beijing Keystone Printing ad in *Beijing Scene*, 8–14 March 1996, p. 3.

129. *qian bushi wannengde, ke meiqian shi wanwan bunengde.*

130. *Liu Yajun youmo manhua shan.* They carried crude cartoon pictures with lines like "I really want to get married but haven't found the right one yet," *henxiang jiehun, dan zhijin meiyou yujian heshide*; "I'm a decent sort, but I always get dumped on," *ren hen shanliang dan lao chikui*; and so on.

131. This information is based on discussions with Kong Yongqian and Wang Youshen and from an interview with Liu Yajun on 19 May 1993. Liu's style of T-shirt was also known as "karaoke T-shirts," *kala wenhua shan.* See Li Jian, "OK! Kala wenhua shan," *Zhongguo qingnian*, 1992:11, pp. 18–19.

132. Bruce Gilley, "Dissident Engages Qian in Repartee," *Eastern Express* (Hong Kong), 13 March 1995; and Bruce Gilley, "Dissident Collared for T-shirt Slogans," *Eastern Express*, 14 March 1995. See also Asia Watch, ed., *Detained in China and Tibet: A Directory of Political and Religious Prisoners* (New York: Human Rights Watch, 1994), pp. 51–52.

133. See Wu Chuming, "Shengshi fengjing yu mochao qingxu," *Minzhu Zhongguo*, 1992:8, p. 79. See also the photographs on the inside cover of *Zhongguo zhi chun*, 1992:1.

134. My thanks to Y. S. Chan and W. J. F. Jenner for bringing this to my notice and to Y. S. for a copy of the stamp itself.

135. The line is spoken by Hunter Chang (Chang Liehu) in act 3 of the opera. See "Zhiqu Weihushan: Shenshan wenku," in *Geming yangbanxi juben huibian diyi ji* (Beijing: Renmin wenxue chubanshe, 1974), p. 18.

136. Zhang Tianwei, "Shinian shouju—dianying xueyuan 82 jie biyesheng juhui," *Beijing qingnian bao*, 11 March 1993.

137. Chen Wei, " 'Zhongpan Aoyun' 1993 Zhongguo wenhuashan sheji dajiangsai juxing," *Beijing wanbao*, 14 April 1993. My thanks to Sang Ye for this information.

138. *he li jiqun, yishan bucang erhu*, and *yijiao buta erchuan*, respectively. Other T-shirts carried lines like "Heroes never miss an opportunity," *yingxiong buchi yanqian kui*; "A Buddha's mouth, heart of a snake," *fokou shexin*; and so on.

139. Liu Xinwu, *Fengguoer* (Beijing: Zhongguo qingnian chubanshe, 1992), p. 16.

140. Wang Shuo et al., *Guanggaoren*, vol. 1, p. 69.

141. "*You xie shiqing ru suhua shuode: ni yue ba ta dang huishi ta jiu yue shi hui shi.*"

Kong's original T-shirt message read *you xiege shi ni yue na ta dang shi ta jiu yue shi ge shi*. See Han Shaogong, "Xing ershangde mishi," *Dushu*, 1994:1, p. 3.

142. Li Xianting, "Dangqian Zhongguo yishude 'wuliaogan'—xi wanshi xianshizhuyi chaoliu," *Ershiyi shiji*, no. 9 (February 1992), p. 69. An expanded version of this article, which included pictures of most of the artists discussed, including Kong Yongqian and images of three of his T-shirts, was published as Hu Cun (Li's pen name), "Hou '89 yishuzhongde wuliaogan he jiegou yishi," *Yishu chaoliu*, vol. 1 (1992), pp. 1–12.

143. See Li Xianting, "Dangqian Zhongguo yishude 'wuliaogan'," pp. 69, 75.

144. Kong has remarked that Liu Xiaodong's painting, that generally depicted the dispirited arty-trendies of the capital, impressed him when he saw it in early 1990. In late 1991, Liu did a portrait of Kong in the nude entitled "Dreaming" (Zuomeng). The painting was included in an exhibition held in Beijing in April 1993.

145. Li Xianting's own analysis was part of the work he did between 1991 and 1993 as a curator for Johnson Chang of T. Z. Hanart in Hong Kong, who launched the exhibition-*cum*-marketing venture of contemporary mainland nonofficial art, "China's New Art, Post-1989," in February 1993. Li Xianting assigned many works to the categories of "cynical realism" and "political pop."

146. Li Xianting, "Dangqian Zhongguo yishude 'wuliaogan'," p. 75.

147. From an interview with Kong Yongqian, 11 November 1991, at Liubukang, Beijing, and from comments to me in April 1993.

148. Here I follow the use of this expression as found in Howard Felperin, *Beyond Deconstruction: The Uses and Abuses of Literary Theory* (Oxford: Clarendon Press, 1985); and David Lehman, *Signs of the Times: Deconstruction and the Fall of Paul de Man* (New York: Poseidon Press, 1991).

149. David Lehman, *Signs of the Times*, p. 119.

150. See Huang Yongyu, *Yongyu sanji*, 3 vols. (Xianggang: Sanlian shudian, 1983). Examples of Huang's sketches can be found in *Seeds of Fire* and *New Ghosts, Old Dreams*.

151. For details, see "Dui hanzide pipan qingxiang," chapter 15 in Lü Peng and Yi Dan, *Zhongguo xiandai yishu shi* (Changsha: Hunan meishu chubanshe, 1992), pp. 288–299.

152. Wu Shanzhuan, "Guanyu 'da shengyi'," *Zhongguo meishubao* no. 11, 13 March 1989; also Barmé and Jaivin, *New Ghosts, Old Dreams*, pp. 279–280; and Geremie Barmé, "Arrière-pensée on an Avant-Garde: The Stars in Retrospect," in *The Stars: 10 Years*, ed. Chang Tsong-zung, Hui Ching-shuen, and Don J. Cohn (Hong Kong: Hanart 2, 1989), p. 82.

153. See Wang Hua, "A Woman's Work . . . and Dreams . . . Are Never Done," *China Today* 40 (8), August 1991, pp. 53–54.

154. The survey results were published in *Zhongguo shibao zhoukan*, March 1993, nos. 61–63.

155. Liu Xiaobo, "Toushi dalu renminde wenhua shenghuo," part 2, *Zhongguo shibao zhoukan*, 7–13 March 1993, table II in sec. II, p. 77.

156. Ibid.

157. Ibid., p. 77.
158. An observation made in conversation with me, March 1993. For an official media view that prefigured Liu Xiaobo's analysis, see Cao Zhiqian's " 'Wenhua shan' de leng sikao."
159. The film was completed in June 1993, but Kong's cameo appearance ended up on the cutting-room floor.
160. See Yan Lieshan, " 'Shan' shangde wenhua," *Jiefang ribao*, 13 June 1993.
161. See "Wenhua shanshang kan wenhua," *Zhonghua zhoumobao*, 3 September 1994.
162. See Yu Genyuan et al., eds., *Xiandai Hanyu xin ciyu cidian* (Beijing: Zhongguo qingnian chubanshe, 1994), p. 947.
163. Lin Xi, "Guanggao shan you huo Jing cheng," *Beijing qingnian bao*, 13 July 1994.
164. In mid-1996, a publisher in Zhejiang Province, one of the centers of the Chinese garment industry, produced a reference volume of commercial T-shirts that reflected the preference for international designs. See He Ping and Lin Yiye, eds., *T xu tu'an* (Hangzhou: Zhejiang kexue jishu chubanshe, 1996).
165. "Iron-on irony" was suggested by the editors of the *Modern Review* in "Ironic shop-o-matic." "Are you embarrassed to wear last year's message T-shirt?" they asked. "The solution is at hand with 'Iron-on Irony.'™ Simply iron-on the inverted commas and, presto! Last year's T-shirt becomes an up-to-the-minute postmodernist statement." See Toby Young, "The Ironic Revival," *Modern Review* 1, no. 9 (June/July 1993), pp. 8–9.

CHAPTER 7

1. See "Deng Xiaoping: Shicha Nanfang fabiao zhongyao tanhua," in Li Fangshi et al., 1993: *Zhongguo renwu nianjian* (Beijing: Huayi chubanshe, 1993), pp. 52–53.
2. See Huangpu Ping, "Gaige kaifang yao you xin silu," *Jiefang ribao*, 2 March 1991; "Kuoda kaifangde yishi yao geng qian xie," *Jiefang ribao*, 22 March 1991; and "Gaige kaifang xuyao dapi decai jianbeide ganbu," *Jiefang ribao*, 22 April 1991.
3. Chen Xitian, "Dongfang feng lai manyuan chun—Deng Xiaoping tongzhi zai Shenzhen jishi," *Shenzhen tequ bao*, 26 March 1992.
4. These books included Committee, ed., *Lishide chaoliu—xuexi Deng Xiaoping nanxun zhongyao jianghua fudao cailiao* (Beijing: Zhongguo renmin daxue, 1992), of which one of the main editors was Yuan Hongbing (see chapter 10, "To Screw Foreigners Is Patriotic"); Zhao Shilin, ed., *Fang "zuo" beiwanglu* (Taiyuan: Shuhai chubanshe, 1992); Wen Yu (the pen name of the Beijing-based sociologist Lu Jianhua), *Zhongguo "zuo" huo* (Beijing: Zhaohua chubanshe, 1993); and Yuan Yongsong and Wang Junwei, eds., *Zuoqing ershi nian—1957–1976* (Beijing: Nongcun duwu chubanshe, 1993).
5. See, for example, Yu Xinyan, *Yu Xinyan zawen xuan xubian* (Beijing: Beijing chubanshe, 1993), pp. 309–376. For more on Yu Xinyan, see chapter 2, "An Iron Fist in a Velvet Glove."
6. This is, of course, not to say that they had been silent following June 1989, but the debate surrounding "*The Abandoned Capital* phenomenon," or incident, did crystallize intellectual opinion in a way not seen for some years.

7. Jia Pingwa, *Feidu* (Beijing: Beijing chubanshe, 1993), pp. 178–179.

8. See also Zha Jianying's comments on the novel in *China Pop: How Soap Operas, Tabloids, and Bestsellers Are Transforming a Culture* (New York: The New Press, 1995), pp. 129–139, 146–164.

9. Xiao Xialin, "Houji," in Xiao Xialin, ed., Feidu *feishei* (Beijing: Xueyuan chubanshe, 1993), p. 289.

10. Xiao Xialin, "Qianyan," in Xiao, Feidu *feishei*, p. 2.

11. Xiao Xialin, Feidu *feishei*, pp. 4, 289.

12. Li Shulei, "Xu: yagen jiu meiyou linghun," in Duo Wei, ed., Feidu *ziwei* (Kaifeng: Henan renmin chubanshe, 1993), p. 2.

13. Zha Jianying, *China Pop*, p. 150.

14. Xi Ning, "Zhonggong zaidu zhengchi chuanmei waifeng," *Zhongguo shibao zhoukan*, 12–18 December 1993, p. 16.

15. Fudan Development Institute (Yang Fujia, Wang Huning, Cheng Tianquan, et al.), ed., *Goujian xin tizhi: 1994 Zhongguo fazhan baogao* (Shanghai: Shanghai renmin chubanshe, 1995), p. 139. See also Geremie R. Barmé, *Shades of Mao: The Posthumous Cult of the Great Leader* (Armonk, N.Y.: Sharpe, 1996), p. 50.

16. "Deng Xiaoping jinianzhang yi faxing wei gongkai," *Shijie ribao* (New York), 18 June 1994.

17. Shi Tao, "1993, Zhongguo changxiaoshu daguan," *Wenhui dushu zhoubao*, 12 March 1994; and "1993 nian Zhongguo dushu chubanjie 10 da xinwen," *Wenhui dushu zhoubao*, 1 January 1994.

18. Ming Xin, "Baoye jingzheng yiqu jilie," *Zhongguo shibao zhoukan*, 20–26 March 1994, p. 21.

19. See Zha Jianying, *China Pop*, pp. 105–111, 117–121.

20. Bob Hawke, the former Labor prime minister of Australia, for example, was on the advisory board of *Strategy and Management*.

21. Zhu Dake, *Ranshaode mijin* (Shanghai: Xue lin chubanshe, 1991), p. 55. There were, however, those persecuted by the People's Democratic Dictatorship for their simple honesty in the face of the state's overwhelming political and cultural hypocrisy.

22. See "Speaking Politics," *China News Analysis* 1553, 1 February 1996, p. 4.

23. The term "spiritual pollution," *jingshen wuran*, was rarely used in the higher realms of government after the 1983–1984 antispiritual pollution campaign. But when employed, it was as a blanket term covering ideas and works that spread, as Deng Xiaoping had put it, "distrust in socialism, communism and the leadership of the Communist Party." See Geremie Barmé and John Minford, eds., *Seeds of Fire: Chinese Voices of Conscience* (Hong Kong: Far Eastern Economic Review, 1986), 2nd ed. (New York: Hill & Wang, 1988), p. 345. Whereas "spiritual pollution" was a code term for cultural anarchy in general, "bourgeois liberalization," *zichanjieji ziyouhua*, denoted, in a political purge, a particular party leader and his bureaucratic allies. Thus the ouster of Party General Secretaries Hu Yaobang in early 1987 and Zhao Ziyang in mid-1989 were referred to in the official media as attacks on bourgeois liberalization.

24. For a list of these up to 1989, see chapter 2, "An Iron Fist in a Velvet Glove," and Barmé and Minford, *Seeds of Fire*, pp. 343–353.

25. See *Zhongguo daobao*, 1993:2, cover; Lao Lin, "Liulang Beijing," pp. 5–11; Zi Ye, "'Xuewei' zhongshengxiang," pp. 14–17; and Dai Hanzhi, "Zhongguo qianwei yishuzhan," pp. 50–55.

26. From comments made to me in late 1991. Other successful, but less media-prominent, coevals of Chen Kaige were seen in a more benign fashion. Take, for example, the case of the middle-aged poet Mang Ke, a founding editor of the nonofficial 1970s' journal *Today* and an old associate of Chen's. By the early 1990s he had achieved the status of Beijing's leading veteran bohemian. Invited to travel internationally, Mang Ke was also an editor of the major mainland unofficial poetry journal *Modern Chinese Poetry* (Xiandai hanshi). In 1994, he even published a fictional account of his early literary career as a dissident poet. See Mang Ke, *Yeshi* (Changsha: Hunan wenyi chubanshe, 1994).

27. Wu explained his three-hour film series of interviews on the Cultural Revolution as presenting a range of narrative perspectives of the period from the point of view of an engaged observer. See Wu Wenguang, "Wode jiyi he wode jilu," *Dongfang*, 1996:4, pp. 80–83. Wu says that originally his elder sister in Yunnan was anxious to see the film and show it to her son, Wu's nephew. Later he discovered that his nephew had taped over the copy of the documentary with some Oscar-winning film (p. 83). The implication is that history is thus obliterated by fashionable, foreign-imported culture. I would venture to guess that the twenty-four-year-old merely subjected Wu's film to the kind of critical treatment it deserved.

28. Called respectively in Chinese, "Guangchang" and "Erzi." See Ian Johnson, "True Grit," *Far Eastern Economic Review*, 11 July 1996, pp. 46–47.

29. See Geremie Barmé, "Arrière-pensée on an Avant-Garde: The Stars in Retrospect," in *The Stars: 10 Years*, ed. Chang Tsong-zung, Hui Ching-shuen, and Don J. Cohn (Hong Kong: Hanart 2, 1989), p. 80; and Bai Jieming (Barmé), "Beijingde yangshalong," *Jiushi niandai yuekan*, 1988:3, 94–95. "Radical Chic: That Party at Lenny's" is collected in Tom Wolfe, *The Purple Decades* (Harmondsworth, Middlesex: Penguin Books, 1984), pp. 181–197. For a time in late 1985 and early 1986, *The Purple Decades* was stocked by the book section of the Beijing Friendship Store.

30. See, for example, Claire Huot, "Anything but Landscapes: The Dazzling Bodies of China's Avant-Garde Art," in *Belief in China: Art and Politics; Deities and Mortality*, ed. Robert Benewick and Stephanie Donald (Brighton, Essex: Green Center for Non-Western Art and Culture at the Royal Pavilion, Art Gallery and Museums, 1996), pp. 53–68.

31. Tony Rayns, "China: Censors, Scapegoats and Bargaining Chips," *Index on Censorship*, 1995:6, p. 79.

32. "Mother" was initially banned from release, although it was eventually screened in China.

33. Dou Wei, the lead singer of the short-lived group Dreaming (Zuomeng), performs a spaced-out rock song that is the high point of the film.

34. See, for example, Tony Rayns's positive evaluation of the film in "The Well Dries Up," *Index on Censorship*, 1997:1, p. 92.

35. See Rey Chow's comments on this in *Primitive Passions: Visuality, Sexuality, Ethnography, and Contemporary Chinese Cinema* (New York: Columbia University Press, 1995), pp. 155–156.

36. Zhang Tianwei of the *Beijing Youth News* was an early example. See Zhang, "Zhang Yuan yu MTV," *Beijing qingnian bao*, 18 July 1992.

37. For a typical example of the hype surrounding Wu Wenguang, see David Blumental's cover story on Wu in the expat English weekly *Beijing Scene*: David Blumental, "Artist on the Edge: Independent Filmmaker Wu Wenguang," *Beijing Scene*, 23–29 February 1996, pp. 8–9.

38. See Lin Xudong, "Zhongguo dianying: 'diwudai' zhi hou, 'diliudai'?" *Jinri xianfeng*, no. 3 (July 1995), pp. 79–90, 124; and Ding Dong and Xie Yong, "Shichang yu ziyou zhuangaoren," *Dongfang*, 1995:4, p. 90. Other examples of this privileged criticism can be found in Beijing, Shanghai, and regional journals. Many of the writers were friends, teachers, or groupies of freelance artists. The potential of the "sixth generation" had been discussed for some years. See, for example, Lao Niu, "Diliudai—yige yuce," *Beijing qingnian bao*, 3 May 1991. For a pen portrait of Dai Jinhua, see Zha Jianying, *China Pop*, pp. 155–156.

39. A number of Beijing journals and newspapers expressed interest in publishing my own Chinese-language critique of Zhang Yuan's and Wu Wenguang's work that appeared in Taiwan and Hong Kong in late 1993. See Bai Jieming, "Dalude yazhimin wenhua," *Zhongguo shibao zhoukan*, 21–27 December 1993. All that was asked was that they be allowed to edit out my observation that the quirks of authoritarian culture on the mainland had engendered a vacuous parallel arts scene. I failed to comply, and the article was not reprinted.

40. Billy Bragg, an English singer, said He Yong was the closest thing to a punk he had seen during his trip to mainland China in early 1989. Bragg saw He Yong perform a song "Take off your clothes and come with me," during which the singer sprayed the audience with beer.

41. When He Yong and I performed a two-man show, "Red Noise," at the Institute of Contemporary Art as part of the London International Festival of Theater in June 1993, we opened it with "Garbage Dump" and closed with "Bell and Drum Towers."

42. Arthur C. Danto, *Encounters and Reflections: Art in the Historical Present* (New York: Farrar, Straus & Giroux, 1990), p. 302.

CHAPTER 8

1. "Reformist Baroque" was included in Don J. Cohn, ed., *Liu Da Hong: Paintings 1986–92* (Hong Kong: Schoeni Fine Oriental Art, 1992); "Export, Exploit, Expropriate: Artful Marketing from China" was published in Valerie C. Doran, ed., *New Art from China, 1989–93* (Hong Kong: Hanart, 1993); "Taiwan: China's Other" was an essay in *Contemporary Taiwan Art* (Taipei: Museum of Modern Art, 1995); "Draco

Volans Est in Coelo" was written for a catalog produced by the Louisiana Museum of Modern Art in Humblebaek, Denmark, which hosted a Cai Guo Qiang installation and exhibition in March and April 1997; and "'MB@Game!'—A Beijing Screensaver" appeared in *Art AsiaPacific*, no. 15 (June 1997), pp. 78–83.

2. Wu Shanzhuan, "Guanyu 'da shengyi'," *Zhongguo meishu bao*, 1989:11, 13 March. This translation is from Geremie Barmé and Linda Jaivin, eds., *New Ghosts, Old Dreams: Chinese Rebel Voices* (New York: Times Books, 1992), pp. 279–280.

3. See Geremie R. Barmé, "The Garden of Perfect Brightness, a Life in Ruins," *East Asian History*, no. 11 (June 1996), pp. 145 ff.

4. From Sang Ye, "Fringe-Dwellers: Down and out in the Yuan Ming Yuan Artists' Village," trans. Geremie R. Barmé, *Art AsiaPacfic*, no. 15 (June 1997), p. 77.

5. Tom Wolfe, *The Painted Word* (New York: Farrar, Straus & Giroux, 1975), pp. 22–23. In the late 1980s, I had the pleasure of being criticized in the Hong Kong press by Yang Manke for organizing a Beijing "foreign salon." Yang referred to an eyewitness account by the dilettante Zhang Langlang. It would appear that my offense was to have invited Langlang to dinner at the home of Jane Macartney, a foreign correspondent, with the acerbic literary critic Liu Xiaobo. See Yang Manke, "Beijing yangshalongde xingxing sese," *Jiushi niandai yuekan*, 1989:1–2, pp. 14–16, an article partially inspired by my own "Beijing yangshalong," *Jiushi niandai yuekan*, 1988:3, pp. 94–95. See also Liu Xiaobo's riposte in his "Yangshalong yu wenhua qinlüe," *Jiefang yuekan*, 1989:3, pp. 79–82.

6. Quoted in Geremie Barmé, "Arrière-pensée on an Avant-Garde: The Stars in Retrospect," in *The Stars: 10 Years*, ed. Chang Tsong-zung, Hui Ching-shuen, and Don J. Cohn (Hong Kong: Hanart 2 Gallery, 1989), pp. 80–81.

7. Sang Ye, "Fringe-Dwellers," pp. 74–75.

8. In 1986–1987, I recall a number of filmmakers who now have established international careers earnestly seeking guidance on this issue from the foreigners of their acquaintance.

9. See Zhang Geng, *Guochao huazheng lu*, in *Hualan congkan*, ed. Yu Anlan (Beijing: Renmin meishu chubanshe, 1960), vol. 2, p. 32.

10. See Norman K. Denzin, "Blue Velvet: Postmodern Contradictions," *Theory, Culture & Society* 5 (1988), p. 471.

11. Some of the political works like "Model Wheel of Life" and "Door Gods" did appear in 1993 in print. See *Dangdai yishu: Bopu qingxiang—dangdai Zhongguo xin keti*, series 5 (Changsha: Hunan meishu chubanshe, 1993), pp. 26, 29.

12. See José Antonio Maravall, *Culture of the Baroque: Analysis of a Historical Structure* (Minneapolis: University of Minnesota Press, 1986).

13. See Lin Yutang, *With Love and Irony* (London: Heinemann, 1942), pp. 53.

14. See Barmé, "Arrière-pensée," p. 82.

15. "The Painting Den: Liu Wei, Fang Lijun Exhibition," held at the Beijing Capital Museum, Wanshou Temple, April 1992.

16. The "New Generation Art" exhibition sponsored by the *Beijing Youth News* was held in the Chinese History Museum on Tiananmen Square, July 1991.

17. See "A Rogue's Words," quoted in Claire Roberts, "New Art from China," from the catalog for the exhibition "Post-Mao Product: New Art from China" (Sydney: Art Gallery of New South Wales, September–October 1992).

18. This was an exhibition organized in 1993 by the Hong Kong art dealer Johnson Chang (Chang Tsong-zung; Zhang Songren) with the support of David Tang, the wealthy proprietor of the neochinoiserie China Club.

19. For the detailed history of these trends and examples of major works, see Lü Peng and Yi Dan, *Zhongguo xiandai yishu shi 1979–1989* (Changsha: Hunan meishu chubanshe, 1992).

20. See Arthur C. Danto, *Beyond the Brillo Box: The Visual Arts in Post-Historical Perspective* (New York: Farrar, Straus & Giroux, 1992), p.10.

21. See the comments on the *Beijing Youth News* in chapter 5, "The Graying of Chinese Culture."

22. My thanks to Gavan McCormack for suggesting this translation.

23. See *Yishu shichang*, 1992:6.

24. Quoted in Xu Hailing, "Guangzhou shouci juban yishu shuangnian zhan," *Zhongguo shibao zhoukan*, 1–7 November 1992, p. 81.

25. Li Xiaoshan, the Nanjing-based critic noted for his fiery attacks on traditional Chinese painting in 1985–1986, was himself enshrined in oil when Mao Yan did a large "A Portrait of Xiaoshan." The painting was exhibited at the Guangzhou Biennial.

26. "Preface by the Editor," *Yishu shichang*, 1992:6, p. 2.

27. Peng De, "Piping yu runge," *Yishu shichang*, 1992:5, p. 49. For details of Peng's "scale of critical worth," see p. 51.

28. Robert Hughes, "Jean-Michel Basquiat: Requiem for a Featherweight," in *Nothing If Not Critical: Selected Essays on Art and Artists* (London: Harvill, 1991), p. 310.

29. See Andrew Ross, "Uses of Camp," in his *No Respect: Intellectuals & Popular Culture* (New York: Routledge, Chapman and Hall, 1989), p. 139; and chapter 5, "The Graying of Chinese Culture."

30. Before their dispersal in mid-1995, members of the Yuan Ming Yuan Artists' Village — Beijing's West Village — claimed they had stocks of paintings in various avant-garde styles that used the image of Deng Xiaoping. According to one artist, they were preparing to flood the international market with these cutting-edge works following the leader's demise. See also Sang Ye, "Fringe-Dwellers," pp. 74–77.

31. Such tea shops and eateries did become more common in Beijing from 1995 with the opening, for example, of the Taiwan Wufu Chadao Teahouse near Di'anmen and the Gengwu Mess Hall in Sanlitun.

32. My thanks to Claire Roberts of the Powerhouse Museum in Sydney and Rhana Devenport of the Queensland Art Gallery in Brisbane for allowing me access to their archival material on Cai Guo Qiang. I am grateful also to John Minford, who first brought to my attention the eighteenth-century Latin translation of the *Book of Changes*, from which the line "draco volans est in coelo" is taken.

33. *wei waixingren zuo jihua.*

34. Cai Guo Qiang, "Project for Extraterrestrials No. 10: Project to Add 10,000 Meters to the Great Wall of China," February 1993, details in *Cai Guo Qiang "From The Pan-Pacific,"* Iwaki City Art Museum, 6–31 March 1994, p. 115.

35. See Arthur Waldron, *The Great Wall of China: From History to Myth* (Cambridge: Cambridge University Press, 1990).

36. This is according to Terry White of the Media Services Branch of the U.S. National Aeronautics and Space Administration in Houston, Texas. My thanks to Linda Jaivin for providing me with a copy of Mr White's comments.

37. From Hou Dejian, "Longde chuanren," translated in Barmé and Jaivin, *New Ghosts, Old Dreams,* p. 154.

38. From Su Xiaokang et al., *River Elegy,* translated in *New Ghosts, Old Dreams,* pp. 153, 155.

39. David Wingrove, *Chung Kuo Book 1: The Middle Kingdom* (New York: Dell, 1990). My thanks to Dru Gladney for bringing this novel to my attention.

40. See Holland Cotter, "A SoHo Sampler: Short List for Prize," *New York Times,* 22 November 1996.

41. C. A. S. Williams, *Outline of Chinese Symbolism and Art Motives: An Alphabetical Compendium of Antique Legends and Beliefs, as Reflected in the Manners and Customs of the Chinese* (Shanghai: Kelly and Walsh, 1941), p. 136.

42. *The I Ching or Book of Changes,* the Richard Wilhelm translation rendered into English by Cary F. Baynes (London: Routledge & Kegan Paul, 1970), pp. 9–10.

43. A number of paintings from the *Video Engame Series* were included in the exhibition MAO GOES POP at the Museum of Contemporary Art in Sydney, June 1993.

44. See Feng Mengbo, *Youxi jieshu: Changzheng, Endgame: Long March* (Hong Kong: Hanart TZ Gallery, 1994), pp. 13–56.

45. Ibid., p. 58.

46. From Feng Mengbo, "Private Paths," trans. Geremie R. Barmé.

47. From ibid. See also Feng Mengbo, "My Private Album," *Grand Street* 63 (1997), p. 27.

48. Feng did not complete this project at the time.

49. See Geremie R. Barmé, *Shades of Mao: The Posthumous Cult of the Great Leader* (Armonk, N.Y.: Sharpe, 1996), pp. 97–99.

50. The 1998 URL for the site was egg.tokyoweb.or.jp/comdex/newcc/new/guide.htm

51. For details regarding the development of the Internet in China, see Geremie R. Barmé and Sang Ye, "The Great Firewall of China," *Wired* (5.06), June 1997, pp. 138–150, 174–178 . In 1997, Feng and his wife moved to a spacious villa to the south of Beijing, commuting to the city in their jeep.

CHAPTER 9

1. Robert Goldman and Stephen Papson, *Sign Wars: The Cluttered Landscape of Advertising* (New York: Guilford Press, 1996), pp. 249–252, 255. The expression "pale-osymbolic" comes from Alvin Gouldner, *The Dialectic of Ideology and Technology* (New York: Oxford University Press, 1982), p. 225.

2.   The names of mainland and Hong Kong pop singers popular in the mid-1980s.

3.   From Liu Xinwu, "A Riot," translated in Geremie Barmé and Linda Jaivin, eds., *New Ghosts, Old Dreams: Chinese Rebel Voices* (New York: Times Books, 1992) pp. 275–276.

4.   James B. Twitchell, ADCULT USA: *The Triumph of Advertising in American Culture* (New York: Columbia University Press, 1996), p. 3; and Tom Vanderbilt, "The Advertised Life," in *Commodify Your Dissent, Salvos from the Baffler*, ed. Thomas Frank and Matt Weiland (New York: Norton, 1997), p. 130.

5.   See Jiwei Ci, *Dialectic of the Chinese Revolution: From Utopianism to Hedonism* (Stanford, Calif.: Stanford University Press, 1994), pp. 166–167.

6.   See, for example, the section "Humanity" in Geremie Barmé and John Minford, eds., *Seeds of Fire: Chinese Voices of Conscience* (Hong Kong: Far Eastern Economic Review, 1986), 2nd ed. (New York: Hill & Wang, 1988), pp. 149–166.

7.   See Zhongguo diyi qiche jituan gongsi, "Hongqi—hecai! jiayou!!!" *Beijing qingnianbao*, 31 January 1997. Prizes offered for winning slogans ranged from 10,000 *yuan* in cash to to-scale models of the new "Red Flag."

8.   See Lauren Langman, "Neon Cages: Shopping for Subjectivity," in *Lifestyle Shopping: The Subject of Consumption*, ed. Rob Shields (London: Routledge, 1992), pp. 40–82.

9.   There is some recognition of this in Zhang Xinying, "Xianggangde liuxing wenhua," *Dushu*, 1996:7, pp. 26–31.

10.   There have even been interesting mainland-essayed fictional investigations of the extreme urban environment of Hong Kong, as witnessed by Wang Anyi's 1993 story "Love and Sentiment in Hong Kong." See Wang Anyi, "Xianggangde qing he ai," *Shanghai wenxue*, 1993:8, discussed by Xiaobing Tang in "New Urban Culture and the Anxiety of Everyday Life in Contemporary China," in *In Pursuit of Contemporary East Asian Culture*, ed. Xiaobing Tang and Stephen Snyder (Boulder, Colo.: Westview Press, 1996), pp. 115–118.

11.   The first local television ad was broadcast in Shanghai on 28 January 1979. It hawked medicinal wine, the traditional snake oil of the nation. This was followed in February of the same year by print ads in the *Shanghai Wenhui Daily* and the *People's Daily* in Beijing. In December 1979, China Central TV (CCTV) broadcast its first advertisement. On this, see Zhou Xing, "Guanggao geile women shenme?" *Dongfang*, 1996:4, p. 98. In January 1980, the station introduced a daily eighty-minute advertising program. The Guanggao jiemu, as it was called, was later extended to 160 minutes. For a history of post-1979 advertising in China, see Chen Peiai, *Zhongwai guangao shi—zhan zai dangdai shijiaode quanmian huigu* (Beijing: Zhongguo wujia chubanshe, 1997), pp. 80–165. Also see Xu Bai Yi, *Marketing to China: One Billion New Customers* (Lincolnwood, Ill.: NTC Business Books, 1991), pp. 71–84; and Randall Stross, "The Return of Advertising in China: A Survey of the Ideological Reversal," *China Quarterly*, no. 123, September 1990, pp. 485–502. My thanks to Miriam Lang for bringing Stross's work to my attention.

12.   Among Zhong's early work, a personal favorite is an ad for the drink Oreon. In December 1993, Zhong told me that the ad was filmed in May 1989 and that the actors were university students who were taking time off from the hunger strike on Tiananmen Square to participate in the shoot. Another representative early advertisement by

Zhong was made for Air China. It features Qin tomb warriors in the loess plains of Shaanxi turning to look as a jet flies overhead. Both ads are featured in the documentary film *The Gate of Heavenly Peace*, directed by Carma Hinton and Richard Gordon (Boston: Long Bow Group, 1995); and see chapter 12, "Totalitarian Nostalgia." Information about other successful ad makers can be found in Du Liancheng, ed., *Zhongguo guanggaoren fengcai* (Beijing: Zhongguo wenlian chuban gongsi, 1995).

13. For a volume of mainland Chinese views of what ads have been successful, see Yu Genyuan et al., eds., *Guanggao, biaoyu, zhaotie . . . yongyu pingxi 400 li* (Beijing: Zhongguo shehui kexue chubanshe, 1992).

14. See "No Sex, No Violence, No News," a one-hour documentary on cable television in Shanghai directed by Susan Lambert and Stephan Moore (Sydney: Film Australia, 1995), screened by the Australian Broadcasting Commission on 9 May 1996. As one of the talking heads in that documentary, I made the case that more TV in China did not necessarily mean greater freedoms or access to "Western values." In many instances, it probably presages nothing so much as more shopping channels and the delirium of retail therapy.

15. The Tianjin Ruida Company was introduced to the Hula Hoop by an American businessman. The Ruida's hoops were promoted via a TV ad that called on viewers to use the hoop to "reclaim that slim you of yesteryear; recall the memories of your childhood." This helped sparked a craze that soon engulfed Beijing and then the whole of China. As reported in *Zhongguo tiyu bao*, 23 February 1992. The fad, not surprisingly, soon fell into abeyance, thus setting the scene for a revival.

16. The rapid growth of Internet access and ISPs in China after 1995 led the authorities to direct considerable resources to developing a modern cyber-identity. See, for example, the design and language of *People's Daily Online* (www.peopledaily.co.cn).

17. Other anniversaries, both national and local, are too numerous to mention. But they include 8 March (International Women's Day), 4 May (Youth Day), 1 June (Children's Day), and 1 August (Army Day).

18. In regard to the late-1996 and 1997 National Quiz Show on HK, see Kevin Kwong, "Facing up to the Facts," in "The Review," *South China Morning Post*, 18 January 1997.

19. See Cheng Manli, "Gonggong guanggao—guanggao jiazude xin chengyuan," *Xiandai guanggao*, 1994:2, pp. 24–25; and Yue Wenhou, "Jingji shenghuo xin fengjing: Gongyi guanggao," *Renmin ribao*, 17 October 1996.

20. For example, large billboards were set up throughout Beijing that carried public service announcements and propaganda slogans in an environment of soft-focus images and slick photographs. Clumsy and wordy exhortations, however, were also common, and they were plastered throughout Chinese cities during the summer and autumn months of 1996.

21. The People's Bank of China, the chief state fiscal institution, for example, created a logo-*cum*-corporate identity marker by combining the design of traditional Chinese coins with the word China/center (Zhong). See *Xiandai guanggao*, 1994:2, p. 32. The publishers mentioned here relied initially on their pre-1949 commercial and revolutionary symbolism, and China Travel gradually evolved a more marketable image.

22. For details on the evolution of the paper's layout, see Zheng Xingdong et al., eds., *Beijing qingnian bao—Beijing qingnian bao xianxiang saomiao, Xinwen chongjibo* (Beijing: Zhongguo renmin daxue, 1994), pp. 234–257.

23. From the late 1980s, when it was a weekly, the paper gradually expanded its reader base from its original target-audience of middle-school students. It also increased the frequency of publication to twice a week in the early 1990s, supplemented by a special weekend edition when such papers became the fashion in 1993, in response to the increased leisure time and disposable income of their readers.

24. Zheng Xingdong, *Beijing qingnian bao*, p. 5.

25. See Li Xianting, "Major Trends in the Development of Contemporary Chinese Art," in *China's New Art, Post-1989*, ed. Valerie C. Doran (Hong Kong: Hanart TZ Gallery, 1993), pp. x–xxii.

26. See Li Xianting, "Pupu zhi hou: yansu huayu yu fanfeng mofang," *Shan yishu*, no. 92, 1997:11, pp. 63–68.

27. See Don J. Cohn, ed., *Liu Da Hong: Paintings 1986–92* (Hong Kong: Schoeni Fine Oriental Art, 1992), pp. 136–139.

28. "Qiangjingde junlü xiongfeng—budui huajia zuopin xuan," *Meishu bao* (Zhongguo Meishu xueyuan, Hangzhou, Zhejiang), 31 July 1995.

29. See Daozi, "Xin jishi: sheying yishude shenmei zhuanxiang," *Dongfang*, 1996:4, pp. 95–97. Daozi was originally from Xi'an and a poet of the 1985 School of the Supreme Ultimate. See Barmé and Minford, *Seeds of Fire*, pp. 409–410.

30. Twitchell, *Adcult USA*, pp. 179–228, esp. pp. 207–213.

31. Arthur C. Danto, *Encounters and Reflections: Art in the Historical Present* (New York: Farrar, Straus & Giroux, 1990), p. 303.

32. Celeste Olalquiaga, *Megalopolis: Contemporary Culture Sensibilities* (Minneapolis: University of Minnesota Press, 1992), p. 51, quoted in Goldman and Papson, *Sign Wars*, p. 258. There were strong indicators that elements of the early-1990s' revival of the Mao cult appealed to certain urbanites because of its "second-degree kitsch."

33. My thanks to Tom Parker for searching out Mr Shen and obtaining this information on my behalf.

34. The expression "attention engineers" comes from Twitchell's *Adcult USA*, p. 33.

35. Mao, "Reply to Comrade Kuo Mo-jo—to the Tune of *Man Chiang Hung*," in Mao Tsetung, *Poems* (Peking: Foreign Languages Press, 1976), p. 47.

36. These ads appeared on Beijing TV in mid-1996. For the use of the image of PLA martyr Lei Feng and an accompanying Mao quotation "Learn from Comrade Lei Feng" for the promotion of the Changsha Municipal Advertising Company, see Geremie R. Barmé, *Shades of Mao: The Posthumous Cult of the Great Leader* (Armonk, N.Y.: Sharpe, 1996), p. 87, fig. 13.

37. *Haicheng xunhu quanxin quanyi wei renmin fuwu.* Billboards with this line (written in white paint on a red background, in imitation of the original propaganda slogans) were situated at the main intersection at Dongdaqiao in Chaoyang District and at the Di'anmen Bridge north of Jingshan Park.

38. "*Zhang Xiaoquande daojian yiwan nian ye buyao gaodiao,*" Mao Zedong, 5 March

1956, from "Jiakuai shougongyede shehuizhuyi gaizao," in Mao Zedong, *Mao Zedong xuanji diwu juan* (Beijing: Renmin chubanshe, 1977), p. 265.

39. For a less-than-optimistic view of state control over general advertising in China, in particular following the promulgation of the 1994 advertising law, see Mark Spence and Stella L. M. So, "Advertising in China," *Access China*, no. 23, October 1996, pp. 13–17, esp. pp. 16–17.

40. John Heileman, "Rouble without a cause," *Modern Review* 1, no. 1 (Autumn 1991), p. 7.

41. Henry A. Giroux, "Benetton's 'World without Borders': Buying Social Change," in *The Subversive Imagination: Artists, Society, and Social Responsibility*, ed. Carol Becker (New York: Routledge, 1994), p. 204.

42. Mihajlo Mihajlov, *Underground Notes*, trans. Maria Mihajlov Ivusic and Christopher W. Ivusic (London: Routledge & Kegan Paul, 1977), p. 34.

43. Twitchell, *Adcult* USA, p. 30.

CHAPTER 10

1. In "Are you ready?" an émigré Chinese interviewee—a prostitute from Nanchang who was plying her trade on the Gold Coast in Queensland, Australia—told the writer Sang Ye that Chinese students and other mainlanders she had encountered thought "that to screw foreign cunt is a kind of patriotism," *cao waiguo bi ye suan aiguo ma*. See Sang Ye, "Are You Ready?" translated by Geremie R. Barmé, with Linda Jaivin, in Sang Ye, *The Year the Dragon Came* (Brisbane: Queensland University Press, 1996), p. 14.

2. Zha Xiduo, "Youse yanjinglide xiyangjing—Beijingrende Niuyue meng," *Jiushi niandai yuekan*, 1994:2, pp. 16–17. Zha Xiduo is the pen name of Jianying Zha, the author of *China Pop*. In relation to the market in and cultural significance of white flesh in contemporary China, see Louisa Schein, "The Consumption of Color and the Politics of White Skin in Post-Mao China," *Social Text*, Winter 1995, pp. 146–147. In the early 1990s, salacious stories about Russian prostitutes and bar girls working in northeast and northern China were common in the Chinese gutter press.

3. Another choice scene occurs in episode 8 when Wang's lover, the Taiwanese restaurateuse Ah Chun, says : "They [the Americans] can quite easily imagine a world without China but could never conceive of a world without themselves." Wang responds angrily: "Fuck them! They were still monkeys up in the trees when we were human beings on the ground. Look at how hairy they are; they're not as evolved as us. Just 'cause they have a bit of money!"

4. At the same time, it should be noted that the series belongs to a tradition in which history or things foreign are manipulated in an attempt to comment on contemporary Chinese political and social realities. The plot and characters of *A Beijing Man in New York* were to a great extent concerned not with the fate of Chinese in the United States as such, but with the Chinese and their machinations. Apart from the elements of the series discussed in this chapter, many other complex issues are raised in it that also relate to contemporary attitudes of self-loathing. That the action of the

piece took place in New York is at times coincidental to the central concerns of what was an often-incoherent and crude production.

5. See my remarks in Linda Jaivin, "Life in a 'Battlefield'," *Asian Wall Street Journal*, 24–25 December 1993.

6. See, for example, Frank Dikötter, *The Discourse of Race in Modern China* (London: Hurst, 1992), pp. 75–77, 107–115; and Frank Dikötter, "Racial Identities in China: Context and Meaning," *China Quarterly*, no. 138, June 1994, pp. 404–412.

7. For some of the basic texts in these century-old debates, see, for example, Committee, ed., *Zhongguo jindai wenhua wenti* (Beijing: Zhonghua shuju, 1989); Chen Song, ed., *"Wusi" qianhou Dong-Xi wenhua wenti lunzhan wenxuan*, enlarged ed. (Beijing: Zhongguo shehui kexue chubanshe, 1989); and, Luo Rongqu, ed., *Cong "xihua" dao xiandaihua* (Beijing: Beijing daxue chubanshe, 1990).

8. This point is made very forcefully by the noted writer and translator Dong Leshan in "Dongfangzhuyi dahechang?" *Dushu*, 1994:5, pp. 99–102. Dong, educated in the liberal arts before 1949, was famed for his translations of George Orwell's *1984* (Guangzhou, 1985) and Arthur Koestler's *Darkness at Noon* (Changsha, 1989). In the context of nationalist and racist views as reflected in the attitudes of pro-reform students, activists, and others, see the revealing studies by Barry Sautman, "Anti-Black Racism in Post-Mao China," and Michael J. Sullivan, "The 1988–89 Nanjing Anti-African Protests: Racial Nationalism or National Racism?" both in *China Quarterly*, no. 138, June 1994, pp. 413–437 and 438–457, respectively.

9. In 1988–1989, a number of articles in the journal *New Enlightenment* (Xin qimeng) and the Shanghai weekly *World Economic Herald* (Shijie jingji daobao), for example, made comparisons between the late Qing and Deng's reform era. In the early 1990s, there was a renewed interest in the late-Qing reforms (*xinzheng*, literally "new political system [reforms]") among intellectuals and the reading public. See, for example, Lu Jia, "Wan-Qing zhengzhire ranshao quan Zhongguo," *Zhongguo shibao*, 29 November 1994; and Yang Ping, "Zeng Guofan xianxiangde qishi," *Beijing qingnian bao*, 28 May 1994. For a range of the academic discussions of this topic, see Douglas R. Reynolds, ed. and trans., *China, 1895–1912: State-Sponsored Reforms and China's Late-Qing Revolution Selected Essays from Zhongguo Jindai Shi (Modern Chinese History, 1840–1919)*, *Chinese Studies in History* 28 (3–4), Spring/Summer 1995, pp. 49–171; and Reynolds's own study of the subject, *China, 1898–1912: The Xinzheng Revolution and Japan* (Cambridge, Mass.: Council on East Asian Studies, Harvard University, 1993); and Xu Jilin, "Zhongguoshide rushi jinyu," in his *Xunqiu yiyi: xiandaihua yu wenhua pipan* (Shanghai: Shanghai Sanlian shudian, 1997), pp. 127–135.

10. See the editorial note to "Zeng Guofan caizhe Xiang jun," *Wenhui dushu zhoubao*, 6 September 1994.

11. This view was expressed by Sun Liping of the sociology department of Beijing University in Lu Jia, "Wan-Qing zhengzhire ranshao quan Zhongguo."

12. This point is made by Tang Haoming, the author of the three-volume biographical novel *Zeng Guofan*. See Shao Yanfeng in conversation with Tang, "Zeng Guofan: shijimode wenren meng," *Beijing qingnian bao*, 4 June 1994.

13. See Liu Xinwu, "A Riot," in Geremie Barmé and Linda Jaivin, eds., *New Ghosts, Old Dreams: Chinese Rebel Voices* (New York: Times Books, 1992), pp. 265–278.

14. See James L. Watson, "The Renegotiation of Chinese Cultural Identity in the Post-Mao Era," in *Popular Protest and Political Culture in Modern China*, ed. Jeffrey N. Wasserstrom and Elizabeth J. Perry (Boulder, Colo.: Westview Press, 1992), pp. 67–84; and Edward Friedman, "Reconstructing China's National Identity: A Southern Alternative to Mao-Era Anti-Imperialist Nationalism," *Journal of Asian Studies* 53 (1), February 1994, pp. 67–91.

15. The expression *guoqing*, literally "national situation," although first used in the classical history *Zhanguo ce*, has a complex history in post-nineteenth-century Chinese cultural and political debate. The term was used variously as a pretext for rejecting the influence of the West last century because Western institutions and practices did not "conform to China's national situation," or as a rationale for opposing Communist ideology in the 1930s because it was "unsuited to China's situation." Meanwhile, Mao Zedong declared that an appreciation of China's *guoqing* was essential to the success of the Communist revolution. See Zhu Yuhe and Yang Hongbo, eds., *Zhongguo jin xiandai guoqing wenti pouxi* (Beijing: Qinghua daxue chubanshe, 1991). In 1981, the party employed the term as a propaganda device, as, at times, did oppositionists, and a formidable literature on the subject developed, particularly in the late 1980s. The official Communist Party definition of *guoqing* is "China is a nation that has successfully established a socialist system that over time has proved superior to capitalism but that, nonetheless, requires further political and economic reform. China is a heavily populated country with a large labor force that can contribute greatly to the national economy but that also, due to its size, is the cause of considerable social and economic problems. Rich in natural and mineral resources, China suffers from an uneven distribution of its population and limited arable land. China has an ancient history that has given birth to numerous positive national traditions and traits. The negative ideological influence of the old society, however, has not been entirely eradicated." For this definition, see Liu Hong et al., eds., *Zhongguo guoqing*, restricted circulation (Beijing: Zhonggong zhongyang dangxiao chubanshe, 1990), pp. 3–8. See also Fei Xiaotong, "Tantan renshi Zhongguo guoqing," *Zhongguo guoqing guoli*, 1992:1, pp. 4–5. The mainland usage of the term generally harks back to Mao Zedong's 1939 dictum: "A clear understanding of the national situation of China [*Zhongguode guoqing*] is the primary basis for appreciating all questions related to the Chinese revolution" (see Mao Zedong's "The Chinese Revolution and the Chinese Communist Party").

16. Ten elements of *guoqing* were encapsulated in the formula of a three-word song, *sanzige*, written in imitation of the Confucian children's primer *The Three Character Classic* (Sanzijing). See Guojia jiaowei jichu jiaoyusi, ed., *Xiaoxuesheng guoqing shi zhidao* (Beijing: Zhongguo shaonian ertong chubanshe, 1990), pp. 62–63. For an overview of the subject of *guoqing* in Chinese, see Lu Nian, "Guoqing zhuanzhu gailan," *Wenhui dushu zhoubao*, 11 August 1990. For a more historical and hysterical overview, see the Taiwanese writer Li Ao's essay, "Gei tan Zhong-Xi wenhuade ren

kankan bing," *Li Ao quanji*, vol. 4 (Taibei: Siji chuban shiye youxian gongsi, 1980), p. 23. See also the short-lived Beijing journal *Guoqing Studies* (Guoqing yanjiu), which was published in 1989, and *China's guoqing and National Power* (Zhongguo guoqing guoli), which started publication in 1992, and Wu Jie et al., eds., *Guoqing jiaoyu shouce* (Beijing: Huaxia chubanshe, 1990). A useful volume of party leader's remarks on the subject is Zhonggong zhongyang zhengce yanjiushi dangjianzu, ed., *Mao Zedong, Deng Xiaoping lun Zhongguo guoqing* (Beijing: Zhonggong zhongyang dangxiao chubanshe, 1992).

17. See Jiang Zemin's speeches on this subject in Zhonggong zhongyang zhengce yanjiushi, ed., *Zai xinde lishi tiaojianxia jicheng he fayang aiguozhuyi chuantong—shiyijie sanzhong quanhui yilai youguan zhongyao wenxian zhaibian* (Beijing: *Hongqi* chubanshe, 1990), pp. 301–309, 319–326, 329–351, 373–381, 387–401. For the party's Department of Propaganda documents on educating workers in China's *guoqing* and on carrying out patriotic and revolutionary education among the young, see Zhongyang xuanchuanbu bangongting, ed., *Dangde xuanchuan gongzuo wenjian xuanbian (1988–1992)*, restricted circulation, vol. 4 (Beijing: Zhonggong zhongyang dangxiao chubanshe, 1994), pp. 1962–1965 and 2078–2081, respectively. As noted in chapter 2, "An Iron Fist in a Velvet Glove," Li Ruihuan, the first post–4 June ideological commissar in the Politburo, started his own campaign to "enhance national culture," both to fit in with the strategic shift in propaganda requirements and to counteract attempts by rabid ideologues to purge the cultural sphere. See Li, "Guanyu hongyang minzu youxiu wenhuade ruogan wenti," *Renmin ribao*, 10 January 1990.

18. See "Zhong xiaoxue jiaqiang Zhongguo jindai, xiandaishi ji guoqing jiaoyude zongti gangyao," *Renmin jiaoyu*, 1991:10, pp. 2–24. In 1993, the party's Department of Propaganda; the State Education Commission; the Ministry of Broadcasting, Film, and Television; and the Ministry of Culture jointly issued a list of films that were to be used in pursuing these educational aims. See "Guanyu yunyong youxiu yingshipian zai quanguo zhong xiaoxue kaizhan aiguozhuyi jiaoyude tongzhi (jiaoji [1993] 17 hao)."

19. See "Aiguozhuyi jiaoyu shishi gangyao," *Renmin ribao*, 6 September 1994. The masses had been introduced to "economic patriotism" long before this. Whenever the state had an excess of a certain crop or consumer item, people would be mobilized to show their patriotism by going shopping. Thus, for example, there were sales of the "patriotic vegetable" *aiguo cai*, in Beijing whenever there was a surplus of the annual cabbage crop. Similarly, when there was an overproduction of pork or tangerines, the authorities would enjoin the populace to buy "patriotic meat," *aiguo rou*, and "patriotic tangerines," *aiguo juzi*.

20. See "Aiguozhuyi jiaoyu shishi gangyao," sec. 1, item 2.

21. See "Zhongxuanbu zhaokai 'Aiguozhuyi jiaoyu shishi gangyao' zuotanhui qiangdiao: Guangfan kaizhan aiguozhuyi jiaoyu tigao quanminzude zhengti suzhi," *Renmin ribao*, 10 September 1994.

22. See Fudan Development Institute (Yang Fujia, Wang Huning, Cheng Tianquan, et al., eds.), Goujian xin tizhi: 1994 Zhongguo fazhan baogao (Shanghai: Shanghai renmin chubanshe, 1995), p. 149.

23. *bainian baijie, bainian baishi, bainian baiye, bainian baizhan, bainian baiyi.*

24. Quan Xin, " 'Zhongguo shiji zhi lu: guoqing bainian aiguozhuyi jiaoyu gongcheng' jinqi tuichu," *Beijing qingnian bao,* 16 October 1994. In relation to this collection of patriotic odds and ends, see the encyclopedic work of Ma Yong et al., eds., *Zhongguo jingshen* (Beijing: Hongqi chubanshe, 1991). For other commercial adaptations of the party's patriotism campaign, see Wang Ying, "Xunzhao zhidian—Beijing aiguozhuyi jiaoyu jishi," *Beijing qingnian bao,* 22 November 1994.

25. See Guowu yuan Xinwen bangongshi, *Zhongguode renquan zhuangkuang* (Beijing: Zhongyang wenxian chubanshe, 1991), pp. 1–3; and Committee, ed., *Zhongguode renquan zhuangkuang (baipishu) xuexi cailiao* (Beijing: Hongqi chubanshe, 1991), p. 3. See also the long article on human rights abuses in the West published in *Guangming ribao,* 11 September 1994.

26. The new Mao cult (ca. 1988–1993) was an extremely complex phenomenon, and the anti-Western dimension of it was arguably peripheral to its significance in terms of Chinese culture, social sentiment, and politics.

27. For a typical example of this kind of propaganda, see "Zhongguorende jingshen neng yishan daohai," *Beijing qingnian bao,* 2 August 1991. The language of such writing is highly reminiscent of Maoist propaganda (such as reports on the construction of the Red Flag canal, Dazhai, and Daqing, and the effects of the 1976 Tangshan earthquake) that spoke constantly of the ability of the Chinese laboring people to overcome all obstacles and refashion the world. After 1989, this style of language was used to promote the Asian Games (1990), to mobilize people to fight the 1991 and 1998 floods in south China and, in 1993, in the competition to secure the 2000 Olympic Games for Beijing.

28. See Nayan Chanda and Lincoln Kaye, "Circling Hawks," *Far Eastern Economic Review,* 7 October 1993, pp. 12–13.

29. Wang Shan, *Disan zhi yanjing kan Zhongguo* (Taiyuan: Shanxi renmin chubanshe, 1994). Attributed to a German author, the book was actually written by Wang Shan, its putative "translator." For details of this, see the introduction written by Wang's literary agent Xu Bing for the Hong Kong edition of the book published in early 1995 by *Ming Pao,* in which Wang Shan's ploy of using a pseudoforeign name to disguise the author's true identity is described as being a "well-intentioned deception."

30. Song Qiong et al., *Zhongguo keyi shuo bu—lengzhan hou shidaide zhengzhi yu qinggan jueze* (Beijing: Zhonghua gongshang lianhe chubanshe, 1996). It is interesting to note that Zhang and Qiao, two of the authors of this histrionic tract, were also avantgarde poets and freelance writers. See Fang Jinyu, "Zhongguo keyi shuo bu ma?—shi xia'aide minzuzhuyi? Haishi xin yidai fan-Mei qingxu?" *Nanfang zhoumo,* 9 August 1996. My thanks to Chris Buckley for this material. For excerpts from *No!,* see Zhang Zang Zang et al., "China Can Say No," in *Index on Censorship,* 1997:1, pp. 60–63.

31. See, for example, Willy Wo-Lap Lam, *China After Deng Xiaoping: The Power Struggle in Beijing Since Tiananmen* (Singapore: Wiley, 1995), pp. 185–191.

32. These lyrics come from the Singaporean singer Dick Lee's pop-rap song "Orientalism," Music & Movement (Singapore) / Dick Lee's Club Asia (Tokyo). In full the song goes: "It's a state of mind / It's peace of mind / If you don't mind / Orientalism. / It's East and

West / Forget the rest / So can you guess? / Orientalism. / It's being near / Your being clear / Of being here / Orientalism. / It's being strong / Your fears are gone / You're turning on to / Orientalism. / . . . [Chorus] Oriental, Orientalism! / Oriental — Paris, Tokyo / Oriental — Dallas, Cairo / Oriental — Zurich, Hong Kong / Oriental — Munich, Saigon / It's quite all right / Be white inside / This is your pride / Orientalism. / It's being new / And feeling new / It's being you / Orientalism. / [Rap] I think it's time to show / That all of us are no / Caricatures or stereotypes, / No token yellows! / We simply have to be / Assertive, make them see / This is the new Asian / Ready for the twenty-first century!" My thanks for Gloria Davies for introducing me to Dick Lee's work.

33. For the comments of a number of noted scholars on the revival of "national studies" in the 1990s and its relevance to the question of cultural nationalism and Western thought, see "Guoxue, chuantong wenhua yu shehuizhuyi shicang jingji" in the feature "Wenhua tanfang lu," *Renmin ribao*, 6 and 27 December 1994.

34. For a review of these magazines, see Cheng Nong, "Fuchu haimian," *Dushu*, 1994:2, pp. 47–52. Numerous other publications both in China and elsewhere, like the Hong Kong–based *Twenty-First Century* which circulated in China, played a significant role in mainland intellectual debates in the early 1990s. For an overview of the leading mainland journals, their background, the sources of their funding, and their significance in the early 1990s, see Wang Desheng, " 'Minjiande' xueshu jingguan — 90 niandai dalu 'xuekan xianxiang'," *Dongfang*, 1994:5, pp. 56–58. Other commentators have remarked that the appearance of these publications was symptomatic of a "second cultural fever," *wenhuare*, of the kind that had developed on the mainland in the 1980s. See Hu Yanhua, " 'Dierci wenhuare' qiaoran shengwen," *Zhonghua dushu bao*, 15 February 1995.

35. The titles of these journals in Chinese are *Zhongguo wenhua, Xueren, Dongfang, Zhonghua dushu zhoubao, Wenlun, Zhanlüe yu guanli*, and *Tianya*, respectively.

36. See, for example, the essays by Li Shenzhi, an American studies specialist with the Chinese Academic of Social Science, "Quanqiuhua shidai Zhongguorende shiming," *Dongfang*, 1994:5, pp. 13–18, and "Yazhou jiazhi yu quanqiu jiazhi," *Dongfang*, 1995:4, pp. 4–9.

37. The Chinese terms for "nationalism" most often used in these discussions were *minzuzhuyi* and, more rarely, *mincuizhuyi*. *Mincuizhuyi* had, however, a more narrow definition and strong connotations of cultural determinism. One writer for *Strategy and Management*, for example, noted the *mincuizhuyi* elements of Maoism and their popular appeal in the economic dislocation of the 1990s. See Hu Weixi, "Zhongguo jin xiandaide shehui zhuanxing yu mincuizhuyi," *Zhanlüe yu guanli*, 1994:5, pp. 26–27.

38. See Shi Zhong, "Weilaide chongtu," *Zhanlüe yu guanli*, 1993:1, pp. 46–50. For Huntington's original article, later expanded into a book, see "The Clash of Civilizations," *Foreign Affairs* 72 (3), Summer 1993, pp. 22–49. Wang was also the English editor of the biannual English-language version of *Strategy and Management* that began appearing in 1995. For Shi Zhong's article in English, see *Strategy and Management* (English ed.), 1995:1, pp. 66–73.

39. Shi Zhong, "Weilaide chongtu," p. 47.

40. Ibid., p. 49. Wang's essay was by no means the only mainland Chinese response to Huntington's work. Also see, for example, the far less phlegmatic comments by Ni Shixiong in "Wo suo liaojiede 'Wenming chongtu'," *Tansuo yu zhengming*, 1994:8, digested in Fudan Development Institute, ed., *Goujian xin tizhi: 1994 Zhongguo fazhan baogao*, p. 145.

41. Bao Mi, *Huanghuo*, 3 vols. (Taibei: Fengyun shidai chuban youxian gongsi, 1991). In particular, Wang used an essay appended to the novel. See Li Ming, "Zongkan Zhongguode weiji," *Huanghuo*, vol. 3, pp. 279–313.

42. The novel was written on the mainland and circulated on computer disk. A version was also published in Taiwan amid considerable fanfare. The author's concerns and reflections were supposed to be a direct response to the events of 1989. The book was itself in the style of the "crisis writings" common on the mainland in the late 1980s. Bao Mi told a Beijing-based reporter for *Time* that his novel was "a philosophical tract against consumerism, not an attack on the Communist regime." Jaime A. FlorCruz, "Secrets of a Hot Novel," *Time*, 30 March 1992. See also chapter 5, "The Graying of Chinese Culture."

43. Qiao Liang, *Mori zhi men* (Beijing: Kunlun chubanshe, 1995); and Xiao Nan, "Jingshi yuyan cong Xianggang kaishi . . . —Zhongguo zuojia xiechude diyi bu 'jinweilai xiaoshuo'," *Mingbao yuekan*, 1996:1, p. 102. Similar science-fantasy war novels were available at bookstalls in many Chinese cities. Also see, for example, the PLA Airforce Captain Dai Xu's two-volume *Blood Sacrifice to Heaven* published by the National Defense University in 1994. Dai Xu, *Yi xie ji tian*, 2 vols. (Beijing: Guofang daxue chubanshe, 1994).

44. Qiao Liang, *Mori zhi men*, pp. 527–528.

45. For examples, see ibid., pp. 41–42, 69–71, 124.

46. At the end of the novel, in a scene set at the funeral of the female protagonist, Chan, James White, the representative of Western conscience, declares that he has lost all hope in the West and that Euro-America was in terminal decline. "As a wise man of the East once said: 'What prospers first will decay first, what prospers later has yet to decline. That which has fallen into desuetude first will be the first to be revived. And thus things alternate every one thousand years.' Now the truth of this aphorism can be found among the descendants of that Eastern holy man. The children of the East are like a dark-haired David who takes up his slingshot and casts his stone, the crystallization of his hopes, into the boundless blue firmament. . . . At present we still cannot tell how far it will travel, although we know one thing for sure: the morning sun that rises now over the earth's horizon will be his and his alone . . . Good night, America! Good morning, Asia!" See Qiao Liang, *Mori zhi men*, pp. 605–606.

47. Ibid., pp. 61 and 126. See also pp. 201, 222, and 272 where the astronaut also bids goodnight to Europe and Africa while greeting Asia, the Pacific, and even Australia with the coming of dawn.

48. Xiao Gongqin, "Minzuzhuyi yu Zhongguo zhuanxing shiqide yishi xingtai," *Zhanlūe yu guanli*, 1994:4, pp. 21–25. Also see Xiao, *Xiao Gongqin ji* (Haerbin: Hei-

longjiang jiaoyu chubanshe, 1995), pp. 87–174. Similar sentiments have been expressed by a number of Chinese analysts and would-be government advisers. See, for example, Wang Shaoguang and Hu Angang's 1993 report on the state of the Chinese economy and central government power discussed by Shuang Yi in "Xuezhe xiance, quanzhe juece," *Zhongguo shibao zhoukan*, 17–23 October 1993, pp. 16–18.

49. Wang Hui and Zhang Tianwei in conversation, "Wenhui pipan lilun yu dangdai Zhongguo minzuzhuyi wenti," *Zhanlüe yu guanli*, 1994:4, p. 19. Wang's work appeared regularly in *Reading*, the editorship of which he was invited to assume in late 1995.

50. See Wang Hui, "Wenhui pipan lilun yu dangdai Zhongguo minzuzhuyi wenti," p. 19. In his comments, Wang uses the dichotomy between political and cultural nationalism in a way that is highly reminiscent of John Hutchinson's work on the subject. See Hutchinson, *The Dynamics of Cultural Nationalism* (London: Allen & Unwin, 1987), pp. 12 ff. Wang made similar points about the political and nationalist nature of commercial culture and postmodernist debate in his essay "Jiushi niandai Zhongguo dalude wenhua yanjiu yu wenhua piping," *Dianying yishu*, 1995:1, summarized in *Dushu*, 1995:5, pp. 151–152. See also his major article "Dangdai Zhongguode sixiang zhuangkuang yu xiandaixing wenti," *Tianya*, 1997:5, pp. 133–150.

51. *wenhua lengzhande dunci.* Xu Jilin, " 'Houzhimin wenhua piping' mianmianguan," *Dongfang*, 1994:4, p. 23.

52. Zhao Yiheng, " 'Houxue' yu Zhongguo xin baoshouzhuyi," *Ershiyi shiji*, 1995:2, pp. 4–15. See also Xu Ben's " 'Disan shijie piping' zai dangjin Zhongguode chujing," in the same issue, pp. 16–27. For a critique of these articles—and a rejection of their approach—by Zhang Yiwu, associate professor in Chinese literature at Peking University and a leading figure in this debate, see Zhang, "Chanshi 'Zhongguo' de jiaolü," *Ershiyi shiji*, 1995:4, pp. 128–135.

53. See Xu Jilin in "Xiandaixing shifou zhende zhongjie," *Shanghai wenlun*, 1995:1, p. 63. Xu's article is a response to an essay by Zhang Yiwu, "Xiandaixingde zhongjie: yige wufa huibide keti," *Zhanlüe yu guanli*, 1994:3, pp. 104–109.

54. This group included the Beijing-based literary critics Chen Xiaoming and Zhang Yiwu, although their fellows were legion. For some of Chen's and Zhang's views see, for example, the record of the roundtable discussion, "Jingshen tuibaizhede kuangwu," *Zhongshan*, 1993:6, pp. 142–162, and "Dongfangzhuyi yu houzhimin wenhua," *Zhongshan*, 1994:1, pp. 126–148.

55. See, in particular, Liu Dong, "Jingti renweide 'yangjingbang xuefeng'," *Ershiyi shiji*, 1995:12, pp. 4–13, and a reply from Gan Yang, "Shei shi Zhongguo yanjiuzhongde 'women'?" *Ershiyi shiji*, 1995:12, pp. 21–25.

56. My thanks to Frank Dikötter for suggesting this retro-translation.

57. Zhang Kuan wrote one of the first reviews of Said's work for *Reading* in 1993. See Zhang Kuan, "Ou-Meiren yanzhongde 'fei wo zulei'," *Dushu*, 1993:9, pp. 3–9, and again in Zhang, "Zai tan Saiyide," *Dushu*, 1994:10, pp. 8–14. Zhang himself had been studying outside China for some years, and the second of his articles was written at Stanford University. He was particularly peeved by Western (presumably U.S.) media representations of China. See "Ou-Meiren yanzhongde 'fei wo zulei'," p. 7.

58. Zhang Kuan, "Sayide 'Dongfangzhuyi' yu Xifangde Hanxue yanjiu," *Liaowang*, no. 27, 1995, reprinted in *Huaxia wenzhai* (*China News Digest-Chinese Magazine*, CND-CM), no. 251, 19 January 1996, translated by David Kelly, with modifications.

59. See, for example, Xu Ben, " 'Women' shi shei?—lun wenhua pipingzhongde gong-tongti shenfen rentong wenti," *Dongfang*, 1996:2, pp. 69–73.

60. Xiaomei Chen, *Occidentalism* (Oxford: Oxford University Press, 1995), p. 58.

61. Ibid., pp. 65–66.

62. Roland Barthes, "Alors, la Chine," *Le Monde*, 24 May 1974, quoted in Simon Leys, *Chinese Shadows* (New York: Penguin Books, 1978), p. 199.

63. He Xin, "Gudu yu tiaozhan—wode fendou yu sikao," *Zixue zazhi*, 1988:10, p. 39, quoted in Barmé and Jaivin, *New Ghosts, Old Dreams*, pp. 213, 254. For an early 1990s' catalog of the ills of the national spirit, see Jia Lusheng, *Wode bing* (Beijing: Guoji wenhua chuban gongsi, 1992).

64. See, for example, Wu Pei-yi, *The Confucian's Progress: Autobiographical Writings in Traditional China* (Princeton, N.J.: Princeton University Press, 1990); and William Theodore deBary, "Individualism and Humanitarianism in Late Ming Thought," in deBary et al., eds., *Self and Society in Ming Thought* (New York: Columbia University Press, 1970), pp. 145–247.

65. Tan Sitong, "Renxue," *Tan Sitong quanji* (Beijing: Sanlian shudian, 1954), p. 73, quoted in Barmé and Jaivin, *New Ghosts, Old Dreams*, p. 117.

66. Xuan Yongguang's *Wangtan-Fenghua* reappeared after an hiatus of many decades. See Xuan Yongguang, *Foolish Talk & Mad Ramblings* (Wangtan-Fenghua), 2 vols. (Beijing: Jinri Zhongguo chubanshe, 1993). Li Zongwu's work was first reprinted on the mainland in 1989, and Li Ao's essays began to appear there the same year. Bo Yang's controversial *The Ugly Chinaman* and Lung-kee Sun's *The "Deep Structure" of Chinese Culture*, influential polemical works in Taiwan and Hong Kong, were eventually published on the mainland in 1986. Long Yingtai's essays (see *Yehuo ji* [Taibei: Yuanshen chubanshe, 1985]), which were highly critical of Taiwan and "Chineseness," had also been available for some years. Ironically, the mainland critic Liu Xiaobo was banned on the mainland, although he was regularly able to publish social and political critiques in the Kong-Tai press following his release from jail in 1991 and until his further incarceration in late 1996. For Li Jie, see chapter 12, "Totalitarian Nostalgia." Of these writers, Bo Yang was the most consistently vociferous critic of the Chinese national character. Some of his 1960s' satirical essays appeared on the mainland in 1993. In those writings he remarked, among other things, that what appears to be Chinese nationalism is little more than a disguised refusal to accept superior institutions and practices that are generally identified as and rejected for being "Western." See Shen Xi, "Meng kan 'jianggang wenhua' de yiba jufu—du Bo Yang zawen xuan *Xichuang suibi*," *Wenhui dushu zhoubao*, 29 January 1994. For a response to Bo Yang's approach by a prominent mainland writer, see Han Shaogong, *93 duanxiang: shei shi chouloude Zhongguoren?* (Xianggang: Tiandi tushu youxian gongsi, 1995).

67. This far-from-exhaustive list of ills is taken for the most part from the many publications dwelling on national crises that appeared on mainland China from the late

1980s. These sources include Lu Yi et al., *Qiuji: yige shijixingde xuanze* (Shanghai: Baijia chubanshe, 1989); Li Ming, ed., *Zhongguode weiji yu sikao*, restricted circulation (Tianjin: Tianjin renmin chubanshe, 1989); He Bochuan, *Shan'aoshangde Zhongguo: wenti, kunjing, tongkude xuanze*, rev. ed. (Xianggang: Sanlian shudian, 1990); Su Ya and Jia Lusheng, *Shei lai chengbao?—Zhonguo jingji xianzhuang toushi* (Guangzhou: Huacheng chubanshe, 1990); Shi Zhongwen, *Zhongguo ren: zouchu sihutong* (Beijing: Zhongguo fazhan chubanshe, 1991); and Qiao Lijun et al., *Zhongguo buneng luan* (Beijing: Zhonggong zhongyang dangxiao chubanshe, 1994).

68. See, for example, the chapter "The Culture of Killing" in Guanlong Cao's *The Attic: Memoir of a Chinese Landlord's Son*, trans. Guanlong Cao and Nancy Moskin (Berkeley and Los Angeles: University of California Press, 1996), pp. 84–96.

69. This expression was common in the late 1980s at the height of crisis awareness. Mao Zedong used this phrase on 30 August 1956 in a speech at the Preparatory Conference for the party's Eighth Congress. He said that if China did not economically outstrip America after five or six decades of socialism, it deserved to be "expelled from the human race."

70. Wang Yiming, *Wo shi Wang Shuo* (Beijing: Guoji wenhua chuban gongsi, 1992), p. 97.

71. Hannah Arendt, "The Aftermath of Nazi Rule: Report from Germany (1950)," in her *Essays in Understanding, 1930–1954*, ed. Jerome Kohn (New York: Harcourt Brace, 1994), p. 250.

72. See W. L. Chong, "Su Xiaokang on His Film 'River Elegy'," *China Information* 4 (3), Winter 1989–1990, p. 46. For an analysis of the series as a form of "counterdiscourse," see also Xiaomei Chen, *Occidentalism*, pp. 27–48.

73. A point forcefully made by Dong Leshan in "Dongfangzhuyi dahechang?" pp. 99–100, 101. The debate surrounding *River Elegy* was revisited in 1995 by Tang Yijie, a leading Beijing University philosopher, when he commented publicly that the series was important in that it represented a major 1980s' current of thought that was critical of the "Chinese tradition." Academics like Tang, it was reported, were concerned that the revival of interest in traditional studies could be manipulated by party conservatives to negate modern Chinese—in particular, reformist—culture. See Zhongyang she (Taibei), "Xuezhe kending 'Heshang' fanxing jiazhi, xuejie chuxian pipan fanxing shengyin," *Shijie ribao* (New York), 13 June 1995.

74. The full title of the later series is *Dongfang—yige weidade wenmingde shengwuxue jiepou*, and it consists of six fifty-minute episodes.

75. Mai Tianshu, "Faxian Dongfang," *Beijing qingnian bao*, 24 April 1994.

76. Shao Yanfeng, " 'Dongfang' de qishi," *Beijing qingnian bao*, 24 April 1994.

77. For a critique of Zhang's work in this regard and its relevance to the debate on the "loss of the humanist spirit" in China that began in late 1993, see Xu Lin and Zhang Hong's comments in Wang Xiaoming et al., "Kuangyeshangde feixu—wenxue he wenren jingshende weiji," *Shanghai wenxue*, 1993:6, pp. 65–66.

78. See Ma Junxiang, "Minzuzhuyi suo suzaode xiandai Zhongguo dianying," in *Minzuzhuyi yu Zhongguo xiandaihua*, ed. Liu Qingfeng (Xianggang: Zhongwen daxue chubanshe, 1994), pp. 521–532.

79. See Jeffrey N. Wasserstrom and Elizabeth J. Perry, eds., *Popular Protest and Political Culture in Modern China* (Boulder, Colo.: Westview Press, 1992); and Geremie Barmé, "Confession, Redemption, and Death: Liu Xiaobo and the Protest Movement of 1989," in *The Broken Mirror: China After Tiananmen*, ed. George Hicks (Essex: Longman, 1990), pp. 70–80.

80. For a Chinese view of this historical pattern in this century, see Yang Xiong, "Cong jijinzhuyi dao minzuzhuyi—shilun Zhongguo qingnian yundongde fazhan dongji jiqi wuqu," *Qingnian yanjiu*, 1991:7, pp. 7–13.

81. *renwen jingshede shiluo*. See Wang Xiaoming et al., "Kuangyeshangde feixu," pp. 63–71. The discussion took place in February 1993, but the record of it was not published until later in the year. For a collection of the main articles published during this debate, see Wang Xiaoming, ed., *Renwen jingshen xunsi lu* (Shanghai: Wenhui chubanshe, 1996). This was by no means the first time such sentiments had been expressed by contemporary Chinese critics. Both Zhu Dake and Liu Xiaobo, for example, were noted for their criticisms of the vacuity of the reformist literature of the 1980s.

82. Mindful of various political and social taboos, these views were generally expressed in an elliptical fashion. See, for example, Xiao Tongqing, "Xunqiu jiazhi mubiao yu lishi jinchengde qihe," *Dongfang*, 1995:1, summarized in *Dushu*, 1995:5, p. 154.

83. See Li Tiangang's comments in Gao Ruiquan et al., "Renwen jingshen xunzong," *Dushu*, 1994:4, p. 75.

84. See Xue Ji, ed., *Yaogun xunmeng—Zhongguo yaogunyue shilu* (Beijing: Zhongguo dianying chubanshe, 1993), pp. 2–3. Chinese rock 'n' rollers, while superficially "Westernized," were often stridently antiforeign in private. See also Andrew F. Jones, "The Politics of Popular Music in Post-Tiananmen China," in Wasserstrom and Perry, *Popular Protest and Political Culture in Modern China*, pp. 158–161.

85. Yuan Hongbing, *Huangyuan feng* (Beijing: Xiandai chubanshe, 1990), p. 127.

86. This Chinese "peace charter," published in translation as an appendix to Human Rights Watch/Asia, "China: New Arrests Linked to Worker Rights," 11 March 1994, is in itself highly revealing. Although one could argue that the authors have purposefully used party-style rhetoric to appeal to a wide audience (and perhaps even the authorities), the egregious nationalistic sentiments and elitism of the document are in marked contrast to the contents of "Charter 77." Yuan's coauthor, Zhou Guoqiang (Aqu Qiangba), who was also detained in early 1994 and subsequently jailed for three years (see chapter 6, "Consuming T-shirts in Beijing"), was released and exiled to the United States in December 1998.

87. See "China's Most Distrusted," *Newsweek*, 21 March 1994, p. 8; and, Ying Fu, "Yuan Hongbing kangyi zhengzhi qishi," *Zhongguo shibao zhoukan*, 5–11 December 1993, p. 17; Human Rights Watch/Asia, "China: New Arrests Linked to Worker Rights," 11 March 1994, pp. 1–2. Official persecution led the nonmainland media to classify Yuan as a "liberal" or "democratic activist."

88. Matei Mihalca, "China's New Heroes Signal New Nationalism," *Asian Wall Street Journal*, 20 December 1994.

89. Committee, ed., *Lishide chaoliu* (Beijing: Zhongguo renmin daxue, 1992). Yuan wrote one of the two introductory essays to the book. See Yuan Hongbing, "Rang lishi buzai beiqi," *Lishide chaoliu*, pp. 13–28. He was reportedly cashiered from Peking University for his involvement with this publication and attempted to sue the University Party Committee for expelling him. See Human Rights Watch/Asia, "China: New Arrests Linked to Worker Rights," p. 2.

90. Yuan Hongbing, "Yi xin shijide mingyi," in Zhao Shilin, ed., *Fang "zuo" beiwanglu* (Taiyuan: Shuhai chubanshe, 1992), p. 252.

91. Ibid., pp. 252, 254.

92. Yuan Hongbing, *Huangyuan feng*.

93. Luo Wen, "Bashezhe, xiong lang, yemanren—*Huangyuan feng* shi zenyang yiben shu?" *Zhongguo tushu pinglun*, 1991:3, p. 8. See also Chen Ping, "Choulou yu ziside linghun—ping *Huangyuan feng* de 'meide zhuti'," *Zhongguo tushu pinglun*, 1991:3, pp. 11–12.

94. See *Zhongguo tushu pinglun*, 1991:3, pp. 8, 11–12. *Zhongguo tushu pinglun* was an official publishing journal.

95. Yuan Hongbing, *Huangyuan feng*, p. 216.

96. Ibid., p. 250.

97. For example, Yuan writes: "On the battlefield of racial competition, the most moving clarion call is the concept of racial superiority. . . . Only the fresh blood of others can prove the strength of one race." Yuan Hongbing, *Huangyuan feng*, p. 193.

98. Quoted in J. Hoberman, "The Fascist Guns in the West," *Aperture: The Return of the Hero*, no. 110, Spring 1988, p. 69.

99. The debate concerning neoauthoritarianism versus mass democracy developed in 1988 and has continued under various guises to the present day. See, for example, Barry Sautman, "Sirens of the Strongman: Neo-Authoritarianism in Recent Chinese Political Theory," *China Quarterly*, no. 129, March 1992, pp. 72–102.

100. This is a summary of the parting words of the author. See Yuan Hongbing, "Yuyun," *Huangyuan feng*, pp. 267–273.

101. As Hannah Arendt puts it, people "have recoiled more and more from the idea of humanity and become more susceptible to the doctrine of race, which denies the very possibility of a common humanity. They instinctively felt that the idea of humanity, whether it appears in a religious or humanistic form, implies the obligation of a general responsibility which they do not wish to assume. For the idea of humanity, when purged of all sentimentality, has the very serious consequence that in one form or another men must assume responsibility for all crimes committed by men and that all nations share the onus of evil committed by all others. Shame at being a human being is the purely individual and still nonpolitical expression of this insight." See Hannah Arendt, "Organized Guilt and Universal Responsibility," in her *Essays in Understanding, 1930–1954*, p. 130.

102. Yuan Hongbing, *Huangyuan feng*, p. 210.

103. See, for example, ibid., pp. 87–96

104. Zhou Lunyou, "Hongse xiezuode jingyi shenru gutou yu zhidu," *Kaifang zazhi*, 1993:8,

pp. 101–102. For the full text, see Zhou, "Hongse xiezuo—1992 yishu xianzhang huo fei xianshi shige yuanze," *Feifei (fukanhao)* (Beijing: N.p., 1992), pp. 1–17.

105. *Beijing Bastards*, Beijing zazhong, was the title of the director Zhang Yuan's 1993 film about Beijing youth culture discussed in chapter 7, "Packaged Dissent." The opening remark in this section was made by Wang Qiming to David McCarthy, his business competitor and rival in love, in episode 9 of *A Beijing Man in New York*. Wang made the comment in English after landing his first order for knitwear sweaters from McCarthy's major buyer. Note that Wang's rival was called McCarthy, a name with anti-Communist and, by extension, anti-Chinese, associations.

106. Although *Beijing People in New York* or a similar rendition would be closer to the lexicographical meaning of "Beijingren zai Niuyue," since the series mainly concerned the fate of Wang Qiming, its male protagonist, *A Beijing Man in New York* appears to be a more accurate translation.

107. See Eric J. Leed, *The Mind of the Traveler: From Gilgamesh to Global Tourism* (New York: Basic Books, 1991), p. 114.

108. Following his work on the series in New York, Jiang Wen expressed a number of strong anti-Western sentiments and stated that among other things, while the Chinese were increasingly being freed from their prejudices about the outside world, foreigners (that is, Americans) remained deeply biased against China. See Jiang Wen and Luo Xueying, "Jiang Wen yanlide shijie," *Wenhui dianying shibao*, 21 September 1992.

109. See James Lull, *China Turned On: Television, Reform, and Resistance* (London: Routledge, 1991), p. 170; and Jin Shui, "Dianshi wenhuade xianzhuang yu quxiang," *Shanghai daxue xuebao (shekeban)*, digested in *Dushu*, 1995:3, pp. 156–157.

110. *Beijing dianshi yishu zhongxin*.

111. For details, see Qian Lijun, "Film Crew Conquers New York" and "Cross-Cultural Exchange" in *Twenty-First Century* (*China Daily*), 13–19 October 1993.

112. Bao Ming, "Huanmie he mengxiang yiyang mei—dianshiju *Beijingren zai Niuyue* hongdong dalu," *Zhongguo shibao zhoukan*, 17–23 October 1993, p. 77.

113. Cao Guilin, *Beijingren zai Niuyue* (Beijing: Zhonguo wenlian chuban gongsi, 1991). The text of the book was serialized in the *Beijing Evening News* (Beijing wanbao) and printed in full in the literary journal *October* (Shiyue), as well as being broadcast on Central People's Radio. For an English version see Glen Cao, *Beijinger in New York*, trans. Ted Wang (San Francisco: China Books, 1994).

114. Cao Laifu, "Jishixing xushuxiade wenhua chongji—du *Beijingren zai Niuyue*," *Wenyi bao*, 30 November 1991.

115. *xin yimin wenxue*. Other terms for this genre are "literature that deals with foreign topics," *yuwai ticai wenxue zuopin*, and "literature of the overseas students," *liuxuesheng wenxue*.

116. See Pan Kaixiong, "Rere naonao beihoude changchang duanduan—guanyu 'xin yimin wenxue' de zaisikao," *Dangdai zuojia pinglun*, 1993:3, pp. 20–23. Other bestselling works of this genre include Liu Guande's *Wode caifu zai Aozhou*, Fan Xiangda's *Shanghairen zai Dongjing*, Ke Yan's *Taxiang mingyue*, Zhou Li's *Manhadunde Zhongguo nüren*, and Wu Li's *Qu ge waiguo nüren zuo taitai*. Writers and academics

at a seminar organized by the Literature Research Institute of the Chinese Academy of Social Sciences and the Chinese Writers' Association in late 1992 extolled the patriotic yearnings, *aiguo qinghuai*, expressed in these best-selling books. See "Yuwai ticai wenxue zuopin chengwei remen duwu," *Wenyi bao*, 26 December 1992; also see Xiaomei Chen's discussion of Zhou Li's *A Chinese Woman in Manhattan* in her *Occidentalism*, pp. 157–167.

117. Zhao Xun, the ideologically conservative head of the book's publishing house and a leading cultural bureaucrat, reportedly commented that Cao's reportage "conforms to our present needs." See Zheng Xinyuan, "Yisheng zhi zhuiqiu mingqi he nüren— *Beijingren zai Niuyue* zuozhe Cao Guilin zhi qi zai Niuyue xuangao pochan," *Zhongguo shibao zhoukan*, 12–18 December 1993, p. 78.

118. Yu Wentao, "TV Series Tells About Beijingers in New York," *China Daily*, 13 October 1993.

119. Wu Hong, "Beijingren, Niuyueren," *Dushu*, 1994:1, p. 84. McCarthy, who according to his parents was a sinicized American, claims in episodes 8 and 11 that the only reason he is now involved with the Chinese was to beat them at their own games of treachery, lying, and moneygrubbing. In the end, however, having failed in business, he returns to Beijing to teach English.

120. Zha Xiduo, "Youse yanjinglide xiyangjing," p. 17.

121. Ibid.

122. See Bao Lai, "Jingshen guizude lunluo—tan dianshiju 'Beijingren zai Niuyue'," *Kaifang zazhi*, 1994:1, p. 95.

123. Xu Jilin, "Wudu zhi houde jiazhi anshi—zai shuo *Beijingren zai Niuyue*," *Wenhui bao*, 13 November 1993. Xu's first criticism of the *pizi*, or "lout," Wang Qiming, was made in "Ancang xuanjide haiwai 'youshi'," *Wenxue bao (shikan)*, 1993:3; reprinted in his *Disanzhong zunyan* (Beijing: Renmin wenxue chubanshe, 1996), pp. 68–73.

124. Xu Jilin, "Wudu zhi houde jiazhi anshi."

125. The conservative critic He Xin, an ideological foe of writers like Xu Jilin, expressed similar views in the mid-1980s. See chapter 4, "The Apotheosis of the *Liumang*."

126. Xu, "Wudu zhi houde jiazhi anshi." This last line, "*wo shi liumang wo pa shei*," was the title of a book devoted to the novelist Wang Shuo. See Xiao Sheng, ed., *Wang Shuo pipan—wo shi liumang wo pa shei* (Changsha: Shuhai chubanshe, 1993).

127. According to the Beijing computer artist Feng Mengbo, February 1996.

128. *papan jiemi sida tianwang zhiyi*.

129. Sang Ye, *Diannao chong*, February 1995. From the manuscript of his oral history of contemporary China, *Chinese Time* (Zhongguo shijian). This passage is from Sang Ye and Geremie R. Barmé, "Computer Insect," *Wired* (4.07), July 1996, p. 84.

130. Liu Qingfeng, the editor of *Twenty-First Century* (see chapter 3, "Traveling Heavy"), calls this "neosinocentrism," *xin huaxia zhongxinzhuyi*. See her "Wenhua gemingzhongde huaxia zhongxinzhuyi," in *Minzuzhuyi yu Zhongguo xiandaihua*, pp. 359–366.

131. Beckoning, too, is the age of what one mainland writer, presumably inspired by Tu Wei-ming's work on "cultural China," called "Pacific Confucianism," Taipingyang

ruxue. See Wu Huailian, "Taipingyang shidai yu Zhonghuazhuyi," *Qingnian tansuo*, 1994:4, pp. 9–11.

132. See, for example, the essays of Wang Xiaobo (d. 1997), *Wode jingshen jiayuan: Wang Xiaobo zawen zixuanji* (Beijing: Wenhua yishu chubanshe, 1997), pp. 88–104.

133. From Robyn Ianssen and Yiyan Wang, eds., *Footprints on Paper: An Anthology of Australian Writing in English and Chinese* (Sydney: Robyn Ianssen Productions, 1996), p. 106.

CHAPTER 11

1. Toby Young, "The End of Irony?" *Modern Review* 1, no. 14 (April/May 1994), p. 6.

2. Suzanne Moore, "Notes on Camp," *Modern Review* 1, no. 3 (Spring 1992), p. 12.

3. B. Austin-Smith, "Into the Heart of Irony," *Canadian Dimension* 27 (7), p. 51.

4. As Deng Xiaoping said when he initiated the anti–bourgeois liberalization campaign in late 1986, "Our socialist construction can only be carried out under leadership, in an orderly way, and in an environment of stability and unity." See Geremie Barmé and John Minford, eds., *Seeds of Fire: Chinese Voices of Conscience* (Hong Kong: Far Eastern Economic Review, 1986), 2nd ed. (New York: Hill & Wang, 1988), p. 379.

5. See Frank Dikötter's remarks on the issue of race and state formation in late-nineteenth-century China in Frank Dikötter, ed., *The Construction of Racial Identities in China and Japan* (London: C. Hurst, 1997), pp. 12–33.

6. *renwen jingshide shiluo*. For the major contributions to this debate, see Wang Xiaoming, ed., *Renwen jingshen xunsi lu* (Shanghai: Wenhui chubanshe, 1996).

7. "Shanghai xueshujie bufen qingnian xuezhe renwei—renwen xueke xianru weiji, renwen jingshen jidai chongjian," *Wenhui dushu zhoubao*, 5 March 1994. For a survey of this period and earlier cultural debates, see Jing Wang, *High Culture Fever: Politics, Aesthetics and Ideology in Deng's China* (Berkeley and Los Angeles: University of California Press, 1996).

8. Zhang Yiwu, "Renwen jingshen: zuihoude shenhua," in Wang Xiaoming, *Renwen jingshen xunsi lu*, p. 139.

9. Nan Fan, "Renwen jingshen: beijing he kuangjia," *Dushu*, 1996:7, p. 11.

10. See, for example, the comments of the poet Daozi and others in Ye Shui, "Renwen jingshen: yige weisuide wenhua yaoan—Zhongguo '85 xinchao yu shinian meishu taolunhui," *Wenyi bao* (Xianggang), no. 3, September 1995, pp. 71–77.

11. Wang Lixiong, "Kewang duoluo—tan zhishifenzide pizihua qingxiang," *Dongfang*, 1994:1, pp. 16–18.

12. Ibid., p. 18.

13. See Geremie R. Barmé, *Shades of Mao: The Posthumous Cult of the Great Leader* (Armonk, N.Y.: Sharpe, 1996), pp. 269–275; and the section "Dreaming of Chairman Mao" in chapter 12.

14. See Zhang Chengzhi, "Shiren, ni wei shenme bu fennu?!" *Wenhui bao*, 7 August 1994. Xu Jilin rebutted Zhang in the same issue of the paper, and the controversy con-

tinued for some weeks. See the feature "Renwen jingshen yu wenren caoshou," *Wenhui bao*, 7 and 21 August 1994, as well as 4 and 18 September 1994.

15. This had, of course, also been true in the 1980s when controversial works by authors like the poet Xu Jingya, Liu Xinwu, and Liu Xiaobo, to mention but a few writers, had been much sought-after items following bans or public criticisms.

16. Wang Meng, "Zuzhibuli xinlaide qingnianren," translated by Geremie Barmé as "The Newcomer," in *Fragrant Weeds—Chinese Short Stories Once Labeled as "Poisonous Weeds,"* ed. W. J. F. Jenner (Hong Kong: Joint Publishing, 1983), pp. 71–116. For a list of Wang's works in translation, see Kam Louie and Louise Edwards, eds., *Bibliography of English Translations and Critiques of Contemporary Chinese Fiction 1945–1992* (Taipei: Center for Chinese Studies, 1993), pp. 62–64.

17. This sobriquet was presumably chosen in ironical contrast to the Maoist slogan that purges should be either like "tempests," *baofeng zhouyu*, or a like "fine rain," *maomao xiyu*.

18. See Geremie Barmé and Linda Jaivin, eds., *New Ghosts, Old Dreams: Chinese Rebel Voices* (New York: Times Books, 1992) , p. 285.

19. This rumor circulated in Beijing literary circles for some years, and it was confirmed by Wang Meng in conversation with me in late 1992.

20. Jin Sheng, "Shetai shijian beiwanglu," *Wenyi bao*, 19 May 1990.

21. Yan Zhaozhu, "Lun wenxue benzhi duoyuanlunde shizhi," originally published in the January 1991 issue of *Wenyi lilun yu piping* and reprinted in *Guangming ribao*, 25 January 1991. It should be noted that Yan was also the author of virulent denunciations of Li Zehou and Liu Zaifu. See, for example, Yan Zhaozhu and Zhang Hua, "Ping gerenzhuyide wenxue jiazhiguan," *Guangming ribao*, 12 March 1991.

22. Zhang Jie, "Rizi," *Huacheng*, 1991:2, p. 13.

23. Although signed "Shen Ping," for readers schooled in the code of the mainland denunciatory style, it was obvious that the letter had a complex political pedigree. Writing for *Cheng Ming* in Hong Kong, Luo Bing suggested that because of its controversial nature, the article was rejected by a number of "leftist" newspapers in Beijing before finally finding a home in the pages of *Literary Gazette*. See "Wang Meng shijian yu He Jingzhi xin gongshi," *Zhengming*, 1991:12, p. 11. Huai Bing suggested that "Shen Ping" may well have been an acronym for "*Carefully* guard against *peaceful* evolution," *Shen fang he ping yanbian*. See Huai Bing, "Zuowang pipan Wang Mengde dejiang xiaoshuo," *Zhengming*, 1991:11, p. 82.

24. See Wang Meng, *Jianyingde xizhou* (Xianggang: Tiandi tushu youxian gongsi, 1992), pp. 95–116 for the story itself, and pp. 117–146 for various related materials.

25. These sentiments were expressed in slogans like "Xiaoping, Xiaoping, a venerable eighty-five, / He may still be walking but his brain's half alive"; "Who says I'm old? I'm just a tad over eighty!"; and "Black cats, white cats—they're all old cats!" See Barmé and Jaivin, *New Ghosts, Old Dreams*, p. 85.

26. Shen Ping, "Duzhe laixin," *Jianyingde xizhou*, pp. 117–119. For some reports on this case in the major Chinese-language Hong Kong journals, see also Meizi, "Feitengde 'xizhou': Wang Meng lizhan zuojiazhuang," *Baixing banyuekan*, 16 November 1991,

pp. 34–35; Lizi, "Dalu wenhuajiede gaoya yu fan gaoya—cong Wang Meng shangsu shuoqi," *Mingbao yuekan*, 1991:12, pp. 45–48; and Bi Hua, "Wang Meng 'Xizhou' an shimo," *Jiushi niandai yuekan*, 1992:2, pp. 88–89.

27. The editorship of the weekly changed hands in late 1989. Cheng Daixi, writing under his pen name Yi Ren (see chapter 2, "An Iron Fist in a Velvet Glove"), had attacked the pre–4 June *Literary Gazette* in a lengthy article published around the time of the purge. See Yi Ren, "Du *Wenyi bao* di 20 qi yougan," *Guangming ribao*, 25 October 1989. One of Wang Meng's sons, Wang Shan, was on the staff of the *Literary Gazette* before the 1989–1990 purge.

28. The "rumor" was also reported in some detail in the Hong Kong press. See Li Yenan, "Lai zi Beijing wentande binfen huaxu," *Mingbao yuekan*, 1992:3, p. 72. For Yan Zhaozhu's attack, see n. 21 above.

29. See "Wang Meng dui 'laixin' de fanbo," *Jianyingde xizhou*, pp. 124–125.

30. See "Minshi qisuzhuang (zhengqiu yijian gao)," in Wang Meng, *Jianyingde xizhou*, pp. 126–130. A copy of the original is given in *Ming Pao Monthly*; see Lizi, "Dalu wenhuajiede gaoya yu fan gaoya," p. 47.

31. "Beijingshi zhongji renmin fayuan minshi caidingshu, (1991) zhongmin shou zi di 2696 hao," dated 22 October 1991. See Wang Meng, *Jianyingde xizhou*, pp. 131–132. A copy of the original can be found in Lizi, "Dalu wenhuajiede gaoya yu fan gaoya," p. 48.

32. Wang Meng, "Wo ai he xizhou," *Nongmin ribao*, 14 November 1991, reprinted in Wang Meng, *Jianyingde xizhou*, pp. 136–139. Wang Meng told me that he published this essay with the help of the Henan novelist Liu Zhenyun, who was an editor with the *Farmer's Daily*.

33. Wang Meng, "Huashuo zhewan 'zhou'," in his *Jianyingde xizhou*, pp. 140–142.

34. Wang got the idea to sue the *Literary Gazette* from the Tianjin woman poet Lin Xi, who took Zheng Bonong to court for a libelous review of her work. The Shanghai critic Wu Liang provided the inspiration to photocopy multiple copies of his letter of complaint, lawsuit, and other essays that had been typed on a word processor.

35. "'Jianyingde xizhou' qi bolan—Wang Meng shangsu Beijing zhongyuan," *Wenhui dushu zhoubao*, 19 October 1991. This weekly, published by the Shanghai *Wenhui Daily*, was a forum for more liberal writers in 1990, and it published a front-page interview with Wang in mid-1990, long before it became fashionable to champion his cause. See Zhou Zhonglin, "Caigan zaiyu jianchi—fang Wang Meng," *Wenhui dushu zhoubao*, 11 August 1990.

36. See, for example, Shan Ren, "'Jianyingde xizhou' shi yipian shenme zuopin?" *Wenyi lilun yu piping*, 1991:2 (published on 24 November 1991); Qian Fan, "Zuozhe ying zhengque duidai duzhede piping," *Wenyi bao*, 31 November 1991; and Chun Yushui, "Wei shenme 'xizhou' hai hui 'jianying' ne?" *Zhongliu*, 1991:10, reprinted in *Wenyi bao*, 6 November 1991.

37. See *Zuopin yu zhengming*, 1991:12.

38. "Guanyu 'Jianyingde xizhou' de yixie qingkuang," published in Wang Meng's *Jianyingde xizhou*, pp. 133–135.

39. Wang Meng, *Jianyingde xizhou* (Xianggang: Tiandi tushu youxian gongsi, 1992). Tiandi, or Cosmos Books, had long-standing relations with many Beijing writers, which it often maintained through the auspices of editors at the Hong Kong branch of the Joint Publishing Company (Sanlian shudian).

40. See Timothy Tung, "Porridge & the Law: Wang Meng Sues," *Human Rights Tribune* (New York) 3 (1), Spring 1992, p. 9. Timothy was the brother of the Beijing translator Dong Leshan.

41. The essays included works by Zong Pu, Shao Yanxiang, Lin Xi (the Tianjin poet mentioned earlier), Zhang Kangkang, Ye Nan, Liu Xinwu, Zhang Jie, and Shen Rong.

42. For details of Wu Zuguang's purge, see Barmé and Minford, *Seeds of Fire*, pp. 370–372.

43. See Wu Zuguang, *Jieyou ji* (Beijing: Zhongwai wenhua chuban gongsi, 1988). Wu had issued a written call for friends to contribute to the volume dated 1 August 1987, the day Hu Qiaomu, the leader dispatched to request that he leave the party, visited him at home. I was also invited to write an essay for that volume. See Bai Jieming, "Yuwai tanjiu," *Jieyou ji*, pp. 317–321. The book's title was inspired by a line from a poem by the general and writer Cao Cao, which runs, "How can one alleviate sorrows / Only through wine," *he yi jie you / wei you Du Kang.*

44. Zhang Jie, "Shanghuo," *Zhongshan*, 1991:5, pp. 25–63. Reprinted by Cosmos Books (Tiandi tushu youxian gongsi) in Hong Kong in the volume *Shanghuo*, 1992.

45. See Li Yenan, "Lai zi Beijing wentande binfen huaxu," p. 73.

46. Xiao Wei, "Zhang Jie bei hecaide hua," *Mingbao yuekan*, 1992:5, p. 16.

47. Ibid.

48. Wang Meng, "Zuojia shujian," *Shouhuo*, 1992:1, p. 92.

49. Wang "Zuojia shujian," p. 93. Malaqinfu's letter had earlier been published by Wang in the Guangzhou essay journal *Suibi* in July 1991, where he prefaced it with an even more biting comment.

50. An excellent example of this was Yu Xing's sarcastic lambasting of Malaqinfu, "Fuli laoji," *Wenhui dushu zhoukan*, 29 February 1992.

51. See Wang Meng, "Manhua wenyi xiaoguo," *Jiefang ribao*, 25 August 1992; "Zai shuo wenyi xiaoguo," *Jiefang ribao*, 3 September 1992; and "Jianshe yu wenyi" in *Jiefang ribao*, 24 September 1992. This last essay declares in no uncertain terms that "revolutionary literature" based on class struggle was outmoded. For an example of Wang's late-1980s polemical essays, see Yang Yu, "Wenxue: Shique hongdong xiaoying yihou," *Renmin ribao*, 9 February 1988.

52. See Ye Zhiqiu, "Beida Weiminghu pan you you wenxue shenghui," *Zhongguo shibao zhoukan*, 11–17 October 1992, p. 89.

53. Wang Meng, "Duobi chonggao," *Dushu*, 1993:1, pp. 10–17.

54. See Tao Dongfang, "Cong 'Wang Meng xianxiang' tandao wenhua jiazhide jiangou," *Wenyi zhengming*, 1995:3, p. 5. Tao was a supporter of Wang's position. For a collection of materials related to this debate, see Ding Dong, and Sun Min, eds., *Shiji zhi jiaode chongzhuang—Wang Meng xianxiang zhengming lu* (Beijing: *Guangming ribao* chubanshe, 1996).

55. Wang Meng, "Renwen jingshen wenti ougan," *Dongfang*, 1994:5, p. 48. Among other things, Wang wrote that ironically, proponents of cultural integrity and independence still expected to be given handouts by the state. In early 1995, Wang continued on this tack and commented on the utter confusion surrounding the "humanist spirit" debate. See Wang Meng, "Hushang sixu lu," collected in Ding Dong and Sun Min, *Shiji zhijiaode chongzhuang*, pp. 74–87. For a satirical lambasting of both Sino-postmodernism and Wang Meng, see Zhu Xueqin's "Chengtou bianhuan erwangqi," *Ershiyi shiji*, 1995:4, pp. 119–122.

56. See also Xiaobing Tang, "New Urban Culture and the Anxiety of Everyday Life in Contemporary China," in *In Pursuit of Contemporary East Asian Culture*, ed. Xiaobing Tang and Stephen Snyder (Boulder, Colo.: Westview Press, 1996), pp. 107–108 and n. 2.

57. See Xu Jilin, Yang Yang, and Xue Yi in conversation, "Pipingde daode yu daodede piping—guanyu Wang Meng, Zhang Chengzhi xianxiang lunzhengde duihua," *Shanghai wenxue*, 1996:5, pp. 75–79.

58. Qi Shuyu, "Wufa huibide chonggao—guanyu jianshe xinde renwenjingshende zhenglun jiqi pingjia," *Wenyi zhengming*, 1995:3, p. 15. See also Yu Kaiwei, "Wang Meng shifou 'zhuanxiang'—dui 'Duobi chonggao' yiwende zhiyi," *Wenyi zhengming*, 1995:3, pp. 18–21.

59. Ding Guo, "Wang Meng pouxi Wang Shuo—cong pizi wenxue kan Shenzhou wentande xin fangxiang," *Mingbao yuekan*, 1995:6, p. 82.

60. Wang Binbin, "Guoyu congmingde Zhongguo zuojia," *Wenyi zhengming*, 1994:6, pp. 65–68.

61. Wang Shuo, "Zuozhede hua," in his *Guo ba yin jiu si* (Beijing: Huayi chubanshe, 1992), p. 5.

62. See Wang Shuo et al., "Xuanzede ziyou yu wenhua taishi," in Wang Xiaoming, *Renwen jingshen xunsi lu*, pp. 84–99.

63. This is based on conversations with Wang Shuo in May 1989, and at various times in 1990 and 1991.

64. In an interview with the Hong Kong press in 1995, Wang Meng went so far as to say that a cultural environment in China that could not tolerate Wang Shuo's style of irreverent humor would be grim indeed. In defense of the satirical badinage that had been popularized by Wang Shuo, Wang Meng said, "After all, Milan Kundera also makes jokes"! Ding Guo, "Wang Meng pouxi Wang Shuo," p. 81.

65. For details of relevant articles that appeared in the 1994–1995 debate, see Xiao Lin, "'Shu wo zhi yan'—'95 wentan xin shishang," *Beijing qingnian bao*, 13 July 1995; and Ding Dong and Sun Min, *Shiji zhijiaode chongzhuang*.

66. Liu Xiaobo, "Lun gudu," *Baijia*, 1988:2, pp. 5–6, quoted in Geremie Barmé, "Confession, Redemption, and Death: Liu Xiaobo and the Protest Movement of 1989," in *The Broken Mirror: China After Tiananmen*, ed. George Hicks (Essex: Longman, 1990), p. 81.

67. See "Wang Meng tan wenyi," *Zhongguo wenhua bao*, 26 November 1986; and Barmé, "Confession, Redemption, and Death," p. 56.

68. I have written a number of pieces on Liu. The first, published in Chinese in 1987, elicited denunciations from the Wang Meng camp. See Bai Jieming, "Zhongguorende jiefang zai ziwo juexing," *Jiushi niandai yuekan*, 1987:3, pp. 61–65; and Bai, "Liu Xiaobode shengshi weiyan—kanchuan Zhongguo xinyide talu pinglunjia," *Dangdai* (Taibei), 1988:10, pp. 4–10. For the philosopher Li Zehou's intemperate response to this second article, see Lin Daoqun, " 'Wusi' yu Zhongguo wenhua taolunde misi—fangwen Li Zehou xiansheng," in Lin Yusheng et al., *Wusi: duoyuande fansi* (Xianggang: Sanlian shudian, 1989), p. 263.

69. He continued his career as a political agitator and, in 1996, was sentenced to three years of labor reform.

70. Wang Meng, "Heima yu heiju," *Xinmin wanbao*, 17 January 1995.

71. In late 1987, for example, Hai Bo, an editor of the PLA *Kunlun* literary journal, was of the opinion that "a fin-de-siècle ambience is beginning to suffuse the literary scene, causing people to become lost and confused in its miasma . . . works of sincerity are increasingly rare." See "Miandui dangjin wentande lengjun chensi," *Wenxue pinglun*, 1988:3, p. 5. It is equally noteworthy that Zhang Xianliang, a popular author of serious fiction in both the mainland and Taiwan, was a self-proclaimed master of insincerity. In 1986, Zhang published an article entitled "Please Buy *Selected Works of Zhang Xianliang*," in which he said although he could be accused of occasional hypocrisy in his writings, it was "sincere hypocrisy," "*zhenchengde xuwei*." See Zhang Xianliang, "Qing mai *Zhang Xianliang zixuan ji*," *Wenhui bao*, 12 May 1986.

72. Li Tuo, an enthusiastic 1980s' "discoverer" of new trends and writers, cried out: "Why can't we Chinese writers stand up straight and hold our heads up high? Why can't we start something new, 'form a faction' [*la shantou*], and create our own school of writing? Even the Japanese have *shikangaku shōsetsu*, why can't we [do something like that]?" See "Miandui dangjin wentande lengjun chensi," p. 8. In tone, this was not unlike the questions being asked by Bo Yang and Sun Kuan-han in Taiwan. In the 1990s, after a period of radicalism in 1989 and self-imposed exile in San Francisco, Li Tuo returned to China to pursue his essentialist agenda.

   Liu Ji, an editor with the Writers' Publishing House, characterized the cultural scene after 1987 as being a "period of exhaustion . . . weariness." He saw the causes of this as being that "the society's aesthetic is becoming more variegated [*duoyanghua*, not *duoyuanhua*]. Also, and more important, "a few years back, theoreticians and writers played around with too many new fads in too short a period; they lost their heads in an orgy of release," and creative impotence was the result. See "Miandui dangjin wentande lengjun chensi," p. 6. Liu Xinwu, though, kept within the parameters of the official dogma concerning the "primary stage of socialism." He claimed that between 1977 and 1980, Chinese literature was in an "embryonic stage," *peitaiqi*, and that since then, it had entered its adolescence, *shaonianqi*. See Liu Xinwu, "Jin shinian Zhongguo wenxuede ruogan texing," *Wenxue pinglun*, 1988:1, pp. 10–12.

73. See Ye Jianming's "Lixingde huanghun—Dui Zhongguo zhishifenzi chujing he xintaide liangxiang diaocha," *Mingbao yuekan*, 1989:2, pp. 15–18.

74. Wang Meng writing again as Yang Yu, the engineer of writers' souls, attempted to con-

front and dismiss these concerns in "Hebi beiguan — Dui yizhong wenxue piping luo-jide zhiyi," *Wenyi bao*, 28 January 1989.

75. "Ruxiao," *Xunzi*, ch. 8. For the Kundera quotation, see his *The Unbearable Lightness of Being*, trans. from Czech by Michael Henry Heim (London: Faber & Faber, 1984), p. 251.

76. Wang Shuo, "Ni bushi yige suren," *Shouhuo*, 1992:2, reprinted in Wang, *Wang Shuo wenji* (Beijing: Huayi chubanshe, 1992), vol. 4, pp. 155–222.

77. Miklós Haraszti, *The Velvet Prison: Artists Under State Socialism*, trans. Katalin and Stephen Landesmann (New York: Basic Books, 1987), pp. 155–156, italics in original.

78. Yi Xiaoqiang, "Zhongshuo fenyun hua wentan," *Zhongliu*, 1995:7, p. 36.

79. Of course, Xia's supporters had their version of the good writer, a philosopher by the name of Gu Zhun (1915–1974), who wrote an extraordinary series of independent critiques of Maoist-socialism during the Cultural Revolution and, most amazingly of all, managed to keep a diary during those dark years. See Gu Zhun, *Gu Zhun wenji* (Guiyang: Guizhou renmin chubanshe, 1994); and Chen Minzhi and Ding Dong, eds., *Gu Zhun riji* (Beijing: *Jingji ribao* chubanshe, 1997).

80. Zhu Wei, "Zhang Chengzhi ji," in Zhang Chengzhi, *Wuyuande sixiang*, ed. Xiao Xialin (Beijing: Huayi chubanshe, 1995), p. 278.

81. See Zhang Chengzhi's "Chairman Mao Grafitti," in Barmé, *Shades of Mao*, p. 269, and chapter 12. According to the U.S.-based filmmaker Liu Yuan, who interviewed the first Red Guards in the early 1990s, the term Zhang had originally employed was "Red Warrior," *hong weishi*. The group who founded the Red Guard movement at the Yuan Ming Yuan in May 1996 decided the term *shi* (warrior or literatus) was too closely associated with the moribund traditional culture, so they replaced it with *bing*, soldier, thus the name *hong weibing*, Red Guard.

82. Zhang Chengzhi, *Wuyuande sixiang*, p. 17; and W. J. F. Jenner, "Tough Guys, Mateship and Honour: Another Chinese Tradition," *East Asian History*, no. 12 (December 1996), p. 28, n. 71.

83. Xiao Xialin, "Shidaide aitongzhe he xingfuzhe—xie zai *Dikang touxiang shuxi* de qianmian," *Wuyuande sixiang*.

84. *pizi geming*, an expression taken from Mao Zedong. See Barmé, *Shades of Mao*, p. 168, n. 11.

85. I have chosen the term "the public" to translate *dazhong*, literally "the masses," so as to distinguish it from the Maoist term "the broad masses," *guangda renmin qunzhong*, and its shortened version, *qunzhong*, an expression with particular pro-party ideological connotations.

86. Xiao Xialin, "Shidaide aitongzhe he xingfuzhe," 3 March 1995, introduction to *Dikang touxiang shuxi*. See Zhang Chengzhi, *Wuyuande sixiang*, p. i.

87. Wang Shuo, "Wode xiaoshuo," *Renmin wenxue*, 1989:3, p. 108.

88. See Chow Kai-wing, "Imagining Boundaries of Blood: Zhang Binglin and the Invention of the Han 'Race' in Modern China," in *The Construction of Racial Identities in China and Japan: Historical and Contemporary Perspectives*, ed. Frank Dikötter (London: Hurst, 1997), pp. 34–52.

89. Xiao Xialin, "Shidaide aitongzhe he xingfuzhe," p. ii.

90. Zhang Chengzhi, *Wuyuande sixiang*, pp. 24–25.

91. Yu Shaowen, "Qie ting Wang Shuo fenjie," *Beijing qingnian bao*, 31 August 1995. This interview was digested and reprinted with a number of commentaries by authors and critics, including Chen Cun, Wang Gan, and Mao Shian in Shanghai, under the heading "Zhongguo wentan: shijimode zhenglun," *Haishang wentan*, 1995:12, pp. 10–19.

92. Wang was merely repeating comments made about Lu Xun in the 1930s. See, for example, Tian Yi, "Neishan Wanzaode mimi," *Shehui xinwen* 7 (16) (May 1935), reprinted in Sun Yu, ed., *Bei xiedude Lu Xun* (Beijing: Qunyan chubanshe, 1994), pp. 164–165.

93. Wang Meng, "Huzhu," in *Ketinglide baozha, Jiduanpian juan, I* (Taibei: Xindi chubanshe, 1988), p. 150.

94. These included *Reading, Orient* (1993–1996), *Frontiers* (Tianya, 1992–), *Today's Avant-Garde* (Jinri xianfeng, 1994–), and *Way* (Fangfa, 1996–), among others.

95. These comments are inspired by the concluding remarks made by Mikhail N. Epstein in "Relativistic Patterns in Totalitarian Thinking: The Linguistic Games of Soviet Ideology," in his *After the Future: The Paradoxes of Postmodernism and Contemporary Russian Culture*, trans. Anesa Miller-Pogacar (Amherst: University of Massachusetts Press, 1995), pp. 161–163.

96. Ewa Kuryluk, "A Plea for Irresponsibility," in *The Subversive Imagination: Artists, Society, and Social Responsibility*, ed. Carol Becker (New York: Routledge, 1994), pp. 18–19. Xu Jilin contrasted writers like Zhang Chengzhi with another former Red Guard novelist, Shi Tiesheng, an idealist whose values were based on the worth of the individual. See Xu, "Shijimode lixiangzhuyi," in his *Xunqiu yiyi: xiandaihua yu wenhua pipan* (Shanghai: Shanghai Sanlian shudian, 1997), pp. 115–123.

97. Deng Youmei, Chen Jiangong, Liu Xinwu, Shen Rong, Zhang Jie, Feng Jicai, and others.

98. Norman Manea, *On Clowns: The Dictator and the Artist* (New York: Grove Press, 1992), pp. 17–18.

99. For the main official documents related to this movement, see *Zhonggong zhongyang guanyu jiaqiang shehuizhuyi jingshen wenming jianshe ruogan zhongyao wentide jueyi* (Beijing: Renmin chubanshe, 1996); and Committee, ed., *Jingshen wenming jianshede lishixing wenxian—xuexi dangde shisi jie liuzhong quanhui jueyi* (Beijing: Xinhua chubanshe, 1996).

100. Zheng Bonong, "Yao jiang zhengzhi, yao zhongshi wenyide yishi xingtaixing," *Zhongliu*, 1996:2, pp. 2–3.

101. See Gong Yizhou, "Wang Meng qiren qishi," *Zhongliu*, 1997:1, pp. 33–39.

102. Qian Liqun, "Fansi santi," *Wenyi bao*, 20 May 1989, trans. in Barmé and Jaivin, *New Ghosts, Old Dreams*, pp. 368–369.

CHAPTER 12

1. Svetlana Boym, *Common Places: Mythologies of Everyday Life in Russia* (Cambridge, Mass.: Harvard University Press, 1994), p. 247. Boym, who acknowledges herself to be

a product of the epoch of totalitarian decadence, the skeptical age of late Brezh-nevism, remarks in her disquisition on totalitarian nostalgia that "I can only develop a genre of nostalgia mediated by irony, which combines estrangement with the longing for the familiar—in my case this happens to be a familiar collective oppression. It offers a good balance between homesickness and the sickness of being home that is necessary for a cultural mythologist." (p. 290).

2.   *Yangguang canlande rizi* (1995), based on Wang Shuo's 1991 novella *Wild Beasts* (Dongwu xiongmeng).

3.   See Johannes Hofer, "Medical Dissertation on Nostalgia," first published in Latin in 1688 and translated into English by Carolyn K. Anspach, *Bulletin of the History of Medicine* 2 (1934), pp. 376–391. See Fred Davis, *Yearning for Yesterday: A Sociology of Nostalgia* (New York: Free Press, 1979), pp. 1–2.

4.   The Chinese expressions were *boluan fanzheng, huan lishi benlai mianmu,* and *ba diandaolede lishi zai diandao guolai,* respectively. See Geremie Barmé, "History for the Masses," in *Using the Past to Serve the Present: Historiography and Politics in Contemporary China,* ed. Jonathan Unger (Armonk, N.Y.: Sharpe, 1993), p. 260.

5.   Dai Qing, "Zhonghua yinglie yu 1986," *Dushu,* 1987:2, p. 124, quoted in Geremie Barmé, "Using the Past to Save the Present: Dai Qing's Historiographical Dissent," *East Asian History,* no. 1 (June 1991), p. 174.

6.   The Chinese Premier Li Peng spoke in such terms at the emergency meeting of civil, party, and military officials on the night of 19 May 1989, as the People's Liberation Army attempted to enter Beijing and bring an end to the student protests. Again, such language was commonly used in official government propaganda regarding the troops and police who died on 3–4 June 1989.

7.   Davis, *Yearning for Yesterday,* pp. 18, 21, 24.

8.   For a comment on nostalgia, fascism, and revolution, see Frederic Jameson, "Walter Benjamin, or Nostalgia," *Salmagundi,* no. 10–11 (Fall/Winter 1969–1970), p. 68.

9.   *jingshen wenming.* An early example of this codified body of materials is Feng Lianhui et al., eds., *Jingshen wenming cishu* (Beijing: Zhongguo zhanwang chubanshe, 1986).

10. For more on this, see Geremie R. Barmé, *Shades of Mao: The Posthumous Cult of the Great Leader* (Armonk, N.Y.: Sharpe, 1996), pp. 14–15 and p. 191, n. 3.

11. Some of this material has appeared in ibid., pp. 15 ff.

12. Boym, *Common Places,* p. 239.

13. Victor Zaslavsky, *The Neo-Stalinist State: Class, Ethnicity, and Consensus in Soviet Society* (Armonk, N.Y.: Sharpe, 1994), pp. 15–16.

14. Alexandre Zinoviev, "Staline et le Stalinisme," *Nous et l'occident* (Lausanne: Editions L'Age d'Homme, 1981), pp. 7–17.

15. Li Jie, "Lun Mao Zedong xianxiang—yige xingcunzhede pipan shouji, zhiwu," *Baijia,* 1989:3, pp. 52 ff. This translation is from Barmé, *Shades of Mao,* pp. 143–145.

16. Zhang Chengzhi (Chō Shōshi), "Mō shuseki gurafiti," *Sekai,* 1994:1, pp. 210–216, translated in Barmé, *Shades of Mao,* pp. 271, 272, 274.

17. J. M. Coetzee, *Giving Offense, Essays on Censorship* (Chicago: University of Chicago Press, 1996), p. 113.

18. From Melamid's comments in Carter Ratcliff, *Komar & Melamid* (New York: Abbeville Press, 1988), p. 30. Two of their best-known works of nostalgic *sots art* are *Stalin and the Muses* and *I Saw Stalin Once When I Was a Child*. Robert Hughes writes of the artists' work:

    "In essence, K&M's work is of the same kidney as Aleksandr Zinoviev's *The Yawning Heights*: a prolonged satire that is bureaucratically realistic; a machine that recycles its own absurdity; above all, a meditation on the entropy of rhetoric, the way clichés wear down and finally deflate one another. . . . One can imagine some good apparatchik responding without irony to K&M's appalling *View of the Kremlin in a Romantic Landscape*, its gold onion domes and pink ramparts and red star floating on a sea like the isle of Cythera itself, framed by a 'classical' Poussinesque clutter of arching trees, fallen columns and pediments and other bric-a-brac. It has the deeply sincere vulgarity of a holy card: an alliance between Aleksandr Gerasimov, Stalin's favorite artist, and Walt Disney.

    " . . . It is the nature of carnivores to get power and then, having disposed of their enemies, to deploy the emollient powers of Great Art to make themselves look like herbivores. Stalinist socialist realism was merely the end of this process, carried out by hacks. After it, the more intelligent of the Beloved Leaders would want radio and television, not painting, as their cosmeticians. We must thank Melamid and Komar for reminding us what heights of awfulness the great lost tradition could reach in pre-electronic days." See Robert Hughes, "Komar and Melamid," in his *Nothing If Not Critical: Selected Essays on Art and Artists* (London: Harvill, 1991), pp. 280–281.

19. James B. Twitchell, *Adcult USA: The Triumph of Advertising in American Culture* (New York: Columbia University Press, 1996), pp. 179–228, esp. pp. 207–213.

20. Arthur C. Danto, *Encounters and Reflections: Art in the Historical Present* (New York: Farrar, Straus & Giroux, 1990), p. 303.

21. See Celeste Olalquiaga, *Megalopolis: Contemporary Culture Sensibilities* (Minneapolis: University of Minnesota Press, 1992), p. 51, quoted in Robert Goldman and Stephen Papson, *Sign Wars: The Cluttered Landscape of Advertising* (New York: Guilford Press, 1996), p. 258.

22. See Mikhail N. Epstein, *After the Future: The Paradoxes of Postmodernism and Contemporary Russian Culture*, trans. Anesa Miller-Pogacar (Amherst: University of Massachusetts Press, 1995), pp. 5–7, 159.

23. Ibid., p. 102.

24. Ibid., p. 119.

25. Ibid., p. 153.

26. Ibid., p. 155.

27. Ibid., p. 156.

28. Ibid., pp. 158–159.

29. *The Gate of Heavenly Peace* was directed by Carma Hinton and Richard Gordon of the Long Bow Group in Boston and written by Geremie R. Barmé and John Crowley. It opened at the New York Film Festival in October 1995. For the full script of the film in Chinese, see Ka Ma, Gao Fugui, et al., *Tiananmen* (Xianggang: Mingjing

chubanshe, 1997); and the Chinese VCD version, *Tiananmen*, Unlimited Film Sensation, Ltd., Hong Kong; or, for the English, see www.nmis.org/gate

30. *Lianhebao.*

31. The Hsüeh material was carried on the Mainland [China] News page of the *World Journal*. It was in two parts entitled, respectively, " 'Tiananmen' jilupian 89 nian xueleipian: Bieren liuxie huanqi tuanjie ziji qiusheng!—qidai Tiananmen liuxue chenghe, Chai Lingde gaobai beican qili" and "Liusi beiju: liji yingxiong wudao qunzhong; Wenge yidu: daode jiazhi dangran wucun," *Shijie ribao*, 26 April 1995.

32. Ibid. The full text of the Chai interview had not been published in Chinese previously. Excerpts had been used in both English and Chinese, but generally these were only partial quotations that were often given in the wrong order. Hsüeh's quotations are taken from the videotape of the interview Philip Cunningham provided to the film-makers. After the interview, Chai gave Cunningham a written request to broadcast the material.

33. The layout of the first issue of the journal *Tiananmen* is itself highly instructive in the context of this discussion. Produced by a number of the less self-reflective 1989 activists, directly as a result of the debate concerning *The Gate of Heavenly Peace*, *Tiananmen* is an example of what could be termed "high Communist propaganda style," reflecting party-style typesetting conventions. The cover features an image of the statue of the "Goddess of Democracy" with the caption "Deeply grieve the victims of 4 June." On the inside cover there is a full-page picture of Wei Jingsheng holding a cigarette in what could be mistaken for a Mao-esque pose with the line: "The Pioneer of the Chinese Democracy Movement: Wei Jingsheng." The editorial, *fakanci*, occupies the next page and in tone and style is reminiscent of similar publication statements in mainland propaganda. On the copyright page, there is a calligraphic inscription in ballpoint pen by a token authority figure, in this case the historian Ying-shih Yü, a sympathizer of the exiles. It reads: "Preserving the Most Accurate Account of the History of Tiananmen." It is dated 25 May 1995, Princeton. The back page features a photograph of the Tiananmen student leaders taken at their July 1991 Paris plenum, and the inside back cover shows a number of them speaking at that gathering. The contents of the magazine are arranged very much in the style of Communist publications. The feature articles are by the "leaders" Chai Ling, Bai Meng, and Zhang Boli, followed by "think pieces" by Ruan Ming and Zheng Yi, which in reality are emotive denunciations of *Gate*. Although Wang Dan's 1995 public reevaluation of the movement, which was critical of the student extremists, is not reproduced, an emotive hunger strike declaration written in December 1994 is included. Hsüeh Hsiao-kuang's "negative text," *fanmian jiaocai*, is placed at the end of the magazine. Because it is a reduced copy of Hsüeh's original, it is all but illegible. This is followed by two further rebuttals of Hsüeh, which are all too clear.

34. Chai Ling, "Qing zunzhong lishi," reprinted in *Tiananmen*, June 1995, inaugural issue, p. 4.

35. Ibid.

36. Ibid.

37. This translation is based on the Long Bow transcript of the Cunningham interview. This quotation also appears in *Gate*.

38. For more details on this controversy, see Richard B. Woodward, "Anatomy of a Massacre," *The Village Voice* 41 (23), 4 June 1996, pp. 29–35.

39. See, for examples, Bai Jieming (Barmé), "Juantu chonglaide zuofeng," *Dangdai* (Taibei), 1990:10, p. 114.

40. See Bai Jieming (Barmé) in " 'Liusi' guanghuanhoude yinying," *Dangdai* (Taibei), 1990:9, pp. 86, 87, 89.

41. See Chi Shizi, "Cong 'wenge yuyan' tanqi," *Zhongliu*, 1993:5, p. 30. Chi Shizi refers in particular to the introduction of Zhao Shilin, ed., *Fang "zuo" beiwanglu* (Taiyuan: Shuhai chubanshe, 1992), pp. 1–3, an essay by Zhou Da, "Yan mei ze xiang mei, yan e ze xiang e," pp. 291–293, and another piece by Yin Shixian, "Wenhua: yao 'geming,' haishi jianshe," pp. 373–379.

42. Zhao Shilin, *Fang "zuo" beiwanglu*, p. 1.

43. See Chai's remarks in Jose Martinez, "China's Most-Wanted Female Criminal Is Living Quietly in Boston," *Philadelphia Inquirer*, 20 July 1995.

44. Bai Meng, "Tiananmen shenpan," *Tiananmen*, 1995:1, June, pp. 7, 10, 11.

45. Ye Ren, "Haiwai minyun tiaobuchu gongchan moshi," *Jiushi niandai yuekan*, 1995:7, p. 88, trans. Carma Hinton.

46. Zheng Yi, "Wei Chai Ling bianhu," *Tiananmen*, June 1995, inaugural issue, p. 30.

47. Ibid., p. 37.

48. From the lead denunciation of the film by a commentator for the *People's Daily*. See "Edude yongxin, beiliede shoufa—pipan Andongni'aoni paishede tiwei 'Zhongguo' de fanhua yingpian," *Hongqi zazhi*, 1974:2, p. 76.

49. Coetzee, *Giving Offense*, p. 101.

50. Ibid., p. 134.

51. Ibid., p. 135, italics in original.

52. Ibid., p. 136.

53. Ratcliff, *Komar & Melamid*, p. 154.

54. Ibid., p. 156.

55. For an interesting essay on this topic by a Hong Kong–based scholar, see Zhu Yaowei, *Hou dongfangzhuyi—Zhong-Xi wenhua piping lunshu celüe* (Taibei: Luotuo chubanshe, 1994). My thanks to Miriam Lang for bringing this book to my attention. See also Dru C. Gladney, "Representing Nationality in China: Refiguring Majority/ Minority Identities," *Journal of Asian Studies* 53 (1), February 1994, pp. 92–123; and Barry Sautman, "Myths of Descent, Racial Nationalism and Ethnic Minorities in the People's Republic of China," in Frank Dikötter, ed., *The Construction of Racial Identities in China and Japan: Historical and Contemporary Perspectives* (London: Hurst, 1997), pp. 75–95.

56. See, for example, Liu Dong, "Jingti renweide 'yangjingbang xuefeng'," *Ershiyi shiji*, 1995:12, pp. 4–13. This is not to deny, however, the value of such insightful historical studies as Mao Haijian's *Collapse of the Celestial Empire—A Reassessment of the Opium War* (Tianchaode bengkui: Yapian zhanzheng) (Beijing: Sanlian shudian, 1995).

57. See Arif Dirlik, "Reversals, Ironies, Hegemonies: Notes on the Contemporary Histo-riography of Modern China," *Modern China: An International Quarterly of History and Social Science* 22 (3), July 1996, p. 278.

58. Boym, *Common Places*, p. 265.

59. These quotations come from Xu Jilin, "Xiwangde chuntian yu juewangde dong-tian—'95 wenhua piping huigu," *Dongfang*, 1996:2, p. 43. Xu had expressed similar ideas in regard to independent intellectuals and their fate in China in the late 1980s. See, for example, Geremie Barmé and Linda Jaivin, eds., *New Ghosts, Old Dreams: Chinese Rebel Voices* (New York: Times Books, 1992), pp. 348–350.

60. For details of these debates, see the articles by Lei Yi, Liu Dong, Gan Yang, Xiao Gongqin, et al., in the pages of *Twenty-First Century* in 1996, 1997, and 1998.

61. This is not to say that the editors of journals that survived the 1996–1997 publication purge did not make similar attempts at maintaining relative independence. This was certainly the case for the Beijing monthly *Reading*, and *Frontiers* (Tianya), published in Hainan Province.

62. See, for example, Xu Jilin's *Zhizhede zunyan* (Shanghai: Xuelin chubanshe, 1991) and his *Xunqiu yiyi: xiandaihua bianqian yu wenhua piping* (Shanghai: Shanghai Sanlian shudian, 1997)

63. Epstein, *After the Future*, p. 158.

64. Boym, *Common Places*, p. 284.

65. Ibid., p. 287.

POSTSCRIPT

1. "Ganchang," written by Guang Yi and Chen Jue, from Chen Jue and Shi Jian, dir., "Tiananmen" (Beijing: CCTV, not broadcast).

2. *shijian shi jianyan zhenlide weiyi biaozhun.* See Tao Kai, Zhang Yide, Dai Qing, et al., *Zouchu xiandai mixin—guanyu zhenli biaozhun wentide da bianlun* (Xianggang: Sanlian shudian, 1989); and Tang Yingwu, ed., *1976 nian yilaide Zhongguo* (Beijing: Jingji ribao chubanshe, 1997), pp. 1–154.

3. Ma Licheng and Ling Zhijun, *Jiaofeng: dangdai Zhongguo sanci sixiang jiefang shilu* (Beijing: Jinri Zhongguo chubanshe, 1998). For details of the internal petitions to the Central Committee, see pp. 242–251 and 276–281. This book offers a somewhat fawning, pro–Jiang Zemin history of post-1977 political thought. Ma was a senior writer for *People's Daily* who had also been an active journalist-protester in 1989. The book was subsequently criticized for revealing too many details of the dissension within the party.

4. *Zhongguo wenti baogao*, edited by Xu Ming and published by *China Today* (Jinri Zhongguo chubanshe), Beijing, in 1997–1998.

5. He Qinglian, *Xiandaihuade xianjing—dangdai Zhongguode jingji shehui wenti* (Bei-jing: Jinri Zhongguo chubanshe, 1998); and Shen Jiru, *Zhongguo budang "Bu xian-sheng"—dangdai Zhongguode guoji zhanlüe wenti* (Beijing: Jinri Zhongguo chuban-she, 1998).

6. Liu Ji, "21 shiji Zhong-Mei guanxide xuanze—zai Hafo daxue Fei Zhengqing Dongya yanjiu zhongxinde yanjiang," *Gongren ribao*, 17 June 1998. My thanks to Scott Hillis of Reuters in Beijing for bringing the published version of this talk to my attention.

7. "Richu jianghua hong sheng huo—Jiang Zemin zhuxi fang Mei zhuizong," dir. Zhuge Hongyun (Beijing: Tianhong yulin guoji wenhua yishu youxian gongsi, 1998).

8. In this context, Chai Ling and her supporters continued to pursue their distorted account of the events depicted in the film *The Gate of Heavenly Peace*. See, for example, "Zhongguo yaowen," *Mingbao*, 20 May 1997; and Carma Hinton's response, Ka Ma, "'Tiananmen' daoyan huiying benbao baodao Chai Ling 'qidai liuxue' bing wu duanzhang quyi," *Mingbao*, 5 June 1997. In 1998, Feng Congde published his own account of the events of 1989.

9. Jiang Zemin, "Zai qingzhu Beijing daxue jianxiao yibai zhounian dahuishangde jianghua," *Renmin ribao*, 5 May 1998.

10. Qian Liqun, "Xiangqi qishiliu nian qiande jinian," *Dushu*, 1998:5, p. 7.

11. Ibid., pp. 8–9.

12. Yu Jie, "Shiluode 'Wusi,'" in his *Huo yu bing—yige Beida guaicaide chouti wenxue* (Beijing: *Jingji ribao* chubanshe, 1998), pp. 185, 187.

13. See the cover of *Fire and Ice*. Li Ao (born 1935) moved to Taiwan with his family in 1948. In the 1960s he began publishing highly erudite satirical essays that made him the bane of the Nationalist authorities. His works began appearing on the mainland in the late 1980s. See Geremie Barmé and Linda Jaivin, eds., *New Ghosts, Old Dreams: Chinese Rebel Voices* (New York: Times Books, 1992), pp. 202–203, inter alia. Wang Xiaobo (1952–1997) taught at Peking University for a time before becoming a professional writer. He was one of the most noted novelists and essayists of the 1990s. See his *Wode jingshen jiayuan—Wang Xiaobo zawen zixuan ji* (Beijing: Wenhua yishu chubanshe, 1997).

14. *sannian ziran zaihai*, the official euphemism for the state-induced famine of 1959–1962 resulting from Mao Zedong and the Communist Party's Great Leap Forward policies.

15. Yu Jie, *Huo yu bing*, pp. 301–302.

16. Ibid., p. 302.

17. Letters of protest to the authorities were common from the mid-1990s. Petitions of this kind written not only by critics of the government in Beijing and Shanghai but also by individuals and groups in other provincial cities generally called for the rehabilitation of the victims of the 4 June massacre and the democratization of China.

18. *Gonggong luncong*, published by Joint Publishers (Sanlian shudian) in Beijing.

19. Yang, a graduate of Harvard University, organized the Chinese League for the Protection of Human Rights with Lu Xun and Soong Ch'ing-ling in 1932. He was assassinated by Nationalist agents the following year.

20. Liu Junning, "Beida chuantong yu jinxiandai Zhongguode ziyouzhuyi," editor's preface to *Beida chuantong yu jindai Zhongguo—ziyouzhuyide xiansheng* (Beijing: Zhongguo renshi chubanshe, 1998), pp. 1–2.

21. Liu Junning, "Beida chuantong yu jinxiandai Zhongguode ziyouzhuyi," p. 11.

22. Wang Hui, "Dangdai Zhongguode sixiang zhuangkuang yu xiandaixing wenti," *Tianya*, 1997:5, p. 145.
23. An observation made by Lincoln Lee via Gloria Davies.
24. Li Tuo, "Rang zhenglun fuchu haimian," *Dushu*, 1997:12, pp. 52–59.
25. Ibid., p. 53.
26. Zhi Ming, "'Lüka' shenfen yu 'xiao huoji' xintai," *Dongfang zhoukan* (Nanjing), 15 May 1998.
27. See Yu Jie, *Huo yu bing*, p. 93.
28. See Zygmunt Bauman, *Globalization, The Human Consequences* (Cambridge: Polity Press, 1998), pp. 85 ff.
29. Wang Shuo, *Wang Shuo zixuan ji* (Beijing: Huayi chubanshe, 1998), p. 4.
30. Ibid., p. 2.
31. Václav Havel, *Living in Truth* (London: Faber & Faber, 1986), p. 65.
32. Thomas Frank, "Liberation Marketing and the Culture Trust," *Conglomerates and the Media* (New York: The New Press, 1997), p. 187.
33. *Mandopop!* no. 9, 14 June 1998.
34. Cui Jian, "Xinxian yaogun Rock 'n' Roll," from his "Wunengde liliang" (Beijing: Zhongguo changpian gongsi, 1998).
35. Christi R. Perkins, "Power of the Powerless: Cui Jian Turns up the Base," *Beijing Scene*, 4, no. 2 (15–28 May 1998), p. 6.
36. Ibid., p. 7. For more on Cui's supposedly "antimaterialist patriotic project," see Gregory B. Lee, *Troubadours, Trumpeters, Trouble Makers: Lyricism, Nationalism and Hybridity in China and Its Others* (Durham, N.C.: Duke University Press, 1996), pp. 171 ff.
37. This is a line about another "cutting-edge" cultural figure from Mike Vago's "Dissed Harmony," *New York Press*, 11, no. 21 (27 May–9 June 1998), p. 20.
38. Although the level of political dissent was still relatively primitive, even in comparison with critics of the party in the 1950s.
39. Václav Havel, *The Art of the Impossible, Politics as Morality in Practice (Speeches and Writings, 1990–1996)*, trans. Paul Wilson (New York: Fromm International, 1998), p. 8.
40. See Zeng Xiaojun and Ai Weiwei, eds., *Huipishu (neibu jiaoliu ziliao)* (Beijing, 1997), p. 11. My thanks to Francesca Dal Lago for securing copies of this publication for me.
41. Ai Weiwei, "Zuochu xuanze," *Huipishu*, p. 10.

APPENDIX

1. Richard Bernstein and Ross H. Munro, *The Coming Conflict with China* (New York: Knopf, 1997).
2. He Xin, *Zhongguo fuxing yu shijie weilai*, 2 vols. (Chengdu: Sichuan renmin chubanshe, 1996).
3. See Christopher Lingle, *The Rise and Decline of the Asian Century: False Starts on the Path to the Global Millennium* (Barcelona: Sirocco, 1997).
4. Shi Zhong, "Xifangren yanzhongde 'Zhongguo minzuzhuyi'," *Zhanlüe yu guanli*, 1996:1, p. 22.

5. Ibid., p. 25. Shi's comments were addressed in particular to the volume *Chinese Na-tionalism*, edited by Jonathan Unger (Armonk, N.Y.: Sharpe, 1996), in which a short-er version of "To Screw Foreigners Is Patriotic" also appeared.

6. Liu Xiguang and Liu Kang, *Yaomohua Zhongguode beihou* (Beijing: Zhongguo she-hui kexue chubanshe, 1997).

7. Xiao Pang, ed., *Zhongguo ruhe duidai Xifang* (Xianggang: Mingjing chubanshe, 1997).

8. Simon Leys, "The China Experts," in his *The Burning Forest: Essays on Chinese Cul-ture and Politics* (New York: Holt, Rinehart and Winston, 1985), p. 194.

9. Reg White and Warren Reed, *The Tyranny of Fortune: Australia's Asian Destiny* (War-riewood, N.S.W.: Business & Professional Publishing, 1997).

10. See Geremie R. Barmé, "The Great Con," *The Australian's Review of Books* 3 (3), April 1998, pp. 8–9.

GLOSSARY

an fen 安分
anding tuanjie 安定团结

ba jingji gao shangqu 把经济搞上去
baobianci 褒贬词
baoyici 褒义词
baozhuang 包装
Beijing bang 北京帮
Beijing tuhua 北京土话
bei pichu minglai 被批出名来
bentuhua 本土化
bianyici 贬义词
bianyuan renwu 边缘人物
Bose qiyi 百色起义
buhui lai shi'r 不会来事儿
bukan ladao 不看拉倒
buzhi bujue, qianyi mohua 不知不觉，潜移默化

cao ni ma! 操你妈！
chao 潮
chaozuo 炒作
chengyu 成语
chishifenzi 吃屎分子
chongchu Yazhou, zou xiang shijie 冲出亚洲，走向世界
chouti wenxue 抽屉文学
chuanqi 传奇
chunqiu bifa 春秋笔法
chun wenxue 纯文学
CI xingxiang CI形象
cong mei zhaoguo shei, ye mei reguo shei 从没招过谁，也没惹过谁

Da chaoliu 大潮流
Da Qing huanglong qi 大清黄龙旗

da gunzi	打棍子
da pipan wenzhang	大批判文章
daban	打扮
damengquan	大梦拳
datsu a	脱亞
dayou shi	打油诗
dazhong	大众
dazhong wenhua	大众文化
de zhi ti	德智体
diannao chong	电脑虫
Dianzi yitiao jie	电子一条街
Dikang touxiang shuxi	抵抗投降书系
disu	低俗
Dongfang bingdu	东方病毒
Dongfang hong	东方红
dongfangzhuyi	东方主义
Donggong xigong	东宫西宫
dongluan	动乱
du Mao zhuxide shu	读毛主席的书,
ting Mao zhuxide hua	听毛主席的话,
zhao Mao zhuxide zhishi banshi	照毛主席的指示办事,
zuo Mao zhuxide hao zhanshi	做毛主席的好战士。
duo shuo haohua	多说好话
Erguotou	二锅头
Erliutang	二流堂
fan	烦
fan'an	翻案
fanmian jiaocai	反面教材
fanrong wenyi	繁荣文艺
fanzhe ne, bie li wo	烦着呢，别理我
fanzheng, laowai budong!	反正，老外不懂！
fei long zai tian	飞龙在天
fei zhuliu	非主流
Feichang Zhongguo	非常中国
feifei	非非
fengxian aixin	奉献爱心
fengyu tongzhou	风雨同舟
fucang long	伏藏龙
gaizao	改造
gaige	改革

ganxiexin	感谢信
gao	搞
gao geming	搞革命
gei Zhongguo yige jihui	给中国一个机会
gemen'r jiemen'r yan'rli wo burou shazi	哥们儿姐们儿眼儿里我不揉沙子
gemen'r yiqi	哥们儿义气
gemen'rbang	哥们儿帮
geming yangbanxi	革命样板戏
geyao	歌谣
gongguan guanggao	公关广告
gongyi guanggao	公益广告
guanbao guan ban guan ding guan kan	官报官办官订官看
guanxi	关系
guo	锅
guominxing	国民性
guoqing	国情
guoqing jiaoyu	国情教育
guoxue	国学
guoyu	国语
guoyu congming	过于聪明
haohan	好汉
haoxia	豪侠
hehe wenhua	合和文化
heiju	黑驹
heima	黑马
Heima congshu	黑马丛书
Heshang	河殇
Hongqi	红旗
hongyang minzu wenhua	弘扬民族文化
houhei	厚黑
houxue	后学
houzhu	后主
hukouben	户口本
huangchong	蝗虫
huanglong	黄龙
huichen buhui ziji paodiao	灰尘不会自己跑掉
huise qingxu	灰色情绪
huitou shi an (shi an)	回头是岸（失暗）
huoyao	火药
jia yangguizi	假洋鬼子

jianghua	僵化
jiang zhengzhi	讲政治
jiayuan	家园
jiegou	解构
jiemen'r	姐们儿
jiemen'rbang	姐们儿帮
jin Jing	进京
Jinlilai	金利来
Jinpingmei	金瓶梅
Jinshu tiantang	金属天堂
jinwan women xiangshi	今晚我们相识
jingshen wenming	精神文明
jingying wenhua	精英文化
Jiao Yulu	焦裕禄
kaichu qiuji	开除球籍
Kaiguo dadian	开国大典
kala OK re	卡拉OK热
kan	侃（砍）
kan renao	看热闹
kang long you hui	亢龙有悔
kejiao xing guo	科教兴国
Kong Laore	孔老惹
Kong Long	恐龙
Kong-Tai (Gang-Tai)	港台
ku	苦
ku (as in "cool")	酷
kui	夔
lajia daikou	拉家带口
la shantou	拉山头
Lao Mao dadi	老毛搭的
laotou shan	老头衫
laowai	老外
laowai hui xihuan ma?	老外会喜欢吗？
lei	累
lianpu	脸谱
liangge ziyou	两个自由
linghun shenchu baofa geming	灵魂深处爆发革命
liumang	流氓
liumang yishi	流氓意识
liu si	六四

long	龙
luan	乱
luosiding jingshen	螺丝钉精神
mangliu yishujia	盲流艺术家
Maocheng ji	猫城记
Meiguo, wo cao ni daye!	美国，我操你大爷！
meisu	媚俗
meiqian	没钱
menglong	朦胧
miansu	免俗
mianzi	面子
minge	民歌
Minnan	闽南
Minnanhua	闽南话
minyao	民谣
mitan	密探
mozhe shitou guo he	摸着石头过河
nanxun	南巡
nanzihan	男子汉
nianhua	年画
nimen bu jiushi juede ni da ma?	你们不就是觉得你大吗？
nimen Taiwanren bu jiushi you jige qian ma?	你们台湾人不就是有几个钱吗？
panlong	蟠龙
Panpan	盼盼
pi-Lin pi-Kong	批林批孔
pian'rjing	片儿警
Pianzi yitiao jie	骗子一条街
pingfan	平反
pingmin xiaoshuo	平民小说
pizi	痞子
popi	泼皮
putonghua	普通话
qi	气
qian	乾
qiangbi	枪毙
qidai	期待
qigong	气功

qingtan	清谈
qiuge	囚歌
qiuhou suanzhang	秋后算帐
qiulong	虬龙
quan min jie shang	全民皆商
re	热
ren	人
renmin	人民
rennai	忍耐
renqing	人情
renqingwei'r	人情味儿
renshu	忍术
ruan zhaolu	软着陆
santi	三T（三替）
sao hui	扫灰
sha ci	杀瓷
sha huilai	杀回来
shandong	煽动
shangpin dachao	商品大潮
shao ganyu, shao jieru	少干预，少介入
shehuizhuyi xinren	社会主义新人
shenlong	神龙
shenru shenghuo	深入生活
shenshi	绅士
shi'r	事儿
Shiji zhi jiaode minzuzhuyi xueshu taolunhui ji '95 Nan-Bei xuezhe duihuahui	世纪之交的民族主义学术讨论会暨 '95南北学者对话会
shijian	事件
shinian le, bie ti ta la!	十年了，别提它啦！
shinian shouju	十年首聚
shisu	世俗
shua liumang	耍流氓
shuishen huore	水深火热
shunkouliu'r	顺口溜儿
si daziyou	四大自由
sida	四大
sihai	四害
sixiang jiefang yundong	思想解放运动
sixiang ziyou, jianrong bingbao	思想自由，兼容并包
su	俗

su buke nai	俗不可耐
suqing	俗情
suren	俗人
sushang	俗尚
T xu	T恤
Taiping tianguo	太平天国
tan'r	摊儿
tazhehua	他者化
te shenchen	特深沉
Tiananmen	天安门
tianlong	天龙
tiaokan	调侃
ting tian you ming	听天由命
tinghua	听话
tongsu	通俗
tongsu wenhua	通俗文化
touxiang	投降
tuo kuzi, ge weiba	脱裤子，割尾巴
Tuoye	陀爷
wan (wan'r)	玩（玩儿）
wan ren sang de, wan wu sang zhi	玩人丧德，玩物丧志
wan'r buzhuan	玩儿不转
wan'r huahuo	玩儿花活
wan'r qu	玩儿去
wan'r wan	玩儿完
wan'r yinde	玩儿阴的
wanshi xianshizhuyi	玩世现实主义
wanzhu	顽主
wangba	王八
Wang Meng bang	王蒙帮
Wangshi	往事
weidade Zhonghua	伟大的中华
wenhua chaozuo	文化炒作
wenhua kuaican	文化快餐
wenhuapai	文化派
wenhua re	文化热
wenhua shan	文化衫
wo yan'rli roubude shazi	我眼儿里揉不得沙子
wo zong biebuzhu pi	我总憋不住屁
wuda	武打
Wunengde liliang	无能的力量

wuqiannian wenhua	五千年文化
wuxia	武侠
xi xin ge mian	洗心革面
xipishi	嬉皮士
xizhou wenxue	稀粥文学
xiake	侠客
xiangsheng	相声
xianxiang	现象
xiao qihou	小气候
xiaojie	消解
xiashi	侠士
xieshou gongjin, rang ninde pinpai shanyao Zhongguo dadi	携手共进，让你的品牌闪耀中国大地
xin	新
xin jishi sheying	新纪实摄影
xin ruxue	新儒学
xin shiqi	新时期
Xinhua wenti	新华文体
xinren	新人
xing "zi" haishi xing "she"	性"资"还是性"社"
xiongdi/jiemei	兄弟/姐妹
xuean	血案
yang lüka	养绿卡
yang shalong	洋沙龙
yangjingbang xuefeng	洋泾浜学风
yansu wenxue	严肃文学
yansu yishu	艳俗艺术
yanyu	谚语
yao	药
yao saochu yiqie hairenchong, quan wu di!	要扫除一切害人虫，全无敌！
yaoya qiechi	咬牙切齿
yapishi	雅皮士
yi bupa ku, er bupa si, ye bupa ni	一不怕苦，二不怕死，也不怕你
yi wu suo you	一无所有
yindao shichang	引导市场
yinglong	应龙
youshui zhi shi	游说之士
youxia	游侠
yuan (Renminbi; RMB)	元（人民币）
yuan hongzhizhuyi	原红旨主义

Yuan Ming Yuan	圆明园
yuanxiao jie	元宵节
yundong	运动
yundong yishi	运动意识
zawen	杂文
zai dalu denglu	在大陆登陆
Zeng Guofan	曾国藩
zhao'an	招安
zhen lei	真累
zhengdun	整顿
zhengduo huayuquan	争夺话语权
zhengzhi bopu (popu)	政治波普
zhishi	知识
zhishifenzi	知识分子
zhizhengdang	执政党
zhongguwei	中顾委
Zhonghua jingshen	中华精神
Zhonghua minzu	中华民族
zhongji guanhuai	终极关怀
zhongpan Ao (Ao) yun	众盼奥（澳）运
zhongsaiwei	中赛委
Zhongyang	中央
zhongzaiqu	重灾区
zhu xuanlü	主旋律
zige	资格
ziran bense	自然本色
zishen yishi	自审意识
ziyou zhishifenzi	自由知识分子
zong shejishi	总设计师
zonghengjia	纵横家
zongxiang lianxi	纵向联系
zou xue	走穴
zouzhe wenxue	奏折文学
zuo laoshi ren	做老实人/
shuo laoshi hua	说老实话/
ban laoshi shi	办老实事/
laolao shishi	老老实实
zuohuai buluan	坐怀不乱
zuzhi	组织

INDEX